GENERAL MOTORS | S-SERIES PICK-UPS & SUVs
1994-99 REPAIR MANUAL

CHILTON'S

Covers all U.S. and Canadian models of Chevrolet S10 and Blazer; GMC Sonoma, Envoy and Jimmy; Oldsmobile Bravada; Isuzu Hombre; 2 and 4 wheel drive

by **Thomas Mellon,** A.S.E., S.A.E.

CHILTON Automotive Books

PUBLISHED BY **HAYNES NORTH AMERICA. Inc.**

Manufactured in USA
© 1999 Haynes North America, Inc.
ISBN 0-8019-9111-0
Library of Congress Catalog Card No. 99-072297
4567890123 9876543210

Haynes Publishing Group
Sparkford Nr Yeovil
Somerset BA22 7JJ England

Haynes North America, Inc
861 Lawrence Drive
Newbury Park
California 91320 USA

ABCDE
FGHIJ
KLMN

Chilton is a registered trademark of W.G. Nichols, Inc., and has been licensed to Haynes North America, Inc.

Contents

Contents

DRIVE TRAIN 7

SUSPENSION AND STEERING 8

BRAKES 9

BODY AND TRIM 10

GLOSSARY

MASTER INDEX

SAFETY NOTICE

Proper service and repair procedures are vital to the safe, reliable operation of all motor vehicles, as well as the personal safety of those performing repairs. This manual outlines procedures for servicing and repairing vehicles using safe, effective methods. The procedures contain many NOTES, CAUTIONS and WARNINGS which should be followed, along with standard procedures to eliminate the possibility of personal injury or improper service which could damage the vehicle or compromise its safety.

It is important to note that repair procedures and techniques, tools and parts for servicing motor vehicles, as well as the skill and experience of the individual performing the work vary widely. It is not possible to anticipate all of the conceivable ways or conditions under which vehicles may be serviced, or to provide cautions as to all possible hazards that may result. Standard and accepted safety precautions and equipment should be used when handling toxic or flammable fluids, and safety goggles or other protection should be used during cutting, grinding, chiseling, prying, or any other process that can cause material removal or projectiles.

Some procedures require the use of tools specially designed for a specific purpose. Before substituting another tool or procedure, you must be completely satisfied that neither your personal safety, nor the performance of the vehicle will be endangered.

Although information in this manual is based on industry sources and is complete as possible at the time of publication, the possibility exists that some car manufacturers made later changes which could not be included here. While striving for total accuracy, the authors or publishers cannot assume responsibility for any errors, changes or omissions that may occur in the compilation of this data.

PART NUMBERS

Part numbers listed in this reference are not recommendations by Haynes North America, Inc. for any product brand name. They are references that can be used with interchange manuals and aftermarket supplier catalogs to locate each brand supplier's discrete part number.

SPECIAL TOOLS

Special tools are recommended by the vehicle manufacturer to perform their specific job. Use has been kept to a minimum, but where absolutely necessary, they are referred to in the text by the part number of the tool manufacturer. These tools can be purchased, under the appropriate part number, from your local dealer or regional distributor, or an equivalent tool can be purchased locally from a tool supplier or parts outlet. Before substituting any tool for the one recommended, read the SAFETY NOTICE at the top of this page.

ACKNOWLEDGMENTS

Portions of materials contained herein have been reprinted with the permission of General Motors Corporation, Service Technology Group.

All rights reserved. No part of this book may be reproduced or transmitted in any form or by any means, electronic or mechanical, including photocopying, recording or by any information storage or retrieval system, without permission in writing from the copyright holder.

While every attempt is made to ensure that the information in this manual is correct, no liability can be accepted by the authors or publishers for loss, damage or injury caused by any errors in, or omissions from, the information given.

1

GENERAL
INFORMATION
AND
MAINTENANCE

HOW TO USE THIS BOOK

Chilton's Total Car Care manual for the 1994–99 Chevrolet and GMC S-series Pick-ups, Sonoma, Bravada, Jimmy and 1996–99 Isuzu Hombre is intended to help you learn more about the inner workings of your vehicle while saving you money on its upkeep and operation.

The beginning of the book will likely be referred to the most, since that is where you will find information for maintenance and tune-up. The other sections deal with the more complex systems of your vehicle. Systems (from engine through brakes) are covered to the extent that the average do-it-yourselfer can attempt. This book will not explain such things as rebuilding a differential because the expertise required and the special tools necessary make this uneconomical. It will, however, give you detailed instructions to help you change your own brake pads and shoes, replace spark plugs, and perform many more jobs that can save you money and help avoid expensive problems.

A secondary purpose of this book is a reference for owners who want to understand their vehicle and/or their mechanics better.

Where to Begin

Before removing any bolts, read through the entire procedure. This will give you the overall view of what tools and supplies will be required. So read ahead and plan ahead. Each operation should be approached logically and all procedures thoroughly understood before attempting any work.

If repair of a component is not considered practical, we tell you how to remove the part and then how to install the new or rebuilt replacement. In this way, you at least save labor costs.

Avoiding Trouble

Many procedures in this book require you to "label and disconnect . . ." a group of lines, hoses or wires. Don't be lulled into thinking you can remember where everything goes—you won't. If you hook up vacuum or fuel lines incorrectly, the vehicle may run poorly, if at all. If you hook up electrical wiring incorrectly, you may instantly learn a very expensive lesson.

You don't need to know the proper name for each hose or line. A piece of masking tape on the hose and a piece on its fitting will allow you to assign your own label. As long as you remember your own code, the lines can be reconnected by matching your tags. Remember that tape will dissolve in gasoline or solvents; if a part is to be washed or cleaned, use another method of identification. A permanent felt-tipped marker or a metal scribe can be very handy for marking metal parts. Remove any tape or paper labels after assembly.

Maintenance or Repair?

Maintenance includes routine inspections, adjustments, and replacement of parts which show signs of normal wear. Maintenance compensates for wear or deterioration. Repair implies that something has broken or is not working. A need for a repair is often caused by lack of maintenance. for example: draining and refilling automatic transmission fluid is maintenance recommended at specific intervals. Failure to do this can shorten the life of the transmission/transaxle, requiring very expensive repairs. While no maintenance program can prevent items from eventually breaking or wearing out, a general rule is true: MAINTENANCE IS CHEAPER THAN REPAIR.

TOOLS AND EQUIPMENT

▶ **See Figures 1 thru 15**

Without the proper tools and equipment it is impossible to properly service your vehicle. It would be virtually impossible to catalog every tool that you would need to perform all of the operations in this book. It would be unwise for the amateur to rush out and buy an expensive set of tools on the theory that he/she may need one or more of them at some time.

The best approach is to proceed slowly, gathering a good quality set of those tools that are used most frequently. Don't be misled by the low cost of bargain tools. It is far better to spend a little more for better quality. Forged wrenches, 6 or 12-point sockets and fine tooth ratchets are by far preferable to their less expensive counterparts. As any good mechanic can tell you, there are few worse experiences than trying to work on a vehicle with bad tools.

Two basic mechanic's rules should be mentioned here. First, whenever the left side of the vehicle or engine is referred to, it means the driver's side. Conversely, the right side of the vehicle means the passenger's side. Second, screws and bolts are removed by turning counterclockwise, and tightened by turning clockwise unless specifically noted.

Safety is always the most important rule. Constantly be aware of the dangers involved in working on an automobile and take the proper precautions. Please refer to the information in this section regarding SERVICING YOUR VEHICLE SAFELY and the SAFETY NOTICE on the acknowledgment page.

Avoiding the Most Common Mistakes

Pay attention to the instructions provided. There are 3 common mistakes in mechanical work:

1. Incorrect order of assembly, disassembly or adjustment. When taking something apart or putting it together, performing steps in the wrong order usually just costs you extra time; however, it CAN break something. Read the entire procedure before beginning. Perform everything in the order in which the instructions say you should, even if you can't see a reason for it. When you're taking apart something that is very intricate, you might want to draw a picture of how it looks when assembled in order to make sure you get everything back in its proper position. When making adjustments, perform them in the proper order. One adjustment possibly will affect another.

2. Overtorquing (or undertorquing). While it is more common for overtorquing to cause damage, undertorquing may allow a fastener to vibrate loose causing serious damage. Especially when dealing with aluminum parts, pay attention to torque specifications and utilize a torque wrench in assembly. If a torque figure is not available, remember that if you are using the right tool to perform the job, you will probably not have to strain yourself to get a fastener tight enough. The pitch of most threads is so slight that the tension you put on the wrench will be multiplied many times in actual force on what you are tightening.

There are many commercial products available for ensuring that fasteners won't come loose, even if they are not torqued just right (a very common brand is Loctite®. If you're worried about getting something together tight enough to hold, but loose enough to avoid mechanical damage during assembly, one of these products might offer substantial insurance. Before choosing a threadlocking compound, read the label on the package and make sure the product is compatible with the materials, fluids, etc. involved.

3. Crossthreading. This occurs when a part such as a bolt is screwed into a nut or casting at the wrong angle and forced. Crossthreading is more likely to occur if access is difficult. It helps to clean and lubricate fasteners, then to start threading the bolt, spark plug, etc. with your fingers. If you encounter resistance, unscrew the part and start over again at a different angle until it can be inserted and turned several times without much effort. Keep in mind that many parts have tapered threads, so that gentle turning will automatically bring the part you're threading to the proper angle. Don't put a wrench on the part until it's been tightened a couple of turns by hand. If you suddenly encounter resistance, and the part has not seated fully, don't force it. Pull it back out to make sure it's clean and threading properly.

Be sure to take your time and be patient, and always plan ahead. Allow yourself ample time to perform repairs and maintenance.

Your monetary savings will be far outweighed by frustration and mangled knuckles.

Begin accumulating those tools that are used most frequently: those associated with routine maintenance and tune-up. In addition to the normal assortment of screwdrivers and pliers, you should have the following tools:

• Wrenches/sockets and combination open end/box end wrenches in sizes from $\frac{1}{8}$–$\frac{3}{4}$ in. or 3–19mm, as well as a $\frac{13}{16}$ in. or $\frac{5}{8}$ in. spark plug socket (depending on plug type).

➡**If possible, buy various length socket drive extensions. Universal-joint and wobble extensions can be extremely useful, but be careful when using them, as they can change the amount of torque applied to the socket.**

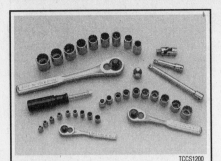

Fig. 1 All but the most basic procedures will require an assortment of ratchets and sockets

TCCS1200

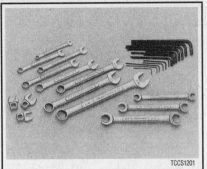

Fig. 2 In addition to ratchets, a good set of wrenches and hex keys will be necessary

TCCS1201

Fig. 3 A hydraulic floor jack and a set of jackstands are essential for lifting and supporting the vehicle

TCCS1202

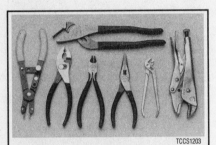

Fig. 4 An assortment of pliers, grippers and cutters will be handy for old rusted parts and stripped bolt heads

TCCS1203

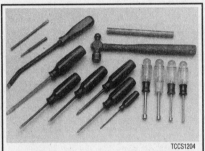

Fig. 5 Various drivers, chisels and prybars are great tools to have in your toolbox

TCCS1204

Fig. 6 Many repairs will require the use of a torque wrench to assure the components are properly fastened

TCCS1205

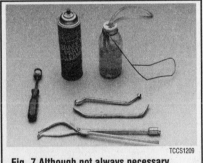

Fig. 7 Although not always necessary, using specialized brake tools will save time

TCCS1209

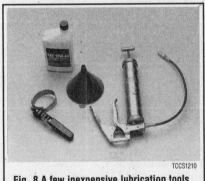

Fig. 8 A few inexpensive lubrication tools will make maintenance easier

TCCS1210

Fig. 9 Various pullers, clamps and separator tools are needed for many larger, more complicated repairs

TCCS1211

- Jackstands for support.
- Oil filter wrench.
- Spout or funnel for pouring fluids.
- Grease gun for chassis lubrication (unless your vehicle is not equipped with any grease fittings)
- Hydrometer for checking the battery (unless equipped with a sealed, maintenance-free battery).
- A container for draining oil and other fluids.
- Rags for wiping up the inevitable mess.

In addition to the above items there are several others that are not absolutely necessary, but handy to have around. These include an equivalent oil absorbent gravel, like cat litter, and the usual supply of lubricants, antifreeze and fluids. This is a basic list for routine maintenance, but only your personal needs and desire can accurately determine your list of tools.

After performing a few projects on the vehicle, you'll be amazed at the other tools and non-tools on your workbench. Some useful household items are: a large turkey baster or siphon, empty coffee cans and ice trays (to store parts), a ball of twine, electrical tape for wiring, small rolls of colored tape for tagging lines or hoses, markers and pens, a note pad, golf tees (for plugging vacuum lines), metal coat hangers or a roll of mechanic's wire (to hold things out of the way), dental pick or similar long, pointed probe, a strong magnet, and a small mirror (to see into recesses and under manifolds).

A more advanced set of tools, suitable for tune-up work, can be drawn up easily. While the tools are slightly more sophisticated, they need not be outrageously expensive. There are several inexpensive tach/dwell meters on the market that are every bit as good for the average mechanic as a professional model. Just be sure that it goes to a least 1200–1500 rpm on the tach scale and that it works on 4, 6 and 8-cylinder engines. The key to these purchases is to make them with an eye towards adaptability and wide range. A basic list of tune-up tools could include:

- Tach/dwell meter.
- Spark plug wrench and gapping tool.
- Feeler gauges for valve adjustment.
- Timing light.

The choice of a timing light should be made carefully. A light which works on the DC current supplied by the vehicle's battery is the best choice; it should have a xenon tube for brightness. On any vehicle with an electronic ignition system, a timing light with an inductive pickup that clamps around the No. 1 spark plug cable is preferred.

In addition to these basic tools, there are several other tools and gauges you may find useful. These include:

- Compression gauge. The screw-in type is slower to use, but eliminates the possibility of a faulty reading due to escaping pressure.
- Manifold vacuum gauge.

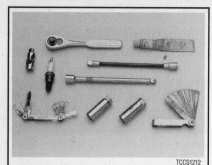

Fig. 10 A variety of tools and gauges should be used for spark plug gapping and installation

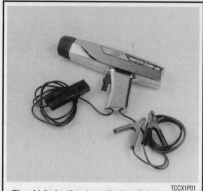

Fig. 11 Inductive type timing light

Fig. 12 A screw-in type compression gauge is recommended for compression testing

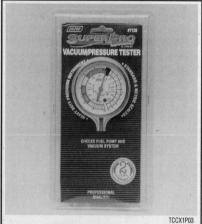

Fig. 13 A vacuum/pressure tester is necessary for many testing procedures

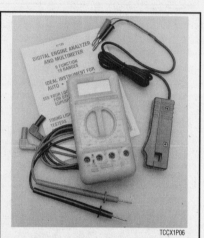

Fig. 14 Most modern automotive multimeters incorporate many helpful features

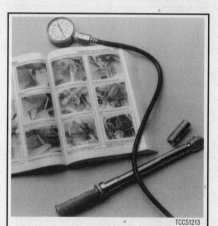

Fig. 15 Proper information is vital, so always have a Chilton Total Car Care manual handy

- 12V test light.
- A combination volt/ohmmeter
- Induction Ammeter. This is used for determining whether or not there is current in a wire. These are handy for use if a wire is broken somewhere in a wiring harness.

As a final note, you will probably find a torque wrench necessary for all but the most basic work. The beam type models are perfectly adequate, although the newer click types (breakaway) are easier to use. The click type torque wrenches tend to be more expensive. Also keep in mind that all types of torque wrenches should be periodically checked and/or recalibrated. You will have to decide for yourself which better fits your pocketbook, and purpose.

SERVICING YOUR VEHICLE SAFELY

▶ See Figures 16, 17 and 18

It is virtually impossible to anticipate all of the hazards involved with automotive maintenance and service, but care and common sense will prevent most accidents.

The rules of safety for mechanics range from "don't smoke around gasoline," to "use the proper tool(s) for the job." The trick to avoiding injuries is to develop safe work habits and to take every possible precaution.

Do's

- Do keep a fire extinguisher and first aid kit handy.
- Do wear safety glasses or goggles when cutting, drilling, grinding or prying, even if you have 20–20 vision. If you wear glasses for the sake of vision, wear safety goggles over your regular glasses.
- Do shield your eyes whenever you work around the battery. Batteries contain sulfuric acid. In case of contact with, flush the area with water or a mixture of water and baking soda, then seek immediate medical attention.

Special Tools

Normally, the use of special factory tools is avoided for repair procedures, since these are not readily available for the do-it-yourself mechanic. When it is possible to perform the job with more commonly available tools, it will be pointed out, but occasionally, a special tool was designed to perform a specific function and should be used. Before substituting another tool, you should be convinced that neither your safety nor the performance of the vehicle will be compromised.

Special tools can usually be purchased from an automotive parts store or from your dealer. In some cases special tools may be available directly from the tool manufacturer.

- Do use safety stands (jackstands) for any undervehicle service. Jacks are for raising vehicles; jackstands are for making sure the vehicle stays raised until you want it to come down.
- Do use adequate ventilation when working with any chemicals or hazardous materials. Like carbon monoxide, the asbestos dust resulting from some brake lining wear can be hazardous in sufficient quantities.
- Do disconnect the negative battery cable when working on the electrical system. The secondary ignition system contains EXTREMELY HIGH VOLTAGE. In some cases it can even exceed 50,000 volts.
- Do follow manufacturer's directions whenever working with potentially hazardous materials. Most chemicals and fluids are poisonous.
- Do properly maintain your tools. Loose hammerheads, mushroomed punches and chisels, frayed or poorly grounded electrical cords, excessively worn screwdrivers, spread wrenches (open end), cracked sockets, slipping ratchets, or faulty droplight sockets can cause accidents.
- Likewise, keep your tools clean; a greasy wrench can slip off a bolt head, ruining the bolt and often harming your knuckles in the process.
- Do use the proper size and type of tool for the job at hand. Do select a

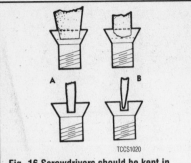

Fig. 16 Screwdrivers should be kept in good condition to prevent injury or damage which could result if the blade slips from the screw

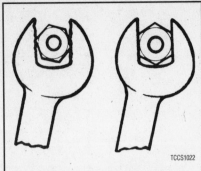

Fig. 17 Using the correct size wrench will help prevent the possibility of rounding off a nut

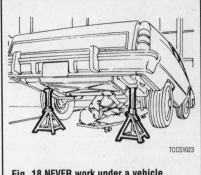

Fig. 18 NEVER work under a vehicle unless it is supported using safety stands (jackstands)

wrench or socket that fits the nut or bolt. The wrench or socket should sit straight, not cocked.

• Do, when possible, pull on a wrench handle rather than push on it, and adjust your stance to prevent a fall.

• Do be sure that adjustable wrenches are tightly closed on the nut or bolt and pulled so that the force is on the side of the fixed jaw.

• Do strike squarely with a hammer; avoid glancing blows.

• Do set the parking brake and block the drive wheels if the work requires a running engine.

Don'ts

• Don't run the engine in a garage or anywhere else without proper ventilation—EVER! Carbon monoxide is poisonous; it takes a long time to leave the human body and you can build up a deadly supply of it in your system by simply breathing in a little at a time. You may not realize you are slowly poisoning yourself. Always use power vents, windows, fans and/or open the garage door.

• Don't work around moving parts while wearing loose clothing. Short sleeves are much safer than long, loose sleeves. Hard-toed shoes with neoprene soles protect your toes and give a better grip on slippery surfaces. Watches and jewelry is not safe working around a vehicle. Long hair should be tied back under a hat or cap.

• Don't use pockets for toolboxes. A fall or bump can drive a screwdriver deep into your body. Even a rag hanging from your back pocket can wrap around a spinning shaft or fan.

• Don't smoke when working around gasoline, cleaning solvent or other flammable material.

• Don't smoke when working around the battery. When the battery is being charged, it gives off explosive hydrogen gas.

• Don't use gasoline to wash your hands; there are excellent soaps available. Gasoline contains dangerous additives which can enter the body through a cut or through your pores. Gasoline also removes all the natural oils from the skin so that bone dry hands will suck up oil and grease.

• Don't service the air conditioning system unless you are equipped with the necessary tools and training. When liquid or compressed gas refrigerant is released to atmospheric pressure it will absorb heat from whatever it contacts. This will chill or freeze anything it touches.

• Don't use screwdrivers for anything other than driving screws! A screwdriver used as an prying tool can snap when you least expect it, causing injuries. At the very least, you'll ruin a good screwdriver.

• Don't use an emergency jack (that little ratchet, scissors, or pantograph jack supplied with the vehicle) for anything other than changing a flat! These jacks are only intended for emergency use out on the road; they are NOT designed as a maintenance tool. If you are serious about maintaining your vehicle yourself, invest in a hydraulic floor jack of at least a 1½ ton capacity, and at least two sturdy jackstands.

FASTENERS, MEASUREMENTS AND CONVERSIONS

Bolts, Nuts and Other Threaded Retainers

▶ **See Figures 19 and 20**

Although there are a great variety of fasteners found in the modern car or truck, the most commonly used retainer is the threaded fastener (nuts, bolts, screws, studs, etc.). Most threaded retainers may be reused, provided that they are not damaged in use or during the repair. Some retainers (such as stretch bolts or torque prevailing nuts) are designed to deform when tightened or in use and should not be reinstalled.

Whenever possible, we will note any special retainers which should be replaced during a procedure. But you should always inspect the condition of a retainer when it is removed and replace any that show signs of damage. Check all threads for rust or corrosion which can increase the torque necessary to achieve the desired clamp load for which that fastener was originally selected. Additionally, be sure that the driver surface of the fastener has not been compromised by rounding or other damage. In some cases a driver surface may become only partially rounded, allowing the driver to catch in only one direction. In many of these occurrences, a fastener may be installed and tightened, but the driver would not be able to grip and loosen the fastener again.

If you must replace a fastener, whether due to design or damage, you must ALWAYS be sure to use the proper replacement. In all cases, a retainer of the same design, material and strength should be used. Markings on the heads of most bolts will help determine the proper strength of the fastener. The same material, thread and pitch must be selected to assure proper installation and safe operation of the vehicle afterwards.

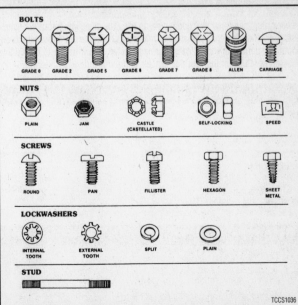

Fig. 19 There are many different types of threaded retainers found on vehicles

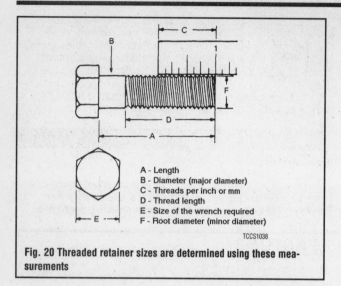

A - Length
B - Diameter (major diameter)
C - Threads per inch or mm
D - Thread length
E - Size of the wrench required
F - Root diameter (minor diameter)

TCCS1038

Fig. 20 Threaded retainer sizes are determined using these measurements

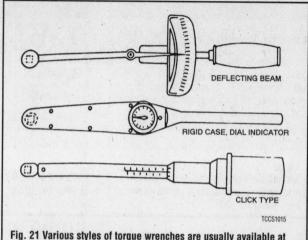

DEFLECTING BEAM

RIGID CASE, DIAL INDICATOR

CLICK TYPE

TCCS1015

Fig. 21 Various styles of torque wrenches are usually available at your local automotive supply store

Thread gauges are available to help measure a bolt or stud's thread. Most automotive and hardware stores keep gauges available to help you select the proper size. In a pinch, you can use another nut or bolt for a thread gauge. If the bolt you are replacing is not too badly damaged, you can select a match by finding another bolt which will thread in its place. If you find a nut which threads properly onto the damaged bolt, then use that nut to help select the replacement bolt.

✳✳ WARNING

Be aware that when you find a bolt with damaged threads, you may also find the nut or drilled hole it was threaded into has also been damaged. If this is the case, you may have to drill and tap the hole, replace the nut or otherwise repair the threads. NEVER try to force a replacement bolt to fit into the damaged threads.

Torque

Torque is defined as the measurement of resistance to turning or rotating. It tends to twist a body about an axis of rotation. A common example of this would be tightening a threaded retainer such as a nut, bolt or screw. Measuring torque is one of the most common ways to help assure that a threaded retainer has been properly fastened.

When tightening a threaded fastener, torque is applied in three distinct areas, the head, the bearing surface and the clamp load. About 50 percent of the measured torque is used in overcoming bearing friction. This is the friction between the bearing surface of the bolt head, screw head or nut face and the base material or washer (the surface on which the fastener is rotating). Approximately 40 percent of the applied torque is used in overcoming thread friction. This leaves only about 10 percent of the applied torque to develop a useful clamp load (the force which holds a joint together). This means that friction can account for as much as 90 percent of the applied torque on a fastener.

TORQUE WRENCHES

▶ See Figure 21

In most applications, a torque wrench can be used to assure proper installation of a fastener. Torque wrenches come in various designs and most automotive supply stores will carry a variety to suit your needs. A torque wrench should be used any time we supply a specific torque value for a fastener. Again, the general rule of "if you are using the right tool for the job, you should not have to strain to tighten a fastener" applies here.

Beam Type

The beam type torque wrench is one of the most popular types. It consists of a pointer attached to the head that runs the length of the flexible beam (shaft) to a scale located near the handle. As the wrench is pulled, the beam bends and the pointer indicates the torque using the scale.

Click (Breakaway) Type

Another popular design of torque wrench is the click type. To use the click type wrench you pre-adjust it to a torque setting. Once the torque is reached, the wrench has a reflex signaling feature that causes a momentary breakaway of the torque wrench body, sending an impulse to the operator's hand.

Pivot Head Type

▶ See Figure 22

Some torque wrenches (usually of the click type) may be equipped with a pivot head which can allow it to be used in areas of limited access. BUT, it must be used properly. To hold a pivot head wrench, grasp the handle lightly, and as you pull on the handle, it should be floated on the pivot point. If the handle comes in contact with the yoke extension during the process of pulling, there is a very good chance the torque readings will be inaccurate because this could alter the wrench loading point. The design of the handle is usually such as to make it inconvenient to deliberately misuse the wrench.

➡️**It should be mentioned that the use of any U-joint, wobble or extension will have an effect on the torque readings, no matter what type of wrench you are using. For the most accurate readings, install the socket directly on the wrench driver. If necessary, straight extensions (which hold a socket directly under the wrench driver) will have the least effect on the torque reading. Avoid any extension that alters the length of the wrench from the handle to the head/driving point (such as a crow's**

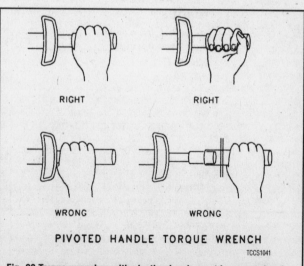

RIGHT

RIGHT

WRONG

WRONG

PIVOTED HANDLE TORQUE WRENCH

TCCS1041

Fig. 22 Torque wrenches with pivoting heads must be grasped and used properly to prevent an incorrect reading

foot). U-joint or wobble extensions can greatly affect the readings; avoid their use at all times.

Rigid Case (Direct Reading)

A rigid case or direct reading torque wrench is equipped with a dial indicator to show torque values. One advantage of these wrenches is that they can be held at any position on the wrench without affecting accuracy. These wrenches are often preferred because they tend to be compact, easy to read and have a great degree of accuracy.

TORQUE ANGLE METERS

Because the frictional characteristics of each fastener or threaded hole will vary, clamp loads which are based strictly on torque will vary as well. In most applications, this variance is not significant enough to cause worry. But, in cer-tain applications, a manufacturer's engineers may determine that more precise clamp loads are necessary (such is the case with many aluminum cylinder heads). In these cases, a torque angle method of installation would be specified. When installing fasteners which are torque angle tightened, a predetermined seating torque and standard torque wrench are usually used first to remove any compliance from the joint. The fastener is then tightened the specified additional portion of a turn measured in degrees. A torque angle gauge (mechanical pro-tractor) is used for these applications.

Standard and Metric Measurements

◗ **See Figure 23**

Throughout this manual, specifications are given to help you determine the condition of various components on your vehicle, or to assist you in their installation. Some of the most common measurements include length (in. or

CONVERSION FACTORS

LENGTH–DISTANCE

Inches (in.)	x 25.4	= Millimeters (mm)	x .0394	= Inches
Feet (ft.)	x .305	= Meters (m)	x 3.281	= Feet
Miles	x 1.609	= Kilometers (km)	x .0621	= Miles

VOLUME

Cubic Inches (in3)	x 16.387	= Cubic Centimeters	x .061	= in3
IMP Pints (IMP pt.)	x .568	= Liters (L)	x 1.76	= IMP pt.
IMP Quarts (IMP qt.)	x 1.137	= Liters (L)	x .88	= IMP qt.
IMP Gallons (IMP gal.)	x 4.546	= Liters (L)	x .22	= IMP gal.
IMP Quarts (IMP qt.)	x 1.201	= US Quarts (US qt.)	x .833	= IMP qt.
IMP Gallons (IMP gal.)	x 1.201	= US Gallons (US gal.)	x .833	= IMP gal.
Fl. Ounces	x 29.573	= Milliliters	x .034	= Ounces
US Pints (US pt.)	x .473	= Liters (L)	x 2.113	= Pints
US Quarts (US qt.)	x .946	= Liters (L)	x 1.057	= Quarts
US Gallons (US gal.)	x 3.785	= Liters (L)	x .264	= Gallons

MASS–WEIGHT

Ounces (oz.)	x 28.35	= Grams (g)	x .035	= Ounces
Pounds (lb.)	x .454	= Kilograms (kg)	x 2.205	= Pounds

PRESSURE

Pounds Per Sq. In. (psi)	x 6.895	= Kilopascals (kPa)	x .145	= psi
Inches of Mercury (Hg)	x .4912	= psi	x 2.036	= Hg
Inches of Mercury (Hg)	x 3.377	= Kilopascals (kPa)	x .2961	= Hg
Inches of Water (H2O)	x .07355	= Inches of Mercury	x 13.783	= H2O
Inches of Water (H2O)	x .03613	= psi	x 27.684	= H2O
Inches of Water (H2O)	x .248	= Kilopascals (kPa)	x 4.026	= H2O

TORQUE

Pounds–Force Inches (in–lb)	x .113	= Newton Meters (N·m)	x 8.85	= in–lb
Pounds–Force Feet (ft–lb)	x 1.356	= Newton Meters (N·m)	x .738	= ft–lb

VELOCITY

Miles Per Hour (MPH)	x 1.609	= Kilometers Per Hour (KPH)	x .621	= MPH

POWER

Horsepower (Hp)	x .745	= Kilowatts	x 1.34	= Horsepower

FUEL CONSUMPTION*

Miles Per Gallon IMP (MPG)	x .354	= Kilometers Per Liter (Km/L)
Kilometers Per Liter (Km/L)	x 2.352	= IMP MPG
Miles Per Gallon US (MPG)	x .425	= Kilometers Per Liter (Km/L)
Kilometers Per Liter (Km/L)	x 2.352	= US MPG

*It is common to covert from miles per gallon (mpg) to liters/100 kilometers (1/100 km), where mpg (IMP) x 1/100 km = 282 and mpg (US) x 1/100 km = 235.

TEMPERATURE

Degree Fahrenheit (°F)	= (°C x 1.8) + 32
Degree Celsius (°C)	= (°F − 32) x .56

TCCS1044

Fig. 23 Standard and metric conversion factors chart

cm/mm), torque (ft. lbs., inch lbs. or Nm) and pressure (psi, in. Hg, kPa or mm Hg). In most cases, we strive to provide the proper measurement as determined by the manufacturer's engineers.

Though, in some cases, that value may not be conveniently measured with what is available in your toolbox. Luckily, many of the measuring devices which are available today will have two scales so the Standard or Metric measurements may easily be taken. If any of the various measuring tools which are available to you do not contain the same scale as listed in the specifications, use the accompanying conversion factors to determine the proper value.

The conversion factor chart is used by taking the given specification and multiplying it by the necessary conversion factor. For instance, looking at the first line, if you have a measurement in inches such as "free-play should be 2 in." but your ruler reads only in millimeters, multiply 2 in. by the conversion factor of 25.4 to get the metric equivalent of 50.8mm. Likewise, if the specification was given only in a Metric measurement, for example in Newton Meters (Nm), then look at the center column first. If the measurement is 100 Nm, multiply it by the conversion factor of 0.738 to get 73.8 ft. lbs.

SERIAL NUMBER IDENTIFICATION

Vehicle

VEHICLE IDENTIFICATION PLATE

▶ **See Figures 24 and 25**

The Vehicle Identification Number (VIN) is stamped on a plate located on the top left hand side of the instrument panel, so it can be seen by looking through the windshield. It is also found on various other anti-theft labels found throughout the vehicle. The VIN is a seventeen digit sequence of numbers and letters which can be important for ordering parts and for servicing. The VIN plate is part of the Federal Vehicle Theft Prevention Standard and cannot be removed or altered in anyway. The 8th digit of the VIN identifies the factory equipped engine while the 10th digit will give the vehicle model year.

SERVICE PARTS IDENTIFICATION LABEL

▶ **See Figure 26**

The service parts identification label has been developed and placed on the vehicle to aid in identifying parts and options which were originally installed on the vehicle. The service parts identification label is located on the inside of the

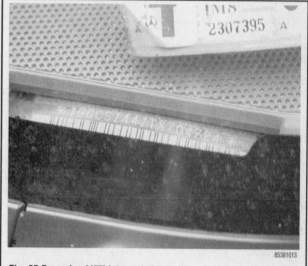

Fig. 25 Example of VIN interpretation

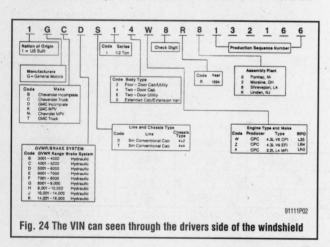

Fig. 24 The VIN can seen through the drivers side of the windshield

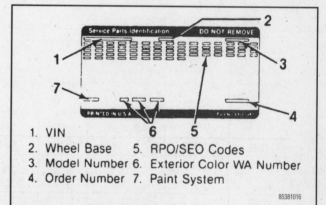

1. VIN
2. Wheel Base
3. Model Number
4. Order Number
5. RPO/SEO Codes
6. Exterior Color WA Number
7. Paint System

Fig. 26 Service parts identification label

VEHICLE IDENTIFICATION CHART

Engine Code						Model Year	
Engine Series (ID/VIN)	Engine Displacement Liters	Cubic Inches	No. of Cylinders	Fuel System	Eng. Mfg.	Code	Year
4	2.2 (2189)	133	4	MFI/SFI	CPC	R	1994
W	4.3 (4293)	262	6	CMFI/CSFI	CPC	S	1995
X	4.3 (4293)	262	6	CSFI	CPC	T	1996
Z	4.3 (4293)	262	6	TBI	CPC	V	1997
						W	1998
						X	1999

91111C01

glove box door. In most cases, the label lists the VIN, wheelbase, paint information and all production options or special equipment on the truck when it was shipped from the factory. Always refer to this information when ordering parts.

VEHICLE CERTIFICATION LABEL

▶ See Figure 27

The certification label shows the Gross Vehicle Weight Rating (GVWR), the front and rear Gross Axle Weight Rating (GAWR) and the Payload Rating.

Gross Vehicle Weight (GVW) is the weight of the originally equipped truck and all items added to it after leaving the factory. The GVW must not exceed the Gross Vehicle Weight Rating (GVWR) of your truck.

The Payload Rating shown on the label is the maximum allowable cargo load (including the weight of the occupants) that the truck can carry. The payload rating is decreased if any accessories or other equipment is added to the truck after delivery from the factory. Deduct the weight of any added accessories from the original payload rating to determine the new payload rating.

Engine

Engine identification can take place using various methods. The VIN, described earlier in this section, contains a code identifying the engine which was originally installed in the vehicle. In most cases, this should be sufficient for determining the engine with which your truck is currently equipped. But, some older vehicles may have had the engine replaced or changed by a previous owner. If this is the case, the first step in identification is to locate an engine serial number and code which is laser etched, stamped on the block or located on adhesive labels that may be present on valve covers or other engine components.

2.2L ENGINE

▶ See Figure 28

The engine identification number is stamped on a flat, machined surface, on the left rear of the engine block, near the flywheel.

4.3L ENGINE

▶ See Figure 29

The engine identification number is stamped either on a flat, machined surface, on the right-front of the engine block, just above the water pump (on some earlier model engines), or on the left-rear side of the engine block, where the transmission is joined to the engine.

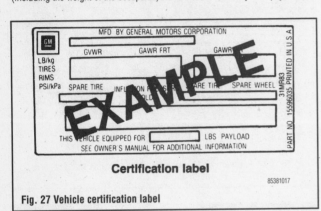

Certification label

Fig. 27 Vehicle certification label

GENERAL ENGINE SPECIFICATIONS

Year	Engine ID/VIN	Engine Displacement Liters (cc)	No. of Cyl.	Fuel System Type	Net Horsepower @ rpm	Net Torque @ rpm (ft. lbs.)	Compression Ratio	Oil Pressure (lbs. @ rpm)
1994	4	2.2 (2189)	4	MFI	118@5200	130@2800	8.85:1	56@3000
	W	4.3 (4293)	6	CMFI	195@4500	260@3600	9.5:1	25-50@1200
	Z	4.3 (4293)	6	TBI	165@4000	235@2400	9.5:1	18@2000
1995	4	2.2 (2189)	4	MFI	118@5200	130@2800	8.85:1	56@3000
	W	4.3 (4293)	6	CMFI	191@4500	260@3600	9.10:1	18@2000
	Z	4.3 (4293)	6	TBI	155@4000	235@2400	9.10:1	18@2000
1996	4	2.2 (2189)	4	SFI	118@5200	130@2800	8.85:1	56@3000
	W	4.3 (4293)	6	CSFI	①	③	9.2:1	18@2000
	X	4.3 (4293)	6	CSFI	②	240@2800	9.2:1	18@2000
1997	4	2.2 (2189)	4	SFI	118@5200	130@2800	8.85:1	56@3000
	W	4.3 (4293)	6	CSFI	①	③	9.2:1	18@2000
	X	4.3 (4293)	6	CSFI	②	240@2800	9.2:1	18@2000
1998	4	2.2 (2189)	4	SFI	118@5200	130@2800	8.85:1	56@3000
	W	4.3 (4293)	6	CSFI	①	③	9.2:1	18@2000
	X	4.3 (4293)	6	CSFI	②	240@2800	9.2:1	18@2000
1999	4	2.2 (2189)	4	SFI	118@5200	130@2800	8.85:1	56@3000
	W	4.3 (4293)	6	CSFI	①	③	9.2:1	18@2000
	X	4.3 (4293)	6	CSFI	②	240@2800	9.2:1	18@2000

MFI–Multi-port Fuel Injection

SFI–Sequential Fuel Injection

TBI–Throttle Body Injection

CMFI–Central Multi-port Fuel Injection

CSFI–Central Sequential Fuel Injection

① 2WD: 180@4400
   4WD: 190@4400

② 2WD: 175@4400
   4WD: 180@4400

③ 2WD: 245@2800
   4WD: 250@2800

91111C02

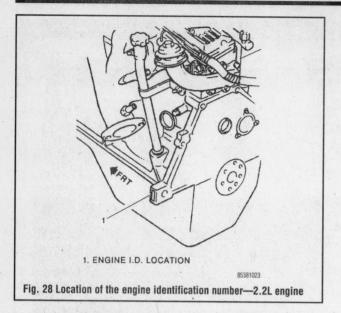

1. ENGINE I.D. LOCATION

85381023

Fig. 28 Location of the engine identification number—2.2L engine

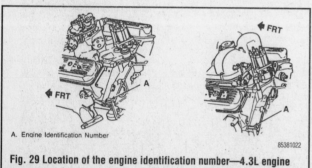

A. Engine Identification Number

85381022

Fig. 29 Location of the engine identification number—4.3L engine

Transmission

MANUAL

▶ **See Figures 30 and 31**

A transmission serial number is stamped on each transmission case or to a plate which is welded to the case. Location of the ID number will vary with the transmission manufacturer. With the Borg Warner T-5 transmission or New Venture Gear 1500/3500, locate the transmission ID number on the front right of the housing.

AUTOMATIC

▶ **See Figure 32**

The identification number for the 4L60-E is stamped on the right rear of the housing just above the pan rail.

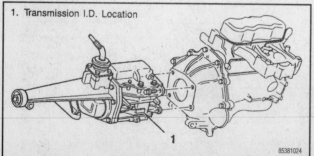

1. Transmission I.D. Location

85381024

Fig. 30 Manual transmission identification number location—Borg Warner T-5

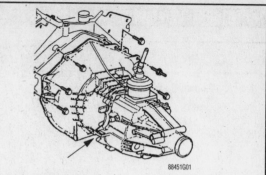

88451G01

Fig. 31 Manual transmission identification number location—New Venture Gear 1500 and 3500

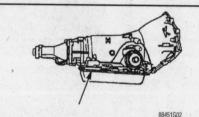

88451G02

Fig. 32 4L60-E automatic transmission identification number location

Drive Axle

▶ **See Figure 33**

On most rear axles, the identification number is stamped on the right-front side of the axle tube, next to the differential. On front axles, the ID number is either stamped on a tag, attached to the differential cover by a cover bolt or is stamped, on the top of the carrier case along the edge of the machined face of the left half.

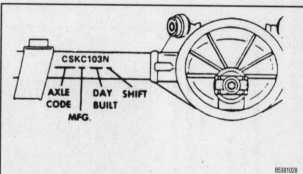

CSKC103N

AXLE CODE   DAY BUILT   SHIFT

MFG.

85381028

Fig. 33 Location and explanation of a common rear axle identification number

Transfer Case

There are a number of different transfer cases used on these models. The New Process 231, New Venture Gear NV231, New Process 233 and the New Venture Gear NV233 transfer cases are used on models with part time four wheel drive. The Borg-Warner 4472 transfer case is used on models with full time four wheel drive.

All transfer cases covered in this manual are equipped with an identification tag which is attached to the rear half of the case; the tag gives the model number, the low range reduction ratio and the assembly part number. If for some reason it becomes dislodged or removed, reattach it with an adhesive sealant.

MAINTENANCE COMPONENT LOCATIONS
4.3L TBI (1994 SHOWN)

1. Brake master cylinder reservoir
2. Brake booster
3. Air filter housing
4. Alternator
5. Upper radiator hose
6. Serpentine belt routing label
7. Emission hose routing label
8. Serpentine belt
9. Radiator cap
10. Battery
11. Coolant recovery tank
12. Engine oil dipstick
13. Engine oil filler cap
14. Manual transmission filler cap
15. Windshield washer fluid reservoir
16. Vehicle emission label

88451P46

UNDERHOOD MAINTENANCE COMPONENT LOCATIONS—2.2L MFI MODELS

1. Engine oil fluid dipstick
   (beside EGR valve)
2. Engine oil fill cap
3. Brake master cylinder
4. Power steering pump reservoir cap
5. Hydraulic clutch master cylinder
6. Windshield washer fluid reservoir
7. Air filter housing
8. Radiator cap
9. Upper radiator hose
10. Battery
11. Coolant recovery reservoir
12. Serpentine belt
13. Heater hoses

91111P99

UNDERHOOD MAINTENANCE COMPONENT LOCATIONS—4.3L CSFI MODELS

1. Brake master cylinder
2. Windshield washer fluid reservoir
3. Air filter housing
4. Upper radiator hose
5. Radiator cap
6. Battery
7. Coolant recovery reservoir
8. Engine oil fluid dipstick
9. Serpentine belt
10. Engine oil fill cap
11. Automatic transmission fluid dipstick
12. Heater hoses
13. Underhood fuse and relay panel
14. Power steering pump reservoir cap

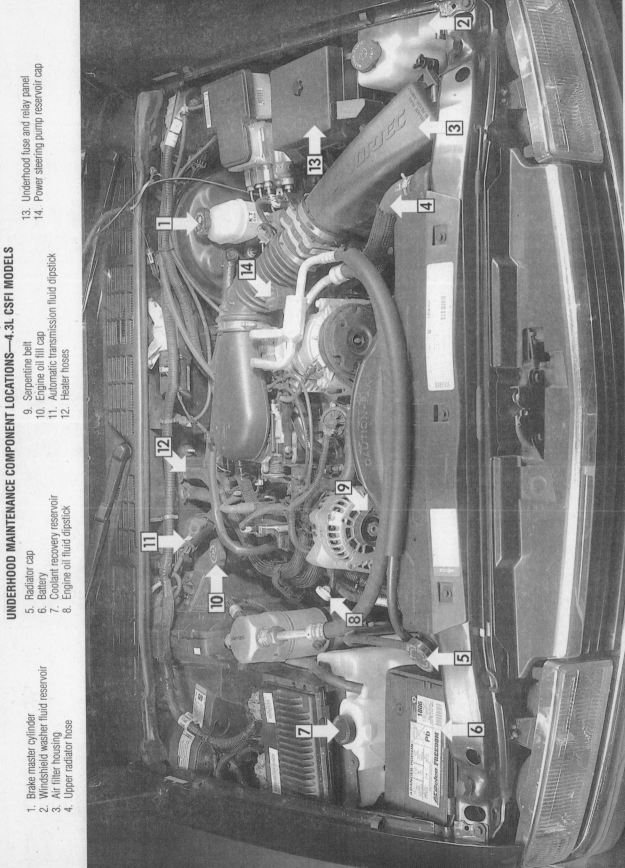

91111PA4

Proper maintenance and tune-up is the key to long and trouble-free vehicle life, and the work can yield its own rewards. Studies have shown that a properly tuned and maintained vehicle can achieve better gas mileage than an out-of-tune vehicle. As a conscientious owner and driver, set aside a Saturday morning, say once a month, to check or replace items which could cause major problems later. Keep your own personal log to jot down which services you performed, how much the parts cost you, the date, and the exact odometer reading at the time. Keep all receipts for such items as engine oil and filters, so that they may be referred to in case of related problems or to determine operating expenses. As a do-it-yourselfer, these receipts are the only proof you have that the required maintenance was performed. In the event of a warranty problem, these receipts will be invaluable.

The literature provided with your vehicle when it was originally delivered includes the factory recommended maintenance schedule. If you no longer have this literature, replacement copies are usually available from the dealer. A maintenance schedule is provided later in this section, in case you do not have the factory literature.

Air Cleaner

The air cleaner has a dual purpose. It not only filters the air, but also acts as a flame arrester if the engine should backfire. The engine should never be run without the air cleaner installed unless an engine maintenance procedure specifically requires the temporary removal of the air cleaner. Operating a vehicle without its air cleaner results in some throaty sounds from the engine giving the impression of increased power but will only cause trouble.

Your truck is equipped with an air cleaner element of the paper cartridge type. The element should be replaced every year or 30,000 miles (48,000 km), whichever comes first. If the truck is operated in heavy traffic or under dusty conditions, replace the element at more frequent intervals.

REMOVAL & INSTALLATION

TBI Models

▶ See Figures 34, 35 and 36

1. If so equipped, unlatch the clamp fasteners around the perimeter of the air cleaner housing.
2. Loosen the wingnut(s) at the center of the air cleaner cover.
3. Remove the cover from the air cleaner assembly, then remove the air cleaner element from the housing.

To install:
4. Using a clean rag, wipe the inside of the air cleaner housing assembly to remove any dirt or debris.
5. Install the air cleaner element to the housing, then position the cover onto the assembly.
6. Secure the cover using the clamp fasteners and/or wingnut(s).

MFI/CMFI/CSFI Models

▶ See Figures 37, 38, 39, 40 and 41

1. Loosen the housing cover retaining clips, nuts or screws and separate the housing cover from the housing.

2. Remove the air filter assembly.
To install:
3. Using a clean rag, wipe the inside of the air cleaner housing assembly to remove any dirt or debris.
4. Install the air filter assembly.
5. Engage the housing cover and fasten the retainers securely.

Fuel Filter

REMOVAL & INSTALLATION

In-line Filter

EXCEPT 1997–99 2.2L ENGINES AND 1999 4.3L ENGINES
▶ See Figure 42

✳✳ CAUTION

Before removing any fuel system component, always relieve pressure from the system. Refer to Section 5 for this procedure

To locate the inline filter, follow the fuel line back from the throttle body unit or fuel rail. In-line filters are often mounted to the frame rail underneath the vehicle. It may be necessary to raise and safely support the vehicle using jackstands in order to access the filter.

1. Properly relieve the fuel system pressure.
2. Using a backup wrench (where applicable) to prevent overtorquing the lines or fittings, loosen and disconnect the fuel lines from the filter. Be sure to

Fig. 34 Remove the wingnuts from the air cleaner cover

Fig. 35 Remove the air cleaner cover

Fig. 36 Remove the old air filter from the housing

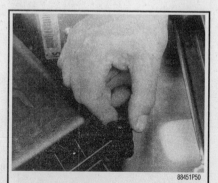
Fig. 37 Unfasten the air cleaner housing retainers—1996 4.3L CSFI model shown

Fig. 38 Remove the air filter from the housing—1996 4.3L CSFI model shown

Fig. 39 Unfasten the air cleaner cover retaining clips–2.2L MFI model shown

Fig. 40 Separate the air cleaner cover from the housing and pull out the filter element–2.2L MFI model shown

Fig. 41 Inspect the filter element for dirt that may cause air flow restrictions, this filter as you can see is saturated with dirt–2.2L MFI model shown

Fig. 42 In-line fuel filter—4.3L engine

1	LEFT FRAME SIDE MEMBER
2	BOLT – TIGHTEN 16 N·m (24 lb. ft.)
3	CLAMP
4	REAR FUEL FEED PIPE TIGHTEN 26 N·m (20 lb. ft.)
5	INTERMEDIATE FUEL FEED PIPE TIGHTEN 26 N·m (20 lb. ft.)
6	IN – LINE FUEL FILTER

position a rag in order to catch any remaining fuel which may escape when the fittings are loosened.

3. Remove the fuel filter from the retainer or mounting bolt. For most filters which are retained by band clamps, loosen the fastener(s) and remove the filter.

For some filters it may be necessary to completely remove the clamp and filter assembly.

To install:

4. Position the filter and retaining bracket with the directional arrow facing away from the fuel tank, towards the throttle body.

➡**The filter has an arrow (fuel flow direction) on the side of the case, be sure to install it correctly in the system, the with arrow facing away from the fuel tank.**

5. Install and tighten the filter/bracket retainer(s), as applicable.
6. Connect the fuel lines to the filter and tighten using a backup wrench to prevent damage.
7. Connect the negative battery cable and tighten the fuel filler cap, then start the engine and check for leaks.

1997–99 2.2L ENGINES AND 1999 4.3L ENGINES

✳✳ CAUTION

Before removing any fuel system component, always relieve pressure from the system. Refer to Section 5 for this procedure

To locate the inline filter, follow the fuel line back from the throttle body unit or fuel rail. In-line filters are often mounted to the frame rail underneath the vehicle. It may be necessary to raise and safely support the vehicle using jackstands in order to access the filter.

1. Properly relieve the fuel system pressure.
2. Remove the fuel filler cap.
3. Seperate the quick connect fittings from the filter. Refer to the quick connect fitting procedure is Section 5 of this manual.
4. Remove the filter feed nut and the clamp bolt.
5. Remove the filter and the clamp from the vehicle.

To install:

6. Position the filter and clamp with the directional arrow facing away from the fuel tank, towards the throttle body.

➡**The filter has an arrow (fuel flow direction) on the side of the case, be sure to install it correctly in the system, the with arrow facing away from the fuel tank.**

7. Attach and tighten the fuel feed nut.
8. Install and tighten the filter clamp assembly bolt.
9. Attach the fuel quick disconnect fittings to the filter. Refer to the quick connect fitting procedure is Section 5 of this manual.
10. Install the filler cap.
11. Connect the negative battery cable, then start the engine and check for leaks.

Positive Crankcase Ventilation (PCV) Valve

♦ See Figures 43 and 44

The PCV system must be operating properly in order to allow evaporation of fuel vapors and water from the crankcase. This system should be serviced and

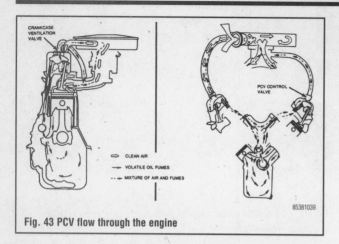

Fig. 43 PCV flow through the engine

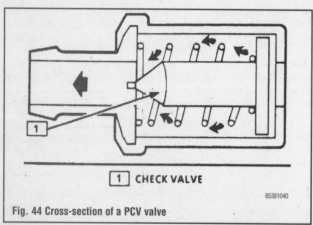

Fig. 44 Cross-section of a PCV valve

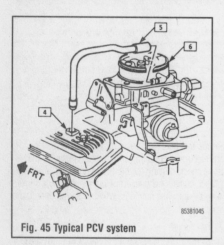

Fig. 45 Typical PCV system

Fig. 46 Remove the PCV valve from the valve cover

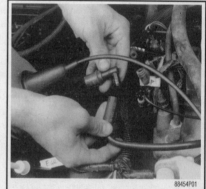

Fig. 47 Removing the PCV valve from the hose

If the new valve doesn't noticeably improve engine idle, the problem might be a restriction in the PCV hose. For further details on PCV valve operation please refer to Section 4 of this manual.

FUNCTIONAL CHECK

▶ **See Figure 45**

If the engine is idling rough, check for a clogged PCV valve, dirty vent filter or air cleaner element, or plugged hose. Test the system using the following procedure and replace components as necessary.

1. Remove the PCV valve from the rocker cover.
2. Run the engine at idle and place your thumb over the end of the valve to check for vacuum. If the engine speed decreases less than 50 rpm, the valve is clogged and should be replaced. If the engine speed decreases much more than 50 rpm, then the valve is good.
3. If no vacuum exists, check for plugged hoses, manifold port.
4. To check the PCV valve, remove the valve from the hose and shake it. If a rattling noise is heard, the valve is good. If no noise is heard, the valve is plugged and replacement is necessary.

REMOVAL & INSTALLATION

▶ **See Figures 46 and 47**

1. Grasp the valve and withdraw it from the valve cover.
2. Holding the valve in one hand and the hose in the other, carefully pull the valve from the hose and remove from the vehicle.

➡**Some PCV valve hoses will be retained to the valve using a clamp. If so, use a pair of pliers to slide the clamp back on the hose until it is clear of the bulged area on the end of PCV valve nipple. With the clamp in this position, the hose should be free to slip from the valve.**

To install:
3. Install the PCV hose to the grommet in the valve cover.
4. Connect the PCV hose to the valve.

both the PCV valve and filter replaced as outlined in the maintenance interval charts at the end of this section. Normal service entails cleaning the passages of the system hoses with solvent, inspecting them for cracks and breaks, and replacing them as necessary. The PCV valve contains a check valve and, when working properly, this valve will make a rattling sound when the outside case is tapped. If it fails to rattle, then it is probably stuck in a closed position and needs to be replaced.

The PCV system is designed to prevent the emission of gases from the crankcase into the atmosphere. It does this by connecting a crankcase outlet (usually the valve cover) to the intake with a hose. The crankcase gases travel through the hose to the intake where they are returned to the combustion chamber to be burned. If maintained properly, this system reduces condensation in the crankcase and the resultant formation of harmful acids and oil dilution. Disconnect the valve from the engine or merely clamp the hose shut. The PCV valve is an inexpensive item and it is suggested that it be replaced, if suspected.

Evaporative Canister

▶ **See Figure 48**

This system is designed to limit gasoline vapor, which normally escapes from the fuel tank and the intake manifold, from discharging into the atmosphere. Vapor absorption is accomplished through the use of the charcoal canister. The canister absorbs fuel vapors and stores them until they can be removed and burned in the combustion process. Removal of the vapors from the canister to the engine is accomplished through a computer controlled canister purge solenoid.

In addition to the canister, the fuel tank requires a non-vented gas cap. This cap does not allow fuel vapor to discharge into the atmosphere. All fuel vapor travels through a vent line (inserted high into the domed fuel tank) directly to the canister.

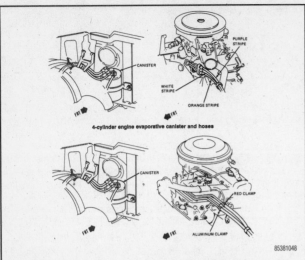

Fig. 48 Example of a common evaporative canister and hose assembly

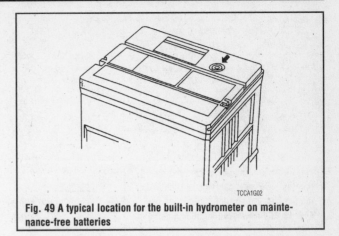

Fig. 49 A typical location for the built-in hydrometer on maintenance-free batteries

SERVICING

Every 30,000 miles (48,000 km) or 24 months, check all fuel, vapor lines and hoses for proper hook-up, routing and condition. If equipped, check that the bowl vent and purge valves work properly. Remove the canister and check for cracks or damage and replace, if necessary.

Battery

PRECAUTIONS

Always use caution when working on or near the battery. Never allow a tool to bridge the gap between the negative and positive battery terminals. Also, be careful not to allow a tool to provide a ground between the positive cable/terminal and any metal component on the vehicle. Either of these conditions will cause a short circuit, leading to sparks and possible personal injury.

Do not smoke, have an open flame or create sparks near a battery; the gases contained in the battery are very explosive and, if ignited, could cause severe injury or death.

All batteries, regardless of type, should be carefully secured by a battery hold-down device. If this is not done, the battery terminals or casing may crack from stress applied to the battery during vehicle operation. A battery which is not secured may allow acid to leak out, making it discharge faster; such leaking corrosive acid can also eat away at components under the hood.

Always visually inspect the battery case for cracks, leakage and corrosion. A white corrosive substance on the battery case or on nearby components would indicate a leaking or cracked battery. If the battery is cracked, it should be replaced immediately.

GENERAL MAINTENANCE

▶ **See Figure 49**

A battery that is not sealed must be checked periodically for electrolyte level. You cannot add water to a sealed maintenance-free battery (though not all maintenance-free batteries are sealed); however, a sealed battery must also be checked for proper electrolyte level, as indicated by the color of the built-in hydrometer "eye."

Always keep the battery cables and terminals free of corrosion. Check these components about once a year. Refer to the removal, installation and cleaning procedures outlined in this section.

Keep the top of the battery clean, as a film of dirt can help completely discharge a battery that is not used for long periods. A solution of baking soda and water may be used for cleaning, but be careful to flush this off with clear water. DO NOT let any of the solution into the filler holes. Baking soda neutralizes battery acid and will de-activate a battery cell.

Batteries in vehicles which are not operated on a regular basis can fall victim to parasitic loads (small current drains which are constantly drawing current from the battery). Normal parasitic loads may drain a battery on a vehicle that is in storage and not used for 6–8 weeks. Vehicles that have additional accessories such as a cellular phone, an alarm system or other devices that increase parasitic load may discharge a battery sooner. If the vehicle is to be stored for 6–8 weeks in a secure area and the alarm system, if present, is not necessary, the negative battery cable should be disconnected at the onset of storage to protect the battery charge.

Remember that constantly discharging and recharging will shorten battery life. Take care not to allow a battery to be needlessly discharged.

BATTERY FLUID

Check the battery electrolyte level at least once a month, or more often in hot weather or during periods of extended vehicle operation. On non-sealed batteries, the level can be checked either through the case on translucent batteries or by removing the cell caps on opaque-cased types. The electrolyte level in each cell should be kept filled to the split ring inside each cell, or the line marked on the outside of the case.

If the level is low, add only distilled water through the opening until the level is correct. Each cell is separate from the others, so each must be checked and filled individually. Distilled water should be used, because the chemicals and minerals found in most drinking water are harmful to the battery and could significantly shorten its life.

If water is added in freezing weather, the vehicle should be driven several miles to allow the water to mix with the electrolyte. Otherwise, the battery could freeze.

Although some maintenance-free batteries have removable cell caps for access to the electrolyte, the electrolyte condition and level on all sealed maintenance-free batteries must be checked using the built-in hydrometer "eye. The exact type of eye varies between battery manufacturers, but most apply a sticker to the battery itself explaining the possible readings. When in doubt, refer to the battery manufacturer's instructions to interpret battery condition using the built-in hydrometer.

➡**Although the readings from built-in hydrometers found in sealed batteries may vary, a green eye usually indicates a properly charged battery with sufficient fluid level. A dark eye is normally an indicator of a battery with sufficient fluid, but one which may be low in charge. And a light or yellow eye is usually an indication that electrolyte supply has dropped below the necessary level for battery (and hydrometer) operation. In this last case, sealed batteries with an insufficient electrolyte level must usually be discarded.**

Checking the Specific Gravity

▶ **See Figures 50, 51 and 52**

A hydrometer is required to check the specific gravity on all batteries that are not maintenance-free. On batteries that are maintenance-free, the specific gravity is checked by observing the built-in hydrometer "eye" on the top of the battery case. Check with your battery's manufacturer for proper interpretation of its built-in hydrometer readings.

Fig. 50 On non-maintenance-free batteries, the fluid level can be checked through the case on translucent models; the cell caps must be removed on other models

Fig. 51 If the fluid level is low, add only distilled water through the opening until the level is correct

Fig. 52 Check the specific gravity of the battery's electrolyte with a hydrometer

✳✳ CAUTION

Battery electrolyte contains sulfuric acid. If you should splash any on your skin or in your eyes, flush the affected area with plenty of clear water. If it lands in your eyes, get medical help immediately.

The fluid (sulfuric acid solution) contained in the battery cells will tell you many things about the condition of the battery. Because the cell plates must be kept submerged below the fluid level in order to operate, maintaining the fluid level is extremely important. And, because the specific gravity of the acid is an indication of electrical charge, testing the fluid can be an aid in determining if the battery must be replaced. A battery in a vehicle with a properly operating charging system should require little maintenance, but careful, periodic inspection should reveal problems before they leave you stranded.

As stated earlier, the specific gravity of a battery's electrolyte level can be used as an indication of battery charge. At least once a year, check the specific gravity of the battery. It should be between 1.20 and 1.26 on the gravity scale. Most auto supply stores carry a variety of inexpensive battery testing hydrometers. These can be used on any non-sealed battery to test the specific gravity in each cell.

The battery testing hydrometer has a squeeze bulb at one end and a nozzle at the other. Battery electrolyte is sucked into the hydrometer until the float is lifted from its seat. The specific gravity is then read by noting the position of the float. If gravity is low in one or more cells, the battery should be slowly charged and checked again to see if the gravity has come up. Generally, if after charging, the specific gravity between any two cells varies more than 50 points (0.50), the battery should be replaced, as it can no longer produce sufficient voltage to guarantee proper operation.

CABLES

▶ **See Figures 53 thru 58**

Once a year (or as necessary), the battery terminals and the cable clamps should be cleaned. Loosen the clamps and remove the cables, negative cable first. On batteries with posts on top, the use of a puller specially made for this purpose is recommended. These are inexpensive and available in most auto parts stores. Side terminal battery cables are secured with a small bolt.

Clean the cable clamps and the battery terminal with a wire brush, until all corrosion, grease, etc., is removed and the metal is shiny. It is especially important to clean the inside of the clamp thoroughly (an old knife is useful here), since a small deposit of foreign material or oxidation there will prevent a sound electrical connection and inhibit either starting or charging. Special tools are available for cleaning these parts, one type for conventional top post batteries and another type for side terminal batteries. It is also a good idea to apply some dielectric grease to the terminal, as this will aid in the prevention of corrosion.

After the clamps and terminals are clean, reinstall the cables, negative cable last; DO NOT hammer the clamps onto battery posts. Tighten the clamps securely, but do not distort them. Give the clamps and terminals a thin external coating of grease after installation, to retard corrosion.

Check the cables at the same time that the terminals are cleaned. If the cable insulation is cracked or broken, or if the ends are frayed, the cable should be replaced with a new cable of the same length and gauge.

CHARGING

✳✳ CAUTION

The chemical reaction which takes place in all batteries generates explosive hydrogen gas. A spark can cause the battery to explode and splash acid. To avoid serious personal injury, be sure there is proper ventilation and take appropriate fire safety precautions when connecting, disconnecting, or charging a battery and when using jumper cables.

A battery should be charged at a slow rate to keep the plates inside from getting too hot. However, if some maintenance-free batteries are allowed to discharge until they are almost "dead," they may have to be charged at a high rate

Fig. 53 Loosen the battery cable retaining nut . . .

Fig. 54 . . . then disconnect the cable from the battery

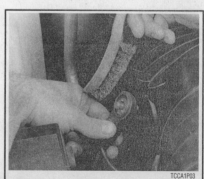

Fig. 55 A wire brush may be used to clean any corrosion or foreign material from the cable

Fig. 56 The wire brush can also be used to remove any corrosion or dirt from the battery terminal

Fig. 57 The battery terminal can also be cleaned using a solution of baking soda and water

Fig. 58 Before connecting the cables, it's a good idea to coat the terminals with a small amount of dielectric grease

to bring them back to "life." Always follow the charger manufacturer's instructions on charging the battery.

REPLACEMENT

When it becomes necessary to replace the battery, select one with an amperage rating equal to or greater than the battery originally installed. Deterioration and just plain aging of the battery cables, starter motor, and associated wires makes the battery's job harder in successive years. The slow increase in electrical resistance over time makes it prudent to install a new battery with a greater capacity than the old.

Belts

INSPECTION

▶ See Figures 59, 60, 61, 62 and 63

Inspect the belts for signs of glazing or cracking. A glazed belt will be perfectly smooth from slippage, while a good belt will have a slight texture of fabric

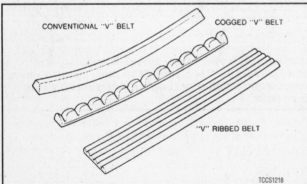

CONVENTIONAL "V" BELT   COGGED "V" BELT

"V" RIBBED BELT

TCCS1218

Fig. 59 There are typically 3 types of accessory drive belts found on vehicles today

visible. Cracks will usually start at the inner edge of the belt and run outward. All worn or damaged drive belts should be replaced immediately. It is best to replace all drive belts at one time, as a preventive maintenance measure, during this service operation.

ADJUSTMENT

▶ See Figure 64

Serpentine belts are automatically tensioned by a system of idler and tensioner pulleys, thus require no adjustment. The serpentine belt tension can be checked by simply observing the belt acceptable belt wear range indicator located on the tensioner spindle. If the belt does not meet the specified range, it must be replaced.

➡ **A belt is considered used after 15 minutes of operation.**

REMOVAL & INSTALLATION

▶ See Figures 65 thru 70

1. On 1994–97 2.2L engines and 1994–96 4.3L engines, using a ½ in. breaker bar and if necessary, with a socket placed on the tensioner pulley bolt, rotate the tensioner counterclockwise to relieve the belt tension. On some 2.2L engines it may be easier to attach the breaker bar to the tensioner arm from under the vehicle.
2. On 1998–99 2.2L engines and 1997–99 4.3L engines, using a ⅜ in. breaker bar, rotate the tensioner counterclockwise to relieve the belt tension. On some 2.2L engines it may be easier to attach the breaker bar to the tensioner arm from under the vehicle.
3. Remove the serpentine belt.
   To install:
4. Route the belt over all the pulleys except the tensioner.
5. Place the breaker bar and if necessary the socket, on the tensioner pulley bolt and rotate the tensioner counterclockwise to the released position.
6. Install the belt and return the pulley slowly to its original position. Do not let the pulley snap back into position as this may damage the belt and pulley.
7. Check that the belt is properly seated in each pulley.

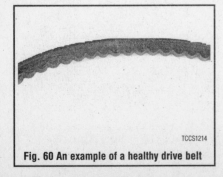

TCCS1214

Fig. 60 An example of a healthy drive belt

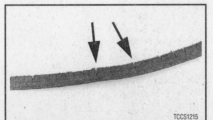

TCCS1215

Fig. 61 Deep cracks in this belt will cause flex, building up heat that will eventually lead to belt failure

TCCS1216

Fig. 62 The cover of this belt is worn, exposing the critical reinforcing cords to excessive wear

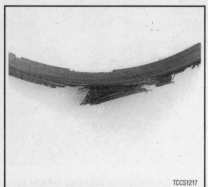

Fig. 63 Installing too wide a belt can result in serious belt wear and/or breakage

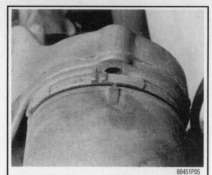

Fig. 64 Check the belt tension by simply observing the range indicator located on the tensioner spindle

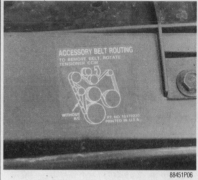

Fig. 65 A decal showing the belt routing may sometimes be found under the hood

Fig. 66 Relieve the belt tension and remove the belt—1994 4.3L model shown

Fig. 67 On some 2.2L engines it may be easier to attach the breaker bar to the tensioner arm from under the vehicle to relieve belt tension

Fig. 68 Relieve the belt tension and remove the belt—1996 4.3L model shown

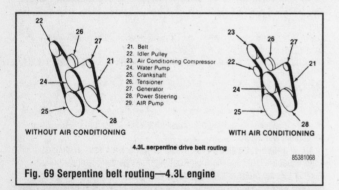

21. Belt
22. Idler Pulley
23. Air Conditioning Compressor
24. Water Pump
25. Crankshaft
26. Tensioner
27. Generator
28. Power Steering
29. AIR Pump

WITHOUT AIR CONDITIONING
WITH AIR CONDITIONING

4.3L serpentine drive belt routing

Fig. 69 Serpentine belt routing—4.3L engine

Hoses

INSPECTION

▶ See Figures 71, 72, 73 and 74

Upper and lower radiator hoses, along with the heater hoses, should be checked for deterioration, leaks and loose hose clamps at least every 15,000 miles (24,000 km). It is also wise to check the hoses periodically in early spring and at the beginning of the fall or winter when you are performing other maintenance. A quick visual inspection could discover a weakened hose which might have left you stranded if it had remained unrepaired.

Whenever you are checking the hoses, make sure the engine and cooling system are cold. Visually inspect for cracking, rotting or collapsed hoses, and replace as necessary. Run your hand along the length of the hose. If a weak or swollen spot is noted when squeezing the hose wall, the hose should be replaced.

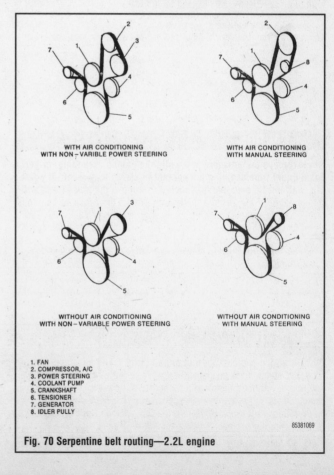

WITH AIR CONDITIONING
WITH NON-VARIBLE POWER STEERING

WITH AIR CONDITIONING
WITH MANUAL STEERING

WITHOUT AIR CONDITIONING
WITH NON-VARIBLE POWER STEERING

WITHOUT AIR CONDITIONING
WITH MANUAL STEERING

1. FAN
2. COMPRESSOR, A/C
3. POWER STEERING
4. COOLANT PUMP
5. CRANKSHAFT
6. TENSIONER
7. GENERATOR
8. IDLER PULLY

Fig. 70 Serpentine belt routing—2.2L engine

Fig. 71 The cracks developing along this hose are a result of age-related hardening

Fig. 72 A hose clamp that is too tight can cause older hoses to separate and tear on either side of the clamp

Fig. 73 A soft spongy hose (identifiable by the swollen section) will eventually burst and should be replaced

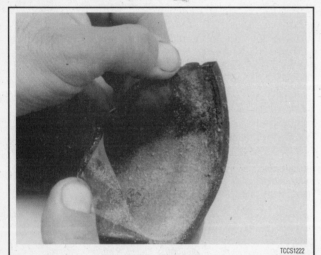

Fig. 74 Hoses are likely to deteriorate from the inside if the cooling system is not periodically flushed

REMOVAL & INSTALLATION

1. Remove the radiator pressure cap.

✶✶ CAUTION

Never remove the pressure cap while the engine is running, or personal injury from scalding hot coolant or steam may result. If possible, wait until the engine has cooled to remove the pressure cap. If this is not possible, wrap a thick cloth around the pressure cap and turn it slowly to the stop. Step back while the pressure is released from the cooling system. When you are sure all the pressure has been released, use the cloth to turn and remove the cap.

2. Position a clean container under the radiator and/or engine draincock or plug, then open the drain and allow the cooling system to drain to an appropriate level. For some upper hoses, only a little coolant must be drained. To remove hoses positioned lower on the engine, such as a lower radiator hose, the entire cooling system must be emptied.

✶✶ CAUTION

When draining coolant, keep in mind that cats and dogs are attracted by ethylene glycol antifreeze, and are quite likely to drink any that is left in an uncovered container or in puddles on the ground. This will prove fatal in sufficient quantity. Always drain coolant into a sealable container. Coolant may be reused unless it is contaminated or several years old.

3. Loosen the hose clamps at each end of the hose requiring replacement. Clamps are usually either of the spring tension type (which require pliers to squeeze the tabs and loosen) or of the screw tension type (which require screw or hex drivers to loosen). Pull the clamps back on the hose away from the connection.

4. Twist, pull and slide the hose off the fitting, taking care not to damage the neck of the component from which the hose is being removed.

➡If the hose is stuck at the connection, do not try to insert a screwdriver or other sharp tool under the hose end in an effort to free it, as the connection and/or hose may become damaged. Heater connections especially may be easily damaged by such a procedure. If the hose is to be replaced, use a single-edged razor blade to make a slice along the portion of the hose which is stuck on the connection, perpendicular to the end of the hose. Do not cut deep so as to prevent damaging the connection. The hose can then be peeled from the connection and discarded.

5. Clean both hose mounting connections. Inspect the condition of the hose clamps and replace them, if necessary.

To install:

6. Dip the ends of the new hose into clean engine coolant to ease installation.

7. Slide the clamps over the replacement hose, then slide the hose ends over the connections into position.

8. Position and secure the clamps at least ¼ in. (6.35mm) from the ends of the hose. Make sure they are located beyond the raised bead of the connector.

9. Close the radiator or engine drains and properly refill the cooling system with the clean drained engine coolant or a suitable mixture of ethylene glycol coolant and water.

10. If available, install a pressure tester and check for leaks. If a pressure tester is not available, run the engine until normal operating temperature is reached (allowing the system to naturally pressurize), then check for leaks.

✶✶ CAUTION

If you are checking for leaks with the system at normal operating temperature, BE EXTREMELY CAREFUL not to touch any moving or hot engine parts. Once temperature has been reached, shut the engine OFF, and check for leaks around the hose fittings and connections which were removed earlier.

CV-Boots

INSPECTION

▶ See Figures 75 and 76

The CV (Constant Velocity) boots should be checked for damage each time the oil is changed and any other time the vehicle is raised for service. These boots keep water, grime, dirt and other damaging matter from entering the CV-joints. Any of these could cause early CV-joint failure which can be expensive to repair. Heavy grease thrown around the inside of the front wheel(s) and on the brake caliper/drum can be an indication of a torn boot. Thoroughly check the boots for missing clamps and tears. If the boot is damaged, it should be replaced immediately. Please refer to Section 7 for procedures.

Spark Plugs

▶ **See Figure 77**

A typical spark plug consists of a metal shell surrounding a ceramic insulator. A metal electrode extends downward through the center of the insulator and protrudes a small distance. Located at the end of the plug and attached to the side of the outer metal shell is the side electrode. The side electrode bends in at a 90° angle so that its tip is just past and parallel to the tip of the center electrode. The distance between these two electrodes (measured in thousandths of an inch or hundredths of a millimeter) is called the spark plug gap.

The spark plug does not produce a spark, but instead provides a gap across which the current can arc. The coil produces anywhere from 20,000 to 50,000 volts (depending on the type and application) which travels through the wires to the spark plugs. The current passes along the center electrode and jumps the gap to the side electrode, and in doing so, ignites the air/fuel mixture in the combustion chamber.

SPARK PLUG HEAT RANGE

▶ **See Figure 78**

Spark plug heat range is the ability of the plug to dissipate heat. The longer the insulator (or the farther it extends into the engine), the hotter the plug will operate; the shorter the insulator (the closer the electrode is to the block's cooling passages) the cooler it will operate. A plug that absorbs little heat and remains too cool will quickly accumulate deposits of oil and carbon since it is not hot enough to burn them off. This leads to plug fouling and consequently to misfiring. A plug that absorbs too much heat will have no deposits but, due to the excessive heat, the electrodes will burn away quickly and might possibly

km). As the gap increases, the plug's voltage requirement also increases. It requires a greater voltage to jump the wider gap and about two to three times as much voltage to fire the plug at high speeds than at idle. The improved air/fuel ratio control of modern fuel injection combined with the higher voltage output of modern ignition systems will often allow an engine to run significantly longer on a set of standard spark plugs, but keep in mind that efficiency will drop as the gap widens (along with fuel economy and power).

When you're removing spark plugs, work on one at a time. Don't start by removing the plug wires all at once, because, unless you number them, they may become mixed up. Take a minute before you begin and number the wires with tape.

1. Disconnect the negative battery cable, and if the vehicle has been run recently, allow the engine to thoroughly cool.

2. Carefully twist the spark plug wire boot to loosen it, then pull upward and remove the boot from the plug. Be sure to pull on the boot and not on the wire, otherwise the connector located inside the boot may become separated.

3. Using compressed air, blow any water or debris from the spark plug well to assure that no harmful contaminants are allowed to enter the combustion chamber when the spark plug is removed. If compressed air is not available, use a rag or a brush to clean the area.

➡ **Remove the spark plugs when the engine is cold, if possible, to prevent damage to the threads. If removal of the plugs is difficult, apply a few drops of penetrating oil or silicone spray to the area around the base of the plug, and allow it a few minutes to work.**

4. Using a spark plug socket that is equipped with a rubber insert to properly hold the plug, turn the spark plug counterclockwise to loosen and remove the spark plug from the bore.

✳✳ WARNING

Be sure not to use a flexible extension on the socket. Use of a flexible extension may allow a shear force to be applied to the plug. A shear force could break the plug off in the cylinder head, leading to costly and frustrating repairs.

Fig. 75 CV-boots must be inspected periodically for damage

Fig. 76 A torn boot should be replaced immediately

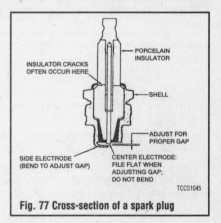

Fig. 77 Cross-section of a spark plug

lead to preignition or other ignition problems. Preignition takes place when plug tips get so hot that they glow sufficiently to ignite the air/fuel mixture before the actual spark occurs. This early ignition will usually cause a pinging during low speeds and heavy loads.

The general rule of thumb for choosing the correct heat range when picking a spark plug is: if most of your driving is long distance, high speed travel, use a colder plug; if most of your driving is stop and go, use a hotter plug. Original equipment plugs are generally a good compromise between the 2 styles and most people never have the need to change their plugs from the factory-recommended heat range.

REMOVAL & INSTALLATION

▶ **See Figures 79, 80 and 81**

A set of spark plugs usually requires replacement after about 20,000–30,000 miles (32,000–48,000 km), depending on your style of driving. In normal operation plug gap increases about 0.001 in (0.025 mm) for every 2500 miles (4000

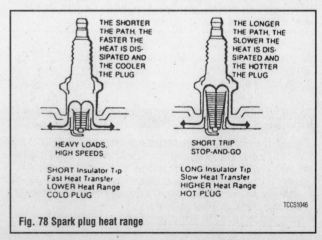

Fig. 78 Spark plug heat range

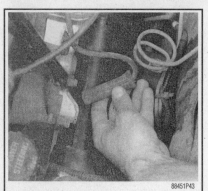

Fig. 79 Remove the spark plug wire by pulling on the boot

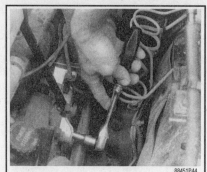

Fig. 80 Using a spark plug socket with a rubber insert, turn the plug counterclockwise to loosen it

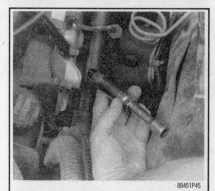

Fig. 81 Remove the spark plug from the bore

To install:

5. Inspect the spark plug boot for tears or damage. If a damaged boot is found, the spark plug wire must be replaced.

6. Using a wire feeler gauge, check and adjust the spark plug gap. When using a gauge, the proper size should pass between the electrodes with a slight drag. The next larger size should not be able to pass while the next smaller size should pass freely.

7. Carefully thread the plug into the bore by hand. If resistance is felt before the plug is almost completely threaded, back the plug out and begin threading again. In small, hard to reach areas, an old spark plug wire and boot could be used as a threading tool. The boot will hold the plug while you twist the end of the wire and the wire is supple enough to twist before it would allow the plug to crossthread.

✳ WARNING

Do not use the spark plug socket to thread the plugs. Always carefully thread the plug by hand or using an old plug wire to prevent the possibility of crossthreading and damaging the cylinder head bore.

8. Carefully tighten the spark plug. If the plug you are installing is equipped with a crush washer, seat the plug, then tighten about ¼ turn to crush the washer. If you are installing a tapered seat plug, tighten the plug to specifications provided by the vehicle or plug manufacturer.

9. Apply a small amount of silicone dielectric compound to the end of the spark plug lead or inside the spark plug boot to prevent sticking, then install the boot to the spark plug and push until it clicks into place. The click may be felt or heard, then gently pull back on the boot to assure proper contact.

INSPECTION & GAPPING

▶ **See Figures 82, 83, 84, 85 and 86**

Check the plugs for deposits and wear. If they are not going to be replaced, clean the plugs thoroughly. Remember that any kind of deposit will decrease the efficiency of the plug. Plugs can be cleaned on a spark plug cleaning machine, which can sometimes be found in service stations, or you can do an acceptable job of cleaning with a stiff brush. If the plugs are cleaned, the electrodes must be filed flat. Use an ignition points file, not an emery board or the like, which will leave deposits. The electrodes must be filed perfectly flat with sharp edges; rounded edges reduce the spark plug voltage by as much as 50%.

A **normally worn** spark plug should have light tan or gray deposits on the firing tip.

A **physically damaged** spark plug may be evidence of severe detonation in that cylinder. Watch that cylinder carefully between services, as a continued detonation will not only damage the plug, but could also damage the engine.

An **oil fouled** spark plug indicates an engine with worn poston rings and/or bad valve seals allowing excessive oil to enter the chamber.

This spark plug has been **left in the engine too long,** as evidenced by the extreme gap- Plugs with such an extreme gap can cause misfiring and stumbling accompanied by a noticeable lack of power.

A **carbon fouled** plug, identified by soft, sooty, black deposits, may indicate an improperly tuned vehicle. Check the air cleaner, ignition components and engine control system.

A **bridged or almost bridged** spark plug, identified by a build-up between the electrodes caused by excessive carbon or oil build-up on the plug.

Fig. 82 Inspect the spark plug to determine engine running conditions

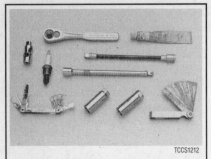

Fig. 83 A variety of tools and gauges are needed for spark plug service

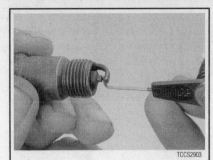

Fig. 84 Checking the spark plug gap with a feeler gauge

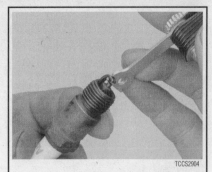

Fig. 85 Adjusting the spark plug gap

Check spark plug gap before installation. The ground electrode (the L-shaped one connected to the body of the plug) must be parallel to the center electrode and the specified size wire gauge (please refer to the Tune-Up Specifications chart for details) must pass between the electrodes with a slight drag.

→**NEVER adjust the gap on a used platinum type spark plug.**

Always check the gap on new plugs as they are not always set correctly at the factory. Do not use a flat feeler gauge when measuring the gap on a used plug, because the reading may be inaccurate. A round-wire type gapping tool is the best way to check the gap. The correct gauge should pass through the electrode gap with a slight drag. If you're in doubt, try one size smaller and one larger. The smaller gauge should go through easily, while the larger one shouldn't go through at all. Wire gapping tools usually have a bending tool attached. Use that to adjust the side electrode until the proper distance is obtained. Absolutely never attempt to bend the center electrode. Also, be careful not to bend the side electrode too far or too often as it may weaken and break off within the engine, requiring removal of the cylinder head to retrieve it.

Spark Plug Wires

TESTING

♦ **See Figure 87**

At every tune-up/inspection, visually check the spark plug cables for burns cuts, or breaks in the insulation. Check the boots and the nipples on the distributor cap and/or coil. Replace any damaged wiring.

Every 50,000 miles (80,000 Km) or 60 months, the resistance of the wires should be checked with an ohmmeter. Wires with excessive resistance will cause misfiring, and may make the engine difficult to start in damp weather.

To check resistance on models with a distributor:

1. Remove the distributor cap, leaving the wires in place.
2. Connect one lead of an ohmmeter to an electrode within the cap.
3. Connect the other lead to the corresponding spark plug terminal (remove it from the spark plug for this test).

4. Replace any wire which shows a resistance over 30,000 ohms. Generally speaking, however, resistance should not be over 25,000 ohms, and 30,000 ohms must be considered the outer limit of acceptability.

It should be remembered that resistance is also a function of length. The longer the wire, the greater the resistance. Thus, if the wires on your truck are longer than the factory originals, the resistance will be higher, possibly outside these limits.

To check resistance on models with a distributor:

5. Tag the wires, then remove the wires one at a time from the spark plug and the coil pack. To access the wires at the coil pack, raise the front passenger side of the vehicle, support it with jackstands and remove the passenger side tire. The coil pack and wires can now be reached through the opening in the wheel well.
6. Connect one lead of an ohmmeter to one end of the wire and the other lead to the other end of the wire.
7. Replace any wire which shows a resistance over 30,000 ohms. Generally speaking, however, resistance should not be over 25,000 ohms, and 30,000 ohms must be considered the outer limit of acceptability.

It should be remembered that resistance is also a function of length. The longer the wire, the greater the resistance. Thus, if the wires on your truck are longer than the factory originals, the resistance will be higher, possibly outside these limits.

REMOVAL & INSTALLATION

♦ **See Figures 88 and 89**

When installing new wires, replace them one at a time to avoid mix-ups. Start by replacing the longest one first.

1. Remove the spark plug wire by gripping the boot firmly and disengaging the wire from the spark plug and the distributor or coil pack. To access the wires at the coil pack, raise the front passenger side of the vehicle, support it with jackstands and remove the passenger side tire. The coil pack and wires can now be reached through the opening in the wheel well.
2. Install the boot of the new wire firmly over the spark plug. Route the wire over the same path as the original.

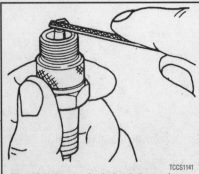

Fig. 86 If the standard plug is in good condition, the electrode may be filed flat—WARNING: do not file platinum plugs

Fig. 87 Checking individual plug wire resistance with a digital ohmmeter

Fig. 88 Removing the spark plug boot from models equipped with a distributor

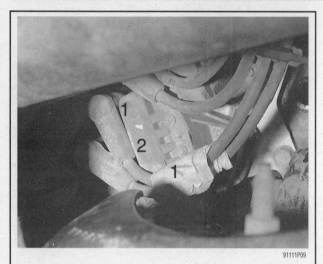

Fig. 89 Mark the spark plug wire and coil pack prior to disconnecting the wire, this will make installation easier—models equipped with a distributorless ignition system

Distributor Cap and Rotor

REMOVAL & INSTALLATION

Except Models Equipped With The HVS System

▶ See Figures 90, 91 and 92

1. Tag and remove the spark plug wires.
2. Loosen the cap retaining fasteners and remove the cap.
3. Remove the rotor from the distributor shaft.
4. Installation is the reverse of removal.

Models Equipped With The HVS System

▶ See Figure 93

➡It is advisable to discard the old distributor cap screws when you remove the distributor cap and replace them wit new screws when re-installing the cap.

1. Tag and disconnect the spark plug wires from the distributor.
2. Unfasten the distributor cap retaining screws and remove the cap.

➡Mark the rotor mounting hole locations before unfastening the screws and removing the rotor. If the rotor is installed in the wrong mounting holes a no start condition may occur.

3. Using a grease pencil, mark the location of the rotor mounting holes.
4. Unfasten the rotor retaining screws and remove the rotor.

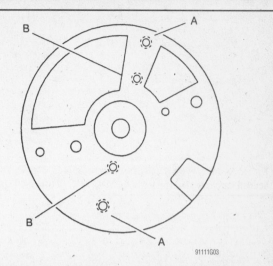

Fig. 93 The rotor mounting holes should be marked before disassembly. A indicates the mounting holes and B indicates the locating holes

To install:

5. Install the rotor making sure to align the rotor screw holes with the marks made earlier to indicate the location of the mounting.
6. Once the rotor is in position, tighten the rotor retaining screws.
7. Place the distributor cap into position and tighten its retaining screws.
8. Attach the spark plug wires to the distributor cap.
9. Start the engine and check for proper operation.

INSPECTION

1. Remove the distributor cap and rotor as described in this section.
2. Check the cap for wear, electrode cracks or damage. Replace if defective.
3. Check the rotor for cracks and wear. Replace if defective.

Ignition Timing

GENERAL INFORMATION

Ignition timing is the measurement, in degrees of crankshaft rotation, of the point at which the spark plugs fire in each of the cylinders. It is measured in degrees before or after Top Dead Center (TDC) of the compression stroke.

Because it takes a fraction of a second for the spark plug to ignite the mixture in the cylinder, the spark plug must fire a little before the piston reaches TDC. Otherwise, the mixture will not be completely ignited as the piston passes TDC and the full power of the explosion will not be used by the engine.

The timing measurement is given in degrees of crankshaft rotation before the piston reaches TDC (BTDC). If the setting for the ignition timing is 5° BTDC,

Fig. 90 Loosen the distributor cap retaining fasteners

Fig. 91 Remove the distributor cap

Fig. 92 Remove the rotor from the distributor shaft

the spark plug must fire 5° before each piston reaches TDC. This only holds true, however, when the engine is at idle speed.

As the engine speed increases, the pistons go faster. The spark plugs have to ignite the fuel even sooner if it is to be completely ignited when the piston reaches TDC. The Electronic Spark Timing (EST) system makes all timing changes electronically based on signals from various sensors. The 1994–97 2.2L engine and 1996–97 4.3L engine uses a distributorless Electronic Ignition (EI) system. Operation of the EI system allows for fully electronic control of the timing.

If the ignition is set too far advanced (BTDC), the ignition and expansion of the fuel in the cylinder will occur too soon and tend to force the piston down while it is still traveling up. This causes engine ping. If the ignition spark is set too far retarded, after TDC (ATDC), the piston will have already passed TDC and started on its way down when the fuel is ignited. This will cause the piston to be forced down for only a portion of its travel. This will result in poor engine performance and lack of power.

Timing marks consist of a notch on the rim of the crankshaft pulley and a scale of degrees attached to the front of the engine (often on the engine front cover). The notch corresponds to the position of the piston in the number 1 cylinder. A stroboscopic (dynamic) timing light is used, which is hooked into the circuit of the No. 1 cylinder spark plug. Every time the spark plug fires, the timing light flashes. By aiming the timing light at the timing marks while the engine is running, the exact position of the piston within the cylinder can be easily read since the stroboscopic flash makes the mark on the pulley appear to be standing still. Proper timing is indicated when the notch is aligned with the correct number on the scale.

➡Never pierce a spark plug wire in order to attach a timing light or perform tests. The pierced insulation will eventually lead to an electrical arc and related ignition troubles.

INSPECTION & ADJUSTMENT

Electronic Ignition (EI) Systems

2.2L ENGINES

On vehicles equipped with this system, the ignition timing is controlled by the Powertrain Control Module (PCM). No adjustment is possible or necessary.

Distributor Ignition (DI) Systems

4.3L ENGINES—1995 (VIN W) MODELS

➡Refer to the underhood label for the proper timing setting.

1. Engage the parking brake, block the wheels and set the transmission in P.
2. Disconnect the Ignition Control (IC) system by disengaging the "set timing connector". This is a single wire sealed connector that has a tan with black stripe lead. This wire comes out of the wiring harness below the heater case.
3. With the ignition switch **OFF**, connect the timing light pickup lead to the No. 1 spark plug wire.
4. Start the engine and point the timing light at the timing mark on the balancer or pulley and check the timing.
5. If the timing is not within specifications (0° Before Top Dead Center), loosen the distributor hold-down bolt. Slowly rotate the distributor until the proper timing setting is achieved.
6. Tighten the hold-down bolt and recheck the timing.
7. Turn the ignition **OFF**, remove the timing light and engage the "set timing" connector.

4.3L ENGINES—1996–99 MODELS

The ignition timing is preset and cannot be adjusted. If the distributor position is moved crossfiring may be induced.

Valve Lash

ADJUSTMENT

2.2L (VIN 4) Engine

This engine utilizes hydraulic valve lifters which means that a valve adjustment is NOT a regular maintenance item.

4.3L Engine

The 4.3L engines may be equipped with either of 2 rocker arm retaining systems. If your engine utilizes screw-in type rocker arm studs with positive stop shoulders, no valve lash adjustment is necessary or possible. If however, you engine utilizes the pressed-in rocker arm studs, use the following procedure to tighten the rocker arm nuts and properly center the pushrod on the hydraulic lifter:

1. To prepare the engine for valve adjustment, rotate the crankshaft until the mark on the damper pulley aligns with the 0° mark on the timing plate and the No. 1 cylinder is on the compression stroke. You will know when the No. 1 piston is on it's compression stroke because both the intake and exhaust valves will remain closed as the crankshaft damper mark approaches the timing scale.

➡Another method to tell when the piston is coming up on the compression stroke is by removing the spark plug and placing your thumb over the hole, you will feel the air being forced out of the spark plug hole. Stop turning the crankshaft when the TDC timing mark on the crankshaft pulley is directly aligned with the timing mark pointer or the zero mark on the scale.

The valve arrangement is as follows:
- E—I—I—E—I—E (right bank—front-to-rear)
- E—I—E—I—I—E (left bank—front-to-rear)

2. With the engine on the compression stroke, adjust the exhaust valves of cylinders No. 1, 5 & 6 and the intake valves of cylinders No. 1, 2 & 3 by performing the following procedures:
   a. Back out the adjusting nut until lash can be felt at the pushrod.
   b. While rotating the pushrod, turn the adjusting nut inward until all of the lash is removed.
   c. When the play has disappeared, turn the adjusting nut inward 1¾ additional turns.
3. Rotate the crankshaft one complete revolution and align the mark on the damper pulley with the 0° mark on the timing plate; the engine is now positioned on the No. 4 firing position. This time the No. 4 cylinder valves remain closed as the timing mark approaches the scale. Adjust the exhaust valves of cylinders No. 2, 3 & 4 and the intake valves of cylinders No. 4, 5 & 6, by performing the following procedures:
   a. Back out the adjusting nut until lash can be felt at the pushrod.
   b. While rotating the pushrod, turn the adjusting nut inward until all of the lash is removed.
   c. When the play has disappeared, turn the adjusting nut inward 1¾ additional turn.
4. Install the remaining components, then start the engine and check for oil leaks.

Idle Speed and Mixture Adjustments

These vehicles are controlled by a computer which supplies the correct amount of fuel during all engine operating conditions and controls idle speed; no adjustment is necessary or possible.

Air Conditioning System

SYSTEM SERVICE & REPAIR

➡It is recommended that the A/C system be serviced by an EPA Section 609 certified automotive technician utilizing a refrigerant recovery/recycling machine.

The do-it-yourselfer should not service his/her own vehicle's A/C system for many reasons, including legal concerns, personal injury, environmental damage and cost. The following are some of the reasons why you may decide not to service your own vehicle's A/C system.

According to the U.S. Clean Air Act, it is a federal crime to service or repair (involving the refrigerant) a Motor Vehicle Air Conditioning (MVAC) system for money without being EPA certified. It is also illegal to vent R-12 and R-134a refrigerants into the atmosphere. Selling or distributing A/C system refrigerant (in a container which contains less than 20 pounds of refrigerant) to any person who is not EPA 609 certified is also not allowed by law.

ENGINE TUNE-UP SPECIFICATIONS

Year	Engine ID/VIN	Engine Displacement Liters (cc)	Spark Plugs Gap (in.)	Ignition Timing (deg.) MT	Ignition Timing (deg.) AT	Fuel Pump (psi)	Idle Speed (rpm) MT	Idle Speed (rpm) AT	Valve Clearance In.	Valve Clearance Ex.
1994	4	2.2 (2189)	0.060	①	①	41-47 ⑤	⑥	⑥	HYD	HYD
	W	4.3 (4293)	0.035	②	②	55-61 ⑤	⑥	⑥	HYD	HYD
	Z	4.3 (4293)	0.035	②	②	9-13 ⑤	⑥	⑥	HYD	HYD
1995	4	2.2 (2189)	0.060	①	①	41-47 ⑤	⑥	⑥	HYD	HYD
	W	4.3 (4293)	0.035	③	③	58-64 ⑤	⑥	⑥	HYD	HYD
	Z	4.3 (4293)	0.035	④	④	9-13 ⑤	⑥	⑥	HYD	HYD
1996	4	2.2 (2189)	0.060	①	①	41-47 ⑤	⑥	⑥	HYD	HYD
	W	4.3 (4293)	0.045	③	③	60-66 ⑤	⑥	⑥	HYD	HYD
	X	4.3 (4293)	0.045	③	③	60-66 ⑤	⑥	⑥	HYD	HYD
1997	4	2.2 (2189)	0.060	①	①	41-47 ⑤	⑥	⑥	HYD	HYD
	W	4.3 (4293)	0.045	③	③	60-66 ⑤	⑥	⑥	HYD	HYD
	X	4.3 (4293)	0.045	③	③	60-66 ⑤	⑥	⑥	HYD	HYD
1998	4	2.2 (2189)	0.060	①	①	41-47 ⑤	⑥	⑥	HYD	HYD
	W	4.3 (4293)	0.045	③	③	60-66 ⑤	⑥	⑥	HYD	HYD
	X	4.3 (4293)	0.045	③	③	60-66 ⑤	⑥	⑥	HYD	HYD
1999	4	2.2 (2189)	0.060	①	①	41-47 ⑤	⑥	⑥	HYD	HYD
	W	4.3 (4293)	0.045	③	③	60-66 ⑤	⑥	⑥	HYD	HYD
	X	4.3 (4293)	0.045	③	③	60-66 ⑤	⑥	⑥	HYD	HYD

NOTE: The Vehicle Emission Control Information label often reflects specification changes made during production. The label figures must be used if they differ from those in this chart.

① Distributorless ignition, no adjustment possible

② 0° disconnect set timing connector (tan with black striped wire taped to engine harness near distributor)

③ Ignition timing is preset and cannot be adjusted

④ Refer to the underhood label for the exact setting

⑤ With key **ON** and engine **OFF**

⑥ Idle speed is computer controlled. No adjustments are necessary or possible

91111C03

State and/or local laws may be more strict than the federal regulations, so be sure to check with your state and/or local authorities for further information. For further federal information on the legality of servicing your A/C system, call the EPA Stratospheric Ozone Hotline.

➡**Federal law dictates that a fine of up to $25,000 may be levied on people convicted of venting refrigerant into the atmosphere. Additionally, the EPA may pay up to $10,000 for information or services leading to a criminal conviction of the violation of these laws.**

When servicing an A/C system you run the risk of handling or coming in contact with refrigerant, which may result in skin or eye irritation or frostbite. Although low in toxicity (due to chemical stability), inhalation of concentrated refrigerant fumes is dangerous and can result in death; cases of fatal cardiac arrhythmia have been reported in people accidentally subjected to high levels of refrigerant. Some early symptoms include loss of concentration and drowsiness.

➡**Generally, the limit for exposure is lower for R-134a than it is for R-12. Exceptional care must be practiced when handling R-134a.**

Also, refrigerants can decompose at high temperatures (near gas heaters or open flame), which may result in hydrofluoric acid, hydrochloric acid and phosgene (a fatal nerve gas).

R-12 refrigerant can damage the environment because it is a Chlorofluorocarbon (CFC), which has been proven to add to ozone layer depletion, leading to increasing levels of UV radiation. UV radiation has been linked with an increase in skin cancer, suppression of the human immune system, an increase in cataracts, damage to crops, damage to aquatic organisms, an increase in ground-level ozone, and increased global warming.

R-134a refrigerant is a greenhouse gas which, if allowed to vent into the atmosphere, will contribute to global warming (the Greenhouse Effect).

It is usually more economically feasible to have a certified MVAC automotive technician perform A/C system service on your vehicle. Some possible reasons for this are as follows:

• While it is illegal to service an A/C system without the proper equipment, the home mechanic would have to purchase an expensive refrigerant recovery/recycling machine to service his/her own vehicle.

• Since only a certified person may purchase refrigerant—according to the Clean Air Act, there are specific restrictions on selling or distributing A/C system refrigerant—it is legally impossible (unless certified) for the home mechanic to service his/her own vehicle. Procuring refrigerant in an illegal fashion exposes one to the risk of paying a $25,000 fine to the EPA.

R-12 Refrigerant Conversion

If your vehicle still uses R-12 refrigerant, one way to save A/C system costs down the road is to investigate the possibility of having your system converted to R-134a. The older R-12 systems can be easily converted to R-134a refrigerant by a certified automotive technician by installing a few new components and changing the system oil.

The cost of R-12 is steadily rising and will continue to increase, because it is no longer imported or manufactured in the United States. Therefore, it is often possible to have an R-12 system converted to R-134a and recharged for less than it would cost to just charge the system with R-12.

If you are interested in having your system converted, contact local automotive service stations for more details and information.

PREVENTIVE MAINTENANCE

▶ **See Figures 94 and 95**

Although the A/C system should not be serviced by the do-it-yourselfer, preventive maintenance can be practiced and A/C system inspections can be performed to help maintain the efficiency of the vehicle's A/C system. For preventive maintenance, perform the following:

• The easiest and most important preventive maintenance for your A/C system is to be sure that it is used on a regular basis. Running the system for five minutes each month (no matter what the season) will help ensure that the seals and all internal components remain lubricated.

➡**Some newer vehicles automatically operate the A/C system compressor whenever the windshield defroster is activated. When running, the compressor lubricates the A/C system components; therefore, the A/C system would not need to be operated each month.**

• In order to prevent heater core freeze-up during A/C operation, it is necessary to maintain proper antifreeze protection. Use a hand-held coolant tester (hydrometer) to periodically check the condition of the antifreeze in your engine's cooling system.

➡**Antifreeze should not be used longer than the manufacturer specifies.**

• For efficient operation of an air conditioned vehicle's cooling system, the radiator cap should have a holding pressure which meets manufacturer's specifications. A cap which fails to hold these pressures should be replaced.

• Any obstruction of or damage to the condenser configuration will restrict air flow which is essential to its efficient operation. It is, therefore, a good rule to keep this unit clean and in proper physical shape.

➡**Bug screens which are mounted in front of the condenser (unless they are original equipment) are regarded as obstructions.**

• The condensation drain tube expels any water which accumulates on the bottom of the evaporator housing into the engine compartment. If this tube is obstructed, the air conditioning performance can be restricted and condensation buildup can spill over onto the vehicle's floor.

SYSTEM INSPECTION

▶ **See Figure 96**

Although the A/C system should not be serviced by the do-it-yourselfer, preventive maintenance can be practiced and A/C system inspections can be performed to help maintain the efficiency of the vehicle's A/C system. For A/C system inspection, perform the following:

The easiest and often most important check for the air conditioning system consists of a visual inspection of the system components. Visually inspect the air conditioning system for refrigerant leaks, damaged compressor clutch, abnormal compressor drive belt tension and/or condition, plugged evaporator drain tube, blocked condenser fins, disconnected or broken wires, blown fuses, corroded connections and poor insulation.

A refrigerant leak will usually appear as an oily residue at the leakage point in the system. The oily residue soon picks up dust or dirt particles from the sur-

rounding air and appears greasy. Through time, this will build up and appear to be a heavy dirt impregnated grease.

For a thorough visual and operational inspection, check the following:

• Check the surface of the radiator and condenser for dirt, leaves or other material which might block air flow.

• Check for kinks in hoses and lines. Check the system for leaks.

• Make sure the drive belt is properly tensioned. When the air conditioning is operating, make sure the drive belt is free of noise or slippage.

• Make sure the blower motor operates at all appropriate positions, then check for distribution of the air from all outlets with the blower on **HIGH** or **MAX**.

➡**Keep in mind that under conditions of high humidity, air discharged from the A/C vents may not feel as cold as expected, even if the system is working properly. This is because vaporized moisture in humid air retains heat more effectively than dry air, thereby making humid air more difficult to cool.**

• Make sure the air passage selection lever is operating correctly. Start the engine and warm it to normal operating temperature, then make sure the temperature selection lever is operating correctly.

Windshield Wipers

ELEMENT (REFILL) CARE & REPLACEMENT

▶ **See Figures 97, 98 and 99**

For maximum effectiveness and longest element life, the windshield and wiper blades should be kept clean. Dirt, tree sap, road tar and so on will cause streaking, smearing and blade deterioration if left on the glass. It is advisable to wash the windshield carefully with a commercial glass cleaner at least once a month. Wipe off the rubber blades with the wet rag afterwards. Do not attempt to move wipers across the windshield by hand; damage to the motor and drive mechanism will result.

To inspect and/or replace the wiper blade elements, place the wiper switch in the **LOW** speed position and the ignition switch in the **ACC** position. When the wiper blades are approximately vertical on the windshield, turn the ignition switch to **OFF**.

Examine the wiper blade elements. If they are found to be cracked, broken or torn, they should be replaced immediately. Replacement intervals will vary with usage, although ozone deterioration usually limits element life to about one year. If the wiper pattern is smeared or streaked, or if the blade chatters across the glass, the elements should be replaced. It is easiest and most sensible to replace the elements in pairs.

If your vehicle is equipped with aftermarket blades, there are several different types of refills and your vehicle might have any kind. Aftermarket blades and arms rarely use the exact same type blade or refill as the original equipment.

Regardless of the type of refill used, be sure to follow the part manufacturer's instructions closely. Make sure that all of the frame jaws are engaged as the refill is pushed into place and locked. If the metal blade holder and frame are allowed to touch the glass during wiper operation, the glass will be scratched.

Fig. 94 A coolant tester can be used to determine the freezing and boiling levels of the coolant in your vehicle

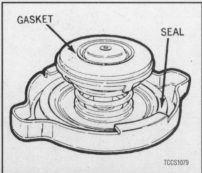

Fig. 95 To ensure efficient cooling system operation, inspect the radiator cap gasket and seal

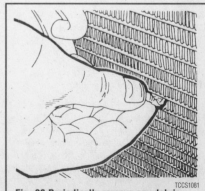

Fig. 96 Periodically remove any debris from the condenser and radiator fins

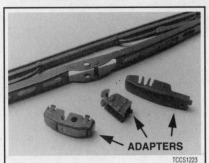

Fig. 97 Most aftermarket blades are available with multiple adapters to fit different vehicles

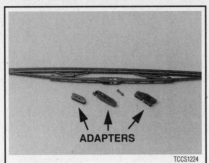

Fig. 98 Choose a blade which will fit your vehicle, and that will be readily available next time you need blades

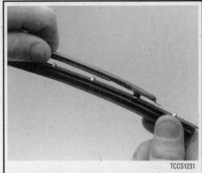

Fig. 99 When installed, be certain the blade is fully inserted into the backing

Tires and Wheels

Common sense and good driving habits will afford maximum tire life. Make sure that you don't overload the vehicle or run with incorrect pressure in the tires. Either of these will increase tread wear. Fast starts, sudden stops and sharp cornering are hard on tires and will shorten their useful life span.

➡**For optimum tire life, keep the tires properly inflated, rotate them often and have the wheel alignment checked periodically.**

Inspect your tires frequently. Be especially careful to watch for bubbles in the tread or sidewall, deep cuts or underinflation. Replace any tires with bubbles in the sidewall. If cuts are so deep that they penetrate to the cords, discard the tire. Any cut in the sidewall of a radial tire renders it unsafe. Also look for uneven tread wear patterns that may indicate the front end is out of alignment or that the tires are out of balance.

TIRE ROTATION

➧ **See Figure 100**

Tires must be rotated periodically to equalize wear patterns that vary with a tire's position on the vehicle. Tires will also wear in an uneven way as the front steering/suspension system wears to the point where the alignment should be reset.

Rotating the tires will ensure maximum life for the tires as a set, so you will not have to discard a tire early due to wear on only part of the tread. Regular rotation is required to equalize wear.

When rotating "unidirectional tires," make sure that they always roll in the same direction. This means that a tire used on the left side of the vehicle must not be switched to the right side and vice-versa. Such tires should only be rotated front-to-rear or rear-to-front, while always remaining on the same side of the vehicle. These tires are marked on the sidewall as to the direction of rotation; observe the marks when reinstalling the tire(s).

Some styled or "mag" wheels may have different offsets front to rear. In these cases, the rear wheels must not be used up front and vice-versa. Furthermore, if these wheels are equipped with unidirectional tires, they cannot be rotated unless the tire is remounted for the proper direction of rotation.

➡**The compact or space-saver spare is strictly for emergency use. It must never be included in the tire rotation or placed on the vehicle for everyday use.**

TIRE DESIGN

➧ **See Figure 101**

For maximum satisfaction, tires should be used in sets of four. Mixing of different brands or types (radial, bias-belted, fiberglass belted) should be avoided. In most cases, the vehicle manufacturer has designated a type of tire on which the vehicle will perform best. Your first choice when replacing tires should be to use the same type of tire that the manufacturer recommends.

When radial tires are used, tire sizes and wheel diameters should be selected to maintain ground clearance and tire load capacity equivalent to the original specified tire. Radial tires should always be used in sets of four.

✷✷ CAUTION

Radial tires should never be used on only the front axle.

When selecting tires, pay attention to the original size as marked on the tire. Most tires are described using an industry size code sometimes referred to as P-Metric. This allows the exact identification of the tire specifications, regardless of the manufacturer. If selecting a different tire size or brand, remember to check the installed tire for any sign of interference with the body or suspension while the vehicle is stopping, turning sharply or heavily loaded.

Snow Tires

Good radial tires can produce a big advantage in slippery weather, but in snow, a street radial tire does not have sufficient tread to provide traction and

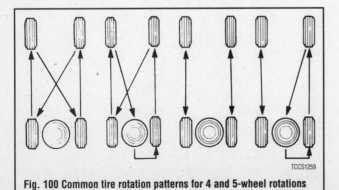

Fig. 100 Common tire rotation patterns for 4 and 5-wheel rotations

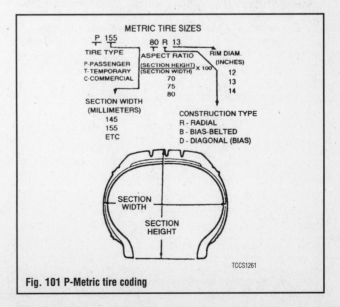

Fig. 101 P-Metric tire coding

control. The small grooves of a street tire quickly pack with snow and the tire behaves like a billiard ball on a marble floor. The more open, chunky tread of a snow tire will self-clean as the tire turns, providing much better grip on snowy surfaces.

To satisfy municipalities requiring snow tires during weather emergencies, most snow tires carry either an M + S designation after the tire size stamped on the sidewall, or the designation "all-season." In general, no change in tire size is necessary when buying snow tires.

Most manufacturers strongly recommend the use of 4 snow tires on their vehicles for reasons of stability. If snow tires are fitted only to the drive wheels, the opposite end of the vehicle may become very unstable when braking or turning on slippery surfaces. This instability can lead to unpleasant endings if the driver can't counteract the slide in time.

Note that snow tires, whether 2 or 4, will affect vehicle handling in all non-snow situations. The stiffer, heavier snow tires will noticeably change the turning and braking characteristics of the vehicle. Once the snow tires are installed, you must re-learn the behavior of the vehicle and drive accordingly.

➡**Consider buying extra wheels on which to mount the snow tires. Once done, the "snow wheels" can be installed and removed as needed. This eliminates the potential damage to tires or wheels from seasonal removal and installation. Even if your vehicle has styled wheels, see if inexpensive steel wheels are available. Although the look of the vehicle will change, the expensive wheels will be protected from salt, curb hits and pothole damage.**

TIRE STORAGE

If they are mounted on wheels, store the tires at proper inflation pressure. All tires should be kept in a cool, dry place. If they are stored in the garage or basement, do not let them stand on a concrete floor; set them on strips of wood, a mat or a large stack of newspaper. Keeping them away from direct moisture is of paramount importance. Tires should not be stored upright, but in a flat position.

INFLATION & INSPECTION

▶ **See Figures 102 thru 107**

The importance of proper tire inflation cannot be overemphasized. A tire employs air as part of its structure. It is designed around the supporting strength of the air at a specified pressure. For this reason, improper inflation drastically reduces the tire's ability to perform as intended. A tire will lose some air in day-to-day use; having to add a few pounds of air periodically is not necessarily a sign of a leaking tire.

Two items should be a permanent fixture in every glove compartment: an accurate tire pressure gauge and a tread depth gauge. Check the tire pres-

TCCS1095

Fig. 102 Tires with deep cuts, or cuts which bulge, should be replaced immediately

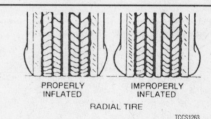

PROPERLY INFLATED   IMPROPERLY INFLATED

RADIAL TIRE

TCCS1263

Fig. 103 Radial tires have a characteristic sidewall bulge; don't try to measure pressure by looking at the tire. Use a quality air pressure gauge

sure (including the spare) regularly with a pocket type gauge. Too often, the gauge on the end of the air hose at your corner garage is not accurate because it suffers too much abuse. Always check tire pressure when the tires are cold, as pressure increases with temperature. If you must move the vehicle to check the tire inflation, do not drive more than a mile before checking. A cold tire is generally one that has not been driven for more than three hours.

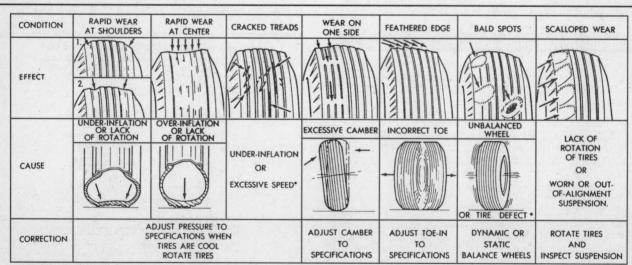

CONDITION	RAPID WEAR AT SHOULDERS	RAPID WEAR AT CENTER	CRACKED TREADS	WEAR ON ONE SIDE	FEATHERED EDGE	BALD SPOTS	SCALLOPED WEAR
EFFECT							
CAUSE	UNDER-INFLATION OR LACK OF ROTATION	OVER-INFLATION OR LACK OF ROTATION	UNDER-INFLATION OR EXCESSIVE SPEED*	EXCESSIVE CAMBER	INCORRECT TOE	UNBALANCED WHEEL OR TIRE DEFECT*	LACK OF ROTATION OF TIRES OR WORN OR OUT-OF-ALIGNMENT SUSPENSION.
CORRECTION	ADJUST PRESSURE TO SPECIFICATIONS WHEN TIRES ARE COOL ROTATE TIRES		UNDER-INFLATION OR EXCESSIVE SPEED*	ADJUST CAMBER TO SPECIFICATIONS	ADJUST TOE-IN TO SPECIFICATIONS	DYNAMIC OR STATIC BALANCE WHEELS	ROTATE TIRES AND INSPECT SUSPENSION

*HAVE TIRE INSPECTED FOR FURTHER USE.

TCCS1267

Fig. 104 Common tire wear patterns and causes

A plate or sticker is normally provided somewhere in the vehicle (door post, hood, tailgate or trunk lid) which shows the proper pressure for the tires. Never counteract excessive pressure build-up by bleeding off air pressure (letting some air out). This will cause the tire to run hotter and wear quicker.

❊❊ CAUTION

Never exceed the maximum tire pressure embossed on the tire! This is the pressure to be used when the tire is at maximum loading, but it is rarely the correct pressure for everyday driving. Consult the owner's manual or the tire pressure sticker for the correct tire pressure.

Once you've maintained the correct tire pressures for several weeks, you'll be familiar with the vehicle's braking and handling personality. Slight adjustments in tire pressures can fine-tune these characteristics, but never change the cold pressure specification by more than 2 psi. A slightly softer tire pres-

sure will give a softer ride but also yield lower fuel mileage. A slightly harder tire will give crisper dry road handling but can cause skidding on wet surfaces. Unless you're fully attuned to the vehicle, stick to the recommended inflation pressures.

All automotive tires have built-in tread wear indicator bars that show up as ½ in. (13mm) wide smooth bands across the tire when 1/16 in. (1.5mm) of tread remains. The appearance of tread wear indicators means that the tires should be replaced. In fact, many states have laws prohibiting the use of tires with less than this amount of tread.

You can check your own tread depth with an inexpensive gauge or by using a Lincoln head penny. Slip the Lincoln penny (with Lincoln's head upside-down) into several tread grooves. If you can see the top of Lincoln's head in 2 adjacent grooves, the tire has less than 1/16 in. (1.5mm) tread left and should be replaced. You can measure snow tires in the same manner by using the "tails" side of the Lincoln penny. If you can see the top of the Lincoln memorial, it's time to replace the snow tire(s).

Fig. 105 Tread wear indicators will appear when the tire is worn

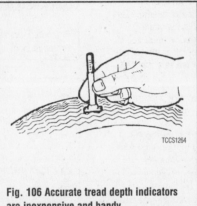

Fig. 106 Accurate tread depth indicators are inexpensive and handy

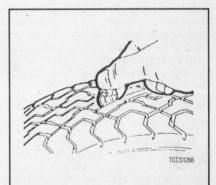

Fig. 107 A penny works well for a quick check of tread depth

FLUIDS AND LUBRICANTS

Fluid Disposal

Used fluids such as engine oil, transmission fluid, antifreeze and brake fluid are hazardous wastes and must be disposed of properly. Before draining any fluids, consult with your local authorities; in many areas, waste oil, antifreeze, etc. is being accepted as a part of recycling programs. A number of service stations and auto parts stores are also accepting waste fluids for recycling.

Be sure of the recycling center's policies before draining any fluids, as many will not accept different fluids that have been mixed together.

Fuel and Oil Recommendations

OIL

▶ See Figures 108 and 109

The Society of Automotive Engineers (SAE) grade number indicates the viscosity of the engine oil; its resistance to flow at a given temperature. The lower the SAE grade number, the lighter the oil. For example, the mono-grade oils begin with SAE 5 weight, which is a thin light oil, and continue in viscosity up to SAE 80 or 90 weight, which are heavy gear lubricants. These oils are also known as "straight weight", meaning they are of a single viscosity, and do not vary with engine temperature.

Multi-viscosity oils offer the important advantage of being adaptable to temperature extremes. These oils have designations such as 10W-40, 20W-50, etc. The 10W-40 means that in winter (the "W" in the designation) the oil acts like a thin 10 weight oil, allowing the engine to spin easily when cold and offering rapid lubrication. Once the engine has warmed up, however, the oil acts like a straight 40 weight, maintaining good lubrication and protection for the engine's internal components. A 20W-50 oil would therefore be slightly heavier than and not as ideal in cold weather as the 10W-40, but would offer better protection at higher rpm and temperatures because when warm it acts like a 50 weight oil.

Whichever oil viscosity you choose when changing the oil, make sure you are anticipating the temperatures your engine will be operating in until the oil is changed again. Refer to the oil viscosity chart for oil recommendations according to temperature.

The American Petroleum Institute (API) designation indicates the classification of engine oil used under certain given operating conditions. Only oils designated for use "Service SG" or greater should be used. Oils of the SG type perform a variety of functions inside the engine in addition to the basic function as a lubricant. Through a balanced system of metallic detergents and polymeric

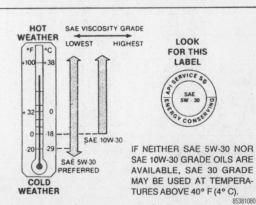

Fig. 108 Recommended SAE engine oil viscosity grades

dispersants, the oil prevents the formation of high and low temperature deposits and also keeps sludge and particles of dirt in suspension. Acids, particularly sulfuric acid, as well as other by-products of combustion, are neutralized. Both the SAE grade number and the APE designation can be found on top of the oil can.

For recommended oil viscosity's, refer to the chart. Note that 10W-30 and 10W-40 grade oils are not recommended for sustained high speed driving when the temperature rises above the indicated limit.

Synthetic Oil

There are many excellent synthetic and fuel-efficient oils currently available that can provide better gas mileage, longer service life and, in some cases, better engine protection. These benefits do not come without a few hitches, however; the main one being the price of synthetic oils, which may be more expensive than the price per quart of conventional oil.

Synthetic oil is not for every car and every type of driving, so you should consider your engine's condition and your type of driving. Also, check your car's warranty conditions regarding the use of synthetic oils.

FUEL

It is important to use fuel of the proper octane rating in your vehicle. Octane rating is based on the quantity of anti-knock compounds added to the fuel and it determines the speed at which the gas will burn. The lower the octane rating, the faster it burns. The higher the octane, the slower the fuel will burn and a greater percentage of compounds in the fuel prevent spark ping (knock), detonation and preignition (dieseling).

As the temperature of the engine increases, the air/fuel mixture exhibits a tendency to ignite before the spark plug is fired. If fuel of an octane rating too low for the engine is used, this will allow combustion to occur before the piston has completed its compression stroke, thereby creating a very high pressure very rapidly.

Fuel of the proper octane rating, for the compression ratio and ignition timing of your truck, will slow the combustion process sufficiently to allow the spark plug enough time to ignite the mixture completely and smoothly. Many non-catalyst models are designed to run on regular fuel. The use of some super-premium fuel is no substitution for a properly tuned and maintained engine. Chances are that if your engine exhibits any signs of spark ping, detonation or pre-ignition when using regular fuel, the ignition timing should be checked against specifications or the cylinder head should be removed for decarbonizing.

Most models are designed to operate using unleaded gasoline with a minimum rating of 87 octane. Use of unleaded gas with octane ratings lower than 87 can cause persistent spark knock which could lead to engine damage.

Light spark knock may be noticed when accelerating or driving up hills. The slight knocking may be considered normal (with 87 octane) because the maximum fuel economy is obtained under condition of occasional light spark knock. Gasoline with an octane rating higher than 87 may be used, but it is not necessary (in most cases) for proper operation.

If spark knock is constant, when using 87 octane, at cruising speeds on level ground, ignition timing adjustment may be required. Refer to this section for the proper procedure

➡Your engine's fuel requirement can change with time, mainly due to carbon buildup, which changes the compression ratio. If your engine pings, knocks or runs on, switch to a higher grade of fuel. Sometimes just changing brands will cure the problem. If it becomes necessary to retard the timing from specifications, don't change it more than a few degrees. Retarded timing will reduce power output and fuel mileage and will increase the engine temperature.

Engine

OIL LEVEL CHECK

◗ **See Figures 110, 111, 112 and 113**

Every time you stop for fuel, check the engine oil making sure the engine has fully warmed and the vehicle is parked on a level surface. If the truck is used for trailer towing or for heavy-duty use, it is recommended to check the oil more frequently. Because it takes a few minutes for all the oil to drain back to the oil pan, you should wait a few minutes before checking your oil. If you are doing this at a fuel stop, first fill the fuel tank, then open the hood and check the oil, but don't get so carried away as to forget to pay for the fuel. Most station attendants won't believe that you forgot.

1. Make sure the truck is parked on level ground.

2. When checking the oil level it is best for the engine to be a normal operating temperature, although checking the oil immediately after stopping will lead to a false reading. Wait a few minutes after turning off the engine to allow the oil to drain back into the crankcase.

3. Open the hood and locate the dipstick which will be in a guide tube mounted in the upper engine block, just below the cylinder head mating surface. The dipstick may be located on the right or left side of the vehicle depending upon your particular engine. Pull the dipstick from its tube, wipe it clean (using a clean, lint free rag) and then reinsert it.

4. Pull the dipstick out again and, holding it horizontally, read the oil level. The oil should be between the FULL and ADD marks on the dipstick. If the oil is below the ADD mark, add oil of the proper viscosity through the capped opening in the top of the cylinder head cover or filler tube, as applicable. See the oil and fuel recommendations listed earlier in this section for the proper viscosity and rating of oil to use.

5. Replace the dipstick and check the oil level again after adding any oil. Approximately one quart of oil will raise the level from the ADD mark to the FULL mark. Be sure not to overfill the crankcase and waste the oil. Excess oil will generally be consumed at an accelerated rate.

OIL & FILTER CHANGE

◗ **See Figures 114 thru 120**

If the vehicle is operated on a daily or semi-daily basis and most trips are for several miles (allowing the engine to properly warm-up), the oil should be changed a minimum of every 12 months or 7500 miles (12,000 Km), whichever comes first.

If however, the vehicle is used to tow a trailer, is made to idle for extended periods of time such as in heavy daily traffic or if used as a service vehicle

Fig. 109 Look for the API oil identification label when choosing your engine oil

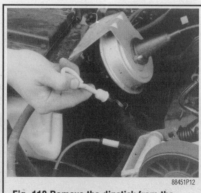

Fig. 110 Remove the dipstick from the tube, wipe it clean, then reinsert it

Fig. 111 Remove the dipstick again and, while holding it horizontally, read the oil level

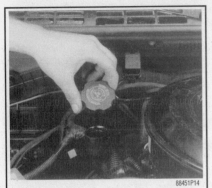

Fig. 112 If oil needs to be added, remove the oil filler cap . . .

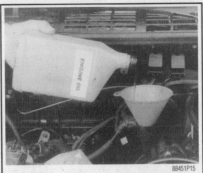

Fig. 113 . . . then using a funnel to avoid spillage, add the correct amount and grade of oil

Fig. 114 Remove the oil pan drain plug (usually a 14mm)

Fig. 115 On some early model 4.3L engines the oil filter is located behind an access panel. If this is the case, open the oil filter access panel located at the front of the vehicle

Fig. 116 Using the proper size oil filter wrench, remove the old oil filter

Fig. 117 Before installing a new oil filter, lightly coat the rubber gasket with clean oil

Fig. 118 Add the proper amount and grade of engine oil to the engine

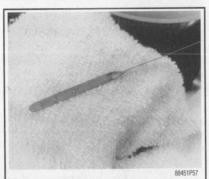

Fig. 119 After adding the oil, check the dipstick to ensure that the crankcase is filled to the proper level

Fig. 120 Remember to always replace the engine oil filler cap after adding oil

(delivery) or the vehicle is used for only short trips in below freezing temperature, the oil change interval should be shortened. Likewise, if your vehicle is used under dusty, polluted or off-road conditions, the oil should be changed more frequently. Under these circumstances oil has a greater chance of building up sludge and contaminants which could damage your engine. If your vehicle use fits into these circumstance, as most do, it is suggested that the oil and filter be changed every 3000 miles (4800 Km) or 3 months, whichever comes first.

Under certain circumstances, Chevrolet and GMC recommend changing both the oil and filter during the first oil change and then only replacing the filter every other oil change thereafter. For the small price of an oil filter, it's cheap insurance to replace the filter at every oil change. One of the larger filter manufacturers points out in its advertisements that not changing the filter leaves one quart of dirty oil in the engine. This claim is true and should be kept in mind when changing your oil.

Oil should always be changed after the engine has been running long enough to bring it up to normal operating temperature. Hot oil will flow easier and more contaminants will be removed along with the oil than if it were drained cold. The oil drain plug is located on the bottom of the oil pan (bottom of the engine, underneath the vehicle). The oil filter is usually located on the left side of the engine and in some cases may be easier to reach through the plastic access flap in the wheel well. On some older 4.3L models, the oil filter is located behind a access panel.

You should have available a container that will hold a minimum of 6 quarts (5.6L) of liquid (to help prevent spilling the oil even after it is drained), a wrench to fit the drain plug, a spout for pouring in new oil and a rag or two, which you will always need. If the filter is being replaced, you will also need a band wrench or a filter wrench that fits the end of the filter.

➥If the engine is equipped with an oil cooler, this will also have to be drained, using the drain plug. Be sure to add enough oil to fill the cooler in addition to the engine.

1. Run the engine until it reaches normal operating temperature, then shut the engine **OFF**, make sure the parking brake is firmly set and block the drive wheels.

2. Clearance may be sufficient to access the drain plug without raising the vehicle. If the truck must be lifted, be sure to support it safely with jackstands and be sure to position the drain plug at a low point under the vehicle.

3. Slide a drain pan of a least 6 quarts (5.6L) capacity under the oil pan. Wipe the drain plug and surrounding area clean using an old rag.

✳✳ CAUTION

The EPA warns that prolonged contact with used engine oil may cause a number of skin disorders, including cancer! You should make every effort to minimize your exposure to used engine oil. Protective gloves should be worn when changing the oil. Wash your hands and any other exposed skin areas as soon as possible after exposure to used engine oil. Soap and water, or waterless hand cleaner should be used.

4. Loosen the drain plug (the plug is usually about 14mm) using a ratchet, short extension and socket or a box-wrench. Turn the plug out by hand, using a rag to shield your fingers from the hot oil. By keeping an inward pressure on the plug as you unscrew it, oil won't escape past the threads and you can remove it without being burned by hot oil.

5. Quickly withdraw the plug and move your hands out of the way, but be careful not to drop the plug into the drain pan as fishing it out can be an unpleasant mess. Allow the oil to drain completely in the pan, then install and carefully tighten the drain plug. Be careful not to overtighten the drain plug, otherwise you'll be buying a new pan or a trick replacement plug for stripped threads.

➥Although some manufacturers have at times recommended changing the oil filter every other oil change, we recommend the filter be changed each time you change your oil. The added benefit of clean oil is quickly lost if the old filter is clogged and the added protection to the heart of your engine far outweighs the few dollars saved by using a old filter.

6. Move the drain pan under the oil filter. Use a strap-type or cap-type filter wrench to loosen the oil filter. Cover your hand with a rag and spin the filter off by hand; turn it slowly. Keep in mind that it's holding about one quart of dirty, hot oil.

✳✳ CAUTION

On most Chevrolet engines, especially the V6s, the oil filter is next to the exhaust pipes. Stay clear of these, since even a passing contact can result in a painful burn. ALSO, on trucks equipped with catalytic converters, stay clear of the converter. The outside temperature of a hot catalytic converter can approach 1200°F.

7. Empty the old filter into the drain pan and properly dispose of the filter.

8. Using a clean rag, wipe off the filter adapter on the engine block. Be sure that the rag doesn't leave any lint which could clog an oil passage.

9. Coat the rubber gasket on the filter with fresh oil, then spin it onto the engine by hand; when the gasket touches the adapter surface, give it another ½–1 turn. No more, or you'll squash the gasket and it will leak.

10. Refill the engine with the correct amount of fresh oil. Please refer to the Capacities chart at the end of this section.

11. Check the oil level on the dipstick. It is normal for the level to be a bit above the full mark until the engine is run and the new filter is filled with oil. Start the engine and allow it to idle for a few minutes.

✳✳ CAUTION

Do not run the engine above idle speed until it has built up oil pressure, as indicated when the oil light goes out.

12. Shut off the engine and allow the oil to flow back to the crankcase for a minute, then recheck the oil level. Check around the filter and drain plug for any leaks, and correct as necessary.

When you have finished this job, you will notice that you now possess four or five quarts of dirty oil. The best thing to do with it is to pour it into plastic jugs, such as milk or antifreeze containers. Then, locate a service station or automotive parts store where you can pour it into their used oil tank for recycling.

✳✳ CAUTION

Pouring used motor oil into a storm drain not only pollutes the environment, it violates Federal law. Dispose of waste oil properly.

Manual Transmission

FLUID RECOMMENDATIONS

On 1994 vehicles equipped with a Borg Warner 5 speed manual transmission, use Dexron® II automatic transmission fluid. On 1995 vehicles equipped with a Borg Warner 5 speed manual transmission, use Dexron® III automatic transmission fluid.

On 1994–99 vehicles equipped with a New Venture Gear 3500/1500 and 1996–97 Borg Warner 5 speed manual transmission, use Synchromesh transmission fluid GM part No. 12345349 or its equivalent.

➥Using the incorrect lubricant in your transmission can lead to significant transmission damage and a costly overhaul.

LEVEL CHECK

◆ See Figures 121, 122, 123, 124 and 125

Remove the filler plug (usually with a 17mm Allen wrench) from the side of the transmission (usually located on the passenger's-side of the housing). If the transmission housing contains 2 plugs, the lower is a drain plug, while the

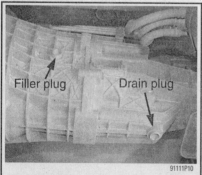
Fig. 121 Location of the manual transmission filler and drain plugs

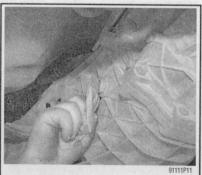
Fig. 122 Clean the area around the filler plug with a rag

Fig. 123 Using a 17mm Allen wrench, remove the filler plug

upper plug is the filler. The oil should be level with the bottom edge of the filler hole. This should be checked at least once every 6000 miles (9600 km) or if leakage or seepage is observed. If the oil level is below the bottom edge of the filler hole, add the recommended lubricant until the proper level is reached. Most parts stores will carry a small, hand operated pump which will greatly ease the task of adding fluid to the transmission.

➥**When checking the fluid, the vehicle must be level. If it was necessary to raise and support the vehicle to access the filler plug, the vehicle must be supported at sufficient points (all wheels or 4 points on the frame) so it is sitting level and is not tilted forward/backward or to one side.**

DRAIN & REFILL

▶ **See Figures 126, 127 and 128**

Under normal conditions, the manual transmission fluid should not need to be changed. However, if the truck is driven in deep water (as high as the transmission casing) it is a good idea to replace the fluid. Little harm can come from a fluid change when you have just purchased a used vehicle, especially since the condition of the transmission fluid is usually not known.

If the fluid is to be drained, it is a good idea to warm the fluid first so it will flow better. This can be accomplished by 15–20 miles (24–32 km) of highway driving. Fluid which is warmed to normal operating temperature will flow faster, drain more completely and remove more contaminants from the housing.

1. Raise and support the vehicle safely using jackstands.
2. Place a fluid catch pan under the transmission.
3. Use a rag to clean any dirt from around the fill plug and the drain plug.
4. Remove the filler plug (usually with a 17mm Allen wrench).
5. Remove the drain plug (usually with a 17mm Allen wrench) from the bottom of the transmission housing and allow the fluid to drain.
6. After all the fluid has drained, install the drain plug. Before installing the drain plug on 1997–99 models, apply Teflon® sealer GM part number 1052080 or its equivalent to the plug threads.

7. Refill the transmission with the specified type of fluid until the fluid is level with the filler hole. Most parts stores will carry a small, hand operated pump which will greatly ease the task of adding fluid to the transmission.
8. Install the filler plug and lower the vehicle.

Automatic Transmission

FLUID RECOMMENDATIONS

When adding fluid or refilling the transmission, always use Dexron® III automatic transmission fluid.

LEVEL CHECK

▶ **See Figures 129, 130 and 131**

Check the automatic transmission fluid level at least every 7500 miles (12,000 km). The dipstick can be found in the rear of the engine compartment. The fluid level should be checked only when the transmission is hot (normal operating temperature). The transmission is considered hot after about 15–20 miles (24–32 km) of highway driving.

➥**Although the transmission should be checked while the fluid is at normal operating temperature, do not check it if it is at the extreme high end of the operating temperature range. Wait at least 30 minutes if you have just be driving the vehicle in ambient temperatures in excess of 90°F (32°C), at highway speeds for a long time, in heavy traffic (especially in hot weather) or have been pulling a trailer.**

1. Park the truck on a level surface with the engine idling, then shift the transmission into Park and firmly set the parking brake.
2. With your foot on the brake pedal, move the selector through each gear range (pausing for about 3 seconds in each gear), then place it in Park. Allow the engine to run at idle about 3 more minutes.

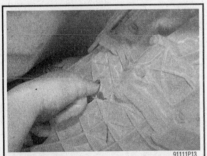
Fig. 124 Insert your pinky finger into the hole (being very careful not to cut yourself on any sharp edges) and check that the fluid is level with the bottom of the hole

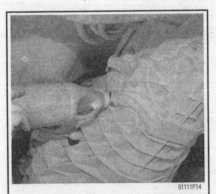
Fig. 125 If the level is incorrect, add fluid until it just starts to seep from the hole

Fig. 126 Using a 17mm Allen wrench, loosen, but do not remove the drain plug

Fig. 127 Unscrew the drain plug by hand, and remove it from the transmission quickly to avoid it running down your arm

Fig. 128 Allow the fluid to completely drain into a suitable container before replacing the drain plug

Fig. 129 Remove the automatic transmission dipstick from the tube

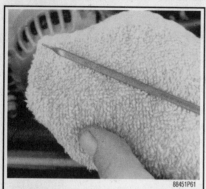

Fig. 130 Check the transmission fluid level on the dipstick

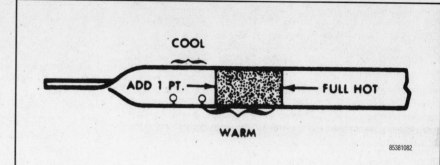

Fig. 131 Automatic transmission dipstick marks; the proper level for a hot transmission is within the shaded area

➡**When moving the selector through each range, DO NOT race the engine.**

3. With the engine running at a low idle, remove the dipstick, wipe it clean and then reinsert it firmly. Be sure that it has been pushed all the way in, then pause 3 seconds. Remove the dipstick again and check the fluid level while holding it horizontally. The fluid level should be between the upper notch and the FULL HOT line. If the fluid must be checked when it is cool, the level should be between the lower 2 notches.

➡**Most of the transmissions for the 4.3L engine are equipped with a flip-top handle on the dipstick. To withdraw these, flip the handle upward, then pull the dipstick from the guide.**

4. If the fluid level is low add DEXRON®III automatic transmission fluid. The fluid must be added through the transmission dipstick tube, which is easily accomplished using a funnel. Add fluid gradually, checking the level often as you are filling the transmission. Be extremely careful not to overfill the transmission, as this will cause slippage, seal damage and overheating. Approximately one pint of ATF will raise the fluid level from one notch/line to the other.

❄❄ WARNING

Always use DEXRON®III ATF. The use of ATF Type F or any other fluid will cause severe damage to the transmission.

The fluid on the dipstick should always be a bright red color. If it is discolored (brown or black), or smells burnt, serious transmission troubles, probably due to overheating, should be suspected. The transmission should be inspected by a qualified technician to locate the cause of the burnt fluid.

DRAIN & REFILL

▶ **See Figures 132 and 133**

➡**The truck should be driven 15–20 miles (24–32 km) to warm the transmission fluid before the pan is removed.**

1. Raise and support the front of vehicle safely using jackstands.
2. Place a drain pan under the transmission housing and fluid pan.
3. On models equipped with a drain plug, remove the transmission oil pan drain plug and allow the fluid to fully drain. After the fluid has drained, install the drain plug and tighten the plug to 13 ft. lbs. (18 Nm), then, unfasten the pan bolts to remove the pan and access the filter.
4. On models not equipped with a drain plug, remove the pan bolts from the front and the sides, then loosen the rear bolts 4 turns.

➡**On some vehicles, it may be necessary to support the transmission tailshaft and remove the crossmember just behind the transmission for pan clearance or access to the pan bolts.**

5. Using a small prybar, carefully pry the pan downward at the front of the transmission. This will allow the pan to partially drain. Remove the remaining pan bolts and lower the pan from the transmission.

➡**If the transmission fluid is dark or has a burnt smell, transmission damage is indicated. Have the transmission checked professionally.**

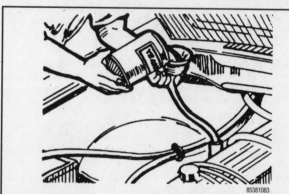

Fig. 132 Fluid may be added to the transmission through the dipstick using a funnel and flexible hose

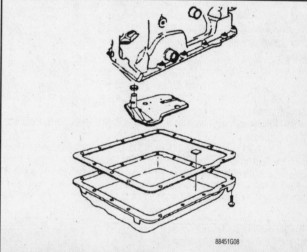

Fig. 133 Exploded view of the automatic transmission oil pan and filter—4L60-E transmission shown

6. Empty the transmission pan of the remaining fluid, then remove the gasket material and clean with a solvent.
7. Using a putty knife, carefully clean the gasket mounting surfaces.
8. Remove the screen and the filter from the valve body. Most screens are retained using a bolt fastener, though some may use an interference fit between the screen tube and valve body.

To install:

9. Install a new filter using a new gasket or O-ring.

➡**If the transmission uses a filter equipped with a fully exposed screen, it may be cleaned and reused.**

10. Use a new gasket and sealant and install the transmission pan. Install and tighten the retaining bolts to 8 ft. lbs. (11 Nm) using a crisscross pattern on 1994–97 models and on 1998–99 models tighten the bolts to 18 ft. lbs. (24 Nm) using a crisscross pattern.

11. Remove the jackstands and carefully lower the vehicle.

12. Immediately refill the transmission housing using Dexron® II automatic transmission fluid. Add the fluid through the filler tube. Please refer to the Capacities chart found later in this section to determine the proper amount of fluid to be added.

⁎⁎ WARNING

DO NOT OVERFILL the transmission. Foaming of the fluid and subsequent transmission damage due to slippage will result.

13. With the gearshift lever in Park, start the engine and let it idle. DO NOT race the engine.

14. Apply the parking brake and move the gearshift lever through each position. Return the lever to Park and check the fluid level with the engine idling. The level should be between the two dimples on the dipstick, about ¼ in. (6mm) below the ADD mark. Add fluid, if necessary.

15. Check the fluid level after the truck has been driven enough to thoroughly warm the transmission.

Transfer Case

FLUID RECOMMENDATIONS

When adding fluid or refilling the transfer case, use Dexron® II E (or its superceding type) on 1994 models and Dexron® III automatic transmission fluid for 1995–99 models covered by this manual. .

LEVEL CHECK

◆ **See Figure 134**

➡**When checking the fluid, the vehicle must be level. If it was necessary to raise and support the vehicle to access the filler plug, the vehicle must be supported at sufficient points (all wheels or 4 points on the frame) so it is sitting level and is not tilted forward/backward or to one side.**

1. If necessary for access to the filler plug, raise and support the vehicle safely using jackstands, but make sure the vehicle is level.

2. Remove the filler plug (upper one of the 2 plugs) from the rear-side of the transfer case.

3. Using your finger, check the fluid level, it should be level with the bottom of the filler hole.

4. If the fluid level is low, use Dexron® III automatic transmission fluid to bring the fluid up to the proper level. Most parts stores will carry a small, hand operated pump which will greatly ease the task of adding fluid to the transfer case.

5. Install and tighten the filler plug.

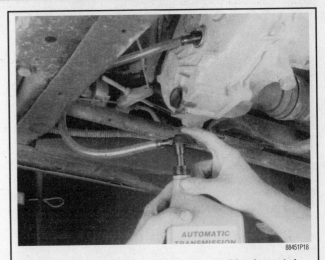

Fig. 134 If it is necessary to add fluid, use a small hand operated pump to add the fluid

DRAIN & REFILL

◆ **See Figures 135, 136 and 137**

1. Operate the vehicle in four wheel drive in order to warm the fluid to normal operating temperature.

2. If necessary for access to the drain and filler plugs, raise and support the vehicle safely using jackstands. Support the truck so it is level; this is necessary to assure the proper fluid level is maintained when the case is refilled.

3. Position drain pan under transfer case.

4. Use a rag to clean any dirt from around the fill and drain plugs.

5. Remove drain and fill plugs, then drain the lubricant into the drain pan.

6. After the fluid has completely drained, install and tighten the drain plug.

7. Remove the drain pan and dump the fluid into a used transmission fluid storage tank, for recycling purposes.

8. Fill transfer case to edge of fill plug opening. Most parts stores will carry a small, hand operated pump which will greatly ease the task of adding fluid to the transfer case.

9. Install and tighten the fill plug.

10. Remove the jackstands and carefully lower the vehicle, then check for proper operation of the transfer case.

Drive Axles

The fluid in both the rear axle and, if equipped, the front drive axle should be checked at each oil change. The fluid in the rear axle should be changed at the truck's first engine oil change and thereafter at intervals of 15,000 miles (24,000 km). Changing the front drive axle fluid on these vehicles usually requires it's removal and partial disassembly. The fluid in the front drive axle should not need to be changed unless the axle is removed for repair.

Fig. 135 Use a wrench to loosen the drain plug

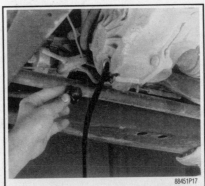

Fig. 136 Remove the drain plug and let the fluid drain

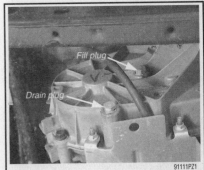

Fig. 137 Location of the transfer case fill and drain plugs. The plug size is usually 18mm

The fluid is checked by removing the filler plug, but keep in mind the truck must be sitting level or an incorrect fluid level will be indicated. Maintain the fluid at a level ⅜ in. (9.5mm) below the filler plug hole.

FLUID RECOMMENDATIONS

Always use SAE 80W-90 GL5 gear lubricant, part number 1052271, or equivalent.

LEVEL CHECK

▶ **See Figures 138, 139, 140 and 141**

➥**When checking the fluid, the vehicle must be level. If it was necessary to raise and support the vehicle to access the filler plug, the vehicle must be supported at sufficient points (all wheels or 4 points on the frame) so it is sitting level and is not tilted forward/backward or to one side.**

1. If necessary for access to the filler plug, raise and support the vehicle safely using jackstands, but make sure the vehicle is level.
2. Use a rag to clean the area around the filler plug.

3. Remove the filler plug, located at the side of the differential carrier.
4. Check the fluid level, it should be ⅜ in. (9.5 mm) below the filler plug hole.
5. If necessary add fluid through the filler plug opening. A suction gun or a squeeze bulb may be used to add fluid. Most parts stores will carry a small, hand operated pump which will greatly ease the task of adding fluid.
6. Install and tighten the filler plug.
7. Remove the jackstands and carefully lower the vehicle.

DRAIN & REFILL

Rear Axle

▶ **See Figures 142, 143, 144, 145 and 146**

1. Run the vehicle until the lubricant reaches operating temperature.
2. If necessary for access, raise and support the vehicle safely using jackstands; but make sure that the vehicle is level.
3. Use a wire brush to clean the area around the differential. This will help prevent dirt from contaminating the differential housing while the cover is removed.
4. Position a drain pan under the rear axle.

Fig. 138 Remove the filler plug from the front drive axle

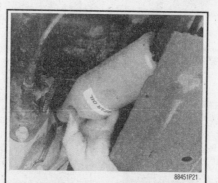
Fig. 139 If necessary, add fluid through the filler plug opening

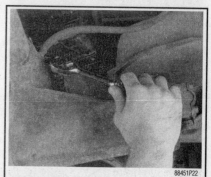
Fig. 140 Remove the filler plug from the rear drive axle

Fig. 141 If necessary, add fluid through the filler plug opening

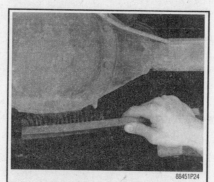
Fig. 142 Clean the area around the rear differential using a wire brush

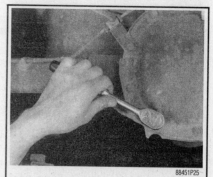
Fig. 143 Remove the rear differential cover retaining bolts

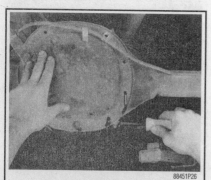
Fig. 144 Use a small prytool to pry the cover away from the axle housing

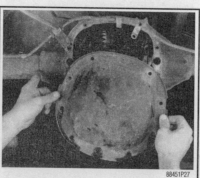
Fig. 145 Remove the rear differential cover

Fig. 146 Clean the old gasket from the surfaces of the cover and axle housing

5. Unscrew the retaining bolts and remove the rear cover. When removing the cover, a small prytool may be used at the base of the cover to gently pry it back from the axle housing, breaking the gasket seal and allowing the lubricant to drain out into the container. Be careful not to use excessive force and damage the cover or housing.

To install:

6. Carefully clean the gasket mating surfaces of the cover and axle housing of any remaining gasket or sealer. A putty knife is a good tool to use for this.

7. Install the rear cover using a new gasket and sealant. Tighten the retaining bolts using a crosswise pattern to 20 ft. lbs. (27 Nm).

➡**Make sure the vehicle is level before attempting to add fluid to the rear axle or an incorrect fluid level will result.**

8. Refill the rear axle housing using the proper grade and quantity of lubricant as detailed earlier in this section. Install the filler plug, operate the vehicle and check for any leaks.

Front Differential

1. Run the vehicle until the lubricant reaches operating temperature.
2. If necessary for access, raise and support the vehicle safely using jackstands; but make sure that the vehicle is level.
3. Using a floor jack, support the front axle. Position a drain pan under the front axle.
4. Remove the drain plug from the right side of the front axle, then drain the lubricant.
5. Remove the filler plug.

To install:

6. Use a sealant on the drain plug, then torque the plug to 24 ft. lbs. (33 Nm).
7. Using a suction gun or a squeeze bulb, install the fluid through the filler plug hole.
8. Using sealant, coat the filler plug threads, then torque the plug to 24 ft. lbs. (33 Nm).

Cooling System

The cooling system was filled at the factory with a high quality coolant solution that is good for year around operation and protects the system from freezing down to -20°F (-29°C) (-32°F/36°C in Canada).

The hot coolant level should be at the FULL HOT mark on the expansion tank and the cold coolant level should be at the FULL COLD mark on the tank. Do not remove the radiator cap to check the coolant level.

FLUID RECOMMENDATIONS

Coolant mixture in 1994–95 pick-ups is 50/50 ethylene glycol and water for year round use. Use a good quality anti-freeze with water pump lubricants, rust inhibitors and other corrosion inhibitors along with acid neutralizers.

The 1996–99 models use a 50/50 mixture of water and DEX-COOL™ coolant. This silicate free coolant is orange in color and does not require maintenance for 5 years or 100,000 miles (166,000 km). If additional coolant needs to be added to the system, use only DEX-COOL™ or a silicate free orange coolant meeting GM spec 6277M. If another coolant type is added, the advantage of the prolonged maintenance period is lost.

FLUID LEVEL CHECK

◆ **See Figures 147, 148, 149 and 150**

1. Check the level on the see-through expansion tank.

☀☀ CAUTION

The radiator coolant is under pressure when hot. To avoid the danger of physical harm, coolant level should be checked or replenished only when the engine is cold. To remove the radiator cap when the engine is hot, first cover the cap with a thick rag, or wear a heavy glove for protection. Press down on the cap slightly and slowly turn it counterclockwise until it reaches the first stop. Allow all the pressure to vent (indicated when the hissing sound stops). When the pressure is released, press down on the cap and continue to rotate it counterclockwise. Some radiator caps have a lever for venting the pressure, but you should still exercise extreme caution when removing the cap.

2. Check the level and, if necessary, add the proper type of coolant (see fluid recommendations) through the expansion tank to the proper level. Anti-

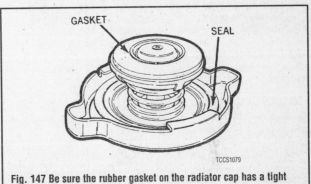

Fig. 147 Be sure the rubber gasket on the radiator cap has a tight seal

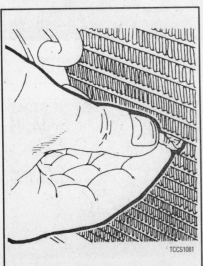

Fig. 148 Periodically remove all debris from the radiator fins

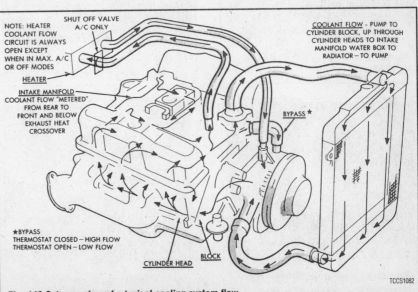

Fig. 149 Cutaway view of a typical cooling system flow

Fig. 150 Cooling systems should be pressure tested for leaks periodically

freeze solutions should be used, even in summer, to prevent rust and to take advantage of the solution's higher boiling point compared to plain water. This is imperative on air conditioned vehicles; the heater core can freeze if it isn't protected. Coolant should be added through the coolant recovery tank, not the radiator filler neck.

✻✻ WARNING

Never add large quantities of cold coolant to a hot engine! A cracked engine block may result!

Each year the cooling system should be serviced as follows:
- Wash the radiator cap and filler neck with clean water.
- Check the coolant for proper level and freeze protection.
- Have the system pressure tested at psi. (103 kPa), If a replacement cap is installed, be sure that it conforms to the original specifications.
- Tighten the hose clamps and inspect all hoses. Replace hoses that are swollen, cracked or otherwise deteriorated.
- Clean the frontal area of the radiator core and the air conditioning condenser, if so equipped.

DRAINING & FLUSHING

▶ **See Figures 151 thru 155**

The cooling system in your vehicle accumulates some internal rust and corrosion in its normal operation. A simple method of keeping the system clean is known as flushing the system. It is performed by circulating a can of radiator flush through the system, and then draining and refilling the system with the normal coolant. Radiator flush is marketed by several different manufacturers, and is available in cans at auto departments, parts stores, and many hardware stores. On 1994–95 models, this operation should be performed every 30,000 miles (48,000 km) or once a year (whichever comes first). On 1996–99 models, this service should be performed every 100,000 miles (166,000 km) or once every 5 years. Keep in mind this holds true only if DEX-COOL™ or a silicate free orange coolant meeting GM spec 6277M has been used. If another type of

coolant has been used in this system, then this operation should be performed every 30,000 miles (48,000 km) or once a year (whichever comes first).

✻✻ CAUTION

Never open, service or drain the radiator or cooling system when hot; serious burns can occur from the steam and hot coolant. Also, when draining engine coolant, keep in mind that cats and dogs are attracted to ethylene glycol antifreeze and could drink any that is left in an uncovered container or in puddles on the ground. This will prove fatal in sufficient quantities. Always drain coolant into a sealable container. Coolant should be reused unless it is contaminated or is several years old.

1. Drain the existing anti-freeze and coolant. Open the radiator and engine drain petcocks (located near the bottom of the radiator and engine block, respectively), or disconnect the bottom radiator hose at the radiator outlet.
2. Close the petcock or reconnect the lower hose and fill the system with water—hot water if the system has just been run.
3. Add a can of quality radiator flush to the radiator or recovery tank, following any special instructions on the can.
4. Idle the engine as long as specified on the can of flush, or until the upper radiator hose gets hot.
5. Drain the system again. There should be quite a bit of scale and rust in the drained water.
6. Repeat this process until the drained water is mostly clear.
7. Close all petcocks and connect all hoses.
8. Flush the coolant recovery reservoir with water and leave empty.
9. Determine the capacity of your truck's cooling system (see the Capacities chart in this guide). Fill the cooling system with the proper type of coolant (refer to fluid recommendations).
10. Run the engine to operating temperature, then stop the engine and check for leaks. Check the coolant level and top up if necessary.
11. Check the protection level of your anti-freeze mix with an anti-freeze tester (a small, inexpensive syringe type device available at any auto parts store). The tester has five or six small colored balls inside, each of which signify a certain temperature rating. Insert the tester in the recovery tank and suck just enough coolant into the syringe to float as many individual balls as you can (without sucking in too much coolant and floating all the balls at once). A table supplied with the tester will explain how many floating balls equal protection down to a certain temperature (three floating balls might mean the coolant will protect your engine down to +5°F (-15°C), for example).

Brake Master Cylinder

FLUID RECOMMENDATIONS

▶ **See Figure 156**

✻✻ CAUTION

Brake fluid contains polyglycol ethers and polyglycols. Avoid contact with the eyes and wash your hands thoroughly after handling

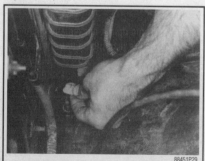

Fig. 151 To drain the cooling system, open the radiator petcock—1994 model shown, others similar

Fig. 152 Remove the radiator cap

Fig. 153 Add a 50/50 mix of ethylene glycol, or other suitable antifreeze and water

Fig. 154 If necessary, add coolant to the recovery tank

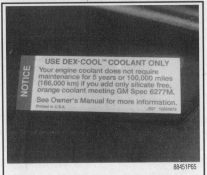

Fig. 155 As this label indicates, 1996 and newer models use DEX-COOL™ coolant

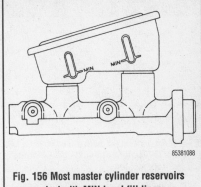

Fig. 156 Most master cylinder reservoirs are marked with MIN level fill lines

brake fluid. If you do get brake fluid in your eyes, flush your eyes with clean, running water for 15 minutes. If eye irritation persists, or if you have taken brake fluid internally, IMMEDIATELY seek medical assistance.

Use only heavy-duty Delco Supreme 11® or DOT-3 brake fluid.

✳✳ WARNING

Clean, high quality brake fluid is essential to the safe and proper operation of the brake system. You should always buy the highest quality brake fluid that is available. If the brake fluid becomes contaminated, drain and flush the system, then refill the master cylinder with new fluid. Never reuse any brake fluid. Any brake fluid that is removed from the system should be discarded. Also, do not allow any brake fluid to come in contact with a painted surface; it will damage the paint.

FLUID LEVEL CHECK

▶ See Figures 157, 158 and 159

It should be obvious how important the brake system is to safe operation of your vehicle. The brake fluid is key to the proper operation of the brake system. Low levels of fluid indicate a need for service (there may be a leak in the system or the brake pads may just be worn and in need of replacement). In any case, the brake fluid level should be inspected at least during every oil change, but more often is desirable. Every time you open the hood is a good time to glance at the master cylinder reservoir.

The master cylinder is mounted to the left side of the firewall.

The brake fluid level can be checked by observing the MIN and MAX marks on the side of the reservoir.

1. Clean all of the dirt from around the cover of the master cylinder.
2. Be sure that the vehicle is resting on a level surface.
3. Pull up on the tabs on the top of the master cylinder to release the cover.
4. The fluid level should be approximately ¼ in. (6mm) from the top of

the master cylinder or at least above the MIN mark. If not, add fluid until the level is correct. Replacement fluid should be Delco Supreme No. 11®, DOT 3, or its equivalent. It is normal for the fluid level to fall as the disc brake pads wear.

✳✳ WARNING

Brake fluid dissolves paint! It also absorbs moisture from the air. Never leave a container or the master cylinder uncovered any longer than necessary!

5. Install the cover of the master cylinder. On most models there is a rubber gasket under the cover, which fits into 2 slots on the cover. Be sure that this is seated properly.
6. Push the cover back into place and be sure that it seats correctly.

Clutch Master Cylinder

FLUID RECOMMENDATIONS

Use only heavy duty Delco Supreme 11® or DOT-3 brake fluid.

FLUID LEVEL CHECK

▶ See Figures 160 and 161

The clutch master cylinder is located on the firewall in the engine compartment.

1. Clean all of the dirt from around the cover of the master cylinder.
2. Be sure that the vehicle is resting on a level surface.
3. Carefully remove the cover from the master cylinder.
4. The fluid level should be approximately ¼ in. (6mm) from the top of the master cylinder or at least above the MIN mark. If not, add fluid until the level is correct. Replacement fluid should be Delco Supreme No. 11®, DOT 3, or its equivalent.
5. Install the cover of the master cylinder.

Fig. 157 The fluid level can be checked by looking at the level marks on the reservoir

Fig. 158 Remove the master cylinder cover

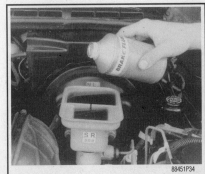

Fig. 159 If necessary, add brake fluid until the level is correct

Power Steering Pump

FLUID RECOMMENDATION

Use GM Power Steering fluid, or its equivalent.

FLUID LEVEL CHECK

▶ **See Figures 162, 163, 164 and 165**

➡**On models equipped with a remote reservoir, the fluid level should be ½–1 in. (13–25.4mm) from the top when the wheels are turned to the extreme left position.**

The power steering pump reservoir is located at the front left-side of the engine.

Check the dipstick in the pump reservoir when the fluid is at operating temperature. The fluid should be between the **HOT** and **COLD** marks. If the fluid is at room temperature, the fluid should be between the **ADD** and **COLD** marks. The fluid does not require periodic changing.

On systems with a remote reservoir, the level should be maintained approximately ½–1 in. (13–25mm) from the top with the wheels in the full left turn position.

Steering Gear

FLUID RECOMMENDATIONS

Use GM Lubricant (part No. 1051052) or equivalent.

FLUID LEVEL CHECK

No lubrication is needed for the life of the gear, except in the event of seal replacement or overhaul, when the gear should be refilled with a 13 oz. container of Steering Gear Lubricant (Part No. 1051052) which meets GM Specification GM 4673M, or its equivalent.

Chassis Greasing

Chassis greasing should be performed every 6 months or 7,500 miles for trucks used in normal/light service. More frequent greasing is recommended for trucks in heavy/severe usage; about every 3 months or 3,000 miles. Greasing can be performed with a commercial pressurized grease gun or at home by using a hand-operated grease gun. Wipe the grease fittings clean before greasing in order to prevent the possibility of forcing any dirt into the component.

The four wheel drive front driveshaft requires special attention for lubrication. The large constant velocity joint at the front of the transfer case has a special grease fitting in the centering ball. A special needle nose adapter for a flush type fitting is required, as well as a special lubricant (GM part No. 1052497). You can only get at this fitting when it is facing up toward the floorboard, so you need a flexible hose, too.

Water resistant EP chassis lubricant (grease) conforming to GM specification 6031-M (GM part No. 1052497) should be used for all chassis grease points.

Every year or 7500 miles (12,067 km) the front suspension ball joints, both upper and lower on each side of the truck, must be greased. Most trucks covered in this guide should be equipped with grease nipples on the ball joints, although some may have plugs which must be removed and nipples fitted.

✴✴ WARNING

Do not pump so much grease into the ball joint that excess grease squeezes out of the rubber boot. This destroys the watertight seal.

1. Raise up the front end of the truck and safely support it with jackstands. Block the rear wheels and firmly apply the parking brake.

2. If the truck has been parked in temperatures below 20°F (-7°C) for any length of time, park it in a heated garage for an hour or so until the ball joints loosen up enough to accept the grease.

3. Depending on which front wheel you work on first, turn the wheel and tire outward, either full-lock right or full-lock left. You now have the ends of the

Fig. 160 Remove the clutch master cylinder cover

Fig. 161 If necessary, add DOT-3 brake fluid to achieve the proper fluid level

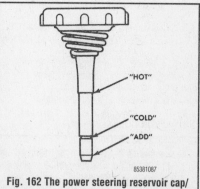

Fig. 162 The power steering reservoir cap/dipstick is marked for proper fluid levels

Fig. 163 Remove the power steering pump dipstick

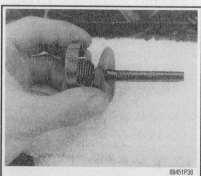

Fig. 164 Check the level of the power steering fluid on the dipstick

Fig. 165 If necessary, add the proper amount of power steering fluid

upper and lower suspension control arms in front of you; the grease nipples are visible pointing up (top ball joint) and down (lower ball joint) through the end of each control arm.

4. If the nipples are not accessible enough, remove the wheel and tire.

5. Wipe all dirt and crud from the nipples or from around the plugs (if installed). If plugs are on the truck, remove them and install grease nipples in the holes (nipples are available in various thread sizes at most auto parts stores).

6. Using a hand operated, low pressure grease gun loaded with a quality chassis grease, grease the ball joint only until the rubber joint boot begins to swell out.

The steering linkage should be greased at the same interval as the ball joints. Grease nipples are installed on the steering tie rod ends on most models.

7. Wipe all dirt and crud from around the nipples at each tie rod end.

8. Using a hand operated, low pressure grease gun loaded with a suitable chassis grease, grease the linkage until the old grease begins to squeeze out around the tie rod ends.

9. Wipe off the nipples and any excess grease. Also grease the nipples on the steering idler arms.

Use chassis grease on the parking brake cable where it contacts the cable guides, levers and linkage.

Apply a small amount of clean engine oil to the kickdown and shift linkage points at 7500 mile (12,000 km) intervals.

Body Lubrication And Maintenance

LOCK CYLINDERS

Apply graphite lubricant sparingly through the key slot. Insert the key and operate the lock several times to be sure that the lubricant is worked into the lock cylinder.

HOOD LATCH AND HINGES

Clean the latch surfaces and apply clean engine oil to the latch pilot bolts and the spring anchor. Also lubricate the hood hinges with engine oil. Use a chassis grease to lubricate all the pivot points in the latch release mechanism.

DOOR HINGES

The gas tank filler door and truck doors should be wiped clean and lubricated with clean engine oil once a year. The door lock cylinders and latch mechanisms should be lubricated periodically with a few drops of graphite lock lubricant or a few shots of silicone spray.

BODY DRAIN HOLES

Be sure that the drain holes in the doors and rocker panels are cleared of obstruction. A small punch, screwdriver or unbent wire coat hanger can be used to clear them of any debris.

Front Wheel Bearings

▶ See Figure 166

Only the front wheel bearings on 2WD models require periodic maintenance. A premium high melting point grease meeting GM part number 1052497 or its equivalent, must be used. Long fiber type greases must not be used. This service is recommended at the intervals in the Maintenance Intervals Chart or whenever the truck has been driven in water up to the hubs.

Before handling the bearings, there are a few things that you should remember to do and not to do.

Remember to do the following:
- Remove all outside dirt from the housing before exposing the bearing.
- Treat a used bearing as gently as you would a new one.
- Work with clean tools in clean surroundings.
- Use clean, dry canvas gloves, or at least clean, dry hands.
- Clean solvents and flushing fluids are a must.
- Use clean paper when laying out the bearings to dry.

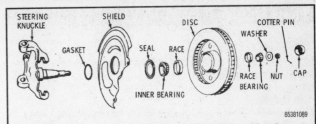

Fig. 166 Exploded view of a common 2WD front hub and bearing assembly

- Protect disassembled bearings from rust and dirt. Cover them up.
- Use clean rags to wipe bearings.
- Keep the bearings in oil-proof paper when they are to be stored or are not in use.
- Clean the inside of the housing before replacing the bearing.

Do not do the following:
- Don't work in dirty surroundings.
- Don't use dirty, chipped or damaged tools.
- Try not to work on wooden work benches or use wooden mallets.
- Don't handle bearings with dirty or moist hands.
- Do not use gasoline for cleaning; use a safe solvent.
- Do not spin-dry bearings with compressed air. They will be damaged.
- Do not spin dirty bearings.
- Avoid using cotton waste or dirty cloths to wipe bearings.
- Try not to scratch or nick bearing surfaces.
- Do not allow the bearing to come in contact with dirt or rust at any time.

REMOVAL, PACKING & INSTALLATION

➡Sodium-based grease is not compatible with lithium-based grease. Read the package labels and be careful not to mix the two types. If there is any doubt as to the type of grease used, completely clean the old grease from the bearing and hub before replacing.

2-Wheel Drive Models

▶ See Figures 167 thru 180

1. Raise and support the front of the vehicle safely using jackstands.

2. Remove the tire and wheel assembly.

3. Remove the brake caliper mounting bolts and carefully remove the caliper (along with the brake pads) from the rotor. Do not disconnect the brake line; instead wire the caliper out of the way with the line still connected. Refer to Section 9 of this manual for this procedure.

4. Carefully pry out the grease cap, then remove the cotter pin, spindle nut, and washer.

Fig. 167 Pry the dust cap from the hub, taking care not to distort or damage its flange

5. Remove the hub, being careful not to drop the outer wheel bearings. As the hub is pulled forward, the outer wheel bearings will often fall forward and they may easily be removed at this time.

6. If not done already, remove the outer roller bearing assembly from the hub. The inner bearing assembly will remain in the hub and may be removed from the rear of the hub after prying out the inner seal with a small prybar. Discard the seal after removal.

To install:

7. Clean all parts in a non-flammable solvent and let them air dry. Never spin-dry a bearing with compressed air! Check for excessive wear and damage.

➡**DO NOT remove the bearing races from the hub, unless they show signs of damage.**

Fig. 168 Once the bent ends are cut, grasp the cotter pin and pull or pry it free of the spindle

8. If it is necessary to remove the wheel bearing races, use the GM front bearing race removal tool No. J-29117 or equivalent, to drive the races from the hub/disc assembly. A hammer and drift may be used to drive the races from the hub, but the race removal tool is quicker.

9. If the bearing races were removed, place the replacement races in the freezer for a few minutes and then install them to the hub:

   a. Lightly lubricate the inside of the hub/disc assembly using wheel bearing grease.

   b. Using the GM seal installation tools No. J-8092 and J-8850 or equivalent, drive the inner bearing race into the hub/disc assembly until it seats. Make sure the race is properly seated against the hub shoulder and is not cocked.

➡**When installing the bearing races, be sure to support the hub/disc assembly with GM tool No. J-9746-02 or equivalent.**

   c. Using the GM seal installation tools No. J-8092 and J-8457 or equivalent, drive the outer race into the hub/disc assembly until it seats.

10. Pack both wheel bearings using high melting point wheel bearing grease for disc brakes. Ordinary grease will melt and ooze out ruining the pads. Bearings should be packed using a cone-type wheel bearing greaser tool. If one is not available they may be packed by hand as follows:

   a. Place a healthy glob of grease in the palm of one hand.

   b. Force the edge of the bearing into it so that the grease fills the bearing. Do this until the whole bearing is packed.

11. Place the inner bearing in the hub, then apply a thin coating of grease to the sealing lip and install a new inner seal, making sure the seal flange faces the bearing cup.

➡**Although a seal installation tool is preferable, a section of pipe with a smooth edge or a suitably sized socket may be used to drive the seal into position. Make sure the seal is flush with the outer surface of the hub assembly.**

12. Carefully install the wheel hub over the spindle.

13. Using your hands, firmly press the outer bearing into the hub.

14. Loosely install the spindle washer and nut, but do not install the cotter pin or dust cap at this time.

Fig. 169 If difficulty is encountered, gently tap on the pliers with a hammer to help free the cotter pin

Fig. 170 Loosen and remove the castellated nut from the spindle

Fig. 171 Remove the washer from the spindle

Fig. 172 With the nut and washer out of the way, the outer bearing may be removed from the hub

Fig. 173 Pull the hub and inner bearing assembly from the spindle

Fig. 174 Use a small prytool to remove the old inner bearing seal

Fig. 175 With the seal removed, the inner bearing may be withdrawn from the hub

Fig. 176 Thoroughly pack the bearing with fresh, high temperature wheel-bearing grease before installation

Fig. 177 Apply a thin coat of fresh grease to the new inner bearing seal lip

Fig. 178 Use a suitably sized driver to install the inner bearing seal to the hub

Fig. 179 Tighten the nut to specifications while gently spinning the wheel, then adjust the bearing

Fig. 180 After the bearings are adjusted, install the dust cap by gently tapping on its flange

15. Install the brake caliper.
16. Install the tire and wheel assembly.

✳✳ WARNING

If you have to cut the cotter pin using a pair of side cutters make sure to wear safety glasses to avoid a piece of the pin breaking off and hitting your eye causing serious damage or blindness.

17. Properly adjust the wheel bearings, then install a new cotter pin. Make sure the ends of the cotter pin
does not interfere with the dust cap. Bend the ends of the cotter pin against the nut and use a pair of side cutters to remove any excess pin length.
18. Install the dust cap.
19. Install the wheel/hub cover, then remove the supports and carefully lower the vehicle.

4-Wheel Drive Models

These axles have integral hub/bearing assemblies. No periodic service is required. See Section 7 for disassembly details.

ADJUSTMENT

1. Raise and support the vehicle safely using a jackstand under the lower control arm.
2. If equipped, remove the wheel/hub cover for access, then remove the dust cap from the hub.
3. Remove the cotter pin and loosen the spindle nut.
4. Spin the wheel forward by hand and tighten the nut to 12 ft. lbs. (16 Nm) in order to fully seat the bearings and remove any burrs from the threads.
5. Back off the nut until it is just loose, then finger-tighten the nut.
6. Loosen the nut ¼-½ turn until either hole in the spindle lines up with a slot in the nut, then install a new cotter pin. This may appear to be too loose, but it is the correct adjustment.

➡**Proper adjustment creates 0.001–0.005 in. (0.025–0.127mm) end-play in the rotor.**

TRAILER TOWING

General Recommendations

Your vehicle was primarily designed to carry passengers and cargo. It is important to remember that towing a trailer will place additional loads on your vehicles engine, drive train, steering, braking and other systems. However, if you decide to tow a trailer, using the prior equipment is a must.

Local laws may require specific equipment such as trailer brakes or fender mounted mirrors. Check your local laws.

Trailer Weight

The weight of the trailer is the most important factor. A good weight-to-horse-power ratio is about 35:1, 35 lbs. of Gross Combined Weight (GCW) for every horsepower your engine develops. Multiply the engine's rated horsepower by 35 and subtract the weight of the vehicle passengers and luggage. The number remaining is the approximate ideal maximum weight you should tow, although a numerically higher axle ratio can help compensate for heavier weight.

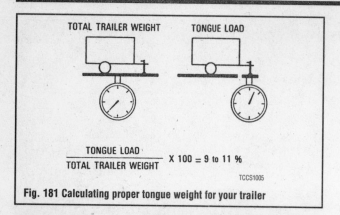

TONGUE LOAD / TOTAL TRAILER WEIGHT X 100 = 9 to 11 %

TCCS1005

Fig. 181 Calculating proper tongue weight for your trailer

Hitch (Tongue) Weight

♦ See Figure 181

Calculate the hitch weight in order to select a proper hitch. The weight of the hitch is usually 9–11% of the trailer gross weight and should be measured with the trailer loaded. Hitches fall into various categories: those that mount on the frame and rear bumper, the bolt-on type, or the weld-on distribution type used for larger trailers. Axle mounted or clamp-on bumper hitches should never be used.

Check the gross weight rating of your trailer. Tongue weight is usually figured as 10% of gross trailer weight. Therefore, a trailer with a maximum gross weight of 99 lbs. will have a maximum tongue weight of 200 lbs. Class I trailers fall into this category. Class II trailers are those with a gross weight rating of 99–3000 lbs., while Class III trailers fall into the 3500–6000 lbs. category. Class IV trailers are those over 6000 lbs. and are for use with fifth wheel trucks, only.

When you've determined the hitch that you'll need, follow the manufacturer's installation instructions, exactly, especially when it comes to fastener torques. The hitch will subjected to a lot of stress and good hitches come with hardened bolts. Never substitute an inferior bolt for a hardened bolt.

Engine

One of the most common, if not THE most common, problems associated with trailer towing is engine overheating. If you have a cooling system without an expansion tank, you'll definitely need to get an aftermarket expansion tank

kit, preferably one with at least a 2 quart capacity. These kits are easily installed on the radiator's overflow hose, and come with a pressure cap designed for expansion tanks.

Aftermarket engine oil coolers are helpful for prolonging engine oil life and reducing overall engine temperatures. Both of these factors increase engine life. While not absolutely necessary in towing Class I and some Class II trailers, they are recommended for heavier Class II and all Class III towing. Engine oil cooler systems usually consist of an adapter, screwed on in place of the oil filter, a remote filter mounting and a multi-tube, finned heat exchanger, which is mounted in front of the radiator or air conditioning condenser.

Transmission

An automatic transmission is usually recommended for trailer towing. Modern automatics have proven reliable and, of course, easy to operate, in trailer towing. The increased load of a trailer, however, causes an increase in the temperature of the automatic transmission fluid. Heat is the worst enemy of an automatic transmission. As the temperature of the fluid increases, the life of the fluid decreases.

It is essential, therefore, that you install an automatic transmission cooler. The cooler, which consists of a multi-tube, finned heat exchanger, is usually installed in front of the radiator or air conditioning compressor, and hooked in-line with the transmission cooler tank inlet line. Follow the cooler manufacturer's installation instructions.

Select a cooler of at least adequate capacity, based upon the combined gross weights of the vehicle and trailer.

Cooler manufacturers recommend that you use an aftermarket cooler in addition to, and not instead of, the present cooling tank in your radiator. If you do want to use it in place of the radiator cooling tank, get a cooler at least two sizes larger than normally necessary.

➥A transmission cooler can, sometimes, cause slow or harsh shifting in the transmission during cold weather, until the fluid has a chance to come up to normal operating temperature. Some coolers can be purchased with or retrofitted with a temperature bypass valve which will allow fluid flow through the cooler only when the fluid has reached above a certain operating temperature.

Handling A Trailer

Towing a trailer with ease and safety requires a certain amount of experience. It's a good idea to learn the feel of a trailer by practicing turning, stopping and backing in an open area such as an empty parking lot.

TOWING THE VEHICLE

General Information

2-WHEEL DRIVE

Chevrolet and GMC Pick-ups can be towed on all four wheels (flat towed) at speeds of less than 35 mph (56 kph), for distances less than 50 miles (80 kph), providing that the axle, driveline and engine/transmission are normally operable. The transmission should be in Neutral, the engine off, the steering unlocked, and the parking brake released.

The rear wheels must be raised off the ground or the driveshaft disconnected when the transmission if not operating properly, or when speeds of over 35 mph (56 kph) will be used or when towing more than 50 miles. (80 kph).

Do not attach chains to the bumpers or bracketing. All attachments must be made to the structural members. Safety chains should be used. It should also be remembered that power steering and brake assists will not be working with the engine off.

4-WHEEL DRIVE

Remember that the power steering and power brakes will not have their power assist with the engine off. The only safe way to tow is with a tow bar. The steering column must be unlocked and the parking brake released. Attachments should be made to the frame and to the bumper or its brackets. Safety chains are also required.

JUMP STARTING A DEAD BATTERY

♦ See Figure 182

Whenever a vehicle is jump started, precautions must be followed in order to prevent the possibility of personal injury. Remember that batteries contain a

small amount of explosive hydrogen gas which is a by-product of battery charging. Sparks should always be avoided when working around batteries, especially when attaching jumper cables. To minimize the possibility of accidental sparks, follow the procedure carefully.

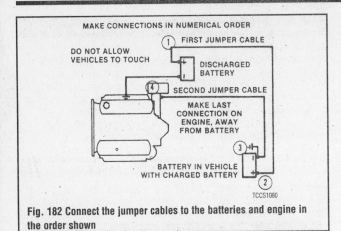

Fig. 182 Connect the jumper cables to the batteries and engine in the order shown

✲✲ CAUTION

NEVER hook the batteries up in a series circuit or the entire electrical system will go up in smoke, including the starter!

Vehicles equipped with a diesel engine may utilize two 12 volt batteries. If so, the batteries are connected in a parallel circuit (positive terminal to positive terminal, negative terminal to negative terminal). Hooking the batteries up in parallel circuit increases battery cranking power without increasing total battery voltage output. Output remains at 12 volts. On the other hand, hooking two 12 volt batteries up in a series circuit (positive terminal to negative terminal, positive terminal to negative terminal) increases total battery output to 24 volts (12 volts plus 12 volts).

Jump Starting Precautions

• Be sure that both batteries are of the same voltage. Vehicles covered by this manual and most vehicles on the road today utilize a 12 volt charging system.
• Be sure that both batteries are of the same polarity (have the same terminal, in most cases NEGATIVE grounded).
• Be sure that the vehicles are not touching or a short could occur.
• On serviceable batteries, be sure the vent cap holes are not obstructed.
• Do not smoke or allow sparks anywhere near the batteries.
• In cold weather, make sure the battery electrolyte is not frozen. This can occur more readily in a battery that has been in a state of discharge.
• Do not allow electrolyte to contact your skin or clothing.

Jump Starting Procedure

1. Make sure that the voltages of the 2 batteries are the same. Most batteries and charging systems are of the 12 volt variety.
2. Pull the jumping vehicle (with the good battery) into a position so the jumper cables can reach the dead battery and that vehicle's engine. Make sure that the vehicles do NOT touch.
3. Place the transmissions/transaxles of both vehicles in **Neutral** (MT) or **P** (AT), as applicable, then firmly set their parking brakes.

➡ **If necessary for safety reasons, the hazard lights on both vehicles may be operated throughout the entire procedure without significantly increasing the difficulty of jumping the dead battery.**

4. Turn all lights and accessories OFF on both vehicles. Make sure the ignition switches on both vehicles are turned to the **OFF** position.
5. Cover the battery cell caps with a rag, but do not cover the terminals.
6. Make sure the terminals on both batteries are clean and free of corrosion or proper electrical connection will be impeded. If necessary, clean the battery terminals before proceeding.
7. Identify the positive (+) and negative (-) terminals on both batteries.
8. Connect the first jumper cable to the positive (+) terminal of the dead battery, then connect the other end of that cable to the positive (+) terminal of the booster (good) battery.
9. Connect one end of the other jumper cable to the negative (-) terminal on the booster battery and the final cable clamp to an engine bolt head, alternator bracket or other solid, metallic point on the engine with the dead battery. Try to pick a ground on the engine that is positioned away from the battery in order to minimize the possibility of the 2 clamps touching should one loosen during the procedure. DO NOT connect this clamp to the negative (–) terminal of the bad battery.

✲✲ CAUTION

Be very careful to keep the jumper cables away from moving parts (cooling fan, belts, etc.) on both engines.

10. Check to make sure that the cables are routed away from any moving parts, then start the donor vehicle's engine. Run the engine at moderate speed for several minutes to allow the dead battery a chance to receive some initial charge.
11. With the donor vehicle's engine still running slightly above idle, try to start the vehicle with the dead battery. Crank the engine for no more than 10 seconds at a time and let the starter cool for at least 20 seconds between tries. If the vehicle does not start in 3 tries, it is likely that something else is also wrong or that the battery needs additional time to charge.
12. Once the vehicle is started, allow it to run at idle for a few seconds to make sure that it is operating properly.
13. Turn ON the headlights, heater blower and, if equipped, the rear defroster of both vehicles in order to reduce the severity of voltage spikes and subsequent risk of damage to the vehicles' electrical systems when the cables are disconnected. This step is especially important to any vehicle equipped with computer control modules.
14. Carefully disconnect the cables in the reverse order of connection. Start with the negative cable that is attached to the engine ground, then the negative cable on the donor battery. Disconnect the positive cable from the donor battery and finally, disconnect the positive cable from the formerly dead battery. Be careful when disconnecting the cables from the positive terminals not to allow the alligator clips to touch any metal on either vehicle or a short and sparks will occur.

JACKING

♦ **See Figures 183, 184, 185, 186 and 187**

Your vehicle was supplied with a jack for emergency road repairs. This jack is fine for changing a flat tire or other short term procedures not requiring you to go beneath the vehicle. If it is used in an emergency situation, carefully follow the instructions provided either with the jack or in your owner's manual. Do not attempt to use the jack on any portions of the vehicle other than specified by the vehicle manufacturer. Always block the diagonally opposite wheel when using a jack.

A more convenient way of jacking is the use of a garage or floor jack. You may use the floor jack at the point shown in the accompanying illustration.

Never place the jack under the radiator, engine or transmission components. Severe and expensive damage will result when the jack is raised. Additionally, never jack under the floorpan or bodywork; the metal will deform.

Whenever you plan to work under the vehicle, you must support it on jackstands or ramps. Never use cinder blocks or stacks of wood to support the vehicle, even if you're only going to be under it for a few minutes. Never crawl under the vehicle when it is supported only by the tire-changing jack or other floor jack.

➡ **Always position a block of wood or small rubber pad on top of the jack or jackstand to protect the lifting point's finish when lifting or supporting the vehicle.**

Small hydraulic, screw, or scissors jacks are satisfactory for raising the vehicle. Drive-on trestles or ramps are also a handy and safe way to both raise and support the vehicle. Be careful though, some ramps may be too steep to drive your vehicle onto without scraping the front bottom panels. Never support the vehicle on any suspension member (unless specifically instructed to do so by a repair manual) or by an underbody panel.

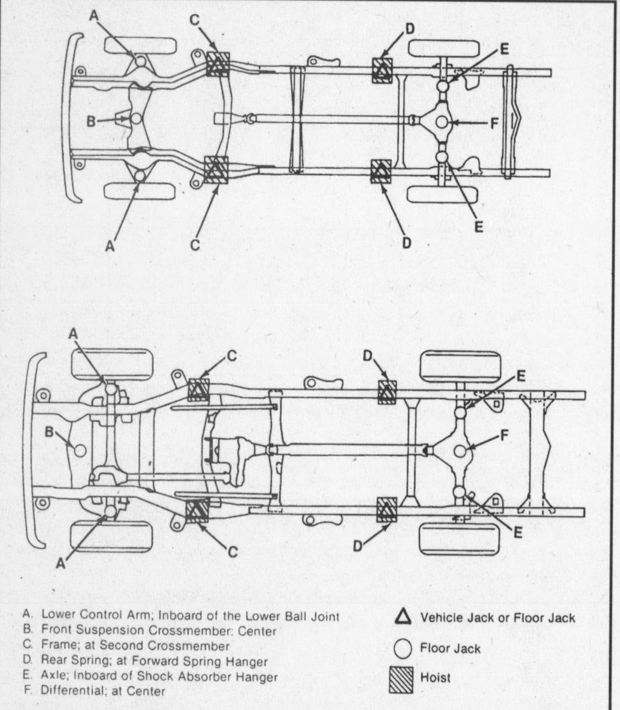

A. Lower Control Arm; Inboard of the Lower Ball Joint
B. Front Suspension Crossmember; Center
C. Frame; at Second Crossmember
D. Rear Spring; at Forward Spring Hanger
E. Axle; Inboard of Shock Absorber Hanger
F. Differential; at Center

△ Vehicle Jack or Floor Jack
○ Floor Jack
▨ Hoist

88451G03

Fig. 183 Recommended vehicle jacking and lifting points. Note that floor jacks may be used on the lined areas, but it is advisable to protect the vehicle's frame using a block of wood

Jacking Precautions

The following safety points cannot be overemphasized:
• Always block the opposite wheel or wheels to keep the vehicle from rolling off the jack.
• When raising the front of the vehicle, firmly apply the parking brake.
• When the drive wheels are to remain on the ground, leave the vehicle in gear to help prevent it from rolling.
• Always use jackstands to support the vehicle when you are working underneath. Place the stands beneath the vehicle's jacking brackets. Before climbing underneath, rock the vehicle a bit to make sure it is firmly supported.

88451P40

Fig. 184 Raising the front of the vehicle using a hydraulic jack

88451P41

Fig. 185 Raising the rear of the vehicle using a hydraulic jack

88451P42

Fig. 186 Place the jackstands along the frame rails to support the front of the vehicle

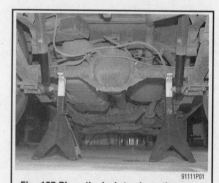

91111P01

Fig. 187 Place the jackstands on the rear axle tube when supporting the rear of the vehicle

CAPACITIES

Year	Model	Engine ID/VIN	Engine Displacement Liters (cc)	Oil with Filter (qts.)	Transmission (pts.) 5-Spd	Transmission (pts.) Auto.	Transfer Case (pts.)	Drive Axle Front (pts.)	Drive Axle Rear (pts.)	Fuel Tank (gal.)	Cooling System (qts.)
1994	S10 Blazer/Jimmy/Bravada	W	4.3 (4293)	4.5	4.4	10.0 ①	–	2.6	3.5	20.0	12.0
	S10 Blazer/Jimmy/Bravada	Z	4.3 (4293)	5.0	4.4	10.0 ①	4.6	2.6	3.5	20.0	12.1
	S10/S15 Pick-up/Sonoma	4	2.2 (2189)	4.0	4.4	10.0 ①	4.6	2.6	3.5	13.0 ②	11.5
	S10/S15 Pick-up/Sonoma	W	4.3 (4293)	4.5	4.4	10.0 ①	4.6	2.6	3.5	20.0	12.0
	S10/S15 Pick-up/Sonoma	Z	4.3 (4293)	5.0	4.4	10.0 ①	4.6	2.6	3.5	20.0	12.0
1995	S10 Blazer/Jimmy/Bravada	W	4.3 (4293)	4.5	4.4	10.0 ①	–	2.6	3.5	20.0	12.0
	S10 Blazer/Jimmy/Bravada	Z	4.3 (4293)	5.0	4.4	10.0 ①	4.6	2.6	3.5	20.0	12.1
	S10/S15 Pick-up/Sonoma	4	2.2 (2189)	4.0	4.4	10.0 ①	4.6	2.6	3.5	13.0 ③	11.5
	S10/S15 Pick-up/Sonoma	W	4.3 (4293)	4.5	4.4	10.0 ①	4.6	2.6	3.5	20.0	12.0
	S10/S15 Pick-up/Sonoma	Z	4.3 (4293)	5.0	4.4	10.0 ①	4.6		3.5	20.0	12.0
1996	S10 Blazer/Jimmy/Bravada	W	4.3 (4293)	5.0	4.4	10.0 ①	2.6	2.6	3.9	20.0	11.9
	S10 Blazer/Jimmy/Bravada	X	4.3 (4293)	5.0	4.4	10.0 ①	2.6	2.6	3.9	20.0	11.9
	S10/S15 Pick-up/Sonoma Hombre	4	2.2 (2189)	4.0	4.4	10.0 ①	2.6	2.6	3.9	13.0 ③	11.5
	S10/S15 Pick-up/Sonoma	W	4.3 (4293)	5.0	4.4	10.0 ①	2.6	2.6	3.9	20.0	11.9
	S10/S15 Pick-up/Sonoma	X	4.3 (4293)	5.0	4.4	10.0 ①	2.6	2.6	3.9	20.0	11.9
1997	S10 Blazer/Jimmy/Bravada	W	4.3 (4293)	5.0	4.4	10.0 ①	2.6	2.6	3.9	20.0	11.9
	S10 Blazer/Jimmy/Bravada	X	4.3 (4293)	5.0	4.4	10.0 ①	2.6	2.6	3.9	20.0	11.9
	S10/S15 Pick-up/Sonoma Hombre	4	2.2 (2189)	4.0	4.4	10.0 ①	2.6	2.6	3.9	13.0 ③	11.5
	S10/S15 Pick-up/Sonoma	W	4.3 (4293)	5.0	4.4	10.0 ①	2.6	2.6	3.9	20.0	11.9
	S10/S15 Pick-up/Sonoma	X	4.3 (4293)	5.0	4.4	10.0 ①	2.6	2.6	3.9	20.0	11.9
1998	S10 Blazer/Jimmy/Bravada/Envoy	W	4.3 (4293)	5.0	④	11.0	2.6	2.6	3.9	20.0	11.9
	S10 Blazer/Jimmy/Bravada/Envoy	X	4.3 (4293)	5.0	④	11.0	2.6	2.6	3.9	20.0	11.9
	S10/S15 Pick-up/Sonoma Hombre	4	2.2 (2189)	4.0	④	11.0	2.6	2.6	3.9	13.0 ③	11.5
	S10/S15 Pick-up/Sonoma Hombre	W	4.3 (4293)	5.0	④	11.0	2.6	2.6	3.9	20.0	11.9
	S10/S15 Pick-up/Sonoma Hombre	X	4.3 (4293)	5.0	④	11.0	2.6	2.6	3.9	20.0	11.9
1999	S10 Blazer/Jimmy/Bravada/Envoy	W	4.3 (4293)	5.0	④	11.0	2.6	2.6	3.9	20.0	11.9
	S10 Blazer/Jimmy/Bravada/Envoy	X	4.3 (4293)	5.0	④	11.0	2.6	2.6	3.9	20.0	11.9
	S10/S15 Pick-up/Sonoma Hombre	4	2.2 (2189)	4.0	④	11.0	2.6	2.6	3.9	13.0 ③	11.5
	S10/S15 Pick-up/Sonoma Hombre	W	4.3 (4293)	5.0	④	11.0	2.6	2.6	3.9	20.0	11.9
	S10/S15 Pick-up/Sonoma Hombre	X	4.3 (4293)	5.0	④	11.0	2.6	2.6	3.9	20.0	11.9

① Figure shown is for pan removal only.

For complete overhaul use 22 pts.

② Available with 31 and 40 gallon tanks

③ Available with 20 gallon tank

④ NVG 1500 : 6 pts.

NVG 3500: 4.5 pts.

91111C04

SCHEDULED MAINTENANCE INTERVALS—1997-99 MODELS

TO BE SERVICED	TYPE OF SERVICE	VEHICLE MILEAGE INTERVAL (x1000)																	
		7.5	15	22.5	30	37.5	45	52.5	60	67.5	75	82.5	90	97.5	100	105	112.5	120	150
Engine oil and filter	R	✓	✓	✓	✓	✓	✓	✓	✓	✓	✓	✓	✓	✓		✓	✓	✓	✓
Accessory drive belt	S/I								✓									✓	
Air cleaner filter & fuel filter	R				✓				✓				✓					✓	✓
Automatic transmission fluid	R	Every 50,000 miles																	
Brake system ①	S/I		✓	✓	✓	✓	✓	✓	✓	✓	✓	✓	✓	✓		✓	✓	✓	✓
Chassis suspension & grease points	L		✓		✓		✓		✓		✓		✓			✓		✓	✓
CV joint boots & axle seals	S/I		✓		✓		✓		✓		✓		✓			✓		✓	✓
Engine coolant system ②	R	Every 50,000 miles																	
Front wheel bearings ③	S/I & L				✓				✓				✓					✓	✓
Fuel tank, cap & lines	S/I								✓									✓	
PCV valve	S/I	Every 100,000 miles																	
Rear/front axle fluid level	S/I		✓		✓		✓		✓		✓		✓			✓		✓	✓
Rotate tires	S/I	✓		✓		✓		✓		✓		✓		✓			✓		
Spark plug wires	S/I	Every 100,000 miles																	
Spark plugs	R	Every 100,000 miles																	

① This should be performed when the tires are removed for rotation
② Drain, flush and refill the cooling system, inspect the system hoses, and clean the radiator and condenser
③ 2-wheel drive models only

R - Replace   S/I - Inspect and service, if needed   L - Lubricate

FREQUENT OPERATION MAINTENANCE (SEVERE SERVICE)

If a vehicle is operated under any of the following conditions it is considered severe service:
- Towing a trailer or using a camper or car-top carrier.
- Repeated short trips of less than 5 miles in temperatures below freezing, or trips of less than 10 miles in any temperature.
- Extensive idling or low-speed driving for long distances as in heavy commercial use, such as delivery, taxi or police cars.
- Operating on rough, muddy or salt-covered roads.
- Operating on unpaved or dusty roads.
- Driving in extremely hot (over 90°) conditions.

Chassis and suspension grease points - lubricate every 3,000 miles
Rear/front axle fluid level - inspect every 3,000 miles
Rotate tires every 6000 miles
Brake system components - inspect every 6000 miles
Front wheel bearings (2 wheel drive models only) - clean, inspect and repack every 15,000 miles
Air cleaner element - inspect every 15,000 miles
Automatic transmission fluid and filter - replace every 15,000 miles

91111C06

SCHEDULED MAINTENANCE INTERVALS—1994-96 MODELS

TO BE SERVICED	TYPE OF SERVICE	VEHICLE MILEAGE INTERVAL (x1000)																	
		7.5	15	22.5	30	37.5	45	52.5	60	67.5	75	82.5	90	97.5	100	105	112.5	120	150
Engine oil and filter	R	✓	✓	✓	✓	✓	✓	✓	✓	✓	✓	✓	✓	✓	✓	✓	✓	✓	✓
Brake/clutch pedal springs & parking brake pedal guides	S/I		✓		✓		✓		✓		✓		✓			✓		✓	✓
Chassis lubrication & CV joints, ball joints & axle seals	S/I	✓	✓	✓	✓	✓	✓	✓	✓	✓	✓	✓	✓	✓		✓	✓	✓	✓
Drive axle, steering linkage & front suspension	S/I		✓		✓		✓		✓		✓		✓			✓		✓	✓
Front/rear axle fluid & transfer case shift linkage (4WD)	S/I		✓		✓		✓		✓		✓		✓			✓		✓	✓
Rotate tires		✓		✓		✓		✓		✓		✓		✓			✓		
Engine coolant strength, hoses & clamps	S/I				✓				✓				✓					✓	✓
Air cleaner filter & fuel filter	R				✓				✓				✓					✓	✓
Automatic transmission fluid & filter ①	R				✓				✓				✓					✓	✓
Engine coolant ②	R														✓				
Spark plugs ③	R														✓				✓
Accessory drive belt	S/I								✓									✓	✓
Exhaust system	S/I								✓									✓	✓
Fuel tank, cap & lines	S/I								✓				✓					✓	✓
Engine timing check ①	S/I																		✓

① 1994-95 models—change every 30,000 miles
1996 models—change only when necessary
② On 1996 models—replace every 100,000 miles. Use O.E. specified (DEX-COOL) coolant only. If any silicat coolant is used, the service interval is 30,000 miles.
1994-95 models—change every 100,000 miles. On 1996 models—replace every 100,000 miles.
③ Check ignition wires, spark plugs.

R - Replace   S/I - Inspect and service, if needed

FREQUENT OPERATION MAINTENANCE (SEVERE SERVICE)

If a vehicle is operated under any of the following conditions it is considered severe service:
- Operating on unpaved or dusty roads.
- 50% or more of the vehicle operation is in 32°C (90°F) or higher temperatures, or constant operation in temperatures below normal operating temperatures).
- Prolonged idling (vehicle operation in stop and go driving).
- Frequent short running periods (engine does not warm to normal operating temperatures).
- Police, taxi, delivery usage or trailer towing usage.
- Operating on rough, muddy or salt-covered roads.

Engine oil and filter - change every 3,000 miles or 3 months, whichever occurs first.
Rotate tires every 6,000 miles, then every 15,000 miles.
Lubricate chassis every 3000 miles.
Drive axle—check every 15,000 miles.
Automatic transmission fluid & filter (1994-95 models—change every 15,000 miles)
Automatic transmission fluid & filter (1996 models—change every 50,000 miles)
Air cleaner element - replace every 15,000 miles.

91111C05

ENGLISH TO METRIC CONVERSION: MASS (WEIGHT)

Current **mass** measurement is expressed in pounds and ounces (lbs. & ozs.). The metric unit of mass (or weight) is the kilogram (kg). Even although this table does not show conversion of masses (weights) larger than 15 lbs, it is easy to calculate larger units by following the data immediately below.

To convert ounces (oz.) to grams (g): multiply th number of ozs. by 28
To convert grams (g) to ounces (oz.): multiply the number of grams by .035

To convert pounds (lbs.) to kilograms (kg): multiply the number of lbs. by .45
To convert kilograms (kg) to pounds (lbs.): multiply the number of kilograms by 2.2

lbs	kg	lbs	kg	oz	kg	oz	kg
0.1	0.04	0.9	0.41	0.1	0.003	0.9	0.024
0.2	0.09	1	0.4	0.2	0.005	1	0.03
0.3	0.14	2	0.9	0.3	0.008	2	0.06
0.4	0.18	3	1.4	0.4	0.011	3	0.08
0.5	0.23	4	1.8	0.5	0.014	4	0.11
0.6	0.27	5	2.3	0.6	0.017	5	0.14
0.7	0.32	10	4.5	0.7	0.020	10	0.28
0.8	0.36	15	6.8	0.8	0.023	15	0.42

ENGLISH TO METRIC CONVERSION: TEMPERATURE

To convert Fahrenheit (°F) to Celsius (°C): take number of °F and subtract 32; multiply result by 5; divide result by 9

To convert Celsius (°C) to Fahrenheit (°F): take number of °C and multiply by 9; divide result by 5; add 32 to total

Fahrenheit (F)	Celsius (C)			Fahrenheit (F)	Celsius (C)			Fahrenheit (F)	Celsius (C)		
°F	°C	°C	°F	°F	°C	°C	°F	°F	°C	°C	°F
−40	−40	−38	−36.4	80	26.7	18	64.4	215	101.7	80	176
−35	−37.2	−36	−32.8	85	29.4	20	68	220	104.4	85	185
−30	−34.4	−34	−29.2	90	32.2	22	71.6	225	107.2	90	194
−25	−31.7	−32	−25.6	95	35.0	24	75.2	230	110.0	95	202
−20	−28.9	−30	−22	100	37.8	26	78.8	235	112.8	100	212
−15	−26.1	−28	−18.4	105	40.6	28	82.4	240	115.6	105	221
−10	−23.3	−26	−14.8	110	43.3	30	86	245	118.3	110	230
−5	−20.6	−24	−11.2	115	46.1	32	89.6	250	121.1	115	239
0	−17.8	−22	−7.6	120	48.9	34	93.2	255	123.9	120	248
1	−17.2	−20	−4	125	51.7	36	96.8	260	126.6	125	257
2	−16.7	−18	−0.4	130	54.4	38	100.4	265	129.4	130	266
3	−16.1	−16	3.2	135	57.2	40	104	270	132.2	135	275
4	−15.6	−14	6.8	140	60.0	42	107.6	275	135.0	140	284
5	−15.0	−12	10.4	145	62.8	44	112.2	280	137.8	145	293
10	−12.2	−10	14	150	65.6	46	114.8	285	140.6	150	302
15	−9.4	−8	17.6	155	68.3	48	118.4	290	143.3	155	311
20	−6.7	−6	21.2	160	71.1	50	122	295	146.1	160	320
25	−3.9	−4	24.8	165	73.9	52	125.6	300	148.9	165	329
30	−1.1	−2	28.4	170	76.7	54	129.2	305	151.7	170	338
35	1.7	0	32	175	79.4	56	132.8	310	154.4	175	347
40	4.4	2	35.6	180	82.2	58	136.4	315	157.2	180	356
45	7.2	4	39.2	185	85.0	60	140	320	160.0	185	365
50	10.0	6	42.8	190	87.8	62	143.6	325	162.8	190	374
55	12.8	8	46.4	195	90.6	64	147.2	330	165.6	195	383
60	15.6	10	50	200	93.3	66	150.8	335	168.3	200	392
65	18.3	12	53.6	205	96.1	68	154.4	340	171.1	205	401
70	21.1	14	57.2	210	98.9	70	158	345	173.9	210	410
75	23.9	16	60.8	212	100.0	75	167	350	176.7	215	414

TCCS1C01

ENGLISH TO METRIC CONVERSION: LENGTH

To convert inches (ins.) to millimeters (mm): multiply number of inches by 25.4

To convert millimeters (mm) to inches (ins.): multiply number of millimeters by .04

Inches		Decimals	Milli-meters	Inches to millimeters inches	mm	Inches		Decimals	Milli-meters	Inches to millimeters inches	mm
	1/64	0.051625	0.3969	0.0001	0.00254		33/64	0.515625	13.0969	0.6	15.24
1/32		0.03125	0.7937	0.0002	0.00508	17/32		0.53125	13.4937	0.7	17.78
	3/64	0.046875	1.1906	0.0003	0.00762		35/64	0.546875	13.8906	0.8	20.32
1/16		0.0625	1.5875	0.0004	0.01016	9/16		0.5625	14.2875	0.9	22.86
	5/64	0.078125	1.9844	0.0005	0.01270		37/64	0.578125	14.6844	1	25.4
3/32		0.09375	2.3812	0.0006	0.01524	19/32		0.59375	15.0812	2	50.8
	7/64	0.109375	2.7781	0.0007	0.01778		39/64	0.609375	15.4781	3	76.2
1/8		0.125	3.1750	0.0008	0.02032	5/8		0.625	15.8750	4	101.6
	9/64	0.140625	3.5719	0.0009	0.02286		41/64	0.640625	16.2719	5	127.0
5/32		0.15625	3.9687	0.001	0.0254	21/32		0.65625	16.6687	6	152.4
	11/64	0.171875	4.3656	0.002	0.0508		43/64	0.671875	17.0656	7	177.8
3/16		0.1875	4.7625	0.003	0.0762	11/16		0.6875	17.4625	8	203.2
	13/64	0.203125	5.1594	0.004	0.1016		45/64	0.703125	17.8594	9	228.6
7/32		0.21875	5.5562	0.005	0.1270	23/32		0.71875	18.2562	10	254.0
	15/64	0.234375	5.9531	0.006	0.1524		47/64	0.734375	18.6531	11	279.4
1/4		0.25	6.3500	0.007	0.1778	3/4		0.75	19.0500	12	304.8
	17/64	0.265625	6.7469	0.008	0.2032		49/64	0.765625	19.4469	13	330.2
9/32		0.28125	7.1437	0.009	0.2286	25/32		0.78125	19.8437	14	355.6
	19/64	0.296875	7.5406	0.01	0.254		51/64	0.796875	20.2406	15	381.0
5/16		0.3125	7.9375	0.02	0.508	13/16		0.8125	20.6375	16	406.4
	21/64	0.328125	8.3344	0.03	0.762		53/64	0.828125	21.0344	17	431.8
11/32		0.34375	8.7312	0.04	1.016	27/32		0.84375	21.4312	18	457.2
	23/64	0.359375	9.1281	0.05	1.270		55/64	0.859375	21.8281	19	482.6
3/8		0.375	9.5250	0.06	1.524	7/8		0.875	22.2250	20	508.0
	25/64	0.390625	9.9219	0.07	1.778		57/64	0.890625	22.6219	21	533.4
13/32		0.40625	10.3187	0.08	2.032	29/32		0.90625	23.0187	22	558.8
	27/64	0.421875	10.7156	0.09	2.286		59/64	0.921875	23.4156	23	584.2
7/16		0.4375	11.1125	0.1	2.54	15/16		0.9375	23.8125	24	609.6
	29/64	0.453125	11.5094	0.2	5.08		61/64	0.953125	24.2094	25	635.0
15/32		0.46875	11.9062	0.3	7.62	31/32		0.96875	24.6062	26	660.4
	31/64	0.484375	12.3031	0.4	10.16		63/64	0.984375	25.0031	27	690.6
1/2		0.5	12.7000	0.5	12.70						

ENGLISH TO METRIC CONVERSION: TORQUE

To convert foot-pounds (ft. lbs.) to Newton-meters: multiply the number of ft. lbs. by 1.3

To convert inch-pounds (in. lbs.) to Newton-meters: multiply the number of in. lbs. by .11

in lbs	N-m	in lbs	N-m	in lbs	N-m	in lbs	N-m	in lbs	N-m
0.1	0.01	1	0.11	10	1.13	19	2.15	28	3.16
0.2	0.02	2	0.23	11	1.24	20	2.26	29	3.28
0.3	0.03	3	0.34	12	1.36	21	2.37	30	3.39
0.4	0.04	4	0.45	13	1.47	22	2.49	31	3.50
0.5	0.06	5	0.56	14	1.58	23	2.60	32	3.62
0.6	0.07	6	0.68	15	1.70	24	2.71	33	3.73
0.7	0.08	7	0.78	16	1.81	25	2.82	34	3.84
0.8	0.09	8	0.90	17	1.92	26	2.94	35	3.95
0.9	0.10	9	1.02	18	2.03	27	3.05	36	4.0

ENGLISH TO METRIC CONVERSION: TORQUE

Torque is now expressed as either foot-pounds (ft./lbs.) or inch-pounds (in./lbs.). The metric measurement unit for torque is the Newton-meter (Nm). This unit—the Nm—will be used for all SI metric torque references, both the present ft./lbs. and in./lbs.

ft lbs	N-m	ft lbs	N-m	ft lbs	N-m	ft lbs	N-m
0.1	0.1	33	44.7	74	100.3	115	155.9
0.2	0.3	34	46.1	75	101.7	116	157.3
0.3	0.4	35	47.4	76	103.0	117	158.6
0.4	0.5	36	48.8	77	104.4	118	160.0
0.5	0.7	37	50.7	78	105.8	119	161.3
0.6	0.8	38	51.5	79	107.1	120	162.7
0.7	1.0	39	52.9	80	108.5	121	164.0
0.8	1.1	40	54.2	81	109.8	122	165.4
0.9	1.2	41	55.6	82	111.2	123	166.8
1	1.3	42	56.9	83	112.5	124	168.1
2	2.7	43	58.3	84	113.9	125	169.5
3	4.1	44	59.7	85	115.2	126	170.8
4	5.4	45	61.0	86	116.6	127	172.2
5	6.8	46	62.4	87	118.0	128	173.5
6	8.1	47	63.7	88	119.3	129	174.9
7	9.5	48	65.1	89	120.7	130	176.2
8	10.8	49	66.4	90	122.0	131	177.6
9	12.2	50	67.8	91	123.4	132	179.0
10	13.6	51	69.2	92	124.7	133	180.3
11	14.9	52	70.5	93	126.1	134	181.7
12	16.3	53	71.9	94	127.4	135	183.0
13	17.6	54	73.2	95	128.8	136	184.4
14	18.9	55	74.6	96	130.2	137	185.7
15	20.3	56	75.9	97	131.5	138	187.1
16	21.7	57	77.3	98	132.9	139	188.5
17	23.0	58	78.6	99	134.2	140	189.8
18	24.4	59	80.0	100	135.6	141	191.2
19	25.8	60	81.4	101	136.9	142	192.5
20	27.1	61	82.7	102	138.3	143	193.9
21	28.5	62	84.1	103	139.6	144	195.2
22	29.8	63	85.4	104	141.0	145	196.6
23	31.2	64	86.8	105	142.4	146	198.0
24	32.5	65	88.1	106	143.7	147	199.3
25	33.9	66	89.5	107	145.1	148	200.7
26	35.2	67	90.8	108	146.4	149	202.0
27	36.6	68	92.2	109	147.8	150	203.4
28	38.0	69	93.6	110	149.1	151	204.7
29	39.3	70	94.9	111	150.5	152	206.1
30	40.7	71	96.3	112	151.8	153	207.4
31	42.0	72	97.6	113	153.2	154	208.8
32	43.4	73	99.0	114	154.6	155	210.2

TCCS1C03

ENGLISH TO METRIC CONVERSION: FORCE

Force is presently measured in pounds (lbs.). This type of measurement is used to measure spring pressure, specifically how many pounds it takes to compress a spring. Our present force unit (the pound) will be replaced in SI metric measurements by the Newton (N). This term will eventually see use in specifications for electric motor brush spring pressures, valve spring pressures, etc.

To convert pounds (lbs.) to Newton (N): multiply the number of lbs. by 4.45

lbs	N	lbs	N	lbs	N	oz	N
0.01	0.04	21	93.4	59	262.4	1	0.3
0.02	0.09	22	97.9	60	266.9	2	0.6
0.03	0.13	23	102.3	61	271.3	3	0.8
0.04	0.18	24	106.8	62	275.8	4	1.1
0.05	0.22	25	111.2	63	280.2	5	1.4
0.06	0.27	26	115.6	64	284.6	6	1.7
0.07	0.31	27	120.1	65	289.1	7	2.0
0.08	0.36	28	124.6	66	293.6	8	2.2
0.09	0.40	29	129.0	67	298.0	9	2.5
0.1	0.4	30	133.4	68	302.5	10	2.8
0.2	0.9	31	137.9	69	306.9	11	3.1
0.3	1.3	32	142.3	70	311.4	12	3.3
0.4	1.8	33	146.8	71	315.8	13	3.6
0.5	2.2	34	151.2	72	320.3	14	3.9
0.6	2.7	35	155.7	73	324.7	15	4.2
0.7	3.1	36	160.1	74	329.2	16	4.4
0.8	3.6	37	164.6	75	333.6	17	4.7
0.9	4.0	38	169.0	76	338.1	18	5.0
1	4.4	39	173.5	77	342.5	19	5.3
2	8.9	40	177.9	78	347.0	20	5.6
3	13.4	41	182.4	79	351.4	21	5.8
4	17.8	42	186.8	80	355.9	22	6.1
5	22.2	43	191.3	81	360.3	23	6.4
6	26.7	44	195.7	82	364.8	24	6.7
7	31.1	45	200.2	83	369.2	25	7.0
8	35.6	46	204.6	84	373.6	26	7.2
9	40.0	47	209.1	85	378.1	27	7.5
10	44.5	48	213.5	86	382.6	28	7.8
11	48.9	49	218.0	87	387.0	29	8.1
12	53.4	50	224.4	88	391.4	30	8.3
13	57.8	51	226.9	89	395.9	31	8.6
14	62.3	52	231.3	90	400.3	32	8.9
15	66.7	53	235.8	91	404.8	33	9.2
16	71.2	54	240.2	92	409.2	34	9.4
17	75.6	55	244.6	93	413.7	35	9.7
18	80.1	56	249.1	94	418.1	36	10.0
19	84.5	57	253.6	95	422.6	37	10.3
20	89.0	58	258.0	96	427.0	38	10.6

TCCS1C04

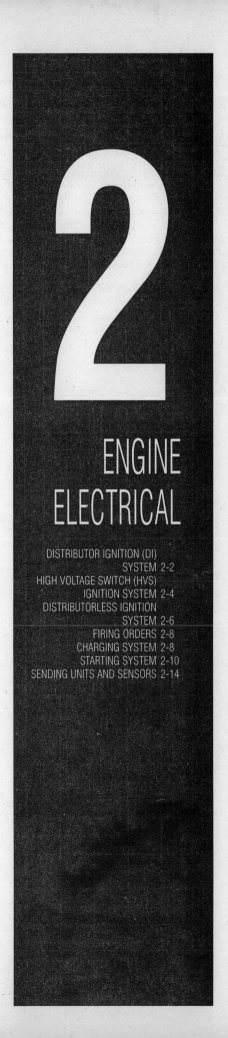

2

ENGINE
ELECTRICAL

DISTRIBUTOR IGNITION (DI) SYSTEM

➡For information on understanding electricity and troubleshooting electrical circuits, please refer to Section 6 of this manual.

General Information

The Distributor Ignition (DI) system consists of the distributor, hall effect switch (camshaft position sensor), ignition coil, secondary wires, spark plugs, knock sensor and the crankshaft position sensor. The system is controlled by the Vehicle Control Module (VCM). The VCM, using information from various engine sensors, controls the spark timing, dwell, and the firing of the ignition coil. It is used on some 4.3L models.

Diagnosis and Testing

The symptoms of a defective component within the DI system are exactly the same as those you would encounter in a conventional or HEI system. Some of these symptoms are:

- Hard or no Starting
- Rough Idle
- Fuel Poor Economy
- Engine misses under load or while accelerating

If you suspect a problem in the ignition system, there are certain preliminary checks which you should carry out before you begin to check the electronic portions of the system. First, it is extremely important to `make sure the vehicle battery is in a good state of charge. A defective or poorly charged battery will cause the various components of the ignition system to read incorrectly when they are being tested. Second, make sure all wiring connections are clean and tight, not only at the battery, but also at the distributor cap, ignition coil, and at the electronic control module.

1. Check the cap for tiny holes and carbon tracks as follows.
    a. Remove the cap and place an ohmmeter lead on the cap terminal.
    b. Use the other lead to probe all the other terminals and the center carbon ball.
2. If the readings are not infinite, the cap must be replaced.

SECONDARY SPARK TEST

It is imperative to check the secondary ignition circuit first. If the secondary circuit checks out properly, then the engine condition is probably not the fault of the ignition system. To check the secondary ignition system, perform a simple spark test.

1. Remove one of the plug wires and insert some sort of extension in the plug socket. An old spark plug with the ground electrode removed makes a good extension.
2. Hold the wire and extension about ¼ in. (0.25mm) away from the block and crank the engine.
3. If a normal spark occurs, then the problem is most likely not in the ignition system. Check for fuel system problems, or fouled spark plugs.
4. If, however, there is no spark or a weak spark, then test the ignition coil and the camshaft and crankshaft position sensors. For testing the camshaft and crankshaft position sensors, refer to Section 4.

Ignition Coil

TESTING

◗ See Figure 1

➡Make sure the ignition switch is OFF

1. Tag and disconnect the wires from the ignition coil.
2. Using a digital ohmmeter set on the high scale, probe the ignition coil as shown in Step 1 of the accompanying illustration.
3. The reading should be infinite. If not replace the coil.
4. Using the low scale of the ohmmeter, probe the ignition coil as shown in Step 2 of the accompanying illustration. The reading should be 0.2–0.5 ohms, if not replace the coil.
5. Using the high scale of the ohmmeter, probe the ignition coil as shown in

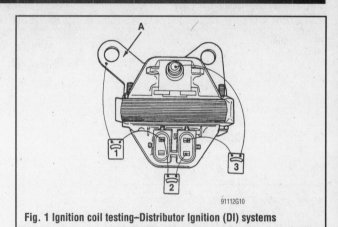

Fig. 1 Ignition coil testing—Distributor Ignition (DI) systems

Step 3 of the accompanying illustration. The reading should be 5k–25k ohms, if not replace the coil.
6. Reconnect the wires to the ignition coil.

REMOVAL & INSTALLATION

1. Tag and disengage the wiring connectors from the coil and the coil wire.
2. Unfasten the retainers securing the coil bracket or coil to the manifold.
3. Remove the coil and bracket and drill out the two rivets securing the coil to the bracket.
4. Remove the coil from the bracket.
To install:

➡The replacement coil kit may come with the two screws to attach the coil to the bracket. If not, you must supply your own screws.

5. Fasten the coil to the bracket using two screws.
6. Fasten the coil bracket or to the manifold. Tighten the retainers to 20 ft. lbs. (27 Nm).
7. Engage the coil wire and the wiring connectors to the coil.

Ignition Module

REMOVAL & INSTALLATION

All 1994 4.3L engines and 1995 4.3L VIN Z Engines

◗ See Figure 2

1. Disconnect the negative battery cable.
2. Remove the distributor cap and rotor.

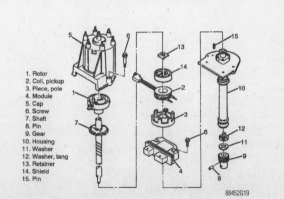

1. Rotor
2. Coil, pickup
3. Piece, pole
4. Module
5. Cap
6. Screw
7. Shaft
8. Pin
9. Gear
10. Housing
11. Washer
12. Washer, tang
13. Retainer
14. Shield
15. Pin

Fig. 2 Exploded view of the distributor and related components—All 1994 4.3L engines and 1995 4.3L VIN Z engines

3. Tag and disengage the connectors from the sealed connectors.
4. Unfasten the module retainers and remove the module.

To install:

5. Coat the base of the base of the replacement module prior to installation.

→**Neglecting to coat the base of the module with heat-sink silicone grease can lead to repeated module failure.**

6. Install the module and fasten the retainers.
7. Attach the module electrical connections.
8. Install the distributor rotor and cap.
9. Connect the negative battery cable.

Distributor

REMOVAL

▶ **See Figures 3, 4, 5 and 6**

1. Disconnect the negative battery cable.
2. If necessary, remove the air cleaner.
3. Tag and remove the spark plug wires and the coil leads from the distributor.
4. Unplug the electrical connector at the base of the distributor.
5. Loosen the distributor cap fasteners and remove the cap.
6. Using a marker, matchmark the rotor-to-housing and housing-to-engine block positions so that they can be matched during installation.
7. Loosen and remove the distributor hold-down bolt.
8. Remove the distributor from the engine.

INSTALLATION

Engine Not Disturbed

1. Install the distributor in the engine making sure that the matchmarks are properly aligned.

2. Install the hold-down bolt and tighten the bolt to 20 ft. lbs. (27 Nm).
3. Install the distributor cap and attach the electrical connector at the base of the distributor.
4. Install the spark plug wires and coil leads.
5. If removed, install the air cleaner assembly.
6. Connect the negative battery cable.

Engine Disturbed

▶ **See Figure 7**

1. Remove the No. 1 cylinder spark plug. Turn the engine using a socket wrench on the large bolt on the front of the crankshaft pulley. Place a finger near the No. 1 spark plug hole and turn the crankshaft until the piston reaches Top Dead Center (TDC). As the engine approaches TDC, you will feel air being expelled by the No. 1 cylinder. If the position is not being met, turn the engine another full turn (360 degree). Once the engine's position is correct, install the spark plug.
2. Using a long screwdriver, align the oil pump drive shaft in the engine in the mating drive tab in the distributor.
3. Install the distributor in the engine.
4. Install the distributor in the engine making sure that the matchmarks are properly aligned.
5. Install the hold-down bolt and tighten the bolt to 20 ft. lbs. (27 Nm).
6. Install the distributor cap and attach the electrical connector at the base of the distributor.
7. Install the spark plug wires and coil leads.
8. If removed, install the air cleaner assembly.
9. Connect the negative battery cable.

Crankshaft and Camshaft Position Sensors

For information on these sensors, please refer to Section 4.

Fig. 3 Disengage the electrical connector from the distributor

Fig. 4 Matchmark the rotor-to-housing and housing-to-engine block positions to aid in installation

Fig. 5 Using a distributor wrench, remove the distributor hold-down bolt

Fig. 6 Remove the distributor from the engine

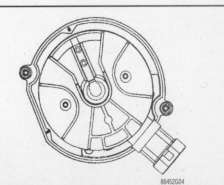

Fig. 7 The rotor segment should be aligned with the pointer cast in the distributor base, when the distributor is fully seated

HIGH VOLTAGE SWITCH (HVS) IGNITION SYSTEM

Description and Operation

▶ **See Figures 8 and 9**

The High Voltage Switch (HVS) ignition system, also known as the Enhanced Ignition (EI) system, is used only on the 1995 4.3L (VIN W) engine and all 1996–99 4.3L engines. Though the names of the system has changed the actual system itself is completely unchanged. The ignition system is controlled by the Vehicle Control Module (VCM). The VCM obtains information from various engine sensors, then uses it to compute the desired spark timing, as well as control the dwell and firing of the ignition coil by way of an ignition control line to the coil driver. The High Voltage Switch (HVS) assembly resembles a distributor, containing both a cap and rotor. But, unlike a distributor ignition system, ignition timing is preset and cannot be adjusted because the HVS is mounted in a fixed position (it cannot be rotated). The HVS provides spark at exactly the right time to ignite the air/fuel mixture producing peak performance and fuel economy. The HVS system is comprised of the following parts:

- Vehicle Control Module (VCM)
- Crankshaft Position Sensor
- Ignition Coil Driver Module
- Ignition Coil
- High Voltage Switch

The Vehicle Control Module (VCM, often referred to in the past as an ECM) is located on the right-hand side fenderwell of the vehicle. It is the control center for fuel emissions, automatic transmission control functions and the anti-lock brake system. The VCM constantly monitors information from sensors in the engine and controls the component systems. It is designed to process the various input information, then send the necessary electrical responses. The ignition module that was used on the Distributor Ignition (DI) system is not used. All Ignition Control (IC) and bypass functions are controlled by the VCM.

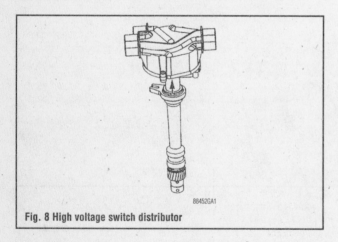

88452GA1

Fig. 8 High voltage switch distributor

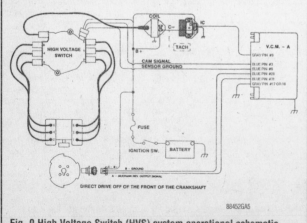

88452GA5

Fig. 9 High Voltage Switch (HVS) system operational schematic

The Crankshaft Position Sensor (CKP) is a digital sensor that provides reference information to the VCM for spark and fuel delivery. It is located in the front timing chain cover and is perpendicular to the crankshaft target wheel. There is an air gap between the sensor and the target wheel which is not adjustable. The target wheel has three slots 60° apart and is keyed to the crankshaft. As the target wheel rotates, the slots passing by the sensor create a change in the magnetic field of the sensor which results in an induced voltage pulse. One revolution of the crankshaft results in three pulses (3x signal). From these pulses, the VCM is able to determine crankshaft position and engine speed. The VCM then activates the fuel injector and provides spark to the High Voltage Switch. There is a very important relationship between the crankshaft position sensor and the target wheel in that the sensor must be perpendicular to the target wheel and have the precise air gap.

The Ignition Coil Driver (ICD) module is mounted on a bracket next to the ignition coil. The ICD controls the communication between the ignition coil and the VCM. The VCM sends a signal to the ICD commanding it to turn current ON and OFF to the ignition coil at the proper times.

The High Voltage Switch (HVS) is an assembly that looks similar to a distributor. It contains the Camshaft Position (CMP) sensor, cap, rotor and shaft. The HVS shaft is driven by the camshaft and rotates like a distributor providing spark to the correct cylinder using the cap and rotor.

The Camshaft Position (CMP) sensor is located within the HVS. It's operation is very similar to the Crankshaft Position (CKP) sensor, but it provides one pulse per camshaft revolution (1x signal). The VCM uses this signal along with the crankshaft position to determine which cylinder(s) are misfiring. It connects to the VCM through the primary engine harness and provides cylinder identification. The VCM controls the dwell and firing of the ignition coil through an ignition control line to the coil driver.

➡ **The Camshaft Position sensor does not have any effect on driveability. It's only purpose is to provide the VCM with cylinder identification and other needed information for misfire diagnostic trouble codes.**

HVS SERVICE PRECAUTIONS

- When making compression checks, disconnect the HVS electrical connector to disable the ignition and fuel injection system. Refer to Section 3 for compression check procedures.
- No periodic lubrication of the high voltage switch is required. Engine oil lubricates the lower bushing and the upper bushing is prelubricated and sealed.
- There is no manual dwell adjustment.
- The spark plug wires are made of a material which is very pliable and soft. It is very important to route the spark plug wires correctly to prevent chafing or cutting.

Inspection and Testing

HIGH VOLTAGE SWITCH INSPECTION

1. Visually inspect the HVS cap for cracks or tiny holes. Replace the cap if it is damaged or worn.
2. Check the metal terminals in the cap for corrosion. If any corrosion is found, scrape the terminals clean with a suitable scraping tool or replace the cap.
3. Inspect the HVS rotor for wear or burning at the outer terminal. A build-up of carbon on the terminal means the rotor has worn and needs to be replaced.
4. Check HVS shaft for shaft-to-bushing looseness. Place the shaft in the housing. If the shaft wobbles, replace the housing and/or shaft.
5. Visually inspect the HVS housing for cracks or damage.

IGNITION COIL TEST

▶ **See Figures 10 and 11**

If the trouble has been narrowed down to one of the components in the ignition system, the following test can help pinpoint the problem. An ohmmeter with both high and low ranges should be used. This test is made with the negative battery cable disconnected.

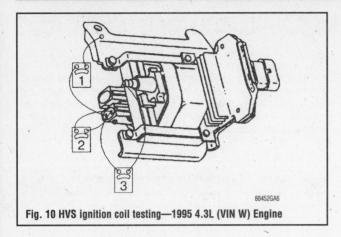

Fig. 10 HVS ignition coil testing—1995 4.3L (VIN W) Engine

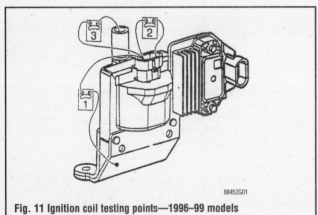

Fig. 11 Ignition coil testing points—1996–99 models

1. Disconnect the high voltage switch lead and the wiring from the ignition coil.

2. Set the ohmmeter to the HIGH scale, then connect it to the coil, as shown in Step 1 of the appropriate illustration. The reading should be infinite. If not, verify a proper test connection to be assured of a true test result and if still not infinite, replace the coil.

3. Set the ohmmeter to the LOW scale, then connect it as shown in Step 2 of the appropriate illustration. The reading should be very low or zero. If not, verify a proper test connection and replace the coil.

4. Set the ohmmeter on the HIGH scale, then connect it to the coil as shown in Step 3 of the appropriate illustration. The ohmmeter should NOT read infinite. If it does, verify the connection and replace the coil.

5. Reconnect the high voltage switch lead and wiring to the coil.

Component Replacement

REMOVAL & INSTALLATION

Ignition Coil

▶ See Figure 12

1. Disconnect the negative battery cable.
2. Disengage the wiring connectors from the side of the coil.
3. Disconnect the coil wire.
4. Disconnect the nuts holding the coil bracket and coil to the engine bracket or manifold.
5. Drill and punch out the two rivets holding the coil to the bracket then remove the coil bracket and the coil.

➡ **A replacement coil kit comes with two screws to attach the coil to the bracket.**

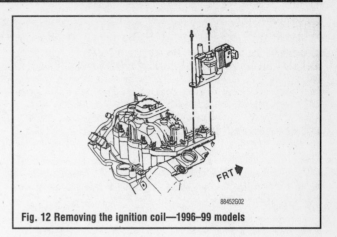

Fig. 12 Removing the ignition coil—1996–99 models

To install:

6. Connect the coil to the bracket with two screws.
7. Connect the coil and bracket to the engine bracket or manifold with studs and nuts.
8. Tighten the coil hold-down nuts to 27 Nm (20 ft. lbs.).
9. Engage the coil wire, then the wiring connectors at the side of the coil.
10. Connect the negative battery cable.

Distributor

REMOVAL

1. Disconnect the negative battery cable.
2. Tag and remove the spark plug wires and the coil leads from the distributor.
3. Disengage the electrical connector from the distributor.
4. Loosen the distributor cap fasteners and remove the cap.
5. Using a marker, matchmark the rotor-to-housing and housing-to-intake manifold positions so that they can be matched during installation.
6. Loosen and remove the distributor hold-down bolt.
7. Remove the distributor from the engine.
8. As the distributor is being removed from the engine the rotor will move in a counterclockwise direction about 42°. This will appear as slightly more than one clock position.
9. Place a second mark on the distributor to mark the position of the rotor segment. This will help to ensure the correct rotor alignment when installing the distributor.

INSTALLATION

Engine Not Disturbed

1. If installing a new distributor, place two marks on the new distributor housing in the same position as the marks on the old distributor housing.
2. Align the rotor with the second mark made on the distributor.
3. Install the distributor in the engine making sure that the mounting hole in the distributor hold-down base is aligned over the mounting hole in the intake manifold.
4. As you are installing the distributor, watch the rotor move in a clockwise direction about 42°.
5. Once the distributor is fully seated, the rotor should be aligned with the first mark made on the distributor housing. If the rotor is not aligned with the first mark made on the housing, the distributor and camshaft teeth have meshed one or more teeth out of alignment. If this is the case, remove the distributor and reinstall it so that all the marks are aligned.
6. Install the hold-down bolt and tighten the bolt to 18 ft. lbs. (25 Nm).
7. Install the distributor cap and engage the electrical connector to the distributor.
8. Install the spark plug wires and coil leads.
9. Connect the negative battery cable.

Engine Disturbed

1. Remove the No. 1 cylinder spark plug. Turn the engine using a socket wrench on the large bolt on the front of the crankshaft pulley. Place a finger near the No. 1 spark plug hole and turn the crankshaft until the piston reaches Top Dead Center (TDC). As the engine approaches TDC, you will feel air being expelled by the No. 1 cylinder. If the position is not being met, turn the engine another full turn (360 degree). Once the engine's position is correct, install the spark plug.

2. Align the cast arrow in the distributor housing, the driven gear roll pin and the pre-drilled indent hole in the distributor driven gear. If the driven gear is installed correctly, the dimple will be approximately 180° opposite the rotor segment when it is installed in the distributor.

➡ **Installing the distributor 180° out of alignment, or locating the rotor in the wrong holes, may cause a no start condition or can cause premature engine damage and wear.**

3. Make sure the rotor is pointing to the cap hold-down mount nearest the flat side of the housing.

4. Using a long screwdriver, align the oil pump drive shaft in the engine in the mating drive tab in the distributor.

5. Install the distributor in the engine. Make sure the spark plug towers are perpendicular to the centerline of the engine.

6. When the distributor is fully seated, the rotor segment should be aligned with the pointer cast in the distributor base. The pointer will have a "6" cast into it indicating a 6 cylinder engine. If the rotor segment is not within a few degrees of the pointer, the distributor gear may be off a tooth or more. If this is the case repeat the process until the rotor aligns with the pointer.

7. Install the cap and fasten the mounting screws.

8. Tighten the distributor mounting bolt to 18 ft. lbs. (25 Nm).

9. Engage the electrical connections and the spark plug wires.

Crankshaft and Camshaft Position Sensors

For information on these sensors, please refer to Section 4.

DISTRIBUTORLESS IGNITION SYSTEM

General Information

♦ **See Figure 13**

The distributorless Electronic Ignition (EI) system is used only on the 2.2L (VIN 4) engine. This electronic system is designed to provide spark for air/fuel combustion in response to timing commands from the Powertrain Control Module (PCM, often referred to in the past as the ECM). System components include the PCM, the Ignition Control Module (ICM) which contains 2 coil packs and the Crankshaft Position (CKP) sensor. Each coil pack is made up of 2 spark towers. Spark plug wires deliver voltage from the towers to the spark plugs located in the cylinder head bores. The ICM receives inputs from the crankshaft position sensor in order to monitor engine position and rotation. The module provides output signals, based on the CKP signal, which are used by the PCM to determine engine timing.

The crankshaft position sensor is mounted in the side of the engine block and protrudes within approximately 0.050 in. (1.27mm) of the crankshaft reluctor ring. The reluctor is a special wheel which is cast into the crankshaft with seven slots that are machined into it. Six of the slots are evenly spaced (60 degrees apart) while a seventh slot is spaced 10 degrees from one of the other slots. As the reluctor rotates with the crankshaft, the slots change the magnetic field of the sensor, creating an induced voltage pulse. The unevenly spaced slot is used as a reference point so the ICM can tell the PCM what cylinder is next approaching TDC.

A distributorless ignition system such as this one operates based on the "waste spark" method of spark distribution. Each cylinder is paired with the cylinder that is opposite it (1 and 4 or 2 and 3) in the firing order. The spark occurs simultaneously in the cylinder coming up on the compression stroke and in the cylinder coming up on the exhaust stroke. Since the cylinder on the exhaust stroke requires very little of the available energy to fire the spark plug, most of the voltage will go to fire the cylinder on compression. As the process is repeated, the cylinders reverse roles.

When the ignition is switched to the **ON** (or **RUN**) position, battery voltage is applied to the ICM but no spark occurs because the CKP sensor shows no engine rotation. When the engine begins to rotate and reference signals are received, the ICM will control spark by triggering each of the 2 ignition coils at a pre-determined interval based only on engine speed. This ignition operation during engine cranking is known as bypass timing mode.

Once engine speed rises above 400 rpm, the PCM will take over control of the ignition control circuit in order to compensate for all driving conditions. This is known as Ignition Control (IC) mode. During normal engine operation in IC mode, the PCM will control spark timing advance or retard according to various sensor inputs, in order to obtain optimum performance. In IC mode the PCM will rely on the following information:

• Engine load (as determined by manifold pressure/vacuum)
• Atmospheric pressure
• Engine temperature
• Manifold air temperature
• Crankshaft position
• Engine speed (rpm)

PCM control of the ignition timing will continue unless a problem occurs and the bypass timing mode is again entered, during which the ICM module will determine engine timing based on preset values. If the vehicle stalls, the engine will cease rotation thus ending CKP reference pulses. The PCM and ICM will cut the ignition. Should this occur, the ICM will not resume plug firing until engine rotation resumes.

Diagnosis

Before beginning any diagnosis and testing procedures, visually inspect the components of the ignition system and engine control systems. Check for the following:

• Discharged battery
• Damaged or loose connections
• Damaged electrical insulation
• Poor coil and spark plug connections
• Ignition module connections
• Blown fuses
• Damaged vacuum hoses
• Damaged spark plugs

Check the spark plug wires and boots for signs of poor insulation that could cause crossfiring. Make sure the battery is fully charged and that all accessories are off during diagnosis and testing. Make sure the idle speed is within specification.

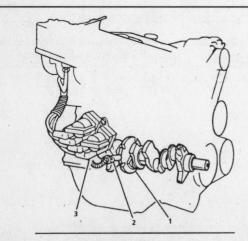

1	CRANKSHAFT RELUCTOR
2	CRANKSHAFT POSITION (CKP) SENSOR
3	IGNITION COIL ASSEMBLY

85382032

Fig. 13 Crankshaft sensor-to-crankshaft reluctor relationship

If an open or ground in the Ignition Control (IC) circuit occurs during engine operation, then engine will continue to run, but using a back-up timing mode (controlled by the ICM) based on preset timing values: The Malfunction Indicator Lamp (MIL) or SERVICE ENGINE SOON light will not illuminate at the first appearance of a break in the circuit. However, if the IC fault is still present once the engine is restarted, a Code 42 will set on OBD 1 systems in the PCM and the MIL will illuminate. Poor performance and fuel economy may be noticed while the engine is running under back-up timing.

When attempting to search for ignition troubles, keep in mind the various sensor inputs which the PCM uses to calculate timing may affect engine performance. The PCM will alter timing based on sensor inputs as follows:
- Low MAP output voltage = More spark advance
- Cold engine = More spark advance
- High MAP output voltage = Less spark advance
- Hot engine = Less spark advance

With this in mind, DETONATION could be caused by low MAP output or high resistance in the coolant sensor circuit. POOR PERFORMANCE could be caused by a high MAP output or low resistance in the coolant sensor circuit.

Ignition Coil Pack

REMOVAL & INSTALLATION

▶ **See Figure 14**

1. Disconnect the negative battery cable.
2. Raise the vehicle and support it with jackstands.
3. Remove the passenger side tire and wheel assembly.
4. Lift up the rubber flap on the wheel well to access the coil pack.
5. Tag and disconnect the spark plug wiring from the coil(s).
6. Remove the coil retaining screws (there are 2 screws per coil).
7. Separate the coil from the ignition module.

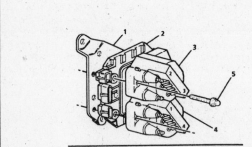

1	BRACKET	4	1-4 IGNITION COIL
2	IGNITION CONTROL MODULE	5	SCREWS (4) 4.5 N·m (40 lb. in.)
3	2-3 IGNITION COIL		

85382037

Fig. 14 Exploded view of the ignition coils and ignition module assembly

To install:

8. Install the coil to the ignition module assembly.
9. Install the coil retaining screws and tighten to 40 inch lbs. (4.5 Nm).
10. Engage the spark plug wire to the coil(s) and noted during removal.
11. Place the rubber flap back in position and lower the vehicle.
12. Connect the negative battery cable.

TESTING

1. Remove the ignition coil(s).
2. Using an ohmmeter, check the resistance between the primary terminals on the underside of the coil. The resistance should be 0.50–0.90 ohms.

3. Check the resistance between the secondary terminals. It should be 5000–10,000 ohms.
4. If the coil failed either test, replace the coil.

Ignition Control Module

REMOVAL & INSTALLATION

▶ **See Figure 15**

1. Disconnect the negative battery cable.
2. Raise the vehicle and support it with jackstands.
3. Remove the passenger side tire and wheel assembly.
4. Lift up the rubber flap on the wheel well to access the module/coil assembly.
5. Unplug the module electrical connectors.
6. Tag and disconnect the spark plug wiring from the coils.
7. Remove the 3 ignition module/coil assembly-to-block retaining bolts, then remove the assembly from the engine.
8. Remove the coils from the ignition module, then separate the module from the assembly plate bracket.

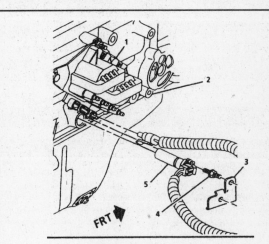

1	IGNITION CONTROL MODULE
2	ENGINE BLOCK
3	BRACKET
4	STUD - TIGHTEN TO 11 N·m (9 lb. ft.)
5	CRANKSHAFT POSITION SENSOR

85382038

Fig. 15 The ignition coil and module assembly is mounted on the side of the engine, just above the crankshaft position sensor

To install:

9. Install the module to the assembly plate bracket, then install the ignition coils.
10. Install the module/coil assembly to the engine block and tighten the retaining bolts to 15–22 ft. lbs. (20–30 Nm).
11. Connect the spark plug cables to the proper coil towers, as noted during removal.
12. Attach the module electrical connectors.
13. Place the rubber flap back in position and lower the vehicle.
14. Connect the negative battery cable.

Crankshaft and Camshaft Position Sensors

For information on these sensors, please refer to Section 4.

FIRING ORDERS

♦ **See Figures 16, 17 and 18**

➥**To avoid confusion, remove and tag the spark plug wires one at a time, for replacement.**

If a distributor is not keyed for installation with only one orientation, it could have been removed previously and rewired. The resultant wiring would hold the correct firing order, but could change the relative placement of the plug towers in relation to the engine. For this reason it is imperative that you label all wires before disconnecting any of them. Also, before removal, compare the current wiring with the accompanying illustrations. If the current wiring does not match, make notes in your book to reflect how your engine is wired.

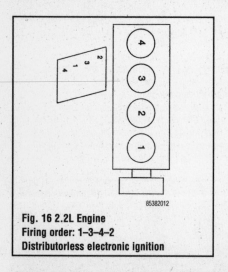

85382012

Fig. 16 2.2L Engine
Firing order: 1–3–4–2
Distributorless electronic ignition

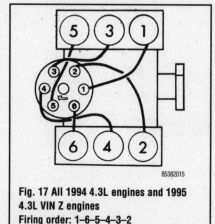

85382015

Fig. 17 All 1994 4.3L engines and 1995 4.3L VIN Z engines
Firing order: 1–6–5–4–3–2
Distributor rotation: clockwise

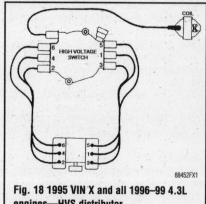

88452FX1

Fig. 18 1995 VIN X and all 1996–99 4.3L engines—HVS distributor
Firing order: 1–6–5–4–3–2
Distributor rotation: clockwise

CHARGING SYSTEM

General Information

The charging system provides electrical power for operation of the vehicle's ignition and starting systems and all the electrical accessories. The battery serves as an electrical surge or storage tank, storing (in chemical form) the energy originally produced by the engine driven generator. The system also provides a means of regulating generator output to protect the battery from being overcharged and to avoid excessive voltage to the accessories.

Alternator Precautions

To prevent damage to the alternator and regulator, the following precautionary measures must be taken when working with the electrical system.
• Never reverse the battery connections. Always check the battery polarity visually. This is to be done before any connections are made to ensure that all of the connections correspond to the battery ground polarity of the car
• Booster batteries must be connected properly. Make sure the positive cable of the booster battery is connected to the positive terminal of the battery which is getting the boost
• Disconnect the battery cables before using a fast charger; the charger has a tendency to force current through the diodes in the opposite direction for which they were designed.
• Never use a fast charger as a booster for starting the vehicle
• Never disconnect the voltage regulator while the engine is running, unless as noted for testing purposes.
• Do not ground the alternator output terminal
• Do not operate the alternator on an open circuit with the field energized
• Do not attempt to polarize the alternator
• Disconnect the battery cables and remove the alternator before using an electric arc welder on the car
• Protect the alternator from excessive moisture. If the engine is to be steam cleaned, cover or remove the alternator

Alternator

TESTING

♦ **See Figure 19**

1. Check drive belt(s) for wear and tension. Check wiring for obvious damage.
2. Go to Step 7 for vehicles without a charge indicator lamp.
3. With the ignition switch **ON** and the engine stopped, the lamp should be ON. If not, detach the wiring harness at the generator and ground the "L" terminal lead.

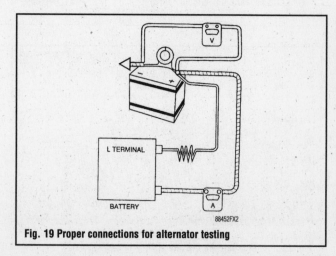

88452FX2

Fig. 19 Proper connections for alternator testing

4. If the lamp illuminates, replace the alternator. If the lamp does not illuminate, locate the open circuit between the grounding lead and the ignition switch. Check the lamp, it may be open.

5. With the ignition switch **ON** and the engine running at moderate speed, the lamp should be OFF. If not, stop the engine, then turn the switch **ON** and detach the wiring harness at the alternator.

6. If the lamp goes out, replace the alternator. If the lamp stays ON, check for a grounded "L" terminal wire in the harness.

7. Determine if the battery is undercharged or overcharged.

• An undercharged battery is evidenced by slow cranking or a dark hydrometer.

• An overcharged battery is evidenced by excessive spewing of electrolyte from the vents.

8. Detach the wiring harness connector from the alternator.

9. With the ignition switch **ON**, and the engine not running, connect a voltmeter from ground to the "L" terminal in the wiring harness, and to the "I" terminal, if used.

10. A zero reading indicates an open circuit between the terminal and the battery. Repair the circuit as necessary.

11. Attach the harness connector to the alternator and run the engine at moderate speed with accessories OFF.

12. Measure the voltage across the battery. If above 16 volts, replace the alternator.

13. Connect an ammeter at the alternator output terminal, run the engine at moderate speed, turn ON all the accessories and load the battery with a carbon pile to obtain maximum amperage. Maintain voltage at 13 volts or above.

14. If the output is within 15 amps of the rated output of the alternator (stamped on the alternator case), the alternator is good. If the output is not within 15 amps, replace the alternator.

REMOVAL & INSTALLATION

Except 2.2L Engine

▶ **See Figures 20, 21, 22, 23 and 24**

1. Disconnect the negative battery cable.
2. Remove the air inlet duct assembly, if necessary.
3. Carefully relieve the serpentine drive belt tension, then remove the belt from the alternator pulley. Do not allow the tensioner to snap back into position once the belt is off the pulley.
4. Remove the nut retaining the radiator hose brace to the back on the alternator.
5. If equipped, unfasten the retainers, then remove the brace from the engine and/or the alternator.
6. Disconnect the battery terminal boot wiring from the back of the alternator, then unplug the regulator wiring connector.
7. Support the alternator and remove the mounting bolts (usually 2) from either side of the alternator, then remove the alternator from the vehicle.

To install:

8. Position the alternator in the vehicle and loosely install using the mounting bolts.
9. If equipped, loosely install the brace to the engine and/or alternator.
10. Tighten the left or front alternator retaining bolts to 36 ft. lbs. (50 Nm), the right or rear alternator bolt to 18 ft. lbs. (25 Nm), the brace bolt to 18 ft. lbs. (25 Nm) and/or the brace nut to 22 ft. lbs. (30 Nm), as applicable.
11. Connect and secure the alternator wiring.
12. Carefully relieve the serpentine drive belt tension and position the belt over the alternator pulley, then slowly release the tensioner into position.

Fig. 20 Remove the air inlet duct assembly

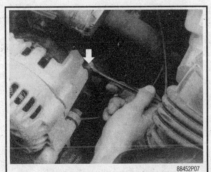

Fig. 21 Unfasten the nut retaining the radiator hose brace to the back on the alternator

Fig. 22 Remove the electrical wire from the rear of the alternator, . . .

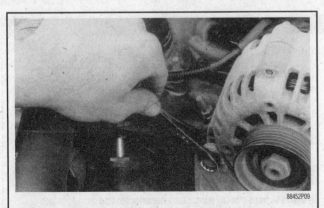

Fig. 23 . . . then remove the alternator's mounting bolts . . .

Fig. 24 . . . and remove the alternator from the vehicle

13. If equipped, install the air inlet duct assembly.
14. Connect the negative battery cable.

2.2L Engine

▶ See Figures 25, 26, 27 and 28

1. Disconnect the negative battery cable.
2. Raise and support the front of the vehicle, then remove the passenger side tire and wheel assembly for access to the rear of the alternator through the wheel well.
3. Working through the wheel well, unfasten the alternator brace-to-block bolt, then remove the brace-to-intake nut and the brace-to-engine stud nut.

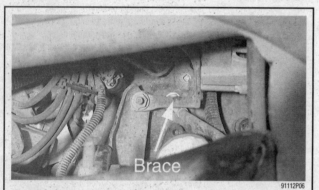

Fig. 25 The alternator brace-to-block bolts and wires are accessible through the passenger side wheel well

4. Unplug the alternator wiring connector, then remove the battery terminal nut and wire.
5. Carefully release the serpentine belt tension and remove the belt from the alternator pulley. Do not allow the tensioner to snap back into position once the belt is off the pulley.
6. Loosen the alternator retaining bolts, then support the alternator and remove the fasteners. Remove the alternator from the vehicle.

To install:

7. Position the alternator in the vehicle and loosely install the retaining bolts.
8. On 1994–98 models, tighten the top alternator bolt to 22 ft. lbs. (30 Nm) and the bottom bolt to 32 ft. lbs. (43 Nm).
9. On 1999 models, tighten the rear bolt to 37 ft. lbs. (50 Nm) and the front bolt to 18 ft. lbs. (25 Nm).
10. On 1994–98 models, install the alternator brace, then tighten the retaining nut(s) and bolts to 22 ft. lbs. (30 Nm).
11. On 1999 models, install the alternator brace, tighten the brace-to-alternator and brace-to-intake retainers to 18 ft. lbs. (25 Nm). Tighten the brace-to-engine stud nut to 37 ft. lbs. (50 Nm).
12. Install the battery terminal wire and tighten the retaining nut, then engage the alternator wiring connector.
13. Hold the serpentine drive belt tensioner, back off the belt while slipping the belt over the alternator pulley. Gradually lower the tensioner into contact with the belt, then check for proper alignment and tension.
14. Connect the negative battery cable.

Regulator

All vehicles covered in this manual were equipped with alternators which have built-in solid state voltage regulators. The regulator is in the end frame (inside) of the alternator. No adjustments are necessary or required on GM internal regulators.

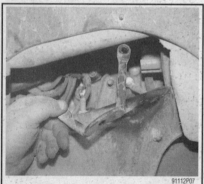

Fig. 26 After unfastening all the retainers, remove the brace through the opening

Fig. 27 The top bolt (1) is removed first from the rear of the alternator and is accessible through the wheel well opening, then remove the bottom mounting bolt (2) from the front

Fig. 28 After the bolts are unfastened, remove the alternator from the engine compartment

STARTING SYSTEM

Starter

The starting motor is a specially designed, direct current electric motor capable of producing a great amount of power for its size. One thing that allows the motor to produce a great deal of power is its tremendous rotating speed. It drives the engine through a tiny pinion gear (attached to the starter's armature), which drives the very large flywheel ring gear at a greatly reduced speed. Another factor allowing it to produce so much power is that only intermittent operation is required of it. Thus, little allowance for air circulation is required, and the windings can be built into a very small space.

The starter is usually located on the lower right-side (4.3L engines) or on the lower left-side (2.2L engines).

TESTING

Before removing the starter for repair or replacement, check the condition of all circuit wiring for damage. Inspect all connection to the starter motor, solenoid, ignition switch, and battery, including all ground connections. Clean and tighten all connections as required.

Check all switches to determine their condition. Vehicles equipped with manual transmission have a clutch safety switch attached to the clutch pedal bracket which closes when the clutch is depressed. Vehicles equipped with automatic transmissions have a manual interlock in the steering column which does not allow the ignition switch to turn to the start position unless the transmission is in the Park or Neutral position.

Check the battery to ensure that it is fully charged. For more information on battery service, please refer to Section 1 of this manual.

Check the battery cables for excessive resistance as follows:

✳✳ CAUTION

To prevent possible injury from a moving vehicle or operating engine, engage the parking brakes, block the drive wheels, place the manual transmission in Neutral or the automatic transmission in Park, and disconnect the battery feed at the distributor before performing these tests.

• Check the voltage drop between the negative battery terminal and the vehicle frame by placing one lead of a voltmeter on the grounded battery post (not the cable clamp) and the other lead on the frame. Turn the ignition key to the START position and note the voltage drop.

• Check the voltage drop between the positive battery terminal (not the cable clamp) and the starter terminal stud. Turn the ignition key to the START position and note the voltage drop.

• Check the voltage drop between the starter housing and the frame. Turn the ignition key to the START position and note the voltage drop.

• If the voltage drop in any of the above is more than 1 volt, there is excessive resistance in the circuit. Clean and retest all cables not within specification. Replace as necessary.

No Load Test

▶ **See Figures 29, 30 and 31**

Make the test connections as shown in the illustration. Close the switch and compare the rpm, current and voltage readings with the accompanying specification illustration.

• Current draw and no load speed within specifications indicates normal condition of the starter motor.

• Low free speed and high current draw indicates worn bearings, a bent armature shaft, a shorted armature or grounded armature fields

• Failure to operate with high current draw indicates a direct ground in the terminal or fields, or frozen bearings.

• Failure to operate with no current draw indicates an open field circuit,

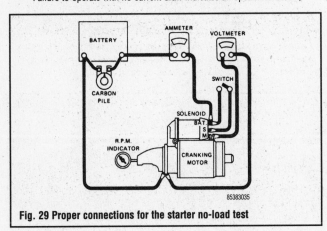

Fig. 29 Proper connections for the starter no-load test

28-MT STARTER MOTOR			
No Load Test @ 10 Volts (includes solenoid current)			
Amps		RPM	
Minimum	Maximum	Minimum	Maximum
125	190	3000	5600

91112G01

Fig. 30 Starter no load test specifications—28-MT series

SD STARTER MOTOR			
No Load Test @ 10 Volts (includes solenoid current)			
Starter	Amps		RPM	
Series	Minimum	Maximum	Minimum	Maximum
SD-210	52	76	6000	12,900
SD-260	50	62	8500	10,700
SD-260	47	70	6500	11,000

91112G02

Fig. 31 Starter no load test specifications—SD series

open armature coils, broken brush springs, worn brushes or other causes which would prevent good contact between the commutator and the brushes.

• A low no load speed and low current draw indicates high internal resistance due to poor connections, defective leads or a dirty commutator.

• High free speed and high current draw usually indicate shorted fields or a shorted armature.

REMOVAL & INSTALLATION

Two Wheel Drive

1994 MODELS

1. Disconnect the negative battery cable.
2. Raise and support the front of the truck safely using jackstands.
3. Remove the cover in order to provide access to the flywheel.
4. Tag and disconnect the solenoid wiring.
5. For the 2.2L engine, remove the attaching bracket-to-engine mount bolt.
6. Remove the starter-to-engine block bolts. When removing the last bolt, be sure to support the starter to keep it from falling and possibly injuring you.
7. Carefully lower the starter and shims (if equipped) from the vehicle.
8. If necessary, remove the bracket (2.2L engine) or the shield (4.3L engine) from the starter assembly.

To install:

9. If removed, install the bracket or shield to the starter, as applicable. Tighten the bracket nuts to 97 inch lbs. (11 Nm) or the shield nuts to 106 inch lbs. (12 Nm).
10. Carefully raise the starter and shims (if equipped) into position in the vehicle and thread one of the retaining bolts to hold it in position.
11. On the 2.2L engine, loosely install the bracket-to-engine mount bolt.
12. Install the remaining starter mounting bolt, then tighten all mounting fasteners to 32 ft. lbs. (43 Nm).
13. Engage the wiring to the solenoid as noted during removal.
14. Install the flywheel cover.
15. Remove the jackstands and carefully lower the truck.
16. Connect the negative battery cable.

1995–97 4.3L MODELS AND 1995–99 2.2L MODELS

▶ **See Figures 32 thru 38**

1. Disconnect the negative battery cable.
2. Raise and support the front of the truck safely using jackstands.

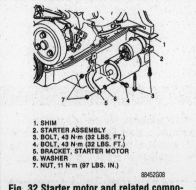

1. SHIM
2. STARTER ASSEMBLY
3. BOLT, 43 N·m (32 LBS. FT.)
4. BOLT, 43 N·m (32 LBS. FT.)
5. BRACKET, STARTER MOTOR
6. WASHER
7. NUT, 11 N·m (97 LBS. IN.)

88452G08

Fig. 32 Starter motor and related components—1996–97 2.2L engine

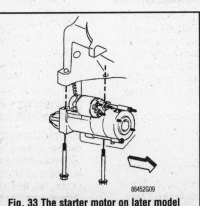

88452G09

Fig. 33 The starter motor on later model 4.3L engines is retained by two long bolts

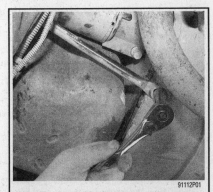

91112P01

Fig. 34 Unfasten the nut that attaches the brace rod to the transmission bellhousing

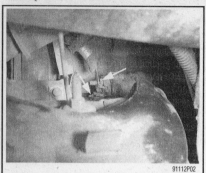

Fig. 35 Remove the drivers side wheel to access the solenoid wires through the opening in the wheel well

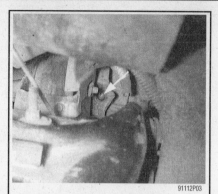

Fig. 36 Location of the starter motor attaching bracket-to-engine bolt

Fig. 37 Location of the starter mounting bolts

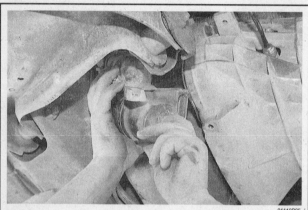

Fig. 38 After all the mounting bolts have been unfastened, slide the starter motor forward, tilt the rear end up and remove the starter motor

3. If necessary for access, disconnect the front exhaust pipe.

4. If equipped, remove the starter heat shield.

5. On the 2.2L engine, remove the brace rod from the front of the engine and the bell housing.

6. On 2.2L engines, remove the drivers side wheel to access the starter motor wires and the starter motor attaching bracket-to-engine bolt through the opening in the wheel well.

7. Disengage the wires from the starter solenoid.

8. On the 2.2L engine, remove the attaching bracket-to-engine mount bolt.

9. Remove the starter-to-engine block bolts. When removing the last bolt, be sure to support the starter to keep it from falling and possibly injuring you.

10. Carefully lower the starter and shims (if equipped) from the vehicle.

11. If necessary, remove the bracket (2.2L engine) or the shield (4.3L engine) from the starter assembly.

To install:

12. If removed, install the bracket or shield to the starter, as applicable. Tighten the bracket nuts to 97 inch lbs. (11 Nm) or the shield nuts to 106 inch lbs. (12 Nm).

13. Carefully raise the starter and shims (if equipped) into position in the vehicle and thread one of the retaining bolts to hold it in position.

14. On the 2.2L engine, loosely install the bracket-to-engine mount bolt.

15. Install the remaining starter mounting bolt, then tighten all mounting fasteners to 32 ft. lbs. (43 Nm).

16. Engage the wiring to the solenoid as noted during removal.

17. On the 2.2L engine, install the brace rod and tighten the retainers.

18. If disconnected for access, install the front exhaust pipe and tighten the fasteners.

19. If equipped, install the starter heat shield.

20. On 2.2L engines, install the drivers side wheel.

21. Remove the jackstands and carefully lower the truck.

22. Connect the negative battery cable.

1998–99 4.3L MODELS

1. Disconnect the negative battery cable.

2. Raise the vehicle and support it with safety stands.

3. Disconnect the wires from the starter solenoid.

4. Unfasten the starter motor mounting bolts.

5. If equipped, note the location of the shims. This will help during reassembly.

6. Remove the starter motor and if equipped, the shims.

To install:

7. Place the starter motor into position.

8. Install the starter motor inboard bolt but do not tighten it at this time. If equipped, install the starter motor shims, then install the outboard starter motor bolt. Tighten the bolts to 32 ft. lbs. (43 Nm).

9. Attach the wires to the solenoid and lower the vehicle.

10. Connect the negative battery cable.

Four Wheel Drive

EXCEPT UTILITY MODELS

1. Disconnect the negative battery cable.

2. In some cases it may be easier to access the starter motor bolts if you raise the vehicle, support it with jackstands and remove the wheel assembly.

3. Unbolt the engine mounts, then raise and support the engine using a suitable lifting device.

4. Unbolt the transmission mount and support the transmission assembly.

5. Remove the starter-to-engine bolts and support the starter.

6. Rotate the starter as necessary for access, then tag and disconnect the solenoid wiring.

7. Carefully lower the starter and shims (if equipped) from the vehicle. Note the location of any shims for installation purposes.

8. If necessary, remove the shield from the starter assembly.

To install:

9. Raise the starter into position in the vehicle along with any shims (making sure they are in their original positions), then tighten the mounting bolts to 32 ft. lbs. (43 Nm).

10. If removed, install the shield to the starter assembly and tighten the retaining nuts to 106 inch lbs. (12 Nm).

11. Engage the wiring to the solenoid as noted during removal.

12. Install the transmission mount and remove the supports.

13. Lower the engine and secure the engine mounts, then remove the lifting device.

14. If removed for access, install the wheel assembly.

15. Connect the negative battery cable.

UTILITY MODELS

1. Disconnect the negative battery cable.

2. Raise the vehicle and support it with jack stands.

3. If equipped, remove the brush end mounting bracket.

4. Disconnect the wiring from the starter solenoid.

5. If equipped, remove the transfer case shield.

6. Unfasten the bolts that attach the brake pipe-to-transmission bracket to the transmission crossmember and remove the brackets.

7. Unfasten the transmission crossmember bolts, (usually three on each side).

8. Unfasten the transmission mount bolts, support the transmission assembly with a transmission jack and slide the transmission crossmember out of the way.

9. Remove the bracket that attaches the transmission cooler lines to the flywheel housing, brace rod to the flywheel housing, and/or the lower flywheel housing as necessary.

10. If equipped, note the location of the shims. This will help during reassembly.

11. Unfasten the starter motor mounting bolts.

12. Remove the starter and if equipped, the starter shims.

To install:

13. If equipped, install the shims in their original locations, then place the starter motor into position.

14. Install the starter motor bolts and tighten them to 33 ft. lbs. (45 Nm).

15. If removed, install the lower flywheel cover.

16. If equipped, attach the transmission line bracket to the housing and the brace rod to the housing.

17. Place the crossmember into position and tighten the retaining bolts.

18. If equipped, install the transfer case shield.

19. Attach the solenoid wiring.

20. If equipped, install the brush end bracket and tighten the nuts to 97 inch lbs. (11 Nm).

21. Connect the negative battery cable and lower the vehicle.

22. Start the vehicle to check for proper operation.

SHIMMING THE STARTER

▶ **See Figures 39 and 40**

Starter noise during cranking and after the engine fires is often a result of too much or tool little distance between the starter pinion gear and the flywheel. A high pitched whine during cranking (before the engine fires) can be caused by the pinion and flywheel being too far apart. Likewise, a whine after the engine starts (as the key is released) is often a result of the pinion-flywheel relationship being too close. In both cases flywheel damage can occur. Shims are available in various sizes to properly adjust the starter on its mount. In order to check and adjust the shims, you will also need a flywheel turning tool, available at most auto parts stores or from any auto tool store or salesperson.

If your car's starter emits the above noises, follow the shimming procedure below:

1. Disconnect the negative battery cable.

2. Raise and support the vehicle safely using jackstands.

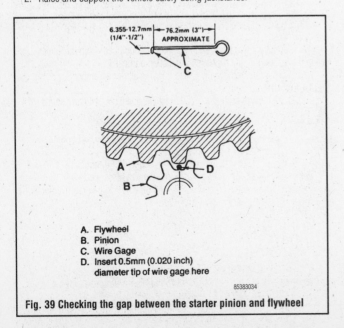

A. Flywheel
B. Pinion
C. Wire Gage
D. Insert 0.5mm (0.020 inch) diameter tip of wire gage here

85383034

Fig. 39 Checking the gap between the starter pinion and flywheel

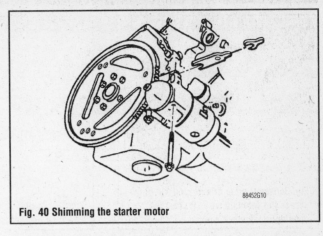

88452G10

Fig. 40 Shimming the starter motor

3. Remove the torque converter/flywheel cover from the bottom of the bell housing.

4. Using the flywheel turning tool, turn the flywheel and examine the flywheel teeth. If damage is evident, the flywheel should be replaced.

➡**Most starters are equipped with an access hole in which a small screwdriver or prybar may be inserted to push the starter pinion outward into contact with the flywheel.**

5. Move the starter pinion and clutch assembly so the pinion and flywheel teeth mesh. If necessary, rotate the flywheel so that a pinion tooth is directly in the center of the two flywheel teeth and on the centerline of the two gears, as shown in the accompanying illustration.

➡**Normal pinion-to-flywheel clearance is about 0.01–0.06 in. (0.5–1.5mm).**

6. Check the pinion-to-flywheel clearance by using a 0.020 in. (0.5mm) wire gauge (a spark plug wire gauge may work here, or you can make your own). Make sure you center the pinion tooth between the flywheel teeth and the gauge—NOT in the corners, as you may get a false reading. If the clearance is under this minimum, shim the starter away from the flywheel by adding 0.04 in. (1mm) shims one at a time to the starter mount. Check clearance after adding each shim, but do not use more than 2 shims.

7. If the clearance is over 0.060 in. (1.5mm), shim the starter towards the flywheel. Broken or severely mangled flywheel teeth are also a good indicator that the clearance here is too great. Shimming the starter towards the flywheel is done by adding shims to the outboard starter mounting pad only. Check the clearance after each shim is added. Add 0.013 in. (0.33mm) shims at this location, one at a time, but do NOT add a total of more than 4 shims.

SOLENOID REPLACEMENT

Most starters covered by this manual are equipped with replaceable solenoids. In all cases, the starter must first be removed from the vehicle for access.

1. Remove the starter and place it on a workbench.

2. Remove the screw and the washer from the motor connector strap terminal.

3. Remove the two solenoid retaining screws.

4. Twist the solenoid housing clockwise to remove the flange key from the keyway in the housing and remove.

To install:

5. Place the return spring on the plunger and place the solenoid body on the drive housing.

6. Turn solenoid counterclockwise to engage the flange key.

7. Install the two retaining screws, then install the screw and washer which secures the strap terminal.

8. Install the starter on the vehicle.

SENDING UNITS AND SENSORS

The sensors covered in this section are not related to engine control. They are for gauges and warning lights only. For sensors related to engine control refer to Electronic Engine Controls in Section 4.

Coolant Temperature Sender

TESTING

1. Remove the sender from the vehicle.
2. Place the sender in a container of water.
3. Connect one lead of a ohmmeter to the sender terminal and the other lead to the sender body.
4. Place a thermometer in the container of water and heat the water.
5. When the water is cool the resistance should be high. As the water temperature increases the resistance should decrease smoothly.
6. If not, the sender is probably faulty.

REMOVAL & INSTALLATION

▶ **See Figures 41 and 42**

1. Disconnect the negative battery cable.
2. Drain the engine cooling system to a level below the sensor.
3. Release the locktab and disengage the sensor connector.
4. Using a special sensor tool or a deep 12-point socket, loosen the sensor, then carefully unthread and remove it from the engine.

88452G11

Fig. 41 Coolant temperature sensor location—1996 2.2L engine

To install:
5. Thread the sensor into the engine by hand, then tighten using the socket or tool. If a replacement sensor came with instructions use a torque wrench to assure proper tightening.

➡**On the 4.3L engine, the manufacturer suggests coating the coolant sensor threads with a sealant such as 1052080, or equivalent.**

6. Engage the sensor wiring harness.
7. Connect the negative battery cable.
8. Properly refill the engine cooling system, then run the engine and check for leaks.

Oil Pressure Sender

OPERATION

The oil pressure sender relays to the dash gauge the oil pressure in the engine. The sensor is usually located on the top left side of the engine on the 2.2L engine and on the top left side near the distributor/high voltage switch on the 4.3L engine.

TESTING

✳✳ WARNING

This test is for testing the sender only. Verify that the engine has sufficient oil pressure before conducting this test.

1. Unplug the sender electrical connection.
2. Connect one lead of a ohmmeter to the sender terminal and the other lead to the sender body.
3. With the engine off the resistance should be approximately 1 ohm.
4. Start the engine. The resistance should increase as the engine speed increases.
5. If not, replace the sender.

REMOVAL & INSTALLATION

▶ **See Figures 43 and 44**

1. Disconnect the negative battery cable and drain the engine oil.
2. Disconnect the sensor electrical lead and unscrew the sensor.
To install:
3. Coat the first two or three threads with sealer. Install the sensor and tighten until snug. Attach the electrical lead.
4. Connect the battery cable and fill the engine with oil.

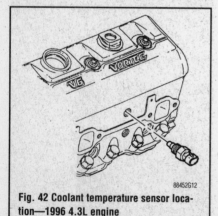

88452G12

Fig. 42 Coolant temperature sensor location—1996 4.3L engine

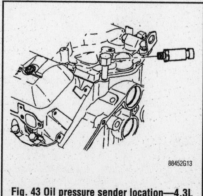

88452G13

Fig. 43 Oil pressure sender location—4.3L engine

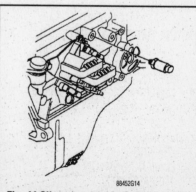

88452G14

Fig. 44 Oil pressure sender location—2.2L engine

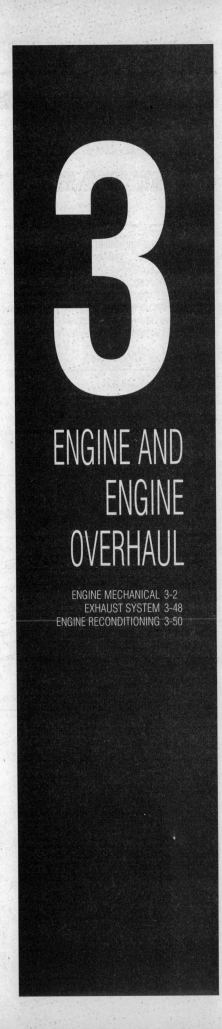

3

ENGINE AND ENGINE OVERHAUL

ENGINE MECHANICAL 3-2
EXHAUST SYSTEM 3-48
ENGINE RECONDITIONING 3-50

ENGINE MECHANICAL

2.2L ENGINE MECHANICAL SPECIFICATIONS

Description			English Specifications	Metric Specifications
General Information				
Engine type			4 cylinder in-line	
Displacement			134	2.2L
Bore			3.50 in.	89mm
Stroke			3.46 in.	88mm
Compression ratio			8.85:1	
Firing order			1-3-4-2	
Cylinder Bore				
Diameter			3.5036-3.5043 in.	88.991-89.009mm
Out-of-round (max.)			0.0005 in.	0.013mm
Taper (max.)			0.0005 in.	0.013mm
Piston				
Clearance to bore			0.0007-0.0017 in.	0.015-0.045mm
Piston Rings				
End gap				
	Compression		0.010-0.020 in.	0.25-0.50mm
	Oil		0.010-0.050 in.	0.25-1.27mm
Groove clearance				
	Compression		0.0019-0.0027 in.	0.05-0.07mm
	Oil		0.0019-0.0082 in.	0.05-0.21mm
Piston Pin				
Diameter			0.8000-0.8002 in.	20.320-20.325mm
Fit in piston			0.0004-0.0009 in.	0.010-0.022mm
Press fit in rod			0.00098-0.0017 in.	0.025-0.045mm
Camshaft				
Lift				
	Intake			
		1994-95 models	0.259 in.	6.60mm
		1996-99 models	0.288 in.	7.31mm
	Exhaust			
		1994-95 models	0.250 in.	6.35mm
		1996-99 models	0.288 in.	7.31mm
Journal diameter			1.867-1.869 in.	47.44-47.49mm
Journal clearance				
	1994-95 models		0.001-0.0039 in.	0.026-0.101mm
	1996-99 models		0.0005-0.0035 in.	0.013-0.089mm
Crankshaft				
Main journal				
	Diameter (all)		2.4945-2.4954 in.	63.360-63.384mm
	Taper (max.)		0.00019 in.	0.005mm
	Out-of-round (max.)		0.00019 in.	0.005mm
Main bearing				
	Clearance (all)		0.0006-0.0019 in.	0.015-0.047mm
Crankshaft end-play			0.002-0.007 in.	0.0511-0.1780mm
Connecting rod				
	Bearing journal			
		Diameter	1.9983-1.9994 in.	50.758-50.784mm
		Taper (max.)	0.00019 in.	0.005mm

2.2L ENGINE MECHANICAL SPECIFICATIONS

Description			English Specifications	Metric Specifications
Crankshaft (cont.)				
Connecting rod (cont.)				
	Out-of-round (max.)		0.00019 in.	0.005mm
	Rod bearing clearance		0.00098-0.0031 in.	0.025-0.079mm
	Rod side clearance		0.0039-0.0149 in.	0.10-0.38mm
Valve System				
Lifter				
	Type		Hydraulic	
	Leak down rate		12-90 seconds with 50 lb. load	
	Body diameter		0.842-0.834 in.	21.38-21.41mm
	Bore diameter		0.8435-0.8447 in.	21.42-21.45mm
	Clearance in bore		0.008-0.0027 in.	0.203-0.068mm
Rocker arm ratio			1.5:1	
Face angle (all)			45°	
Seat angle (all)			46°	
Seat run-out			0.002 in.	0.05mm
Face run-out (max. all)			0.0012 in.	0.03mm
Seat width				
	Intake			
		1994-97 models	0.049-0.059 in.	1.25-1.50mm
		1998-99 models	0.110 in.	2.80mm
	Exhaust			
		1994-97 models	0.063-0.075 in.	1.60-1.90mm
		1998-99 models	0.138 in.	3.51mm
Valve margin (min.)			0.031 in.	0.08mm
Stem-to-guide				
	Clearance			
		Intake		
		1994-97 models	0.0010-0.002 in.	0.028-0.066mm
		1998-99 models	0.0007-0.0020 in.	0.00020mm
		Exhaust		
		1994-97 models	0.001-0.003 in.	0.035-0.081mm
		1998-99 models	0.001-0.002 in.	0.035-0.076mm
Valve spring				
	Free length			
		1994-95 models	1.89 in.	48mm
		1996-99 models	1.94 in.	49mm
	Load			
		Closed		
		1994-95 models	79-85 lbs. @ 1.637 in.	350-380 N @ 41.58mm
		1996-97 models	78 lbs. @ 1.710 in.	347 N @ 43.43mm
		1998-99 models	81.2-72.8 lbs. @ 1.600 in.	361-324 N @ 40.64mm
		Open		
		1994-95 models	225-233 lbs. @ 1.247 in.	956-1036 N @ 31.67mm
		1996-97 models	228 lbs. @ 1.278 in.	1014 N @ 32.461mm
		1998-99 models	215-201 lbs. @ 1.175 in.	957-893 N @ 29.845mm

91113C01

2.2L ENGINE MECHANICAL SPECIFICATIONS

Description	English Specifications	Metric Specifications
Oil Pump		
Pressure @ 3000 rpm 150° F (65° C)	56 psi	348 kPa
Gear lash	0.004-0.008 in.	0.094-0.195mm
Gear pocket		
Depth	1.195-1.198 in.	30.36-30.44mm
Diameter	1.503-1.506 in.	38.18-38.25mm
Gear		
Length		
Drive gear	1.199-1.20 in.	30.45-30.48mm
Idler	1.199-1.20 in.	30.45-30.48mm
Diameter		
Drive gear	1.498-1.5 in.	38.05-38.10mm
Idler	1.498-1.5 in.	38.05-38.10mm
Side clearance		
Drive gear	0.0015-0.004 in.	0.038-0.102mm
Idler	0.0015-0.004 in.	0.038-0.102mm
End clearance	0.002-0.007 in.	0.05-0.18mm
Valve-to-bore		
Clearance	0.0015-0.0035mm	0.038-0.089mm

91113C03

4.3L VIN Z ENGINE MECHANICAL SPECIFICATIONS—1994-95 MODELS

Description	English Specifications	Metric Specifications
General Information		
Engine type	V6	
Displacement	4.3L	262
Bore	4.00 in.	101.64mm
Stroke	3.480 in.	88.89mm
Compression ratio		
1994 models	9.5:1	
1995 models	9.10:1	
Firing order	1-6-5-4-3-2	
Oil pressure		
1994 models	42-60 PSI @ 2400-5000 RPM	
1995 models	6 PSI @ 1000 RPM; 18 PSI @ 2000 RPM	
Cylinder Bore		
Diameter	4.0007-4.0017 in.	101.618-101.643mm
Out-of-round (max.)		
Production	0.001 in.	0.02mm
Service	0.002 in.	0.050mm
Taper		
Production		
Thrust side (max.)	0.0005 in.	0.012mm
Relief side (max.)	0.001 in.	0.02mm
Service limit (max.)	0.001 in.	0.02mm
Piston		
Clearance		
Production		
1994 models	0.0007-0.0017 in.	0.0177-0.0431mm
1995 models	0.0007-0.0024 in.	0.0177-0.0609mm
Service limit (max.)		
1994 models	0.0027 in.	0.068mm
1995 models	0.0024 in.	0.0609mm
Piston Ring		
Compression rings		
Groove clearance		
Production		
Top	0.0012-0.0032 in.	0.0304-0.0812mm
Second	0.0012-0.0032 in.	0.0304-0.0812mm
Service limit (max.)	0.0042 in.	0.1066mm
Gap		
Production		
Top	0.010-0.020 in.	0.254-0.508mm
Second	0.010-0.025 in.	0.254-0.635mm
Service limit (max.)	0.035 in.	0.889mm
Oil rings		
Production		
Groove clearance	0.002-0.007 in.	0.050-0.177mm
Gap	0.015-0.055 in.	0.381-1.397mm
Service limit (max.)	0.065 in.	1.651mm

91113C04

4.3L VIN Z ENGINE MECHANICAL SPECIFICATIONS—1994-95 MODELS

Description	English Specifications	Metric Specifications
Piston Pin		
Diameter	0.9270-0.9273 in.	23.545-23.548mm
Clearance in piston	0.0002-0.0007 in.	0.0050-0.0177mm
Fit in rod (interference)	0.0008-0.0016 in.	0.0203-0.0406mm
Exhaust Manifold		
Surface flatness (max.)	0.010 in.	0.254mm
Inlet Manifold		
Surface flatness (max.)	0.010 in.	0.254mm
Cylinder Head		
Surface flatness (overall)	0.004 in.	0.101mm
Balance Shaft		
Front bearing journal diameter	2.1648-2.1654 in.	54.985-55.001mm
Rear bearing journal diameter	1.4994-1.500 in.	38.084-38.100mm
Rear bearing clearance	0.001-0.0036 in.	0.0254-0.0914mm
Crankshaft		
Main journal		
Diameter		
No. 1	2.4484-2.4493 in.	62.189-62.212mm
Nos. 2 and 3	2.4481-2.4490 in.	62.18162.204mm
No. 4	2.4479-2.4488 in.	62.176-62.199mm
Taper		
Production (max.)	0.0002 in.	0.0050mm
Service limit (max.)	0.001 in.	0.0254mm
Out-of-round		
Production (max.)	0.0002 in.	0.0050mm
Service limit (max.)	0.001 in.	0.0254mm
Main bearing clearance		
Production		
No. 1	0.0008-0.0020 in.	0.0203-0.0508mm
Nos. 2 and 3	0.0011-0.0023 in.	0.0279-0.05842mm
No. 4	0.0017-0.0032 in.	0.04318-0.08128mm
Service limit (max.)		
No. 1	0.0010-0.0015 in.	0.0254-0.0381mm
Nos. 2 and 3	0.0010-0.0025 in.	0.0254-0.0635mm
No. 4	0.0025-0.0035 in.	0.0635-0.0889mm
Crankshaft end-play		
1994 models	0.002-0.007 in.	0.050-0.177mm
1995 models	0.005-0.018 in.	0.127-0.457mm
Crankshaft run-out (max.)	0.001 in.	0.0254mm
Crankpin		
Taper		
Production		
1994 models	0.0002 in.	0.0050mm
1995 models	0.005 in.	0.0127mm
Service limit (max.)	0.001 in.	0.0254mm

91113C05

4.3L VIN Z ENGINE MECHANICAL SPECIFICATIONS—1994-95 MODELS

Description	English Specifications	Metric Specifications
Crankshaft (cont.)		
Crankpin		
Out-of-round		
Production		
1994 models	0.0002 in.	0.0050mm
1995 models	0.0002 in.	0.0050mm
Service limit (max.)	0.005 in.	0.0127mm
Rod bearing clearance	0.001 in.	0.0254mm
Production	0.0013-0.0035 in.	0.03302-0.0889mm
Service limit	0.0030 in.	0.0762mm
Rod side clearance		
1994 models	0.006-0.014 in.	0.152-0.355mm
1995 models	0.006-0.014 in.	0.152-0.355mm
Service limit (max.)	0.015-0.046 in.	0.381-1.168mm
Camshaft		
Lobe lift		
Intake	0.232-0.236 in.	5.892-5.994mm
Exhaust	0.255-0.259 in.	6.477-6.578mm
Journal diameter	1.8682-1.8692 in.	47.452-47.477mm
Camshaft end-play	0.004-0.012 in.	0.101-0.304mm
Valve System		
Lifter	Hydraulic	
Rocker arm ratio	1.50:1	
Valve lash		
Non-adjustable		
Intake/Exhaust	①	①
Adjustable		
Intake/Exhaust	②	②
Face angle		
Intake/Exhaust	45°	45°
Seat angle		
Intake/Exhaust	46°	46°
Seat run-out (max.)		
Intake/Exhaust	0.002 in.	0.0508mm
Seat width		
Intake	0.035-0.060 in.	0.889-1.524mm
Exhaust	0.062-0.093 in.	1.5748-2.3622mm
Stem clearance		
Production		
Intake	0.0010-0.0027 in.	0.0254-0.0685mm
Exhaust	0.0010-0.0027 in.	0.0254-0.0685mm
Service (high limit production)		
Intake	+0.001 in.	+0.0254mm
Exhaust	+0.002 in.	+0.0508mm

91113C06

4.3L VIN Z ENGINE MECHANICAL SPECIFICATIONS—1994-95 MODELS

Description	English Specifications	Metric Specifications
Valve System (cont.)		
Valve spring (outer)		
Free length	2.03 in.	51.562mm
Pressure		
Closed	76-84 lbs. @ 1.70 in.	338-374 N @ 43mm
Open	194-206 lbs. @ 1.25 in.	863-916.7 N @ 31.75mm
Installed height	1.690-1.710 in.	42.926-43.434mm
Valve spring damper		
Free length	1.86 in.	47.244mm
Approximate number of coils	4	

91113C07

4.3L VIN W ENGINE MECHANICAL SPECIFICATIONS—1994-95 MODELS

Description	English Specifications	Metric Specifications
General Information		
Engine type	V6	
Displacement	4.3L	262
Bore	4.00 in.	101.64mm
Stroke	3.480 in.	88.89mm
Compression ratio		
1994 models	9.5:1	
1995 models	9.10:1	
Firing order	1-6-5-4-3-2	
Oil pressure	42-60 PSI @ 2400-5000 RPM	
1994 models	6 PSI @ 1000 RPM; 18 PSI @ 2000 RPM	
1995 models		
Cylinder Bore		
Diameter	4.0007-4.0017 in.	101.618-101.643mm
Out-of-round (max.)		
Production	0.001 in.	0.02mm
Service	0.002 in.	0.050mm
Taper		
Production		
Thrust side (max.)	0.0005 in.	0.012mm
Relief side (max.)	0.001 in.	0.02mm
Service limit (max.)	0.001 in.	0.02mm
Piston		
Clearance		
Production		
1994 models	0.0007-0.0017 in.	0.0177-0.0431mm
1995 models	0.0007-0.0024 in.	0.0177-0.0609mm
Service limit (max.)		
1994 models	0.0027 in.	0.068mm
1995 models	0.0024 in.	0.0609mm
Piston Ring		
Compression rings		
Groove clearance		
Production		
Top	0.0014-0.0032 in.	0.0355-0.0812mm
Second	0.0014-0.0032 in.	0.0355-0.0812mm
Service limit (max.)	0.0042 in.	0.1066mm
Gap		
Production		
Top	0.010-0.020 in.	0.254-0.508mm
Second		
1994 models	0.010-0.025 in.	0.2540.635mm
1995 models	0.018-0.026 in.	0.457-0.660mm
Service limit (max.)	0.035 in.	0.889mm

91113C08

4.3L VIN W ENGINE MECHANICAL SPECIFICATIONS—1994-95 MODELS

Description	English Specifications	Metric Specifications
Crankshaft (cont.)		
No. 4	0.0025-0.0035 in.	0.0635-0.0889mm
Crankshaft end-play		
1994 models	0.002-0.007 in.	0.050-0.177mm
1995 models	0.005-0.018 in.	0.127-0.457mm
Crankshaft run-out (max.)	0.001 in.	0.0254mm
Crankpin		
Taper		
Production	0.0002 in.	0.0050mm
Service limit (max.)	0.001 in.	0.0254mm
Out-of-round		
Production	0.0002 in.	0.0050mm
Service limit (max.)	0.001 in.	0.0254mm
Rod bearing clearance		
Production	0.0013-0.0035 in.	0.03302-0.0889mm
Service limit	0.0030 in.	0.0762mm
Rod side clearance		
1994 models	0.006-0.014 in.	0.152-0.355mm
1995 models	0.015-0.046 in.	0.381-1.168mm
Camshaft		
Lobe lift		
Intake	0.286-0.290 in.	7.264-7.366mm
Exhaust	0.292-0.296 in.	7.416-7.518mm
Journal diameter	1.8682-1.8692 in.	47.452-47.477mm
Camshaft end-play	0.001-0.009 in.	0.025-0.228mm
Valve System		
Lifter	Hydraulic	
Rocker arm ratio	1.50:1	
Valve lash		
Non-adjustable		
Intake/Exhaust	①	
Adjustable		
Intake/Exhaust	②	
Face angle		
Intake/Exhaust	45°	
Seat angle		
Intake/Exhaust	46°	
Seat run-out (max.)		
Intake/Exhaust	0.002 in.	0.0508mm
Seat width		
Intake	0.035-0.060 in.	0.889-1.524mm
Exhaust	0.062-0.093 in.	1.5748-2.3622mm

91113C10

4.3L VIN W ENGINE MECHANICAL SPECIFICATIONS—1994-95 MODELS

Description	English Specifications	Metric Specifications
Piston Ring (cont.)		
Oil rings		
Production		
Groove clearance	0.0014-0.0032 in.	0.0355-0.0812mm
Gap	0.015-0.055 in.	0.381-1.397mm
Service limit (max.)	0.065 in.	1.651mm
Piston Pin		
Diameter		
1994 models	0.9270-0.9271 in.	23.545-23.548mm
1995 models	0.9270-0.9273 in.	23.545-23.553mm
Clearance in piston		
1994 models	0.0004-0.0008 in.	0.0101-0.0203mm
1995 models	0.0002-0.0007 in.	0.0050-0.0177mm
Fit in rod (interference)		
1994 models	0.0013-0.0019 in.	0.0013-0.0482mm
1995 models	0.0008-0.0016 in.	0.0203-0.0406mm
Exhaust Manifold		
Surface flatness (max.)	0.010 in.	0.254mm
Inlet Manifold		
Surface flatness (max.)	0.010 in.	0.254mm
Cylinder Head		
Surface flatness (overall)	0.004 in.	0.101mm
Balance Shaft		
Front bearing journal diameter	2.1648-2.1654 in.	54.985-55.001mm
Rear bearing journal diameter	1.4994-1.500 in.	38.084-38.100mm
Rear bearing clearance	0.001-0.0036 in.	0.0254-0.0914mm
Crankshaft		
Main journal		
Diameter		
No.1	2.4488-2.4495 in.	62.199-62.217mm
Nos. 2 and 3	2.4485-2.4494 in.	62.1919-62.2147mm
No.4	2.4480-2.4489 in.	62.179-62.202mm
Taper		
Production (max.)	0.0002 in.	0.0050mm
Service limit (max.)	0.001 in.	0.0254mm
Out-of-round		
Production (max.)	0.0002 in.	0.0050mm
Service limit (max.)	0.001 in.	0.0254mm
Main bearing clearance		
Production		
No.1	0.0008-0.0020 in.	0.0203-0.0508mm
Nos. 2 and 3	0.0011-0.0023 in.	0.0279-0.05842mm
No.4	0.0017-0.0032 in.	0.04318-0.08128mm
Service limit (max.)		
No.1	0.0010-0.0015 in.	0.0254-0.0381mm
Nos. 2 and 3	0.0010-0.0025 in.	0.0254-0.0635mm

91113C09

4.3L VIN W ENGINE MECHANICAL SPECIFICATIONS—1994-95 MODELS

Description	English Specifications	Metric Specifications
Valve System (cont.)		
Stem clearance		
Production		
Intake	0.0011-0.0027 in.	0.0279-0.0685mm
Exhaust	0.0011-0.0027 in.	0.0279-0.0685mm
Service (high limit production)		
Intake	+0.001 in.	+0.0254mm
Exhaust	+0.002 in.	+0.0508mm
Valve spring (outer)		
Free length	2.03 in.	51.562mm
Pressure		
Closed	76-84 lbs. @ 1.70 in.	338-374 N @ 43mm
Open	194-206 lbs. @ 1.25 in.	863-916.7 N @ 31.75mm
Installed height	1.690-1.710 in.	42.926-43.434mm
Valve spring damper		
Free length	1.86 in.	47.244mm
Approximate number of coils	4	
Valve lift		
Intake	0.432 in.	10.927mm
Exhaust	0.441 in.	11.201mm

① Tighten the rocker arm nut to 20 ft. lbs. (27 Nm)
② Zero lash + 1 3/4 turn

91113C11

4.3L VINS W & X ENGINE MECHANICAL SPECIFICATIONS—1996 MODELS

Description	English Specifications	Metric Specifications
General Information		
Engine type	V6	
Displacement	4.3L	262
Bore	4.00 in.	101.64mm
Stroke	3.480 in.	88.89mm
Compression ratio	9.2:1	
Firing order	1-6-5-4-3-2	
Oil pressure	6 PSI @ 1000 RPM; 18 PSI @ 2000 RPM	
Cylinder Bore		
Diameter	4.0007-4.0017 in.	101.618-101.643mm
Out-of-round (max.)	0.002 in.	0.050mm
Taper	0.001 in.	0.02mm
Piston		
Clearance	0.0024 in.	0.0609mm
Piston Ring		
Compression rings		
Groove clearance	0.0042 in.	0.1066mm
Gap	0.035 in.	0.889mm
Oil rings		
Groove clearance	0.008 in.	0.2032mm
Gap	0.065 in.	1.651mm
Oil Pan		
Engine block clearance		
Tolerance (max.)	0.010 in.	0.254mm
Piston Pin		
Diameter	0.927-0.926 in.	23.545-23.548mm
Clearance in piston	0.001 in.	0.0254mm
Fit in rod (interference)	0.0008-0.0016 in.	0.0203-0.0406mm
Exhaust Manifold		
Surface flatness (max.)	0.010 in.	0.254mm
Inlet Manifold		
Surface flatness (max.)	0.010 in.	0.254mm
Cylinder Head		
Surface flatness (overall)	0.004 in.	0.101mm
Balance Shaft		
Front bearing journal diameter	2.1648-2.1654 in.	54.985-55.001mm
Rear bearing journal diameter	1.4994-1.500 in.	38.084-38.100mm
Rear bearing clearance	0.001-0.0036 in.	0.0254-0.0914mm
Crankshaft		
Main journal		
Diameter		
No.1	2.4488-2.4495 in.	62.199-62.217mm
Nos. 2 and 3	2.4485-2.4494 in.	62.1919-62.2147mm
No.4	2.4480-2.4489 in.	62.179-62.202mm
Taper (max.)	0.001 in.	0.0254mm
Out-of-round (max.)	0.0010 in.	0.025mm

91113C12

4.3L VINS W & X ENGINE MECHANICAL SPECIFICATIONS—1996 MODELS

Description	English Specifications	Metric Specifications
Crankshaft (cont.)		
Main bearing clearance		
No. 1	0.0010-0.0015 in.	0.0254-0.0381mm
Nos. 2 and 3	0.0010-0.0025 in.	0.0254-0.0635mm
No. 4	0.0025-0.0035 in.	0.0635-0.0889mm
Crankshaft end-play	0.002-0.008 in.	0.050-0.203mm
Connecting Rod		
Connecting rod journal		
Diameter	2.2487-2.2497 in.	57.117-57.142mm
Taper	0.001 in.	0.0254mm
Out-of-round	0.001 in.	0.0254mm
Rod bearing clearance	0.0010-0.0030 in.	0.0254-0.0762mm
Rod side clearance	0.006-0.017 in.	0.152-0.431mm
Camshaft		
Lobe lift	plus or minus 0.002 in.	plus or minus 0.05mm
Intake	0.2763 in.	0.7180mm
Exhaust	0.2855 in.	0.7252mm
Journal diameter	1.8677-1.8697 in.	47.440-47.490mm
Camshaft end-play	0.001-0.009 in.	0.025-0.228mm
Valve System		
Lifter	Hydraulic	
Rocker arm ratio	1.50:1	
Valve lash	Non-adjustable	
Face angle		
Intake/Exhaust	45°	
Seat angle		
Intake/Exhaust	46°	
Seat run-out (max.)		
Intake/Exhaust	0.002 in.	0.0508mm
Seat width		
Intake	0.040-0.065 in.	1.016-1.651mm
Exhaust	0.065-0.098 in.	1.651-2.489mm
Stem clearance		
High limit production		
Intake	+ 0.001 in.	+ 0.0254mm
Exhaust	+ 0.002 in.	+ 0.0508mm
Valve spring		
Free length	2.03 in.	52mm
Pressure		
Closed	76-84 lbs. @ 1.70 in.	338-374 N @ 43mm
Open	187-203 lbs. @ 1.27 in.	832-903 N @ 32mm
Installed height	1.690-1.710 in.	42.926-43.434mm
Valve lift		
Intake	0.414 in.	10.51mm
Exhaust	0.428 in.	10.87mm

91113C13

4.3L VINS W & X ENGINE MECHANICAL SPECIFICATIONS—1997-99 MODELS

Description	English Specifications	Metric Specifications
General Information		
Engine type	V6	
Displacement	4.3L	262
Bore	4.00 in.	101.64mm
Stroke	3.480 in.	88.89mm
Compression ratio	9.2:1	
Firing order	1-6-5-4-3-2	
Oil pressure	6 PSI @ 1000 RPM; 18 PSI @ 99 RPM	
Spark plug gap	0.060 in.	1.24mm
Oil Pan		
Engine block clearance		
Tolerance (max.)	0.011 in.	0.3mm
Exhaust Manifold		
Surface flatness (max.)		
1997-98 models	0.010 in.	0.254mm
1999 models	0.002 in.	0.05mm
Intake Manifold		
Surface flatness (max.)		
1997-98 models	0.010 in.	0.254mm
1999 models	0.004 in.	0.101mm
Cylinder Head		
Surface flatness (overall)	0.004 in.	0.101mm
Cylinder Bore		
Diameter	4.0007-4.0017 in.	101.618-101.643mm
Out-of-round		
Production (max.)		
1997-98 models	0.0001 in.	0.02mm
1999 models	0.0005 in.	0.0127mm
Service limit (max.)	0.002 in.	0.05mm
Taper		
Production (max.)		
Thrust side	0.0005 in.	0.012mm
Relief side	0.001 in.	0.025mm
Service limit (max.)	0.001 in.	0.025mm
Piston		
Piston bore clearance		
Production	0.0007-0.002 in.	0.018-0.061mm
Service limit (max.)	0.0024 in.	0.070mm
Piston Ring (end gap measured in the cylinder bore)		
Compression rings		
Groove clearance		
Production		
Top		
1997-98 models	0.02-0.06 in.	0.050-0.15mm
1999 models	0.0012-0.0027 in.	0.030-0.070mm
Second		
1997-98 models	0.04-0.08 in.	0.10-0.20mm
1999 models	0.0015-0.0031 in.	0.040-0.080mm
Service limit (max.)		
1997-98 models	0.0042 in.	0.107mm
1999 models	0.0033 in.	0.085mm

91113C14

4.3L VINS W & X ENGINE MECHANICAL SPECIFICATIONS—1997-99 MODELS

Description	English Specifications	Metric Specifications
Connecting Rod (cont.)		
Journal diameter	1.8682-1.8692 in.	47.452-47.478mm
Camshaft end-play	0.001-0.009 in.	0.025-0.228mm
Lobe lift		
Intake	0.286-0.290 in.	0.0726-0.0736mm
Exhaust	0.292-0.296 in.	0.0741-0.0751mm
Balance Shaft		
Front bearing journal diameter	2.1648-2.1654 in.	54.985-55.001mm
Rear bearing journal diameter	1.4994-1.500 in.	38.084-38.100mm
Rear bearing clearance	0.001-0.0036 in.	0.0254-0.0914mm
Valve System		
Lifter	Hydraulic roller type	
Rocker arm ratio	1.50:1	
Valve lash	Non-adjustable	
Face angle		
Intake/Exhaust	45°	
Seat angle		
Intake/Exhaust	46°	
Seat run-out (max.)		
Intake/Exhaust	0.002 in.	0.0508mm
Seat width		
Intake	0.030-0.050 in.	0.76-1.27mm
Exhaust	0.065-0.098 in.	1.651-2.489mm
Stem clearance		
Intake		
Production (max.)	0.0011-0.0027 in.	0.025-0.069mm
Service limit (max.)	0.001 in.	0.0257mm
Exhaust		
Production (max.)	0.0011-0.0027 in.	0.025-0.069mm
Service limit (max.)	0.002 in.	0.0508mm
Valve spring		
Free length	2.03 in.	52mm
Pressure		
Closed	76-84 lbs. @ 1.70 in.	338-374 N @ 43mm
Open	187-203 lbs. @ 1.27 in.	832-903 N @ 32mm
Installed height	1.78 in.	45.2mm
Intake		
Exhaust	1.690-1.710 in.	42.926-43.434mm
Valve lift		
Intake	0.414 in.	10.51mm
Exhaust	0.428 in.	10.87mm

91113C16

4.3L VINS W & X ENGINE MECHANICAL SPECIFICATIONS—1997-99 MODELS

Description	English Specifications	Metric Specifications
Piston Ring (cont.)		
Gap		
Production		
Top	0.010-0.016 in.	0.25-0.40mm
Second	0.018-0.026 in.	0.46-0.66mm
Service limit (max.)	0.06-0.035 in.	0.25-0.88mm
Oil rings		
Production		
Groove clearance	0.002-0.007 in.	0.050-0.177mm
Gap	0.015-0.050 in.	0.003-0.0127mm
Service limit (max.)		
Groove clearance	0.002-0.008 in.	0.051-0.20mm
Gap	0.009-0.065 in.	0.25-1.65mm
Piston Pin		
Diameter	0.926-0.927 in.	23.545-23.548mm
Clearance in piston		
Production	0.0002-0.0007 in.	0.009-0.0024mm
Service limit (max.)	0.001 in.	0.0254mm
Fit in rod (interference)	0.0008-0.0016 in.	0.0203-0.0406mm
Crankshaft		
Main journal		
Diameter		
No.1	2.4488-2.4495 in.	62.199-62.217mm
Nos. 2 and 3	2.4485-2.4494 in.	62.1919-62.2147mm
No. 4	2.4480-2.4489 in.	62.179-62.202mm
Taper		
Production (max.)	0.0003 in.	0.0076mm
Out-of-round		
Production (max.)	0.0002 in.	0.005mm
Service limit (max.)	0.001 in.	0.025mm
Main bearing clearance		
Production (max.)		
No.1	0.0008-0.0020 in.	0.020-0.050mm
Nos. 2, 3 and 4	0.0009-0.0024 in.	0.22-0.061mm
Service limit (max.)		
No.1	0.0010-0.0020 in.	0.025-0.05mm
Nos. 2, 3 and 4	0.0010-0.0025 in.	0.025-0.06mm
Crankshaft end-play	0.002-0.008 in.	0.050-0.203mm
Crankshaft run-out	0.001 in.	0.025mm
Connecting Rod		
Connecting rod journal		
Diameter	2.2487-2.2497 in.	57.117-57.142mm
Taper		
Production (max.)	0.0003 in.	0.007mm
Service limit (max.)	0.001 in.	0.0254mm
Out-of-round		
Production (max.)	0.0002 in.	0.007mm
Service limit (max.)	0.001 in.	0.0254mm
Rod bearing clearance		
Production (max.)	0.0013-0.0035 in.	0.033-0.088mm
Service limit (max.)	0.0010-0.0030 in.	0.025-0.076mm
Rod side clearance	0.006-0.017 in.	0.152-0.431mm

91113C15

Engine

REMOVAL & INSTALLATION

◆ See Figure 1

In the process of removing the engine, you will come across a number of steps which call for the removal of a separate component or system, such as "disconnect the exhaust system" or "remove the radiator." In most instances, a detailed removal procedure can be found elsewhere in this manual.

It is virtually impossible to list each individual wire and hose which must be disconnected, simply because so many different model and engine combinations have been manufactured. Careful observation and common sense are the best possible approaches to any repair procedure.

Removal and installation of the engine can be made easier if you follow these basic points:

• If you have to drain any of the fluids, use a suitable container.

• Always tag any wires or hoses and, if possible, the components they came from before disconnecting them.

• Because there are so many bolts and fasteners involved, store and label the retainers from components separately in muffin pans, jars or coffee cans. This will prevent confusion during installation.

• After unbolting the transmission or transaxle, always make sure it is properly supported.

• If it is necessary to disconnect the air conditioning system, have this service performed by a qualified technician using a recovery/recycling station. If the system does not have to be disconnected, unbolt the compressor and set it aside.

• When unbolting the engine mounts, always make sure the engine is properly supported. When removing the engine, make sure that any lifting devices are properly attached to the engine. It is recommended that if your engine is supplied with lifting hooks, your lifting apparatus be attached to them.

• Lift the engine from its compartment slowly, checking that no hoses, wires or other components are still connected.

• After the engine is clear of the compartment, place it on an engine stand or workbench.

• After the engine has been removed, you can perform a partial or full teardown of the engine using the

Fig. 1 When removing nuts, bolts and other parts, place them in a tray or similar container

TCCS3111

4.3L Engines

1. Disconnect the negative battery cable and properly relieve the fuel system pressure.

2. Disconnect the vacuum reservoir and/or the underhood light from the hood (as equipped), then remove the outer cowl vent grilles.

3. Matchmark and remove the hood from the vehicle.

4. Raise and support the front of the vehicle safely using jackstands. It will be most convenient if the truck can be supported so underhood access is still possible. Otherwise, the truck will have to be raised and lowered multiple times during the procedure for the necessary access.

5. Drain the engine cooling system and the engine oil into separate drain pans.

6. Disconnect the oxygen sensor and/or wiring.

7. Disconnect the exhaust at the manifolds and loosen the hanger at the catalytic converter. This is necessary to remove the rear catalytic converter cushion mounts for removal of the exhaust assembly.

8. If equipped, remove the skid plate.

9. Remove the pencil braces from the engine to the transmission.

10. If equipped, remove the slave cylinder and position aside.

11. Disconnect the line clamp at the bellhousing.

12. Tag and disconnect the wiring from the starter, remove the flywheel cover and remove the starter from the vehicle.

13. On some 1998–99 4WD models, remove the transfer case.

14. Remove the oil filter.

15. Remove the engine mount through-bolts.

16. Remove the rear engine mount crossbar nut and washer.

17. Unfasten all of the bellhousing bolts, except the upper left bolt.

18. Disconnect the battery ground (negative) cable from the engine.

19. On 4WD vehicles, remove the front drive axle bolts and roll the axle downward.

20. Remove the air cleaner assembly and duct work.

21. Remove the upper radiator shroud, then remove the fan assembly.

22. Remove the multi-ribbed serpentine drive belt, then remove the water pump pulley.

23. Disconnect the upper radiator hose, then remove the A/C compressor (if equipped) and position aside with the lines intact.

24. Disconnect the lower radiator hose, then disconnect the oil cooler and overflow lines from the radiator. Plug the cooler line openings to prevent system contamination or excessive fluid loss.

25. Remove the radiator from the vehicle, then remove the lower radiator shroud.

26. Disconnect the power steering hoses from the steering gear, then cap the openings to prevent system contamination or excessive fluid loss.

27. Disconnect the heater hoses from the intake manifold and the water pump.

28. Tag, disconnect and remove the wiring harness and vacuum lines from the engine. On some later model vehicles, remove the distributor assembly from the engine.

29. Disconnect the throttle cables, then remove the distributor cap.

30. Support the transmission with a jack and remove the remaining bolt from the bellhousing.

31. Disconnect the fuel lines and remove the bracket.

32. Remove the ground strap(s) from the rear of the cylinder head.

33. On 4WD vehicles, loosen the front body mount bolts.

34. Support the transmission using a jack.

35. Install a suitable lifting device and carefully lift the engine from the vehicle. Pause several times while lifting the engine to make sure no wires or hoses have become snagged.

To install:

36. Carefully lower the engine into the vehicle.

37. On 4WD vehicles, tighten the front body mount bolts.

38. Install the ground strap(s) to the rear of the cylinder head.

39. Connect the fuel lines and install the bracket.

40. Install the upper left bellhousing bolt and remove the jack supporting the transmission.

41. If removed, install the distributor, then install the distributor cap and wires.

42. Connect the throttle cables.

43. Attach the vacuum lines and wiring harness connectors as noted during removal.

44. Attach the heater hoses, then uncap and connect the power steering hoses.

45. Install the lower shroud, then install the radiator.

46. Uncap and attach the oil cooler lines to the radiator, then connect the overflow hose.

47. Connect the lower radiator hose, then if equipped, reposition and secure the A/C compressor to the engine.

48. Attach the upper radiator hose, then install the water pump pulley.

49. Install the serpentine drive belt, then install the fan assembly.
50. Install the upper radiator shroud.
51. Install the air cleaner and ducts.
52. For 4WD vehicles, roll the front axle up into position, then install and tighten the retaining bolts.
53. Connect the battery ground strap to the engine block.
54. Install the remaining bellhousing bolts.
55. Install the engine mount through-bolts and tighten to 49 ft. lbs. (66 Nm).
56. Install the rear engine mount crossbar nut and washer. Tighten the nut to 33 ft. lbs. (45 Nm).
57. If removed on some 1998–99 4WD models, install the transfer case.
58. Install a new oil filter.
59. Install the starter motor.
60. Install the line clamp at the bellhousing.
61. Install the flywheel cover.
62. If equipped, reposition and secure the clutch slave cylinder.
63. Install the pencil brace and the skid plate, as equipped.
64. Install the catalytic converter Y-pipe assembly and hangers.
65. Remove the jackstands and carefully lower the truck.
66. Align the marks made during removal and install the hood.
67. Install the outer cowl vent grilles, then connect the vacuum reservoir and/or the underhood light to the hood (as equipped).
68. Check all powertrain fluid levels and add, as necessary. Be sure to properly fill the engine crankcase with clean engine oil.
69. Connect the negative battery cable and properly fill the engine cooling system.
70. Start and run the engine, then check for leaks.

2.2L (VIN 4) Engines

✳✳ CAUTION

Never open, service or drain the radiator or cooling system when hot; serious burns can occur from the steam and hot coolant. Also, when draining engine coolant, keep in mind that cats and dogs are attracted to ethylene glycol antifreeze and could drink any that is left in an uncovered container or in puddles on the ground. This will prove fatal in sufficient quantities. Always drain coolant into a sealable container. Coolant should be reused unless it is contaminated or is several years old.

➡ **In certain cases on some models the A/C system will have to be evacuated because the compressor may need to be removed from the vehicle to allow clearance for engine removal. On other models you maybe able to set the compressor and lines to one side and still have enough clearance to remove the engine. In this case the system does not have to be evacuated because the lines do not have to be disconnected from the compressor. To check if your system has to be evacuated, unplug the electrical connectors from the compressor, then unbolt the compressor assembly. Unfasten any brackets holding the refrigerant lines and try to set the components aside so that you will have enough clearance for engine removal. If there is not enough clearance for engine removal you must have the refrigerant recovered from the A/C system by a facility equipped with an approved recovery station before attempting to remove the engine from your vehicle. DO NOT attempt this without the proper equipment. R-134a should NOT be mixed with R-12 refrigerant and, depending on your local laws, attempting to service this system could be illegal.**

1. Disconnect the negative battery cable and properly relieve the fuel system pressure.
2. Drain the engine cooling system and the engine oil into separate drain pans.
3. Matchmark and remove the hood from the vehicle.
4. On 1997 models, remove the battery.
5. Raise and support the front of the vehicle safely using jackstands. It will be most convenient if the truck can be supported so underhood access is still possible. Otherwise, the truck will have to be raised and lowered multiple times during the procedure for the necessary access.
6. Unplug the Oxygen sensor electrical connection.

7. Disconnect the exhaust pipe from the manifold. On some models it may also be necessary to disconnect the catalytic converter from the exhaust pipe.
8. Remove the braces from the engine and the transmission (if equipped).
9. On 1998–99 models, remove the starter motor.
10. Unbolt the transmission and separate it from the engine or, if necessary, remove it from the vehicle.
11. If necessary for clearance on 1998–99 models, remove the alternator rear brace by unfastening the bolt and nuts.
12. Disconnect the ground straps from the engine block and remove the drive belt.
13. On 1997 models, GM recommends that you remove the water pump. We here at Chilton have removed quite a few of these engines and as of yet, we still have not had to remove the water pump when removing the engine. However, if you feel that there is not enough clearance to remove the engine without causing damage, then by all means remove the pump. It is always better to be careful so that you won't have to buy any unnecessary replacement parts, because we all know how expensive they can be.
14. Remove the A/C compressor and bracket. If possible, set the compressor and bracket to one side without disconnecting the lines.
15. Tag and disconnect the hoses and transmission coolant lines engaged to the radiator, then remove the radiator.
16. Remove the power steering pump and cap the power steering lines to avoid contamination.
17. Tag and disengage the heater hoses from the heater core in the bulkhead or from the manifold.
18. Disconnect the 12 volt supply from the mega fuse, if necessary.
19. Tag and unplug all electrical connections and wiring harnesses.
20. Tag and unplug all vacuum lines.
21. Disengage the throttle cable, and if equipped the cruise control cable.
22. If necessary for clearance on 1998–99 models, remove the EGR pipe and the EGR valve.
23. Disconnect the fuel lines.
24. Install a suitable lifting device to the engine.
25. Remove the engine mount bolts and carefully lift the engine from the vehicle. Pause several times while lifting the engine to make sure no wires or hoses have become snagged.

To install:
26. Carefully lower the engine into the vehicle and install the engine mount bolts. Remove the engine lifting device.
27. Connect the fuel lines.
28. If removed, connect the 12 volt supply to the mega fuse.
29. Attach all vacuum lines, electrical connections and wiring harnesses that were tagged and

   disconnected during the removal process.
30. If removed for clearance on 1998–99 models, install the EGR valve and pipe.
31. Connect the throttle and if equipped, the cruise control cable.
32. Connect the heater hoses to the heater core in the bulkhead or to the manifold.
33. Install the power steering pump and attach the lines.
34. Install the A/C compressor.
35. Install the radiator and attach all hoses and fluid cooler lines.
36. If removed for clearance on 1997 models, install the water pump.
37. Install the drive belt.
38. Connect the ground strap to the engine.
39. If removed for clearance on 1998–99 models, install the alternator rear brace and tighten the bolt and nuts.
40. Engage the transmission to the engine.
41. On 1998–99 models, install the starter motor.
42. Install the braces to the engine and the transmission (if equipped).
43. Connect the exhaust pipe to the manifold. If removed connect the catalytic converter to the exhaust pipe.
44. Attach the oxygen sensor electrical connection.
45. Remove the jackstands and carefully lower the truck.
46. Install the battery.
47. Align the marks made during removal and install the hood.
48. Check all powertrain fluid levels and add, as necessary. Be sure to properly fill the engine crankcase with clean engine oil.
49. Connect the battery cables and properly fill the engine cooling system.
50. Start and run the engine, then check for leaks.

Rocker Arm (Valve) Cover

REMOVAL & INSTALLATION

2.2L Engine

1994–97 MODELS

▶ See Figures 2 thru 15

1. Disconnect the negative battery cable and remove the air duct assembly.
2. Disconnect the throttle cable and remove the cable support linkage.
3. If equipped, disconnect the cruise control cable assembly.
4. Remove the PCV valve and pipe assembly.
5. Tag and disconnect the spark plug wires and move them out of the way.

6. Disconnect the power brake booster vacuum hose.
7. Loosen and remove the rocker cover retaining bolts, then remove the cover from the engine.

➡ DO NOT pry on the cover to remove it. If it sticks, use your palm or a rubber mallet to bump it rearwards, from the front.

8. Using a putty knife, carefully clean the gasket mounting surfaces. Keep debris out of the engine.

To install:

9. Install the rocker arm cover to the engine using a new gasket, then tighten the retainers to 89 inch lbs. (10 Nm). Be careful not to overtighten the fasteners and either distort the valve cover (causing and leak) or break the fastener (causing more work).
10. Connect the spark plug wires.
11. Install the PCV valve and pipe assembly.
12. Connect the brake booster vacuum hose.

Fig. 2 Unfasten the throttle linkage cover retaining bolt . . .

Fig. 3 . . . and remove the cover

Fig. 4 Disconnect the throttle cable from the linkage

Fig. 5 Use a suitable prytool to pry the cable retaining clip from the cable support bracket and slide the cable out of the bracket

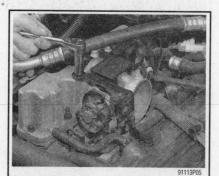

Fig. 6 Unfasten the retainers attaching the front cable support bracket from the upper intake manifold and the valve cover

Fig. 7 Unfasten the rear cable support bracket bolt and set the cable and bracket aside

Fig. 8 Unscrew the crankcase vent valve retainer . . .

Fig. 9 . . . and pull the pipe and valve assembly from the valve cover

Fig. 10 Disconnect the PCV valve hose from the valve

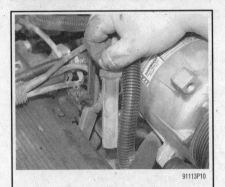

Fig. 11 Disconnect the spark plug wires and move them aside

Fig. 12 Disconnect the brake booster vacuum hose clamp using pliers . . .

Fig. 13 . . . and disconnect the hose, then set the hose assembly aside

Fig. 14 Remove the valve cover retaining bolts

Fig. 15 Lift the valve cover and move it backwards until it clears the hoses at the front of the engine, then remove the valve cover

13. If equipped, install the cruise control cable assembly.

14. Connect the throttle cable and secure the cable support linkage. Tighten the bracket bolts to 10 ft. lbs. (25 Nm) and the bracket nut to 22 ft. lbs. (30 Nm).

15. Connect the air duct to the inlet, then connect the negative battery cable.

1998-99 MODELS

▶ See Figure 16

1. Disconnect the negative battery cable and remove the air cleaner outlet resonator.

2. Disconnect the vacuum brake booster hose.

3. Disconnect the throttle cable and cruise control cables.

4. Tag and disconnect the spark plug wires from the spark plugs, then remove the spark plug wire retainer from the heater hose pipe.

5. Remove the PCV valve hose.

6. Remove the throttle body assembly.

7. Unfasten the heater hose pipe bracket-to-air cleaner outlet resonator bracket bolt.

8. Remove the air cleaner resonator bracket.

9. Remove the engine wiring harness bracket by unfastening the bolt at the rear of the cylinder head and the two bolts that attach the bracket to the valve cover, then slide the bracket off the bolt at the rear of the cylinder head.

10. Note the location of the studs before removal , then loosen and remove the rocker cover retaining bolts and studs. Remove the cover from the engine.

➡DO NOT pry on the cover to remove it. If it sticks, use your palm or a rubber mallet to bump it rearwards, from the front.

11. Using a putty knife, carefully clean the gasket mounting surfaces. Keep debris out of the engine.

To install:

12. Install the rocker arm cover to the engine using a new gasket, then tighten the retainers to 89 inch lbs. (10 Nm) in the sequence illustrated. Be careful not to overtighten the fasteners and either distort the valve cover (causing and leak) or break the fastener (causing more work).

13. Install the wiring harness bracket and its retainers. Tighten the bracket-

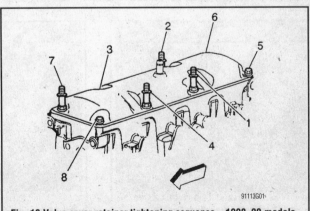

Fig. 16 Valve cover retainer tightening sequence—1998-99 models

to-valve bracket bolts to 89 inch lbs. (10 Nm) and the bolt at the rear of the cylinder head to 18 ft. lbs. (25 Nm).

14. Install the air cleaner resonator bracket. Tighten the nuts to 97 inch lbs. (11 Nm).

15. Attach the heater hose bracket to the air cleaner resonator and tighten the bolt to 10 ft. lbs. (14 Nm).

16. Install the throttle body assembly.

17. Install the spark plug wire retainer and attach the spark plug wires to the plugs.

18. Install the PCV valve hose.

19. Connect the throttle cable and cruise control cable.

20. Connect the vacuum brake booster hose.

21. Install the air cleaner outlet resonator and connect the negative battery cable.

4.3L Engine

RIGHT SIDE—1994–95 MODELS

▶ **See Figures 17, 18, 19 and 20**

1. Disconnect the negative battery cable.
2. Remove the air cleaner.
3. On 1995 (VIN W) engines, remove the PCV valve and pipe assembly.
4. On 1995 (VIN W) engines, remove the coil with the bracket and lay to one side.
5. Remove the EGR controller and MAP sensor bracket.
6. Tag and disconnect the necessary vacuum lines.

Fig. 17 Tag and disengage the necessary electrical connections and vacuum lines

7. Remove the wiring harness from the retaining clips and lay it aside.
8. Remove the rocker arm cover bolts, then remove the cover from the cylinder head.

➡**DO NOT pry on the cover to remove it. If it sticks, use your palm or a rubber mallet to bump it rearwards, from the front.**

9. Using a putty knife, carefully clean the gasket mounting surfaces. Keep debris out of the engine.

To install:

10. Install the rocker arm cover to the engine using a new gasket, then tighten the retainers to 89 inch lbs. (10 Nm). Be careful not to overtighten the fasteners and either distort the valve cover (causing and leak) or break the fastener (causing more work).

11. Install the EGR controller and MAP sensor bracket.
12. Connect the vacuum lines as noted during removal.
13. On 1995 (VIN W) engines, install the coil with the bracket.
14. On 1995 (VIN W) engines, install the PCV valve and pipe assembly.
15. Position and secure electrical wiring harness in the retaining clips.
16. Install the air cleaner.
17. Connect the negative battery cable.

LEFT SIDE—1994–95 MODELS

1. Disconnect the negative battery cable.
2. Remove the air cleaner assembly.
3. If necessary, remove the crankcase ventilation pipe.
4. If equipped, remove the pencil brace, then disconnect the power brake vacuum line at the booster.
5. Remove the rocker arm cover bolts, then remove the cover.

➡**DO NOT pry on the cover to remove it. If it sticks, use your palm or a rubber mallet to bump it rearwards, from the front.**

6. Using a putty knife, carefully clean the gasket mounting surfaces. Keep debris out of the engine.

⁑ **CAUTION**

The EPA warns that prolonged contact with used engine oil may cause a number of skin disorders, including cancer! You should make every effort to minimize you exposure to used engine oil. Protective gloves should be worn when changing the oil. Wash your hands and any other exposed skin areas as soon as possible after exposure to used engine oil. Soap and water, or waterless hand cleaner should be used.

To install:

7. Install the rocker arm cover to the engine using a new gasket, then tighten the retainers to 89 inch lbs. (10 Nm). Be careful not to overtighten the fasteners and either distort the valve cover (causing and leak) or break the fastener (causing more work).

8. Connect the power brake booster vacuum line to the booster.
9. If equipped, install the pencil brace.
10. If removed, install the crankcase ventilation pipe

Fig. 18 Unfasten the rocker arm cover bolts

Fig. 19 Remove the rocker arm cover from the engine

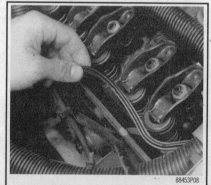

Fig. 20 Remove the old rocker arm cover gasket

11. Install the air cleaner assembly.

12. Connect the negative battery cable.

RIGHT SIDE—1996–98 MODELS

1. Disconnect the negative battery cable.
2. Remove the air cleaner assembly.
3. Tag and disconnect the spark plug wires.
4. If equipped, remove the vent tube.
5. Disconnect the wiring bracket at the generator bracket.
6. Unfasten the oil level dipstick tube brace bolt, then move the heater hoses aside
7. Unfasten the rocker arm cover bolts.
8. Remove the rocker arm cover and gasket.
9. Using a putty knife, carefully clean the gasket mounting surfaces. Keep debris out of the engine.

To install:

10. Install the rocker arm cover to the engine using a new gasket.
11. Install new bolt grommets, then tighten the retainers to 106 inch lbs. (12 Nm). Be careful not to overtighten the fasteners and either distort the valve cover (causing and leak) or break the fastener (causing more work).
12. Engage the wiring bracket to the generator bracket.
13. Install the vent tube and engage the spark plug wires.
14. Install the air cleaner assembly.
15. Connect the negative battery cable.

RIGHT SIDE—1999 MODELS

1. Disconnect the negative battery cable.
2. Remove the PCV tube from the valve cover and air inlet duct.
3. Tag and disconnect the spark plug wires from the plugs.
4. Remove the EVAP canister purge solenoid valve.
5. Unfasten the heater hose retainer above the valve cover.
6. Move the heater hoses to one side and wire them aside so that they stay there.
7. Unfasten the bolt attaching the engine wiring harness bracket to the alternator.
8. Unplug the Crankshaft Position (CKP) sensor electrical connection, then move the wiring harness aside.
9. Unfasten the rocker arm cover bolts.
10. Remove the rocker arm cover and gasket.
11. Using a putty knife, carefully clean the gasket mounting surfaces. Keep debris out of the engine.

To install:

12. Install the rocker arm cover to the engine using a new gasket.
13. Install new bolt grommets, then tighten the retainers to 106 inch lbs. (12 Nm). Be careful not to overtighten the fasteners and either distort the valve cover (causing and leak) or break the fastener (causing more work).
14. Place the wiring harness into position, then attach CKP sensor electrical connection.
15. Place the heater hoses into position and fasten the heater hose retainer.
16. Attach the EVAP canister purge solenoid valve.
17. Connect the spark plug wires.
18. Install the PCV tube.
19. Connect the negative battery cable.

LEFT SIDE—1996–99 MODELS

1. Disconnect the negative battery cable and disconnect the air duct from the inlet.
2. If necessary on 1996 models, disengage the A/C compressor and bracket and move the compressor to one side.
3. Remove the PCV valve and pipe assembly.
4. Tag and disconnect the spark plug wires from the spark plugs.
5. On 1999 and later models, unplug the Engine Coolant Temperature (ECT) sensor electrical connection.
6. On 1999 and later models, partially drain the coolant, then disconnect the radiator inlet hose from the thermostat housing outlet.
7. On 1999 and later models, remove the EGR valve inlet pipe from the exhaust and intake manifolds.
8. Unfasten the rocker arm cover bolts.
9. Remove the rocker arm cover and gasket.
10. Using a putty knife, carefully clean the gasket mounting surfaces. Keep debris out of the engine.

To install:

11. Install the rocker arm cover to the engine using a new gasket.
12. Install new bolt grommets, then tighten the retainers to 106 inch lbs. (12 Nm). Be careful not to overtighten the fasteners and either distort the valve cover (causing and leak) or break the fastener (causing more work).
13. On 1999 and later models, attach the EGR valve inlet pipe from the exhaust and intake manifolds. Tighten the pipe-to-intake manifold nut to 18 ft. lbs. (25 Nm), the pipe-to-exhaust manifold nut to 22 ft. lbs. (30 Nm) and the pipe clamp bolt to 18 ft. lbs. (25 Nm).
14. On 1999 and later models, connect the radiator inlet hose to the thermostat housing outlet and fill the cooling system.
15.. On 1999 and later models, attach the ECT sensor electrical connection.
16. Connect the spark plug wires.
17. On 1996 models, if removed, install the A/C compressor bracket and compressor.
18. Install the PCV valve and pipe assembly.
19. Engage the air duct to the inlet and connect the negative battery cable.

Rocker Arms

REMOVAL & INSTALLATION

2.2L Engine

▶ See Figures 21, 22, 23, 24 and 25

1. Remove the rocker arm cover from the cylinder head.
2. Unfasten the rocker arm retaining nut, then remove the arm and ball. If necessary, withdraw the pushrod form the cylinder head.

➡**Valve train components which are to be reused MUST be installed in their original positions. If removed, be sure to tag or arrange all rocker arms and pushrods to assure proper installation.**

To install:

3. Inspect the rocker arms, balls and pushrods for damage or wear and replace, as necessary:

   a. Check the rocker arms, balls and their mating surfaces. Make sure the surfaces are smooth and free from scoring or other damage.

   b. Check the rocker arm areas that contact the valve stems and the sockets that contact the pushrods, make sure these areas are smooth and free of both damage and wear.

   c. Make sure the pushrods are not bent; this can be determined by rolling them on a flat surface. Check the ends of the pushrods for scoring or roughness.

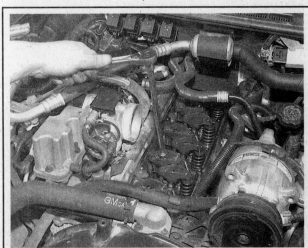

91113P15

Fig. 21 Unfasten the rocker arm retaining nut. A long extension may be needed to avoid hitting your hand on any of the surrounding components

Fig. 22 Once the nut is loosened, remove it from the rocker arm stud

Fig. 23 Remove the rocker ball and washer (which should be inside the rocker arm). Be careful not to loose the ball

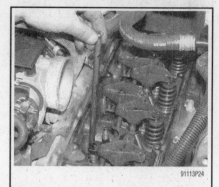

Fig. 24 If necessary, remove the pushrod

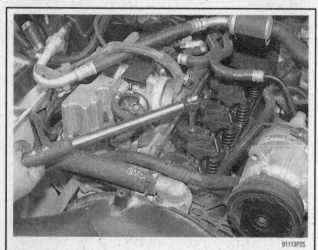

Fig. 25 Use a torque wrench to tighten the rocker arm nuts to specification

d. Inspect the rocker arm bolts for thread damage. Check the rocker arm bolts in the shoulder area for contact damage with the rocker arm.

4. If removed, install the pushrods making sure they are seated within the lifters.

5. If installing new rocker arms and balls, coat the friction surfaces using Dri-Slide Molykote® or an equivalent pre-lube.

➡When tightening the rocker arm retainers, make sure the lifter for that valve is resting on the base circle of the camshaft NOT on the lobe. DO NOT overtighten the retainers.

6. Install the rocker arms and ball, then tighten the retaining nuts to 22 ft. lbs. (30 Nm) on 1994–97 models and 19 ft. lbs. (25 Nm) on 1998–99 models.

➡Valve lash is NOT adjustable on the 2.2L gasoline engine.

7. Install the rocker arm cover, then start and run the engine to check for leaks.

4.3L Engine

▶ See Figures 26, 27, 28, 29 and 30

1. Remove the rocker arm cover(s) from the cylinder head.
2. Remove the rocker arm nut, the rocker arm and the ball washer.

➡If only the pushrod is to be removed, loosen the rocker arm nut, swing the rocker arm to the side and remove the pushrod.

3. Valve train components which are to be reused MUST be installed in their original positions. If removed, be sure to tag or arrange all rocker arms and pushrods to assure proper installation.

4. Withdraw the pushrod from the cylinder head.

To install:

5. Inspect and replace components if worn or damaged.

6. Coat the bearing surfaces of the rocker arms and the rocker arm ball washers with Molykote® or equivalent pre-lube.

7. Install the pushrods making sure that they seat properly in the lifter.

8. Install the rocker arms, ball washers and the nuts.

9. For the 4.3L engines which are equipped with screw-in type rocker arm studs with positive stop shoulders, tighten the rocker arm adjusting nuts against the stop shoulders to 20 ft. lbs. (27 Nm) on 1994–96 models and 18 ft. lbs. (25 Nm) on 1997–99 models. No further adjustment is necessary, or possible.

10. For most 4.3L engines which are not equipped with screw-in type rocker arm studs and positive stop shoulders, properly adjust the valve lash. For details on valve lash adjustment, please refer to the procedure in Section 1.

11. Install the rocker arm cover(s) to the cylinder head.

12. Start and run the engine, then check for leaks and for proper ignition timing adjustment.

Fig. 26 Unfasten the rocker arm nut

Fig. 27 Remove the ball washer . . . .

Fig. 28 . . . . then remove the rocker arm

Fig. 29 Remove the pushrod from the cylinder head

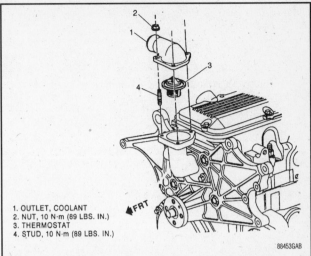

1. OUTLET, COOLANT
2. NUT, 10 N·m (89 LBS. IN.)
3. THERMOSTAT
4. STUD, 10 N·m (89 LBS. IN.)

Fig. 31 View of the thermostat and related components—2.2L engine

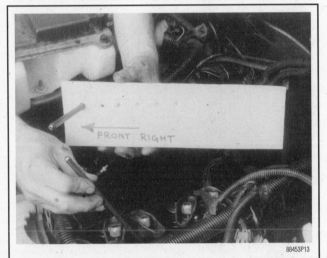

FRONT RIGHT

Fig. 30 A piece of cardboard may be used to hold the pushrods in order

Fig. 32 Use pliers to disconnect the clamp that attaches the upper radiator hose to the water outlet . . .

Thermostat

REMOVAL & INSTALLATION

2.2L Engine

▶ See Figures 31 thru 36

The thermostat is located in a housing protruding from the front of the engine, just above the water pump assembly.

❊❊ CAUTION

Never open, service or drain the radiator or cooling system when hot; serious burns can occur from the steam and hot coolant. Also, when draining engine coolant, keep in mind that cats and dogs are attracted to ethylene glycol antifreeze and could drink any that is left in an uncovered container or in puddles on the ground. This will prove fatal in sufficient quantities. Always drain coolant into a sealable container. Coolant should be reused unless it is contaminated or is several years old.

Fig. 33 . . . then disconnect the hose from the outlet

Fig. 34 Location of the water outlet retainers

Fig. 35 Unfasten the retainers and remove the water outlet assembly

Fig. 36 Note the orientation of the thermostat and remove it from the housing

1. Drain the engine cooling system to a level just below the thermostat.
2. Loosen the clamp that attaches the upper radiator hose to the water outlet and disconnect the hose from the outlet.
3. Remove the water outlet retainers, then lift the outlet from the housing.
4. Remove the thermostat from the housing, noting the orientation for installation purposes.

To install:

5. Carefully clean the all traces of the old gasket or sealer from the housing and outlet.
6. Install the thermostat to the housing, oriented as noted during removal, then position a new gasket (if used).
7. Place a ⅛ in. (3mm) bead of RTV sealant in the groove on the water outlet sealing surface, then install the outlet while the sealer is still wet.
8. Install the outlet retainers and tighten to 18 ft. lbs. (25 Nm) on 1994 models and 89 inch lbs. (10 Nm) on 1995–99 models.
9. Attach the upper radiator hose to the water outlet and securely fasten the clamp.
10. Properly fill the engine cooling system and check for leaks.

4.3L Engine

▶ See Figures 37, 38 and 39

The thermostat is located between the water outlet and a housing built into the intake manifold.

⁑⁑ CAUTION

Never open, service or drain the radiator or cooling system when hot; serious burns can occur from the steam and hot coolant. Also, when draining engine coolant, keep in mind that cats and dogs are attracted to ethylene glycol antifreeze and could drink any that is left in an uncovered container or in puddles on the ground. This will prove fatal in sufficient quantities. Always drain coolant into a sealable container. Coolant should be reused unless it is contaminated or is several years old.

1. Disconnect the negative battery cable.
2. Remove the air inlet duct.
3. Drain the cooling system to a level below the thermostat.
4. Remove the thermostat outlet-to-engine retainers (usually either 2 bolts or 1 bolt and 1 stud), then remove outlet from the intake manifold.
5. Remove the thermostat from the housing, noting the orientation for installation purposes.

To install:

6. Carefully clean the all traces of the old gasket or sealer from the housing and outlet.
7. Install the thermostat to the housing, oriented as noted during removal, then position a new gasket (if used).
8. Place a ⅛ in. bead of RTV sealant in the groove on the water outlet sealing surface, then install the outlet while the sealer is still wet.
9. Install the outlet retainers and tighten to 21 ft. lbs. (28 Nm) for the 4.3L 19–96 models or to 14 ft. lbs. (19 Nm) for the 1997–99 models.
10. Properly fill the engine cooling system and check for leaks.
11. Install the air inlet duct.

Intake Manifold

REMOVAL & INSTALLATION

1994–97 2.2L Engines

UPPER MANIFOLD

▶ See Figures 40 thru 45

The 2.2L (VIN 4) engine was introduced in 1994 and utilizes a Multi-Port Fuel Injection (MFI) system. The intake manifold is an assembly of separate components, an upper and a lower manifold.

1. Properly release the fuel system pressure (if the lower manifold assembly is being removed) and disconnect the negative battery cable.

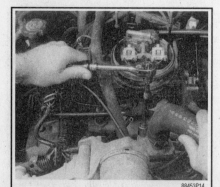

Fig. 37 Unfasten the thermostat outlet-to-engine bolts

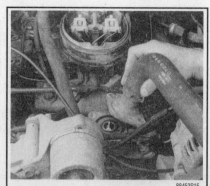

Fig. 38 Remove the outlet from the intake manifold

Fig. 39 Remove the thermostat from the housing

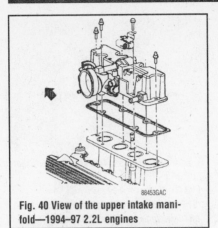

Fig. 40 View of the upper intake manifold—1994–97 2.2L engines

Fig. 41 Disconnect the vacuum hoses assembly from the throttle body assembly by unfastening the clips

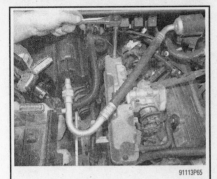

Fig. 42 Remove the upper intake manifold retainers . . .

Fig. 43 . . . then separate the upper manifold from the lower manifold

Fig. 44 Remove the injector EGR valve from the lower intake manifold

Fig. 45 Use a scraper to clean any gasket material from the upper manifold mating surfaces

2. Remove the air cleaner ducts.

3. Disconnect the throttle cable support bracket and cable from the manifold.

4. Remove the MAP sensor and the EGR solenoid valve from the upper intake manifold and engine (if the upper manifold is not being replaced, simply unplug the wiring and hoses).

5. Tag and disengage all wiring and vacuum hoses from the upper intake manifold.

6. Loosen the retainers, then remove the upper intake manifold from the engine and lower manifold assembly.

To install:

7. Install the upper intake manifold using a new gasket, then tighten the retainers to 22 ft. lbs. (30 Nm).

8. Attach the wiring connectors and vacuum hoses to the upper intake manifold assembly.

9. Install the MAP sensor and EGR solenoid valve.

10. Install and secure the throttle cable support and cable. Tighten the cable bracket bolts to 18 ft. lbs. (25 Nm).

11. Install the air cleaner ducts.

12. Connect the negative battery cable, then start and run the engine to check for leaks.

LOWER MANIFOLD

▶ See Figures 46 thru 57

1. Remove the upper intake manifold.

2. Raise and support the front of the vehicle and remove the passenger side wheel.

3. Remove the brackets that attach the wiring and heater hose to the side of the manifold.

4. Disconnect the fuel lines from the rear of the manifold and from the fuel pressure regulator. On some models, the fuel line connected to the regulator may also be attached to the underside of the manifold by a nut and washer. This nut is accessible through a opening on the passengers side wheel well. Locate and loosen the nut, then slide fuel line from under the washer.

Fig. 46 Remove the brackets that attach the wiring . .

Fig. 47 . . . and heater hose to the side of the manifold

Fig. 48 Unplug the vacuum tree hose from underneath the manifold and remove the vacuum tree

Fig. 49 Disconnect the right side heater hose at the firewall

Fig. 50 Disconnect the heater hose from the water outlet by pressing the tabs and pulling on the pipe

Fig. 51 Remove the bracket that attaches the fuel line to the rear of the manifold and disconnect the fuel line from the manifold

Fig. 52 Unfasten the lower intake manifold retainers

Fig. 53 On some models equipped with A/C, you may have to remove the manifold studs because there is not enough clearance to get the manifold past the evaporator core case

Fig. 54 Remove the lower intake manifold from the engine compartment

Fig. 55 Remove the intake manifold gasket

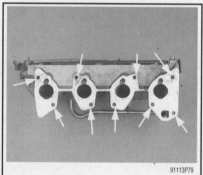

Fig. 56 Location of the lower intake manifold bolt holes

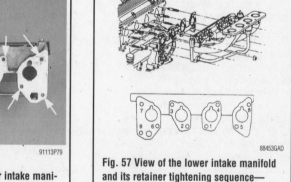

Fig. 57 View of the lower intake manifold and its retainer tightening sequence— 1994–97 2.2L engines

5. If applicable, disconnect the heater hose on the right side of the intake manifold.

6. Remove the EGR inlet pipe, if necessary.

7. Tag and disconnect the spark plug wires from the plugs, then pull the spark plug wires through a opening in the manifold until are all underneath the manifold.

8. If necessary, remove the alternator pencil brace. The brace is accessible through the opening in the passenger side wheel well.

9. On 1997 models, remove the fuel injector retainer bracket and disconnect the fuel pressure regulator from the lower intake manifold.

10. On 1997 models, remove the fuel injectors and disconnect the fuel pressure connection fitting.

11. Remove the lower intake manifold retaining nuts.

12. On some models equipped with A/C, the manifold upper studs may have to be removed because the manifold hits the evaporator case, this does not allow enough clearance for manifold removal. Remove the studs using a Torx socket.

13. Remove the lower intake manifold and gasket.

To install:

14. Carefully remove all traces of gasket material from the mating surfaces. If the EGR pipe was removed, check the EGR passage to be sure it is free of excessive carbon deposits and clean, as necessary.

15. Install the lower intake manifold using a new gasket.

16. If removed, install the manifold studs.

17. Install and tighten the retaining nut to 24 ft. lbs. (33 Nm) using the sequence illustrated.

18. On 1997 models, connect the fuel pressure connection fitting and install the injectors.

19. On 1997 models, connect the fuel pressure regulator to the lower intake manifold and install the fuel injector bracket.

20. If removed, install the alternator pencil brace.

21. Feed the spark plug wires back up through the opening in the manifold and connect them to the plugs.

22. If removed, install the EGR inlet pipe.

23. If applicable, connect the heater hose on the right side of the intake manifold.

24. Install the brackets that attach the wiring and heater hose to the side of the manifold.

25. Connect the fuel lines. If the fuel line was attached underneath the manifold, don't forget to place the line in position and tighten the nut until snug.

26. Install the upper intake manifold.

1998–99 2.2L Engines

▶ **See Figures 58 and 59**

1. Disconnect the negative battery cable and remove the air cleaner resonator.

2. Tag and unplug the three vacuum hoses from the throttle body.

3. Remove the throttle cable support bracket and the throttle body assembly.

4. If necessary, remove the upper fan shroud and disconnect the vacuum brake booster hose.

5. If necessary, unfasten the EGR pipe-to-manifold bolts and the EGR pipe-to-EGR adapter bolt, then remove the EGR pipe.

6. If necessary, remove the EGR adapter.

7. Unplug the electrical connections from the following components:
   a. Idle Air Control (IAC) motor
   b. Manifold Absolute Pressure (MAP) sensor
   c. Throttle Position (TP) sensor
   d. Fuel injector harness connector

8. Remove the right fender wheelhouse extension.

9. Remove the retainers from the engine harness bracket, the transmission filler tube (if equipped) and the fuel system evaporator pipe.

10. Disconnect the fuel pipes from the fuel rail.

11. Disconnect the accelerator cable and if equipped, the cruise control cable.

12. Tag and disconnect the spark plug wires from the plugs.

13. Remove the spark plug wire harness retainer from the heater hose pipe and set aside the harness.

14. If necessary, remove the alternator rear brace by accessing the retaining nuts and bolts through the wheelhouse.

15. If equipped, remove the engine wiring harness bracket located at the rear of the cylinder head, by unfastening the bracket-to-valve cover and bracket-to-cylinder head retainers, then slide the bracket off the bolt at the rear of the cylinder head.

16. Unfasten the intake manifold bolts.

17. Remove the fuel rail bracket.

18. Remove the intake manifold and gasket.

To install:

19. Carefully remove all traces of gasket material from the mating surfaces. Check the EGR passage to be sure it is free of excessive carbon deposits and clean, as necessary.

20. Install the lower intake manifold using a new gasket, then tighten the retaining bolts to 17 ft. lbs. (24 Nm) using the sequence illustrated.

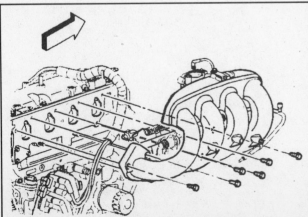

Fig. 58 Typical intake manifold mounting—1998–99 models

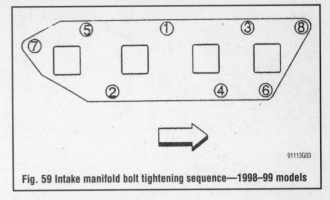

Fig. 59 Intake manifold bolt tightening sequence—1998–99 models

21. If removed, install the engine wiring harness bracket. Tighten the bracket-to-valve cover bolts to 88 inch lbs. (10 Nm) and the bracket-to-cylinder head bolt to 18 ft. lbs. (25 Nm).

22. If removed, install the generator rear brace. Tighten the nuts and bolts to 18 ft. lbs. (25 Nm).

23. Install the spark plug wire harness and retainer and attach the spark plug wires to the plugs.

24. Install the throttle body assembly, if removed and the throttle cable support bracket.

25. Attach the three vacuum lines to the throttle body.

26. Attach the accelerator cable and if equipped, the cruise control cable.

27. Connect the fuel lines.

28. Install and tighten the retainers to the engine harness bracket, the transmission filler tube (if equipped) and the fuel system evaporator pipe.

29. Attach the following electrical connections:
   a. Idle Air Control (IAC) motor
   b. Manifold Absolute Pressure (MAP) sensor
   c. Throttle Position (TP) sensor
   d. Fuel injector harness connector

30. If removed, install the wheelhouse extension.

31. If removed, install the EGR adapter and tighten the retainers to 97 inch lbs. (11 Nm).

32. Install the EGR pipe to the EGR adapter and tighten the bolt to 18 ft. lbs. (25 Nm).

33. Install the EGR pipe-to-intake manifold bolts and tighten the bolts to 89 inch lbs. (10 Nm).

34. If removed, install the upper fan shroud and the brake booster hose.

35. Install the air cleaner resonator and connect the negative battery cable.

36. Start the engine and check for leaks.

1994–95 VIN Z 4.3L Engines

▶ **See Figures 60 and 61**

✳✳ CAUTION

Never open, service or drain the radiator or cooling system when hot; serious burns can occur from the steam and hot coolant. Also, when draining engine coolant, keep in mind that cats and dogs are attracted to ethylene glycol antifreeze and could drink any that is left in an uncovered container or in puddles on the ground. This will prove fatal in sufficient quantities. Always drain coolant into a sealable container. Coolant should be reused unless it is contaminated or is several years old.

1. Disconnect the negative battery cable and properly relieve the fuel system pressure.

2. Drain the cooling system.

3. Remove the air cleaner and heat stove tube.

4. Remove the two braces at the rear of the serpentine drive belt tensioner.

5. Disconnect the upper radiator hose.

6. Remove the emissions relays along with the bracket, then disengage the wiring harness from the retaining clips and position aside. Disconnect the ground cable from the intake manifold stud.

7. Remove the power brake vacuum pipe, then disconnect the heater hose pipe at the manifold and fuel lines at the TBI unit.

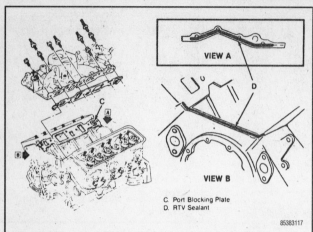

Fig. 60 Intake manifold mounting—1994 4.3L (VIN Z) engine; note the bolt/stud usage may vary

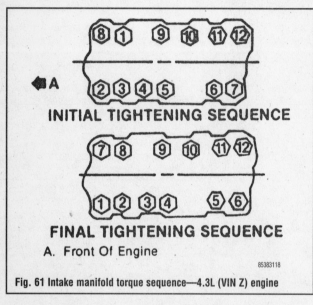

INITIAL TIGHTENING SEQUENCE

FINAL TIGHTENING SEQUENCE

A. Front Of Engine

Fig. 61 Intake manifold torque sequence—4.3L (VIN Z) engine

8. Remove the ignition coil, then disengage the electrical connectors at the sensors on the manifold.

9. Matchmark and remove the distributor from the engine. For details, please refer to the procedure in Section 2.

➡For ease of installation, DO NOT crank the engine with the distributor removed.

10. Tag and disengage the wires and hoses from the TBI unit.

11. Disconnect the EGR hose, then disengage the throttle, TVS and cruise control cables (as equipped).

12. Unfasten the intake manifold retaining studs and/or bolts, then remove the manifold and gaskets.

To install:

✳✳ CAUTION

The EPA warns that prolonged contact with used engine oil may cause a number of skin disorders, including cancer! You should make every effort to minimize you exposure to used engine oil. Protective gloves should be worn when changing the oil. Wash your hands and any other exposed skin areas as soon as possible after exposure to used engine oil. Soap and water, or waterless hand cleaner should be used.

13. Using a putty knife, carefully clean the gasket mounting surfaces. Be sure to inspect the manifold for warpage and/or cracks; if necessary, replace it.

14. Position the gaskets to the cylinder head with the port blocking plates to the rear, then apply a ³⁄₁₆ in. (5mm) bead of RTV sealant to the front and rear of the engine block at the block-to-manifold mating surface. Extend the bead ½ in. (13mm) up each cylinder head to seal and retain the gaskets.

15. Install the intake manifold taking care not to disturb the gaskets, then tighten the manifold retainers to 35 ft. lbs. (48 Nm) using the proper torque sequence.

16. Engage the TVS, cruise control and/or throttle cables, as equipped.

17. Connect the EGR hose then engage the wires and hoses at the TBI unit as noted during removal

18. Align and install the distributor assembly.

19. Install the ignition coil, then connect the fuel pipes.

20. Connect the heater hose pipe and the power brake vacuum pipe.

21. Connect the ground cable to the intake manifold stud, then position and secure the wiring harness using the clips.

22. Install the emissions relays along with their bracket, then connect the upper radiator hose.

23. Install the brace at the rear of the drive belt tensioner, then install the air cleaner and heat stove tube.

24. Connect the negative battery cable, then properly refill the engine cooling system.

25. Run the engine and check for leaks.

1994–95 VIN W 4.3L Engines

UPPER INTAKE MANIFOLD

▶ See Figures 62 thru 68

✳✳ CAUTION

Never open, service or drain the radiator or cooling system when hot; serious burns can occur from the steam and hot coolant. Also, when draining engine coolant, keep in mind that cats and dogs are

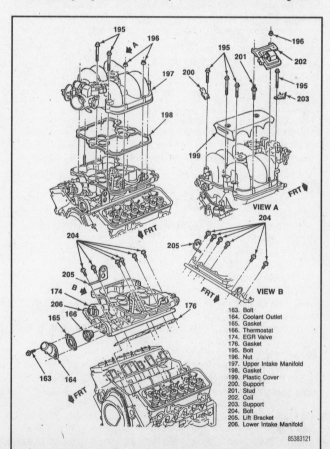

163. Bolt
164. Coolant Outlet
165. Gasket
166. Thermostat
174. EGR Valve
176. Gasket
195. Bolt
196. Nut
197. Upper Intake Manifold
198. Gasket
199. Plastic Cover
200. Support
201. Stud
202. Coil
203. Support
204. Bolt
205. Lift Bracket
206. Lower Intake Manifold

Fig. 62 Exploded view of the intake manifold assembly—4.3L VIN Z engine

Fig. 63 Matchmark the rotor and distributor-to-engine location. This will aid in installation

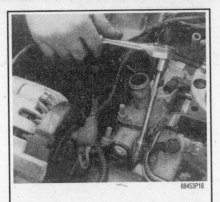

Fig. 64 Unfasten the intake manifold bolts

Fig. 65 Remove the intake manifold from the vehicle

Fig. 66 Insert shop towels to prevent dirt from entering open ports and passages

Fig. 67 Clean the old gasket from the intake manifold mating surfaces using a gasket scraper or putty knife

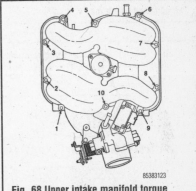

Fig. 68 Upper intake manifold torque sequence—4.3L VIN Z engine

attracted to ethylene glycol antifreeze and could drink any that is left in an uncovered container or in puddles on the ground. This will prove fatal in sufficient quantities. Always drain coolant into a sealable container. Coolant should be reused unless it is contaminated or is several years old.

➡If only the upper intake manifold is being removed, the fuel system pressure does not need to be released. ALWAYS release the pressure before disconnecting any fuel lines.

1. Remove the plastic cover, then properly relieve the fuel system pressure and disconnect the negative battery cable.
2. Drain the engine cooling system, then remove the air cleaner and air inlet duct.
3. Disengage the wiring harness from the necessary upper intake components including:
   - Throttle Position (TP) sensor
   - Idle Air Control (IAC) motor
   - Manifold Absolute Pressure (MAP) sensor
   - Intake Manifold Tuning Valve (IMTV)
4. Disengage the throttle linkage from the upper intake manifold, then remove the ignition coil.
5. Disconnect the PCV hose at the rear of the upper intake manifold, then tag and disengage the vacuum hoses from both the front and rear of the upper intake.
6. Remove the upper intake manifold bolts and studs, making sure to note or mark the location of all studs to assure proper installation. Remove the upper intake manifold from the engine.
7. Using a putty knife, carefully clean the gasket mounting surfaces. Be sure to inspect the manifold for warpage and/or cracks; if necessary, replace it.

To install:

8. Position a new upper intake manifold gasket on the engine, making sure the green sealing lines are facing upward.
9. Install the upper intake manifold being careful not to pinch the fuel injector wires between the manifolds.

10. Install the manifold retainers, making sure the studs are properly positioned, then tighten them using the proper sequence to 124 inch lbs. (14 Nm).
11. Connect the PCV hose to the rear of the upper intake manifold and the vacuum hoses to both the front and rear of the manifold assembly.
12. Connect the throttle linkage to the upper intake, then install the ignition coil.
13. Engage the necessary wiring to the upper intake components including the TP sensor, IAC motor, MAP sensor and the IMTV.
14. Install the plastic cover, the air cleaner and air inlet duct.
15. Connect the negative battery cable, then properly refill the engine cooling system.

LOWER INTAKE MANIFOLD

♦ See Figure 69

1. Remove the upper intake manifold.
2. Disengage the distributor wiring and matchmark the distributor, then remove the assembly from the engine.
3. Disconnect the upper radiator hose at the thermostat housing and the heater hose at the lower intake manifold.
4. Disconnect the fuel supply and return lines at the rear of the lower intake manifold.
5. Remove the pencil brace (A/C compressor bracket-to-lower intake manifold).
6. Disengage the wiring harness connectors from the necessary lower intake components including:
   - Fuel injector
   - Exhaust Gas Recirculation (EGR) valve
   - Engine Coolant Temperature (ECT) sensor
7. Remove the lower intake manifold retaining bolts, then remove the manifold from the engine.

To install:

8. Using a putty knife, carefully clean the gasket mounting surfaces. Be sure to inspect the manifold for warpage and/or cracks; if necessary, replace it.
9. Position the gaskets to the cylinder head with the port blocking plates to

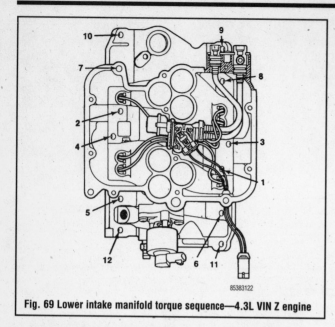

Fig. 69 Lower intake manifold torque sequence—4.3L VIN Z engine

the rear and the "this side up" stamps facing upward, then apply a ³⁄₁₆ in. (5mm) bead of RTV sealant to the front and rear of the engine block at the block-to-manifold mating surface. Extend the bead ½ in. (13mm) up each cylinder head to seal and retain the gaskets.

10. Install the lower intake manifold taking care not to disturb the gaskets, then tighten the manifold retainers to 35 ft. lbs. (48 Nm) using the proper torque sequence.

11. Engage the wiring harness to the lower manifold components, including the injector, EGR valve and ECT sensor.

12. Install the pencil brace to the A/C compressor bracket and the lower intake manifold.

13. Connect the fuel supply and return lines to the rear of the lower intake. Temporarily reconnect the negative battery cable, then pressurize the fuel system (by cycling the ignition without starting the engine) and check for leaks. Disconnect the negative battery cable and continue installation.

14. Connect the heater hose to the lower intake and the upper radiator hose to the thermostat housing.

15. Align the matchmarks and install the distributor assembly, then engage the wiring.

1996–99 4.3L Engines

UPPER INTAKE MANIFOLD

♦ See Figure 70

❊❊ CAUTION

Never open, service or drain the radiator or cooling system when hot; serious burns can occur from the steam and hot coolant. Also, when draining engine coolant, keep in mind that cats and dogs are attracted to ethylene glycol antifreeze and could drink any that is left in an uncovered container or in puddles on the ground. This will prove fatal in sufficient quantities. Always drain coolant into a sealable container. Coolant should be reused unless it is contaminated or is several years old.

1. Disconnect the negative battery cable and properly relieve the fuel system pressure.

2. Drain the cooling system.

3. Remove the air intake duct.

4. Tag and unplug any necessary wiring harness connectors and move any necessary brackets to one side.

5. Disconnect the throttle cable and if equipped the cruise control cable, then remove the throttle cable bracket from the upper intake.

6. Disconnect the fuel lines and move the brackets from the rear of the lower intake.

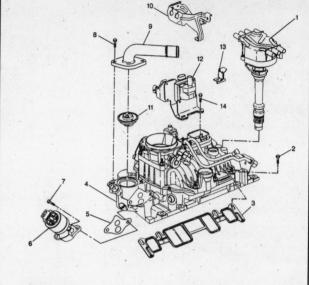

1. DISTRIBUTOR	8. BOLT, WATER OUTLET
2. BOLT, LOWER INTAKE MANIFOLD	9. OUTLET, WATER
3. GASKET, INTAKE	10. BRACKET, THROTTLE CABLE
4. MANIFOLD, INTAKE	11. THERMOSTAT, ENGINE
5. GASKET, EGR	12. COIL, IGNITION
6. VALVE, EGR	13. BRACKET, EVAP PURGE SOLENOID
7. BOLT, EGR VALVE	14. BOLT, IGNITION COIL

Fig. 70 View of the upper intake manifold and related components—1996–99 4.3L engine

7. Disconnect the brake booster vacuum hose and PCV hose from the upper manifold, then remove the ignition coil and bracket.

8. Remove the purge solenoid and bracket, then unfasten the upper intake manifold bolts and studs. Mark the location of the studs to aid in installation.

9. Remove the upper intake manifold.

To install:

10. Position a new upper intake manifold gasket on the engine, making sure the sealing lines are facing upward.

➡**Install two stud type bolts into the lower manifold diagonally opposite each other will help in positioning the upper manifold to the lower manifold.**

11. Install the upper intake manifold being careful not to pinch the fuel injector wires between the manifolds.

12. Install the manifold retainers, making sure the studs are properly positioned, then tighten them to 44 inch lbs. (5 Nm) on the first pass and to 88 inch lbs. (10 Nm) on the final pass.

13. Install the purge solenoid and bracket.

14. Install the ignition coil and bracket, the brake booster vacuum hose and PCV hose.

15. Install the fuel lines and the throttle linkage, cruise control linkage (if equipped) and the throttle cable bracket.

16. Engage the wiring harness connectors and brackets.

17. Install the air cleaner intake duct, then connect the negative battery cable.

18. Start the vehicle and check for leaks.

LOWER INTAKE MANIFOLD

♦ See Figure 71

1. Remove the upper intake manifold.

2. Disengage the distributor wiring and matchmark the distributor, then remove the assembly from the engine.

3. Disconnect the upper radiator hose at the thermostat housing and the heater hose at the lower intake manifold.

4. On automatic transmission equipped vehicles, if necessary, disconnect the transmission dipstick tube.

5. Remove the throttle cable and bracket from the throttle body assembly and set them to one side.

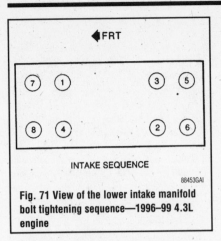

Fig. 71 View of the lower intake manifold bolt tightening sequence—1996–99 4.3L engine

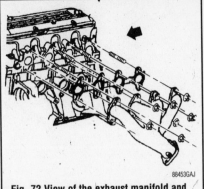

Fig. 72 View of the exhaust manifold and related components—2.2L engine

Fig. 73 Unfasten the nut that attaches the oil fill tube assembly to the manifold stud

6. Remove the EGR tube, clamp and bolt.

7. Disconnect the fuel pipes from the rear of the manifold

8. Disengage the A/C compressor and bracket and move it to one side.

9. Tag and disengage all necessary electrical connections and brackets that would interfere with manifold removal.

10. If necessary for clearance, remove the alternator bracket bolt located next to the thermostat housing.

11. Remove the PCV valve.

12. Remove the lower intake manifold retaining bolts, then remove the manifold from the engine.

13. Using a putty knife, carefully clean the gasket mounting surfaces. Be sure to inspect the manifold for warpage and/or cracks; if necessary, replace it.

To install:

14. Position the gaskets to the cylinder head with the port blocking plates to the rear and the "this side up" stamps facing upward, then apply a ³⁄₁₆ in. (5mm) bead of RTV sealant to the front and rear of the engine block at the block-to-manifold mating surface. Extend the bead ½ in. (13mm) up each cylinder head to seal and retain the gaskets.

15. Install the lower intake manifold taking care not to disturb the gaskets, then tighten the manifold retainers in three steps following the sequence shown in the accompanying illustration as follows.

 a. First pass tighten to 26 inch lbs. (3 Nm)

 b. Second pass tighten to 106 inch lbs. (12 Nm)

 c. Final pass tighten to 11 ft. lbs. (15 Nm)

16. If removed, fasten the alternator bracket bolt located next to the thermostat housing.

17. Install the EGR tube, clamp and bolt.

18. Attach all the electrical connectors that were unplugged and install all brackets that were removed to allow access for manifold removal.

19. Attach the fuel lines.

20. Install the A/C compressor and bracket.

21. If removed, install the automatic transmission dipstick tube.

22. Install the throttle linkage and bracket.

23. Connect the heater hose to the lower intake and the upper radiator hose to the thermostat housing.

24. Align the matchmarks and install the distributor assembly, then attach the wiring.

25. Install the vacuum hoses.

26. Install the upper intake manifold.

Exhaust Manifold

✳✳ CAUTION

ALWAYS use extreme caution when working around the exhaust system. Make sure the engine has had time to thoroughly cool or personal injury from exhaust system burns may occur. Also, be sure to wear safety goggles when working on exhaust parts and they are likely to rust and loose particle will be falling from them during the procedure.

REMOVAL & INSTALLATION

2.2L Engine

♦ See Figures 72 thru 79

1. Disconnect the negative battery cable, then remove the air cleaner and duct work.

2. Unplug the oxygen sensor electrical connection. If the manifold or sensor is to be replaced, remove the sensor.

3. Remove the drive belt.

4. Raise the vehicle, support it with jackstands and disconnect the exhaust pipe from the manifold.

5. Unfasten the nut that attaches the oil fill tube assembly to the manifold and if necessary, remove the pipe.

6. If necessary, remove the heater hose brace.

7. If applicable, remove the power steering pump pencil brace and the heater hose brace and set the pump aside.

8. If applicable, remove the A/C compressor pencil and rear brace and set the compressor aside without disconnecting the lines.

9. Loosen and remove the exhaust manifold retaining nuts, then remove the manifold from the engine.

To install:

10. Carefully clean the threads of the exhaust manifold retainers, then remove all remaining traces of gasket from the mating surfaces.

11. Install the manifold to the engine using a new gasket, then tighten the manifold nuts to 115 inch lbs. (13 Nm). Connect the pipe to the manifold and tighten the retainers.

12. If removed, install the A/C compressor pencil and rear brace.

Fig. 74 Unfasten the nut that attaches the A/C compressor pencil brace (1) and the power steering pump and heater hose pencil braces (2) to the exhaust manifold studs, then remove the braces from the rear of the compressor and pump

Fig. 75 Remove the exhaust manifold nuts and studs

Fig. 76 Remove the exhaust manifold from the engine compartment

Fig. 77 If equipped, remove the smaller gasket pieces first . . .

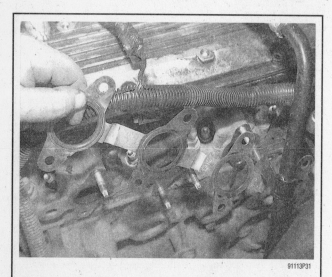

Fig. 78 . . . then remove the main manifold gasket

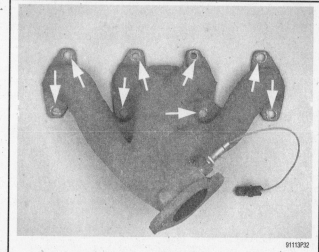

Fig. 79 The exhaust manifold attaches to the engine with nuts and studs at these locations

13. If removed, install the power steering pump brace and the heater hose brace.

14. If removed, install the heater hose brace.

15. Install the oil fill tube assembly.

16. Either install the oxygen sensor or engage the wiring, as applicable. If the sensor or manifold was replaced, tighten the oxygen sensor to 31 ft. lbs. (42 Nm).

17. Install the drive belt.

18. Install the air cleaner and duct work.

19. Connect the negative battery cable.

4.3L Engine

1994–95 MODELS

▶ See Figures 80, 81 and 82

1. Disconnect the negative battery cable, then raise and support the front of the vehicle safely using jackstands.

➡It will be easier if the vehicle is only supported to a height where underhood access is still possible, the vehicle may be left in position

Fig. 80 Unfasten the exhaust manifold retaining bolts and studs then . . .

Fig. 81 . . . remove the bolts and studs

Fig. 82 Remove the exhaust manifold from the engine

for the entire procedure. If the vehicle is raised too high for underhood access, it will have to lowered, raised and lowered again during the procedure.

2. Disconnect the exhaust pipe from the exhaust manifold.

3. If necessary for underhood access, remove the jackstands and lower the vehicle.

4. Tag and disconnect the spark plug wires from the plugs and from the retaining clips.

5. If removing the left side manifold:

   a. Remove the air cleaner with heat stove pipe and cold air intake pipe.

   b. Remove the power steering/alternator rear bracket.

   c. Check for sufficient clearance between the manifold and the intermediate steering shaft. On some models it will be necessary to disconnect the intermediate shaft from the steering gear in order to reposition the shaft for clearance.

6. If necessary when removing the right side manifold, unbolt the A/C compressor and bracket, then position the assembly aside. DO NOT disconnect the lines or allow them to become kinked or otherwise damaged.

7. If necessary for the right side manifold, remove the spark plugs, dipstick tube and wiring.

8. Unbend the locktangs then unfasten the exhaust manifold retaining bolts, washers and tab washers.

9. Disengage the exhaust manifold, then remove and discard the old gaskets.

To install:

10. Using a putty knife, clean the gasket mounting surfaces. Inspect the exhaust manifold for distortion, cracks or damage; replace if necessary.

11. Install the exhaust manifold to the cylinder using a new gasket, then tighten the exhaust manifold-to-cylinder head bolts to 26 ft. lbs. (36 Nm) on the center exhaust tube and to 20 ft. lbs. (28 Nm) on the front and rear exhaust tubes. Once the bolts are tightened, bend the tabs on the washers back over the heads of all bolts in order to lock them in position.

12. If removed on the right side, install the spark plugs, dipstick tube and wiring.

13. If unbolted, reposition and secure the A/C compressor and bracket assembly.

14. If the left manifold was removed:

   a. If unbolted, reconnect the intermediate shaft to the steering gear.

   b. Install the power steering/alternator rear bracket.

   c. Install the air cleaner along with the heat stove pipe and cold air intake pipe.

15. Connect the spark plug wires to the retainer clips and to the plugs as noted during removal.

16. If lowered for underhood access, raise and support the front of the vehicle again using the jackstands.

17. Connect the exhaust pipe to the manifold.

18. Remove the jackstands and carefully lower the vehicle, then connect the negative battery cable.

1996–99 MODELS

♦ **See Figures 83 and 84**

1. Disconnect the negative battery cable, then raise and support the front of the vehicle safely using jackstands.

➡**It will be easier if the vehicle is only supported to a height where underhood access is still possible, the vehicle may be left in position for the entire procedure. If the vehicle is raised too high for underhood access, it will have to lowered, raised and lowered again during the procedure.**

2. Disconnect the exhaust pipe from the exhaust manifold. It may be necessary to remove the tires to gain access to the rear manifold bolts.

3. If removing the right side manifold on 1999 and later models, unfasten the engine oil dipstick tube bolt.

4. Remove the EGR inlet pipe from the left side manifold, if necessary.

5. On 1998 and later models after removing the EGR inlet pipe, unplug the Engine Coolant Temperature (ECT) sensor electrical connection and remove the upper radiator support hose and nut.

6. If removing the left side manifold on 1999 and later models, remove the steering intermediate shaft.

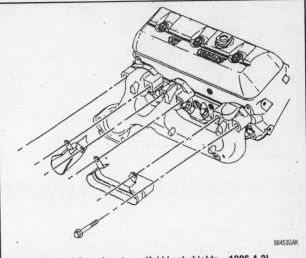

Fig. 83 View of the exhaust manifold heat shields—1996 4.3L engine

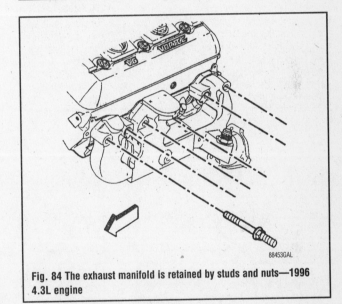

Fig. 84 The exhaust manifold is retained by studs and nuts—1996 4.3L engine

7. If removing the left side manifold on 1999 and later models, remove the wheel house extension.

8. Tag and disconnect the spark plugs wires from the plugs.

9. If equipped, on 1999 and later models, unfasten the nuts attaching the secondary air injection pipe to the manifold, then remove the pipe and gasket.

10. Unbend the locktangs then remove the exhaust manifold retaining bolts, washers and tab washers. Remove the heat shields.

11. Remove the exhaust manifold and if equipped.

12. Remove and discard the old gaskets.

To install:

13. Using a putty knife, clean the gasket mounting surfaces. Inspect the exhaust manifold for distortion, cracks or damage; replace if necessary.

14. On 1996 models, install the exhaust manifold to the cylinder using a new gasket, then tighten the bolts to 22 ft. lbs. (30 Nm). Once the bolts are tightened, bend the tabs on the washers back over the heads of all bolts in order to lock them in position.

15. On 1998 and later models, apply a threadlock such as GM 12345493 or its equivalent to the threads of the manifold retainers prior to installation.

16. On 1997–99 models, install the exhaust manifold to the cylinder using a new gasket, then tighten the center bolts to 11 ft. lbs. (15 Nm) and the front and rear manifold bolts to 22 ft. lbs. (30 Nm). Once the bolts are tightened, bend the tabs on the washers back over the heads of all bolts in order to lock them in position.

17. Attach the spark plug wires to the plugs.

18. If removed on 1999 and later models, install the fender wheelhouse extension and the tire assembly.

19. If removed on 1999 and later models, install the secondary air injection pipe with a NEW gasket to the manifold, tighten the nuts to 18 ft. lbs. (25 Nm).

20. If removed, install the EGR inlet pipe, attach the ECT sensor electrical connection and install the upper radiator hose support and nut.

21. If removed on 1999 and later models (left side manifold only), install the steering intermediate shaft.

22. If removed from the right side manifold on 1999 and later models, fasten the engine oil dipstick tube bolt to 106 inch lbs. (12 Nm).

23. Engage the exhaust pipe to the manifold and lower the vehicle.

24. Connect the negative battery cable.

Radiator

REMOVAL & INSTALLATION

▶ **See Figures 85 thru 95**

✳✳✳ CAUTION

Never open, service or drain the radiator or cooling system when hot; serious burns can occur from the steam and hot coolant. Also, when draining engine coolant, keep in mind that cats and dogs are attracted to ethylene glycol antifreeze and could drink any that is left in an uncovered container or in puddles on the ground. This will prove fatal in sufficient quantities. Always drain coolant into a sealable container. Coolant should be reused unless it is contaminated or is several years old.

1. Disconnect the negative battery cable.

2. Drain the engine cooling system.

3. If equipped, remove the air inlet duct.

4. Disconnect the overflow hose from the radiator, then disconnect the upper and lower radiator hoses.

5. If equipped with A/C, it may be necessary to remove the A/C hose retaining clip and reposition the hose for shroud and/or radiator removal. DO NOT disconnect any refrigerant fittings.

➡**If equipped with a 1 piece shroud, then shroud may be unbolted from the radiator support and pushed back over the cooling fan instead of removing it completely.**

6. If equipped with a 2 piece radiator/fan shroud, remove the upper fan shroud-to-radiator support bolts and the upper fan shroud-to-lower fan shroud retainers. Remove the upper shroud from the vehicle.

7. If equipped with an A/T, disconnect and plug the fluid cooler lines at the radiator. Plug all openings to prevent system contamination or excessive fluid loss.

8. If equipped with a factory engine oil cooler which is integral to the radiator, disconnect and plug the oil cooler lines at the radiator. Plug all openings to prevent system contamination or excessive fluid loss. Plug all openings to prevent system contamination or excessive fluid loss.

9. If equipped, remove the lower fan shroud.

10. Lift the radiator straight upward from the supports and from the vehicle. Be careful to lift the radiator straight upward and not to tilt it excessively as the radiator will still contain a significant amount of coolant and, if applicable, transmission fluid/engine oil.

To install:

11. Lower the radiator into position on the supports.

12. If equipped, install the lower fan shroud.

13. If equipped, remove the plugs, then connect the engine oil cooler lines and tighten the fittings.

14. If equipped with an A/T, remove the plugs, then connect the transmission fluid cooler lines and tighten the fittings.

15. Install the upper fan shroud and secure using the support and lower shroud retainers.

Fig. 85 Place a suitable container beneath the radiator petcock and open the petcock to drain the coolant

Fig. 86 Use pliers to remove the upper radiator hose clamp and then disconnect the hose from the radiator

Fig. 87 The air inlet duct assembly is retained by plastic pins.

Fig. 88 Remove the upper air duct assembly

Fig. 89 Remove the upper shroud bolts

Fig. 90 The upper shroud is attached to the lower shroud with bolts

Fig. 91 After unfastening the bolts, separate the upper shroud from the lower shroud

Fig. 92 The top of the lower shroud will have to be tilted inward to clear the cooling fan to remove the shroud

Fig. 93 The lower shroud clips into the bottom of the radiator

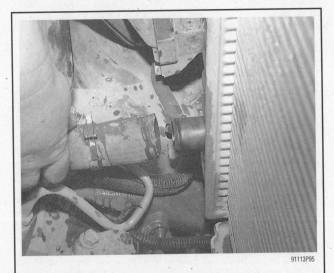

Fig. 94 Disconnect the lower hose from the radiator

Fig. 95 Remove the radiator from the engine compartment

16. If applicable, reposition the A/C refrigerant hose and secure using the retaining clip.
17. Connect the overflow hose, upper and lower radiator hoses.
18. If equipped, install the air inlet duct.
19. Properly refill the engine cooling system.

Engine Cooling Fan

The vehicles covered by this manual are either equipped with a standard cooling fan (early models) or a clutch fan assembly (most later model vehicles). Standard cooling fans are simply bolted to the water pump hub, while on clutch fans, the fan blade assembly is bolted to a clutch assembly which is secured to water pump hub studs. Both fans are removed in a similar manner, but the clutch assembly requires a little more effort.

REMOVAL & INSTALLATION

▶ See Figures 96, 97, 98, 99 and 100

➡DO NOT use or repair a damaged fan assembly. An unbalanced fan assembly could fly apart and cause personal injury or property damage. Replace damaged assemblies with new ones.

Fig. 96 Unfasten the cooling fan retaining bolts. . . .

Fig. 97 . . . then remove the fan and clutch assembly from the vehicle

Fig. 98 Unfasten the fan clutch-to-fan bolts and separate the fan and clutch assembly

Fig. 99 View of the fan-to-fan clutch mounting—typical 2.2L engine without A/C

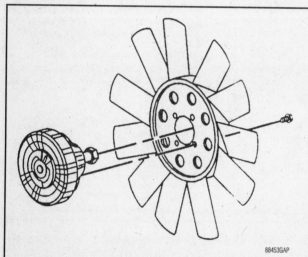

Fig. 100 View of the fan-to-fan clutch mounting—typical 4.3L engine with A/C

1. Disconnect the negative battery cable.
2. Remove the upper radiator shroud and, if desired for additional clearance, remove the radiator from the vehicle.

➡️**Although it is not necessary in most cases, the radiator may be removed from the vehicle for easier access to the fan retainers. If the radiator is left in place, use extra caution to prevent damage to the fragile radiator fins.**

3. Remove the fan assembly attaching nuts, then remove the fan assembly from the engine.

➡️**Some vehicles use a spacer between the fan and the water pump pulley. If used, be sure to retain the spacer for installation.**

4. If necessary, the clutch may be removed from the fan by removing the attaching nuts or bolts (as applicable).
   To install:
5. If removed, install the fan to the clutch and secure using the fasteners. Tighten the fasteners to 24 ft. lbs. (33 Nm).
6. If equipped, align the yellow paint mark on the fan clutch hub with the yellow paint mark on the water pump hub. This will help maintain a balanced fan assembly.
7. Position the spacer (if used) and fan assembly to the water pump pulley and secure using the fasteners. Tighten the fasteners to 17 ft. lbs. (24 Nm) on 1994–97 models and 24 ft. lbs. (33 Nm) on 1998–99 models.

8. If removed for clearance, install the radiator.
9. Install the upper fan shroud.
10. Connect the negative battery cable.
11. If the radiator was removed, properly refill the engine cooling system.

Water Pump

REMOVAL & INSTALLATION

▶ See Figures 101 thru 113

✳️ CAUTION

Never open, service or drain the radiator or cooling system when hot; serious burns can occur from the steam and hot coolant. Also, when draining engine coolant, keep in mind that cats and dogs are attracted to ethylene glycol antifreeze and could drink any that is left in an uncovered container or in puddles on the ground. This will prove fatal in sufficient quantities. Always drain coolant into a sealable container. Coolant should be reused unless it is contaminated or is several years old.

1. Disconnect the negative battery cable, then drain the engine cooling system.
2. Relieve the belt tension, then remove the drive belt.
3. Remove the upper fan shroud, then remove the fan or fan and clutch assembly, as applicable.
4. Remove the water pump pulley.
5. If applicable, loosen the clamp(s) and disconnect the coolant hose(s) from the water pump.
6. Unfasten the retainers, then remove the water pump from the engine. Note the positions of all retainers as some engines will utilize different length fasteners in different locations and/or bolts and studs in different locations.
   To install:
7. Using a putty knife, carefully clean the gasket mounting surfaces.

➡️**The water pumps on some of the engines covered by this manual, may have been installed using sealer only, no gasket, at the factory. If a gasket is supplied with the replacement part, it should be used. Otherwise, a ⅛ in. (.125mm) bead of RTV sealer should be used around the sealing surface of the pump.**

8. Apply 1052080 or an equivalent sealant to the threads of the water pump retainers. Install the water pump to the engine using a new gasket, then thread the retainers in order to hold it in position.
9. Tighten the water pump retainers to specification:
   a. For the 2.2L engines tighten the water pump-to-engine retainers to 18 ft. lbs. (25 Nm).

Fig. 101 After removing the cooling fan assembly, remove the water pump pulley—4.3L engine

Fig. 102 Location the water pump pulley bolts—2.2L engine

Fig. 103 If the pulley turns when you try to loosen the bolts, attach sockets and ratchets to two of the bolts, insert a prybar to hold the pulley in place and loosen the bolts—2.2L engine

Fig. 104 Once all the bolts are unfastened, remove the water pump pulley—2.2L engine

Fig. 105 Disconnect all hoses attached to the water pump assembly—4.3L engine

Fig. 106 Unfasten and remove the water pump retaining bolts—4.3L engine

Fig. 107 The water pump is retained by four bolts—2.2L engine

Fig. 108 Remove the water pump from the vehicle—4.3L engine

Fig. 109 Removing the water pump from the engine block—2.2L engine

Fig. 110 Use a scraper to clean the old gasket material from the water pump . . .

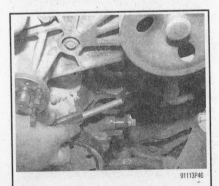

Fig. 111 . . . and the water pump-to-engine mating surface

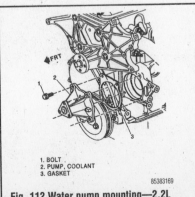

1. BOLT
2. PUMP, COOLANT
3. GASKET

85383169

Fig. 112 Water pump mounting—2.2L gasoline engine

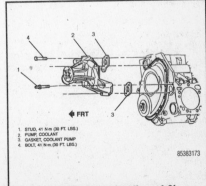

1. STUD, 41 N·m (30 FT. LBS.)
2. PUMP, COOLANT
3. GASKET, COOLANT PUMP
4. BOLT, 41 N·m (30 FT. LBS.)

85383173

Fig. 113 Water pump mounting—4.3L engine (note that stud locations may vary)

b. For the 4.3L engine, tighten the bolts and studs to 30 ft. lbs. (41 Nm).

10. If removed, connect the coolant hose(s) and secure using the retaining clamp(s).

11. Install the water pump pulley, then install the fan or fan and clutch assembly.

12. Position the serpentine belt over the pulleys, then carefully allow the tensioner back into contact with the belt.

13. Install the upper fan shroud, then connect the negative battery cable.

14. Properly refill the engine cooling system, then run the engine and check for leaks.

Cylinder Head

REMOVAL & INSTALLATION

2.2L Engine

♦ See Figures 114 thru 124

✳✳ CAUTION

Never open, service or drain the radiator or cooling system when hot; serious burns can occur from the steam and hot coolant. Also, when draining engine coolant, keep in mind that cats and dogs are attracted to ethylene glycol antifreeze and could drink any that is left in an uncovered container or in puddles on the ground. This will prove fatal in sufficient quantities. Always drain coolant into a sealable container. Coolant should be reused unless it is contaminated or is several years old.

1. Properly relieve the fuel system pressure, then disconnect the negative battery cable.

2. Drain the engine cooling system, then disconnect the air duct from the air inlet.

3. Disconnect the upper radiator hose, then remove the upper fan shroud.

4. Remove the radiator assembly, then remove the lower fan shroud.

5. Remove the fan assembly, then remove the serpentine drive belt.

6. Remove the water pump.

7. Disconnect the heater hose from the intake manifold and the thermostat housing, then remove the thermostat housing.

8. Remove the alternator support brace and disengage the alternator wiring.

9. If equipped, remove the A/C compressor with brackets, then position them aside. DO NOT disconnect the refrigerant lines, but be careful not to kink and damage them. In some cases the A/C compressor can remain attached to the accessory bracket as long as the rear pencil brace is removed. This will enable the compressor to be sat aside when sitting the accessory bracket aside.

10. Disconnect and reposition the accessory bracket along with the alternator and P/S pump and if possible, the A/C compressor still attached. Be careful not to damage the steering pump or A/C lines.

11. Disconnect the throttle cable and cable support linkage, then disconnect the heater hose from the water pump.

12. If necessary, remove the oil fill tube.

13. Disconnect the exhaust pipe and unplug the oxygen sensor electrical connection.

14. Unfasten the exhaust manifold bolts, then remove the manifold.

15. Tag and disconnect both the electrical wiring and the vacuum hoses from the upper intake manifold.

16. Remove the upper intake manifold, then tag and disconnect the wiring from the lower intake manifold.

17. Disconnect the fuel lines, then tag and disengage the spark plug wires.

18. Remove the lower intake manifold from the engine.

19. If equipped, remove the EGR adapter.

20. Remove the rocker arm cover from the cylinder head.

21. Remove the rocker arms and pushrods.

22. Disconnect the engine lift bracket from the rear of the engine.

23. Remove the cylinder head bolts and studs, then carefully lift the cylinder head from the engine.

To install:

24. Carefully clean and inspect cylinder head and the gasket mounting sur-

Fig. 114 Location of the accessory bracket bolts (1) and the water outlet assembly bolts (2)

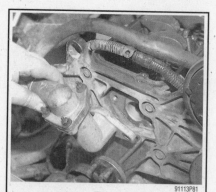

Fig. 115 Remove the water outlet assembly from the engine

Fig. 116 Move the accessory bracket to one side with the A/C compressor and power steering pump still attached. Do not disconnect either of the components lines

Fig. 117 Location of the cylinder head retaining bolt holes

Fig. 118 After unfasten the cylinder head bolts, remove it from the engine block

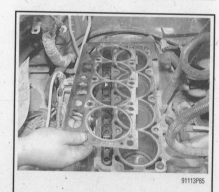

Fig. 119 Remove and discard the old cylinder head gasket

Fig. 120 Use a scraper to remove the old gasket material from the block and the cylinder head

Fig. 121 A new gasket will marked on one side to tell you which side should be facing up

Fig. 122 You must use a torque wrench . . .

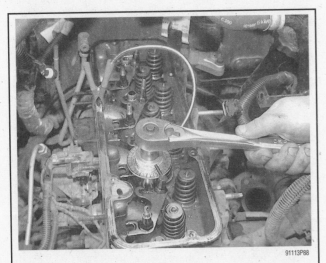
Fig. 123 . . . and a torque angle meter to properly tighten the head bolts to specification

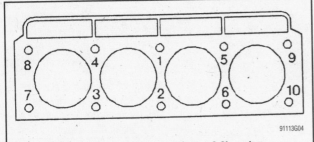
Fig. 124 Cylinder head bolt torque sequence—2.2L engine

faces. Refer to the ENGINE RECONDITIONING procedures at the end of this section.

➡The gasket surfaces on both the head and block must be clean of any foreign matter and free of nicks or heavy scratches. The cylinder bolt threads in the block and thread on the bolts must be cleaned (dirt will affect the bolt torque).

25. Place a new gasket over the dowel pins (DO NOT use any sealer on the gasket), then position the cylinder head over the gasket and dowels.

26. Apply a coating of 1052080 or equivalent sealer to the cylinder head bolt threads. Install the cylinder head bolts (within 15 minutes of sealer application), then tighten them in the proper sequence first to a torque of 46 ft. lbs. (63 Nm) for long bolts or to 43 ft. lbs. (58 Nm) for short bolts and then tighten all bolts an additional 90 degree turn using a torque angle meter.

27. Install the engine lift bracket.

28. Install the rocker arms and pushrods.

29. Install the rocker arm cover.

30. Install the lower intake manifold. Refer to the procedure earlier in this section for specifications.

31. If equipped, install the EGR adapter.

32. Connect the spark plug wires and the fuel lines.

33. Attach the wiring to the lower intake manifold.

34. Install the upper intake manifold. Refer to the procedure earlier in this section for specifications.

35. Connect the vacuum hoses and electrical wiring to the upper intake, as tagged during removal.

36. Install the oil fill tube assembly.

37. Install the exhaust manifold, then connect the exhaust pipe and oxygen sensor.

38. Connect the heater hose to the water pump, then connect the throttle cable support and throttle cable.

39. Install the accessory support bracket and components.

40. If not already done, reposition and secure the A/C compressor.

41. Install the power steering support brace and the alternator support brace. Engage the alternator wiring.

42. Install the thermostat housing, then connect the heater hose to the housing.

43. Install the water pump pulley and the serpentine drive belt.

44. Install the fan assembly, then engage the radiator and the lower fan shroud.

45. Install the upper fan shroud, then connect the upper radiator hose.

46. Engage the air inlet duct work, then connect the negative battery cable.

47. Properly refill the engine cooling system and check for leaks.

4.3L Engine

1994–95 MODELS

◆ See Figures 125 thru 130

☀☀ CAUTION

Never open, service or drain the radiator or cooling system when hot; serious burns can occur from the steam and hot coolant. Also, when draining engine coolant, keep in mind that cats and dogs are attracted to ethylene glycol antifreeze and could drink any that is left in an uncovered container or in puddles on the ground. This will prove fatal in sufficient quantities. Always drain coolant into a sealable container. Coolant should be reused unless it is contaminated or is several years old.

1. Properly relieve the fuel system pressure, then disconnect the negative battery cable.

2. Drain the engine cooling system.

3. Remove the rocker arm cover.

4. Remove the intake manifold.

5. Remove the exhaust manifold.

6. If removing the right cylinder head, remove or disconnect:

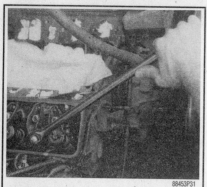

Fig. 125 Loosen the cylinder head bolts in the reverse order of the torque sequence

Fig. 126 Remove the cylinder head from the engine

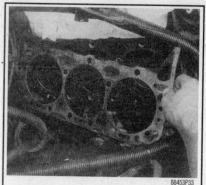

Fig. 127 Remove and discard the old cylinder head gasket

Fig. 128 Place rags or shop towels in the combustion chambers before cleaning the old gasket from the block

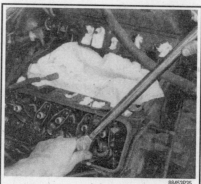

Fig. 129 Tighten the cylinder head bolts in sequence using a torque wrench

Fig. 130 Cylinder head bolt torque sequence—4.3L engine

- Electrical connector at the sensor.
- Dipstick tube at the cylinder head bracket.
- Air conditioning compressor (position it aside with the refrigerant lines attached), if equipped.
- A/C compressor (if equipped)/belt tensioner bracket.

7. If removing the left cylinder head, remove or disconnect:
- Alternator (position it aside).
- Left side engine accessory bracket with power steering pump (position the pump aside with the lines attached) and brackets, if equipped.

8. Tag and disconnect the wiring from the spark plugs. If necessary, remove the spark plugs from the cylinder head.

9. Loosen the rocker arms and remove the pushrods.

➡️**If valve train components, such as the rocker arms or pushrods, are to be reused, they must be tagged or arranged to insure installation in their original locations.**

10. Unfasten the cylinder head bolts by loosening them in the reverse of the torque sequence, then carefully remove the cylinder head.

To install:

11. Carefully clean and inspect the cylinder head and the gasket mounting surfaces. Refer to the ENGINE RECONDITIONING procedures at the end of this section.

➡️**The gasket surfaces on both the head and block must be clean of any foreign matter and free of nicks or heavy scratches. The cylinder bolt threads in the block and thread on the bolts must be cleaned (dirt will affect the bolt torque).**

➡️**DO NOT apply sealer to composition steel-asbestos gaskets.**

12. If using a steel only gasket, apply a thin and even coat of sealer to both sides of the gaskets.

13. Place a new gasket over the dowel pins with the bead or the words "This Side Up" facing upwards (as applicable), then carefully lower the cylinder head into position over the gasket and dowels.

14. Apply a coating of 1052080 or equivalent sealer to the threads of the

cylinder head bolts, then thread the bolts into position until finger-tight. Using the proper torque sequence, tighten the bolts in 3 steps:
- First, tighten the bolts to 25 ft. lbs. (34 Nm).
- Next, tighten the bolts to 45 ft. lbs. (61 Nm).
- Finally, tighten the bolts to 65 ft. lbs. (90 Nm).

15. Install the pushrods, secure the rocker arms and adjust the valves.

16. If removed, install the spark plugs. Engage the spark plug wires.

17. If the left cylinder head was removed, reposition and secure the engine accessory bracket with the power steering pump and brackets, as equipped. Install the alternator.

18. If the right cylinder head was removed, install the A/C compressor (if equipped) and A/C compressor/belt tensioner bracket, then install the dipstick tube bracket and engage the sensor electrical connector.

19. Install the exhaust manifold.

20. Install the intake manifold.

21. Install the rocker arm cover.

22. Connect the negative battery cable, then properly refill the engine cooling system.

23. Run the engine to check for leaks, then check and/or adjust the ignition timing.

1996–99 MODELS

▸ See Figure 130

⁂ CAUTION

Relieve the pressure on the fuel system before disconnecting any fuel line connection. Please refer to Section 5 of this manual for the proper procedures.

1. Properly relieve the fuel system pressure, then disconnect the negative battery cable.

2. Drain the engine cooling system.

3. Remove the intake manifold.

4. Remove the exhaust manifold.

5. If removing the right cylinder head, remove the alternator and bracket.

6. On 1999 and later models, remove the cooling fan assembly.

7. If removing the left cylinder head, remove the air conditioning compressor (position it aside with the refrigerant lines attached), if equipped.

8. If removing the left cylinder head, on 1999 and later models, if equipped remove the air pipe bracket and nut from the rear of the power steering pump.

9. If removing the left cylinder head, remove the engine accessory bracket with power steering pump (position the pump aside with the lines attached) and brackets, if equipped.

10. Tag and disengage the wiring harness and clip from the rear of the cylinder head.

11. Disconnect the coolant sensor wire.

12. Tag and disconnect the wiring from the spark plugs. If necessary, remove the spark plugs from the cylinder head.

13. On 1999 and later models, remove the ground wires and if necessary, the fuel line bracket from the rear of the cylinder head

14. Remove the rocker arm cover.

15. Loosen the rocker arms and remove the pushrods.

➡ **If valve train components, such as the rocker arms or pushrods, are to be reused, they must be tagged or arranged to insure installation in their original locations.**

16. Unfasten the cylinder head bolts by loosening them in the reverse of the torque sequence, then carefully remove the cylinder head.

To install:

17. Carefully clean and inspect the cylinder head and the gasket mounting surfaces. Refer to the ENGINE RECONDITIONING procedures at the end of this section.

➡ **The gasket surfaces on both the head and block must be clean of any foreign matter and free of nicks or heavy scratches. The cylinder bolt threads in the block and thread on the bolts must be cleaned (dirt will affect the bolt torque).**

➡ **DO NOT apply sealer to composition steel-asbestos gaskets.**

18. If using a steel only gasket, apply a thin and even coat of sealer to both sides of the gaskets.

19. Place a new gasket over the dowel pins with the bead or the words "This Side Up" facing upwards (as applicable), then carefully lower the cylinder head into position over the gasket and dowels.

20. Apply a coating of 12346004 or equivalent sealer to the threads of the cylinder head bolts, then thread the bolts into position until finger-tight.

21. Install the bolts in sequence to 22 ft. lbs. (30 Nm). The bolts must then be tightened again in sequence in the following order:

  a. Short length bolts: (11, 7, 3, 2, 6, 10) 55 degrees

  b. Medium length bolts: (12, 13) 65 degrees

  c. Long length bolts: (1, 4, 8, 5, 9) 75 degrees

22. Install the pushrods, secure the rocker arms and adjust the valves.

23. Install the rocker arm cover.

24. If removed, install the spark plugs. Engage the spark plug wires.

25. On 1999 models, attach the fuel line bracket (if removed) and ground wires to the rear of the head and tighten the bolts to 22 ft. lbs. (30 Nm).

26. If the left cylinder head was removed, reposition and secure the air conditioning compressor and bracket.

27. If the right cylinder head was removed, install the alternator and bracket.

28. If the left cylinder head was removed, install the engine accessory bracket with power steering pump.

29. If the left side cylinder head was removed on 1999 models, attach the air pipe bracket and nut to the rear of the power steering pump (if equipped). Tighten the nut to 30 ft. lbs. (41 Nm).

30. If the left cylinder head was removed, install the A/C compressor.

31. If the left side cylinder head was removed on 1999 models, install the cooling fan assembly.

32. Engage the wiring harness and clip from the rear of the cylinder head.

33. Connect the coolant sensor wire.

34. Install the exhaust manifold.

35. Install the intake manifold.

36. Connect the negative battery cable, then properly refill the engine cooling system.

37. Run the engine to check for leaks.

Oil Pan

Pan removal is possible with the engine in the vehicle on some of the powertrain combinations covered by this manual. If it is possible, it will often require the removal or repositioning of components including, the steering linkage assembly, the forward drive axle and crossmember (4WD) and/or the engine mounts. It is a difficult and tedious task to remove the oil pan with the engine in the vehicle. The chances of contaminating the bearing surfaces or damaging other internal engine components is great. Also, working under the vehicle with the engine jacked up in the frame puts you at great risk for great personal injury. Therefore, it is desirable in most cases to remove the engine in order to gain access to the oil pan.

REMOVAL & INSTALLATION

2.2L Engine

➡ **See Figure 131**

1. Remove the engine assembly from the vehicle.

2. If equipped, remove the clutch pressure plate and disc from the engine.

3. Remove the flywheel.

4. Remove the oil pan nuts and bolts, then remove the pan from the bottom of the block.

To install:

5. Carefully clean the gasket mating surfaces of any remaining old gasket or sealer material.

6. Position a new gasket and seal onto the oil pan. Use a thin bead of sealant at either side of the sealer (as shown in the illustration). Use a thin bead of sealant to the oil pan side flanges and the pan surface that contacts the engine front cover.

7. Install the oil pan and tighten the retaining bolts to 89 inch. lbs. (10 Nm).

8. Install the flywheel.

9. If equipped, install the pressure plate and disc.

10. Install the engine to the vehicle.

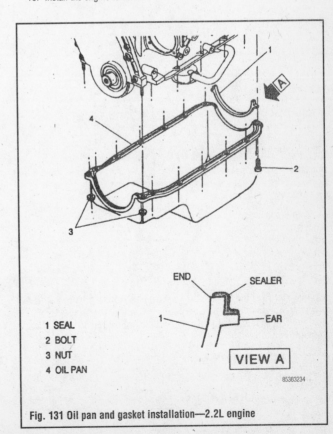

1 SEAL
2 BOLT
3 NUT
4 OIL PAN

85383234

Fig. 131 Oil pan and gasket installation—2.2L engine

2 Wheel Drive 4.3L Engines

♦ **See Figure 132**

1. Remove the engine from the vehicle.
2. Remove the oil pan retainers (nuts, studs and/or bolts) and rail reinforcements, if equipped.
3. Remove the rubber bell housing plugs, if equipped.
4. Remove the oil pan from the block.

To install:

5. Using a putty knife, clean the gasket mounting surfaces. Make sure that all sealing surfaces are clean and free of oil.
6. Apply 1052080 or an equivalent sealant to the oil pan rail where it contacts the timing cover-to-block joint (front) and the crankshaft rear seal retainer-to-block joint (rear). Continue the bead of sealant about 1 in. (25mm) in both directions from each of the four corners.
7. Using a new gasket, install the oil pan, reinforcements (if equipped) and retainers.

➡**On 1996–99 models the alignment between the rear of the pan and rear of the block is critical. The two surfaces must be flush to allow for proper alignment with the transmission housing.**

8. On 1996–99 models, use a feeler gauge to check the clearance between the oil pan-to-transmission contacts. If clearance exceeds 0.011 inch (0.3mm) at any of the three contact points, readjust the pan until the clearance is within specification.
9. Once the pan is in its correct position tighten the retainers to specification:
On 1994–95 models.
- Bolts: 100 inch lbs. (11 Nm).
- Nuts at corners: 17 ft. lbs. (23 Nm)

On 1996–99 models.
- Bolts and studs in the sequence illustrated: 18 ft. lbs. (25 Nm)
10. Install the engine into the vehicle. Refill the crankcase with fresh oil. Start the engine, establish normal operating temperatures and check for leaks.

1994–97 4 Wheel Drive Models

♦ **See Figures 132, 133, 134 and 135**

1. Disconnect the negative battery cable.
2. Remove the dipstick tube.
3. Raise and support the front of the vehicle safely using jackstands.
4. Remove the drive belt splash shield, the front axle shield, and the transfer case shield.
5. Remove the front skid plate and drain the engine crankcase oil, then remove the flywheel cover.
6. If applicable, disengage the wiring harness bracket at the right side of the oil pan.
7. Remove the left and right motor mount through-bolts.
8. Raise the engine using a suitable lifting device and block in position. This may be accomplished using large wooden blocks between the motor mounts and brackets.

➡**Use extreme caution when blocking the engine in position. Get out from underneath the truck and rock the engine slightly once the blocks are in place to be sure the engine is properly supported.**

9. Disconnect the oil cooler line, then remove the oil filter adapter.
10. Remove the pitman arm bolt, then disconnect the pitman arm.
11. Remove the idler arm bolts, then disconnect the idler arm.
12. Remove the front differential through-bolts, then disconnect or remove the front driveshaft (as necessary).
13. Roll the differential assembly forward for clearance.
14. Remove the starter motor retaining bolts, then lower the starter and either remove it from the vehicle or suspend it out of the way using mechanic's wire.
15. Remove the oil pan bolts, nuts and reinforcements, then lower the oil pan and gasket from the vehicle.

To install:

16. Using a putty knife, clean the gasket mounting surfaces. Make sure that all sealing surfaces are clean and free of oil.
17. Apply 1052080, or an equivalent sealant to the oil pan rail where it contacts the timing cover-to-block joint (front) and the crankshaft rear seal retainer-to-block joint (rear). Continue the bead of sealant about 1 in. (25mm) in both directions from each of the four corners.
18. Using a new gasket, install the oil pan, reinforcements and retainers. Tighten the bolts to 100 inch lbs. (11 Nm) and the nuts at the corners to 17 ft. lbs. (23 Nm) on 1994–95 models and 18 ft. lbs. (25 Nm) on 1996–97 models in the sequence illustrated.

※ **CAUTION**

Use a feeler gauge to check the clearance between the three oil pan-to-transmission bell housing contact points. if the clearance exceeds 0.011 in. (0.3mm) at any of the points, move the pan until the clearance is within specifications.

88453GAQ

Fig. 132 Oil pan bolt tightening sequence—1996–99 4.3L engine

88453P40

Fig. 133 Drain the engine oil from the crankcase

88453P41

Fig. 134 After unfastening the oil pan bolts remove the oil pan

88453P42

Fig. 135 Remove and discard the old oil pan gasket

19. Install the starter motor and secure using the mounting bolts.
20. Roll the differential back into position, then install/connect the front driveshaft. Install the front differential through-bolts.
21. Connect the idler arm and secure using the retaining bolts, then connect the pitman arm and secure using the bolts.
22. Install the transfer case shield.
23. Install the flywheel cover, then install the front skid plate.
24. Install the front axle shield, then install the drive belt splash shield.
25. If applicable, engage the wiring harness bracket at the right side of the oil pan.
26. Remove the jackstands and carefully lower the truck.
27. Install the dipstick, then properly refill the engine crankcase.
28. Connect the negative battery cable.
29. Start the engine, establish normal operating temperatures and check for leaks.

1998–99 4 Wheel Drive Models

▶ **See Figure 132**

1. Remove the battery and battery tray.
2. Disconnect the shift cable at the actuator.
3. Raise the vehicle and support it with safety stands.
4. Remove the splash shields from the steering linkage and the oil pan.
5. Drain the engine oil and remove the starter motor.
6. Remove the oil cooler pipes.
7. Remove the front wheels.
8. Unplug the electrical connector at the shift cable housing.
9. Remove the wiring harness bracket from the shift cable housing.
10. Unfasten the shift cable housing bolts and disconnect the shift cable from the differential carrier.
11. Remove both drive axles and the differential.
12. Unfasten the oil pan retainers, then lower the oil pan and gasket from the vehicle.

To install:

13. Using a putty knife, clean the gasket mounting surfaces. Make sure that all sealing surfaces are clean and free of oil.
14. Apply 12346141, or an equivalent sealant to the oil pan rail where it contacts the timing cover-to-block joint (front) and the crankshaft rear seal retainer-to-block joint (rear). Continue the bead of sealant about 1 in. (25mm) in both directions from each of the four corners.
15. Using a new gasket, install the oil pan and retainers. Tighten the bolts to 18 ft. lbs. (25 Nm) in the sequence illustrated.

✳✳ CAUTION

Use a feeler gauge to check the clearance between the three oil pan-to-transmission bell housing contact points. if the clearance exceeds 0.011 in. (0.3mm) at any of the points, move the pan until the clearance is within specifications.

16. Install the differential and the drive axles.
17. Attach the shift cable to the differential carrier and install the shift cable housing bolts.
18. Install the wiring harness bracket at the shift cable housing.
19. Attach the electrical connector at the shift cable housing.
20. Install the front wheels and the oil cooler lines.
21. Install the starter motor and secure using the mounting bolts.
22. Install the splash shields and lower the vehicle.
23. Attach the shift cable at the actuator.
24. Install the battery and battery tray.
25. Properly refill the engine crankcase.
26. Start the engine, establish normal operating temperatures and check for leaks.

Oil Pump

REMOVAL & INSTALLATION

▶ **See Figures 136 and 137**

1. Remove the oil pan.
2. Remove the oil pump attaching bolt and, if equipped, the pickup tube nut/bolt then remove the pump along with the pickup tube and shaft, as necessary.
3. If necessary for the 2.2L engine, remove the extension shaft and retainer (being careful not the crack the retainer) from the pump.

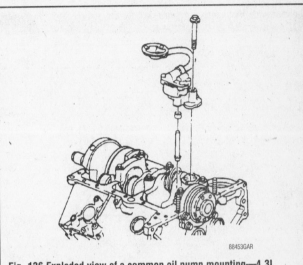

Fig. 136 Exploded view of a common oil pump mounting—4.3L engine shown

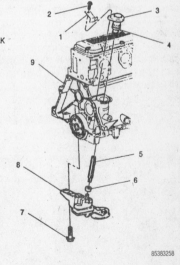

1. BRACKET
2. BOLT
3. OIL PUMP DRIVE ASSEMBLY
4. O–RING
5. SHAFT
6. RETAINER; HEAT AND WATER SOAK PRIOR TO INSTALLATION
7. BOLT
8. OIL PUMP
9. CYLINDER BLOCK

Fig. 137 Exploded view of a common oil pump mounting—2.2L engine shown

To install:

4. For the 2.2L engine, if the extension shaft was removed, heat the extension shaft retainer in hot water, then install the shaft and retainer to the oil pump. Make sure the retainer does not crack during installation.

5. Ensure that the pump pickup tube is tight in the pump body. If the tube should come loose, oil pressure will be lost and oil starvation will occur. If the pickup tube is loose it should be replaced.

6. Install the pump aligning the pump shaft with the distributor drive gear as necessary. Tighten the oil pump/pickup tube retainer(s) to specification:
- 2.2L engine: 32 ft. lbs. (44 Nm)
- 4.3L engine: 65 ft. lbs. (90 Nm)

7. Install the oil pan and refill the engine crankcase. Start the engine and make sure oil pressure builds immediately or engine damage could occur.

Crankshaft Damper/Pulley

REMOVAL & INSTALLATION

4.3L Engines

▶ See Figures 138, 139 and 140

Most of the 4.3L engines covered in this manual are equipped with a crankshaft hub and pulley assembly. The pulley is usually mounted to the hub using 3 or so bolts around the inner circle of the pulley. The center mounting bolt is used to retain the hub to the crankshaft, but may also be used to retain the pulley. If the center mounting bolt also retains the pulley, a washer can normally be seen between the bolt head and the inner lip of the pulley.

1. Disconnect the negative battery cable.

2. Loosen and remove the accessory drive belts or serpentine drive belt from the crankshaft damper.

3. If necessary for access on certain models, remove the fan assembly.

4. Remove the pulley mounting bolts from the pulley and damper assembly. If the center mounting bolt is not used to retain the pulley, it may be separated from the hub at this time and removed from the engine.

5. Spray the damper bolt with penetrating oil and allow it to soak in for at least a few minutes. Loosen and remove the center crankshaft damper bolt. If the pulley was not removed earlier, it should be free now.

➥ **If damper bolt removal is difficult, various methods may be used to hold the crankshaft while loosening or tightening the bolt. One method involves installing a flywheel holding fixture to prevent the crankshaft from turning. A holding tool may be available for some dampers which threads into the pulley bolt holes. But most importantly of all, allow the penetrating oil to do the work when loosening an old damper bolt and reapply oil, as necessary. If you have the time, you might even want the oil to sit overnight.**

6. Remove the damper from the end of the crankshaft using a suitable threaded damper puller, NOT a jawed-type puller which would most likely destroy dampers with bonded hubs.

✳✳ WARNING

The use of any other type of puller, such as a universal claw type which pulls on the outside of the hub, can destroy the balancer on some of these engines. Many of the vehicles covered in this manual use a balancer, the outside ring of which is bonded in rubber to the hub. Pulling on the outside will break the bond.

To install:

7. If removal of the damper was difficult, check the damper inner diameter and the crankshaft outer diameter for corrosion. A small amount of corrosion may be removed using steel wool, then the surface may be lubricated lightly using clean engine oil.

8. Coat the front cover seal contact edge of the damper lightly with clean engine oil, then apply a small amount of RTV sealant to the keyway in the damper hub. Install the damper on the end of the crankshaft (along with the pulley if the share the center retaining bolt), but DO NOT hammer it into position, instead use a damper installation tool to slowly draw the hub into position. If the damper can be positioned far enough over the end of the crankshaft, the damper bolt may be used to draw it into position, but be careful that sufficient threads are in contact to prevent stripping the bolt or crankshaft.

9. Once the damper is fully seated, install and tighten the retaining bolt to 74 ft. lbs. (100 Nm).

10. If not done earlier, install the pulley and secure using the outer retaining bolts. tighten the pulley bolts to 43 ft. lbs. (58 Nm).

11. If removed for access, install the fan assembly.

12. Install the drive belt(s) to the crankshaft pulley.

13. Connect the negative battery cable.

2.2L Engines

▶ See Figures 141, 142 and 143

1. Disconnect the negative battery cable.
2. Remove the serpentine drive belt.
3. Remove the fan shroud and the engine cooling fan.
4. Raise the vehicle and support it with jackstands.
5. Remove the crankshaft pulley bolts.
6. Unfasten the hub bolt and remove the pulley.
7. Attach a suitable puller tool to the crankshaft hub.
8. Turn the center screw of the puller clockwise until it forces the hub from the crankshaft.
9. Inspect the hub for damage and replace it as necessary.
10. Inspect the crankshaft key for damage and replace as necessary.

To install:

11. Coat the front cover seal with clean engine oil.

12. If removed, apply a suitable RTV sealer to the key on the crankshaft and install the key.

13. Place the hub onto the crankshaft making sure to align the key with the notch on the inside diameter of the hub.

14. Using either crankshaft hub installation tool J 29113, its equivalent, or

Fig. 138 Unfasten the pulley mounting bolts

88453P46

Fig. 139 Unfasten the center pulley bolts and remove the pulley from the vehicle

88453P47

Fig. 140 Using a suitable puller, disengage the damper from the crankshaft

88453P48

Fig. 141 Location of the crankshaft pulley bolts (1) and the hub bolt (2)

Fig. 142 Unfasten all the pulley and hub bolts, remove the pulley and install a suitable pulley on the crankshaft hub

Fig. 143 Use the pulley to draw the hub off the crankshaft and remove the hub from the engine compartment

the pulley hub bolt, pull the hub into position. If you use the pulley hub bolt to install the be careful that the hub goes in straight. Once the hub is fully seated, screw two of the pulley bolts into the hub, use a prybar between the bolts to stop the hub from turning and loosen the hub pulley hub bolt.

15. Remove the two pulley bolts and install the pulley.

16. Install the pulley hub bolts and the center hub bolt. Tighten the pulley bolts to 37 ft. lbs. (50 Nm) and the pulley hub bolt to 77 ft. lbs. (105 Nm).

17. Lower the vehicle.

18. Install the cooling fan and the radiator shroud.

19. Install the serpentine drive belt and connect the negative battery cable.

Timing Chain Cover and Seal

REMOVAL & INSTALLATION

2.2L Engine

1994–95 MODELS

1. Disconnect the negative battery cable.

2. Remove the power steering fluid reservoir from the radiator shroud, then remove the upper fan shroud.

3. Carefully release the belt tension, then remove the serpentine drive belt.

4. Remove the alternator and brackets from the engine, then position them aside.

5. Remove the crankshaft pulley and hub. For details, please refer to the procedure located earlier in this section.

6. As necessary, disconnect the lower radiator hose clamp at the water pump, then loosen and/or remove the oil pan.

➡There may be bolts attaching the front of the oil pan to the timing cover. If so, make sure they are removed before attempting to remove the cover.

7. Unfasten the crankcase (timing) front cover bolts, then disengage cover from the engine. Make sure all bolts are removed and be careful not to force and damage the cover.

8. Carefully remove the old crankshaft seal from the cover using a suitable prytool. Be very careful not to distort the front cover or to score the end of the crankshaft.

To install:

9. Carefully remove all traces of gasket or sealant from the mating surfaces.

10. Lubricate the lips of a new seal with clean engine oil, then use a seal centering tool (such as J-35468 or equivalent) to install the seal to the front cover. Leave the tool in position in the seal until the cover is installed.

11. Apply a ⅜ in. (10mm) wide by ⁵⁄₁₆ (5mm) thick bead of RTV sealer to the oil pan at the front crankcase cover sealing surface. Then apply a ¼ in. (6mm) by ⅛ in. (3mm) thick bead of RTV to the crankcase front cover at the block sealing surface.

12. Install the crankcase front cover to the engine using the seal tool to assure it is properly centered and prevent damage to the hub. Tighten the cover retaining bolts to 97 inch lbs. (11 Nm), then remove the seal centering tool.

13. Install the lower radiator hose clamp at the water pump, then install and secure the oil pan, as applicable.

14. If removed, install the oil pan.

15. Install the crankshaft pulley and hub.

16. Reposition and secure the alternator with brackets.

17. Install the serpentine drive belt, then install the upper fan shroud.

18. Reposition and secure the power steering reservoir.

19. Connect the negative battery cable.

1996–99 MODELS

♦ See Figures 144 thru 151

1. Disconnect the negative battery cable.

2. Carefully release the belt tension, then remove the serpentine drive belt.

3. Remove the cooling fan assembly and pulley.

4. Remove the crankshaft pulley and hub.

5. Remove the belt tensioner/idler pulley assembly.

Fig. 144 The belt tensioner assembly is attached to the engine by three bolts located on the side of the unit

Fig. 145 Unfasten the three bolts and remove the tensioner assembly

Fig. 146 Raise the vehicle, support it with jackstands and remove the front two oil pan nuts

Fig. 147 The front cover is attached to the engine with a number of small bolts

Fig. 148 After unfastening the front cover bolts, remove the cover. You may have to gently pry between the cover and oil pan to break the seal to get the cover off

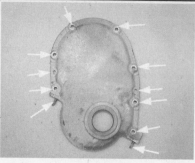

Fig. 149 Location of the front cover retaining bolt holes and studs

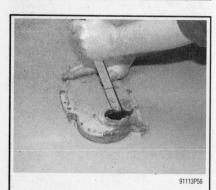

Fig. 150 Use a suitable puller to remove the oil seal

Fig. 151 A sealer driver and a hammer can be used to install a new seal

Fig. 152 Remove the timing cover retaining bolts

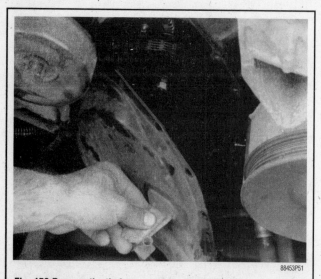

Fig. 153 Remove the timing cover from the vehicle

6. Remove the front oil pan-to-front cover nuts or studs.
7. Remove the starter.
8. If necessary, remove the alternator and brackets from the engine, then position them aside.
9. Loosen but do not remove the oil pan bolts.
10. Unfasten the crankcase (timing) front cover bolts, then remove cover from the engine. Make sure all bolts are removed and be careful not to force and damage the cover.
11. Carefully remove the old crankshaft seal from the cover using a suitable prytool. Be very careful not to distort the front cover or to score the end of the crankshaft.

To install:
12. Carefully remove all traces of gasket or sealant from the mating surfaces.
13. Lubricate the lips of a new seal with clean engine oil, then use a seal centering tool (such as J-35468 or equivalent) to install the seal to the front cover. Leave the tool in position in the seal until the cover is installed.
14. Apply a 3/8 in. (10mm) wide by 5/16 in. (5mm) thick bead of RTV sealer to the oil pan at the front crankcase cover sealing surface. Then apply a 1/4 in. (6mm) by 1/8 in. (3mm) thick bead of RTV to the crankcase front cover at the block sealing surface.
15. Install the crankcase front cover to the engine using the seal tool to assure it is properly centered and prevent damage to the hub. Tighten the cover retaining bolts to 97 inch lbs. (11 Nm), then remove the seal centering tool.
16. Install and secure the oil pan, as applicable.
17. Install the starter.
18. If removed, reposition and secure the alternator with brackets.
19. Install the belt tensioner/idler pulley assembly.
20. Install the belt assembly.
21. Install the crankshaft pulley and hub.
22. Install the cooling fan assembly and pulley.
23. Connect the negative battery cable.

4.3L Engine

▶ See Figures 152, 153 and 154

☀☀ CAUTION

Never open, service or drain the radiator or cooling system when hot; serious burns can occur from the steam and hot coolant. Also, when draining engine coolant, keep in mind that cats and dogs are attracted to ethylene glycol antifreeze and could drink any that is left in an uncovered container or in puddles on the ground. This will prove fatal in sufficient quantities. Always drain coolant into a sealable container. Coolant should be reused unless it is contaminated or is several years old.

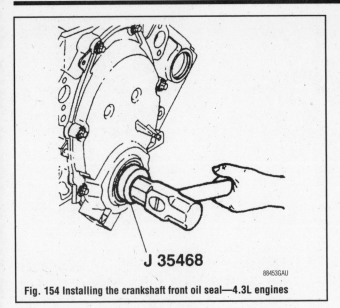

Fig. 154 Installing the crankshaft front oil seal—4.3L engines

1. Disconnect the negative battery cable and drain the engine cooling system.
2. Remove the crankshaft pulley and damper.

✳✳ WARNING

The outer ring (weight) of the torsional damper is bonded to the hub with rubber. The damper must be removed with a puller which acts on the inner hub only. Pulling on the outer portion of the damper will break the rubber bond or destroy the tuning of the unit.

3. Remove the water pump assembly.
4. Loosen the oil pan.
5. If applicable, remove the crankshaft position sensor.
6. Remove the front cover bolts and, if equipped, the reinforcements, then remove the front cover from the engine.
7. Pry the seal out of the front cover using a small prytool. Be very careful not to distort the front cover or to score the end of the crankshaft.

To install:

➡ On 1995–99 models, anytime the front cover is removed, the cover must be replaced upon reassembly. If you reuse the old cover, oil leaks may develop.

8. Clean the gasket mating surfaces of the engine and cover of all remaining gasket or sealer material. Be careful not to score or damage the surfaces.

➡ The manufacturer suggests you wait until the front cover is mounted to the engine before you install the replacement crankshaft oil seal. This assures the cover is properly supported.

9. Position a new front cover gasket to the engine or cover using gasket cement to hold it in position. Lubricate the front of the oil pan seal with engine oil to aid in reassembly.
10. Install the front cover to the engine. Take care while engaging the front of the oil pan seal with the bottom of the cover. On 1998–99 models, apply sealer 12346141, or an equivalent sealant to the oil pan rail where it contacts the timing cover-to-block joint (front) and the crankshaft rear seal retainer-to-block joint (rear). Continue the bead of sealant about 1 in. (25mm) in both directions from each of the four corners.
11. Install front cover retaining bolts and tighten to 124 inch lbs. (14 Nm) on 1994–95 models and 106 inch. lbs. (12 Nm) on 1996–99 models.
12. Lightly coat the lips of the replacement crankshaft seal with clean engine oil, then position the seal with the open end facing inward the engine. Use a suitable seal installation driver to position the seal in the front cover.
13. If removed, install a new crankshaft position sensor O-ring, then install the sensor.
14. Secure the oil pan.
15. Install the water pump.
16. Install the crankshaft damper and pulley.
17. Connect the negative battery cable, then properly refill the engine cooling system.
18. Run the engine until normal operating temperature has been reached, then check for leaks.

Timing Chain and Gears

REMOVAL & INSTALLATION

2.2L Engine

▶ **See Figures 155 thru 162**

1. Disconnect the negative battery cable.
2. Remove the crankcase (timing) front cover from the engine.
3. Turn the crankshaft until the timing marks on the sprockets are in alignment. The marks should also be in alignment with the tabs on the tensioner.
4. Remove the tensioner retaining bolts.
5. Unfasten the camshaft sprocket retaining bolts, then remove the sprocket and timing chain at the same time.
6. Remove the tensioner assembly.
7. If applicable, remove the crankshaft position sensor.
8. If necessary, remove the crankshaft sprocket using J-22888-20 or an equivalent puller.

To install:

9. If removed, install the crankshaft sprocket using a suitable installer such as J-5590 or its equivalent. Make sure the sprocket is fully seated against the crankshaft.
10. Compress the tensioner spring and insert a cotter pin or nail in the hole provided to hold the tensioner in position.
11. Loosely install the tensioner retaining bolts.
12. Position the camshaft sprocket in the timing chain, position the chain under the crankshaft sprocket and the camshaft sprocket to the camshaft.
13. Verify that the timing marks are all properly aligned, then loosely install the camshaft sprocket bolt.

Fig. 155 The timing marks on the sprockets should be in alignment. If not, turn the crankshaft until the marks are aligned

Fig. 156 The timing chain tensioner is retained by a Torx head bolt (1) and a regular hex head bolt (2)

Fig. 157 Unfasten the camshaft sprocket bolt

Fig. 158 Remove the camshaft sprocket and the timing chain at the same time . . .

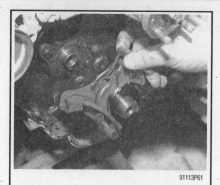

Fig. 159 . . . then remove the tensioner assembly

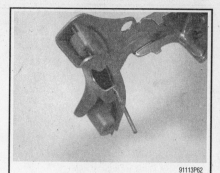

Fig. 160 Compress the tensioner spring and insert a cotter pin or nail in the hole provided to hold the tensioner in position

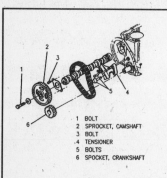

1 BOLT
2 SPROCKET, CAMSHAFT
3 BOLT
4 TENSIONER
5 BOLTS
6 SPROCKET, CRANKSHAFT

A ALIGN TABS ON TENSIONER WITH MARKS ON CAMSHAFT & CRANKSHAFT SPROCKETS.

85383289

Fig. 161 Timing chain, sprocket and camshaft mounting—2.2L engine

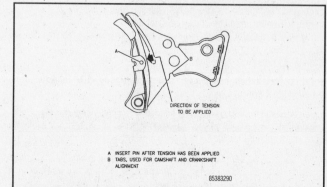

DIRECTION OF TENSION TO BE APPLIED

A INSERT PIN AFTER TENSION HAS BEEN APPLIED
B TABS, USED FOR CAMSHAFT AND CRANKSHAFT ALIGNMENT

85383290

Fig. 162 Locking the timing chain tensioner into position for chain installation—2.2L engine

14. If applicable, install the camshaft position sensor.

15. Tighten the tensioner bolts to 18 ft. lbs. (24 Nm), then tighten the camshaft sprocket bolt to 96 ft. lbs. (130 Nm).

16. Remove the cotter pin or nail holding the tensioner in position off the chain.

17. Install the timing cover to the engine.

4.3L Engine

▶ See Figures 163 thru 168

➡The following procedure requires the use of the Crankshaft Sprocket Removal tool No. J-5825-A or equivalent, and the Crankshaft Sprocket Installation tool No. J-5590 or equivalent.

1. Remove the timing cover from the engine.

2. Rotate the crankshaft until the No. 4 cylinder is on the TDC of its compression stroke and the camshaft sprocket mark aligns with the mark on the crankshaft sprocket (facing each other at a point closest together in their travel) and in line with the shaft centers.

3. If applicable, remove the crankshaft position sensor reluctor ring.

4. Remove the camshaft sprocket-to-camshaft nut and/or bolts, then remove the camshaft sprocket (along with the timing chain). If the sprocket is difficult to remove, use a plastic mallet to bump the sprocket from the camshaft.

➡The camshaft sprocket (located by a dowel) is lightly pressed onto the camshaft and should come off easily. The chain comes off with the camshaft sprocket.

5. If necessary use J-5825-A or an equivalent crankshaft sprocket removal tool to free the timing sprocket from the crankshaft.

6. If necessary, remove the crankshaft sprocket key.

To install:

7. Inspect the timing chain and the timing sprockets for wear or damage, replace the damaged parts as necessary.

Fig. 163 Make sure the marks camshaft and crankshaft sprockets are aligned

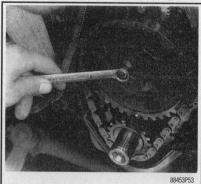

Fig. 164 Unfasten the camshaft sprocket retainers

Fig. 165 Remove the camshaft sprocket and the timing chain together

Fig. 166 Using a suitable puller, remove the crankshaft sprocket

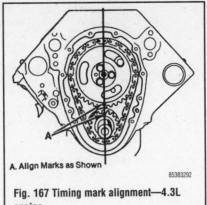

A. Align Marks as Shown

Fig. 167 Timing mark alignment—4.3L engine

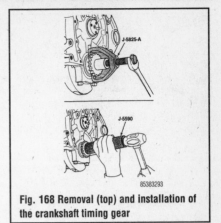

Fig. 168 Removal (top) and installation of the crankshaft timing gear

8. Using a putty knife, clean the gasket mounting surfaces. Using solvent, clean the oil and grease from the gasket mounting surfaces.

9. If removed, install the crankshaft sprocket key.

10. If removed, use J-5590, or an equivalent crankshaft sprocket installation tool and a hammer to drive the crankshaft sprocket onto the crankshaft, without disturbing the position of the engine.

➡**During installation, coat the thrust surfaces lightly with Molykote® or an equivalent pre-lube.**

11. Position the timing chain over the camshaft sprocket. Arrange the camshaft sprocket in such a way that the timing marks will align between the shaft centers and the camshaft locating dowel will enter the dowel hole in the cam sprocket.

12. Position the chain under the crankshaft sprocket, then place the cam sprocket, with the chain still mounted over it, in position on the front of the camshaft. Install and tighten the camshaft sprocket-to-camshaft retainers to 21 ft. lbs. (28 Nm) on 1994–96 models and 18 ft. lbs. (25 Nm) on 1997–99 models.

13. With the timing chain installed, turn the crankshaft two complete revolutions, then check to make certain that the timing marks are in correct alignment between the shaft centers.

14. If applicable, install the crankshaft position sensor reluctor ring.

15. Install the timing cover.

Camshaft and Bearings

REMOVAL & INSTALLATION

On all engines equipped with lifters, a complete new set of lifters must be installed whenever the camshaft is replaced in order to prolong the new camshaft's service life.

2.2L Engine

▶ See Figure 169

✳✳ CAUTION

Never open, service or drain the radiator or cooling system when hot; serious burns can occur from the steam and hot coolant. Also, when draining engine coolant, keep in mind that cats and dogs are attracted to ethylene glycol antifreeze and could drink any that is left in an uncovered container or in puddles on the ground. This will prove fatal in sufficient quantities. Always drain coolant into a sealable container. Coolant should be reused unless it is contaminated or is several years old.

1. If equipped, have the air conditioning system discharged by a qualified technician using a proper refrigerant recovery/recycling station.

2. Properly relieve the fuel system pressure, then disconnect the negative battery cable.

3. Drain the engine cooling system and the engine oil.

4. Remove the air duct from the air inlet.

5. Remove the upper radiator shroud, then disengage the oil and transmission cooler lines at the radiator.

6. Tag and disengage all hoses from the radiator.

7. If necessary for clearance, remove the radiator and air conditioning condenser from the vehicle.

8. Remove the serpentine drive belt.

9. Remove the rocker arm cover.

10. Remove the cylinder head.

11. Unfasten the anti-rotation bracket bolts and brackets, then remove the valve lifters.

12. Unfasten the oil pump drive retaining bolt, then remove the drive by lifting and twisting.

13. If equipped, remove the Camshaft Position (CMP) sensor.

14. Remove the crankshaft pulley and hub.

15. Remove the serpentine drive belt idler pulley.

16. Remove the timing cover from the engine.

17. Remove the timing chain and camshaft sprocket.

18. Unfasten the camshaft thrust plate retaining bolts, then remove the plate from the block.

19. Install the sprocket bolts or longer bolts of the same thread into the end of the camshaft as a handle, then pull the camshaft straight out of the engine, turning slightly as it is withdrawn and taking care not to damage the bearings.

20. If removal of camshaft bearings is necessary, use the following procedure:

a. Install a camshaft bearing removal/installation tool with the shoulder toward the bearing. Ensure that enough threads are engaged.

b. Using two wrenches, hold the puller screw while turning the nut. When the bearing has been released from the bore, remove the tool.

c. Assemble the tool on the driver to remove the front and rear bearings.

d. Install the bearings (outer bearings first) so that the oil holes in the block and the bearing align.

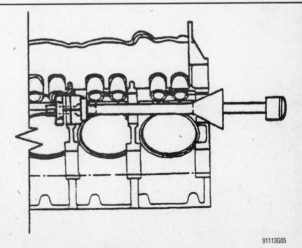

Fig. 169 A suitable camshaft bearing removal/installation tool is required when replacing the bearings

e. Install a fresh camshaft bearing rear cover using sealant.

To install:

21. Inspect the camshaft, journals and lobes for wear and replace, if necessary.

22. Inspect the bearings for scratches, pits or a loose fit in their bores and replace, if necessary.

23. Coat the camshaft lobes and journals with a high viscosity oil with zinc such as No. 12345501, or equivalent.

24. Carefully insert the camshaft in the engine, turning it slightly from side to side and it is inserted.

25. Install the thrust plate and tighten the retaining bolts to 106 inch lbs. (12 Nm).

26. If equipped, install the CMP sensor.

27. Install the timing chain and camshaft sprocket.

28. Install the timing cover to the engine.

29. Install the serpentine drive belt idler pulley.

30. Install the crankshaft pulley and hub.

31. Install the oil pump drive by inserting while twisting, then install the retaining bolt and tighten to 18 ft. lbs. (25 Nm).

32. Install the valve lifters and the anti-rotation brackets.

33. Install the cylinder head.

34. Install the rocker arm cover.

35. Install the air conditioning condenser and the radiator assemblies. Engage all hoses removed from the radiator.

36. Engage the oil and transmission cooler lines at the radiator, then install the radiator shroud.

37. Install the serpentine drive belt.

38. Engage the air cleaner assembly and connect the negative battery cable.

39. Fill the crankcase with the correct grade and amount of oil.

40. Fill the cooling system with coolant.

41. Connect the negative battery cable.

42. Have the air conditioning system charged by a qualified technician using a proper refrigerant recovery/recycling station.

4.3L Engines

▶ See Figures 170, 171 and 172

> **❄❄ CAUTION**
>
> **Never open, service or drain the radiator or cooling system when hot; serious burns can occur from the steam and hot coolant. Also, when draining engine coolant, keep in mind that cats and dogs are attracted to ethylene glycol antifreeze and could drink any that is left in an uncovered container or in puddles on the ground. This will prove fatal in sufficient quantities. Always drain coolant into a sealable container. Coolant should be reused unless it is contaminated or is several years old.**

1. If equipped, have the air conditioning system discharged by a qualified technician using a proper refrigerant recovery/recycling station.

2. Properly relieve the fuel system pressure, then disconnect the negative battery cable.

3. Disconnect the air intake duct, if applicable.

4. Drain the engine cooling system.

5. If necessary for clearance, remove the radiator and air conditioning condenser from the vehicle.

6. Remove the rocker arm covers from the engine.

7. Remove the intake manifold assembly.

8. Remove the rocker arms, pushrods and lifters.

9. Remove the crankshaft pulley and hub.

10. Remove the engine front (timing) cover.

11. Align the timing marks on the crankshaft and camshaft sprockets.

12. Unfasten the balance shaft drive gear bolt and remove the gear to allow clearance for camshaft removal.

13. Remove the camshaft sprocket and timing chain.

14. If necessary, remove the crankshaft position sensor reluctor ring and sprocket.

15. Remove the thrust plate screws, then remove the thrust plate.

16. Install the sprocket bolts or longer bolts of the same thread into the end of the camshaft as a handle, then remove the camshaft front the front of the engine while turning slightly from side to side, as necessary. Take care not to damage the camshaft bearings when removing the camshaft.

17. If removal of camshaft bearings is necessary, use the following procedure:

a. Install a camshaft bearing removal/installation tool with the shoulder toward the bearing. Ensure that enough threads are engaged.

b. Using two wrenches, hold the puller screw while turning the nut. When the bearing has been released from the bore, remove the tool.

c. Assemble the tool on the driver to remove the front and rear bearings.

d. Install the bearings so that the oil holes in the block and the bearing align.

e. Install a fresh camshaft bearing rear cover using sealant.

To install:

18. Lubricate the camshaft journals with clean engine oil or a suitable prelube, then install the camshaft into the block being extremely careful not to contact the bearings with the cam lobes.

19. Install the camshaft thrust plate and tighten the bolts to 106 inch lbs. (12 Nm).

20. Install the timing chain, camshaft sprocket and balance shaft drive gear.

21. Install the engine front (timing) cover.

22. Install the crankshaft pulley and hub.

23. Install the valve lifters, then install the pushrods and rocker arms. Properly adjust the valve clearance.

24. Install the intake manifold assembly.

25. Install the rocker arm covers to the engine.

26. Install the air conditioning condenser and the radiator assemblies. Engage all hoses removed from the radiator.

27. Connect the negative battery cable and properly refill the engine cooling system.

INSPECTION

▶ See Figures 173 and 174

Using solvent, degrease the camshaft and clean out all of the oil holes. Visually inspect the cam lobes and bearing journals for excessive wear. If a lobe is questionable, check all of the lobes as indicated. If a journal or lobe is worn, the camshaft MUST BE reground or replaced.

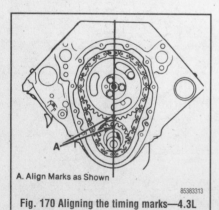

A. Align Marks as Shown

85383313

Fig. 170 Aligning the timing marks—4.3L engine

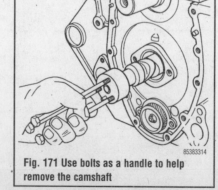

85383314

Fig. 171 Use bolts as a handle to help remove the camshaft

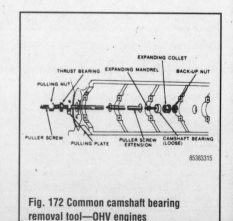

85383315

Fig. 172 Common camshaft bearing removal tool—OHV engines

➡️If a journal is worn, there is a good chance that the bearings are worn and need replacement.

If the lobes and journals appear intact, place the front and rear journals in V-blocks and rest a dial indicator on the center journal. Rotate the camshaft to check the straightness. If deviation exceeds 0.001 in. (0.0254mm), the camshaft should likely be replaced.

➡️On most engines lobe lift can be measured with the camshaft still installed. Simply remove the rocker cover and rocker arm, then use a dial gauge on the end of the pushrod. When the pushrod is at the bottom of its travel, set the dial gauge to "0" then turn the engine and note the gauge's highest reading.

Check the camshaft lobes with a micrometer, by measuring the across the lobe centerline from the nose to the base and again at the centerline across the diameter at 90° from the first measurement (see illustration). The lobe lift is determined by subtracting the second measurement (diameter) from the first (diameter plug lobe lift). If the lobes vary from specification, the camshaft must be reground or replace.

Balance Shaft

REMOVAL & INSTALLATION

▶ See Figures 175, 176, 177 and 178

✳️ CAUTION

Never open, service or drain the radiator or cooling system when hot; serious burns can occur from the steam and hot coolant. Also, when draining engine coolant, keep in mind that cats and dogs are attracted to ethylene glycol antifreeze and could drink any that is left in an uncovered container or in puddles on the ground. This will

prove fatal in sufficient quantities. Always drain coolant into a sealable container. Coolant should be reused unless it is contaminated or is several years old.

1. Have the air conditioning system discharged by a qualified technician using a proper refrigerant recovery/recycling station.
2. Properly relieve the fuel system pressure, then disconnect the negative battery cable.
3. Disconnect the air cleaner intake duct.
4. Drain the engine cooling system.
5. Remove the upper radiator shroud, then disengage the oil and transmission cooler lines at the radiator.
6. Tag and disengage all hoses from the radiator.
7. Remove the radiator and air conditioning condenser from the vehicle.
8. Remove the fan assembly.
9. Carefully release the belt tension, then remove the serpentine drive belt.
10. If equipped, unfasten the pencil brace at the coolant pump, then remove the coolant pump.
11. Remove the crankshaft pulley and damper.
12. If necessary, remove the flywheel inspection cover.
13. Remove the front cover.
14. Unfasten the balance shaft gear bolt, then remove the gear.
15. Remove the timing chain and sprockets.
16. Remove the balance shaft retainer.
17. Remove the intake manifold assembly.
18. Remove the lifter retainer.
19. Remove the balance shaft and front bearing by gently driving them out using a soft faced mallet.
20. Using a balance shaft service kit J–38834 or its equivalent, remove the balance shaft rear bearing.

➡️The balance shaft and drive and driven gears are serviced only as a set, including the gear bolt. The balance shaft and front bearing are serviced as a package.

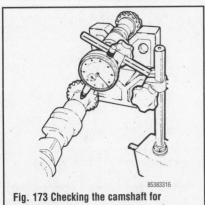

Fig. 173 Checking the camshaft for straightness

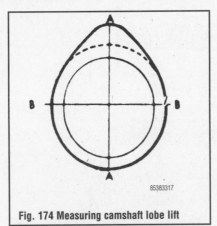

Fig. 174 Measuring camshaft lobe lift

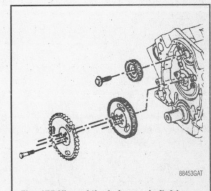

Fig. 175 View of the balance shaft drive and driven gears

Fig. 176 View of the balance shaft location—1994 4.3L engine

Fig. 177 Unfasten the balance shaft gear bolt . . .

Fig. 178 . . . then remove the gear

✳✳ WARNING

The front bearing must not be removed from the balance shaft

To install:

21. Inspect the balance shaft gears for damage, such as nicks and burrs.

22. Using a putty knife, clean the gasket mounting surfaces. Using solvent, clean the oil and grease from the gasket mounting surfaces.

23. Lubricate the balance shaft rear bearing with clean engine oil, then install the bearing using tool J–38834 or its equivalent.

24. Lubricate the balance shaft with clean engine oil, then install the balance shaft into the block.

25. Install the balance shaft bearing retainer and bolts. Tighten the bolts to 124 inch. lbs. (14 Nm).

26. Install the balance shaft driven gear and bolt. Tighten the bolt to 15 ft. lbs. (20 Nm) plus an additional 35° using a torque/angle meter.

27. Install the lifter retainer, then rotate the balance shaft by hand and check that there is clearance between the balance shaft and the lifter retainer.

28. Temporarily install the balance shaft drive gear so that the timing mark on the gear points straight up, then remove the drive gear, turn the balance shaft so the timing mark on the driven gear is facing straight down.

29. Install the drive gear and make sure the timing marks on both gears line up (dot-to-dot).

30. Install the drive gear retaining bolt and tighten to 12 ft. lbs. (16 Nm).

31. Install the intake manifold assembly.

32. Install the timing chain and sprocket assemblies.

33. Install the front cover, seal, bolts and the oil pan assembly.

34. Install the flywheel inspection cover, then using tool J–39046 or its equivalent engage the crankshaft pulley and damper.

35. Install the coolant pump, then engage the pencil brace to the pump.

36. Install the serpentine drive belt.

37. Install the fan assembly.

38. Install the air conditioning condenser and the radiator assemblies. Engage all hoses removed from the radiator.

39. Engage the oil and transmission cooler lines at the radiator, then install the radiator shroud.

40. Install the air cleaner assembly and connect the negative battery cable.

41. Fill the crankcase with the correct grade and amount of oil.

42. Fill the cooling system with coolant.

43. Start the vehicle and check for leaks.

44. Have the air conditioning system charged by a qualified technician using a proper refrigerant recovery/recycling station.

Rear Main Oil Seal

Replacing a rear main seal is a formidable task. Before replacing the seal, care should be taken in determining the exact source of the leak. Various manufacturers produce a fluorescent die oil additive which can be added to your crankcase. The engine is run, allowing the dyed oil to leak from the same source, then a black light is used to illuminate the leak so it can be traced.

REPLACEMENT

2.2L Engines

▶ **See Figures 179, 180, 181 and 182**

➡ **The following procedure requires the use of a seal installation tool such as J-34686 or equivalent.**

1. Remove the transmission assembly.
2. If equipped, remove the clutch.
3. Remove the flywheel and verify the rear main seal is leaking.
4. Remove the seal by inserting a small prybar through the dust lip at an angle and prying the seal out. Be careful not to score the crankshaft sealing surface.

To install:

5. Check the crankshaft and seal bore for nicks or damage. Repair as necessary.

6. Lightly coat the inner diameter of the seal with clean engine oil.

7. Position the seal over the mandrel of the J-34686 or an equivalent installation tool. Make sure the dust lip (back of seal) is bottomed squarely against the collar of the tool.

Fig. 179 View of the rear main seal

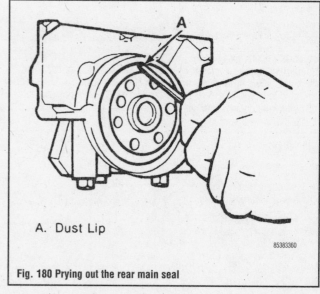

A. Dust Lip

Fig. 180 Prying out the rear main seal

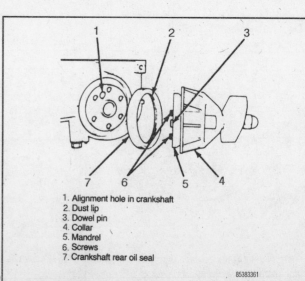

1. Alignment hole in crankshaft
2. Dust lip
3. Dowel pin
4. Collar
5. Mandrel
6. Screws
7. Crankshaft rear oil seal

Fig. 181 Installing the rear main seal

Fig. 182 The rear main seal may be installed using a suitable seal driver tool and a hammer

8. Lightly coat the outer diameter of the seal using clean engine oil, then position the tool to the crankshaft while aligning the tool dowel pin with the crankshaft dowel pin hole. Tighten the screws to attach the tool and assure proper seal installation.

9. Turn the handle of the tool until the collar is tight against the case and the seal has been completely seated.

10. Turn the handle of the tool out until it stops, then remove the tool and verify that the seal is seated squarely in the bore.

11. Install the flywheel.

12. If equipped, install the clutch.

13. Install the transmission assembly.

4.3L Engine

▶ **See Figure 183**

➡**The following procedure requires the use of a seal installation tool (such as J-35621) or equivalent.**

1. Remove the transmission assembly.

2. If equipped, remove the clutch assembly.

3. Remove the flywheel and verify the rear main seal is leaking.

4. Remove the seal by inserting a small prybar into the notches provided in the seal retainer and pry the seal out. Be careful not to score the crankshaft sealing surface.

To install:

5. Check the crankshaft and seal bore for nicks or damage. Repair as necessary.

6. Lightly coat the inner and outer diameters of the seal with clean engine oil, then position the seal on the installation tool.

7. Position the tool to the crankshaft and thread the tool's screws into the tapped holes. Tighten the screws securely using a screwdriver to attach the tool and assure proper seal installation.

8. Turn the handle of the tool until it bottoms and the seal has been completely seated.

9. Turn the handle of the tool out until it stops, then remove the tool and verify that the seal is seated squarely in the bore.

10. Install the flywheel to the engine.

11. If equipped, install the clutch assembly.

12. Install the transmission assembly.

Flywheel

On most of the engines covered by this manual the flywheel and the ring gear are machined from one piece of metal and cannot be separated. On some of the 4.3L engines the ring gear is a separate piece and can be driven from the flywheel once the gear is heated using a torch.

REMOVAL & INSTALLATION

▶ **See Figures 184 thru 190**

1. Remove the transmission assembly from the vehicle.

2. If equipped with a manual transmission, remove the clutch and pressure plate assembly.

3. If equipped, remove the flywheel cover.

4. Remove the flywheel-to-crankshaft bolts, then remove the flywheel and spacer (if used) from the engine.

To install:

5. Inspect the flywheel for cracks, and inspect the ring gear for burrs or worn teeth. Replace the flywheel if any damage is apparent. Remove burrs with a mill file. Remove ant thread sealer from the flywheel bolts.

6. Install the spacer (if used) and the flywheel. Most flywheels will only attach to the crankshaft in one position, as the bolt holes are unevenly spaced and/or the crankshaft is fitted with a dowel pin.

7. On 1998–99 2.2L engines, apply Loctite® 271 or equivalent to the flywheel bolts. Follow the instructions supplied with the thread locking compound to ensure proper bolt retention.

Install the bolts and tighten to 55 ft. lbs. (75 Nm) on 2.2L engines and 75 ft. lbs. (100 Nm) on 4.3L engines using a crisscross pattern.

8. If equipped, install the clutch and pressure plate assembly.

9. Install the transmission assembly.

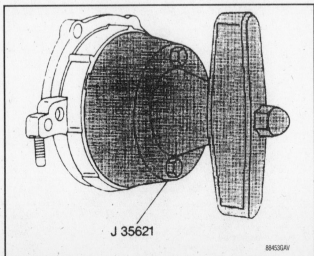

Fig. 183 Installing the rear oil seal using seal installation tool J–35621

Fig. 184 Installing the flywheel in the vehicle

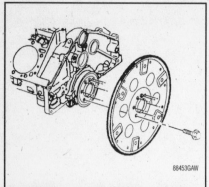

Fig. 185 View of the flywheel and related components (automatic transmission)

88453GAW

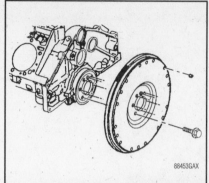

Fig. 186 View of the flywheel and related components (manual transmission)

88453GAX

91113P19

Fig. 187 If a flywheel holding tool is not available install one of the transmission retaining bolts, then use a crowbar to prevent the flywheel from turning while loosening its bolts

91113P20

Fig. 188 After all the bolts have been unfastened, remove the flywheel

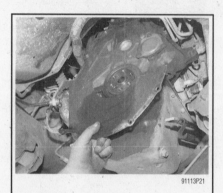

91113P21

Fig. 189 Remove the spacer or clutch housing cover (if equipped)

91113P18

Fig. 190 Use a torque wrench to tighten the flywheel bolts to specification

RING GEAR REPLACEMENT

1. Remove the flywheel from the vehicle. Refer to the procedure outlined in this section.
2. Make certain that the ring gear is a separate piece, then using a torch, uniformly heat it around the entire circumference. DO NOT heat the gear until it is red hot as this will change the metal structure.
3. When the ring gear is hot enough, drive it off the flywheel using a hammer.

To install:

4. Using a torch, heat the ring gear uniformly until it expands enough to be installed on the flywheel.

✳✳ CAUTION

Never heat the ring gear to a temperature above 400°F (204°C) as this will weaken the structure of the metal.

5. When the ring gear and flywheel have cooled sufficiently, install the flywheel on the vehicle.

EXHAUST SYSTEM

Inspection

▶ See Figures 191, 192 and 193

➡Safety glasses should be worn at all times when working on or near the exhaust system. Older exhaust systems will almost always be covered with loose rust particles which will shower you when disturbed. These particles are more than a nuisance and could injure your eye.

✳✳ CAUTION

DO NOT perform exhaust repairs or inspection with the engine or exhaust hot. Allow the system to cool completely before attempting any work. Exhaust systems are noted for sharp edges, flaking metal and rusted bolts. Gloves and eye protection are required. A healthy supply of penetrating oil and rags is highly recommended.

Your vehicle must be raised and supported safely to inspect the exhaust system properly. By placing 4 safety stands under the vehicle for support should provide enough room for you to slide under the vehicle and inspect the

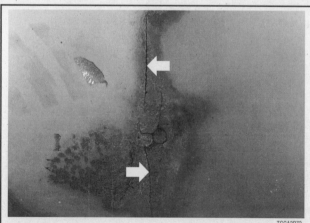

TCCA3P73

Fig. 191 Cracks in the muffler are a guaranteed leak

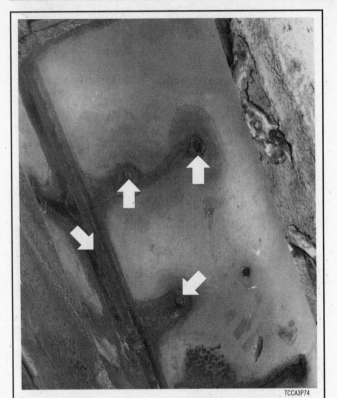

Fig. 192 Check the muffler for rotted spot welds and seams

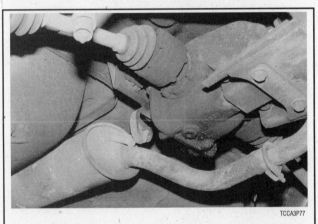

Fig. 193 Make sure the exhaust components are not contacting the body or suspension

system completely. Start the inspection at the exhaust manifold or turbocharger pipe where the header pipe is attached and work your way to the back of the vehicle. On dual exhaust systems, remember to inspect both sides of the vehicle. Check the complete exhaust system for open seams, holes loose connections, or other deterioration which could permit exhaust fumes to seep into the passenger compartment. Inspect all mounting brackets and hangers for deterioration, some models may have rubber O-rings that can be overstretched and non-supportive. These components will need to be replaced if found. It has always been a practice to use a pointed tool to poke up into the exhaust system where the deterioration spots are to see whether or not they crumble. Some models may have heat shield covering certain parts of the exhaust system , it will be necessary to remove these shields to have the exhaust visible for inspection also.

REPLACEMENT

▶ See Figure 194

There are basically two types of exhaust systems. One is the flange type where the component ends are attached with bolts and a gasket in-between. The other exhaust system is the slip joint type. These components slip into one another using clamps to retain them together.

❊❊ CAUTION

Allow the exhaust system to cool sufficiently before spraying a solvent exhaust fasteners. Some solvents are highly flammable and could ignite when sprayed on hot exhaust components.

Before removing any component of the exhaust system, ALWAYS squirt a liquid rust dissolving agent onto the fasteners for ease of removal. A lot of knuckle skin will be saved by following this rule. It may even be wise to spray the fasteners and allow them to sit overnight.

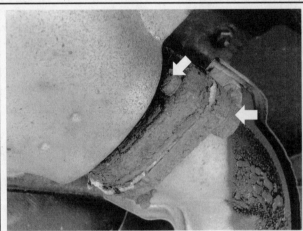

Fig. 194 Nuts and bolts will be extremely difficult to remove when deteriorated with rust

Flange Type
▶ See Figure 195

❊❊ CAUTION

Do NOT perform exhaust repairs or inspection with the engine or exhaust hot. Allow the system to cool completely before attempting any work. Exhaust systems are noted for sharp edges, flaking metal and rusted bolts. Gloves and eye protection are required. A healthy supply of penetrating oil and rags is highly recommended. Never spray liquid rust dissolving agent onto a hot exhaust component.

Before removing any component on a flange type system, ALWAYS squirt a liquid rust dissolving agent onto the fasteners for ease of removal. Start by unbolting the exhaust piece at both ends (if required). When unbolting the headpipe from the manifold, make sure that the bolts are free before trying to remove them. if you snap a stud in the exhaust manifold, the stud will have to be removed with a bolt extractor, which often means removal of the manifold itself. Next, disconnect the component from the mounting; slight twisting and turning may be required to remove the component completely from the vehicle. You may need to tap on the component with a rubber mallet to loosen the component. If all else fails, use a hacksaw to separate the parts. An oxy-acetylene cutting torch may be faster but the sparks are DANGEROUS near the fuel tank, and at the very least, accidents could happen, resulting in damage to the under-car parts, not to mention yourself.

Fig. 195 Example of a flange type exhaust system joint

Slip Joint Type

▶ **See Figure 196**

Before removing any component on the slip joint type exhaust system, ALWAYS squirt a liquid rust dissolving agent onto the fasteners for ease of removal. Start by unbolting the exhaust piece at both ends (if required). When unbolting the headpipe from the manifold, make sure that the bolts are free

Fig. 196 Example of a common slip joint type system

before trying to remove them. If you snap a stud in the exhaust manifold, the stud will have to be removed with a bolt extractor, which often means removal of the manifold itself. Next, remove the mounting U-bolts from around the exhaust pipe you are extracting from the vehicle. Don't be surprised if the U-bolts break while removing the nuts. Loosen the exhaust pipe from any mounting brackets retaining it to the floor pan and separate the components.

ENGINE RECONDITIONING

Determining Engine Condition

Anything that generates heat and/or friction will eventually burn or wear out (for example, a light bulb generates heat, therefore its life span is limited). With this in mind, a running engine generates tremendous amounts of both; friction is encountered by the moving and rotating parts inside the engine and heat is created by friction and combustion of the fuel. However, the engine has systems designed to help reduce the effects of heat and friction and provide added longevity. The oiling system reduces the amount of friction encountered by the moving parts inside the engine, while the cooling system reduces heat created by friction and combustion. If either system is not maintained, a break-down will be inevitable. Therefore, you can see how regular maintenance can affect the service life of your vehicle. If you do not drain, flush and refill your cooling system at the proper intervals, deposits will begin to accumulate in the radiator, thereby reducing the amount of heat it can extract from the coolant. The same applies to your oil and filter; if it is not changed often enough it becomes laden with contaminates and is unable to properly lubricate the engine. This increases friction and wear.

There are a number of methods for evaluating the condition of your engine. A compression test can reveal the condition of your pistons, piston rings, cylinder bores, head gasket(s), valves and valve seats. An oil pressure test can warn you of possible engine bearing, or oil pump failures. Excessive oil consumption, evidence of oil in the engine air intake area and/or bluish smoke from the tailpipe may indicate worn piston rings, worn valve guides and/or valve seals. As a general rule, an engine that uses no more than one quart of oil every 1000 miles is in good condition. Engines that use one quart of oil or more in less than 1000 miles should first be checked for oil leaks. If any oil leaks are present, have them fixed before determining how much oil is consumed by the engine, especially if blue smoke is not visible at the tailpipe.

COMPRESSION TEST

▶ **See Figure 197**

A noticeable lack of engine power, excessive oil consumption and/or poor fuel mileage measured over an extended period are all indicators of internal engine wear. Worn piston rings, scored or worn cylinder bores, blown head gaskets, sticking or burnt valves, and worn valve seats are all possible culprits. A check of each cylinder's compression will help locate the problem.

➡ **A screw-in type compression gauge is more accurate than the type you simply hold against the spark plug hole. Although it takes slightly longer to use, it's worth the effort to obtain a more accurate reading.**

1. Make sure that the proper amount and viscosity of engine oil is in the crankcase, then ensure the battery is fully charged.
2. Warm-up the engine to normal operating temperature, then shut the engine **OFF**.
3. Disable the ignition system.
4. Label and disconnect all of the spark plug wires from the plugs.
5. Thoroughly clean the cylinder head area around the spark plug ports, then remove the spark plugs.
6. Set the throttle plate to the fully open (wide-open throttle) position. You can block the accelerator linkage open for this, or you can have an assistant fully depress the accelerator pedal.

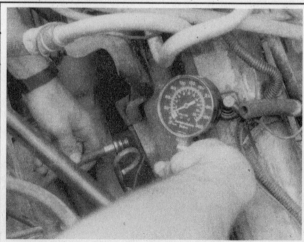

Fig. 197 A screw-in type compression gauge is more accurate and easier to use without an assistant

7. Install a screw-in type compression gauge into the No. 1 spark plug hole until the fitting is snug.

☀☀ WARNING

Be careful not to crossthread the spark plug hole.

8. According to the tool manufacturer's instructions, connect a remote starting switch to the starting circuit.

9. With the ignition switch in the **OFF** position, use the remote starting switch to crank the engine through at least five compression strokes (approximately 5 seconds of cranking) and record the highest reading on the gauge.

10. Repeat the test on each cylinder, cranking the engine approximately the same number of compression strokes and/or time as the first.

11. Compare the highest readings from each cylinder to that of the others. The indicated compression pressures are considered within specifications if the lowest reading cylinder is within 75 percent of the pressure recorded for the highest reading cylinder. For example, if your highest reading cylinder pressure was 150 psi (1034 kPa), then 75 percent of that would be 113 psi (779 kPa). So the lowest reading cylinder should be no less than 113 psi (779 kPa).

12. If a cylinder exhibits an unusually low compression reading, pour a tablespoon of clean engine oil into the cylinder through the spark plug hole and repeat the compression test. If the compression rises after adding oil, it means that the cylinder's piston rings and/or cylinder bore are damaged or worn. If the pressure remains low, the valves may not be seating properly (a valve job is needed), or the head gasket may be blown near that cylinder. If compression in any two adjacent cylinders is low, and if the addition of oil doesn't help raise compression, there is leakage past the head gasket. Oil and coolant in the combustion chamber, combined with blue or constant white smoke from the tailpipe, are symptoms of this problem. However, don't be alarmed by the normal white smoke emitted from the tailpipe during engine warm-up or from cold weather driving. There may be evidence of water droplets on the engine dipstick and/or oil droplets in the cooling system if a head gasket is blown.

OIL PRESSURE TEST

Check for proper oil pressure at the sending unit passage with an externally mounted mechanical oil pressure gauge (as opposed to relying on a factory installed dash-mounted gauge). A tachometer may also be needed, as some specifications may require running the engine at a specific rpm.

1. With the engine cold, locate and remove the oil pressure sending unit.

2. Following the manufacturer's instructions, connect a mechanical oil pressure gauge and, if necessary, a tachometer to the engine.

3. Start the engine and allow it to idle.

4. Check the oil pressure reading when cold and record the number. You may need to run the engine at a specified rpm, so check the specifications.

5. Run the engine until normal operating temperature is reached (upper radiator hose will feel warm).

6. Check the oil pressure reading again with the engine hot and record the number. Turn the engine **OFF**.

7. Compare your hot oil pressure reading to that given in the chart. If the reading is low, check the cold pressure reading against the chart. If the cold pressure is well above the specification, and the hot reading was lower than the specification, you may have the wrong viscosity oil in the engine. Change the oil, making sure to use the proper grade and quantity, then repeat the test.

Low oil pressure readings could be attributed to internal component wear, pump related problems, a low oil level, or oil viscosity that is too low. High oil pressure readings could be caused by an overfilled crankcase, too high of an oil viscosity or a faulty pressure relief valve.

Buy or Rebuild?

Now that you have determined that your engine is worn out, you must make some decisions. The question of whether or not an engine is worth rebuilding is largely a subjective matter and one of personal worth. Is the engine a popular one, or is it an obsolete model? Are parts available? Will it get acceptable gas mileage once it is rebuilt? Is the car it's being put into worth keeping? Would it be less expensive to buy a new engine, have your engine rebuilt by a pro, rebuild it yourself or buy a used engine from a salvage yard? Or would it be simpler and less expensive to buy another car? If you have considered all these matters and more, and have still decided to rebuild the engine, then it is time to decide how you will rebuild it.

➡ The editors at Chilton feel that most engine machining should be performed by a professional machine shop. Don't think of it as wasting money, rather, as an assurance that the job has been done right the first time. There are many expensive and specialized tools required to perform such tasks as boring and honing an engine block or having a valve job done on a cylinder head. Even inspecting the parts requires expensive micrometers and gauges to properly measure wear and clearances. Also, a machine shop can deliver to you clean, and ready to assemble parts, saving you time and aggravation. Your maximum savings will come from performing the removal, disassembly, assembly and installation of the engine and purchasing or renting only the tools required to perform the above tasks. Depending on the particular circumstances, you may save 40 to 60 percent of the cost doing these yourself.

A complete rebuild or overhaul of an engine involves replacing all of the moving parts (pistons, rods, crankshaft, camshaft, etc.) with new ones and machining the non-moving wearing surfaces of the block and heads. Unfortunately, this may not be cost effective. For instance, your crankshaft may have been damaged or worn, but it can be machined undersize for a minimal fee.

So, as you can see, you can replace everything inside the engine, but, it is wiser to replace only those parts which are really needed, and, if possible, repair the more expensive ones. Later in this section, we will break the engine down into its two main components: the cylinder head and the engine block. We will discuss each component, and the recommended parts to replace during a rebuild on each.

Engine Overhaul Tips

Most engine overhaul procedures are fairly standard. In addition to specific parts replacement procedures and specifications for your individual engine, this section is also a guide to acceptable rebuilding procedures. Examples of standard rebuilding practice are given and should be used along with specific details concerning your particular engine.

Competent and accurate machine shop services will ensure maximum performance, reliability and engine life. In most instances it is more profitable for the do-it-yourself mechanic to remove, clean and inspect the component, buy the necessary parts and deliver these to a shop for actual machine work.

Much of the assembly work (crankshaft, bearings, piston rods, and other components) is well within the scope of the do-it-yourself mechanic's tools and abilities. You will have to decide for yourself the depth of involvement you desire in an engine repair or rebuild.

TOOLS

The tools required for an engine overhaul or parts replacement will depend on the depth of your involvement. With a few exceptions, they will be the tools found in a mechanic's tool kit (see Section 1 of this manual). More in-depth work will require some or all of the following:

- A dial indicator (reading in thousandths) mounted on a universal base
- Micrometers and telescope gauges
- Jaw and screw-type pullers
- Scraper
- Valve spring compressor
- Ring groove cleaner
- Piston ring expander and compressor
- Ridge reamer
- Cylinder hone or glaze breaker
- Plastigage®
- Engine stand

The use of most of these tools is illustrated in this section. Many can be rented for a one-time use from a local parts jobber or tool supply house specializing in automotive work.

Occasionally, the use of special tools is called for. See the information on Special Tools and the Safety Notice in the front of this book before substituting another tool.

OVERHAUL TIPS

Aluminum has become extremely popular for use in engines, due to its low weight. Observe the following precautions when handling aluminum parts:
- Never hot tank aluminum parts (the caustic hot tank solution will eat the aluminum.
- Remove all aluminum parts (identification tag, etc.) from engine parts prior to the tanking.
- Always coat threads lightly with engine oil or anti-seize compounds before installation, to prevent seizure.
- Never overtighten bolts or spark plugs especially in aluminum threads.

When assembling the engine, any parts that will be exposed to frictional contact must be prelubed to provide lubrication at initial start-up. Any product specifically formulated for this purpose can be used, but engine oil is not recommended as a prelube in most cases.

When semi-permanent (locked, but removable) installation of bolts or nuts is desired, threads should be cleaned and coated with Loctite® or another similar, commercial non-hardening sealant.

CLEANING

▶ **See Figures 198, 199, 200, 201**

Before the engine and its components are inspected, they must be thoroughly cleaned. You will need to remove any engine varnish, oil sludge and/or carbon deposits from all of the components to insure an accurate inspection. A crack in the engine block or cylinder head can easily become overlooked if hidden by a layer of sludge or carbon.

Most of the cleaning process can be carried out with common hand tools and readily available solvents or solutions. Carbon deposits can be chipped away using a hammer and a hard wooden chisel. Old gasket material and varnish or sludge can usually be removed using a scraper and/or cleaning solvent. Extremely stubborn deposits may require the use of a power drill with a wire brush. If using a wire brush, use extreme care around any critical machined surfaces (such as the gasket surfaces, bearing saddles, cylinder bores, etc.). Use of a wire brush is NOT RECOMMENDED on any aluminum components. Always follow any safety recommendations given by the manufacturer of the tool and/or solvent. You should always wear eye protection during any cleaning process involving scraping, chipping or spraying of solvents.

An alternative to the mess and hassle of cleaning the parts yourself is to drop them off at a local garage or machine shop. They will, more than likely, have the necessary equipment to properly clean all of the parts for a nominal fee.

※ CAUTION

Always wear eye protection during any cleaning process involving scraping, chipping or spraying of solvents.

Remove any oil galley plugs, freeze plugs and/or pressed-in bearings and carefully wash and degrease all of the engine components including the fasteners and bolts. Small parts such as the valves, springs, etc., should be placed in a metal basket and allowed to soak. Use pipe cleaner type brushes, and clean all passageways in the components. Use a ring expander and remove the rings from the pistons. Clean the piston ring grooves with a special tool or a piece of broken ring. Scrape the carbon off of the top of the piston. You should never use a wire brush on the pistons. After preparing all of the piston assemblies in this manner, wash and degrease them again.

※ WARNING

Use extreme care when cleaning around the cylinder head valve seats. A mistake or slip may cost you a new seat.

When cleaning the cylinder head, remove carbon from the combustion chamber with the valves installed. This will avoid damaging the valve seats.

REPAIRING DAMAGED THREADS

▶ **See Figures 202, 203, 204, 205 and 206**

Several methods of repairing damaged threads are available. Heli-Coil® (shown here), Keenserts® and Microdot® are among the most widely used. All involve basically the same principle—drilling out stripped threads, tapping the

Fig. 198 Use a gasket scraper to remove the old gasket material from the mating surfaces

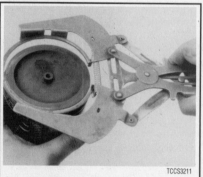

Fig. 199 Use a ring expander tool to remove the piston rings

Fig. 200 Clean the piston ring grooves using a ring groove cleaner tool, or . . .

Fig. 201 . . . use a piece of an old ring to clean the grooves. Be careful, the ring can be quite sharp

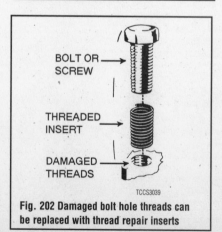

Fig. 202 Damaged bolt hole threads can be replaced with thread repair inserts

Fig. 203 Standard thread repair insert (left), and spark plug thread insert

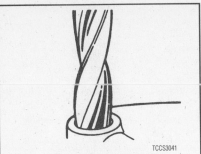

Fig. 204 Drill out the damaged threads with the specified size bit. Be sure to drill completely through the hole or to the bottom of a blind hole

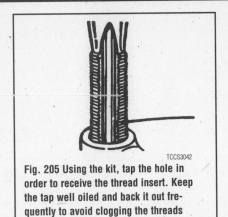

Fig. 205 Using the kit, tap the hole in order to receive the thread insert. Keep the tap well oiled and back it out frequently to avoid clogging the threads

Fig. 206 Screw the insert onto the installer tool until the tang engages the slot. Thread the insert into the hole until it is ¼–½ turn below the top surface, then remove the tool and break off the tang using a punch

hole and installing a prewound insert—making welding, plugging and oversize fasteners unnecessary.

Two types of thread repair inserts are usually supplied: a standard type for most inch coarse, inch fine, metric course and metric fine thread sizes and a spark lug type to fit most spark plug port sizes. Consult the individual tool manufacturer's catalog to determine exact applications. Typical thread repair kits will contain a selection of prewound threaded inserts, a tap (corresponding to the outside diameter threads of the insert) and an installation tool. Spark plug inserts usually differ because they require a tap equipped with pilot threads and a combined reamer/tap section. Most manufacturers also supply blister-packed thread repair inserts separately in addition to a master kit containing a variety of taps and inserts plus installation tools.

Before attempting to repair a threaded hole, remove any snapped, broken or damaged bolts or studs. Penetrating oil can be used to free frozen threads. The offending item can usually be removed with locking pliers or using a screw/stud extractor. After the hole is clear, the thread can be repaired, as shown in the series of accompanying illustrations and in the kit manufacturer's instructions.

Engine Preparation

To properly rebuild an engine, you must first remove it from the vehicle, then disassemble and diagnose it. Ideally you should place your engine on an engine stand. This affords you the best access to the engine components. Follow the manufacturer's directions for using the stand with your particular engine. Remove the flywheel or flexplate before installing the engine to the stand.

Now that you have the engine on a stand, and assuming that you have drained the oil and coolant from the engine, it's time to strip it of all but the necessary components. Before you start disassembling the engine, you may want to take a moment to draw some pictures, or fabricate some labels or containers to mark the locations of various components and the bolts and/or studs which fasten them. Modern day engines use a lot of little brackets and clips which hold wiring harnesses and such, and these holders are often mounted on studs and/or bolts that can be easily mixed up. The manufacturer spent a lot of time and money designing your vehicle, and they wouldn't have wasted any of it by haphazardly placing brackets, clips or fasteners on the vehicle. If it's present when you disassemble it, put it back when you assemble, you will regret not remembering that little bracket which holds a wire harness out of the path of a rotating part.

You should begin by unbolting any accessories still attached to the engine, such as the water pump, power steering pump, alternator, etc. Then, unfasten any manifolds (intake or exhaust) which were not removed during the engine removal procedure. Finally, remove any covers remaining on the engine such as the rocker arm, front or timing cover and oil pan. Some front covers may require the vibration damper and/or crank pulley to be removed beforehand. The idea is to reduce the engine to the bare necessities (cylinder head(s), valve train, engine block, crankshaft, pistons and connecting rods), plus any other 'in block' components such as oil pumps, balance shafts and auxiliary shafts.

Finally, remove the cylinder head(s) from the engine block and carefully place on a bench. Disassembly instructions for each component follow later in this section.

Cylinder Head

There are two basic types of cylinder heads used on today's automobiles: the Overhead Valve (OHV) and the Overhead Camshaft (OHC). The latter can also be broken down into two subgroups: the Single Overhead Camshaft (SOHC) and the Dual Overhead Camshaft (DOHC). Generally, if there is only a single camshaft on a head, it is just referred to as an OHC head. Also, an engine with an OHV cylinder head is also known as a pushrod engine.

Most cylinder heads these days are made of an aluminum alloy due to its light weight, durability and heat transfer qualities. However, cast iron was the material of choice in the past, and is still used on many vehicles today. Whether made from aluminum or iron, all cylinder heads have valves and seats. Some use two valves per cylinder, while the more hi-tech engines will utilize a multi-valve configuration using 3, 4 and even 5 valves per cylinder. When the valve contacts the seat, it does so on precision machined surfaces, which seals the combustion chamber. All cylinder heads have a valve guide for each valve. The guide centers the valve to the seat and allows it to move up and down within it. The clearance between the valve and guide can be critical. Too much clearance and the engine may consume oil, lose vacuum and/or damage the seat. Too little, and the valve can stick in the guide causing the engine to run poorly if at all, and possibly causing severe damage. The last component all cylinder heads have are valve springs. The spring holds the valve against its seat. It also returns the valve to this position when the valve has been opened by the valve train or camshaft. The spring is fastened to the valve by a retainer and valve locks (sometimes called keepers). Aluminum heads will also have a valve spring shim to keep the spring from wearing away the aluminum.

An ideal method of rebuilding the cylinder head would involve replacing all of the valves, guides, seats, springs, etc. with new ones. However, depending on how the engine was maintained, often this is not necessary. A major cause of valve, guide and seat wear is an improperly tuned engine. An engine that is running too rich, will often wash the lubricating oil out of the guide with gasoline, causing it to wear rapidly. Conversely, an engine which is running too lean will place higher combustion temperatures on the valves and seats allowing them to wear or even burn. Springs fall victim to the driving habits of the individual. A driver who often runs the engine rpm to the redline will wear out or break the springs faster then one that stays well below it. Unfortunately, mileage takes it toll on all of the parts. Generally, the valves, guides, springs and seats in a cylinder head can be machined and re-used, saving you money. However, if a valve is burnt, it may be wise to replace all of the valves, since they were all operating in the same environment. The same goes for any other component on the cylinder head. Think of it as an insurance policy against future problems related to that component.

Unfortunately, the only way to find out which components need replacing, is to disassemble and carefully check each piece. After the cylinder head(s) are disassembled, thoroughly clean all of the components.

DISASSEMBLY

◆ See Figures 207 thru 212

Before disassembling the cylinder head, you may want to fabricate some containers to hold the various parts, as some of them can be quite small (such as keepers) and easily lost. Also keeping yourself and the components organized will aid in assembly and reduce confusion. Where possible, try to maintain a components original location; this is especially important if there is not going to be any machine work performed on the components.

1. If you haven't already removed the rocker arms and/or shafts, do so now.
2. Position the head so that the springs are easily accessed.
3. Use a valve spring compressor tool, and relieve spring tension from the retainer.

➥Due to engine varnish, the retainer may stick to the valve locks. A gentle tap with a hammer may help to break it loose.

4. Remove the valve locks from the valve tip and/or retainer. A small magnet may help in removing the locks.
5. Lift the valve spring, tool and all, off of the valve stem.
6. If equipped, remove the valve seal. If the seal is difficult to remove with the valve in place, try removing the valve first, then the seal. Follow the steps below for valve removal.
7. Position the head to allow access for withdrawing the valve.

➥Cylinder heads that have seen a lot of miles and/or abuse may have mushroomed the valve lock grove and/or tip, causing difficulty in removal of the valve. If this has happened, use a metal file to carefully remove the high spots around the lock grooves and/or tip. Only file it enough to allow removal.

8. Remove the valve from the cylinder head.
9. If equipped, remove the valve spring shim. A small magnetic tool or screwdriver will aid in removal.
10. Repeat Steps 3 though 9 until all of the valves have been removed.

INSPECTION

Now that all of the cylinder head components are clean, it's time to inspect them for wear and/or damage. To accurately inspect them, you will need some specialized tools:

- A 0–1 in. micrometer for the valves
- A dial indicator or inside diameter gauge for the valve guides
- A spring pressure test gauge

If you do not have access to the proper tools, you may want to bring the components to a shop that does.

Valves

◆ See Figures 213 and 214

The first thing to inspect are the valve heads. Look closely at the head, margin and face for any cracks, excessive wear or burning. The margin is the best place to look for burning. It should have a squared edge with an even width all around the diameter. When a valve burns, the margin will look melted and the edges rounded. Also inspect the valve head for any signs of tulipping. This will show as a lifting of the edges or dishing in the center of the head and will usually not occur to all of the valves. All of the heads should look the same, any that seem dished more than others are probably bad. Next, inspect the valve lock grooves and valve tips. Check for any burrs around the lock grooves, especially if you had to file them to remove the valve. Valve tips should appear flat, although slight rounding with high mileage engines is normal. Slightly worn valve tips will need to be machined flat. Last, measure the valve stem diameter with the micrometer. Measure the area that rides within the guide, especially towards the tip where most of the wear occurs. Take several measurements along its length and compare them to each other. Wear should be even along the length with little to no taper. If no minimum diameter is given in the specifications, then the stem should not read more than 0.001 in. (0.025mm) below the unworn area of the valve stem. Any valves that fail these inspections should be replaced.

Fig. 207 When removing an OHV valve spring, use a compressor tool to relieve the tension from the retainer

Fig. 208 A small magnet will help in removal of the valve locks

Fig. 209 Be careful not to lose the small valve locks (keepers)

Fig. 210 Remove the valve seal from the valve stem—O-ring type seal shown

Fig. 211 Removing an umbrella/positive type seal

Fig. 212 Invert the cylinder head and withdraw the valve from the valve guide bore

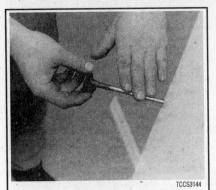

Fig. 213 Valve stems may be rolled on a flat surface to check for bends

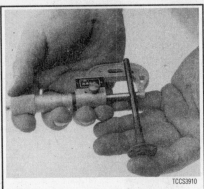

Fig. 214 Use a micrometer to check the valve stem diameter

Fig. 215 Use a caliper to check the valve spring free-length

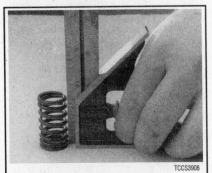

Fig. 216 Check the valve spring for squareness on a flat surface; a carpenter's square can be used

Fig. 217 A dial gauge may be used to check valve stem-to-guide clearance; read the gauge while moving the valve stem

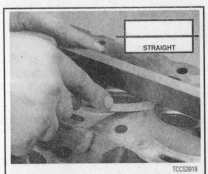

Fig. 218 Check the head for flatness across the center of the head surface using a straightedge and feeler gauge

Springs, Retainers and Valve Locks

♦ See Figures 215 and 216

The first thing to check is the most obvious, broken springs. Next check the free length and squareness of each spring. If applicable, insure to distinguish between intake and exhaust springs. Use a ruler and/or carpenter's square to measure the length. A carpenter's square should be used to check the springs for squareness. If a spring pressure test gauge is available, check each springs rating and compare to the specifications chart. Check the readings against the specifications given. Any springs that fail these inspections should be replaced.

The spring retainers rarely need replacing, however they should still be checked as a precaution. Inspect the spring mating surface and the valve lock retention area for any signs of excessive wear. Also check for any signs of cracking. Replace any retainers that are questionable.

Valve locks should be inspected for excessive wear on the outside contact area as well as on the inner notched surface. Any locks which appear worn or broken and its respective valve should be replaced.

Cylinder Head

There are several things to check on the cylinder head: valve guides, seats, cylinder head surface flatness, cracks and physical damage.

VALVE GUIDES

♦ See Figure 217

Now that you know the valves are good, you can use them to check the guides, although a new valve, if available, is preferred. Before you measure anything, look at the guides carefully and inspect them for any cracks, chips or breakage. Also if the guide is a removable style (as in most aluminum heads), check them for any looseness or evidence of movement. All of the guides should appear to be at the same height from the spring seat. If any seem lower (or higher) from another, the guide has moved. Mount a dial indicator onto the spring side of the cylinder head. Lightly oil the valve stem and insert it into the cylinder head. Position the dial indicator against the valve stem near the tip and zero the gauge. Grasp the valve stem and wiggle towards and away from the dial indicator and observe the readings. Mount the dial indicator 90 degrees from the initial point and zero the gauge and again take a reading. Compare the two readings for a out of round condition. Check the readings against the specifications given. An Inside Diameter (I.D.) gauge designed for valve guides will give you an accurate valve guide bore measurement. If the I.D. gauge is used, compare the readings with the specifications given. Any guides that fail these inspections should be replaced or machined.

VALVE SEATS

A visual inspection of the valve seats should show a slightly worn and pitted surface where the valve face contacts the seat. Inspect the seat carefully for severe pitting or cracks. Also, a seat that is badly worn will be recessed into the cylinder head. A severely worn or recessed seat may need to be replaced. All cracked seats must be replaced. A seat concentricity gauge, if available, should be used to check the seat run-out. If run-out exceeds specifications the seat must be machined (if no specification is given use 0.002 in. or 0.051mm).

CYLINDER HEAD SURFACE FLATNESS

♦ See Figures 218 and 219

After you have cleaned the gasket surface of the cylinder head of any old gasket material, check the head for flatness.

Place a straightedge across the gasket surface. Using feeler gauges, determine the clearance at the center of the straightedge and across the cylinder head at several points. Check along the centerline and diagonally on the head surface. If the warpage exceeds 0.003 in. (0.076mm) within a 6.0 in. (15.2cm) span, or 0.006 in. (0.152mm) over the total length of the head, the cylinder head must be resurfaced. After resurfacing the heads of a V-type engine, the intake manifold flange surface should be checked, and if necessary, milled proportionally to allow for the change in its mounting position.

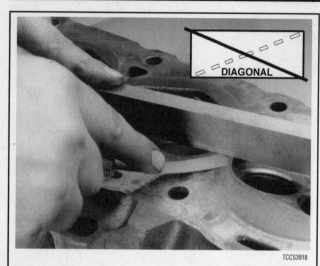

TCCS3918

Fig. 219 Checks should also be made along both diagonals of the head surface

CRACKS AND PHYSICAL DAMAGE

Generally, cracks are limited to the combustion chamber, however, it is not uncommon for the head to crack in a spark plug hole, port, outside of the head or in the valve spring/rocker arm area. The first area to inspect is always the hottest: the exhaust seat/port area.

A visual inspection should be performed, but just because you don't see a crack does not mean it is not there. Some more reliable methods for inspecting for cracks include Magnaflux®, a magnetic process or Zyglo®, a dye penetrant. Magnaflux® is used only on ferrous metal (cast iron) heads. Zyglo® uses a spray on fluorescent mixture along with a black light to reveal the cracks. It is strongly recommended to have your cylinder head checked professionally for cracks, especially if the engine was known to have overheated and/or leaked or consumed coolant. Contact a local shop for availability and pricing of these services.

Physical damage is usually very evident. For example, a broken mounting ear from dropping the head or a bent or broken stud and/or bolt. All of these defects should be fixed or, if unrepairable, the head should be replaced.

REFINISHING & REPAIRING

Many of the procedures given for refinishing and repairing the cylinder head components must be performed by a machine shop. Certain steps, if the inspected part is not worn, can be performed yourself inexpensively. However, you spent a lot of time and effort so far, why risk trying to save a couple bucks if you might have to do it all over again?

Valves

Any valves that were not replaced should be refaced and the tips ground flat. Unless you have access to a valve grinding machine, this should be done by a machine shop. If the valves are in extremely good condition, as well as the valve seats and guides, they may be lapped in without performing machine work.

It is a recommended practice to lap the valves even after machine work has been performed and/or new valves have been purchased. This insures a positive seal between the valve and seat.

LAPPING THE VALVES

➥Before lapping the valves to the seats, read the rest of the cylinder head section to insure that any related parts are in acceptable enough condition to continue.

➥Before any valve seat machining and/or lapping can be performed, the guides must be within factory recommended specifications.

1. Invert the cylinder head.
2. Lightly lubricate the valve stems and insert them into the cylinder head in their numbered order.
3. Raise the valve from the seat and apply a small amount of fine lapping compound to the seat.

4. Moisten the suction head of a hand-lapping tool and attach it to the head of the valve.
5. Rotate the tool between the palms of both hands, changing the position of the valve on the valve seat and lifting the tool often to prevent grooving.
6. Lap the valve until a smooth, polished circle is evident on the valve and seat.
7. Remove the tool and the valve. Wipe away all traces of the grinding compound and store the valve to maintain its lapped location.

✳✳ WARNING

Do not get the valves out of order after they have been lapped. They must be put back with the same valve seat with which they were lapped.

Springs, Retainers and Valve Locks

There is no repair or refinishing possible with the springs, retainers and valve locks. If they are found to be worn or defective, they must be replaced with new (or known good) parts.

Cylinder Head

Most refinishing procedures dealing with the cylinder head must be performed by a machine shop. Read the sections below and review your inspection data to determine whether or not machining is necessary.

VALVE GUIDE

➥If any machining or replacements are made to the valve guides, the seats must be machined.

Unless the valve guides need machining or replacing, the only service to perform is to thoroughly clean them of any dirt or oil residue.

There are only two types of valve guides used on automobile engines: the replaceable-type (all aluminum heads) and the cast-in integral-type (most cast iron heads). There are four recommended methods for repairing worn guides.
- Knurling
- Inserts
- Reaming oversize
- Replacing

Knurling is a process in which metal is displaced and raised, thereby reducing clearance, giving a true center, and providing oil control. It is the least expensive way of repairing the valve guides. However, it is not necessarily the best, and in some cases, a knurled valve guide will not stand up for more than a short time. It requires a special knurlizer and precision reaming tools to obtain proper clearances. It would not be cost effective to purchase these tools, unless you plan on rebuilding several of the same cylinder head.

Installing a guide insert involves machining the guide to accept a bronze insert. One style is the coil-type which is installed into a threaded guide. Another is the thin-walled insert where the guide is reamed oversize to accept a split-sleeve insert. After the insert is installed, a special tool is then run through the guide to expand the insert, locking it to the guide. The insert is then reamed to the standard size for proper valve clearance.

Reaming for oversize valves restores normal clearances and provides a true valve seat. Most cast-in type guides can be reamed to accept an valve with an oversize stem. The cost factor for this can become quite high as you will need to purchase the reamer and new, oversize stem valves for all guides which were reamed. Oversizes are generally 0.003 to 0.030 in. (0.076 to 0.762mm), with 0.015 in. (0.381mm) being the most common.

To replace cast-in type valve guides, they must be drilled out, then reamed to accept replacement guides. This must be done on a fixture which will allow centering and leveling off of the original valve seat or guide, otherwise a serious guide-to-seat misalignment may occur making it impossible to properly machine the seat.

Replaceable-type guides are pressed into the cylinder head. A hammer and a stepped drift or punch may be used to install and remove the guides. Before removing the guides, measure the protrusion on the spring side of the head and record it for installation. Use the stepped drift to hammer out the old guide from the combustion chamber side of the head. When installing, determine whether or not the guide also seals a water jacket in the head, and if it does, use the recommended sealing agent. If there is no water jacket, grease the valve guide and its bore. Use the stepped drift, and hammer the new guide into the cylinder head from the spring side of the cylinder head. A stack of washers the same thickness as the measured protrusion may help the installation process.

VALVE SEATS

➤**Before any valve seat machining can be performed, the guides must be within factory recommended specifications.**

➤**If any machining or replacements were made to the valve guides, the seats must be machined.**

If the seats are in good condition, the valves can be lapped to the seats, and the cylinder head assembled. See the valves section for instructions on lapping.

If the valve seats are worn, cracked or damaged, they must be serviced by a machine shop. The valve seat must be perfectly centered to the valve guide, which requires very accurate machining.

CYLINDER HEAD SURFACE

If the cylinder head is warped, it must be machined flat. If the warpage is extremely severe, the head may need to be replaced. In some instances, it may be possible to straighten a warped head enough to allow machining. In either case, contact a professional machine shop for service.

CRACKS AND PHYSICAL DAMAGE

Certain cracks can be repaired in both cast iron and aluminum heads. For cast iron, a tapered threaded insert is installed along the length of the crack. Aluminum can also use the tapered inserts, however welding is the preferred method. Some physical damage can be repaired through brazing or welding. Contact a machine shop to get expert advice for your particular dilemma.

ASSEMBLY

The first step for any assembly job is to have a clean area in which to work. Next, thoroughly clean all of the parts and components that are to be assembled. Finally, place all of the components onto a suitable work space and, if necessary, arrange the parts to their respective positions.

1. Lightly lubricate the valve stems and insert all of the valves into the cylinder head. If possible, maintain their original locations.
2. If equipped, install any valve spring shims which were removed.
3. If equipped, install the new valve seals, keeping the following in mind:
  • If the valve seal presses over the guide, lightly lubricate the outer guide surfaces.
  • If the seal is an O-ring type, it is installed just after compressing the spring but before the valve locks.
4. Place the valve spring and retainer over the stem.
5. Position the spring compressor tool and compress the spring.
6. Assemble the valve locks to the stem.
7. Relieve the spring pressure slowly and insure that neither valve lock becomes dislodged by the retainer.
8. Remove the spring compressor tool.
9. Repeat Steps 2 through 8 until all of the springs have been installed.

Engine Block

GENERAL INFORMATION

A thorough overhaul or rebuild of an engine block would include replacing the pistons, rings, bearings, timing belt/chain assembly and oil pump. For OHV engines also include a new camshaft and lifters. The block would then have the cylinders bored and honed oversize (or if using removable cylinder sleeves, new sleeves installed) and the crankshaft would be cut undersize to provide new wearing surfaces and perfect clearances. However, your particular engine may not have everything worn out. What if only the piston rings have worn out and the clearances on everything else are still within factory specifications? Well, you could just replace the rings and put it back together, but this would be a very rare example. Chances are, if one component in your engine is worn, other components are sure to follow, and soon. At the very least, you should always replace the rings, bearings and oil pump. This is what is commonly called a "freshen up".

Cylinder Ridge Removal

Because the top piston ring does not travel to the very top of the cylinder, a ridge is built up between the end of the travel and the top of the cylinder bore.

Pushing the piston and connecting rod assembly past the ridge can be difficult, and damage to the piston ring lands could occur. If the ridge is not removed before installing a new piston or not removed at all, piston ring breakage and piston damage may occur.

➤**It is always recommended that you remove any cylinder ridges before removing the piston and connecting rod assemblies. If you know that new pistons are going to be installed and the engine block will be bored oversize, you may be able to forego this step. However, some ridges may actually prevent the assemblies from being removed, necessitating its removal.**

There are several different types of ridge reamers on the market, none of which are inexpensive. Unless a great deal of engine rebuilding is anticipated, borrow or rent a reamer.

1. Turn the crankshaft until the piston is at the bottom of its travel.
2. Cover the head of the piston with a rag.
3. Follow the tool manufacturers instructions and cut away the ridge, exercising extreme care to avoid cutting too deeply.
4. Remove the ridge reamer, the rag and as many of the cuttings as possible. Continue until all of the cylinder ridges have been removed.

DISASSEMBLY

♦ **See Figures 220 and 221**

The engine disassembly instructions following assume that you have the engine mounted on an engine stand. If not, it is easiest to disassemble the engine on a bench or the floor with it resting on the bell housing or transmission mounting surface. You must be able to access the connecting rod fasteners and turn the crankshaft during disassembly. Also, all engine covers (timing, front, side, oil pan, whatever) should have already been removed. Engines which are seized or locked up may not be able to be completely disassembled, and a core (salvage yard) engine should be purchased.

If not done during the cylinder head removal, remove the pushrods and lifters, keeping them in order for assembly. Remove the timing gears and/or timing chain assembly, then remove the oil pump drive assembly and withdraw the camshaft from the engine block. Remove the oil pick-up and pump assembly. If equipped, remove any balance or auxiliary shafts. If necessary, remove the cylinder ridge from the top of the bore. See the cylinder ridge removal procedure earlier in this section.

Rotate the engine over so that the crankshaft is exposed. Use a number punch or scribe and mark each connecting rod with its respective cylinder num-

TCCS3803

Fig. 220 Place rubber hose over the connecting rod studs to protect the crankshaft and cylinder bores from damage

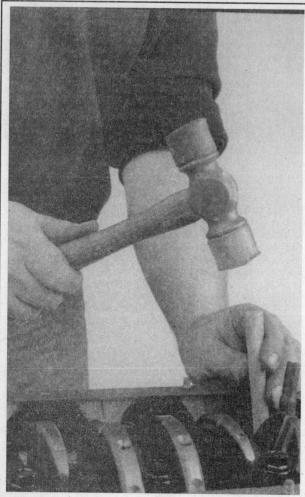

TCCS3804

Fig. 221 Carefully tap the piston out of the bore using a wooden dowel

ber. The cylinder closest to the front of the engine is always number 1. However, depending on the engine placement, the front of the engine could either be the flywheel or damper/pulley end. Generally the front of the engine faces the front of the vehicle. Use a number punch or scribe and also mark the main bearing caps from front to rear with the front most cap being number 1 (if there are five caps, mark them 1 through 5, front to rear).

❊❊ WARNING

Take special care when pushing the connecting rod up from the crankshaft because the sharp threads of the rod bolts/studs will score the crankshaft journal. Insure that special plastic caps are installed over them, or cut two pieces of rubber hose to do the same:

Again, rotate the engine, this time to position the number one cylinder bore (head surface) up. Turn the crankshaft until the number one piston is at the bottom of its travel, this should allow the maximum access to its connecting rod. Remove the number one connecting rods fasteners and cap and place two lengths of rubber hose over the rod bolts/studs to protect the crankshaft from damage. Using a sturdy wooden dowel and a hammer, push the connecting rod up about 1 in. (25mm) from the crankshaft and remove the upper bearing insert. Continue pushing or tapping the connecting rod up until the piston rings are out of the cylinder bore. Remove the piston and rod by hand, put the upper half of the bearing insert back into the rod, install the cap with its bearing insert installed, and hand-tighten the cap fasteners. If the parts are kept in order in this manner, they will not get lost and you will be able to tell which bearings came

form what cylinder if any problems are discovered and diagnosis is necessary. Remove all the other piston assemblies in the same manner. On V-style engines, remove all of the pistons from one bank, then reposition the engine with the other cylinder bank head surface up, and remove that banks piston assemblies.

The only remaining component in the engine block should now be the crankshaft. Loosen the main bearing caps evenly until the fasteners can be turned by hand, then remove them and the caps. Remove the crankshaft from the engine block. Thoroughly clean all of the components.

INSPECTION

Now that the engine block and all of its components are clean, it's time to inspect them for wear and/or damage. To accurately inspect them, you will need some specialized tools:
- Two or three separate micrometers to measure the pistons and crankshaft journals
- A dial indicator
- Telescoping gauges for the cylinder bores
- A rod alignment fixture to check for bent connecting rods

If you do not have access to the proper tools, you may want to bring the components to a shop that does.

Generally, you shouldn't expect cracks in the engine block or its components unless it was known to leak, consume or mix engine fluids, it was severely overheated, or there was evidence of bad bearings and/or crankshaft damage. A visual inspection should be performed on all of the components, but just because you don't see a crack does not mean it is not there. Some more reliable methods for inspecting for cracks include Magnaflux®, a magnetic process or Zyglo®, a dye penetrant. Magnaflux® is used only on ferrous metal (cast iron). Zyglo® uses a spray on fluorescent mixture along with a black light to reveal the cracks. It is strongly recommended to have your engine block checked professionally for cracks, especially if the engine was known to have overheated and/or leaked or consumed coolant. Contact a local shop for availability and pricing of these services.

Engine Block

ENGINE BLOCK BEARING ALIGNMENT

Remove the main bearing caps and, if still installed, the main bearing inserts. Inspect all of the main bearing saddles and caps for damage, burrs or high spots. If damage is found, and it is caused from a spun main bearing, the block will need to be align-bored or, if severe enough, replacement. Any burrs or high spots should be carefully removed with a metal file.

Place a straightedge on the bearing saddles, in the engine block, along the centerline of the crankshaft. If any clearance exists between the straightedge and the saddles, the block must be align-bored.

Align-boring consists of machining the main bearing saddles and caps by means of a flycutter that runs through the bearing saddles.

DECK FLATNESS

The top of the engine block where the cylinder head mounts is called the deck. Insure that the deck surface is clean of dirt, carbon deposits and old gasket material. Place a straightedge across the surface of the deck along its centerline and, using feeler gauges, check the clearance along several points. Repeat the checking procedure with the straightedge placed along both diagonals of the deck surface. If the reading exceeds 0.003 in. (0.076mm) within a 6.0 in. (15.2cm) span, or 0.006 in. (0.152mm) over the total length of the deck, it must be machined.

CYLINDER BORES

♦ **See Figure 222**

The cylinder bores house the pistons and are slightly larger than the pistons themselves. A common piston-to-bore clearance is 0.0015–0.0025 in. (0.0381mm–0.0635mm). Inspect and measure the cylinder bores. The bore should be checked for out-of-roundness, taper and size. The results of this inspection will determine whether the cylinder can be used in its existing size and condition, or a rebore to the next oversize is required (or in the case of removable sleeves, have replacements installed).

The amount of cylinder wall wear is always greater at the top of the cylinder than at the bottom. This wear is known as taper. Any cylinder that has a taper of

Fig. 222 Use a telescoping gauge to measure the cylinder bore diameter—take several readings within the same bore

0.0012 in. (0.305mm) or more, must be rebored. Measurements are taken at a number of positions in each cylinder: at the top, middle and bottom and at two points at each position; that is, at a point 90 degrees from the crankshaft centerline, as well as a point parallel to the crankshaft centerline. The measurements are made with either a special dial indicator or a telescopic gauge and micrometer. If the necessary precision tools to check the bore are not available, take the block to a machine shop and have them mike it. Also if you don't have the tools to check the cylinder bores, chances are you will not have the necessary devices to check the pistons, connecting rods and crankshaft. Take these components with you and save yourself an extra trip.

For our procedures, we will use a telescopic gauge and a micrometer. You will need one of each, with a measuring range which covers your cylinder bore size.

1. Position the telescopic gauge in the cylinder bore, loosen the gauges lock and allow it to expand.

➡**Your first two readings will be at the top of the cylinder bore, then proceed to the middle and finally the bottom, making a total of six measurements.**

2. Hold the gauge square in the bore, 90 degrees from the crankshaft centerline, and gently tighten the lock. Tilt the gauge back to remove it from the bore.

3. Measure the gauge with the micrometer and record the reading.

4. Again, hold the gauge square in the bore, this time parallel to the crankshaft centerline, and gently tighten the lock. Again, you will tilt the gauge back to remove it from the bore.

5. Measure the gauge with the micrometer and record this reading. The difference between these two readings is the out-of-round measurement of the cylinder.

6. Repeat steps 1 through 5, each time going to the next lower position, until you reach the bottom of the cylinder. Then go to the next cylinder, and continue until all of the cylinders have been measured.

The difference between these measurements will tell you all about the wear in your cylinders. The measurements which were taken 90 degrees from the crankshaft centerline will always reflect the most wear. That is because at this position is where the engine power presses the piston against the cylinder bore the hardest. This is known as thrust wear. Take your top, 90 degree measurement and compare it to your bottom, 90 degree measurement. The difference between them is the taper. When you measure your pistons, you will compare these readings to your piston sizes and determine piston-to-wall clearance.

Crankshaft

Inspect the crankshaft for visible signs of wear or damage. All of the journals should be perfectly round and smooth. Slight scores are normal for a used crankshaft, but you should hardly feel them with your fingernail. When measuring the crankshaft with a micrometer, you will take readings at the front and rear of each journal, then turn the micrometer 90 degrees and take two more read-

ings, front and rear. The difference between the front-to-rear readings is the journal taper and the first-to-90 degree reading is the out-of-round measurement. Generally, there should be no taper or out-of-roundness found, however, up to 0.0005 in. (0.0127mm) for either can be overlooked. Also, the readings should fall within the factory specifications for journal diameters.

If the crankshaft journals fall within specifications, it is recommended that it be polished before being returned to service. Polishing the crankshaft insures that any minor burrs or high spots are smoothed, thereby reducing the chance of scoring the new bearings.

Pistons and Connecting Rods

PISTONS

▶ **See Figure 223**

The piston should be visually inspected for any signs of cracking or burning (caused by hot spots or detonation), and scuffing or excessive wear on the skirts. The wrist pin attaches the piston to the connecting rod. The piston should move freely on the wrist pin, both sliding and pivoting. Grasp the connecting rod securely, or mount it in a vise, and try to rock the piston back and forth along the centerline of the wrist pin. There should not be any excessive play evident between the piston and the pin. If there are C-clips retaining the pin in the piston then you have wrist pin bushings in the rods. There should not be any excessive play between the wrist pin and the rod bushing. Normal clearance for the wrist pin is approx. 0.001–0.002 in. (0.025mm–0.051mm).

Use a micrometer and measure the diameter of the piston, perpendicular to the wrist pin, on the skirt. Compare the reading to its original cylinder measurement obtained earlier. The difference between the two readings is the piston-to-wall clearance. If the clearance is within specifications, the piston may be used as is. If the piston is out of specification, but the bore is not, you will need a new piston. If both are out of specification, you will need the cylinder rebored and oversize pistons installed. Generally if two or more pistons/bores are out of specification, it is best to rebore the entire block and purchase a complete set of oversize pistons.

Fig. 223 Measure the piston's outer diameter, perpendicular to the wrist pin, with a micrometer

CONNECTING ROD

You should have the connecting rod checked for straightness at a machine shop. If the connecting rod is bent, it will unevenly wear the bearing and piston, as well as place greater stress on these components. Any bent or twisted connecting rods must be replaced. If the rods are straight and the wrist pin clearance is within specifications, then only the bearing end of the rod need be checked. Place the connecting rod into a vice, with the bearing inserts in place, install the cap to the rod and torque the fasteners to specifications. Use a telescoping gauge and carefully measure the inside diameter of the bearings. Compare this reading to the rods original crankshaft journal diameter measurement. The difference is the oil clearance. If the oil clearance is not within specifications, install new bearings in the rod and take another measurement. If the

Fig. 224 Use a ball type cylinder hone to remove any glaze and provide a new surface for seating the piston rings

Fig. 225 Most pistons are marked to indicate positioning in the engine (usually a mark means the side facing the front)

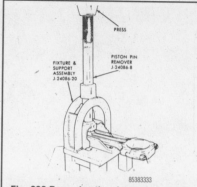
Fig. 226 Removing the piston pin from the assembly—press fit pistons assemblies

clearance is still out of specifications, and the crankshaft is not, the rod will need to be reconditioned by a machine shop.

➡You can also use Plastigage® to check the bearing clearances. The assembling section has complete instructions on its use.

Camshaft

Inspect the camshaft and lifters/followers as described earlier in this section.

Bearings

All of the engine bearings should be visually inspected for wear and/or damage. The bearing should look evenly worn all around with no deep scores or pits. If the bearing is severely worn, scored, pitted or heat blued, then the bearing, and the components that use it, should be brought to a machine shop for inspection. Full-circle bearings (used on most camshafts, auxiliary shafts, balance shafts, etc.) require specialized tools for removal and installation, and should be brought to a machine shop for service.

Oil Pump

➡The oil pump is responsible for providing constant lubrication to the whole engine and so it is recommended that a new oil pump be installed when rebuilding the engine.

Completely disassemble the oil pump and thoroughly clean all of the components. Inspect the oil pump gears and housing for wear and/or damage. Insure that the pressure relief valve operates properly and there is no binding or sticking due to varnish or debris. If all of the parts are in proper working condition, lubricate the gears and relief valve, and assemble the pump.

REFINISHING

◆ See Figure 224

Almost all engine block refinishing must be performed by a machine shop. If the cylinders are not to be rebored, then the cylinder glaze can be removed with a ball hone. When removing cylinder glaze with a ball hone, use a light or penetrating type oil to lubricate the hone. Do not allow the hone to run dry as this may cause excessive scoring of the cylinder bores and wear on the hone. If new pistons are required, they will need to be installed to the connecting rods. This should be performed by a machine shop as the pistons must be installed in the correct relationship to the rod or engine damage can occur.

Pistons and Connecting Rods

◆ See Figures 225 and 226

Only pistons with the wrist pin retained by C-clips are serviceable by the home-mechanic. Press fit pistons require special presses and/or heaters to remove/install the connecting rod and should only be performed by a machine shop.

All pistons will have a mark indicating the direction to the front of the engine and the must be installed into the engine in that manner. Usually it is a notch or arrow on the top of the piston, or it may be the letter F cast or stamped into the piston.

ASSEMBLY

Before you begin assembling the engine, first give yourself a clean, dirt free work area. Next, clean every engine component again. The key to a good assembly is cleanliness.

Mount the engine block into the engine stand and wash it one last time using water and detergent (dishwashing detergent works well). While washing it, scrub the cylinder bores with a soft bristle brush and thoroughly clean all of the oil passages. Completely dry the engine and spray the entire assembly down with an anti-rust solution such as WD-40® or similar product. Take a clean lint-free rag and wipe up any excess anti-rust solution from the bores, bearing saddles, etc. Repeat the final cleaning process on the crankshaft. Replace any freeze or oil galley plugs which were removed during disassembly.

Crankshaft

◆ See Figures 227, 228, 229 and 230

1. Remove the main bearing inserts from the block and bearing caps.
2. If the crankshaft main bearing journals have been refinished to a definite undersize, install the correct undersize bearing. Be sure that the bearing inserts and bearing bores are clean. Foreign material under inserts will distort bearing and cause failure.
3. Place the upper main bearing inserts in bores with tang in slot.

➡The oil holes in the bearing inserts must be aligned with the oil holes in the cylinder block.

4. Install the lower main bearing inserts in bearing caps.
5. Clean the mating surfaces of block and rear main bearing cap.
6. Carefully lower the crankshaft into place. Be careful not to damage bearing surfaces.
7. Check the clearance of each main bearing by using the following procedure:

   a. Place a piece of Plastigage® or its equivalent, on bearing surface across full width of bearing cap and about ¼ in. off center.

   b. Install cap and tighten bolts to specifications. Do not turn crankshaft while Plastigage® is in place.

   c. Remove the cap. Using the supplied Plastigage® scale, check width of Plastigage® at widest point to get maximum clearance. Difference between readings is taper of journal.

   d. If clearance exceeds specified limits, try a 0.001 in. or 0.002 in. undersize bearing in combination with the standard bearing. Bearing clearance must be within specified limits. If standard and 0.002 in. undersize bearing does not bring clearance within desired limits, refinish crankshaft journal, then install undersize bearings.

8. After the bearings have been fitted, apply a light coat of engine oil to the journals and bearings. Install the rear main bearing cap. Install all bearing caps except the thrust bearing cap. Be sure that main bearing caps are installed in original locations. Tighten the bearing cap bolts to specifications.
9. Install the thrust bearing cap with bolts finger-tight.
10. Pry the crankshaft forward against the thrust surface of upper half of bearing.
11. Hold the crankshaft forward and pry the thrust bearing cap to the rear. This aligns the thrust surfaces of both halves of the bearing.

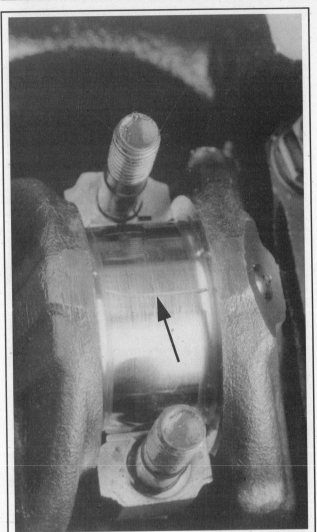

Fig. 227 Apply a strip of gauging material to the bearing journal, then install and torque the cap

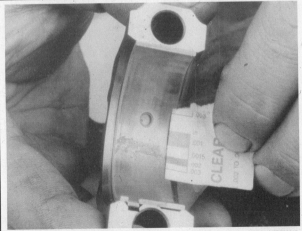

Fig. 228 After the cap is removed again, use the scale supplied with the gauging material to check the clearance

Fig. 229 A dial gauge may be used to check crankshaft end-play

Fig. 230 Carefully pry the crankshaft back and forth while reading the dial gauge for end-play

12. Retain the forward pressure on the crankshaft. Tighten the cap bolts to specifications.

13. Measure the crankshaft end-play as follows:

   a. Mount a dial gauge to the engine block and position the tip of the gauge to read from the crankshaft end.

   b. Carefully pry the crankshaft toward the rear of the engine and hold it there while you zero the gauge.

   c. Carefully pry the crankshaft toward the front of the engine and read the gauge.

   d. Confirm that the reading is within specifications. If not, install a new thrust bearing and repeat the procedure. If the reading is still out of specifications with a new bearing, have a machine shop inspect the thrust surfaces of the crankshaft, and if possible, repair it.

14. Rotate the crankshaft so as to position the first rod journal to the bottom of its stroke.

15. Install the rear main seal.

Pistons and Connecting Rods

▶ See Figures 231 thru 236

1. Before installing the piston/connecting rod assembly, oil the pistons, piston rings and the cylinder walls with light engine oil. Install connecting rod

Fig. 231 Checking the piston ring-to-ring groove side clearance using the ring and a feeler gauge

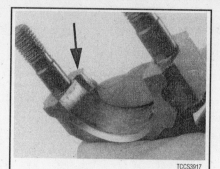

Fig. 232 The notch on the side of the bearing cap matches the tang on the bearing insert

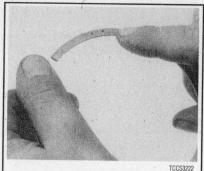

Fig. 233 Most rings are marked to show which side of the ring should face up when installed to the piston

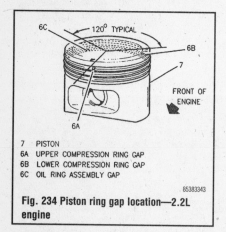

7 PISTON
6A UPPER COMPRESSION RING GAP
6B LOWER COMPRESSION RING GAP
6C OIL RING ASSEMBLY GAP

Fig. 234 Piston ring gap location—2.2L engine

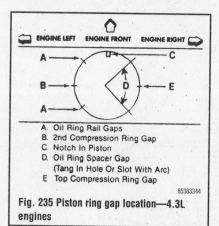

A. Oil Ring Rail Gaps
B. 2nd Compression Ring Gap
C. Notch In Piston
D. Oil Ring Spacer Gap
   (Tang In Hole Or Slot With Arc)
E. Top Compression Ring Gap

Fig. 235 Piston ring gap location—4.3L engines

Fig. 236 Install the piston and rod assembly into the block using a ring compressor and the handle of a hammer

bolt protectors or rubber hose onto the connecting rod bolts/studs. Also perform the following:

   a. Select the proper ring set for the size cylinder bore.

   b. Position the ring in the bore in which it is going to be used.

   c. Push the ring down into the bore area where normal ring wear is not encountered.

   d. Use the head of the piston to position the ring in the bore so that the ring is square with the cylinder wall. Use caution to avoid damage to the ring or cylinder bore.

   e. Measure the gap between the ends of the ring with a feeler gauge. Ring gap in a worn cylinder is normally greater than specification. If the ring gap is greater than the specified limits, try an oversize ring set.

   f. Check the ring side clearance of the compression rings with a feeler gauge inserted between the ring and its lower land according to specification. The gauge should slide freely around the entire ring circumference without binding. Any wear that occurs will form a step at the inner portion of the lower land. If the lower lands have high steps, the piston should be replaced.

2. Unless new pistons are installed, be sure to install the pistons in the cylinders from which they were removed. The numbers on the connecting rod and bearing cap must be on the same side when installed in the cylinder bore. If a connecting rod is ever transposed from one engine or cylinder to another, new bearings should be fitted and the connecting rod should be numbered to correspond with the new cylinder number. The notch on the piston head goes toward the front of the engine.

3. Install all of the rod bearing inserts into the rods and caps.

4. Install the rings to the pistons. Install the oil control ring first, then the second compression ring and finally the top compression ring. Use a piston ring expander tool to aid in installation and to help reduce the chance of breakage.

5. Make sure the ring gaps are properly spaced around the circumference of the piston. Fit a piston ring compressor around the piston and slide the piston and connecting rod assembly down into the cylinder bore, pushing it in with the wooden hammer handle. Push the piston down until it is only slightly below the top of the cylinder bore. Guide the connecting rod onto the crankshaft bearing journal carefully, to avoid damaging the crankshaft.

6. Check the bearing clearance of all the rod bearings, fitting them to the crankshaft bearing journals. Follow the procedure in the crankshaft installation above.

7. After the bearings have been fitted, apply a light coating of assembly oil to the journals and bearings.

8. Turn the crankshaft until the appropriate bearing journal is at the bottom of its stroke, then push the piston assembly all the way down until the connecting rod bearing seats on the crankshaft journal. Be careful not to allow the bearing cap screws to strike the crankshaft bearing journals and damage them.

9. After the piston and connecting rod assemblies have been installed, check the connecting rod side clearance on each crankshaft journal.

10. Prime and install the oil pump and the oil pump intake tube.

11. Install the balance shaft.

12. Install the camshaft.

13. Install the lifters/followers into their bores.

14. Install the timing gears/chain assembly.

15. Install the cylinder head(s) using new gaskets.

16. Assemble the rest of the valve train (pushrods and rocker arms and/or shafts).

Install the timing cover(s) and oil pan. Refer to your notes and drawings made prior to disassembly and install all of the components that were removed. Install the engine into the vehicle.

Engine Start-up and Break-in

STARTING THE ENGINE

Now that the engine is installed and every wire and hose is properly connected, go back and double check that all coolant and vacuum hoses are connected. Check that your oil drain plug is installed and properly tightened. If not already done, install a new oil filter onto the engine. Fill the crankcase with the proper amount and grade of engine oil. Fill the cooling system with a 50/50 mixture of coolant/water.

1. Connect the vehicle battery.

2. Start the engine. Keep your eye on your oil pressure indicator; if it does not indicate oil pressure within 10 seconds of starting, turn the vehicle off.

✳✳ WARNING

Damage to the engine can result if it is allowed to run with no oil pressure. Check the engine oil level to make sure that it is full. Check for any leaks and if found, repair the leaks before continuing. If there is still no indication of oil pressure, you may need to prime the system.

3. Confirm that there are no fluid leaks (oil or other).

4. Allow the engine to reach normal operating temperature (the upper radiator hose will be hot to the touch).

5. At this point you can perform any necessary checks or adjustments, such as checking the ignition timing.

6. Install any remaining components or body panels which were removed.

BREAKING IT IN

Make the first miles on the new engine, easy ones. Vary the speed but do not accelerate hard. Most importantly, do not lug the engine, and avoid sustained high speeds until at least 100 miles. Check the engine oil and coolant levels frequently. Expect the engine to use a little oil until the rings seat. Change the oil and filter at 500 miles, 1500 miles, then every 3000 miles past that.

KEEP IT MAINTAINED

Now that you have just gone through all of that hard work, keep yourself from doing it all over again by thoroughly maintaining it. Not that you may not have maintained it before, heck you could have had one to two hundred thousand miles on it before doing this. However, you may have bought the vehicle used, and the previous owner did not keep up on maintenance. Which is why you just went through all of that hard work. See?

TORQUE SPECIFICATIONS

Components	Ft. Lbs.	Nm
Rocker Arm (Valve) Cover		
2.2L engines		
1994-97 models		
Rocker arm cover retainers	89 inch lbs.	10
Throttle cable bracket		
Bolts	10	25
Nut	22	30
1998-99 models		
Rocker arm cover	89 inch lbs.	10
Wiring harness bracket		
Bracket-to-valve bolts	89 inch lbs.	10
Bolt at the rear of the cylinder head	18	25
Air cleaner resonator bracket nuts	97 inch lbs.	11
Heater hose bracket bolt	10	14
4.3L engines		
1994-95 models		
Rocker arm cover retainers	89 inch lbs.	10
1996-99 models		
Rocker arm cover retainers	106 inch lbs.	12
Rocker Arms and Pushrods		
2.2L engines		
Rocker arm retaining nuts		
1994-97 models	22	30
1998-99 models	19	25
4.3L engines		
Engines equipped with screw-in type rocker arm studs		
1994-96 models	20	27
1997-99 models	18	25
Thermostat		
Thermostat outlet retainers		
2.2L engines		
1994 models	18	25
1995-99 models	89 inch lbs.	10
4.3L engines		
1994-96 models	21	28
1997-99 models	14	19
Intake Manifold		
2.2L engines		
1994-97 models		
Lower intake manifold retainers	24 [1]	33 [1]
Upper intake manifold retainers	22	20
Throttle cable bracket bolts	18	25
1998-99 models		
Lower intake manifold retainers	17 [1]	24 [1]
Engines wiring harness bracket		
Bracket-to-valve cover bolts	88 inch lbs.	10
Bracket-to-cylinder head bolt	18	25

91113C17

TORQUE SPECIFICATIONS

Components	Ft. Lbs.	Nm
Intake Manifold (cont.)		
2.2L engines (cont.)		
1994-97 models (cont.)		
Alternator rear brace nuts and bolts	18	25
EGR adapter retainers	97 inch lbs.	11
EGR pipe-to-EGR adapter bolt	18	25
EGR pipe-to-intake manifold bolts	89 inch lbs.	10
4.3L engines		
1994-95 models		
VIN Z		
Intake manifold retainers	35 [1]	48 [1]
VIN W		
Upper intake manifold	124 inch lbs. [1]	14 [1]
Lower intake manifold	35 [1]	48 [1]
1996-99 models		
Upper intake manifold retainers		
First pass	44 inch lbs.	5
Final pass	88 inch lbs.	10
Lower intake manifold		
Intake manifold retainers		
First pass	26 inch lbs. [1]	3 [1]
Second pass	106 inch lbs. [1]	12 [1]
Final pass	11 [1]	15 [1]
Exhaust Manifold		
2.2L engines		
Manifold nuts	115 inch lbs.	13
4.3L engines		
1994-95 models		
Exhaust manifold bolts		
Center exhaust tube	26	36
Front and rear exhaust tubes	20	28
1996 models		
Exhaust manifold bolts	22	30
1997-99 models		
Exhaust manifold bolts		
Center bolts	11	15
Front and rear bolts	22	30
Secondary air injection pipe nuts (1999 and later models)	18	25
Engines Cooling Fan/Clutch Fan		
Fan-to-clutch fasteners	24	33
Fan assembly-to-water pump pulley fasteners		
1994-97 models	17	24
1998-99 models	24	33

91113C18

TORQUE SPECIFICATIONS

Components	Ft. Lbs.	Nm
Water Pump		
Water pump retainers		
2.2L engines	18	25
4.3L engines	30	41
Cylinder Head		
Cylinder head bolts		
2.2L engines		
4.3L engines	②	②
1994-95 models	③	③
1996-99 models	④	④
Connecting Rods		
2.2L engines		
Cap nuts	38	52
4.3L engines		
Cap nuts	⑥	⑥
Oil Pan		
2.2L engines		
Oil pan bolts	89 inch lbs.	100
4.3L engines		
2 wheel drive models		
1994-95 models		
Bolts	100 inch lbs.	11
Nuts at corners	17	23
1996-97 models		
Bolts and studs	18 ①	25 ①
4 wheel drive models		
1994-97 models		
Oil pan		
Bolts	100 inch lbs.	11
Nuts at the corners		
1994-95 models	17	23
1996-99 models	18 ①	25 ①
Oil Pump		
Oil pump/pickup tube retainer(s)		
2.2L engines	32	44
4.3L engines	65	90
Crankshaft Damper/Pulley		
Damper bolt		
2.2L engines	77	105
4.3L engines	74	100
Timing Chain Cover and Seal		
2.2L engines		
Timing cover bolts	97 inch lbs.	11

91113C19

TORQUE SPECIFICATIONS

Components	Ft. Lbs.	Nm
Timing Chain Cover and Seal (cont.)		
4.3L engines		
Timing cover bolts		
1994-95 models	124 inch lbs.	14
1996-99 models	106 inch lbs.	12
Timing Chain and Gears		
2.2L engines		
Tensioner bolts	18	25
Camshaft sprocket bolt	96	130
4.3L engines		
Camshaft sprocket-to-camshaft retainers		
1994-96 models	21	28
1997-99 models	18	25
Camshaft		
2.2L engines		
Thrust plate bolts	106 inch lbs.	12
Oil pump drive bolt	18	25
4.3L engines		
Thrust plate bolts	106 inch lbs.	12
Valve Lifter		
2.2L engines		
Anti-rotation bracket bolts	97 inch lbs.	11
4.3L engines		
Lifters restrictors and/or retainer bolts	12	16
Balance Shaft		
Balance shaft bearing retainer bolts	124 inch lbs.	14
Balance shaft driven gear bolt	⑤	⑤
Drive gear bolt	12	16
Flywheel		
Flywheel bolts		
2.2L engines	55	75
4.3L engines	75	100

① Tighten the retainers in the sequence illustrated

② First pass

Long bolts 46 ft. lbs. (63 Nm)

Short bolts 43 ft. lbs. (58 Nm)

Final pass

Tighten all bolts an additional 90 degree turn

③ First pass 25 ft. lbs. (34 Nm).

Second pass 45 ft. lbs. (61 Nm).

Final pass 65 ft. lbs. (90 Nm).

④ First pass

All bolts in sequence to 22 ft. lbs. (30 Nm)

Second pass

Short length bolts: (11, 7, 3, 2, 6, 10) 55 degrees

Medium length bolts: (12, 13) 65 degrees

Long length bolts: (1, 4, 8, 5, 9) 75 degrees

⑤ Tighten bolt to 15 ft. lbs. (20 Nm) plus an additional 35°

⑥ Tighten bolt to 20 ft. lbs. (27 Nm) plus an additional 70°

91113C20

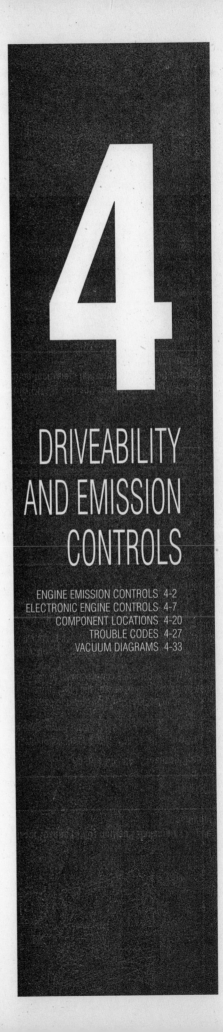

4

DRIVEABILITY AND EMISSION CONTROLS

ENGINE EMISSION CONTROLS

Positive Crankcase Ventilation

OPERATION

▶ See Figure 1

The Positive Crankcase Ventilation (PCV) system is used to evacuate the crankcase vapors. Outside vehicle air is routed through the air cleaner to the crankcase where it mixes with the blow-by gases and is passed through the PCV valve. It is then routed into the intake manifold. The PCV valve meters the air flow rate which varies under engine operation depending on manifold vacuum. In order to maintain idle quality, the PCV valve limits the air flow when intake manifold vacuum is high. If abnormal operating conditions occur, the system will allow excessive blow-by gases to back flow through the crankcase vent tube into the air cleaner. These blow-by gases will then be burned by normal combustion.

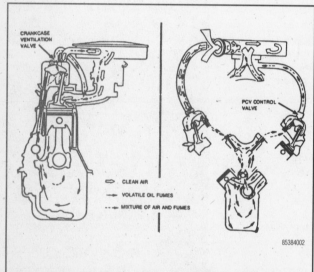

Fig. 1 Positive Crankcase Ventilation (PCV) system schematic

A plugged PCV valve or hose may cause rough idle, stalling or slow idle speed, oil leaks, oil in the air cleaner or sludge in the engine. A leaking PCV valve or hose could cause rough idle, stalling or high idle speed.

Other than checking and replacing the PCV valve and associated hoses, there is no service required. Engine operating conditions that would direct suspicion to the PCV system are rough idle, oil present in the air cleaner, oil leaks and excessive oil sludging or dilution. If any of the above conditions exist, remove the PCV valve and shake it. A clicking sound indicates that the valve is free. If no clicking sound is heard, replace the valve. Inspect the PCV breather in the air cleaner. Replace the breather if it is so dirty that it will not allow gases to pass through. Check all the PCV hoses for condition and tight connections. Replace any hoses that have deteriorated.

TESTING

▶ See Figure 2

1. Remove the PCV valve from the rocker arm cover, but leave the vacuum hose attached.
2. Operate the engine at idle speed.
3. Place your thumb over the end of the valve to check for vacuum. If no vacuum exists, check the valve, the hoses or the manifold port for a plugged condition.
4. Remove the valve from the hose(s), then shake it and listen for a rattling of the check needle (inside the valve); the rattle means the valve is working. If no rattle is heard the valve is stuck, and should be replaced.

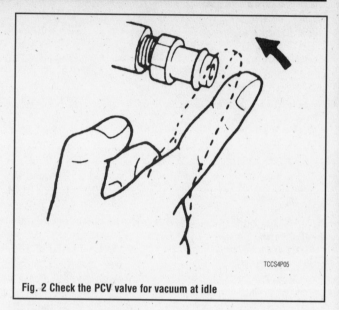

TCCS4P05

Fig. 2 Check the PCV valve for vacuum at idle

REMOVAL & INSTALLATION

Refer to Section 1 of this manual for PCV valve removal and installation.

PCV Breather

Most breathers are located inside the air cleaner assembly, though they may be mounted directly to a valve cover. Although a breather may in some cases be removed and cleaned, it is an inexpensive part and it is wise to replace it if dirty. Breathers which are mounted directly to the valve cover may be simply grasped and pulled from the cover grommet. For breathers which are mounted inside the air cleaner follow the procedure listed below.

1. Loosen the wing nut or release the retainers, then remove the top of the air cleaner assembly.
2. Slide the rubber coupling that joins the tube coming from the valve cover to the breather off the breather nipple.
3. Slide the spring clamp off the breather nipple (if equipped) which is protruding from the air cleaner housing, then withdraw the breather from inside the air cleaner assembly.
4. Inspect the rubber grommet in the valve cover and the rubber coupling for brittleness or cracking. Replace parts as necessary.
   To install:
5. Insert the new PCV breather through the hole in the air cleaner with the open portion of the breather upward. Make sure that the breather is fully seated in the air cleaner housing.
6. If equipped, install a new spring clamp onto the nipple. Make sure the clamp goes under the ridge on the breather nipple all the way around.
7. Reconnect the rubber coupling.
8. Install the air cleaner cover and secure.

Evaporative Emission Control System (EECS)

OPERATION

The Evaporative Emission Control System (EECS) is designed to prevent fuel tank vapors from being emitted into the atmosphere. Gasoline vapors are absorbed and stored by a fuel vapor charcoal canister. The charcoal canister absorbs the gasoline vapors and stores them until certain engine conditions are met, then the vapors are purged and burned in the combustion process.

The charcoal canister purge cycle is normally controlled either by a thermostatic vacuum switch or by a timed vacuum source, though some models may use electronic regulation in the form of a purge control solenoid. The thermostatic vacuum switch is installed in a coolant passage and prevents canister purge when engine operating temperature is below approximately 115°F (46°C). A timed vacuum source uses a manifold vacuum-controlled diaphragm to control canister purge. When the engine is running, full manifold vacuum is applied to the top tube of the purge valve which lifts the valve diaphragm and opens the valve. If equipped with a purge solenoid, under proper engine operating conditions the ECM will signal the solenoid which will then open the vacuum line allowing manifold vacuum to control the purge diaphragm. Most solenoids used on these vehicles are normally closed and will open when the ECM provides a ground signal energizing the solenoid.

➡️Remember that the fuel tank filler cap is an integral part of the system in that it is designed to seal in fuel vapors. If it is lost or damaged, make sure the replacement is of the correct size and fit so a proper seal can be obtained.

A vent, located in the fuel tank, allows fuel vapors to flow to the charcoal canister. A tank pressure control valve, used on high altitude applications, prevents canister purge when the engine is not running. The fuel tank cap does not normally vent to the atmosphere but is designed to provide both vacuum and pressure relief.

Poor engine idle, stalling and poor driveability can be caused by a damaged canister or split, damaged or improperly connected hoses.

Evidence of fuel loss or fuel vapor odor can be caused by a liquid fuel leak; a cracked or damaged vapor canister; disconnected, misrouted, kinked or damaged vapor pipe or canister hoses; a damaged air cleaner or improperly seated air cleaner gasket.

TESTING

Charcoal Canister and Purge Valve

▶ See Figures 3 and 4

The fuel vapor canister is used to absorb and store fuel vapors from the fuel tank. Vacuum sources are generally ported, either through an internal or remote mounted purge control valve. Engines employing the timed vacuum source purge system usually use a canister purge valve which is integral to the vapor canister. The valve consists of a housing and tube molded into the canister cover, valve assembly, diaphragm and valve spring. The diaphragm cover has a built-in control vacuum signal tube.

1. Remove the vacuum hose from the lower tube of the purge valve and install a short length of tube, then try to blow through it (little or no air should

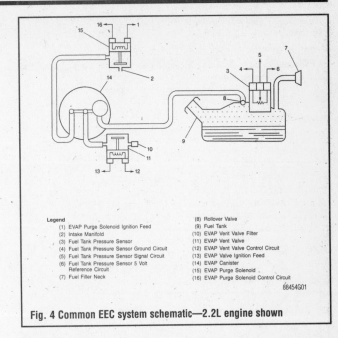

Legend

(1) EVAP Purge Solenoid Ignition Feed
(2) Intake Manifold
(3) Fuel Tank Pressure Sensor
(4) Fuel Tank Pressure Sensor Ground Circuit
(5) Fuel Tank Pressure Sensor Signal Circuit
(6) Fuel Tank Pressure Sensor 5 Volt
    Reference Circuit
(7) Fuel Filler Neck

(8) Rollover Valve
(9) Fuel Tank
(10) EVAP Vent Valve Filter
(11) EVAP Vent Valve
(12) EVAP Vent Valve Control Circuit
(13) EVAP Valve Ignition Feed
(14) EVAP Canister
(15) EVAP Purge Solenoid
(16) EVAP Purge Solenoid Control Circuit

88454G01

Fig. 4 Common EEC system schematic—2.2L engine shown

pass, though a small amount may pass if the vehicles is equipped with a constant purge hole).

2. Using a vacuum source such as a hand vacuum pump, apply 15 in. Hg (51 kPa) to the upper tube of the purge valve. The diaphragm should hold the vacuum for at least 20 seconds, if not replace the purge valve (remote mounted) or canister (internal mounted valve), as applicable.

3. While holding the vacuum on the upper tube, blow through the lower tube (an increased volume of air should now pass); if not, replace the valve or canister, as necessary.

➡️When testing valves by blowing air through them, be careful that you are blowing in the proper direction of flow. Many valves are designed to only allow air to flow in one direction and a proper working valve may seem defective if it is tested with air flow only in the wrong direction.

Thermostatic Vacuum Switch (TVS)

▶ See Figure 5

➡️The number stamped on the base of the switch (valve) is the calibration temperature.

1. With engine temperature below 100°F (38°C), apply vacuum to the manifold side of the switch. The switch should hold vacuum.

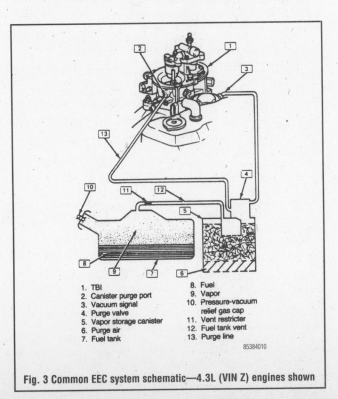

1. TBI
2. Canister purge port
3. Vacuum signal
4. Purge valve
5. Vapor storage canister
6. Purge air
7. Fuel tank
8. Fuel
9. Vapor
10. Pressure-vacuum relief gas cap
11. Vent restricter
12. Fuel tank vent
13. Purge line

85384010

Fig. 3 Common EEC system schematic—4.3L (VIN Z) engines shown

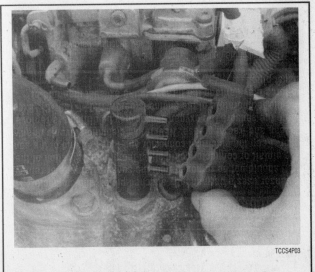

TCCS4P03

Fig. 5 Disconnecting the hoses from the thermal vacuum valve

2. As the engine temperature increases above 122°F (50°C), vacuum should drop off.

3. Replace the switch if it fails either test.

➡ **A leakage of up to 2 in. Hg (13 kPa)/2 min. is allowable and does not mean that the valve is defective.**

Canister Purge Control Solenoid

♦ **See Figure 6**

As stated earlier, most solenoids found on these vehicles use a normally closed solenoid valve. This means that when the solenoid is de-energized it is closed or, when it is energized it will open allowing vacuum to pass. On most vehicles equipped with this solenoid, fused ignition voltage is applied to the solenoid through one of it's terminals. When the ECM recognizes proper engine operating conditions, it will provide a ground through the other solenoid terminal in order to energize the solenoid.

To test a normally closed solenoid valve, try blowing air through the valve fittings when the engine is **OFF**, air should not flow. When the engine is running the solenoid should de-energize during engine warm-up and energize once it has reached normal operating temperature and proper running conditions.

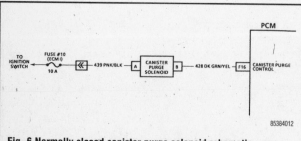

Fig. 6 Normally closed canister purge solenoid schematic—normally found on California emissions vehicles

REMOVAL & INSTALLATION

Charcoal Canister

1. Tag and disconnect them from the canister assembly.

➡ **If access to the vapor hoses is difficult with the canister installed, wait until the canister is released from the bracket or mounting, then reposition the canister for better access.**

2. Loosen the screw(s) fastening the canister retaining bracket to the vehicle.

3. Carefully remove the canister or canister and bracket assembly, as applicable.

To install:

4. Position the canister in the vehicle.

5. If the hoses cannot be accessed once the canister is secured, connect them now as tagged during removal.

6. Install the canister to the retaining bracket and secure using the retaining screw(s).

7. If not done earlier, connect the lines to the canister assembly as tagged during removal.

Thermostatic Vacuum Switch (TVS)

♦ **See Figure 7**

The TVS is located near the engine coolant outlet housing.

1. Drain the engine cooling system to a level below the TVS.

2. Disconnect the vacuum hose manifold from the TVS. If the hoses are not connected to a single manifold, be sure to tag them before removal to assure proper installation.

3. Using a wrench, unthread and remove the TVS from the engine.

To install:

4. Apply a soft setting sealant to the TVS threads.

➡ **DO NOT apply sealant to the sensor end of the TVS.**

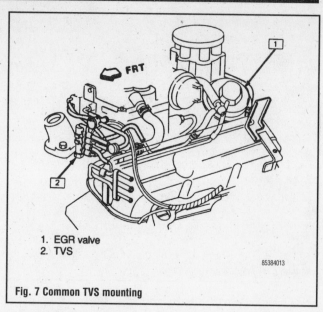

1. EGR valve
2. TVS

Fig. 7 Common TVS mounting

5. Install and tighten the TVS.

6. Reconnect the vacuum hoses.

7. Properly refill the engine cooling system, then run the engine and check for leaks.

Exhaust Gas Recirculation (EGR)

OPERATION

The EGR system's purpose is to control oxides of nitrogen which are formed during the peak combustion temperatures. The end products of combustion are relatively inert gases derived from the exhaust gases which are directed into the EGR valve to help lower peak combustion temperatures.

The port EGR valve is controlled by a flexible diaphragm which is spring loaded to hold the valve closed. Vacuum applied to the top side of the diaphragm overcomes the spring pressure and opens the valve which allows exhaust gas to be pulled into the intake manifold and enter the engine cylinders.

The negative backpressure EGR valve has bleed valve spring below the diaphragm, and the valve is normally closed. The valve varies the amount of exhaust flow into the manifold depending on manifold vacuum and variations in exhaust backpressure.

The diaphragm on this valve has an internal air bleed hole which is held closed by a small spring when there is no exhaust backpressure. Engine vacuum opens the EGR valve against the pressure of a large. When manifold vacuum combines with negative exhaust backpressure, the vacuum bleed hole opens and the EGR valve closes. This valve will open if vacuum is applied with the engine not running.

The linear EGR valve is operated exclusively by the control module command. The control module monitors various engine parameters:

- Throttle Position Sensor (TPS)
- Manifold Absolute Pressure (MAP)
- Engine Coolant Temperature (ECT) sensor
- Pintle position sensor

Output messages are then sent to the EGR system indicating the proper amount of exhaust gas recirculation necessary to lower combustion temperatures.

Refer to the accompanying illustrations to identify the EGR valve used in your vehicle.

TESTING

♦ **See Figures 8 thru 14**

Refer to the appropriate chart for diagnosis the EGR system. On linear EGR systems, an OBD-II compliant scan tool will be needed.

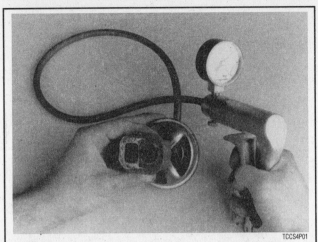

Fig. 8 Some EGR valves may be tested using a vacuum pump by watching for diaphragm movement

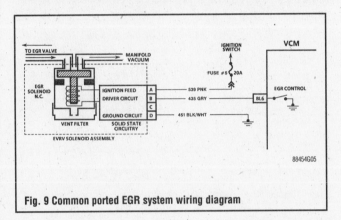

Fig. 9 Common ported EGR system wiring diagram

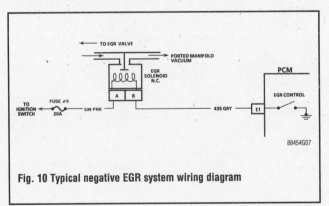

Fig. 10 Typical negative EGR system wiring diagram

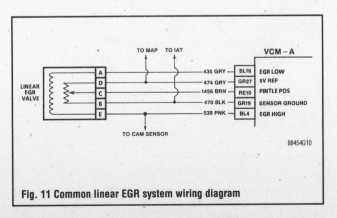

Fig. 11 Common linear EGR system wiring diagram

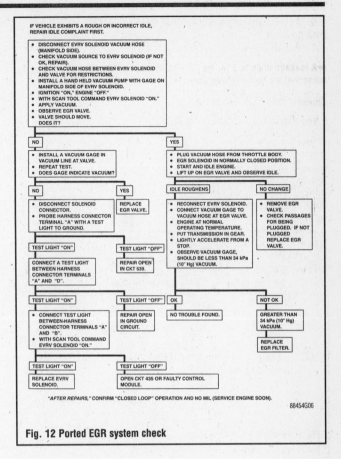

Fig. 12 Ported EGR system check

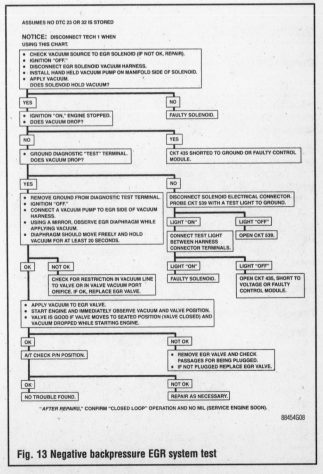

Fig. 13 Negative backpressure EGR system test

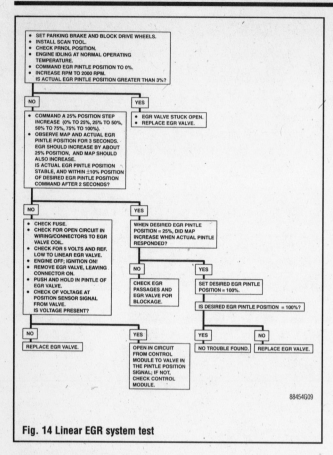

Fig. 14 Linear EGR system test

REMOVAL & INSTALLATION

Except Linear EGR Valve

▶ See Figures 15 and 16

1. Disconnect the negative battery cable.
2. Remove the air cleaner assembly from the engine.
3. If equipped, unplug the valve electrical connection.
4. Remove the EGR valve vacuum tube from the valve.

Fig. 15 Unfasten the EGR valve retaining bolts. . .

Fig. 16 . . . then remove the EGR valve from the vehicle

5. Remove the EGR bolts and/or nuts and remove the EGR valve and gasket.

To install:

6. Install a new gasket to the EGR valve and install the EGR valve to the manifold.
7. Install the nuts and/or bolts. Tighten the bolts to 17 ft. lbs. (24 Nm) and the nuts to 15 ft. lbs. (20 Nm).
8. Connect the vacuum tube to the EGR valve.
9. If equipped, attach the valve electrical connection.
10. Install the air cleaner and connect the negative battery cable.

Linear EGR Valve

1. Disconnect the negative battery cable.

➡**Note the position of the EGR valve prior to removal. Do not rotate the valve 180°.**

2. Unplug the valve electrical connection..
3. Unfasten the valve retainers, then remove the valve and the gasket.

To install:

4. Clean all gasket residue from the gasket mating surfaces.
5. Install a new gasket and the valve.
6. Install the valve retainers.
7. On 1994–97 2.2L engines and 1994–95 4.3L engines, tighten the valve retainers to 17 ft. lbs. (24 Nm). On 1998–99 2.2L models, tighten the retainers to 19 ft. lbs. (26 Nm).
8. On 1996–99 4.3L models, tighten the retainers on the first pass to 89 inch lbs. (10 Nm) and on the final pass to 18 ft. lbs. (25 Nm).
9. Attach the valve electrical connections and connect the negative battery cable.

EGR Solenoid

1. Disconnect the negative battery cable.
2. Remove the air cleaner, as required.
3. Unplug the electrical connector at the solenoid.
4. Disconnect the vacuum hoses.
5. Remove the retaining bolts and the solenoid.
6. Remove the filter, as required.

To install:

7. If removed, install the filter.
8. Install the solenoid and retaining bolts.
9. Connect the vacuum hoses.
10. Engage the electrical connector.
11. If removed, install the air cleaner.
12. Connect the negative battery cable.

ELECTRONIC ENGINE CONTROLS

Vehicle Control Module (VCM)

OPERATION

➡When the term Vehicle Control Module (VCM) is used in this manual it will refer to the engine control computer regardless that it may be a Electronic Control Module (ECM), Powertrain Control Module (PCM) or Vehicle Control Module (VCM).

The Vehicle Control Module (VCM) is required to maintain the exhaust emissions at acceptable levels. The module is a small, solid state computer which receives signals from many sources and sensors; it uses these data to make judgments about operating conditions and then control output signals to the fuel and emission systems to match the current requirements.

Engines coupled to electronically controlled transmissions employ a Powertrain Control Module (PCM) or Vehicle Control Module (VCM) to oversee both engine and transmission operation. The integrated functions of engine and transmission control allow accurate gear selection and improved fuel economy.

In the event of an VCM failure, the system will default to a pre-programmed set of values. These are compromise values which allow the engine to operate, although at a reduced efficiency. This is variously known as the default, limp-in or back-up mode. Driveability is almost always affected when the VCM enters this mode.

The location of the VCM and application varies from model-to-model. The VCM is usually located in the engine compartment, behind a kick panel on the passenger side, or under the dash panel below the glove box.

The models equipped with a PCM are as follows:
- 1994–99 2.2L models
- 1994–95 4.3L VIN Z pick-up and utility with A/T and M/T
- 1994–95 4.3L VIN W pick-up and utility with A/T only

The models equipped with a ECM are as follows:
- 1994 4.3L VIN W pick-up M/T only

The models equipped with a VCM-A are as follows:
- 1995 4.3L VIN W pick-up and utility with A/T and M/T

The models equipped with a VCM are as follows:
- 1994–1995 4.3L VIN Z pick-up with M/T
- 1996–99 4.3L models

REMOVAL & INSTALLATION

1994 Vehicles Equipped With A PCM

UTILITY MODELS

1. Disconnect the negative battery cable.
2. Remove the passenger side kick panel.
3. If equipped, remove the hush panel.
4. Unfasten the PCM retaining screw. Unplug the Vehicle Speed Sensor (VSS) buffer connector and rotate to the PCM to ease PCM removal.
5. Unplug the PCM harness connector.

6. Remove all necessary brackets and modules to complete PCM removal.
To install:
7. If removed, attach all brackets and modules to the PCM prior to installation.
8. Attach the PCM harness and VSS connections to the PCM.
9. Rotate the PCM counterclockwise as you install it, this will ease installation.
10. Install the PCM retainer.
11. If equipped, install the hush panel.
12. Install the kick panel and connect the negative battery cable.

1994–95 Vehicles Equipped With A PCM

PICK-UP MODELS AND UTILITY MODELS

1. Disconnect the negative battery cable.
2. Remove the dash panel below the glove box.
3. Unfasten the PCM retaining screw and unplug the PCM electrical connection.
4. If equipped, unplug the Vehicle Speed Sensor (VSS) buffer connector.
5. Remove all necessary brackets and modules to complete PCM removal.
To install:
6. If removed, attach all brackets and modules to the PCM prior to installation.
7. Attach the PCM harness connection to the PCM.
8. If equipped, attach the VSS buffer connection.
9. Install the PCM retainer.
10. Install the dash panel below the glove box and connect the negative battery cable.

1994–95 Vehicles Equipped With A ECM

1. Disconnect the negative battery cable.
2. Remove the dash panel below the glove box.
3. Unfasten the ECM retainers and remove the ECM mounting hardware.
4. Unplug the ECM electrical connection.
5. Remove the ECM.
To install:
6. Place the ECM into position.
7. Attach the ECM harness connection to the ECM.
8. Attach all mounting hardware and retainers.
9. Install the dash panel below the glove box and connect the negative battery cable.

1994–97 Models Equipped With A VCM-A Or VCM and 1996–99 Models Equipped With A PCM

▶ See Figures 17 thru 25

1. Disconnect the negative battery cable.
2. Unfasten and remove the retainers.
3. Unplug the connectors from the VCM.

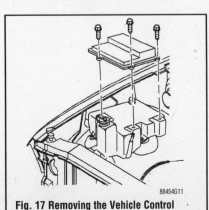

Fig. 17 Removing the Vehicle Control Module (VCM)

Fig. 18 The PCM shown here is mounted on the passenger side of the engine compartment and is retained by three bolts

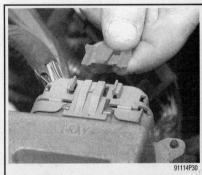

Fig. 19 Remove the PCM electrical connector retainer from the top two connectors . . .

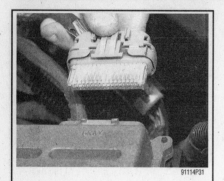

Fig. 20 . . . and unplug both the electrical connections

Fig. 21 Tilt the PCM upwards to access the lower electrical connection and unplug it, then remove the PCM from the vehicle

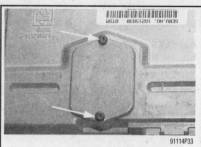

Fig. 22 On this particular PCM the Knock Sensor (KS) module is easily replaced. The module is located under a plate on the PCM and is retained by two Allen head screws

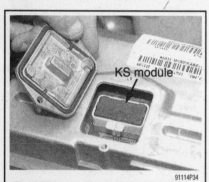

Fig. 23 Unfasten the screws and remove the module cover plate to access the KS module

Fig. 24 Squeeze the module retaining tabs . . .

Fig. 25 . . .and withdraw the module from the PCM

4. Remove the VCM.
5. If necessary, remove the VCM from the bracket.

To install:

6. If necessary, attach the VCM to the bracket, then install the VCM.
7. Attach the electrical connectors and fasten the retainers.
8. Connect the negative battery cable.

1998–99 Models Equipped With A VCM

1. Disconnect the negative battery cable.
2. Pull the spring retainer up and over the VCM rail.
3. Slide the VCM out of the bracket at a angle.
4. Unplug the connectors from the VCM.
5. Remove the VCM.

To install:

6. Attach the electrical connectors to the VCM.
7. Slide the VCM into the bracket at an angle and pull the spring retaining back to its original position.
8. Connect the negative battery cable.

Oxygen Sensor

OPERATION

▶ See Figure 26

There are two types of oxygen sensor's used in these vehicles. They are the single wire oxygen sensor (02S) and the heated oxygen sensor (H02S). The oxygen sensor is a spark plug shaped device that is screwed into the exhaust manifold. It monitors the oxygen content of the exhaust gases and sends a voltage signal to the Vehicle Control Module (VCM). The VCM monitors this voltage and, depending on the value of the received signal, issues a command to the mixture control solenoid to adjust for rich or lean conditions.

The heated oxygen sensor has a heating element incorporated into the sensor to aid in the warm up to the proper operating temperature and to maintain that temperature.

The proper operation of the oxygen sensor depends upon four basic conditions:

1. Good electrical connections. Since the sensor generates low currents, good clean electrical connections at the sensor are a must.
2. Outside air supply. Air must circulate to the internal portion of the sensor. When servicing the sensor, do not restrict the air passages.
3. Proper operating temperatures. The VCM will not recognize the sensor's signals until the sensor reaches approximately 600°F (316°C).

Fig. 26 The oxygen sensor is screwed into the exhaust manifold and/or into the exhaust pipe under the vehicle. The sensor tip protrudes into the exhaust stream to monitor the oxygen content in the exhaust gases

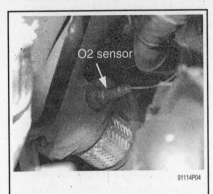

Fig. 27 The oxygen sensor is screwed into the exhaust pipe or manifold

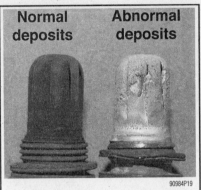

Normal deposits **Abnormal deposits**

Fig. 28 Inspect the oxygen sensor tip for abnormal deposits

Fig. 29 Connect jumper wires to the oxygen sensor terminal and harness so that the sensor may be tested with engine running

4. Non-leaded fuel. The use of leaded gasoline will damage the sensor very quickly.

TESTING

Single Wire Sensor

▶ See Figures 27, 28, 29 and 30

1. Perform a visual inspection on the sensor as follows:
  a. Remove the sensor from the exhaust.
  b. If the sensor tip has a black/sooty deposit, this may indicate a rich fuel mixture.
  c. If the sensor tip has a white gritty deposit, this may indicate an internal anti-freeze leak.
  d. If the sensor tip has a brown deposit, this could indicate oil consumption.

➡ All these contaminates can destroy the sensor, if the problem is not repaired the new sensor will also be damaged.

2. Reinstall the sensor.
3. Start the engine and bring it to normal operating temperature, then run the engine above 1200 rpm for two minutes.
4. Backprobe with a high impedance averaging voltmeter (set to the DC voltage scale) between the oxygen sensor (02S) and battery ground.
5. Verify that the 02S voltage fluctuates rapidly between 0.40–0.60 volts.
6. If the 02S voltage is stabilized at the middle of the specified range (approximately 0.45–0.55 volts) or if the 02S voltage fluctuates very slowly between the specified range (02S signal crosses 0.5 volts less than 5 times in ten seconds), the 02S may be faulty.
7. If the 02S voltage stabilizes at either end of the specified range, the VCM is probably not able to compensate for a mechanical problem such as a vacuum leak or a faulty pressure regulator. These types of mechanical problems will cause the 02S to sense a constant lean or constant rich mixture. The mechanical problem will first have to be repaired and then the 02S test repeated.

8. Pull a vacuum hose located after the throttle plate. Voltage should drop to approximately 0.12 volts (while still fluctuating rapidly). This tests the ability of the 02S to detect a lean mixture condition. Reattach the vacuum hose.
9. Richen the mixture using a propane enrichment tool. Voltage should rise to approximately 0.90 volts (while still fluctuating rapidly). This tests the ability of the 02S to detect a rich mixture condition.
10. If the 02S voltage is above or below the specified range, the 02S and/or the 02S wiring may be faulty. Check the wiring for any breaks, repair as necessary and repeat the test.

Heated Oxygen Sensor

▶ See Figures 28 and 31

1. Perform a visual inspection on the sensor as follows:
  a. Remove the sensor from the exhaust.
  b. If the sensor tip has a black/sooty deposit, this may indicate a rich fuel mixture.
  c. If the sensor tip has a white gritty deposit, this may indicate an internal anti-freeze leak.
  d. If the sensor tip has a brown deposit, this could indicate oil consumption.

➡ All these contaminates can destroy the sensor, if the problem is not repaired the new sensor will also be damaged.

2. Reinstall the sensor.
3. Start the engine and bring it to normal operating temperature, then run the engine above 1200 rpm for two minutes.
4. Turn the ignition **OFF** and disengage the H02S harness connector.
5. Connect a test light between harness terminals **A** and **B**. With the ignition switch **ON** and the engine off, verify that the test light is lit. If the test light is not lit, either the supply voltage to the H02S heater or the ground circuit of the H02S heater is faulty. Check the H02S wiring and the fuse.
6. Next, connect a high impedance ohmmeter between the H02S terminals **B** and **A** and verify that the resistance is 3.5–14.0 ohms.
7. If the H02S heater resistance is not as specified, the H02S may be faulty.

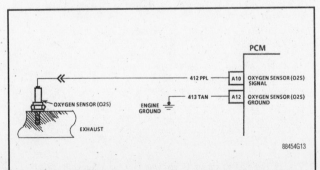

Fig. 30 Typical signal wire oxygen sensor (02S) wiring diagram (wire color, terminal identification/location may vary on certain models)

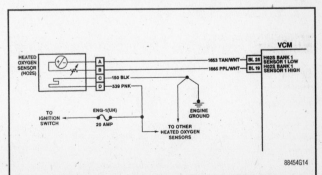

Fig. 31 Common multiple wire Heated Oxygen Sensor (H02S) wiring diagram (wire color, terminal identification/location may vary on certain models)

8. Start the engine and bring it to normal operating temperature, then run the engine above 1200 rpm for two minutes.

9. Backprobe with a high impedance averaging voltmeter (set to the DC voltage scale) between the oxygen sensor (02S) and battery ground.

10. Verify that the 02S voltage fluctuates rapidly between 0.40–0.60 volts.

11. If the 02S voltage is stabilized at the middle of the specified range (approximately 0.45–0.55 volts) or if the 02S voltage fluctuates very slowly between the specified range (02S signal crosses 0.5 volts less than 5 times in ten seconds), the 02S may be faulty.

12. If the 02S voltage stabilizes at either end of the specified range, the VCM is probably not able to compensate for a mechanical problem such as a vacuum leak or a faulty fuel pressure regulator. These types of mechanical problems will cause the 02S to sense a constant lean or constant rich mixture. The mechanical problem will first have to be repaired and then the 02S test repeated.

13. Pull a vacuum hose located after the throttle plate. Voltage should drop to approximately 0.12 volts (while still fluctuating rapidly). This tests the ability of the 02S to detect a lean mixture condition. Reattach the vacuum hose.

14. Richen the mixture using a propane enrichment tool. Voltage should rise to approximately 0.90 volts (while still fluctuating rapidly). This tests the ability of the 02S to detect a rich mixture condition.

15. If the 02S voltage is above or below the specified range, the 02S and/or the 02S wiring may be faulty. Check the wiring for any breaks, repair as necessary and repeat the test.

REMOVAL & INSTALLATION

✸✸ WARNING

The sensor uses a permanently attached pigtail and connector. This pigtail should not be removed from the sensor. Damage or removal of the pigtail or connector could affect the proper operation of the sensor. Keep the electrical connector and louvered end of the sensor clean and free of grease. NEVER use cleaning solvents of any type on the sensor! The oxygen sensor may be difficult to remove when the temperature of the engine is below 120∞F (49∞C). Excessive force may damage the threads in the exhaust manifold or exhaust pipe.

1. Disconnect the negative battery cable.
2. Unplug the electrical connector and any attaching hardware.
3. Remove the sensor.
To install:
4. Coat the threads of the sensor with a GM anti-seize compound, part number 5613695, or its equivalent, before installation. New sensors are pre-coated with this compound.

➡**The GM anti-seize compound is NOT a conventional anti-seize paste. The use of a regular paste may electrically insulate the sensor, rendering it useless. The threads MUST be coated with the proper electrically conductive anti-seize compound.**

5. Install the sensor and tighten to 30 ft. lbs. (40 Nm). Use care in making sure the silicone boot is in the correct position to avoid melting it during operation.
6. Attach the electrical connector.
7. Connect the negative battery cable.

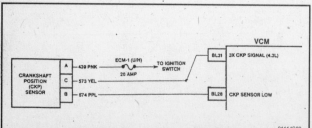

Fig. 32 Typical Crankshaft Position (CKP) sensor wiring diagram— late model 4.3L engines (wire color, terminal identification/location may vary on certain models)

Crankshaft Position (CKP) Sensor

OPERATION

The Crankshaft Position (CKP) sensor provides a signal through the ignition module which the VCM uses as a reference to calculate rpm and crankshaft position.

TESTING

4.3L Engines

▶ **See Figures 32 and 33**

1. Disconnect the CKP sensor harness. Connect an LED test light between battery ground and CKP harness terminal **A**.
2. With the ignition **ON** and the engine off, verify that the test light illuminates.
3. If not as specified, repair or replace the fuse and/or wiring.
4. Carefully connect the test light between CKP harness terminal **A** and **B**. Verify that the test light illuminates.
5. If not as specified, repair the CKP harness ground circuit (terminal **B**).
6. Turn the ignition **OFF** and disconnect the test light.

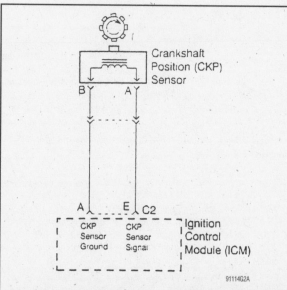

Fig. 33 Typical Crankshaft Position (CKP) sensor wiring diagram— late model 4.3L engines (wire color, terminal identification/location may vary on certain models)

7. Next, connect suitable jumper wires between the CKP sensor and CKP sensor harness. Connect a duty cycle meter to the jumper wire corresponding to CKP terminal **C** and battery ground.

8. Crank the engine and verify that the duty cycle signal is between 40–60%.

9. If it is not as specified, the CKP sensor may be faulty.

10. Next, connect a AC volt meter to the jumper wire corresponding to CKP terminal **C** and battery ground.

11. Crank the engine and verify that the AC voltage signal is at least 10.0 volts.

12. If not as specified the CKP sensor may be faulty.

2.2L Engine

▶ **See Figures 34 and 35**

1. Turn the ignition key **OFF**.
2. Unplug the sensor electrical harness and check the terminals for corrosion and damage.

3. Check the sensor wiring harness wires for continuity and repair as necessary.

4. Attach the sensor harness making sure it is firmly engaged.

5. Using a Digital Volt Ohm Meter (DVOM) set on the DC scale, backprobe the sensor signal terminal (terminal A) with the positive lead of the meter and backprobe the sensor ground terminal (terminal B) with the negative lead of the meter.

6. Have an assistant crank the engine and observe the meter.

7. You should have approximately a 5 volt reference signal pulse. If not the sensor may be defective.

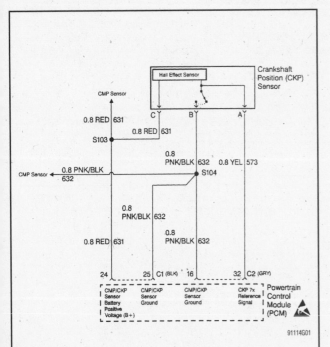

Fig. 34 Common Crankshaft Position (CKP) sensor wiring schematic—2.2L engines (wire color, terminal identification/location may vary on certain models)

Fig. 35 Attach suitable jumper wires between the CKP sensor and CKP sensor harness. A DC volt meter can then be attached to the necessary terminals to test the sensor as the engine is being cranked

REMOVAL & INSTALLATION

▶ See Figures 36, 37, 38, 39 and 40

1. Disconnect the negative battery cable.
2. Raise the vehicle and support it with jackstands.
3. If equipped on 4.3L engines, remove the steering linkage shield to access the sensor.
4. Unplug the sensor harness connector at the sensor.
5. Unfasten the retaining bolt, then remove the sensor from the front cover on 4.3L engines, or from below the coil pack on 2.2L engines. Inspect the sensor O-ring for wear, cracks or leakage and replace if necessary.

To install:

6. Lubricate the O-ring with clean engine oil, then place it on the sensor. Install the sensor into the front cover (4.3L) or below the coil pack (2.2L).
7. Install the sensor and tighten the retaining bolt.
8. Attach the sensor harness connector.
9. If removed, install the steering linkage shield.
10. Lower the vehicle.
11. Connect the negative battery cable.

Camshaft Position (CMP) Sensor

OPERATION

▶ See Figure 41

The VCM uses the camshaft signal to determine the position of the No. 1 cylinder piston during its power stroke. The signal is used by the VCM to calculate fuel injection mode of operation.

If the cam signal is lost while the engine is running, the fuel injection system will shift to a calculated fuel injected mode based on the last fuel injection pulse, and the engine will continue to run.

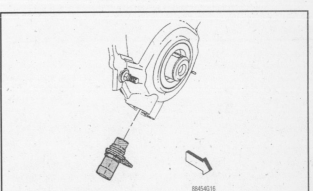

Fig. 36 View of the Crankshaft Position Sensor (CKP) location—1996–99 4.3L engines

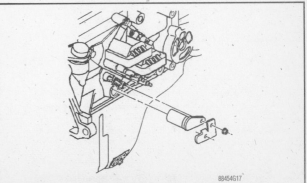

Fig. 37 View of the Crankshaft Position Sensor (CKP) location—1996–99 2.2L engines

Fig. 38 The Crankshaft Position (CKP) sensor is located on the passenger side of the engine block below the coil pack and is accessible when the vehicle is raised and supported with jackstands—2.2L engines

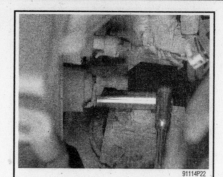

Fig. 39 Unfasten the Crankshaft Position (CKP) sensor retaining bolt—2.2L engine shown

Fig. 40 After the Crankshaft Position (CKP) sensor retaining bolt has been removed, grasp the sensor and pull it from its bore in the engine block using a slight twisting motion—2.2L engine shown

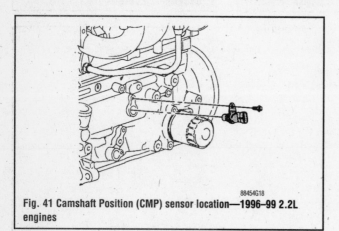

Fig. 41 Camshaft Position (CMP) sensor location—1996–99 2.2L engines

TESTING

▶ See Figures 42, 43, 44 and 45

1. Remove the ECM fuse to prevent the engine from starting. Removal of the ECM fuse does not disable the sensor power supply and allows testing of this sensor safely.

2. Disconnect the CMP sensor wiring harness and attach suitable jumper wires between the CMP sensor and CMP sensor harness. Connect a DC volt meter to the jumper wires corresponding to CMP IGN or PWR terminal and sensor ground.

3. With the ignition **ON** and the engine off, verify that the voltage is approximately battery voltage. The supply voltage should be slightly less than battery voltage.

4. If not as specified, repair or replace the fuse and/or wiring.

5. Connect a DC volt meter to the jumper wires corresponding to CMP signal terminal and sensor ground.

6. Place a socket and breaker bar or the crankshaft pulley bolt and rotate the engine slowly by hand. Observe the volt meter and verify that the voltage signal varies from approximately zero volts to slightly less than supply voltage. The voltage will switch on when the target passes the sensor and will show little or no voltage when the target is past the sensor.

7. If it is not as specified, the CMP sensor may be faulty.

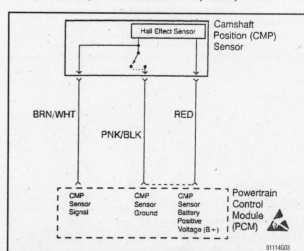

Fig. 43 Common Camshaft Position (CMP) sensor wiring schematic—2.2L engines (wire color, terminal identification/location may vary on certain models)

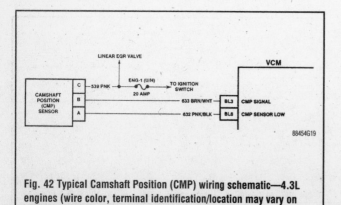

Fig. 42 Typical Camshaft Position (CMP) wiring schematic—4.3L engines (wire color, terminal identification/location may vary on certain models)

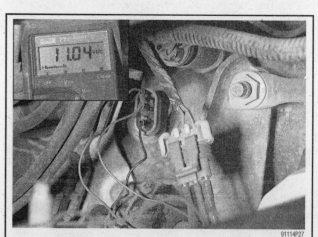

Fig. 44 Attach suitable jumper wires between the CMP sensor and CMP sensor harness. Connect a DC volt meter to the jumper wires corresponding to IGN and sensor ground terminals and note the reading

Fig. 45 Connect the volt meter to the jumper wire corresponding to signal and sensor ground terminals, rotate the engine and observe the volt meter and verify that the voltage signal varies from approximately zero volts to slightly less than supply voltage

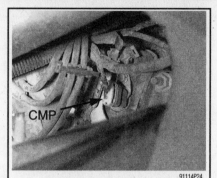

Fig. 46 The Camshaft Position (CMP) sensor is located on the passenger side of the engine and is accessible after removing the right front tire—2.2L engine

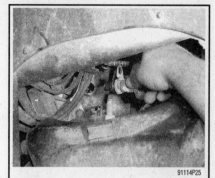

Fig. 47 Unplug CMP sensor electrical connection and unfasten the sensor retainer, then remove the sensor from its bore in the block—2.2L engine

REMOVAL & INSTALLATION

2.2L Engines

◗ See Figures 46 and 47

1. Disconnect the negative battery cable.
2. Raise the vehicle and support it with safety stands.
3. Remove the right hand tire assembly.
4. Unplug the sensor harness connector at the sensor.
5. Unfasten the retaining bolt, then remove the sensor from the camshaft housing.

To install:
6. Place the sensor into position.
7. Install the CMP sensor retaining bolt, then tighten to 88 inch lbs. (10 Nm).
8. Attach the sensor harness connector.
9. Istall the tire assembly and lower the vehicle.
10. Connect the negative battery cable.

4.3L Engines

MODELS EQUIPPED WITH A DISTRIBUTOR IGNITION (DI) OR HIGH VOLTAGE SWITCH (HVS) SYSTEM

The Camshaft Position (CMP) sensor is located in the distributor assembly.
1. Disconnect the negative battery cable.
2. Unplug the electrical connection from the CMP sensor.
3. Remove the distributor cap and rotor.
4. Unfasten the CMP sensor retainer(s).

➡️If equipped, the square cut hole in the vane wheel must be aligned with the sensor in order for the sensor to be removed.

5. Remove the sensor from the distributor.
To install:
6. If equipped, line up the square cut hole in the vane wheel with the sensor and install the sensor.
7. Install the sensor and its retainers. Do not overtighten the retainers as the plastic base may strip.
8. Install the rotor and cap, then attach all necessary electrical connections.
9. Connect the negative battery cable.

Mass Air Flow (MAF) Sensor

OPERATION

◗ See Figure 48

The Mass Air Flow (MAF) Sensor measures the amount of air entering the engine during a given time. The VCM uses the mass airflow information for fuel delivery calculations. A large quantity of air entering the engine indicates an acceleration or high load situation, while a small quantity of air indicates deceleration or idle.

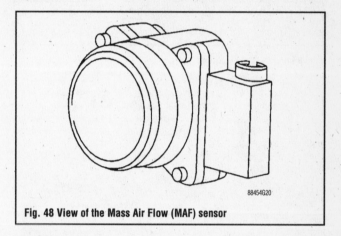

Fig. 48 View of the Mass Air Flow (MAF) sensor

TESTING

◗ See Figure 49

1. Backprobe with a high impedance voltmeter between MAF sensor terminals **C** and **B**.
2. With the ignition **ON** engine off, verify that battery voltage is present.
3. If the voltage is not as specified, either the wiring to the MAF sensor, the fuse, or the VCM may be faulty. Correct any wiring or VCM faults before continuing test.
4. Disconnect the voltmeter and backprobe with a frequency meter between MAF sensor terminals **A** and **B**.
5. Start the engine and wait until it reaches normal idle speed and verify that the MAF sensor output is approximately 99 Hz.
6. Slowly raise engine speed up to maximum recommended rpm and verify that the MAF sensor output rises smoothly to approximately 8000 Hz.
7. If MAF sensor output is not as specified the sensor may be faulty.

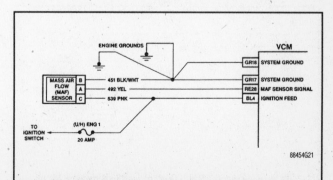

Fig. 49 Typical Mass Airflow (MAF) sensor wiring diagram (wire color, terminal identification/location may vary on certain models)

REMOVAL & INSTALLATION

1. Disconnect the negative battery cable.
2. Unplug the electrical connector.
3. Remove the air intake hoses from the sensor, then remove the sensor.
4. Installation is the reverse of removal.

Engine Coolant Temperature (ECT) Sensor

OPERATION

The Engine Coolant Temperature (ECT) sensor is mounted in the intake manifold and sends engine temperature information to the VCM. The VCM supplies 5 volts to the coolant temperature sensor circuit. The sensor is a thermistor which changes internal resistance as temperature changes. When the sensor is cold (internal resistance high), the VCM monitors a high signal voltage which it interprets as a cold engine. As the sensor warms (internal resistance low), the VCM monitors a low signal voltage which it interprets as warm engine.

TESTING

▶ See Figures 50, 51 and 52

1. Remove the ECT sensor from the vehicle.
2. Immerse the tip of the sensor in container of water.
3. Connect a digital ohmmeter to the two terminals of the sensor.
4. Using a calibrated thermometer, compare the resistance of the sensor to the temperature of the water. Refer to the engine coolant sensor temperature vs. resistance illustration.
5. Repeat the test at two other temperature points, heating or cooling the water as necessary.
6. If the sensor does not met specification shown in the temperature versus resistance chart, it must be replaced.
7. The sensor may also be checked in the vehicle. Unplug the sensor and attach a digital ohmmeter to the two terminals of the sensor.
8. Using a calibrated thermometer, compare the resistance of the sensor to the ambient air temperature.

Fig. 50 Testing the Engine Coolant Temperature (ECT) sensor resistance

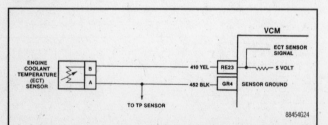

Fig. 51 Engine Coolant Temperature (ECT) sensor wiring diagram (wire color, terminal identification/location may vary on certain models)

ENGINE COOLANT SENSOR		
TEMPERATURE VS. RESISTANCE VALUES (APPROXIMATE)		
°C	°F	OHMS
100	212	177
90	194	241
80	176	332
70	158	467
60	140	667
50	122	973
45	113	1188
40	104	1459
35	95	1802
30	86	2238
25	77	2796
20	68	3520
15	59	4450
10	50	5670
5	41	7280
0	32	9420
-5	23	12300
-10	14	16180
-15	5	21450
-20	-4	28680
-30	-22	52700
-40	-40	100700

Fig. 52 Engine Coolant Temperature (ECT) sensor temperature vs. resistance values

9. Repeat the test at two other temperature points, heating or cooling the water as necessary.
10. If the sensor does not met specification shown in the temperature versus resistance chart, it must be replaced.

REMOVAL & INSTALLATION

1. Disconnect the negative battery cable.
2. Drain the cooling system below the level of the sensor and unplug the sensor electrical connection.
3. Remove the coolant sensor.
To install:
4. On 1998–99 models, coat the threads of the sensor with a suitable water resistant sealer such a sealer 9985253 or its equivalent.
5. Install the sensor and engage the electrical connector.
6. Refill the cooling system and connect the negative battery cable.

Intake Air Temperature (IAT) Sensor

OPERATION

The Intake Air Temperature (IAT) sensor is a thermistor which changes value based on the temperature of the air entering the engine. Low temperature produces a high resistance, while a high temperature causes a low resistance. The VCM supplies a 5 volt signal to the sensor through a resistor in the VCM and measures the voltage. The voltage will be high when the incoming air is cold, and low when the air is hot. By measuring the voltage, the VCM calculates the incoming air temperature.

the IAT sensor signal is used to adjust spark timing according to incoming air density.

TESTING

▶ See Figures 53, 54 and 55

1. Remove the Intake Air Temperature (IAT) sensor.
2. Connect a digital ohmmeter to the two terminals of the sensor.

3. Using a calibrated thermometer, compare the resistance of the sensor to the temperature of the ambient air. Refer to the temperature vs. resistance illustration.

4. Repeat the test at two other temperature points, heating or cooling the air as necessary with a hair dryer or other suitable tool.

5. If the sensor does not meet specification, it must be replaced.

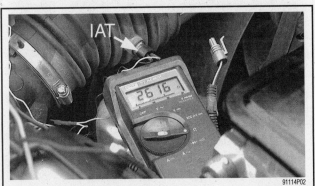

Fig. 53 Measuring the Intake Air Temperature (IAT) sensor resistance

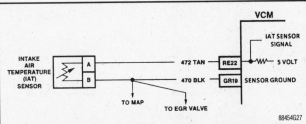

Fig. 54 Common Intake Air Temperature (IAT) sensor wiring diagram (wire color, terminal identification/location may vary on certain models)

INTAKE AIR SENSOR		
TEMPERATURE VS. RESISTANCE VALUES (APPROXIMATE)		
°C	°F	OHMS
100	212	177
90	194	241
80	176	332
70	158	467
60	140	667
50	122	973
45	113	1188
40	104	1459
35	95	1802
30	86	2238
25	77	2796
20	68	3520
15	59	4450
10	50	5670
5	41	7280
0	32	9420
-5	23	12300
-10	14	16180
-15	5	21450
-20	-4	28680
-30	-22	52700
-40	-40	100700

Fig. 55 Intake Air Temperature (IAT) sensor temperature vs. resistance values

REMOVAL & INSTALLATION

▶ See Figures 56 and 57

1. Disconnect the negative battery cable.
2. Unplug the sensor electrical connection.
3. Loosen and remove the IAT sensor.
4. Installation is the reverse of removal.

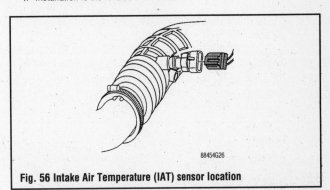

Fig. 56 Intake Air Temperature (IAT) sensor location

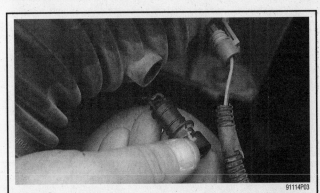

Fig. 57 Use a twisting and pulling motion to remove the Intake Air Temperature (IAT) sensor

Throttle Position Sensor (TPS)

OPERATION

The Throttle Position Sensor (TPS) is connected to the throttle shaft on the throttle body. It is a potentiometer with one end connected to 5 volts from the VCM and the other to ground.

A third wire is connected to the VCM to measure the voltage from the TPS. As the throttle valve angle is changed (accelerator pedal moved), the output of the TPS also changes. At a closed throttle position, the output of the TPS is low (approximately 0.5 volts). As the throttle valve opens, the output increases so that, at wide-open throttle, the output voltage should be approximately 4.5 volts.

By monitoring the output voltage from the TPS, the VCM can determine fuel delivery based on throttle valve angle (driver demand).

TESTING

▶ See Figures 58, 59 and 60

1. Backprobe with a high impedance voltmeter at TPS ground terminal and 5 volt reference signal terminal.
2. With the key **ON** and engine off, the voltmeter reading should be approximately 5.0 volts.
3. If the voltage is not as specified, either the wiring to the TPS or the VCM may be faulty. Correct any wiring or VCM faults before continuing test.
4. Backprobe with a high impedance voltmeter at the TP signal terminal and the sensor ground terminal.
5. With the key **ON** and engine off and the throttle closed, the TPS voltage should be approximately 0.5–1.2 volts.

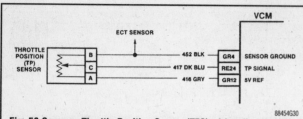

Fig. 58 Common Throttle Position Sensor (TPS) wiring diagram (wire color, terminal identification/location may vary on certain models)

6. Verify that the TPS voltage increases or decreases smoothly as the throttle is opened or closed. Make sure to open and close the throttle very slowly in order to detect any abnormalities in the TPS voltage reading.

7. If the sensor voltage is not as specified, replace the sensor.

REMOVAL & INSTALLATION

Except 1998–99 2.2L Engines

▶ See Figure 61

1. Disconnect the negative battery cable and remove the air cleaner and if equipped, the gasket and bracket.
2. Disengage the electrical connector.
3. Unfasten the two TPS attaching screw assemblies.
4. Remove the TPS from the throttle body assembly.
5. Remove the TPS seal.

To install:

6. Install the TPS seal over the throttle shaft.
7. With the throttle valve closed, install the TPS on the throttle shaft. Rotate it counterclockwise, to align the mounting holes.
8. Install the two TPS attaching screws. Tighten the screws to 18 inch lbs. (2 Nm).
9. Engage the electrical connector.
10. If equipped, install the bracket and gasket air cleaner and gasket.
11. Connect the negative battery cable.

1998–99 2.2L Engines

1. Disconnect the negative battery cable and remove the air cleaner outlet resonator.
2. Remove the throttle body assembly.
3. Unfasten the two TPS attaching screw assemblies.
4. Remove the TPS from the throttle body assembly.

To install:

5. With the throttle valve closed, install the TPS on the throttle body.
6. Install the two TPS attaching screws. Tighten the screws to 27 inch lbs. (3 Nm).
7. Install the throttle body.
8. Install the air cleaner outlet resonator.
9. Connect the negative battery cable.

Idle Air Control (IAC) Valve

OPERATION

The engine idle speed is controlled by the VCM through the Idle Air Control (IAC) valve mounted on the throttle body. The VCM sends voltage pulses to the IAC motor causing the IAC motor shaft and pintle to move in or out a given distance (number of steps) for each pulse, (called counts).

This movement controls air flow around the throttle plate, which in turn, controls engine idle speed, either cold or hot. IAC valve pintle position counts can be seen using a scan tool. Zero counts corresponds to a fully closed passage, while 140 or more counts (depending on the application) corresponds to full flow.

TESTING

▶ See Figures 62, 63 and 64

1. Disengage the IAC electrical connector.
2. Using an ohmmeter, measure the resistance between IAC terminals **A** and **B**. Next measure the resistance between terminals **C** and **D**.
3. Verify that the resistance between both sets of IAC terminals is 20–80 ohms. If the resistance is not as specified, the IAC may be faulty.
4. Measure the resistance between IAC terminals **B** and **C**. Next measure the resistance between terminals **A** and **D**.
5. Verify that the resistance between both sets of IAC terminals is infinite. If the resistance is not infinite, the IAC may be faulty.
6. Also, with a small mirror, inspect IAC air inlet passage and pintle for debris. Clean as necessary, as this can cause IAC malfunction.

REMOVAL & INSTALLATION

▶ See Figures 65, 66, 67, 68 and 69

1. Disconnect the negative battery cable.
2. Remove the air cleaner assembly or resonator as necessary.
3. Unplug the electrical connection.
4. Remove the IAC valve. On thread-mounted units, use 1¼ in. (32mm) wrench and on flange-mounted units, remove the screw assemblies.
5. Remove the IAC valve gasket or O-ring and discard it.

To install:

6. Clean the old gasket material from the surface of the throttle body assembly on the thread mounted valve. On the flange-mounted valve clean the surface to ensure proper O-ring sealing
7. If installing a new IAC valve, measure the distance between the tip of the valve pintle and the mounting flange. If the distance is greater than 1.10 inch (28mm), use finger pressure to slowly retract the pintle until the measurement is within specification (refer to the accompanying illustration).
8. Install the valve with a new gasket or O-ring. Tighten the thread mounted assembly 13 ft. lbs. (18 Nm) and tighten the flange mounted attaching screws to 28 inch. lbs. (3 Nm).
9. Engage the electrical connector to the IAC valve.
10. Connect the negative battery cable.

Fig. 59 Using jumper wires and high impedance voltmeter, test between the sensor ground and reference terminals, the voltage should be approximately 5 volts

Fig. 60 Next test between the sensor signal and ground terminals, verify that the TPS voltage increases or decreases smoothly as the throttle is opened or closed

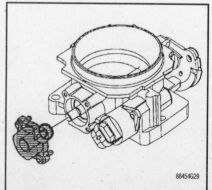

Fig. 61 Common Throttle Position Sensor (TPS)

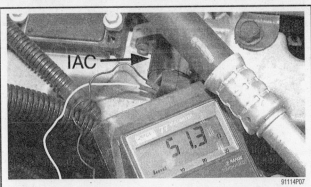

Fig. 62 Test the Idle Air Control (IAC) valve resistance between A and B and terminals C and D. The resistance should be 20–80 ohms

Fig. 63 Test the Idle Air Control (IAC) valve resistance between B and C and terminals A and D. The resistance should be infinite

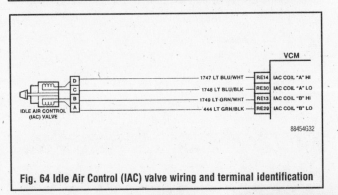

Fig. 64 Idle Air Control (IAC) valve wiring and terminal identification

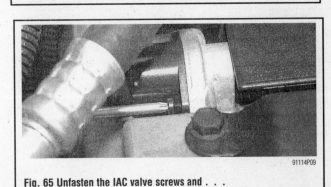

Fig. 65 Unfasten the IAC valve screws and . . .

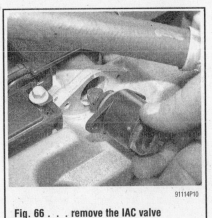

Fig. 66 . . . remove the IAC valve

Fig. 67 When installing a new IAC valve, measure the distance between the tip of the valve pintle and the mounting flange. The distance should be 1.10 inch (28mm)

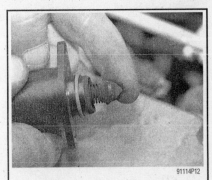

Fig. 68 Use finger pressure to slowly retract the pintle until the measurement is within specification

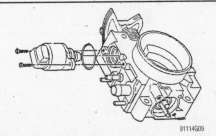

Fig. 69 If installing a new IAC valve, measure the distance between the valve pintle and mounting flange. If adjustment is required, use finger pressure to retract the pintle until the measurement is within specification

11. If removed, install the air cleaner or resonator.

12. On 1998–99 models to set the pintle position, turn the ignition key to the **ON** engine **OFF** for five seconds. Turn the ignition key to the **OFF** position for ten seconds, then start the engine and check for proper idle operation.

Manifold Absolute Pressure (MAP) Sensor

OPERATION

The Manifold Absolute Pressure (MAP) sensor measures the changes in intake manifold pressure, which result from the engine load and speed changes, and converts this to a voltage output.

A closed throttle on engine coastdown will produce a low MAP output, while a wide-open throttle will produce a high output. This high output is produced because the pressure inside the manifold is the same as outside the manifold, so 100 percent of the outside air pressure is measured.

The MAP sensor reading is the opposite of what you would measure on a vacuum gauge. When manifold pressure is high, vacuum is low. The MAP sensor is also used to measure barometric pressure under certain conditions, which allows the VCM to automatically adjust for different altitudes.

The VCM sends a 5 volt reference signal to the MAP sensor. As the manifold pressure changes, the electrical resistance of the sensor also changes. By monitoring the sensor output voltage, the VCM knows the manifold pressure. A higher pressure, low vacuum (high voltage) requires more fuel, while a lower pressure, higher vacuum (low voltage) requires less fuel.

The VCM uses the MAP sensor to control fuel delivery and ignition timing.

TESTING

♦ See Figures 70, 71 and 72

1. Backprobe with a high impedance voltmeter at MAP sensor terminals **A** and **C**.
2. With the key **ON** and engine off, the voltmeter reading should be approximately 5.0 volts.
3. If the voltage is not as specified, either the wiring to the MAP sensor or the VCM may be faulty. Correct any wiring or VCM faults before continuing test.
4. Backprobe with the high impedance voltmeter at MAP sensor terminals **B** and **A**.
5. Verify that the sensor voltage is approximately 0.5 volts with the engine not running (at sea level).
6. Record MAP sensor voltage with the key **ON** and engine off.
7. Start the vehicle.
8. Verify that the sensor voltage is greater than 1.5 volts (above the recorded reading) at idle.

9. Verify that the sensor voltage increases to approximately 4.5 volts (above the recorded reading) at Wide Open Throttle (WOT).
10. If the sensor voltage is as specified, the sensor is functioning properly.
11. If the sensor voltage is not as specified, check the sensor and the sensor vacuum source for a leak or a restriction. If no leaks or restrictions are found, the sensor may be defective and should be replaced.

REMOVAL & INSTALLATION

Except 1998–99 2.2L Models

♦ See Figures 73, 74 and 75

1. Disconnect the negative battery cable.
2. Tag and disconnect the vacuum harness assembly.
3. Unplug the electrical connector.
4. To remove the sensor, release the locktabs, or unfasten the bolts or simply pull the sensor from the grommet, whichever applies to your vehicle.
5. Installation is the reverse of removal.

1998–99 2.2L Models

1. Disconnect the negative battery cable.
2. Unplug the electrical connection and vacuum hose.
3. Unfasten the bracket retaining screw and remove the bracket.
4. Remove the sensor from the intake manifold.
5. Installation is the reverse of removal.

Vehicle Speed Sensor (VSS)

OPERATION

The vehicle speed sensor is made up of a coil mounted on the transmission and a tooth rotor mounted to the output shaft of the transmission. As each tooth nears the coil, the coil produces an AC voltage pulse. As the vehicle speed increases the number of voltage pulses per second increases.

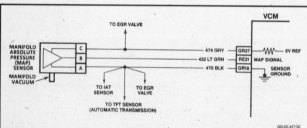

Fig. 70 Typical Manifold Absolute Pressure (MAP) sensor wiring diagram (wire color, terminal identification/location may vary on certain models)

Fig. 71 Using jumper wires and a high impedance voltmeter test between MAP sensor terminals A and C with the key ON and engine off. The voltage should be approximately 5 volts

Fig. 72 Next test between MAP sensor terminals A and B with the key ON and engine off. The voltage should be approximately 0.5 volts

Fig. 73 Unplug the Manifold Absolute Pressure (MAP) sensor electrical connection

Fig. 74 Unfasten the Manifold Absolute Pressure (MAP) sensor retainers . . .

Fig. 75 . . . then remove the MAP sensor

TESTING

▶ See Figures 76 and 77

1. To test the VSS, backprobe the VSS terminals with a high impedance voltmeter (set at the AC voltage scale).
2. Safely raise and support the entire vehicle using jackstands. Make absolutely sure the vehicle is stable.
3. Start the vehicle and place it in gear.
4. Verify that the VSS voltage increases as the drive shaft speed increases.
5. If the VSS voltage is not as specified the VSS may be faulty.

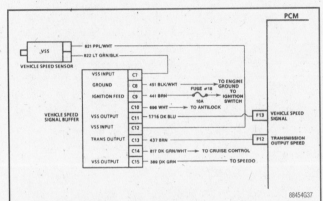

Fig. 76 Common Vehicle Speed Sensor (VSS) and vehicle speed signal buffer wiring diagram, models equipped with a PCM

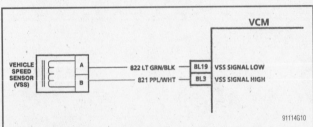

Fig. 77 Typical Vehicle Speed Sensor (VSS) wiring diagram, except models equipped with a PCM

REMOVAL & INSTALLATION

▶ See Figures 78 and 79

1. Disconnect the negative battery cable.
2. Disengage the electrical connection.
3. Unfasten the sensor retainers.
4. On models with a automatic transmission, attach VSS removal/installation tool J 38417 or its equivalent to the sensor.
5. Remove the sensor and gasket or O-ring.

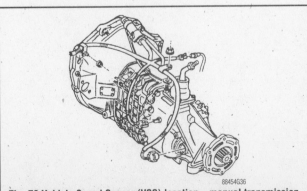

Fig. 78 Vehicle Speed Sensor (VSS) location—manual transmission equipped vehicles

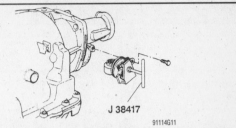

Fig. 79 On models with a automatic transmission, use tool J 38417 or its equivalent to remove/install the VSS

To install:

6. Coat the new O-ring with transmission fluid.
7. On models with a automatic transmission, attach VSS removal/installation tool J 38417 or its equivalent to the sensor.
8. Install the sensor with a new gasket or O-ring.
9. On models with a automatic transmission, remove VSS removal/installation tool J 38417 or its equivalent from the sensor.
10. Fasten the sensor retainers.
11. Engage the electrical connections.
12. Connect the negative battery cable.

Knock Sensor

OPERATION

Located in the engine block, the knock sensor retards ignition timing during a spark knock condition to allow the VCM to maintain maximum timing advance under most conditions.

TESTING

▶ See Figure 80

1. Connect a timing light to the vehicle and start the engine.
2. Check that the timing is correct before testing knock sensor operation.
3. If timing is correct, tap on the front of the engine block with a metal object while observing the timing to see if the timing retards.
4. If the timing does not retard the knock sensor may be defective.

REMOVAL & INSTALLATION

1. Disconnect the negative battery cable.
2. Disengage the wiring harness connector from the knock sensor.
3. Remove the knock sensor from the engine block.

To install:

4. Apply a water base caulk to the knock sensor threads and install the sensor in the engine block.

❊❊ WARNING

Do not use silicon tape to coat the knock sensor threads as this will insulate the sensor from the engine block.

5. Engage the wiring harness connector.
6. Connect the negative battery cable.

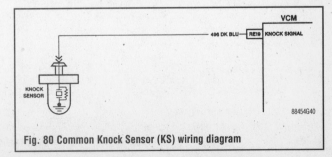

Fig. 80 Common Knock Sensor (KS) wiring diagram

COMPONENT LOCATIONS

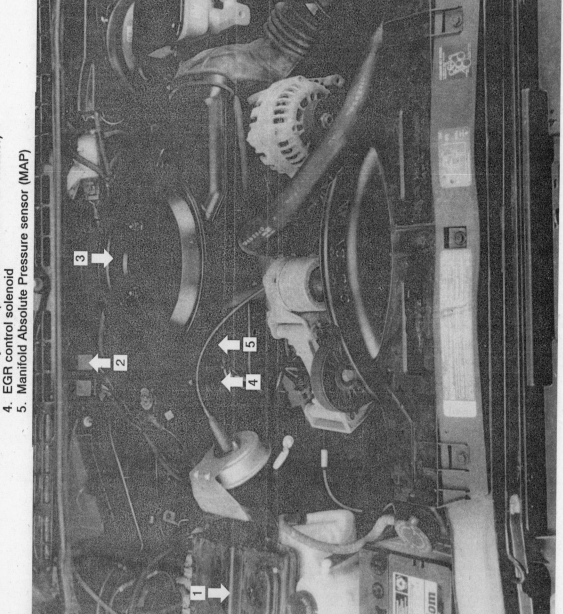

ENGINE ELECTRONIC COMPONENT LOCATIONS—4.3L TBI ENGINE

1. Powertrain Control Module (PCM)
2. Relays
3. Fuel injectors (located under the air cleaner)
4. EGR control solenoid
5. Manifold Absolute Pressure sensor (MAP)

ENGINE ELECTRONIC COMPONENT LOCATIONS—4.3L CSFI ENGINE

1. Powertrain Control Module (PCM)
2. Relays
3. Intake Air Temperature Sensor (IAT)
4. Mass Airflow Sensor (MAF)
5. EGR solenoid
6. Idle Air Control (IAC)
7. Ignition control module
8. Camshaft position sensor (located in the distributor)
9. Fuel injectors (located under the air cleaner)

88454PX2

ENGINE ELECTRONIC EMISSION COMPONENT LOCATIONS—2.2L MFI MODELS

1. Exhaust Gas Recirculation (EGR) valve
2. Intake Air Temperature (IAT) sensor
3. Powertrain Control Module (PCM)
4. Manifold Absolute Pressure (MAP) sensor
5. Idle Air Control (IAC) valve
6. Throttle Position (TP) sensor

ENGINE ELECTRONIC EMISSION COMPONENT LOCATIONS—4.3L CSFI MODELS

1. Camshaft Position (CMP) sensor (located in the distributor)
2. Throttle Position (TP) sensor
3. Idle Air Control (IAC) valve
4. Mass Air Flow (MAF) sensor
5. Exhaust Gas Recirculation (EGR) valve
6. Ignition Control Module (ICM)
7. Vehicle Control Module (VCM)
8. Throttle body assembly

91114PA3

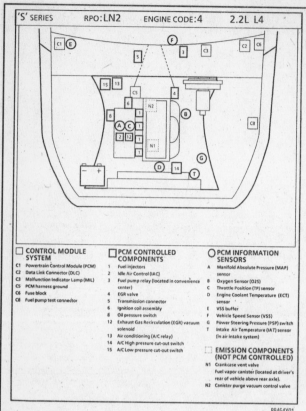

Fig. 81 Component locations—1994 2.2L (VIN 4) engine with automatic and manual transmissions

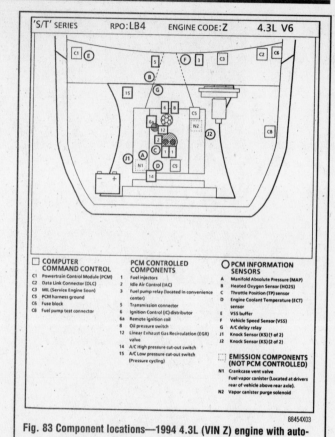

Fig. 83 Component locations—1994 4.3L (VIN Z) engine with automatic transmission (California emissions)

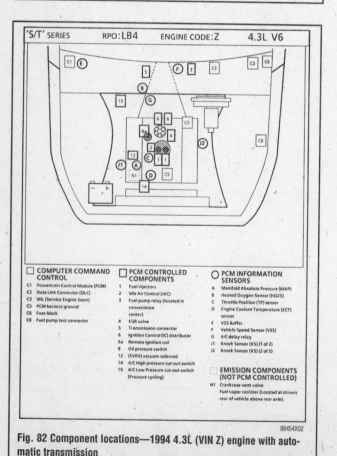

Fig. 82 Component locations—1994 4.3L (VIN Z) engine with automatic transmission

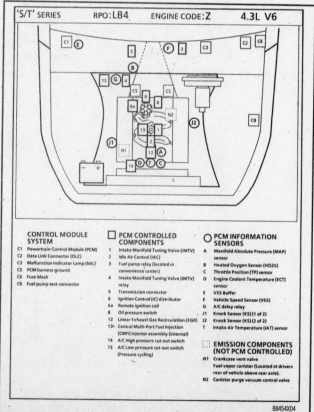

Fig. 84 Component locations—1994 4.3L (VIN W) engine with automatic transmission

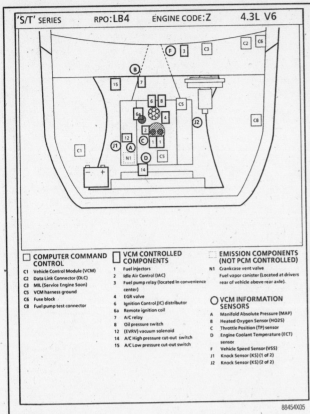

'S/T' SERIES RPO: LB4 ENGINE CODE: Z 4.3L V6

☐ COMPUTER COMMAND CONTROL

C1 Vehicle Control Module (VCM)
C2 Data Link Connector (DLC)
C3 MIL (Service Engine Soon)
C5 VCM harness ground
C6 Fuse block
C8 Fuel pump test connector

☐ VCM CONTROLLED COMPONENTS

1 Fuel injectors
2 Idle Air Control (IAC)
3 Fuel pump relay (located in convenience center)
4 EGR valve
5 Ignition Control (IC) distributor
6a Remote ignition coil
7 A/C relay
8 Oil pressure switch
12 (EVRV) vacuum solenoid
14 A/C High pressure cut-out switch
15 A/C Low pressure cut-out switch

○ VCM INFORMATION SENSORS

A Manifold Absolute Pressure (MAP) sensor
B Heated Oxygen Sensor (HO2S)
C Throttle Position (TP) sensor
D Engine Coolant Temperature (ECT) sensor
F Vehicle Speed Sensor (VSS)
J1 Knock Sensor (KS) (1 of 2)
J2 Knock Sensor (KS) (2 of 2)

⬚ EMISSION COMPONENTS (NOT PCM CONTROLLED)

N1 Crankcase vent valve
Fuel vapor canister (Located at drivers rear of vehicle above rear axle).

88454X05

Fig. 85 Component locations—1994 4.3L (VIN Z) engine with manual transmission

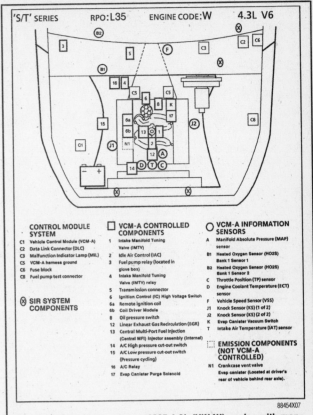

'S/T' SERIES RPO: L35 ENGINE CODE: W 4.3L V6

☐ CONTROL MODULE SYSTEM

C1 Vehicle Control Module (VCM-A)
C2 Data Link Connector (DLC)
C3 Malfunction Indicator Lamp (MIL)
C5 VCM-A harness ground
C6 Fuse block
C8 Fuel pump test connector

⊗ SIR SYSTEM COMPONENTS

☐ VCM-A CONTROLLED COMPONENTS

1 Intake Manifold Tuning Valve (IMTV)
2 Idle Air Control (IAC)
3 Fuel pump relay (located in glove box)
4 Intake Manifold Tuning Valve (IMTV) relay
5 Transmission connector
6 Ignition Control (IC) High Voltage Switch
6a Remote ignition coil
6b Coil Driver Module
8 Oil pressure switch
12 Linear Exhaust Gas Recirculation (EGR)
13 Central Multi-Port Fuel Injection (Central MFI) injector assembly (internal)
14 A/C High pressure cut-out switch
15 A/C Low pressure cut-out switch (Pressure cycling)
16 A/C Relay
17 Evap Canister Purge Solenoid

○ VCM-A INFORMATION SENSORS

A Manifold Absolute Pressure (MAP) sensor
B1 Heated Oxygen Sensor (HO2S) Bank 1 Sensor 1
B2 Heated Oxygen Sensor (HO2S) Bank 1 Sensor 2
C Throttle Position (TP) sensor
D Engine Coolant Temperature (ECT) sensor
F Vehicle Speed Sensor (VSS)
J1 Knock Sensor (KS) (1 of 2)
J2 Knock Sensor (KS) (2 of 2)
K Evap Canister Vacuum Switch
T Intake Air Temperature (IAT) sensor

⬚ EMISSION COMPONENTS (NOT VCM-A CONTROLLED)

N1 Crankcase vent valve
Evap canister (Located at driver's rear of vehicle behind rear axle).

88454X07

Fig. 87 Component locations—1995 4.3L (VIN W) engine with manual transmission

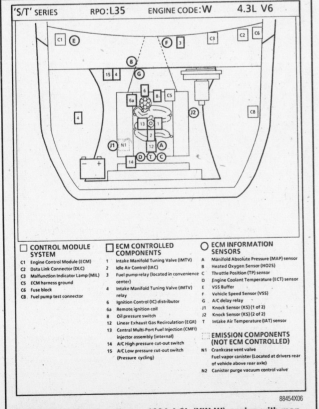

'S/T' SERIES RPO: L35 ENGINE CODE: W 4.3L V6

☐ CONTROL MODULE SYSTEM

C1 Engine Control Module (ECM)
C2 Data Link Connector (DLC)
C3 Malfunction Indicator Lamp (MIL)
C5 ECM harness ground
C6 Fuse block
C8 Fuel pump test connector

☐ ECM CONTROLLED COMPONENTS

1 Intake Manifold Tuning Valve (IMTV)
2 Idle Air Control (IAC)
3 Fuel pump relay (located in convenience center)
4 Intake Manifold Tuning Valve (IMTV) relay
6 Ignition Control (IC) distributor
6a Remote ignition coil
8 Oil pressure switch
12 Linear Exhaust Gas Recirculation (EGR)
13 Central Multi-Port Fuel Injection (CMFI) injector assembly (internal)
14 A/C High pressure cut-out switch
15 A/C Low pressure cut-out switch (Pressure cycling)

○ ECM INFORMATION SENSORS

A Manifold Absolute Pressure (MAP) sensor
B Heated Oxygen Sensor (HO2S)
C Throttle Position (TP) sensor
D Engine Coolant Temperature (ECT) sensor
E VSS Buffer
F Vehicle Speed Sensor (VSS)
G A/C delay relay
J1 Knock Sensor (KS) (1 of 2)
J2 Knock Sensor (KS) (2 of 2)
T Intake Air Temperature (IAT) sensor

⬚ EMISSION COMPONENTS (NOT ECM CONTROLLED)

N1 Crankcase vent valve
Fuel vapor canister (Located at drivers rear of vehicle above rear axle)
N2 Canister purge vacuum control valve

88454X06

Fig. 86 Component locations—1994 4.3L (VIN W) engine with manual transmission

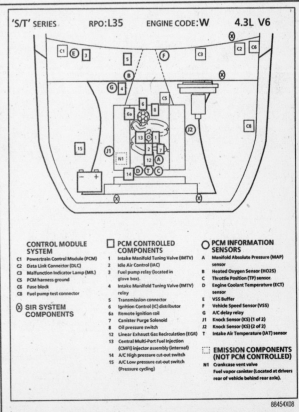

'S/T' SERIES RPO: L35 ENGINE CODE: W 4.3L V6

☐ CONTROL MODULE SYSTEM

C1 Powertrain Control Module (PCM)
C2 Data Link Connector (DLC)
C3 Malfunction Indicator Lamp (MIL)
C5 PCM harness ground
C6 Fuse block
C8 Fuel pump test connector

⊗ SIR SYSTEM COMPONENTS

☐ PCM CONTROLLED COMPONENTS

1 Intake Manifold Tuning Valve (IMTV)
2 Idle Air Control (IAC)
3 Fuel pump relay (located in glove box)
4 Intake Manifold Tuning Valve (IMTV) relay
5 Transmission connector
6 Ignition Control (IC) distributor
6a Remote ignition coil
7 Canister Purge Solenoid
8 Oil pressure switch
12 Linear Exhaust Gas Recirculation (EGR)
13 Central Multi-Port Fuel Injection (CMFI) injector assembly (internal)
14 A/C High pressure cut-out switch
15 A/C Low pressure cut-out switch (Pressure cycling)

○ PCM INFORMATION SENSORS

A Manifold Absolute Pressure (MAP) sensor
B Heated Oxygen Sensor (HO2S)
C Throttle Position (TP) sensor
D Engine Coolant Temperature (ECT) sensor
E VSS Buffer
F Vehicle Speed Sensor (VSS)
G A/C delay relay
J1 Knock Sensor (KS) (1 of 2)
J2 Knock Sensor (KS) (2 of 2)
T Intake Air Temperature (IAT) sensor

⬚ EMISSION COMPONENTS (NOT PCM CONTROLLED)

N1 Crankcase vent valve
Fuel vapor canister (Located at drivers rear of vehicle behind rear axle).

88454X08

Fig. 88 Component locations—1995 4.3L (VIN W) engine with automatic transmission

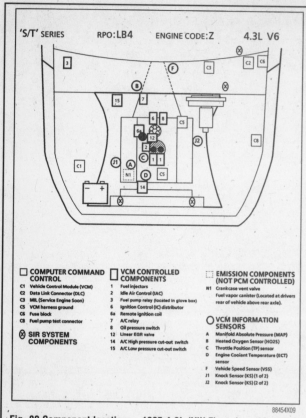

'S/T' SERIES   RPO:LB4   ENGINE CODE:Z   4.3L V6

COMPUTER COMMAND CONTROL
C1 Vehicle Control Module (VCM)
C2 Data Link Connector (DLC)
C3 MIL (Service Engine Soon)
C5 VCM harness ground
C6 Fuse block
C8 Fuel pump test connector

SIR SYSTEM COMPONENTS

VCM CONTROLLED COMPONENTS
1 Fuel injectors
2 Idle Air Control (IAC)
3 Fuel pump relay (located in glove box)
6 Ignition Control (IC) distributor
6a Remote ignition coil
7 A/C relay
8 Oil pressure switch
12 Linear EGR valve
14 A/C High pressure cut-out switch
15 A/C Low pressure cut-out switch

EMISSION COMPONENTS (NOT PCM CONTROLLED)
N1 Crankcase vent valve
    Fuel vapor canister (Located at drivers rear of vehicle above rear axle)

VCM INFORMATION SENSORS
A Manifold Absolute Pressure (MAP)
B Heated Oxygen Sensor (HO2S)
C Throttle Position (TP) sensor
D Engine Coolant Temperature (ECT) sensor
F Vehicle Speed Sensor (VSS)
J1 Knock Sensor (KS) (1 of 2)
J2 Knock Sensor (KS) (2 of 2)

88454X09

Fig. 89 Component locations—1995 4.3L (VIN Z) engine with manual transmission

'S/T' SERIES   RPO:LB4   ENGINE CODE:Z   4.3L V6

COMPUTER COMMAND CONTROL
C1 Powertrain Control Module (PCM)
C2 Data Link Connector (DLC)
C3 MIL (Service Engine Soon)
C5 PCM harness ground
C6 Fuse block
C8 Fuel pump test connector

SIR SYSTEM COMPONENTS

PCM CONTROLLED COMPONENTS
1 Fuel injectors
2 Idle Air Control (IAC)
3 Fuel pump relay (located in glove box)
5 Transmission connector
6 Ignition Control (IC) distributor
6a Remote ignition coil
8 Oil pressure switch
12 Linear Exhaust Gas Recirculation (EGR) valve
14 A/C High pressure cut-out switch
15 A/C Low pressure cut-out switch (Pressure cycling)
16 A/C delay relay
17 Evap canister purge solenoid

PCM INFORMATION SENSORS
A Manifold Absolute Pressure (MAP)
B Heated Oxygen Sensor (HO2S)
C Throttle Position (TP) sensor
D Engine Coolant Temperature (ECT) sensor
E VSS buffer
F Vehicle Speed Sensor (VSS)
J1 Knock Sensor (KS) (1 of 2)
J2 Knock Sensor (KS) (2 of 2)

EMISSION COMPONENTS (NOT PCM CONTROLLED)
N1 Crankcase vent valve
    Evap canister (Located at drivers rear of vehicle above rear axle).

88454X10

Fig. 90 Component locations—1995 4.3L (VIN Z) engine with automatic transmission

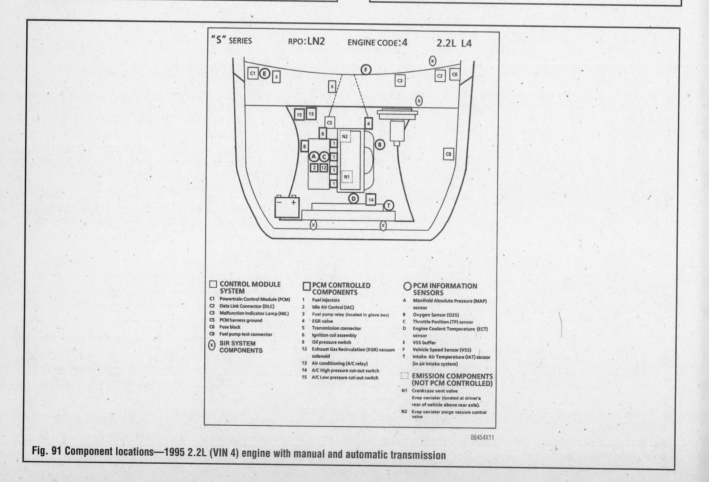

"S" SERIES   RPO:LN2   ENGINE CODE:4   2.2L L4

CONTROL MODULE SYSTEM
C1 Powertrain Control Module (PCM)
C2 Data Link Connector (DLC)
C3 Malfunction Indicator Lamp (MIL)
C5 PCM harness ground
C6 Fuse block
C8 Fuel pump test connector

SIR SYSTEM COMPONENTS

PCM CONTROLLED COMPONENTS
1 Fuel injectors
2 Idle Air Control (IAC)
3 Fuel pump relay (located in glove box)
4 EGR valve
5 Transmission connector
6 Ignition coil assembly
8 Oil pressure switch
12 Exhaust Gas Recirculation (EGR) vacuum solenoid
13 Air conditioning (A/C relay)
14 A/C High pressure cut-out switch
15 A/C Low pressure cut-out switch

PCM INFORMATION SENSORS
A Manifold Absolute Pressure (MAP) sensor
B Oxygen Sensor (O2S)
C Throttle Position (TP) sensor
D Engine Coolant Temperature (ECT) sensor
E VSS buffer
F Vehicle Speed Sensor (VSS)
T Intake Air Temperature (IAT) sensor (in air intake system)

EMISSION COMPONENTS (NOT PCM CONTROLLED)
N1 Crankcase vent valve
    Evap canister (located at driver's rear of vehicle above rear axle).
N2 Evap canister purge vacuum control valve

88454X11

Fig. 91 Component locations—1995 2.2L (VIN 4) engine with manual and automatic transmission

TROUBLE CODES

General Information

Since the control module is programmed to recognize the presence and value of electrical inputs, it will also note the lack of a signal or a radical change in values. It will, for example, react to the loss of signal from the vehicle speed sensor or note that engine coolant temperature has risen beyond acceptable (programmed) limits. Once a fault is recognized, a numeric code is assigned and held in memory. The dashboard warning lamp: CHECK ENGINE or SERVICE ENGINE SOON (SES), will illuminate to advise the operator that the system has detected a fault. This lamp is also known as the Malfunction Indicator Lamp (MIL).

More than one code may be stored. Keep in mind not every engine uses every code. Additionally, the same code may carry different meanings relative to each engine or engine family.

In the event of an computer control module failure, the system will default to a pre-programmed set of values. These are compromise values which allow the engine to operate, although possibly at reduced efficiency. This is variously known as the default, limp-in or back-up mode. Driveability is almost always affected when the VCM enters this mode.

SCAN TOOLS

▶ See Figures 92 and 93

On 1994 and some 1995 models, the stored codes may be read with only the use of a small jumper wire, however the use of a hand-held scan tool such as GM's TECH-1® or equivalent is recommended. On some 1995 and all 1996–99 models, an OBD-II compliant scan tool must be used. There are many manufacturers of these tools; a purchaser must be certain that the tool is proper for the intended use. If you own a scan type tool, it probably came with comprehensive instructions on proper use. Be sure to follow the instructions that came with your unit if they differ from what is given here; this is a general guide with useful information included.

The scan tool allows any stored codes to be read from the VCM or PCM memory. The tool also allows the operator to view the data being sent to the computer control module while the engine is running. This ability has obvious diagnostic advantages; the use of the scan tool is frequently required for component testing. The scan tool makes collecting information easier; the data must be correctly interpreted by an operator familiar with the system.

An example of the usefulness of the scan tool may be seen in the case of a temperature sensor which has changed its electrical characteristics. The VCM is reacting to an apparently warmer engine (causing a driveability problem), but the sensor's voltage has not changed enough to set a fault code. Connecting the scan tool, the voltage signal being sent to the VCM may be viewed; comparison to normal values or a known good vehicle reveals the problem quickly.

Fig. 92 Some inexpensive scan tools, such as the Auto Xray®, can interface with GM vehicles

"SCAN" Position	Units Displayed	Typical Data Value
Engine Speed	Rpm	± 50 RPM from desired rpm in drive (A/T) ± 100 RPM from desired rpm in neutral (M/T)
Desired Idle	Rpm	ECM idle command (varies with temp.)
Coolant Temperature	Degrees Celsius	85° - 105°
IAT/MAT	Degrees Celsius	10° - 90° (varies with underhood temp. and sensor location)
MAP	kPa/Volts	29-48 kPa/1 - 2 volts (varies with manifold and barometric pressures)
Open/Closed Loop	Open/Closed	"Closed Loop" (may enter "Open Loop" with extended idle)
Throt Position	Volts	.30 - 1.33
Throttle Angle	0 - 100%	0
Oxygen Sensor	Millivolts	100 - 999 (varies continuously)
Inj. Pulse Width	Milliseconds	.8 - 3.0
Spark Advance	Degrees	Varies
Engine Speed	Rpm	± 50 RPM from desired rpm in drive (A/T) ± 100 RPM from desired rpm in neutral (M/T)
Fuel Integrator	Counts	110-145
Block Learn	Counts	118-138
Idle Air Control	Counts (steps)	1 - 50
P/N Switch	P-N and R-D-L	Park/Neutral (P/N)
MPH/KPH	0-255	0
TCC	"ON"/"OFF"	"OFF"
Crank Rpm	Rpm	) 796
Ign/Batt Voltage	Volts	13.5 - 14.5
Cooling Fan Relay	"ON"/"OFF"	"OFF" (coolant temperature below 102°C)
A/C Request	"YES"/"NO"	No
A/C Clutch	"ON"/"OFF"	"OFF"
Power Steering	Normal/High Pressure	Normal
Shift Light (M/T)	"ON"/"OFF"	"OFF"

88454G42

Fig. 93 Example of scan tool data and typical or baseline values

ELECTRICAL TOOLS

The most commonly required electrical diagnostic tool is the digital multimeter, allowing voltage, ohmage (resistance) and amperage to be read by one instrument. The multimeter must be a high-impedance unit, with 10 megohms of impedance in the voltmeter. This type of meter will not place an additional load on the circuit it is testing; this is extremely important in low voltage circuits. The multimeter must be of high quality in all respects. It should be handled carefully and protected from impact or damage. Replace batteries frequently in the unit.

Other necessary tools include an unpowered test light, a quality tachometer with an inductive (clip-on) pick up, and the proper tools for releasing GM's Metri-Pack, Weather Pack and Micro-Pack terminals as necessary. The Micro-Pack connectors are used at the VCM electrical connector. A vacuum pump/gauge may also be required for checking sensors, solenoids and valves.

Diagnosis and Testing

Diagnosis of a driveablility and/or emissions problems requires attention to detail and following the diagnostic procedures in the correct order. Resist the temptation to perform any repairs before performing the preliminary diagnostic steps. In many cases this will shorten diagnostic time and often cure the problem without electronic testing.

The proper troubleshooting procedure for these vehicles is as follows:

VISUAL/PHYSICAL INSPECTION

This is possibly the most critical step of diagnosis and should be performed immediately after retrieving any codes. A detailed examination of connectors, wiring and vacuum hoses can often lead to a repair without further diagnosis. Performance of this step relies on the skill of the technician performing it; a careful inspector will check the undersides of hoses as well as the integrity of hard-to-reach hoses blocked by the air cleaner or other component. Wiring should be checked carefully for any sign of strain, burning, crimping, or terminal pull-out from a connector. Checking connectors at components or in harnesses is required; usually, pushing them together will reveal a loose fit.

TCCS4P12

INTERMITTENTS

If a fault occurs intermittently, such as a loose connector pin breaking contact as the vehicle hits a bump, the VCM will note the fault as it occurs and energize the dash warning lamp. If the problem self-corrects, as with the terminal pin again making contact, the dash lamp will extinguish after 10 seconds but a code will remain stored in the computer control module's memory.

When an unexpected code appears during diagnostics, it may have been set during an intermittent failure that self-corrected; the codes are still useful in diagnosis and should not be discounted.

CIRCUIT/COMPONENT REPAIR

The fault codes and the scan tool data will lead to diagnosis and checking of a particular circuit. It is important to note that the fault code indicates a fault or loss of signal in an VCM-controlled system, not necessarily in the specific component.

Refer to the appropriate Diagnostic Code chart to determine the codes meaning. The component may then be tested following the appropriate component test procedures found in this section. If the component is OK, check the wiring for shorts or opens. Further diagnoses should be left to an experienced driveability technician.

If a code indicates the VCM to be faulty and the VCM is replaced, but does not correct the problem, one of the following may be the reason:

• There is a problem with the VCM terminal connections: The terminals may have to be removed from the connector in order to check them properly.

• The VCM or PROM is not correct for the application: The incorrect VCM or PROM may cause a malfunction and may or may not set a code.

• The problem is intermittent: This means that the problem is not present at the time the system is being checked. In this case, make a careful physical inspection of all portions of the system involved.

• Shorted solenoid, relay coil or harness: Solenoids and relays are turned on and off by the VCM using internal electronic switches called drivers. Each driver is part of a group of four called Quad-Drivers. A shorted solenoid, relay coil or harness may cause an VCM to fail, and a replacement VCM to fail when it is installed. Use a short tester, J34696, BT 8405, or equivalent, as a fast, accurate means of checking for a short circuit.

• The Programmable Read Only Memory (PROM) may be faulty: Although the PROM rarely fails, it operates as part of the VCM. Therefore, it could be the cause of the problem. Substitute a known good PROM.

• The replacement VCM may be faulty: After the VCM is replaced, the system should be rechecked for proper operation. If the diagnostic code again indicates the VCM is the problem, substitute a known good VCM. Although this is a very rare condition, it could happen.

Reading Codes

OBD I SYSTEMS

▶ **See Figures 94 thru 101**

Listings of the trouble for the various engine control system covered in this manual are located in this section. Remember that a code only points to the faulty circuit NOT necessarily to a faulty component. Loose, damaged or corroded connections may contribute to a fault code on a circuit when the sensor or component is operating properly. Be sure that the components are faulty before replacing them, especially the expensive ones.

The Assembly Line Diagnostic Link (ALDL) connector or Data Link Connector (DLC) may be located under the dash and sometimes covered with a plastic cover labeled DIAGNOSTIC CONNECTOR.

1. On all 1994 models the diagnostic trouble codes can be read by grounding test terminal **B**. The terminal is most easily grounded by connecting it to terminal **A** (internal ECM ground). This is the terminal to the right of terminal B on the top row of the ALDL connector.

2. Only 1995 models equipped with a PCM use the OBD I system. All other 1995 and later models use the OBD II system. The diagnostic trouble codes on 1995 OBD I systems can be read by grounding test terminal **6**. The terminal is most easily grounded by connecting it to terminal **5** (internal ECM ground).

3. Once the terminals have been connected, the ignition switch must be moved to the **ON** position with the engine not running.

4. The Service Engine Soon or Check Engine light should be flashing. If it isn't, turn the ignition **OFF** and remove the jumper wire. Turn the ignition **ON** and confirm that light is now on. If it is not, replace the bulb and try again. If the bulb still will not light, or if it does not flash with the test terminal grounded, the system should be diagnosed by an experienced driveability technician. If the light is OK, proceed as follows.

5. The code(s) stored in memory may be read through counting the flashes of the dashboard warning lamp. The dash warning lamp should begin to flash Code 12. The code will display as one flash, a pause and two flashes. Code 12 is not a fault code. It is used as a system acknowledgment or handshake code; its presence indicates that the VCM can communicate as requested. Code 12 is used to begin every diagnostic sequence. Some vehicles also use Code 12 after all diagnostic codes have been sent.

6. After Code 12 has been transmitted 3 times, the fault codes, if any, will each be transmitted 3 times. The codes are stored and transmitted in numeric order from lowest to highest.

➡ **The order of codes in the memory does not indicate the order of occurrence.**

7. If there are no codes stored, but a driveability or emissions problem is evident, the system should be diagnosed by an experienced driveability technician.

8. If one or more codes are stored, record them. Refer to the applicable Diagnostic Code chart in this section.

9. Switch the ignition **OFF** when finished with code retrieval or scan tool readings.

➡ **After making repairs, clear the trouble codes and operate the vehicle to see if it will reset, indicating further problems.**

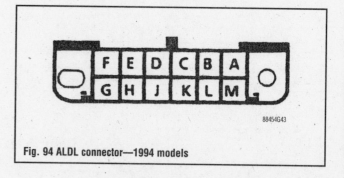

88454G43

Fig. 94 ALDL connector—1994 models

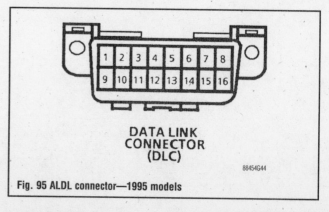

DATA LINK CONNECTOR (DLC)

88454G44

Fig. 95 ALDL connector—1995 models

DTC	DESCRIPTION
13	Oxygen Sensor (02S) Circuit (Open Circuit)
14	Engine Coolant Temperature (ECT) Sensor Circuit (High Temperature Indicated)
15	Engine Coolant Temperature (ECT) Sensor Circuit (Low Temperature Indicated)
21	Throttle Position (TP) Sensor Circuit (Signal Voltage High)
22	Throttle Position (TP) Sensor Circuit (Signal Voltage Low)
23	Intake Air Temperature (IAT) Sensor Circuit (Low Temperature Indicated)
24	Vehicle Speed Sensor (VSS)
25	Intake Air Temperature (IAT) Sensor Circuit (High Temperature Indicated)
32	Exhaust Gas Recirculation (EGR) System
33	Manifold Absolute Pressure (MAP) Sensor Circuit (Signal Voltage High-Low Vacuum)
34	Manifold Absolute Pressure (MAP) Sensor Circuit (Signal Voltage Low-High Vacuum)
35	Idle Air Control (IAC) System
42	Ignition Control (IC)
43	Knock Sensor (KS) Circuit
44	Oxygen Sensor (02S) Circuit (Lean Exhaust Indicated)
45	Oxygen Sensor (02S) Circuit (Rich Exhaust Indicated)
51	Faulty PROM (CAL-PAK)
53	System Over Voltage
54	Fuel Pump Circuit (Low Voltage)
55	Faulty ECM

88454G50

Fig. 96 DTC chart for 1994 ECM models

DTC	DESCRIPTION
13	Oxygen 02S Sensor Circuit (Open Circuit)
14	Engine Coolant Temperature (ECT) Sensor Circuit Low (High Temperature Indicated)
15	Engine Coolant Temperature (ECT) Sensor Circuit High (Low Temperature Indicated)
16	Vehicle Speed Signal (VSS) Buffer Fault (Vehicle Speed Signal)
21	Throttle Position (TP) Sensor Circuit High (Signal Voltage High)
22	Throttle Position (TP) Sensor Circuit Low (Signal Voltage Low)
23	Intake Air Temperature (IAT) Sensor Circuit High (Low Temperature Indicated)
24	Vehicle Speed Sensor (VSS) Circuit Low (Trans Output Speed Signal)
25	Intake Air Temperature (IAT) Sensor Circuit Low (High Temperature Indicated)
28	Transmission Range (TR) Pressure Switch Assembly
32	Exhaust Gas Recirculation (EGR) System
33	Manifold Absolute Pressure (MAP) Sensor Circuit High (Low Vacuum)
34	Manifold Absolute Pressure (MAP) Sensor Circuit Low (High Vacuum)
35	IAC Error
37	Brake Switch Stuck "ON"
38	Brake Switch Stuck "OFF"
41	IX Signal Error
42	Ignition Control (IC) Error
43	Knock Sensor (KS) Circuit
44	Lean Exhaust
45	Rich Exhaust
51	PROM Error (MEL-CAL)
52	System Voltage High Long
53	System Voltage High
54	Fuel Pump Relay Circuit (Low Voltage)
55	Faulty PCM
58	Transmission Fluid Temperature (TFT) Sensor Circuit Low (High Temperature Indicated)
59	Transmission Fluid Temperature (TFT) Sensor Circuit High (Low Temperature Indicated)
66	3-2 Control Solenoid Circuit Fault
67	Torque Converter Clutch (TCC) Solenoid Circuit Fault
69	Torque Converter Clutch (TCC) Stuck "ON"
72	Vehicle Speed Sensor (VSS) Circuit Loss (Trans Output Speed Signal)
73	Pressure Control Solenoid (PCS) Fault (Current Error)
75	System Voltage Low
79	Transmission Fluid Over Temp
81	2-3 Shift Solenoid Circuit Fault
82	1-2 Shift Solenoid Circuit Fault

88454G51

Fig. 97 DTC chart for 1994 PCM models

DTC	DESCRIPTION
P0107	Manifold Absolute Pressure (MAP) Sensor Circuit (Signal Voltage Low-High Vacuum)
P0108	Manifold Absolute Pressure (MAP) Sensor Circuit (Signal Voltage High-Low Vacuum)
P0117	Engine Coolant Temperature (ECT) Sensor Circuit High (Low Temperature Indicated)
P0118	Engine Coolant Temperature (ECT) Sensor Circuit Low (High Temperature Indicated)
P0122	Throttle Position (TP) Sensor Circuit Low (Signal Voltage Low)
P0123	Throttle Position (TP) Sensor Circuit High (Signal Voltage High)
P0139	Heated Oxygen Sensor (H02S) Circuit (Open Circuit)
P0171	Lean Exhaust
P0172	Rich Exhaust
P0320	Ignition Control (IC) Error
P0327	Knock Sensor (KS) Circuit Grounded
P0328	Knock Sensor (KS) Circuit Open
P0400	Exhaust Gas Recirculation (EGR) Error
P0500	Vehicle Speed Sensor (VSS) Error
P1222	Fuel Pump Relay Circuit (Low Voltage)
P1632	System Voltage High

88454G52

Fig. 98 DTC chart for 1994—95 VCM models

DTC	DESCRIPTION
13	Oxygen O2S Sensor Circuit (Open Circuit)
14	Engine Coolant Temperature (ECT) Sensor Circuit Low (High Temperature Indicated)
15	Engine Coolant Temperature (ECT) Sensor Circuit High (Low Temperature Indicated)
16	Vehicle Speed Signal (VSS) Buffer Fault (Vehicle Speed Signal)
21	Throttle Position (TP) Sensor Circuit High (Signal Voltage High)
22	Throttle Position (TP) Sensor Circuit Low (Signal Voltage Low)
23	Intake Air Temperature (IAT) Sensor Circuit High (Low Temperature Indicated)
24	Vehicle Speed Sensor (VSS) Circuit Low (Trans Output Speed Signal)
25	Intake Air Temperature (IAT) Sensor Circuit Low (High Temperature Indicated)
28	Transmission Range (TR) Pressure Switch Assembly
32	Exhaust Gas Recirculation (EGR) System
33	Manifold Absolute Pressure (MAP) Sensor Circuit High (Low Vacuum)
34	Manifold Absolute Pressure (MAP) Sensor Circuit Low (High Vacuum)
35	IAC Error
37	Brake Switch Stuck "ON"
38	Brake Switch Stuck "OFF"
41	IX Signal Error
42	Ignition Control (IC) Error
43	Knock Sensor (KS) Circuit
44	Lean Exhaust
45	Rich Exhaust
51	PROM Error (MEL-CAL)
52	System Voltage High Long
53	System Voltage High
54	Fuel Pump Relay Circuit (Low Voltage)
55	Faulty PCM
58	Transmission Fluid Temperature (TFT) Sensor Circuit Low (High Temperature Indicated)
59	Transmission Fluid Temperature (TFT) Sensor Circuit High (Low Temperature Indicated)
66	3-2 Control Solenoid Circuit Fault
67	Torque Converter Clutch (TCC) Solenoid Circuit Fault
69	Torque Converter Clutch (TCC) Stuck "ON"
72	Vehicle Speed Sensor (VSS) Circuit Loss (Trans Output Speed Signal)
73	Pressure Control Solenoid (PCS) Fault (Current Error)
75	System Voltage Low
79	Transmission Fluid Over Temp
81	2-3 Shift Solenoid Circuit Fault
82	1-2 Shift Solenoid Circuit Fault
83	TCC PWM SOL

Fig. 99 DTC chart for 1995 PCM models

DTC	DESCRIPTION
P0106	Manifold Absolute Pressure (MAP) Sensor Circuit Range Problem
P0107	Manifold Absolute Pressure (MAP) Sensor Circuit - Low Input
P0108	Manifold Absolute Pressure (MAP) Sensor Circuit - High Input
P0112	Intake Air Temperature (IAT) Sensor Circuit - Low Input
P0113	Intake Air Temperature (IAT) Sensor Circuit - High Input
P0117	Engine Coolant Temperature (ECT) Sensor Circuit - Low Input
P0118	Engine Coolant Temperature (ECT) Sensor Circuit - High Input
P0121	Throttle Position (TP) Sensor Circuit Range/Performance Problem
P0122	Throttle Position (TP) Sensor Circuit - Low Input
P0123	Throttle Position (TP) Sensor Circuit - High Input
P0125	Engine Coolant Temperature (ECT) Sensor - Engine Coolant Temperature Excessive Time to "Closed Loop"
P0131	Heated Oxygen Sensor (HO2S 1) Circuit Low Voltage (Bank 1, Sensor 1)
P0132	Heated Oxygen Sensor (HO2S 1) Circuit High Voltage (Bank 1, Sensor 1)
P0133	HO2S Circuit Slow Response (Bank 1, Sensor 1)
P0134	Heated Oxygen Sensor (HO2S 1) Circuit No Activity Detected (Bank 1, Sensor 1)
P0135	HO2S Heater Circuit Malfunction (Bank 1, Sensor 1)
P0137	HO2S Circuit Low Voltage (Bank 1, Sensor 2) (Catalyst Monitor)
P0138	HO2S Circuit High Voltage (Bank 1, Sensor 2) (Catalyst Monitor)
P0140	Heated Oxygen Sensor (HO2S 2) Circuit - No Activity Detected (Bank 1, Sensor 2) (Catalyst Monitor)
P0141	HO2S Heater Malfunction (Bank 1, Sensor 2) (Catalyst Monitor)
P0171	System Too Lean (Bank 1, Sensor 1) (1 of 2)
P0172	System Too Rich (Bank 1, Sensor 1) (1 of 2)
P0300	Random Misfire Detected
P0301	Cylinder 1 Misfire Detected
P0302	Cylinder 2 Misfire Detected
P0303	Cylinder 3 Misfire Detected
P0304	Cylinder 4 Misfire Detected
P0305	Cylinder 5 Misfire Detected
P0306	Cylinder 6 Misfire Detected
P0325	Knock Sensor (KS) Circuit Short or Open
P0326	Knock Sensor (KS) Circuit Range/Rationality
P0337	Crankshaft Position Sensor Circuit - Low Input
P0338	Crankshaft Position Sensor Circuit - High Input
P0340	Camshaft Position Sensor Circuit Malfunction
P0341	Camshaft Position Sensor Circuit - Range/Rationality
P0401	Exhaust Gas Recirculation (EGR) Insufficient Flow Detected
P0420	Catalyst System - Efficiency Below Threshold (Bank 1)
P0441	Evaporative Emissions Control System Incorrect Purge Flow
P0500	Vehicle Speed Sensor (VSS) Error
P0506	Idle Speed Lower Than Expected
P0507	Idle Speed Higher Than Expected
P1106	Manifold Absolute Pressure (MAP) Sensor Circuit - Intermittent High Input
P1107	Manifold Absolute Pressure (MAP) Sensor Circuit - Intermittent Low Input
P1111	Intake Air Temperature (IAT) Circuit - Intermittent High Input
P1112	Intake Air Temperature (IAT) Circuit - Intermittent Low Input
P1114	Engine Coolant Temperature (ECT) Sensor Circuit - Intermittent Low Input
P1115	Engine Coolant Temperature (ECT) Sensor Circuit - Intermittent High Input
P1121	Throttle Position (TP) Sensor Circuit - Intermittent High Input
P1122	Throttle Position (TP) Sensor Circuit - Intermittent Low Input
P1133	HO2S System Fault - Too Few Rich/Lean or Lean/Rich Transitions, Insufficient Activity (Bank 1, Sensor 1)
P1221	Fuel Pump Secondary System Circuit Low

Fig. 100 DTC chart for 1995 VCM-A models

DTC	DESCRIPTION
P1345	Camshaft Sensor Misinstalled
P1351	EST Output High or Pulses Detected When Open
P1361	EST Not Toggling After Enable
P1406	Exhaust Gas Recirculation (EGR) System Pintle Position Error (1 of 2)
P1441	Evaporative Emissions System Continuous Open Purge Flow
P1442	Purge Solenoid Switch Static Test Malfunction
P1508	Idle Air Control Counts Low
P1509	Idle Air Control Counts High

88454G55

Fig. 101 DTC chart for 1995 VCM–A models

OBD II SYSTEMS

▶ **See Figures 102 thru 107**

All 1995 models not equipped with a PCM and all 1996–99 models, an OBD-II compliant scan tool must be used to retrieve the trouble codes. Follow the scan tool manufacturer's instructions on how to connect the scan tool to the vehicle and how to retrieve the codes.

The following is a list of trouble codes for the 1996–99 models with the OBD II system

P0101 Mass or Volume Air Flow Circuit Range/Performance Problem
P0102 Mass or Volume Air Flow Circuit Low Input
P0103 Mass or Volume Air Flow Circuit High Input
P0106 Manifold Absolute Pressure/Barometric Pressure Circuit Range/Performance Problem
P0107 Manifold Absolute Pressure/Barometric Pressure Circuit Low Input
P0108 Manifold Absolute Pressure/Barometric Pressure Circuit High Input
P0112 Intake Air Temperature Circuit Low Input
P0113 Intake Air Temperature Circuit High Input
P0117 Engine Coolant Temperature Circuit Low Input
P0118 Engine Coolant Temperature Circuit High Input
P0121 Throttle/Pedal Position Sensor/Switch "A" Circuit Range/Performance Problem
P0122 Throttle/Pedal Position Sensor/Switch "A" Circuit Low Input
P0123 Throttle/Pedal Position Sensor/Switch "A" Circuit High Input
P0125 Insufficient Coolant Temperature For Closed Loop Fuel Control
P0131 O2 Sensor Circuit Low Voltage (Bank no. 1 Sensor no. 1)
P0132 O2 Sensor Circuit High Voltage (Bank no. 1 Sensor no. 1)

P0133 O2 Sensor Circuit Slow Response (Bank no. 1 Sensor no. 1)
P0134 O2 Sensor Circuit No Activity Detected (Bank no. 1 Sensor no. 1)
P0135 O2 Sensor Heater Circuit Malfunction (Bank no. 1 Sensor no. 1)
P0137 O2 Sensor Circuit Low Voltage (Bank no. 1 Sensor no. 2)
P0138 O2 Sensor Circuit High Voltage (Bank no. 1 Sensor no. 2)
P0139 O2 Sensor Circuit Slow Response (Bank no. 1 Sensor no. 2)
P0140 O2 Sensor Circuit No Activity Detected (Bank no. 1 Sensor no. 2)
P0141 O2 Sensor Heater Circuit Malfunction (Bank no. 1 Sensor no. 2)
P0143 O2 Sensor Circuit Low Voltage (Bank no. 1 Sensor no. 3)
P0144 O2 Sensor Circuit High Voltage (Bank no. 1 Sensor no. 3)
P0146 O2 Sensor Circuit No Activity Detected (Bank no. 1 Sensor no. 3)
P0147 O2 Sensor Heater Circuit Malfunction (Bank no. 1 Sensor no. 3)
P0151 O2 Sensor Circuit Low Voltage (Bank no. 2 Sensor no. 1)
P0152 O2 Sensor Circuit High Voltage (Bank no. 2 Sensor no. 1)
P0153 O2 Sensor Circuit Slow Response (Bank no. 2 Sensor no. 1)
P0154 O2 Sensor Circuit No Activity Detected (Bank no. 2 Sensor no. 1)
P0155 O2 Sensor Heater Circuit Malfunction (Bank no. 2 Sensor no. 1)
P0171 System Too Lean (Bank no. 1)
P0172 System Too Rich (Bank no. 1)
P0174 System Too Lean (Bank no. 2)
P0175 System Too Rich (Bank no. 2)
P0200 Injector Circuit Malfunction
P0300 Random/Multiple Cylinder Misfire Detected
P0301 Cylinder no. 1—Misfire Detected
P0302 Cylinder no. 2—Misfire Detected
P0303 Cylinder no. 3—Misfire Detected
P0304 Cylinder no. 4—Misfire Detected
P0305 Cylinder no. 5—Misfire Detected

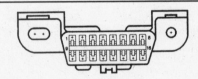

** Cavities which are not listed are not used.

CAVITY	WIRE COLOR	WIRE SIZE	CKT	DESCRIPTION
2	PPL	0.8	1807	SERIAL DATA SIGNAL - PRIMARY
4	BLK	0.8	150	GROUND
5	BLK/WHT	0.8	151	GROUND
8	BLK/WHT	0.8	1455	KEYLESS ENTRY PROGRAM ENABLE (EXCEPT BASE PICKUP)
9	TAN	0.8	800	SERIAL DATA SIGNAL - PRIMARY
12	TAN/WHT	0.8	799	ABS DIAGNOSTIC SIGNAL (PICKUP ONLY)
13	ORN	0.8	1568	TRANSFER CASE SHIFT CONTROL MODULE (W/ 4WD W/ ELECTRIC SHIFT NP1)
16	ORN	1	840	BATTERY - FUSED

88454G45

Fig. 102 ALDL connector—1996 models

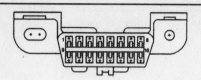

Connector Part Information	• 12110250 • 16 - Way F Metri-Pack 150 Series (Black)		
Pin	Wire Color	Circuit No.	Function
1	—	—	Not Used
2	PPL	1807	Serial data signal - Class II
3	—	—	Not Used
4	BLK	150	Ground
5	BLK/WHT	151	Ground
6	—	—	Not Used
7	—	—	Not Used
8	—	—	Not Used
9	TAN	800	Serial data signal - Primary (SIR)
10	—	—	Not Used
11	—	—	Not Used
12	TAN/WHT	799	Antilock Brake System diagnostic request
13	—	—	Not Used
14	—	—	Not Used
15	—	—	Not Used
16	ORN	840	Battery - fused

88454G46

Fig. 103 ALDL connector—1997–99 base pickup models

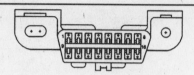

Connector Part Information	• 12110250 • 16 - Way F Metri-Pack 150 Series (Black)		
Pin	Wire Color	Circuit No.	Function
1	—	—	Not Used
2	PPL	1807	Serial data signal - Class II
3	—	—	Not Used
4	BLK	150	Ground
5	BLK/WHT	151	Ground
6	—	—	Not Used
7	—	—	Not Used
8	BLK/WHT	1455	Keyless entry program enable
9	TAN	800	Serial data signal - Primary (SIR)
10	—	—	Not Used
11	—	—	Not Used
12	TAN/WHT	799	Antilock Brake System diagnostic request
13	—	—	Not Used
14	—	—	Not Used
15	—	—	Not Used
16	ORN	840	Battery - fused

88454G48

Fig. 105 ALDL connector—1997–99 4.3L engines without electric shift 4WD

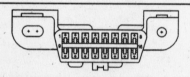

Connector Part Information	• 12110250 • 16 - Way F Metri-Pack 150 Series (Black)		
Pin	Wire Color	Circuit No.	Function
1	—	—	Not Used
2	PPL	1807	Serial data signal - Class II
3	—	—	Not Used
4	BLK	150	Ground
5	BLK/WHT	151	Ground
6	—	—	Not Used
7	—	—	Not Used
8	BLK/WHT	1455	Keyless entry program enable
9	TAN	800	Serial data signal - Primary (SIR)
10	—	—	Not Used
11	—	—	Not Used
12	TAN/WHT	799	Antilock Brake System diagnostic request
13	—	—	Not Used
14	—	—	Not Used
15	—	—	Not Used
16	ORN	840	Battery - fused

88454G47

Fig. 104 ALDL connector—1997–99 non-base pickup with 2.2L engine

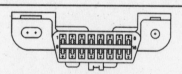

Connector Part Information	• 12110250 • 16 - Way F Metri-Pack 150 Series (Black)		
Pin	Wire Color	Circuit No.	Function
1	—	—	Not Used
2	PPL	1807	Serial data signal - Class II
3	—	—	Not Used
4	BLK	150	Ground
5	BLK/WHT	151	Ground
6	—	—	Not Used
7	—	—	Not Used
8	BLK/WHT	1455	Keyless entry program enable
9	TAN	800	Serial data signal - Primary (SIR)
10	—	—	Not Used
11	—	—	Not Used
12	TAN/WHT	799	Antilock Brake System diagnostic request
13	ORN	1568	Transfer Case Shift Control Module diagnostic request
14	—	—	Not Used
15	—	—	Not Used
16	ORN	840	Battery - fused

88454G49

Fig. 106 ALDL connector—1997–99 4.3L engines with electric shift 4WD

Fig. 107 The ALDL connector is usually located under the dash to the left of the steering column

P0306 Cylinder no. 6—Misfire Detected
P0325 Knock Sensor no. 1—Circuit Malfunction (Bank no. 1 or Single Sensor)
P0327 Knock Sensor no. 1—Circuit Low Input (Bank no. 1 or Single Sensor)
P0334 Knock Sensor no. 2—Circuit Input Intermittent (Bank no. 2)
P0335 Crankshaft Position Sensor "A" Circuit Malfunction
P0336 Crankshaft Position Sensor "A" Circuit Range/Performance
P0337 Crankshaft Position Sensor "A" Circuit Low Input
P0338 Crankshaft Position Sensor "A" Circuit High Input
P0339 Crankshaft Position Sensor "A" Circuit Intermittent
P0340 Camshaft Position Sensor Circuit Malfunction
P0341 Camshaft Position Sensor Circuit Range/Performance
P0342 Camshaft Position Sensor Circuit Low Input
P0401 Exhaust Gas Recirculation Flow Insufficient Detected
P0404 Exhaust Gas Recirculation Circuit Range/Performance
P0405 Exhaust Gas Recirculation Sensor "A" Circuit Low
P0420 Catalyst System Efficiency Below Threshold (Bank no. 1)
P0440 Evaporative Emission Control System Malfunction
P0442 Evaporative Emission Control System Leak Detected (Small Leak)
P0446 Evaporative Emission Control System Vent Control Circuit Malfunction
P0452 Evaporative Emission Control System Pressure Sensor Low Input
P0453 Evaporative Emission Control System Pressure Sensor High Input
P0460 Fuel Level Sensor Circuit Malfunction
P0461 Fuel Level Sensor Circuit Range/Performance
P0462 Fuel Level Sensor Circuit Low Input
P0463 Fuel Level Sensor Circuit High Input
P0500 Vehicle Speed Sensor Malfunction
P0502 Vehicle Speed Sensor Circuit Low Input
P0506 Idle Control System RPM Lower Than Expected
P0507 Idle Control System RPM Higher Than Expected
P0530 A/C Refrigerant Pressure Sensor Circuit Malfunction
P0562 System Voltage Low
P0563 System Voltage High
P0600 Serial Communication Link Malfunction
P0601 Internal Control Module Memory Check Sum Error
P0602 Control Module Programming Error
P0603 Internal Control Module Keep Alive Memory (KAM) Error
P0604 Internal Control Module Random Access Memory (RAM) Error

P0605 Internal Control Module Read Only Memory (ROM) Error
P0704 Clutch Switch Input Circuit Malfunction
P0705 Transmission Range Sensor Circuit Malfunction (PRNDL Input)
P1106 MAP Sensor Voltage Intermittently High
P1107 MAP Sensor Voltage Intermittently Low
P1111 IAT Sensor Circuit Intermittent High Voltage
P1112 IAT Sensor Circuit Intermittent Low Voltage
P1114 ECT Sensor Circuit Intermittent Low Voltage
P1115 ECT Sensor Circuit Intermittent High Voltage
P1121 TP Sensor Voltage Intermittently High
P1122 TP Sensor Voltage Intermittently Low
P1133 HO_2S Insufficient Switching Bank #1, Sensor #1
P1134 HO_2S Transition Time Ratio Bank #1, Sensor #1
P1153 HO_2S Insufficient Switching Sensor Bank #2, Sensor #1
P1154 HO_2S Transition Time Ratio Bank #2, Sensor #1
P1171 Fuel system lean during acceleration
P1336 CKP system variation not learned
P1345 Crankshaft/Camshaft (CKP/CMP) Correlation
P1351 Ignition Control (IC) Circuit High Voltage
P1361 Ignition Control (IC) Circuit Not Toggling
P1361 Ignition Control (IC) Circuit Low Voltage
P1374 3X Reference circuit
P1380 Electronic Brake Control Module (EBCM) DTC Detected Rough Road Data Unusable
P1381 Misfire Detected, No EBCM/PCM/VCM Serial Data
P1404 EGR valve closed pintle position
P1406 EGR Pintle Position Circuit Fault
P1441 EVAP Control System Flow During Non-Purge
P1508 IAC System Low RPM **P1509** IAC System High RPM
P1520 PNP Circuit
P1621 PCM memory performance
P1626 Theft deterrent system fuel enable CKT
P1631 Theft deterrent password incorrect
P1632 Theft deterrent system fuel disabled
U1000 No class 2 communication learned
U1026 Loss of ATCM communication
U1041 Loss of EBCM communication
U1064 Loss of TBC/BCM and/or VTD communication

Clearing Codes

Stored fault codes may be erased from memory at any time by removing power from the VCM for at least 30 seconds. It may be necessary to clear stored codes during diagnosis to check for any recurrence during a test drive, but the stored codes must be written down when retrieved. The codes may still be required for subsequent troubleshooting. Whenever a repair is complete, the stored codes must be erased and the vehicle test driven to confirm correct operation and repair.

✸✸ WARNING

The ignition switch must be OFF any time power is disconnected or restored to the VCM. Severe damage may result if this precaution is not observed.

Depending on the electrical distribution of the particular vehicle, power to the VCM may be disconnected by removing the VCM fuse in the fusebox, disconnecting the in-line fuse holder near the positive battery terminal or disconnecting the VCM power lead at the battery terminal. Disconnecting the negative battery cable to clear codes is not recommended as this will also clear other memory data in the vehicle such as radio presets.

VACUUM DIAGRAMS

Following is a listing of vacuum diagrams for many of the engine and emissions package combinations covered by this manual. Because vacuum circuits will vary based on various engine and vehicle options, always refer first to the vehicle emission control information label. Should the label be missing, or should the vehicle be equipped with a different engine from the original equipment, refer to the diagrams below for the same or similar configuration.

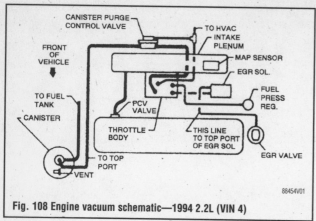

Fig. 108 Engine vacuum schematic—1994 2.2L (VIN 4)

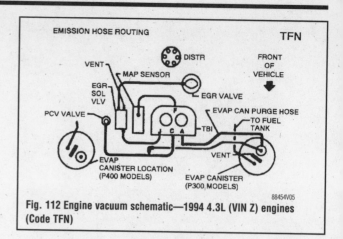

Fig. 112 Engine vacuum schematic—1994 4.3L (VIN Z) engines (Code TFN)

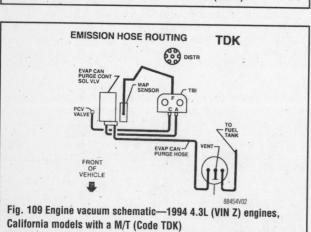

Fig. 109 Engine vacuum schematic—1994 4.3L (VIN Z) engines, California models with a M/T (Code TDK)

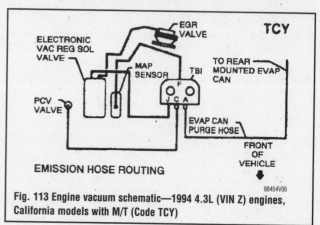

Fig. 113 Engine vacuum schematic—1994 4.3L (VIN Z) engines, California models with M/T (Code TCY)

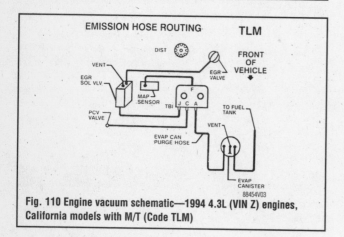

Fig. 110 Engine vacuum schematic—1994 4.3L (VIN Z) engines, California models with M/T (Code TLM)

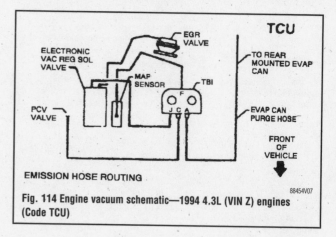

Fig. 114 Engine vacuum schematic—1994 4.3L (VIN Z) engines (Code TCU)

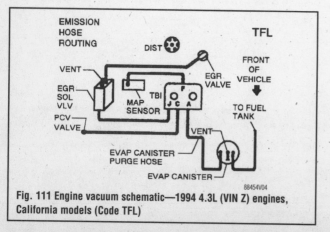

Fig. 111 Engine vacuum schematic—1994 4.3L (VIN Z) engines, California models (Code TFL)

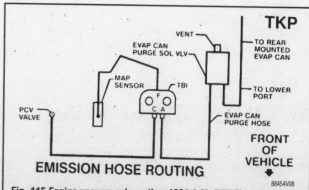

Fig. 115 Engine vacuum schematic—1994 4.3L (VIN Z) engines, California models with A/T (Code TKP)

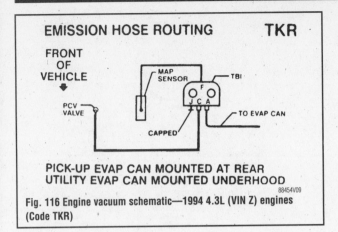

Fig. 116 Engine vacuum schematic—1994 4.3L (VIN Z) engines (Code TKR)

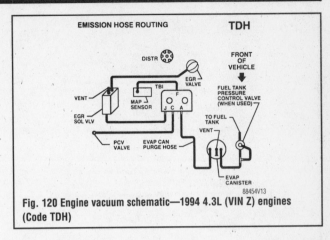

Fig. 120 Engine vacuum schematic—1994 4.3L (VIN Z) engines (Code TDH)

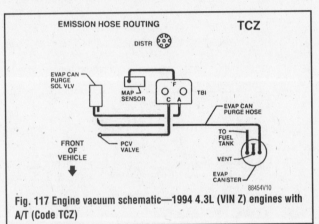

Fig. 117 Engine vacuum schematic—1994 4.3L (VIN Z) engines with A/T (Code TCZ)

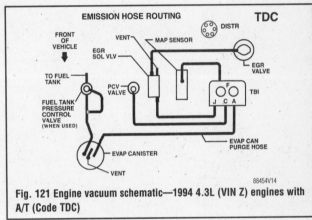

Fig. 121 Engine vacuum schematic—1994 4.3L (VIN Z) engines with A/T (Code TDC)

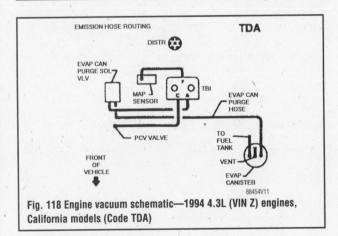

Fig. 118 Engine vacuum schematic—1994 4.3L (VIN Z) engines, California models (Code TDA)

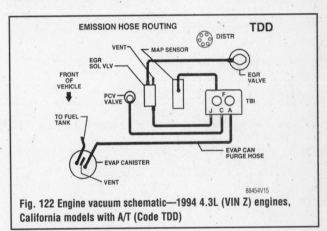

Fig. 122 Engine vacuum schematic—1994 4.3L (VIN Z) engines, California models with A/T (Code TDD)

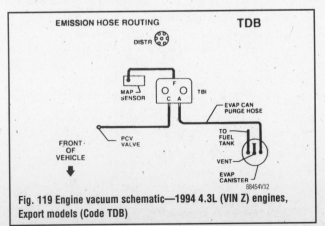

Fig. 119 Engine vacuum schematic—1994 4.3L (VIN Z) engines, Export models (Code TDB)

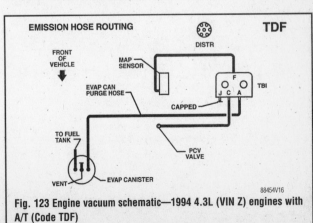

Fig. 123 Engine vacuum schematic—1994 4.3L (VIN Z) engines with A/T (Code TDF)

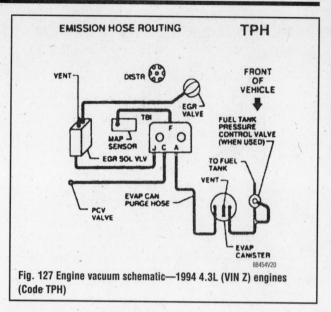

Fig. 124 Engine vacuum schematic—1994 4.3L (VIN Z) engines with A/T (Code TFU)

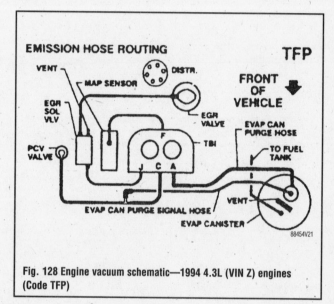

Fig. 127 Engine vacuum schematic—1994 4.3L (VIN Z) engines (Code TPH)

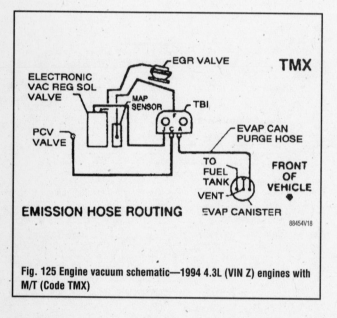

Fig. 125 Engine vacuum schematic—1994 4.3L (VIN Z) engines with M/T (Code TMX)

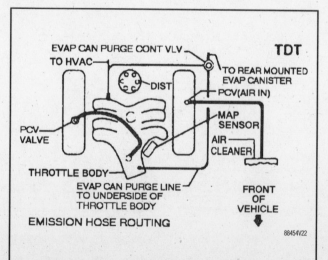

Fig. 128 Engine vacuum schematic—1994 4.3L (VIN Z) engines (Code TFP)

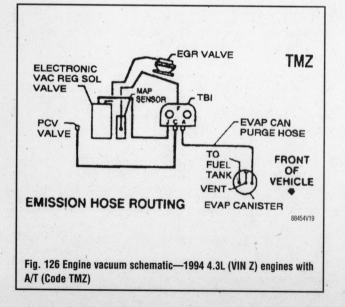

Fig. 126 Engine vacuum schematic—1994 4.3L (VIN Z) engines with A/T (Code TMZ)

Fig. 129 Engine vacuum schematic—1994 4.3L (VIN W) engines, California models with M/T (Code TDT)

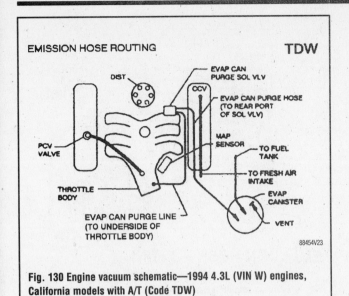

EMISSION HOSE ROUTING   TDW

Fig. 130 Engine vacuum schematic—1994 4.3L (VIN W) engines, California models with A/T (Code TDW)

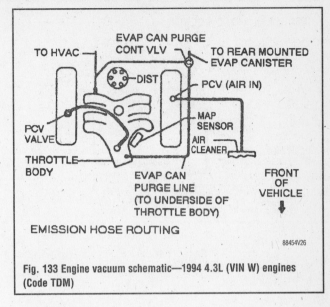

EMISSION HOSE ROUTING

Fig. 133 Engine vacuum schematic—1994 4.3L (VIN W) engines (Code TDM)

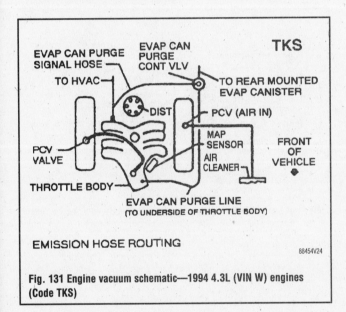

EMISSION HOSE ROUTING

Fig. 131 Engine vacuum schematic—1994 4.3L (VIN W) engines (Code TKS)

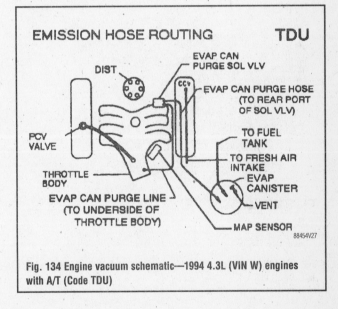

EMISSION HOSE ROUTING   TDU

Fig. 134 Engine vacuum schematic—1994 4.3L (VIN W) engines with A/T (Code TDU)

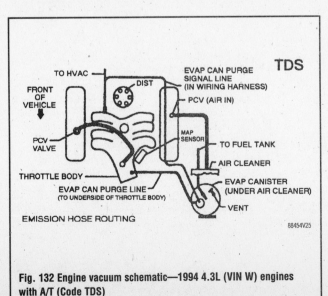

EMISSION HOSE ROUTING

Fig. 132 Engine vacuum schematic—1994 4.3L (VIN W) engines with A/T (Code TDS)

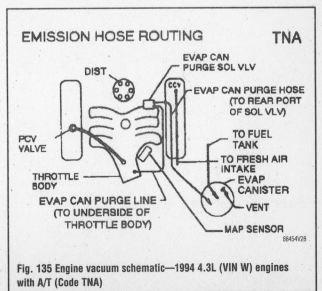

EMISSION HOSE ROUTING   TNA

Fig. 135 Engine vacuum schematic—1994 4.3L (VIN W) engines with A/T (Code TNA)

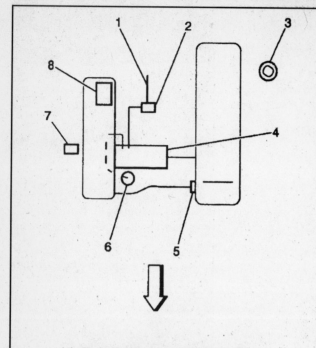

(1) To Rear Mounted EVAP Canister
(2) EVAP Canister Purge Solenoid
(3) EGR Valve
(4) Throttle Body
(5) PCV Valve
(6) Fuel Pressure Regulator Valve
(7) Service Port
(8) MAP Sensor

88454V29

Fig. 136 Engine vacuum schematic—1995–99 2.2L (VIN 4) engines

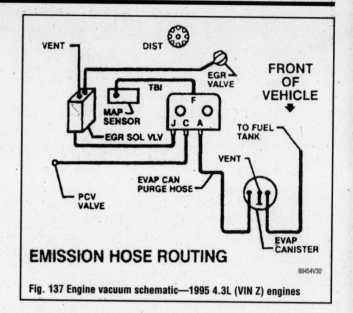

EMISSION HOSE ROUTING

88454V30

Fig. 137 Engine vacuum schematic—1995 4.3L (VIN Z) engines

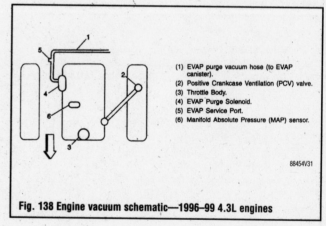

(1) EVAP purge vacuum hose (to EVAP canister).
(2) Positive Crankcase Ventilation (PCV) valve.
(3) Throttle Body.
(4) EVAP Purge Solenoid.
(5) EVAP Service Port.
(6) Manifold Absolute Pressure (MAP) sensor.

88454V31

Fig. 138 Engine vacuum schematic—1996–99 4.3L engines

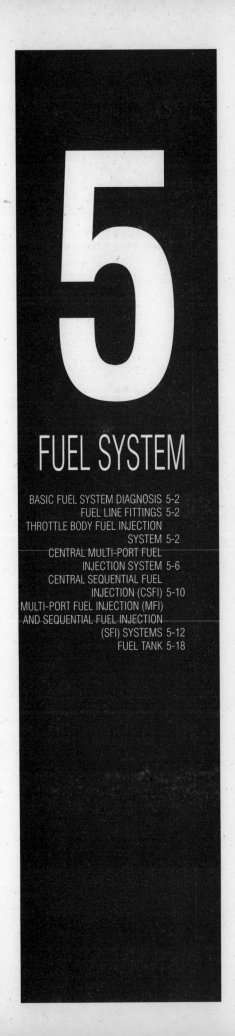

5

FUEL SYSTEM

BASIC FUEL SYSTEM DIAGNOSIS

When there is a problem starting or driving a vehicle, two of the most important checks involve the ignition and the fuel systems. The questions most mechanics attempt to answer first, "is there spark?" and "is there fuel?" will often lead to solving most basic problems. For ignition system diagnosis and testing, please refer to the information on engine electrical components and ignition systems found earlier in this manual. If the ignition system checks out (there is spark), then you must determine if the fuel system is operating properly (is there fuel?).

FUEL LINE FITTINGS

Quick-Connect Fittings

REMOVAL & INSTALLATION

▶ **See Figure 1**

➡ **This procedure requires Tool Set J37088–A or its equivalent fuel line quick-connect separator.**

1. Grasp both sides of the fitting. Twist the female connector ¼ turn in each direction to loosen any dirt within the fittings. Using compressed air, blow out the dirt from the quick-connect fittings at the end of the fittings.

✳✳ CAUTION

Safety glasses MUST be worn when using compressed air to avoid eye injury due to flying dirt particles!

2. For plastic (hand releasable) fittings, squeeze the plastic retainer release tabs, then pull the connection apart.
3. For metal fittings, choose the correct tool from kit J37088–A or its equivalent for the size of the fitting to be disconnected. Insert the proper tool into the female connector, then push inward to release the locking tabs. Pull the connection apart.
4. If it is necessary to remove rust or burrs from the male tube end of a quick-connect fitting, use emery cloth in a radial motion with the tube end to prevent damage to the O-ring sealing surfaces. Using a clean shop towel, wipe off the male tube ends. Inspect all connectors for dirt and burrs. Clean and/or replace if required.

To install:

5. Apply a few drops of clean engine oil to the male tube end of the fitting.
6. Push the connectors together to cause the retaining tabs/fingers to snap into place.
7. Once installed, pull on both ends of each connection to make sure they are secure and check for leaks.

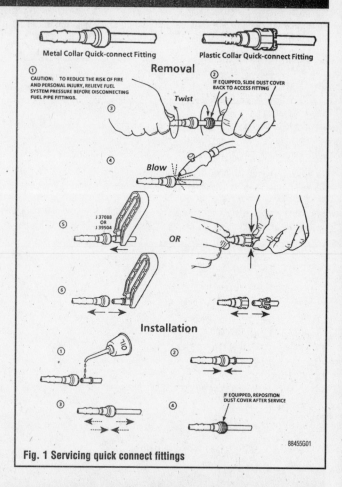

Fig. 1 Servicing quick connect fittings

THROTTLE BODY FUEL INJECTION SYSTEM

General Information

▶ **See Figure 2**

Some 1994–95 fuel injected vehicles were equipped with a Throttle Body Injection (TBI) system. The system uses a TBI unit mounted centrally on the intake manifold where a carburetor would normally be found on older vehicles. The throttle body assembly is equipped with electronic fuel injectors in order to supply fuel to regulate the air/fuel mixture. All fuel injection and ignition functions are controlled by the computer control module, which is sometimes referred to as the ECM, PCM or VCM, depending on the application. It accepts inputs from various sensors and switches, calculates the optimum air/fuel mixture and operates the various output devices to provide peak performance within specific emissions limits. The module will attempt to maintain the ideal air/fuel mixture of 14.7:1 in order to optimize catalytic converter operation. If a system failure occurs that is not serious enough to stop the engine, the module will illuminate the CHECK ENGINE or SERVICE ENGINE SOON light (as applicable) and will continue to operate the engine, although it may need to operate in a backup or fail-safe mode.

Fuel is supplied to the injector(s) through an electric fuel pump assembly

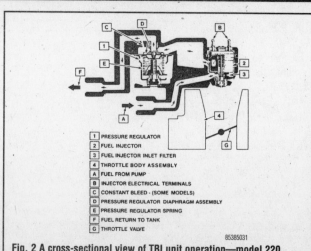

1	PRESSURE REGULATOR
2	FUEL INJECTOR
3	FUEL INJECTOR INLET FILTER
4	THROTTLE BODY ASSEMBLY
5	FUEL FROM PUMP
B	INJECTOR ELECTRICAL TERMINALS
C	CONSTANT BLEED - (SOME MODELS)
D	PRESSURE REGULATOR DIAPHRAGM ASSEMBLY
E	PRESSURE REGULATOR SPRING
F	FUEL RETURN TO TANK
G	THROTTLE VALVE

Fig. 2 A cross-sectional view of TBI unit operation—model 220 found on V6 engines

which is mounted in the vehicle's fuel tank. The module provides a signal to operate the fuel pump though the fuel pump relay and oil pressure switch.

Fuel Pressure Relief

Prior to servicing any component of the fuel injection system, the fuel pressure must be relieved. If fuel pressure is not relieved, serious injury could result.

☼☼ CAUTION

To reduce the chance of personal injury when disconnecting a fuel line, always cover the fuel line with cloth to collect escaping fuel, then place the cloth in an approved container.

1. Disconnect the negative battery cable.
2. Loosen fuel filler cap to relieve fuel tank pressure.
3. The internal constant bleed feature of the Model 220 TBI unit relieves fuel pump system pressure when the engine is turned **OFF**. Therefore, no further action is required.

➡**Allow the engine to sit for 5–10 minutes; this will allow the orifice (in the fuel system) to bleed off the pressure.**

4. When fuel service is finished, tighten the fuel filler cap and connect the negative battery cable.

Electric Fuel Pump

▶ **See Figure 3**

The electric fuel pump is attached to the fuel sending unit, located in the fuel tank.

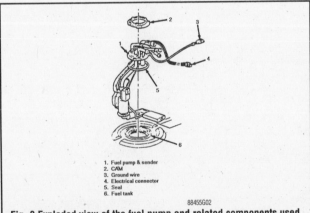

1. Fuel pump & sender
2. CAM
3. Ground wire
4. Electrical connector
5. Seal
6. Fuel tank

88455G02

Fig. 3 Exploded view of the fuel pump and related components used on TBI equipped models

TESTING

▶ **See Figures 4, 5 and 6**

1. Properly relieve the fuel system pressure.
2. If necessary for access, remove the air cleaner assembly and plug the vacuum port(s).
3. Disconnect the flexible fuel supply line, located in the engine compartment between the fuel filter and throttle body.
4. Install a fuel pressure gauge, such as J-29658 or equivalent, in-line between the fuel filter and throttle body unit (between the steel line and flexible hose). If necessary use an adapter or T fitting in order to connect the gauge and complete the fuel circuit.

➡**A T fitting may be fabricated for this purpose. Depending on the fuel pressure gauge, short lengths of steel tubing, appropriately sized flare nuts and a flare nut adapter may be used.**

5. If the engine will run, start the engine and allow it to run at normal idle speed. The fuel pressure should be 9–13 psi (62–90 kPa).

TCCS4P04

Fig. 4 Fuel pressure can be checked using an inexpensive pressure/vacuum gauge

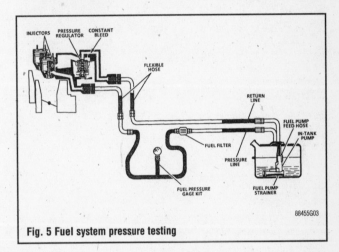

88455G03

Fig. 5 Fuel system pressure testing

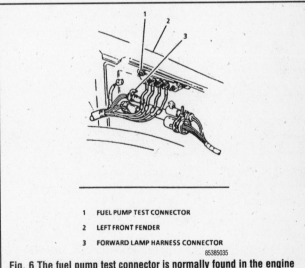

1	FUEL PUMP TEST CONNECTOR
2	LEFT FRONT FENDER
3	FORWARD LAMP HARNESS CONNECTOR

85385035

Fig. 6 The fuel pump test connector is normally found in the engine compartment, on the left fender

6. If the engine does not run, turn the ignition **ON**, but do not attempt to start the engine. Listen for the fuel pump to run. Within 2 seconds of turning the ignition **ON** pressure should be 9–13 psi (62–90 kPa). If necessary, cycle the ignition **OFF**, then **ON** again, in order to build up system pressure.

7. If the fuel pump did not run or system pressure did not reach specification, locate the fuel pump test connector. The test connector is usually found on the driver's side of the engine compartment (on or near the fender), with a single wire (usually red) leading from the relay to the connector. Using a jumper wire, apply battery voltage to the test connector in order to energize and run the fuel pump. The pump should run and produce fuel pressure of

9–13 psi (62–90 kPa). If the pump does not run, check the relay and fuel pump wiring.

8. If the pump pressure was lower than specification, first check for a restricted fuel line or filter and replace, as necessary. If no restrictions can be found, restrict the fuel supply line between the pressure gauge and the TBI unit (a flexible hose may be temporarily clamped to produce the restriction), then apply voltage to the test connector again. If pressure is now above 13 psi (90 kPa), replace the faulty pressure regulator. If pressure remains below 9 psi (62 kPa), then the problem is located in the fuel tank (the fuel pump, coupling hose or inlet filter).

9. If during Step 7, the pressure was higher than specification, unplug the injector connector, then disconnect the fuel return line flexible hose which connects the line from the throttle body to the tank line. Attach a 5⁄16 ID flex hose to the fuel line from the throttle body and place the other end into an approved gasoline container. Cycle the ignition in order to energize the fuel pump and watch system pressure. If pressure is still higher, check for restrictions in the throttle body return line. Repair or replace the line if restrictions are found or replace the faulty pressure regulator if no other causes of high pressure are identified. If fuel pressure is normal only with the flexible hose-to-fuel tank line out of the circuit, check that line for restrictions and repair or replace, as necessary.

10. Once the test is completed, depressurize the fuel system and remove the gauge.

11. Secure the fuel lines and check for leaks.

12. If removed, install the air cleaner assembly.

REMOVAL & INSTALLATION

▶ **See Figures 7, 8 and 9**

1. Properly relieve the fuel system pressure.
2. Connect the negative battery cable.

➡**Be sure to keep a Class B (dry chemical) fire extinguisher nearby.**

✳✳ CAUTION

Due to the possibility of fire or explosion, never drain or store gasoline in an open container.

3. Drain the fuel tank, then remove it from the vehicle. Refer to the procedure found later in this section for details.
4. Using the GM fuel gauge sending unit retaining cam tool No. J-24187, J-36608 (or equivalent) or a brass drift and a hammer, remove the cam locking ring (fuel sending unit) by twisting counterclockwise. With the locking ring released, carefully lift the sending unit from the fuel tank.
5. Remove the fuel pump from the fuel sending unit, by performing the following procedures:
   a. Pull the fuel pump up into the mounting tube, while pulling outward (away) from the bottom support.

➡**When removing the fuel pump from the sending unit, be careful not to damage the rubber insulator and the strainer.**

b. When the pump assembly is clear of the bottom support, pull it out of the rubber connector.

To install:

6. Inspect the fuel pump hose and bottom sound insulator for signs of deterioration, then replace, as necessary.
7. Push the fuel pump onto the sending tube.
8. Using a new sending unit-to-fuel tank O-ring, carefully lower the sending unit/fuel pump assembly into the fuel tank.

➡**When installing the sending unit, be careful not to fold or twist the fuel strainer or it may restrict the fuel flow.**

9. Secure the sending unit by turning or driving the lockring clockwise and into position under the tabs.
10. Install the fuel tank assembly to the vehicle.
11. Connect the negative battery cable and check for proper pump operation.

Throttle Body

REMOVAL & INSTALLATION

▶ **See Figures 10, 11, 12 and 13**

1. Properly relieve the fuel system pressure, then disconnect the negative battery cable.
2. Remove the air cleaner assembly.
3. Unplug the electrical connectors from the idle air control valve, the throttle position sensor and the fuel injector(s). When unplugging the injector connectors, squeeze the plastic tabs and pull straight upward.
4. If applicable, remove the grommet with wires from the throttle body.
5. Disconnect the throttle return spring(s) and linkage (including cruise control and/or throttle valve (as equipped).
6. Tag and disconnect the vacuum hoses from the throttle body.

➡**ALWAYS use a backup wrench on the TBI fuel line inlet nuts when disconnecting the fuel lines.**

7. Place a rag (to catch the excess fuel) under the fuel line-to-throttle body connection, then disconnect the fuel lines from the throttle body. Remove and discard the old O-rings from the lines.
8. Unfasten the TBI unit-to-manifold attaching hardware, then remove the throttle body and discard the old gasket.

➡**Be sure to place a cloth or plastic cover over the intake manifold opening to prevent dirt from entering the engine.**

To install:

9. Clean the gasket mating surfaces taking great care to prevent debris from entering the engine and to make sure the surfaces are not scored or damaged.
10. Position the throttle body to the intake manifold using a new gasket, then thread the retainers and tighten to 12 ft. lbs. (16 Nm).

➡**ALWAYS use a backup wrench on the TBI fuel line inlet nuts when connecting the fuel lines.**

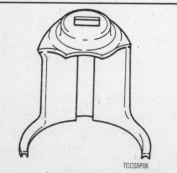

TCCS5P06

Fig. 7 A special tool is usually available to remove or install the fuel pump locking cam

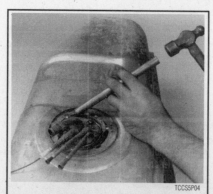

TCCS5P04

Fig. 8 A brass drift and a hammer can be used to loosen the fuel pump locking cam

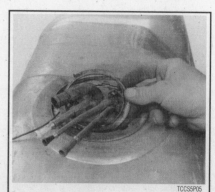

TCCS5P05

Fig. 9 Once the locking cam is released it can be removed to free the fuel pump

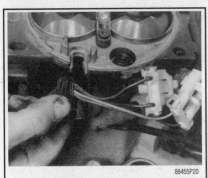

Fig. 10 Unplug the injector connectors and remove the grommet with wires from the throttle body

Fig. 11 Disconnect the throttle linkage

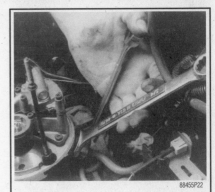

Fig. 12 Disengage the fuel lines from the throttle body

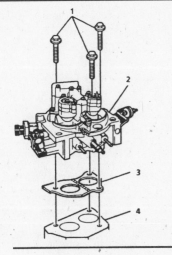

1	BOLT
2	TBI UNIT
3	GASKET (MUST BE INSTALLED WITH STRIPE FACING UP)
4	ENGINE INTAKE MANIFOLD

85385044

Fig. 13 Model 220 TBI unit mounting—4.3L engine

11. Using new O-rings, connect and tighten the fuel line fittings to 20 ft. lbs. (26 Nm).

12. Connect the vacuum hoses to the throttle body, as tagged during removal.

13. Attach the throttle return spring(s) and linkage (including cruise control and/or throttle valve (as equipped).

14. If applicable, install the grommet with wires to the throttle body.

15. Attach the electrical connectors to the idle air control valve, the throttle position sensor and the fuel injector(s).

16. Install the air cleaner assembly.

17. Connect the negative battery cable.

18. Depress the accelerator pedal to the floor and release it, to see if the pedal returns freely. Turn the ignition switch **ON** and check for fuel leaks.

Fuel Injector

REMOVAL & INSTALLATION

▶ See Figures 14 thru 20

✳✳ CAUTION

When removing the injector(s), be careful not to damage the electrical connector pins (on top of the injector), the injector fuel filter and the nozzle. The fuel injector is serviced as a complete assembly ONLY, it is an electrical component and should not be immersed in any kind of cleaner.

1. Properly relieve the fuel system pressure, then disconnect the negative battery cable.

2. Remove the air cleaner assembly.

3. At the injector connector(s), squeeze the two tabs together and pull straight up to unplug the connector from the injector.

4. Loosen the fuel meter cover retaining screws, then remove the cover from the fuel meter body, but leave the cover gasket in place.

5. Using a small pry bar and a round fulcrum, carefully pry the injector until it is free, then remove the injector from the fuel meter body.

6. Remove the small O-ring from the nozzle end of the injector. If equipped and removal is necessary, carefully rotate the injector's fuel filter back and forth to remove it from the base of the injector.

Fig. 14 Unplug the injector electrical connection

Fig. 15 Unfasten the fuel meter cover retaining screws . . .

Fig. 16 . . . then remove the fuel meter cover

Fig. 17 Using a metal dowel as a fulcrum and a prytool to remove the injectors from their bores

Fig. 18 Remove the injectors . . .

Fig. 19 Remove and discard the O-ring seals

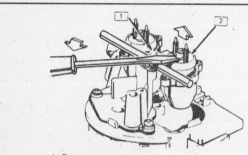

1. Fuel meter cover gasket
2. Removing fuel injector

Fig. 20 Removing the injectors from the model 220 TBI unit—4.3L engine

7. Remove and discard the fuel meter cover gasket.

8. Remove the large O-ring and back-up washer (if equipped) from the top of the counterbore of the fuel meter body injector cavity.

To install:

9. If removed, with the larger end of the filter facing the injector (so that the filter covers the raised rib of the injector base) install the filter by twisting it into position on the injector.

10. Lubricate the new O-rings with clean automatic transmission fluid, then install the small O-ring on the nozzle end of the injector. Be sure the O-ring is pressed up against the injector or injector filter (as applicable).

11. Install the steel backup washer (if equipped) in the top counterbore of the fuel meter body's injector cavity, then install the new large O-ring directly over the backup washer. Make sure the O-ring is properly seated in the cavity and is flush with the top of the fuel meter body casting surface.

➥If the backup washer and large O-ring are not properly installed BEFORE the fuel injector, a fuel leak will likely result.

12. Install the fuel injector into the cavity by aligning the raised lug on the injector base with the cast notch in the fuel meter body cavity. Once the injector is aligned, carefully push down on the injector by hand until it is fully seated in the cavity. When properly aligned and installed, the injector terminals will be approximately parallel to the throttle shaft.

13. Position a new fuel meter cover gasket, then install the cover to the body, making sure the gasket remains in position. Using a suitable threadlocking compound, install and tighten the cover retainers to 30 inch lbs. (4 Nm).

14. Attach the injector electrical connector(s).

15. Connect the negative battery cable, then turn the ignition key to the **ON** position to pressurize the fuel system and check for leaks.

16. Install the air cleaner assembly, then start the engine and check for leaks.

TESTING

1. Unplug the electrical connection from the injector.

2. Have a assistant crank the engine with the electrical connection still unplugged. If there is fuel spray from one or both injectors, the injector seal may be leaking or the injector itself could be faulty.

3. Attach a injector test light (noid light) to one of the injector electrical connections.

4. Have a assistant crank the engine and observe the test light. If the light blinks, the electrical connection is working properly. If the light does not blink, check the injector connection for damage and the wiring for continuity, repair as necessary.

5. Perform the test on both injector electrical connections.

6. Attach the injector electrical connections and have your assistant crank the engine, both injectors should spray fuel. If only one injector sprays fuel, the other injector is probably faulty. If neither injector sprays fuel, check the fuel system pressure. Refer to the fuel pump test procedure in this section. Repair the fuel pump system as necessary and repeat the test.

CENTRAL MULTI-PORT FUEL INJECTION SYSTEM

General Information

▶ See Figures 21, 22 and 23

The Central Multi-port Fuel Injection (CMFI) system, found on 1994–95 4.3L models, functions similarly to the TBI system in that an injection assembly (CMFI unit) is centrally mounted on the engine intake manifold. The major differences come in the incorporation of a split (upper and lower) intake manifold assembly with a variable tuned plenum (using an intake manifold tuning valve) and the CMFI unit's single fuel injector which feeds 6 poppet valves (1 for each individual cylinder).

The non-repairable CMFI assembly or injection unit consists of a fuel meter body, gasket seal, fuel pressure regulator, fuel injector and six poppet nozzles with fuel tubes. The assembly is housed in the lower intake manifold. Should a

failure occur in the CMFI assembly, the entire component must be replaced as a unit.

Fuel is supplied to the injector through an electric fuel pump assembly which is mounted in the vehicle's fuel tank. The module provides a signal to operate the fuel pump though the fuel pump relay and oil pressure switch. The CMFI unit internal pressure regulator maintains a system pressure of approximately 58–64 psi (400–440 kPa). When the injector is energized by the control module, an armature lifts allowing pressurized fuel to travel down the 6 fuel tubes to the poppet valves. In the poppet valves, fuel pressure (working against the extension spring force) will cause the nozzle ball to open from its seat and fuel will flow from the nozzle. It takes approximately 51 psi (350 kPa) to force fuel from the poppet nozzle. Once the module de-energizes the injector, the armature will close, allowing fuel pressure in the tubes to drop and the spring force will close off fuel flow.

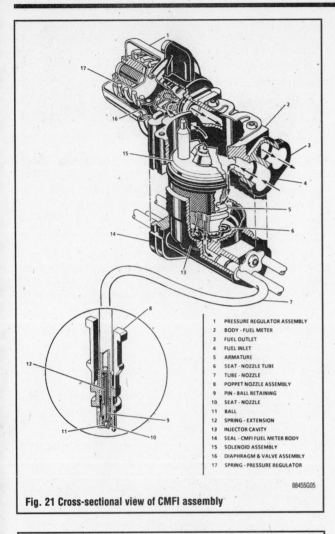

Fig. 21 Cross-sectional view of CMFI assembly

1	PRESSURE REGULATOR ASSEMBLY
2	BODY - FUEL METER
3	FUEL OUTLET
4	FUEL INLET
5	ARMATURE
6	SEAT - NOZZLE TUBE
7	TUBE - NOZZLE
8	POPPET NOZZLE ASSEMBLY
9	PIN - BALL RETAINING
10	SEAT - NOZZLE
11	BALL
12	SPRING - EXTENSION
13	INJECTOR CAVITY
14	SEAL - CMFI FUEL METER BODY
15	SOLENOID ASSEMBLY
16	DIAPHRAGM & VALVE ASSEMBLY
17	SPRING - PRESSURE REGULATOR

88455G05

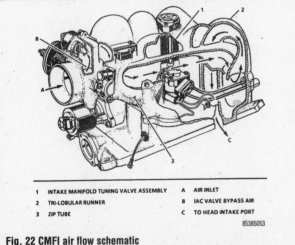

1	INTAKE MANIFOLD TUNING VALVE ASSEMBLY	A	AIR INLET
2	TRI-LOBULAR RUNNER	B	IAC VALVE BYPASS AIR
3	ZIP TUBE	C	TO HEAD INTAKE PORT

85385053

Fig. 22 CMFI air flow schematic

Fuel Pressure Relief

▶ See Figure 24

Prior to servicing any component of the fuel injection system, the fuel pressure must be relieved. If fuel pressure is not relieved, serious injury could result.

A Schrader valve is provided on this fuel system in order to conveniently test or release the fuel system pressure. A fuel pressure gauge and adapter will be necessary to connect the gauge to the fitting. The CMFI system covered here

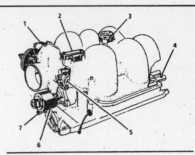

1	VALVE ASSEMBLY - IDLE AIR CONTROL (IAC)
2	SENSOR - MANIFOLD ABSOLUTE PRESSURE (MAP)
3	VALVE ASSEMBLY - INTAKE MANIFOLD TUNING
4	CONNECTION - FUEL PRESSURE
5	SENSOR - THROTTLE POSITION (TP)
6	VALVE ASSEMBLY - EXHAUST GAS RECIRCULATION (EGR)
7	SENSOR - ENGINE COOLANT TEMPERATURE

85385054

Fig. 23 Various CMFI engine components are mounted to the intake manifolds (the CMFI unit is located under the upper intake)

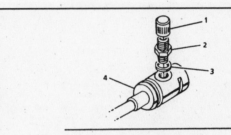

1	CAP - FUEL PRESSURE CONNECTION
2	CONNECTION ASSEMBLY - FUEL PRESSURE
3	SEAL - FUEL PRESSURE CONNECTION
4	PIPE ASSEMBLY - FUEL INJECTION FUEL INLET

85385056

Fig. 24 Fuel pressure connection

uses a valve located on the inlet pipe fitting, immediately before it enters the CMFI assembly (towards the rear of the engine).

1. Disconnect the negative battery cable to assure the prevention of fuel spillage if the ignition switch is accidentally turned **ON** while a fitting is still disconnected.
2. Loosen the fuel filter cap to release the fuel tank pressure.
3. Make sure the release valve on the fuel gauge is closed, then connect the fuel gauge to the pressure fitting located on the inlet fuel pipe fitting.

➡When connecting the gauge to the fitting, be sure to wrap a rag around the fitting to avoid spillage. After repairs, place the rag in an approved container.

4. Install the bleed hose portion of the fuel gauge assembly into an approved container, then open the gauge release valve and bleed the fuel pressure from the system.
5. When the gauge is removed, be sure to open the bleed valve and drain all fuel from the gauge assembly.

Electric Fuel Pump

The electric pump is attached to the fuel sending unit, located in the fuel tank.

TESTING

▶ See Figure 25

1. Properly relieve the fuel system pressure.
2. Leave the gauge attached to the pressure fitting on the fuel inlet pipe.

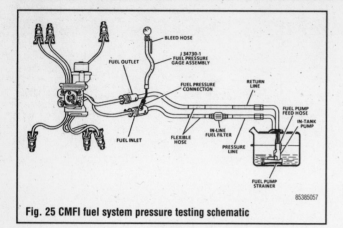

Fig. 25 CMFI fuel system pressure testing schematic

3. If disconnected during the fuel pressure relief procedure, reconnect the negative battery terminal.

4. If the engine will run, start the engine and allow it to run at normal idle speed. The fuel pressure should be 58–64 psi (400–440 kPa). Once the engine is at normal operating temperature, open the throttle quickly while noting fuel pressure; it should quickly approach 64 psi (440 kPa) if all components are operating properly (there is no need to proceed further). If the pressure was in specification before, but does not approach 64 psi (440 kPa) on acceleration, the pressure regulator in the CMFI unit is faulty and the assembly should be replaced.

5. If the engine does not run, turn the ignition **ON**, but do not attempt to start the engine. Listen for the fuel pump to run. Within 2 seconds of turning the ignition **ON** pressure should be 58–64 psi (400–440 kPa) while the pump is running. Once the pump stops, pressure may vary by several pounds, then it should hold steady. If the pressure does not hold steady, wait 10 seconds and repeat this step, but pinch the fuel pressure line flexible hose and watch if the pressure holds. If it still does not hold, the CMFI unit should be replaced. If the pressure holds with the pressure line pinched, check for a partially disconnected fuel dampener (pulsator) or faulty in-tank fuel pump.

6. If the fuel pump did not run or system pressure did not reach specification, locate the fuel pump test connector. The test connector is usually found on the driver's side of the engine compartment (on or near the fender), with a single wire (usually red) leading from the relay to the connector. Using a 10 amp fused jumper wire, apply battery voltage to the test connector in order to energize and run the fuel pump. The pump should run and produce fuel pressure of 58–64 psi (400–440 kPa). If the pump does not run, check the relay and fuel pump wiring.

7. If the pump pressure was lower than specification, first check for a restricted fuel line, filter or a disconnected fuel pulse dampener (pulsator) and repair/replace, as necessary. If no restrictions can be found, restrict the flexible fuel return line (by gradually pinching it) until the pressure rises above 64 psi (440 kPa), but DO NOT allow pressure to exceed 75 psi (517 kPa). If the fuel pressure rises above specification with the return line restricted, then the pressure regulator is faulty and the CMFI assembly should be replaced. If pressure still does not reach specification, check for a faulty fuel pump, partially disconnected fuel pulse dampener (pulsator), partially restricted pump strainer or an incorrect pump.

8. If during the previous steps, the fuel pressure was higher than specification, relieve the system pressure, then disconnect the engine compartment fuel return line. Attach a 5/16 ID flex hose to the fuel line from the throttle body and place the other end into an approved gasoline container. Cycle the ignition in order to energize the fuel pump and watch system pressure. If pressure is still higher, check for restrictions in the line between the pressure regulator and the point where it was disconnected. Repair or replace the line if restrictions are found or replace the CMFI assembly with the faulty internal pressure regulator if no other causes of high pressure are identified. If fuel pressure is normal only with the rest of the return line out of the circuit, check that remaining line for restrictions and repair or replace, as necessary.

9. Once the test is completed, depressurize the fuel system and remove the gauge.

REMOVAL & INSTALLATION

Removal and installation of the fuel pump and sending unit assembly is the same on CMFI vehicles as it is for TBI vehicles. Please refer to the TBI procedure earlier in this section for electric fuel pump replacement.

CMFI Assembly

REMOVAL & INSTALLATION

▶ **See Figures 26 and 27**

The CMFI assembly is mounted to the lower intake manifold. The upper intake manifold assembly must be removed for access. The CMFI assembly includes a fuel meter body, gasket seal, fuel pressure regulator, fuel injector and six poppet nozzles with fuel tubes. Should a failure occur in any components of the CMFI unit, the entire assembly must be replaced.

1. Remove the plastic cover and properly relieve the fuel system pressure.
2. Disconnect the negative battery cable, then remove the air cleaner and air inlet duct.
3. Unplug the wiring harness from the necessary upper intake components including:
 • Throttle Position (TP) sensor
 • Idle Air Control (IAC) motor
 • Manifold Absolute Pressure (MAP) sensor
 • Intake Manifold Tuning Valve (IMTV)
4. Disconnect the throttle linkage from the upper intake manifold, then remove the ignition coil.
5. Disconnect the PCV hose at the rear of the upper intake manifold, then

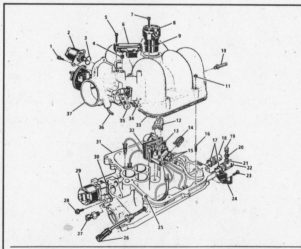

1	BOLT/SCREW - IDLE AIR CONTROL VALVE	14	CLIP - FUEL INJECTION FUEL FEED AND RETURN PIPE	26	HARNESS ASSEMBLY - CENTRAL MULTIPORT FUEL INJECTOR WIRING
2	VALVE ASSEMBLY - IDLE AIR CONTROL (IAC)	15	SEAL - FUEL INJECTION FUEL FEED AND RETURN PIPE (O-RING)	27	SENSOR ASSEMBLY - ENGINE COOLANT TEMPERATURE (ECT)
3	SEAL - IDLE AIR CONTROL VALVE (O-RING)	16	STUD - UPPER INTAKE MANIFOLD	28	BOLT/SCREW - EGR VALVE
4	SEAL - MAP SENSOR	17	SEAL - LOWER INTAKE MANIFOLD FUEL FEED AND RETURN PIPE (O-RING)	29	VALVE ASSEMBLY - EGR
5	BOLT/SCREW - MAP SENSOR	18	PIPE ASSEMBLY - FUEL INJECTION FUEL RETURN	30	GASKET - EGR VALVE
6	SENSOR ASSEMBLY - MANIFOLD ABSOLUTE PRESSURE (MAP)	19	CAP - FUEL PRESSURE CONNECTION	31	MANIFOLD ASSEMBLY - LOWER INTAKE
7	BOLT/SCREW - INTAKE MANIFOLD TUNING VALVE	20	FUEL PRESSURE CONNECTION ASSEMBLY	32	SEAL - CENTRAL MULTIPORT FUEL INJECTOR (CMFI)
8	VALVE ASSEMBLY - INTAKE MANIFOLD TUNING	21	SEAL - FUEL PRESSURE CONNECTION	33	GASKET - UPPER INTAKE MANIFOLD
9	SEAL - INTAKE MANIFOLD VALVE (O-RING)	22	PIPE ASSEMBLY - FUEL INJECTION FUEL FEED	34	BOLT/SCREW - THROTTLE POSITION SENSOR
10	FITTING - POWER BRAKE BOOSTER VACUUM	23	BOLT/SCREW - FUEL INJECTION FUEL FEED AND RETURN PIPE RETAINER	35	SENSOR ASSEMBLY - THROTTLE POSITION (TP) SENSOR
11	NUT - UPPER INTAKE MANIFOLD	24	RETAINER - FUEL INJECTION FUEL FEED AND RETURN PIPE	36	TUBE - FUEL VAPOR CANISTER PURGE
12	CONNECTOR ASSEMBLY - CENTRAL MULTIPORT FUEL INJECTOR WIRING HARNESS	25	PIN - UPPER INTAKE MANIFOLD LOCATING	37	MANIFOLD ASSEMBLY - UPPER INTAKE (WITH THROTTLE BODY)
13	INJECTOR ASSEMBLY - CENTRAL MULTIPORT FUEL INJECTOR (CMFI)				

85385059

Fig. 26 Exploded view of the upper and lower intake manifolds and the CMFI system components

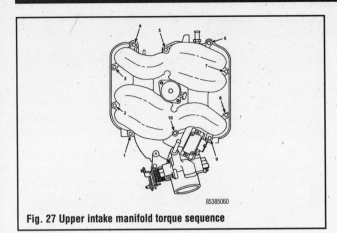

Fig. 27 Upper intake manifold torque sequence

tag and unplug the vacuum hoses from both the front and rear of the upper intake.

6. Remove the upper intake manifold bolts and studs, making sure to note or mark the location of all studs to assure proper installation. Remove the upper intake manifold from the engine.

7. Unplug the injector wiring harness connector at the CMFI assembly.

8. Remove and discard the fuel fitting clip.

9. Disconnect the fuel inlet and return tube and fitting assembly. Discard the old O-rings.

10. Squeeze the poppet nozzle locktabs together while lifting each nozzle out of the casting socket. Once all six nozzles are released, carefully lift the CMFI assembly out of the casting.

To install:

11. Align the CMFI assembly grommet with the casting grommet slots and push downward until it is seated in the bottom guide hole.

✷✷ CAUTION

To reduce the risk of fire and personal injury, be ABSOLUTELY SURE that the poppet nozzles are firmly seated and locked into their casting sockets. An unlocked poppet nozzle could work loose from its socket resulting in a dangerous fuel leak.

12. Carefully insert the poppet nozzles into the casting sockets. Make sure they are FIRMLY SEATED and locked into the casting sockets.

13. Position new O-ring seals (lightly coated with clean engine oil), then connect the fuel inlet and return tube and fitting assembly.

14. Install a new fuel fitting clip.

15. Temporarily connect the negative battery cable, then pressurize the fuel system by cycling the ignition switch **ON** for 2 seconds, then **OFF** for 10 seconds and repeating, as necessary. Once the fuel system is pressurized, check for leaks.

16. Disconnect the negative battery cable.

17. Position a new upper intake manifold gasket on the engine, making sure the green sealing lines are facing upward.

18. Install the upper intake manifold being careful not to pinch the fuel injector wires between the manifolds.

19. Install the manifold retainers, making sure the studs are properly positioned, then tighten them using the proper sequence to specifications. Refer to Section 3 of this manual for the manifold specification.

20. Connect the PCV hose to the rear of the upper intake manifold and the vacuum hoses to both the front and rear of the manifold assembly.

21. Connect the throttle linkage to the upper intake, then install the ignition coil.

22. Attach the necessary wiring to the upper intake components including the TP sensor, IAC motor, MAP sensor and the IMTV.

23. Install the plastic cover, the air cleaner and air inlet duct.

24. Connect the negative battery cable.

Intake Manifold Tuning Valve

▶ **See Figure 28**

The upper intake manifold on the CMFI engine is of a variable tuned split plenum design. The manifold using a centrally mounted tuning valve to equalize pressure in the side by side inlet plenums. The valve is electronically operated by the computer control module.

REMOVAL & INSTALLATION

1. Disconnect the negative battery cable.
2. Unplug the tuning valve electrical connection.
3. Remove the tuning valve attaching screws.
4. Remove the tuning valve from the top of the upper intake manifold assembly.
5. Remove and discard the old O-ring seal.

To install:

6. Lubricate the new O-ring seal with clean engine oil.
7. Make sure the threads of the retaining screws are coated with LoctiteÆ 262, or an equivalent threadlocking compound.
8. Position the tuning valve to the upper intake manifold, then carefully thread the retaining screws.

➡ **To avoid breaking the valve mounting ears, alternately tighten the attaching screws until they engage the mounting ear surface, then carefully tighten the screws to specification.**

9. Tighten the retaining screws to 18 inch lbs. (2 Nm).
10. Engage the valve electrical connector, then connect the negative battery cable.

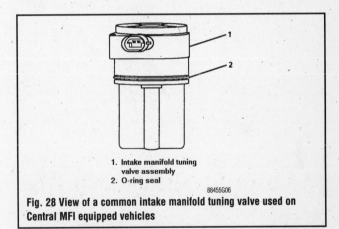

1. Intake manifold tuning valve assembly
2. O-ring seal

Fig. 28 View of a common intake manifold tuning valve used on Central MFI equipped vehicles

Pressure Relief Valve

REMOVAL & INSTALLATION

▶ **See Figure 24**

1. Disconnect the negative batter cable.
2. Relieve the fuel system pressure.
3. Use an appropriate size wrench to unfasten the valve assembly. Discard the seal.

To install:

4. Position a new seal on the valve and thread the valve into the fuel rail. Tighten the valve to 88 inch lbs. (10 Nm).
5. Connect the negative battery cable, start the engine and check for fuel leaks.

CENTRAL SEQUENTIAL FUEL INJECTION (CSFI)

General Information

The 1996–99 4.3L models are equipped with the Central Sequential Fuel Injection (CSFI) system. Fuel is delivered to the engine by individual fuel injectors and poppet nozzles mounted in the intake manifold near each cylinder. Each is fired sequentially for accuracy and precise metering control.

Relieving Fuel System Pressure

➥Fuel pressure gauge J 34730-1A or its equivalent is required to perform this procedure

1. Disconnect the negative battery cable.
2. Loosen the fuel filler cap to relieve fuel tank pressure.
3. Attach the fuel pressure gauge to the fuel pressure connection. Wrap a shop towel around the fitting while connecting the gauge to prevent spillage.
4. Install the bleed hose into an approved container and open the valve to bleed the system. The system is now safe for servicing.
5. Drain any fuel remaining in the gauge into an approved container.

Electric Fuel Pump

▶ See Figure 29

All Chevrolet/GMC Central Sequential Fuel Injection (CSFI) fuel-injected vehicles are equipped with an electric fuel pump. For a fuel injection system to work properly, the pump must develop pressures well above those of a mechanical fuel pump. This high pressure is maintained within the lines even when the engine is OFF. Extreme caution must be used to safely release the pressurized fuel before any work is begun.

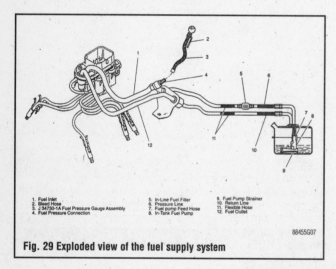

1. Fuel Inlet
2. Bleed Hose
3. J 34730-1A Fuel Pressure Gauge Assembly
4. Fuel Pressure Connection
5. In-Line Fuel Filter
6. Pressure Line
7. Fuel pump Feed Hose
8. In-Tank Fuel Pump
9. Fuel Pump Strainer
10. Return Line
11. Flexible Hose
12. Fuel Outlet

88455G07

Fig. 29 Exploded view of the fuel supply system

❋❋ CAUTION

Always relieve the fuel pressure within the system before any work is begun on any fuel component. Failure to safely relieve the pressure may result in fire and/or serious injury.

TESTING

1. Turn the ignition OFF for 10 seconds.
2. Attach fuel pressure gauge J 34730-1A or its equivalent and relieve the fuel system pressure. Wrap a shop towel around the fitting while connecting the gauge to prevent spillage.
3. With the gauge still attached, turn the ignition ON but not start the engine. The pump should operate for 2 seconds.
4. Bleed the air out of the gauge into a suitable container.
5. Turn the ignition OFF for 10 seconds.
6. Turn the ignition ON but not start the engine.
7. Monitor the fuel pressure with the pump running. The pressure should be 60–66 psi (415–455 kPa).

➥The ignition may have to be cycled ON more than once to obtain the maximum fuel pressure.

8. If the fuel pressure is not as specified, check for a restricted fuel filter of fuel line and repair as necessary, then recheck the fuel pressure.
9. If the pump does not operate, connect a 12 volt fused jumper wire to the fuel pump test terminal located near the fuel pump relay. The pump should operate.
10. If the pump does not operate, unplug the fuel pump harness connector at the tank.
11. Connect a 12 volt fused jumper wire to the fuel pump test terminal.
12. Using a test light connected to ground, probe the fuel pump feed circuit.
13. If the light does not illuminate, use a test light connected to the fuel pump ground (tank side) and probe the fuel pump feed circuit.
14. If the light illuminates the pump is defective and must be replaced.
15. If the light does not illuminate, there is an open between the fuel pump test terminal and the fuel pump feed circuit that must be repaired.

REMOVAL & INSTALLATION

▶ See Figures 30, 31 and 32

1. Disconnect the negative battery cable.
2. Relieve the fuel system pressure. Refer to the fuel system relief procedure in this section.
3. Raise the vehicle and support it safely with jackstands.
4. Drain the fuel system and remove the fuel tank. Refer to the fuel tank removal procedure in this section.
5. Remove the fuel sender assembly turning it counterclockwise using tool J 36608 or J 39765 or their equivalents.

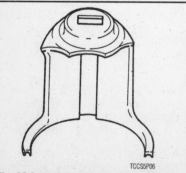

TCCS5P06

Fig. 30 A special tool is usually available to remove or install the fuel pump locking cam

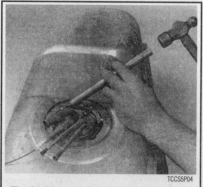

TCCS5P04

Fig. 31 A brass drift and a hammer can be used to loosen the fuel pump locking cam

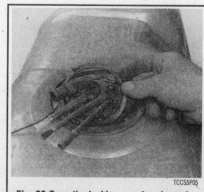

TCCS5P05

Fig. 32 Once the locking cam is released it can be removed to free the fuel pump

6. Remove the fuel pump from the sender assembly. Pull the pump up into the attaching hose while pulling outward from the bottom support. Do not damage the rubber insulator or the strainer.

7. Inspect the fuel pump attaching hose and the rubber sound insulation for signs of deterioration.

8. Inspect the strainer for blockage and damage.

To install:

9. Install the fuel pump assembly into the attaching hose.

➡**Be careful not to bend or fold over the fuel strainer when installing the fuel sender as this will restrict fuel flow.**

10. Install the fuel sender into the fuel tank. Insert a new o-ring seal.

11. Install the camlock assembly turning it clockwise to lock it.

12. Install the fuel tank. Refer to the fuel tank installation procedure in this section.

13. Connect the negative battery cable.

Throttle Body

REMOVAL & INSTALLATION

1. Disconnect the negative battery cable.
2. Remove the air inlet fastener and duct.
3. Unplug the Idle Air Control (IAC) valve and the Throttle Position Sensor (TPS) electrical connectors.
4. Disconnect the throttle and cruise control cables.
5. Disconnect the accelerator cable bracket bolts and nuts.
6. If necessary, remove the wiring harness fastener nut.
7. Unfasten the throttle body retaining nuts and remove the throttle body.
8. Remove and discard the flange gasket.
9. Clean both gasket mating surfaces.

➡**When cleaning the old gasket from the machined aluminum surfaces be careful as sharp tools may damage the sealing surfaces**

To install:

10. Install the new flange gasket and the throttle body assembly.
11. Tighten the throttle body attaching nuts to 18 ft. lbs. (25 Nm) on 1994–98 models and 80 inch lbs. (9 Nm) on 1999 models.
12. Install the accelerator cable bracket bolts and nuts and tighten to 18 ft. lbs. (25 Nm) on 1994–98 models and 108 inch lbs. (12 Nm) on 1999 models.
13. Connect the throttle and cruise control cables.
14. Attach the IAC valve and the TPS electrical connectors.
15. Install the air inlet fastener and duct. Connect the negative battery cable.

Fuel Injectors

REMOVAL & INSTALLATION

▶ **See Figures 33 and 34**

1. Disconnect the negative battery cable.
2. Relieve the fuel system pressure. Refer to the fuel system relief procedure in this section.
3. Unplug the fuel meter body electrical connection and the fuel feed and return hoses from the engine fuel pipes.
4. Remove the upper intake manifold assembly.
5. Tag and remove the poppet nozzle out of the casting socket.
6. Remove the fuel meter body by releasing the locktabs.

➡**Each injector is calibrated. When replacing the fuel injectors, be sure to replace it with the correct injector.**

7. Disassemble the lower hold-down plate and nuts.
8. While pulling the poppet nozzle tube downward, push with a small screwdriver down between the injector terminals and remove the injectors.

To install:

9. Lubricate the new injector O-rings with clean engine oil, then install the O-rings on the injector assembly.

10. Assemble the CSFI injector assembly into the fuel meter body injector socket.

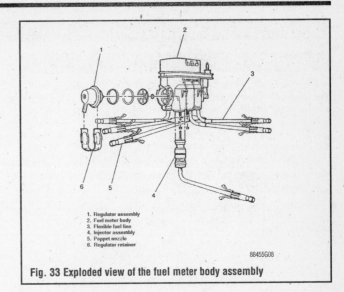

1. Regulator assembly
2. Fuel meter body
3. Flexible fuel line
4. Injector assembly
5. Poppet nozzle
6. Regulator retainer

88455G08

Fig. 33 Exploded view of the fuel meter body assembly

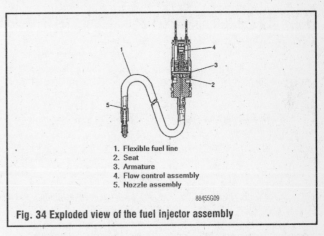

1. Flexible fuel line
2. Seat
3. Armature
4. Flow control assembly
5. Nozzle assembly

88455G09

Fig. 34 Exploded view of the fuel injector assembly

11. Assemble the lower hold-down plate and nuts. Tighten the nuts to 27 inch lbs. (3 Nm).

12. Install the fuel meter body assembly into the intake manifold and tighten the fuel meter bracket retainer bolts to 88 inch. lbs. (10 Nm).

✳✳ CAUTION

To reduce the risk of fire or injury ensure that the poppet nozzles are properly seated and locked in their casting sockets

13. Install the fuel meter body into the bracket and lock all the tabs in place.

14. Install the poppet nozzles into the casting sockets.

15. Engage the electrical connections and install new o-ring seals on the fuel return and feed hoses.

16. Install the fuel feed and return hoses and tighten the fuel pipe nuts to 22 ft. lbs. (30 Nm).

17. Connect the negative battery cable.

18. Turn the ignition **ON** for 2 seconds and then turn it **OFF** for 10 seconds. Again turn the ignition **ON** and check for leaks.

19. Install the upper intake manifold.

TESTING

▶ **See Figure 35**

➡**This test requires the use of fuel injector tester J 39021 or its equivalent.**

1. Disconnect the fuel injector harness and attach a noid light in order to test for injector pulse.

2. With the engine cool and the ignition turned **OFF**, install the fuel pres-

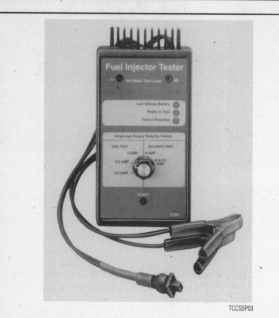

Fig. 35 Fuel injector testers can be purchased or sometimes rented

TCCS5P03

sure gauge to the fuel pressure connection. Wrap a shop towel around the fitting while connecting the gauge to prevent spillage.

3. Turn **ON** the ignition and record the fuel gauge pressure with the pump running.

4. Turn **OFF** the ignition. Pressure should drop and hold steady at this point.

5. To perform this test, set the selector switch to the balance test 2.5 amp position.

6. Turn the injector **ON** by depressing the button on the injector tester. Note this pressure reading the instant the gauge needle stops.

7. Repeat the balance test on the remaining injectors and record the pressure drop on each.

8. Start the engine to clear fuel from the intake. Retest the injectors that appear faulty. Any injector that has a plus or minus 1.5 psi (10 kPa) difference from the other injectors is suspect.

Fuel Pressure Regulator

REMOVAL & INSTALLATION

1. Disconnect the negative battery cable.
2. Relieve the fuel system pressure. Refer to the fuel system relief procedure in this section.
3. Remove the upper intake manifold assembly.
4. Remove the fuel pressure regulator vacuum tube.
5. Disassemble the fuel pressure regulator snapring retainer.
6. Remove the fuel pressure regulator assembly and the O-rings. Discard the O-rings, filter and back-up O-rings.

To install:

7. Lubricate the O-rings with clean engine oil.
8. Install the back-up O-ring, the large O-ring, the filter and the small O-ring.
9. Install the fuel pressure regulator with the vacuum tube facing down into the snapring retainer and attach the vacuum tube.
10. Install the snapring retainer.
11. Install the upper manifold assembly.
12. Connect the negative battery cable.

Fuel Pressure Connection

The fuel pressure connection is non-replaceable, but is serviceable.

SERVICE

1. Disconnect the negative battery cable.
2. Relieve the fuel system pressure. Refer to the fuel system relief procedure in this section.
3. Remove the fuel pressure connection cap.
4. Using a valve core removal tool remove the valve core assembly and discard it.

To install:

5. Install a new valve core assembly using a valve core removal tool.
6. Connect the negative battery cable.
7. Turn the ignition **ON** for 2 seconds and then turn it **OFF** for 10 seconds. Again turn the ignition **ON** and check for leaks.
8. Install the fuel pressure connection cap.

MULTI-PORT FUEL INJECTION (MFI) AND SEQUENTIAL FUEL INJECTION (SFI) SYSTEMS

General Information

▶ **See Figures 36 and 37**

The MFI/SFI system functions with electronic engine control like most fuel injection systems. The MFI system was used on 1994–95 2.2L engines and on 1996–99 2.2L engines a SFI system was introduced. Though the names are different the components and functions of the systems are basically the same except that the injectors are fired (energized) in a different manner. On MFI systems the injectors are fired in pairs (two at a time). On SFI systems the injectors are fired sequentially (one at a time) as each piston is on its intake stroke. A throttle body is used to meter intake air (the throttle body is integral with the upper intake manifold on 1994–97 2.2L engines), but unlike TBI systems, the fuel is delivered further downstream of the air flow. The defining feature of a MFI system is that a separate fuel injector is used for each cylinder. A 2-piece intake manifold assembly is used. on 1994–97 models, the "fuel rail" is incorporated into the lower intake manifold. Fuel is supplied through a passage in the lower intake to each of the bottom feed fuel injectors. On 1998–99 models, the system uses a external type fuel rail that can be removed from the vehicle.

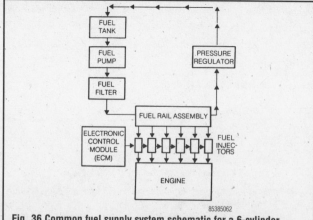

Fig. 36 Common fuel supply system schematic for a 6-cylinder engine (4-cylinder similar, but uses fewer injectors)

85385062

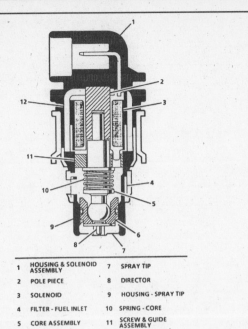

1	HOUSING & SOLENOID ASSEMBLY	7	SPRAY TIP
2	POLE PIECE	8	DIRECTOR
3	SOLENOID	9	HOUSING - SPRAY TIP
4	FILTER - FUEL INLET	10	SPRING - CORE
5	CORE ASSEMBLY	11	SCREW & GUIDE ASSEMBLY
6	CORE SEAT	12	SOLENOID BODY

85385063

Fig. 37 Cross-sectional view of a bottom feed fuel injector used on the 2.2L engine

Fuel Pressure Relief

1994–96 MODELS

Prior to servicing any component of the fuel injection system, the fuel pressure must be relieved. If fuel pressure is not relieved, serious injury could result.

A valve is provided on these fuel systems in order to conveniently test or release the fuel system pressure. A fuel pressure gauge and adapter will be necessary to connect to the fitting. The 2.2L system is equipped with a valve located on the fuel feed inlet fitting, on the opposite end of the lower intake from the pressure regulator.

1. Disconnect the negative battery cable to assure the prevention of fuel spillage if the ignition switch is accidentally turned **ON** while a fitting is still disconnected.
2. Loosen the fuel filter cap to release the fuel tank pressure.
3. Make sure the release valve on the fuel gauge is closed, then connect the fuel gauge to the pressure fitting located on the inlet fuel pipe fitting.

➡When connecting the gauge to the fitting, be sure to wrap a rag around the fitting to avoid spillage. After repairs, place the rag in an approved container.

4. Install the bleed hose portion of the fuel gauge assembly into an approved container, then open the gauge release valve and bleed the fuel pressure from the system.
5. When the gauge is removed, be sure to open the bleed valve and drain all fuel from the gauge assembly.

1997 MODELS

1. Loosen the fuel filler cap.
2. Raise the vehicle and support it with jackstands.
3. Unplug the fuel pump electrical connection and lower the vehicle.
4. Start the engine and let it run until it stalls, then try to start the engine again once or twice to make sure that all the fuel supply and pressure has been depleted.
5. Raise the vehicle and support it with jackstands.
6. Attach the fuel pump electrical connection and lower the vehicle.
7. Tighten the fuel filler cap.
8. Disconnect the negative battery cable to avoid any possible fuel discharge in case somebody accidentally attempts to start the engine.
9. After all necessary repairs have been performed you must reset the system as follows:
   a. Make sure the negative battery cable has been disconnected for more than 10 seconds, then attach the cable to the battery.
   b. Turn the ignition **ON** engine **OFF** for 5 seconds.
   c. Turn the ignition **OFF** for 10 seconds. The fuel system should now be fully charged.

1998 MODELS

▶ **See Figures 38 and 39**

1. Remove the fuel pump relay as follows:
   a. Open the glove box door to access the relay cover.
   b. Unfasten the relay cover screw (if equipped) and remove the cover.
   c. Grasp the relay and gently pull it to remove it.
2. Start the engine and let it run until it stalls, then try to start the engine again once or twice to make sure that all the fuel supply and pressure has been depleted.
3. Reinstall the relay and its cover.
4. Disconnect the negative battery cable to avoid any possible fuel discharge in case somebody accidentally attempts to start the engine.

1999 MODELS

▶ **See Figure 40**

1. Disconnect the negative battery cable and make sure the ignition key is in the **OFF** position.
2. Loosen the fuel filler cap.
3. Attach fuel pressure gauge J 34730-1A or its equivalent to the fuel pressure connection.

➡When connecting the gauge to the fitting, be sure to wrap a rag around the fitting to avoid spillage. After repairs, place the rag in an approved container.

Fig. 38 On later models vehicles, the fuel pump relay is located in the glove box under a cover

Fig. 39 Remove the cover to access the relay

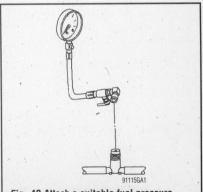

Fig. 40 Attach a suitable fuel pressure gauge to the fuel pressure connection

4. Install the bleed hose portion of the fuel gauge assembly into an approved container, then open the gauge release valve and bleed the fuel pressure from the system.

5. When the gauge is removed, be sure to open the bleed valve and drain all fuel from the gauge assembly.

Electric Fuel Pump

The electric pump is attached to the fuel sending unit, located in the fuel tank.

TESTING

▶ See Figures 41, 42, 43, 44 and 45

1. Properly relieve the fuel system pressure.
2. Leave the gauge attached to the pressure fitting on the fuel inlet pipe.
3. If disconnected during the fuel pressure relief procedure, reconnect the negative battery terminal.
4. Turn the ignition **ON** and listen for the pump to run (is should run for 2 seconds). If necessary, cycle the ignition **OFF** for 10 seconds and then **ON** again in order to build maximum system pressure. Check that pressure is at specification:

a. Note the fuel pressure with the pump RUNNING, it should be 41–47 psi (284–325 kPa). When the pump stops pressure may vary slightly, then should hold steady. If not, refer to the accompanying fuel system diagnosis charts.

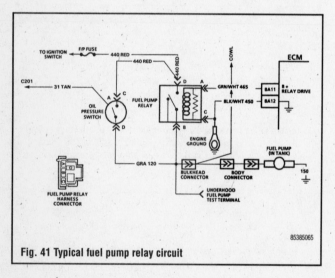

Fig. 41 Typical fuel pump relay circuit

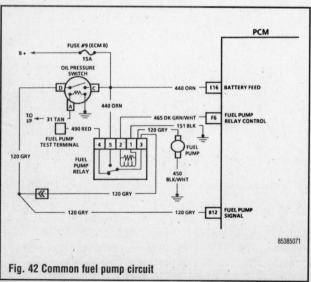

Fig. 42 Common fuel pump circuit

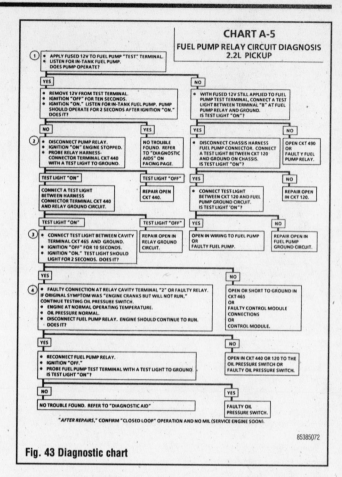

Fig. 43 Diagnostic chart

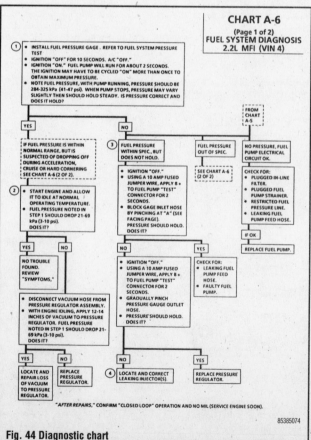

Fig. 44 Diagnostic chart

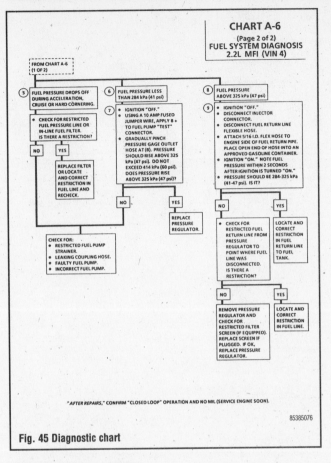

Fig. 45 Diagnostic chart

REMOVAL & INSTALLATION

Removal and installation of the fuel pump and sending unit assembly is the same on MFI/SFI vehicles as it is for TBI vehicles. Please refer to the TBI procedures earlier in this section for electric fuel pump replacement.

Throttle Body

REMOVAL & INSTALLATION

1994–97 models

On the 1994–97 2.2L MFI engine, the throttle body is an integral part of the cast upper intake manifold assembly. For removal and installation procedures, please refer to Section 3 of this manual.

1998–99 Models

1. Disconnect the negative battery cable.
2. Remove the air cleaner resonator.
3. Unplug the electrical connections from the Throttle Position (TP) sensor and the Idle Air Control (IAC) valve.
4. Tag and disconnect the vacuum hoses from the throttle body.
5. Disconnect the throttle, cruise and transmission cables.
6. Remove the throttle cable bracket.
7. Unfasten the throttle body retainers and remove the throttle body.
To install:
8. Place the throttle body into position and install the retainers. Tighten the retainers to 89 inch lbs. (10 Nm).
9. Install the throttle cable bracket.
10. Attach the throttle, cruise and transmission cables.
11. Connect the vacuum hoses to the throttle body.
12. Attach the TP and IAC electrical connections.
13. Install the air cleaner resonator.
14. With the engine **OFF**, check to see if the accelerator pedal is free by depressing the pedal to the floor and then releasing it.
15. Connect the negative battery cable.
16. Turn the ignition switch to the **ON** position.
17. Turn the ignition switch **OFF** for ten seconds.
18. Start the engine and check for proper operation.

Fuel Injectors

REMOVAL & INSTALLATION

1994–97 Models

▶ See Figures 46 thru 52

The bottom feed fuel injectors on the 2.2L MFI engine are installed to the lower intake manifold assembly. For access, the upper intake must first be removed.

➡**Take care when servicing the lower intake and fuel injectors to prevent dirt or contaminants from entering the fuel system. ALL openings in the fuel lines and passages should be capped or plugged while disconnected.**

1. Properly relieve the fuel system pressure, then disconnect the negative battery cable.
2. Remove the accelerator bracket retaining bolts/nuts, then remove or reposition the bracket.
3. Remove the upper intake manifold assembly. For details, please refer to the intake manifold procedures found in Section 3 of this manual.
4. Remove the fuel return line bracket nut, then remove the return line retaining bracket and position it away from the pressure regulator.
5. Remove the fuel pressure regulator assembly. For details, please refer to the procedure later in this section.

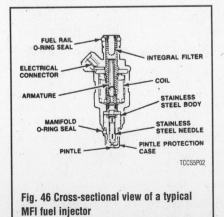

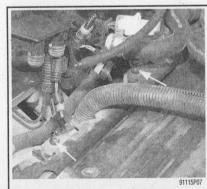

Fig. 46 Cross-sectional view of a typical MFI fuel injector

Fig. 47 Remove the fuel injector retainer bracket attaching screws (arrows)

Fig. 48 Remove the bracket by carefully sliding it off to clear the injector slots

91115P09

Fig. 49 Unplug the injector electrical connectors

91115P10

Fig. 50 Remove the fuel injectors from the lower intake manifold assembly

91115P11

Fig. 51 Remove the injector O-rings and discard them

91115P12

Fig. 52 You may need to use a pick to remove the O-rings as the are sometimes hard to get a hold of

➡**DO NOT attempt to remove the injectors from their bores while lifting upward on the retaining bracket or damage may occur. DO NOT attempt to remove the bracket without first removing the pressure regulator.**

6. Remove the fuel injector retainer bracket attaching screws, then remove the bracket by carefully sliding it off to clear the injector slots.

7. Tag and unplug the injector electrical connectors.

8. Remove the fuel injectors from the lower intake manifold assembly, then remove and discard the old O-rings.

   To install:

➡**Because each injector is calibrated for a specific flow rate, make sure you only replace fuel injectors using an IDENTICAL part number to the old injectors.**

9. Lubricate the new O-ring seals with clean engine oil, then position them on the injectors.

10. Carefully install the injectors assemblies into the lower manifold sockets, making sure the electrical connectors are facing inward.

11. Position the injector bracket to the retaining slots and regulator are aligned with the bracket slots.

12. Engage the injector electrical connectors as tagged during removal.

13. Install the fuel pressure regulator assembly.

14. Make sure the threads of the injector retainer bracket screws are coated with a suitable threadlocking compound such as Loctite®262 or equivalent, then install and tighten them to 31 inch lbs. (3.5 Nm).

15. Install the upper intake manifold assembly. Please refer to the procedure in Section 3 of this manual.

16. If not done already, install the accelerator cable bracket. Tighten the retaining nut to 22 ft. lbs. (30 Nm) and the retaining bolts to 18 ft. lbs. (25 Nm).

17. Connect the negative battery cable.

18. Pressurize the fuel system by cycling the ignition (without attempting to start the engine), then check for leaks.

19. If not done already, install the air inlet duct

1998–99 Models

1. Relieve the fuel system pressure and disconnect the negative battery cable.
2. Remove the fuel rail.
3. Remove the fuel injector retaining clip.
4. Remove the injector.

➡**Because each injector is calibrated for a specific flow rate, make sure you only replace fuel injectors using an IDENTICAL part number to the old injectors.**

   To install:

➡**When installing the injector care should be taken not to tear or misalign O-rings.**

5. Lubricate the injector O-ring seals with clean engine oil and install them injector.

6. Install the upper O-ring, lower back-up O-ring and lower O-ring.
7. Attach the fuel injector to the fuel rail.
8. Install the injector retaining clip and install the fuel rail.
9. Connect the negative battery cable.
10. Inspect for leaks as follows:
  a. Turn the switch to the **ON** position for 2 seconds.
  b. Turn the ignition switch **OFF** for 10 seconds.
  c. Turn the ignition switch to the **ON** position and check for leaks.

Fuel Rail

REMOVAL & INSTALLATION

1998–99 Models

1. Relieve the fuel system pressure and disconnect the negative battery cable.
2. If necessary, remove the intake manifold assembly.
3. Unplug the fuel injector electrical connections by pushing in the wire connector clip and gently pulling on the connector.
4. Disconnect the fuel feed inlet pipe from the rail. Refer to the quick connect fitting removal & installation procedure at the beginning of this section.

➡**Use a back-up wrench on the fuel rail return fitting to prevent it from turning.**

5. Disconnect the fuel return pipe from the fuel pressure regulator.
6. Remove the fuel pressure regulator.
7. Unfasten the fuel rail attaching bolts and lift the fuel rail assembly from the cylinder head.
8. Remove the fuel rail by moving the rail towards the front of the engine.
   To install:
9. Install the fuel rail and insert it into the cylinder head. Install the retaining bolts and tighten to 18 ft. lbs. (25 Nm).
10. Install the fuel pressure regulator.

➡**Use a back-up wrench on the fuel rail return fitting to prevent it from turning.**

11. Connect the return pipe to the fuel pressure regulator. Tighten the fuel pipe nut to 22 ft. lbs. (30 Nm).

12. Connect the fuel feed inlet pipe to rail. Refer to the quick connect fitting removal & installation procedure at the beginning of this section.

➡**Rotate the fuel injectors as necessary to avoid stretching the wire harness.**

13. Attach the injector electrical connections.
14. If removed, install the intake manifold.
15. Connect the negative battery cable.
16. Inspect for leaks as follows:
    a. Turn the switch to the **ON** position for 2 seconds.
    b. Turn the ignition switch **OFF** for 10 seconds.
    c. Turn the ignition switch to the **ON** position and check for leaks.

Fuel Pressure Regulator

REMOVAL & INSTALLATION

1994–97 Models

▶ **See Figures 53, 54, 55, 56 and 57**

1. Properly relieve the fuel system pressure and disconnect the negative battery cable.
2. Remove the fuel return pipe from the regulator and discard the old O-ring.
3. Disconnect the vacuum hose from the regulator.
4. Remove the fuel return pipe clamp.
5. Remove the pressure regulator attaching screw, then remove the regulator and discard the O-ring.
To install:
6. If the old pressure regulator is being installed, check the filter screen (if equipped) for contamination and replace, if necessary.

7. Lubricate the new O-rings with clean engine oil, then install them on the pressure regulator and fuel pipe.
8. Install the pressure regulator onto the manifold.
9. Make sure the regulator attaching screw threads are covered with Loctite®262 or an equivalent threadlocking compound, then install and tighten the screws to 31 inch lbs. (3.5 Nm).
10. Connect the vacuum hose to the regulator.
11. Make sure the new O-ring is in position, then connect the fuel return pipe to the pressure regulator and tighten to 22 ft. lbs. (30 Nm).
12. Install the fuel return pipe clamp and attaching nut to the lower intake manifold assembly.
13. Connect the negative battery cable, then pressurize the fuel system by cycling the ignition (without attempting to start the engine) and check for leaks.

1998–99 Models

1. Properly relieve the fuel system pressure and disconnect the negative battery cable.
2. Disconnect the vacuum hose form the regulator.
3. Unfasten the pressure regulator attaching screw.
4. Remove the regulator and O-ring. Discard the O-ring.
To install:
5. If the old pressure regulator is being installed, check the filter screen (if equipped) for contamination and replace, if necessary.
6. Lubricate the new O-ring with clean engine oil, then install it on the pressure regulator.
7. Position the regulator on the fuel.
8. Make sure the regulator attaching screw threads are covered with Loctite®262 or an equivalent threadlocking compound, then install and tighten the screw to 106 inch lbs. (12 Nm).
9. Connect the negative battery cable.
10. Inspect for leaks as follows:
    a. Turn the switch to the **ON** position for 2 seconds.
    b. Turn the ignition switch **OFF** for 10 seconds.
    c. Turn the ignition switch to the **ON** position and check for leaks.

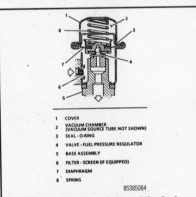

1 COVER
2 VACUUM CHAMBER (VACUUM SOURCE TUBE NOT SHOWN)
3 SEAL - O-RING
4 VALVE - FUEL PRESSURE REGULATOR
5 BASE ASSEMBLY
6 FILTER - SCREEN (IF EQUIPPED)
7 DIAPHRAGM
8 SPRING

85385084

Fig. 53 Cross-sectional view of the fuel pressure regulator—1994–97 I engines

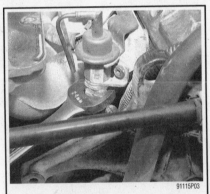

91115P03

Fig. 54 Use a wrench to unfasten the fuel line-to-regulator fitting

91115P04

Fig. 55 Disconnect the vacuum hose from the regulator

91115P05

Fig. 56 Remove the pressure regulator attaching screw

91115P06

Fig. 57 Remove the regulator from the manifold and discard the O-ring

FUEL TANK

Tank Assembly

REMOVAL & INSTALLATION

▶ **See Figures 58 and 59**

Except With Shield Package

1. Properly drain the fuel tank, then disconnect the negative battery cable.
2. If not done already, raise and support the rear of the truck safely using jackstands.
3. If equipped on late-model vehicles, loosen and remove the tank plastic shield.
4. Loosen the retaining clamp and disconnect the tank filler hose from the tank neck.

➡**If fuel and vapor hoses or pump/sending unit wiring can be accessed at this time, they may be tagged and disconnected. If not, wait for the retaining straps to be loosened and lower the tank slightly for access.**

5. Tag and disconnect and accessible wiring or hoses from the top of the fuel tank.
6. Have and assistant support the fuel tank, then remove the fuel tank-to-vehicle straps and, if equipped, the isolation strips. If no assistant is available, position a floor jack to support the tank while the straps are removed.
7. Lower the tank slightly, then remove the sending unit or sending unit/pump wires, hoses and ground strap. Be sure to label all connections to ease installation.
8. Carefully lower the fuel tank from the vehicle and store in a safe place.

To install:

9. Raise the tank partially into position in the vehicle. If you are working without an assistant, you may wish to loosely install one of the retaining straps and use a floor jack to support the tank at an angle so there is access to the sending unit or sending unit/pump assembly (as applicable).
10. Connect the fuel/vapor hoses and wiring to the top of the fuel tank, as tagged during removal.
11. Carefully raise the fuel tank so it is fully into position and loosely secure the retaining straps. Make sure the wires and hoses are not pinched or damaged when raising the tank. Also, be sure that the isolation strips (if used) are positioned between the retaining straps and the fuel tank.
12. It may be easier to connect the fuel filler hose to the tank neck at this time. If desired, connect the hose and secure the clamp.
13. Tighten the fuel tank retaining strap fasteners to specification. Tighten the strap nuts to 33 ft. lbs. (45 Nm).
14. If not done earlier, connect the tank filler hose to the tank neck and secure using the clamp.
15. If equipped, install and secure the tank plastic shield.
16. Remove the jackstands and carefully lower the rear of the truck.
17. Refill the fuel tank and install the filler cap, then check for leaks.
18. Connect the negative battery cable.

Equipped With Shield Package

1. Properly drain the fuel tank, then disconnect the negative battery cable.
2. Raise and support the rear of the truck safely using jackstands.
3. Remove the shield forward support and bracket.
4. While supporting the shield and tank assembly with the help of both an assistant and a floor jack, remove the remaining bolts holding the assembly to the frame, then lower it sufficiently for access to the hoses and wires.
5. Tag and disengage the hoses and wires from the sending unit assembly.
6. Carefully lower the fuel tank and shield from the vehicle, then if necessary for service or replacement, separate the tank from the shield.

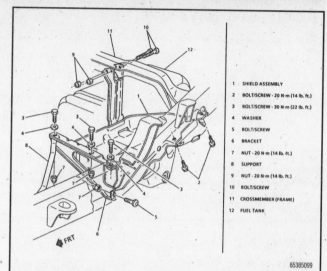

1	SHIELD ASSEMBLY
2	BOLT/SCREW - 20 N·m (14 lb. ft.)
3	BOLT/SCREW - 30 N·m (22 lb. ft.)
4	WASHER
5	BOLT/SCREW
6	BRACKET
7	NUT - 20 N·m (14 lb. ft.)
8	SUPPORT
9	NUT - 20 N·m (14 lb. ft.)
10	BOLT/SCREW
11	CROSSMEMBER (FRAME)
12	FUEL TANK

85385099

Fig. 58 Fuel tank mounting—vehicles equipped with shield package

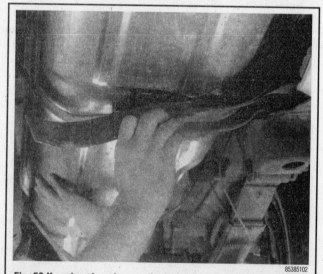

85385102

Fig. 59 If equipped, make sure the isolators are positioned between the straps and tank

To install:

7. If separated, install the tank to the shield.
8. Carefully raise the tank and shield assembly partially into position with the help of an assistant and a floor jack.
9. Connect the wiring and hoses to the sending unit assembly, as tagged during removal.
10. Raise the tank and shield assembly fully into position, then secure to the frame using the lower retaining bolts.
11. Install the shield forward support bracket.
12. Remove the jackstands and carefully lower the rear of the truck.
13. Refill the fuel tank and install the filler cap, then check for leaks.
14. Connect the negative battery cable.

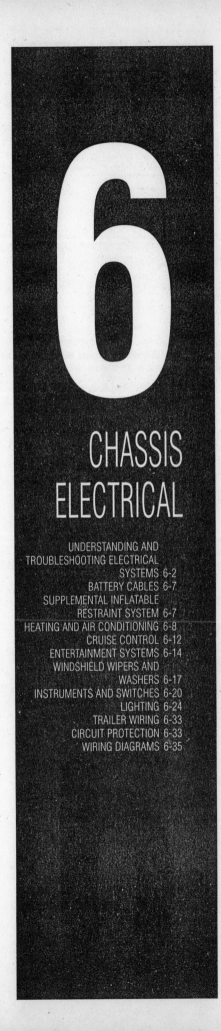

6

CHASSIS ELECTRICAL

UNDERSTANDING AND TROUBLESHOOTING ELECTRICAL SYSTEMS

Basic Electrical Theory

♦ See Figure 1

For any 12 volt, negative ground, electrical system to operate, the electricity must travel in a complete circuit. This simply means that current (power) from the positive (+) terminal of the battery must eventually return to the negative (–) terminal of the battery. Along the way, this current will travel through wires, fuses, switches and components. If, for any reason, the flow of current through the circuit is interrupted, the component fed by that circuit will cease to function properly.

Perhaps the easiest way to visualize a circuit is to think of connecting a light bulb (with two wires attached to it) to the battery—one wire attached to the negative (–) terminal of the battery and the other wire to the positive (+) terminal. With the two wires touching the battery terminals, the circuit would be complete and the light bulb would illuminate. Electricity would follow a path from the battery to the bulb and back to the battery. It's easy to see that with longer wires on our light bulb, it could be mounted anywhere. Further, one wire could be fitted with a switch so that the light could be turned on and off.

The normal automotive circuit differs from this simple example in two ways. First, instead of having a return wire from the bulb to the battery, the current travels through the frame of the vehicle. Since the negative (–) battery cable is attached to the frame (made of electrically conductive metal), the frame of the vehicle can serve as a ground wire to complete the circuit. Secondly, most automotive circuits contain multiple components which receive power from a single circuit. This lessens the amount of wire needed to power components on the vehicle.

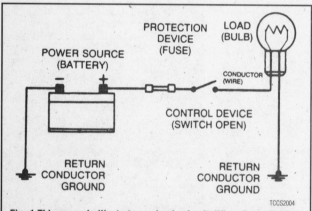

Fig. 1 This example illustrates a simple circuit. When the switch is closed, power from the positive (+) battery terminal flows through the fuse and the switch, and then to the light bulb. The light illuminates and the circuit is completed through the ground wire back to the negative (ñ) battery terminal. In reality, the two ground points shown in the illustration are attached to the metal frame of the vehicle, which completes the circuit back to the battery

HOW DOES ELECTRICITY WORK: THE WATER ANALOGY

Electricity is the flow of electrons—the subatomic particles that constitute the outer shell of an atom. Electrons spin in an orbit around the center core of an atom. The center core is comprised of protons (positive charge) and neutrons (neutral charge). Electrons have a negative charge and balance out the positive charge of the protons. When an outside force causes the number of electrons to unbalance the charge of the protons, the electrons will split off the atom and look for another atom to balance out. If this imbalance is kept up, electrons will continue to move and an electrical flow will exist.

Many people have been taught electrical theory using an analogy with water. In a comparison with water flowing through a pipe, the electrons would be the water and the wire is the pipe.

The flow of electricity can be measured much like the flow of water through a pipe. The unit of measurement used is amperes, frequently abbreviated as amps (a). You can compare amperage to the volume of water flowing through a pipe. When connected to a circuit, an ammeter will measure the actual amount of current flowing through the circuit. When relatively few electrons flow through a circuit, the amperage is low. When many electrons flow, the amperage is high.

Water pressure is measured in units such as pounds per square inch (psi); The electrical pressure is measured in units called volts (v). When a voltmeter is connected to a circuit, it is measuring the electrical pressure.

The actual flow of electricity depends not only on voltage and amperage, but also on the resistance of the circuit. The higher the resistance, the higher the force necessary to push the current through the circuit. The standard unit for measuring resistance is an ohm. Resistance in a circuit varies depending on the amount and type of components used in the circuit. The main factors which determine resistance are:

• Material—some materials have more resistance than others. Those with high resistance are said to be insulators. Rubber materials (or rubber-like plastics) are some of the most common insulators used in vehicles as they have a very high resistance to electricity. Very low resistance materials are said to be conductors. Copper wire is among the best conductors. Silver is actually a superior conductor to copper and is used in some relay contacts, but its high cost prohibits its use as common wiring. Most automotive wiring is made of copper.

• Size—the larger the wire size being used, the less resistance the wire will have. This is why components which use large amounts of electricity usually have large wires supplying current to them.

• Length—for a given thickness of wire, the longer the wire, the greater the resistance. The shorter the wire, the less the resistance. When determining the proper wire for a circuit, both size and length must be considered to design a circuit that can handle the current needs of the component.

• Temperature—with many materials, the higher the temperature, the greater the resistance (positive temperature coefficient). Some materials exhibit the opposite trait of lower resistance with higher temperatures (negative temperature coefficient). These principles are used in many of the sensors on the engine.

OHM'S LAW

There is a direct relationship between current, voltage and resistance. The relationship between current, voltage and resistance can be summed up by a statement known as Ohm's law.

Voltage (E) is equal to amperage (I) times resistance (R): $E = I \times R$
Other forms of the formula are $R = E/I$ and $I = E/R$

In each of these formulas, E is the voltage in volts, I is the current in amps and R is the resistance in ohms. The basic point to remember is that as the resistance of a circuit goes up, the amount of current that flows in the circuit will go down, if voltage remains the same.

The amount of work that the electricity can perform is expressed as power. The unit of power is the watt (w). The relationship between power, voltage and current is expressed as:

Power (w) is equal to amperage (I) times voltage (E): $W = I \times E$

This is only true for direct current (DC) circuits; The alternating current formula is a tad different, but since the electrical circuits in most vehicles are DC type, we need not get into AC circuit theory.

Electrical Components

POWER SOURCE

Power is supplied to the vehicle by two devices: The battery and the alternator. The battery supplies electrical power during starting or during periods when the current demand of the vehicle's electrical system exceeds the output capacity of the alternator. The alternator supplies electrical current when the engine is running. Just not does the alternator supply the current needs of the vehicle, but it recharges the battery.

The Battery

In most modern vehicles, the battery is a lead/acid electrochemical device consisting of six 2 volt subsections (cells) connected in series, so that the unit is capable of producing approximately 12 volts of electrical pressure. Each subsection consists of a series of positive and negative plates held a short distance apart in a solution of sulfuric acid and water.

The two types of plates are of dissimilar metals. This sets up a chemical reaction, and it is this reaction which produces current flow from the battery when its positive and negative terminals are connected to an electrical load. The power removed from the battery is replaced by the alternator, restoring the battery to its original chemical state.

The Alternator

On some vehicles there isn't an alternator, but a generator. The difference is that an alternator supplies alternating current which is then changed to direct current for use on the vehicle, while a generator produces direct current. Alternators tend to be more efficient and that is why they are used.

Alternators and generators are devices that consist of coils of wires wound together making big electromagnets. One group of coils spins within another set and the interaction of the magnetic fields causes a current to flow. This current is then drawn off the coils and fed into the vehicles electrical system.

GROUND

Two types of grounds are used in automotive electric circuits. Direct ground components are grounded to the frame through their mounting points. All other components use some sort of ground wire which is attached to the frame or chassis of the vehicle. The electrical current runs through the chassis of the vehicle and returns to the battery through the ground (–) cable; if you look, you'll see that the battery ground cable connects between the battery and the frame or chassis of the vehicle.

➡ **It should be noted that a good percentage of electrical problems can be traced to bad grounds.**

PROTECTIVE DEVICES

▸ **See Figure 2**

It is possible for large surges of current to pass through the electrical system of your vehicle. If this surge of current were to reach the load in the circuit, the surge could burn it out or severely damage it. It can also overload the wiring, causing the harness to get hot and melt the insulation. To prevent this, fuses, circuit breakers and/or fusible links are connected into the supply wires of the electrical system. These items are nothing more than a built-in weak spot in the

system. When an abnormal amount of current flows through the system, these protective devices work as follows to protect the circuit:

- Fuse—when an excessive electrical current passes through a fuse, the fuse "blows" (the conductor melts) and opens the circuit, preventing the passage of current.
- Circuit Breaker—a circuit breaker is basically a self-repairing fuse. It will open the circuit in the same fashion as a fuse, but when the surge subsides, the circuit breaker can be reset and does not need replacement.
- Fusible Link—a fusible link (fuse link or main link) is a short length of special, high temperature insulated wire that acts as a fuse. When an excessive electrical current passes through a fusible link, the thin gauge wire inside the link melts, creating an intentional open to protect the circuit. To repair the circuit, the link must be replaced. Some newer type fusible links are housed in plug-in modules, which are simply replaced like a fuse, while older type fusible links must be cut and spliced if they melt. Since this link is very early in the electrical path, it's the first place to look if nothing on the vehicle works, yet the battery seems to be charged and is properly connected.

✹✹ CAUTION

Always replace fuses, circuit breakers and fusible links with identically rated components. Under no circumstances should a component of higher or lower amperage rating be substituted.

SWITCHES & RELAYS

▸ **See Figures 3 and 4**

Switches are used in electrical circuits to control the passage of current. The most common use is to open and close circuits between the battery and the various electric devices in the system. Switches are rated according to the amount of amperage they can handle. If a sufficient amperage rated switch is not used in a circuit, the switch could overload and cause damage.

Some electrical components which require a large amount of current to operate use a special switch called a relay. Since these circuits carry a large amount of current, the thickness of the wire in the circuit is also greater. If this large wire were connected from the load to the control switch, the switch would have to carry the high amperage load and the fairing or dash would be twice as large to accommodate the increased size of the wiring harness. To prevent these problems, a relay is used.

Relays are composed of a coil and a set of contacts. When the coil has a current passed though it, a magnetic field is formed and this field causes the contacts to move together, completing the circuit. Most relays are normally open, preventing current from passing through the circuit, but they can take any electrical form depending on the job they are intended to do. Relays can be considered "remote control switches." They allow a smaller current to operate devices that require higher amperages. When a small current operates the coil, a larger current is

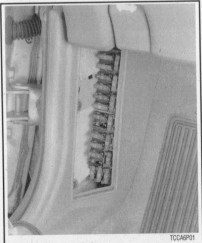

Fig. 2 Most vehicles use one or more fuse panels. This one is located on the driver's side kick panel

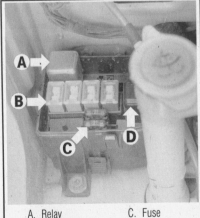

A. Relay   C. Fuse
B. Fusible link   D. Flasher

Fig. 3 The underhood fuse and relay panel usually contains fuses, relays, flashers and fusible links

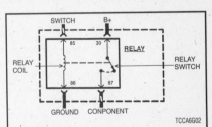

Fig. 4 Relays are composed of a coil and a switch. These two components are linked together so that when one operates, the other operates at the same time. The large wires in the circuit are connected from the battery to one side of the relay switch (B+) and from the opposite side of the relay switch to the load (component). Smaller wires are connected from the relay coil to the control switch for the circuit and from the opposite side of the relay coil to ground

allowed to pass by the contacts. Some common circuits which may use relays are the horn, headlights, starter, electric fuel pump and other high draw circuits.

LOAD

Every electrical circuit must include a "load" (something to use the electricity coming from the source). Without this load, the battery would attempt to deliver its entire power supply from one pole to another. This is called a "short circuit." All this electricity would take a short cut to ground and cause a great amount of damage to other components in the circuit by developing a tremendous amount of heat. This condition could develop sufficient heat to melt the insulation on all the surrounding wires and reduce a multiple wire cable to a lump of plastic and copper.

WIRING & HARNESSES

The average vehicle contains meters and meters of wiring, with hundreds of individual connections. To protect the many wires from damage and to keep them from becoming a confusing tangle, they are organized into bundles, enclosed in plastic or taped together and called wiring harnesses. Different harnesses serve different parts of the vehicle. Individual wires are color coded to help trace them through a harness where sections are hidden from view.

Automotive wiring or circuit conductors can be either single strand wire, multi-strand wire or printed circuitry. Single strand wire has a solid metal core and is usually used inside such components as alternators, motors, relays and other devices. Multi-strand wire has a core made of many small strands of wire twisted together into a single conductor. Most of the wiring in an automotive electrical system is made up of multi-strand wire, either as a single conductor or grouped together in a harness. All wiring is color coded on the insulator, either as a solid color or as a colored wire with an identification stripe. A printed circuit is a thin film of copper or other conductor that is printed on an insulator backing. Occasionally, a printed circuit is sandwiched between two sheets of plastic for more protection and flexibility. A complete printed circuit, consisting of conductors, insulating material and connectors for lamps or other components is called a printed circuit board. Printed circuitry is used in place of individual wires or harnesses in places where space is limited, such as behind instrument panels.

Since automotive electrical systems are very sensitive to changes in resistance, the selection of properly sized wires is critical when systems are repaired. A loose or corroded connection or a replacement wire that is too small for the circuit will add extra resistance and an additional voltage drop to the circuit.

The wire gauge number is an expression of the cross-section area of the conductor. Vehicles from countries that use the metric system will typically describe the wire size as its cross-sectional area in square millimeters. In this method, the larger the wire, the greater the number. Another common system for expressing wire size is the American Wire Gauge (AWG) system. As gauge number increases, area decreases and the wire becomes smaller. An 18 gauge wire is smaller than a 4 gauge wire. A wire with a higher gauge number will carry less current than a wire with a lower gauge number. Gauge wire size refers to the size of the strands of the conductor, not the size of the complete wire with insulator. It is possible, therefore, to have two wires of the same gauge with different diameters because one may have thicker insulation than the other.

It is essential to understand how a circuit works before trying to figure out why it doesn't. An electrical schematic shows the electrical current paths when a circuit is operating properly. Schematics break the entire electrical system down into individual circuits. In a schematic, usually no attempt is made to represent wiring and components as they physically appear on the vehicle; switches and other components are shown as simply as possible. Face views of harness connectors show the cavity or terminal locations in all multi-pin connectors to help locate test points.

CONNECTORS

▶ See Figures 5 and 6

Three types of connectors are commonly used in automotive applications—weatherproof, molded and hard shell.

• Weatherproof—these connectors are most commonly used where the connector is exposed to the elements. Terminals are protected against moisture and dirt by sealing rings which provide a weathertight seal. All repairs require the use of a special terminal and the tool required to service it. Unlike standard blade type terminals, these weatherproof terminals cannot be straightened once they are bent. Make certain that the connectors are properly seated and all of the sealing rings are in place when connecting leads.

• Molded—these connectors require complete replacement of the connector if found to be defective. This means splicing a new connector assembly into the harness. All splices should be soldered to insure proper contact. Use care when probing the connections or replacing terminals in them, as it is possible to create a short circuit between opposite terminals. If this happens to the wrong terminal pair, it is possible to damage certain components. Always use jumper wires between connectors for circuit checking and NEVER probe through weatherproof seals.

• Hard Shell—unlike molded connectors, the terminal contacts in hard-shell connectors can be replaced. Replacement usually involves the use of a special terminal removal tool that depresses the locking tangs (barbs) on the connector terminal and allows the connector to be removed from the rear of the shell. The connector shell should be replaced if it shows any evidence of burning, melting, cracks, or breaks. Replace individual terminals that are burnt, corroded, distorted or loose.

Test Equipment

Pinpointing the exact cause of trouble in an electrical circuit is most times accomplished by the use of special test equipment. The following describes different types of commonly used test equipment and briefly explains how to use them in diagnosis. In addition to the information covered below, the tool manufacturer's instructions booklet (provided with the tester) should be read and clearly understood before attempting any test procedures.

JUMPER WIRES

✵✵ CAUTION

Never use jumper wires made from a thinner gauge wire than the circuit being tested. If the jumper wire is of too small a gauge, it may overheat and possibly melt. Never use jumpers to bypass high resistance loads in a circuit. Bypassing resistances, in effect, creates a short circuit. This may, in turn, cause damage and fire. Jumper wires should only be used to bypass lengths of wire or to simulate switches.

Jumper wires are simple, yet extremely valuable, pieces of test equipment. They are basically test wires which are used to bypass sections of a circuit. Although jumper wires can be purchased, they are usually fabricated from lengths of standard automotive wire and whatever type of connector (alligator clip, spade connector or pin connector) that is required for the particular application being tested. In cramped, hard-to-reach areas, it is advisable to have insulated boots over the jumper wire terminals in order to prevent accidental grounding. It is also advisable to include a standard automotive fuse in any jumper wire. This is commonly referred to as a "fused jumper". By inserting an in-line fuse holder between a set of test leads, a fused jumper wire can be used for bypassing open circuits. Use a 5 amp fuse to provide protection against voltage spikes.

Jumper wires are used primarily to locate open electrical circuits, on either the ground (–) side of the circuit or on the power (+) side. If an electrical component fails to operate, connect the jumper wire between the component and a good ground. If the component operates only with the jumper installed, the ground circuit is open. If the ground circuit is good, but the component does not operate, the circuit between the power feed and component may be open. By moving the jumper wire successively back from the component toward the power source, you can isolate the area of the circuit where the open is located. When the component stops functioning, or the power is cut off, the open is in the segment of wire between the jumper and the point previously tested.

You can sometimes connect the jumper wire directly from the battery to the "hot" terminal of the component, but first make sure the component uses 12 volts in operation. Some electrical components, such as fuel injectors or sensors, are designed to operate on about 4 to 5 volts, and running 12 volts directly to these components will cause damage.

TEST LIGHTS

▶ See Figure 7

The test light is used to check circuits and components while electrical current is flowing through them. It is used for voltage and ground tests. To use a 12 volt test light, connect the ground clip to a good ground and probe wherever

Fig. 5 Hard shell (left) and weatherproof (right) connectors have replaceable terminals

Fig. 6 Weatherproof connectors are most commonly used in the engine compartment or where the connector is exposed to the elements

Fig. 7 A 12 volt test light is used to detect the presence of voltage in a circuit

necessary with the pick. The test light will illuminate when voltage is detected. This does not necessarily mean that 12 volts (or any particular amount of voltage) is present; it only means that some voltage is present. It is advisable before using the test light to touch its ground clip and probe across the battery posts or terminals to make sure the light is operating properly.

✶✶ WARNING

Do not use a test light to probe electronic ignition, spark plug or coil wires. Never use a pick-type test light to probe wiring on computer controlled systems unless specifically instructed to do so. Any wire insulation that is pierced by the test light probe should be taped and sealed with silicone after testing.

Like the jumper wire, the 12 volt test light is used to isolate opens in circuits. But, whereas the jumper wire is used to bypass the open to operate the load, the 12 volt test light is used to locate the presence of voltage in a circuit. If the test light illuminates, there is power up to that point in the circuit; if the test light does not illuminate, there is an open circuit (no power). Move the test light in successive steps back toward the power source until the light in the handle illuminates. The open is between the probe and a point which was previously probed.

The self-powered test light is similar in design to the 12 volt test light, but contains a 1.5 volt penlight battery in the handle. It is most often used in place of a multimeter to check for open or short circuits when power is isolated from the circuit (continuity test).

The battery in a self-powered test light does not provide much current. A weak battery may not provide enough power to illuminate the test light even when a complete circuit is made (especially if there is high resistance in the circuit). Always make sure that the test battery is strong. To check the battery, briefly touch the ground clip to the probe; if the light glows brightly, the battery is strong enough for testing.

➡ **A self-powered test light should not be used on any computer controlled system or component. The small amount of electricity transmitted by the test light is enough to damage many electronic automotive components.**

MULTIMETERS

Multimeters are an extremely useful tool for troubleshooting electrical problems. They can be purchased in either analog or digital form and have a price range to suit any budget. A multimeter is a voltmeter, ammeter and ohmmeter (along with other features) combined into one instrument. It is often used when testing solid state circuits because of its high input impedance (usually 10 megaohms or more). A brief description of the multimeter main test functions follows:

• Voltmeter—the voltmeter is used to measure voltage at any point in a circuit, or to measure the voltage drop across any part of a circuit. Voltmeters usually have various scales and a selector switch to allow the reading of different voltage ranges. The voltmeter has a positive and a negative lead. To avoid damage to the meter, always connect the negative lead to the negative (–) side of the circuit (to ground or nearest the ground side of the circuit) and connect the positive lead to the positive (+) side of the circuit (to the power source or the nearest

power source). Note that the negative voltmeter lead will always be black and that the positive voltmeter will always be some color other than black (usually red).

• Ohmmeter—the ohmmeter is designed to read resistance (measured in ohms) in a circuit or component. Most ohmmeters will have a selector switch which permits the measurement of different ranges of resistance (usually the selector switch allows the multiplication of the meter reading by 10, 100, 1,000 and 10,000). Some ohmmeters are "auto-ranging" which means the meter itself will determine which scale to use. Since the meters are powered by an internal battery, the ohmmeter can be used like a self-powered test light. When the ohmmeter is connected, current from the ohmmeter flows through the circuit or component being tested. Since the ohmmeter's internal resistance and voltage are known values, the amount of current flow through the meter depends on the resistance of the circuit or component being tested. The ohmmeter can also be used to perform a continuity test for suspected open circuits. In using the meter for making continuity checks, do not be concerned with the actual resistance readings. Zero resistance, or any ohm reading, indicates continuity in the circuit. Infinite resistance indicates an opening in the circuit. A high resistance reading where there should be none indicates a problem in the circuit. Checks for short circuits are made in the same manner as checks for open circuits, except that the circuit must be isolated from both power and normal ground. Infinite resistance indicates no continuity, while zero resistance indicates a dead short.

✶✶ WARNING

Never use an ohmmeter to check the resistance of a component or wire while there is voltage applied to the circuit.

• Ammeter—an ammeter measures the amount of current flowing through a circuit in units called amperes or amps. At normal operating voltage, most circuits have a characteristic amount of amperes, called "current draw" which can be measured using an ammeter. By referring to a specified current draw rating, then measuring the amperes and comparing the two values, one can determine what is happening within the circuit to aid in diagnosis. An open circuit, for example, will not allow any current to flow, so the ammeter reading will be zero. A damaged component or circuit will have an increased current draw, so the reading will be high. The ammeter is always connected in series with the circuit being tested. All of the current that normally flows through the circuit must also flow through the ammeter; if there is any other path for the current to follow, the ammeter reading will not be accurate. The ammeter itself has very little resistance to current flow and, therefore, will not affect the circuit, but it will measure current draw only when the circuit is closed and electricity is flowing. Excessive current draw can blow fuses and drain the battery, while a reduced current draw can cause motors to run slowly, lights to dim and other components to not operate properly.

Troubleshooting Electrical Systems

When diagnosing a specific problem, organized troubleshooting is a must. The complexity of a modern automotive vehicle demands that you approach any problem in a logical, organized manner. There are certain troubleshooting techniques, however, which are standard:

• Establish when the problem occurs. Does the problem appear only under certain conditions? Were there any noises, odors or other unusual symptoms?

Isolate the problem area. To do this, make some simple tests and observations, then eliminate the systems that are working properly. Check for obvious problems, such as broken wires and loose or dirty connections. Always check the obvious before assuming something complicated is the cause.

• Test for problems systematically to determine the cause once the problem area is isolated. Are all the components functioning properly? Is there power going to electrical switches and motors. Performing careful, systematic checks will often turn up most causes on the first inspection, without wasting time checking components that have little or no relationship to the problem.

• Test all repairs after the work is done to make sure that the problem is fixed. Some causes can be traced to more than one component, so a careful verification of repair work is important in order to pick up additional malfunctions that may cause a problem to reappear or a different problem to arise. A blown fuse, for example, is a simple problem that may require more than another fuse to repair. If you don't look for a problem that caused a fuse to blow, a shorted wire (for example) may go undetected.

Experience has shown that most problems tend to be the result of a fairly simple and obvious cause, such as loose or corroded connectors, bad grounds or damaged wire insulation which causes a short. This makes careful visual inspection of components during testing essential to quick and accurate troubleshooting.

Testing

OPEN CIRCUITS

▶ **See Figure 8**

This test already assumes the existence of an open in the circuit and it is used to help locate the open portion.

1. Isolate the circuit from power and ground.
2. Connect the self-powered test light or ohmmeter ground clip to the ground side of the circuit and probe sections of the circuit sequentially.
3. If the light is out or there is infinite resistance, the open is between the probe and the circuit ground.
4. If the light is on or the meter shows continuity, the open is between the probe and the end of the circuit toward the power source.

SHORT CIRCUITS

➡ **Never use a self-powered test light to perform checks for opens or shorts when power is applied to the circuit under test. The test light can be damaged by outside power.**

1. Isolate the circuit from power and ground.
2. Connect the self-powered test light or ohmmeter ground clip to a good ground and probe any easy-to-reach point in the circuit.
3. If the light comes on or there is continuity, there is a short somewhere in the circuit.
4. To isolate the short, probe a test point at either end of the isolated circuit (the light should be on or the meter should indicate continuity).
5. Leave the test light probe engaged and sequentially open connectors or switches, remove parts, etc. until the light goes out or continuity is broken.

6. When the light goes out, the short is between the last two circuit components which were opened.

VOLTAGE

This test determines voltage available from the battery and should be the first step in any electrical troubleshooting procedure after visual inspection. Many electrical problems, especially on computer controlled systems, can be caused by a low state of charge in the battery. Excessive corrosion at the battery cable terminals can cause poor contact that will prevent proper charging and full battery current flow.

1. Set the voltmeter selector switch to the 20V position.
2. Connect the multimeter negative lead to the battery's negative (–) post or terminal and the positive lead to the battery's positive (+) post or terminal.
3. Turn the ignition switch **ON** to provide a load.
4. A well charged battery should register over 12 volts. If the meter reads below 11.5 volts, the battery power may be insufficient to operate the electrical system properly.

VOLTAGE DROP

▶ **See Figure 9**

When current flows through a load, the voltage beyond the load drops. This voltage drop is due to the resistance created by the load and also by small resistances created by corrosion at the connectors and damaged insulation on the wires. The maximum allowable voltage drop under load is critical, especially if there is more than one load in the circuit, since all voltage drops are cumulative.

1. Set the voltmeter selector switch to the 20 volt position.
2. Connect the multimeter negative lead to a good ground.
3. Operate the circuit and check the voltage prior to the first component (load).
4. There should be little or no voltage drop in the circuit prior to the first component. If a voltage drop exists, the wire or connectors in the circuit are suspect.
5. While operating the first component in the circuit, probe the ground side of the component with the positive meter lead and observe the voltage readings. A small voltage drop should be noticed. This voltage drop is caused by the resistance of the component.
6. Repeat the test for each component (load) down the circuit.
7. If a large voltage drop is noticed, the preceding component, wire or connector is suspect.

RESISTANCE

▶ **See Figures 10 and 11**

❊❊ WARNING

Never use an ohmmeter with power applied to the circuit. The ohmmeter is designed to operate on its own power supply. The normal 12 volt electrical system voltage could damage the meter!

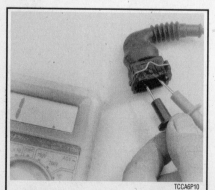

Fig. 8 The infinite reading on this multimeter indicates that the circuit is open

TCCA6P10

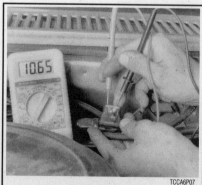

Fig. 9 This voltage drop test revealed high resistance (low voltage) in the circuit

TCCA6P07

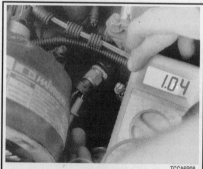

Fig. 10 Checking the resistance of a coolant temperature sensor with an ohmmeter. Reading is 1.04 kilohms

TCCA6P08

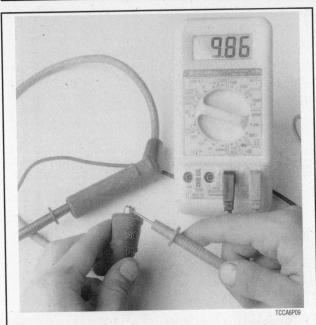

Fig. 11 Spark plug wires can be checked for excessive resistance using an ohmmeter

1. Isolate the circuit from the vehicle's power source.
2. Ensure that the ignition key is **OFF** when disconnecting any components or the battery.
3. Where necessary, also isolate at least one side of the circuit to be checked, in order to avoid reading parallel resistances. Parallel circuit resistances will always give a lower reading than the actual resistance of either of the branches.
4. Connect the meter leads to both sides of the circuit (wire or component) and read the actual measured ohms on the meter scale. Make sure the selector switch is set to the proper ohm scale for the circuit being tested, to avoid misreading the ohmmeter test value.

Wire and Connector Repair

Almost anyone can replace damaged wires, as long as the proper tools and parts are available. Wire and terminals are available to fit almost any need. Even the specialized weatherproof, molded and hard shell connectors are now available from aftermarket suppliers.

Be sure the ends of all the wires are fitted with the proper terminal hardware and connectors. Wrapping a wire around a stud is never a permanent solution and will only cause trouble later. Replace wires one at a time to avoid confusion. Always route wires exactly the same as the factory.

➡ **If connector repair is necessary, only attempt it if you have the proper tools. Weatherproof and hard shell connectors require special tools to release the pins inside the connector. Attempting to repair these connectors with conventional hand tools will damage them.**

BATTERY CABLES

Disconnecting the Cables

When working on any electrical component on the vehicle, it is always a good idea to disconnect the negative (−) battery cable. This will prevent potential damage to many sensitive electrical components such as the Engine Control Module (ECM), radio, alternator, etc.

➡ **Any time you disengage the battery cables, it is recommended that you disconnect the negative (−) battery cable first. This will prevent your accidentally grounding the positive (+) terminal to the body of the vehi-**

cle when disconnecting it, thereby preventing damage to the above mentioned components.

Before you disconnect the cable(s), first turn the ignition to the **OFF** position. This will prevent a draw on the battery which could cause arcing (electricity trying to ground itself to the body of a vehicle, just like a spark plug jumping the gap) and, of course, damaging some components such as the alternator diodes.

When the battery cable(s) are reconnected (negative cable last), be sure to check that your lights, windshield wipers and other electrically operated safety components are all working correctly. If your vehicle contains an Electronically Tuned Radio (ETR), don't forget to also reset your radio stations. Ditto for the clock.

SUPPLEMENTAL INFLATABLE RESTRAINT SYSTEM

General Information

The Supplemental Inflatable Restraint (SIR) system offers protection in addition to that provided by the driver's seat belt by deploying an air bag from the center of the steering wheel. The air bag deploys when the vehicle is involved in a frontal crash of sufficient force up to 30° off the centerline of the vehicle. To further absorb the crash energy, there is also a knee bolster located beneath the instrument panel in the driver's area and the steering wheel is collapsible.

The system has an energy reserve, which can store a large enough electrical charge to deploy the air bag(s) for up to ten minutes after the battery has been disconnected or damaged. The system **MUST** be disabled before any service is performed on or around SIR components or SIR wiring.

SERVICE PRECAUTIONS

▶ **See Figure 12**

- When performing service around the SIR system components or wiring, the SIR system **MUST** be disabled. Failure to do so could result in possible air bag deployment, personal injury or unneeded SIR system repairs.
- When carrying a live inflator module, make sure that the bag and trim cover are pointed away from you. Never carry the inflator module by the wires or

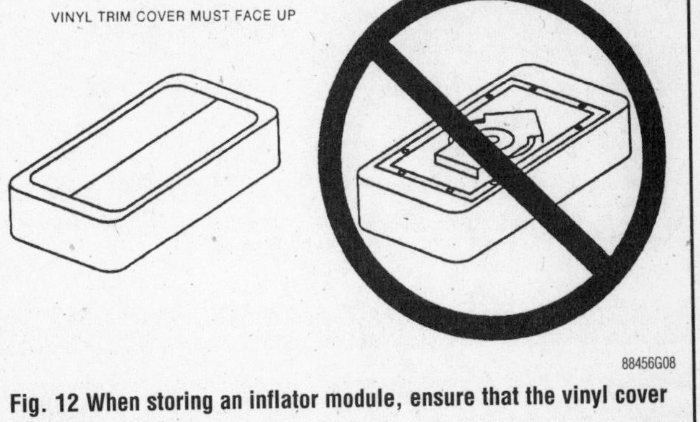

VINYL TRIM COVER MUST FACE UP

Fig. 12 When storing an inflator module, ensure that the vinyl cover faces up

connector on the underside of the module. In case of accidental deployment, the bag will then deploy with minimal chance of injury.

- When placing a live inflator module on a bench or other surface, always face the bag and trim cover up, away from the surface.

Fig. 13 Remove the fuse panel cover

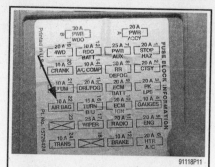

Fig. 14 Look at the diagram on the back of the fuse panel cover to identify the location of the air bag fuse

Fig. 15 Once located, remove the air bag fuse from the panel

Fig. 16 Remove the lower left hand instrument panel knee bolster to access the Connector Position Assurance (CPA) 2-way connector located at the base of the steering column

Fig. 17 Remove the clip that prevents the CPA from being accidentally disconnected . . .

Fig. 18 Unplug the CPA connector

DISABLING THE SYSTEM

▶ See Figures 13 thru 18

1. Turn the steering wheel so that the vehicle's wheels are pointing straight ahead.
2. Turn the ignition switch to **LOCK**, remove the key, then disconnect the negative battery cable.
3. Remove the AIR BAG fuse from the fuse block.
4. Remove the steering column filler panel or knee bolster.
5. Unplug the Connector Position Assurance (CPA) and yellow two way connector at the base of the steering column.
6. On 1998–99 models, remove the Connector Position Assurance (CPA) from the passenger yellow two way connector located behind the glove box.
7. On 1998–99 models, unplug the yellow two way connector located behind the glove box.
8. Connect the negative battery cable.

➡ With the AIR BAG fuse removed, the battery cable connected and the ignition in the ON position, the AIR BAG warning lamp will be ON. This is normal and does not indicate a system malfunction.

ENABLING THE SYSTEM

1. Disconnect the negative battery cable.
2. On 1998–99 models, attach the yellow two way connector located behind the glove box.
3. On 1998–99 models, install the Connector Position Assurance (CPA) to the passenger yellow two way connector located behind the glove box.
4. Turn the ignition switch to **LOCK**, then remove the key.
5. Attach the two way connector at the base of the steering column and the Connector Position Assurance (CPA).
6. Install the steering column filler panel or knee bolster.
7. Install the AIR BAG fuse to the fuse block.
8. Connect the negative battery cable.
9. From the passenger seat, turn the ignition switch to **RUN** and make sure that the AIR BAG warning lamp flashes seven times and then shuts off. If the warning lamp does not shut off, make sure that the wiring is properly connected. If the light remains on, take the vehicle to a reputable repair facility for service.

HEATING AND AIR CONDITIONING

Blower Motor

REMOVAL & INSTALLATION

Pick-Up models

▶ See Figures 19, 20, 21, 22 and 23

1. Disconnect the negative battery cable.
2. If equipped, remove the Vehicle Control Module (VCM) from the engine compartment.

3. Remove the coolant recovery reservoir.
4. Disconnect the blower motor cooling tube.
5. Unplug the electrical connector(s) from the blower motor, as necessary.
6. Remove the blower motor-to-case screws, then carefully withdraw the blower motor from the case.

To install:

7. Install the blower motor to the case and secure using the retaining screws.
8. Engage the electrical connector(s) to the motor, as necessary.
9. If moved on early model vehicles, reposition and secure the A/C vacuum tank.

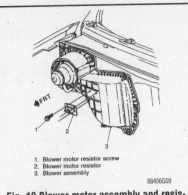

1. Blower motor resistor screw
2. Blower motor resistor
3. Blower assembly

88456G09

Fig. 19 Blower motor assembly and resistor locations

88456P01

Fig. 20 If equipped, remove the VCM from the engine compartment

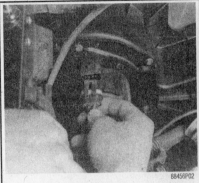

88456P02

Fig. 21 Disengage the blower motor electrical connection

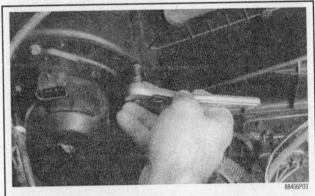

88456P03

Fig. 22 Unfasten and remove the blower motor retainers

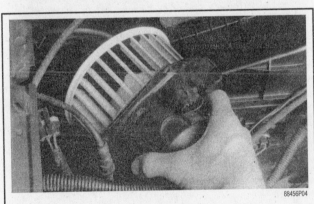

88456P04

Fig. 23 Remove the blower motor from the housing assembly

10. Connect the blower motor cooling tube.
11. Install the coolant recovery reservoir, then if equipped, install the VCM.
12. Connect the negative battery cable.

Utility Models

▶ See Figure 24

1. Disconnect the negative battery cable.
2. If equipped, remove the Vehicle Control Module (VCM) from the engine compartment.
3. Remove the coolant recovery reservoir.
4. Disconnect the blower motor cooling tube.

5. Unplug the electrical connector(s) from the blower motor, as necessary.
6. Remove the blower motor-to-case screws (the lower screw is on the bottom front of the cover).
7. Disconnect the harness from the blower motor.
8. Use a razor or utility knife to cut through the cover on the cut line as neatly as possible because the access cover has to be reinstalled.
9. Starting with upper half of the cover, tear the remaining part of the access cover from the remaining portion. Then remove the lower half of the cover in the same manner.
10. Remove the blower motor assembly.

To install:
11. Install the blower motor assembly.
12. Connect the two halves of the access cover together using the three flange clips.
13. Using black duct tape, place a piece of the tape along the bottom lower edge of the lower half of the lower cover only. The tape has to be the full width of the cover.
14. Install the access cover onto the case.
15. Install the screw and align the cut areas.
16. Seal the cut areas using black weatherstrip adhesive. Do not use RTV to seal the assembly. The weatherstrip adhesive bead should be as straight as possible to ensure a neat and professional finish to the cover. Allow the adhesive to set at least 15 minutes until it skins over.
17. Attach the electrical connections.
18. Attach the cooling tube and install the coolant recovery reservoir.
19. If removed, install the VCM.
20. Connect the negative battery cable and refill the coolant reservoir to the proper level.

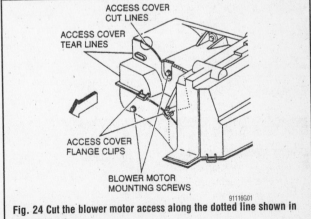

ACCESS COVER
CUT LINES

ACCESS COVER
TEAR LINES

ACCESS COVER
FLANGE CLIPS

BLOWER MOTOR
MOUNTING SCREWS

91116G01

Fig. 24 Cut the blower motor access along the dotted line shown in this illustration

Heater Core

REMOVAL & INSTALLATION

1994–97 Vehicles

♦ **See Figure 25**

1. Disconnect the negative battery cable and properly drain the engine cooling system to a level below the heater core.
2. Disconnect the heater hoses from the core tubes near the cowl.

➡**The instrument panel carrier is designed not only to provide access to parts through removal of the carrier components, but the carrier will also tilt downward as a complete assembly to allow access from the top. If this is desired, remove the retainer screws along the top and bottom of the carrier assembly (refer to the figure). The instrument panel will then tilt as an assembly into the cab. It is necessary to unbolt and lower the steering column from the carrier to allow for maximum movement of the instrument panel.**

3. The instrument panel must be removed or repositioned for access to the heater core case. Unbolt and either tilt the instrument panel forward or disengage the instrument panel components and remove the panel from the vehicle. In most cases, tilting the panel forward should be sufficient for the necessary access, but if necessary remove the panel refer to Section 10 in this manual.
4. Unfasten the heater core rear case retaining screws, then remove the rear case for access to the heater core.
5. Loosen the retainers and remove the heater core retaining straps.
6. Remove the heater core and seals.

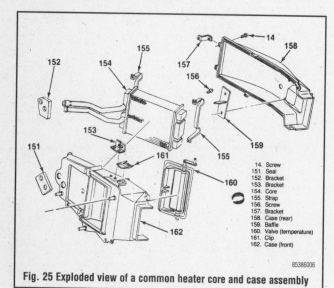

14. Screw
151. Seal
152. Bracket
153. Bracket
154. Core
155. Strap
156. Screw
157. Bracket
158. Case (rear)
159. Baffle
160. Valve (temperature)
161. Clip
162. Case (front)

85386006

Fig. 25 Exploded view of a common heater core and case assembly

To install:

7. Install the heater core and seals, taking care not to damage the core tubes when inserting them through the cowl.
8. Install and secure the core retaining straps.
9. Install the rear case and secure using the screws.
10. Reposition and secure the instrument panel and components. Tighten the cowl screws to 17 inch lbs. (1.9 Nm) and the lower instrument panel screws to 66 inch lbs. (7.5 Nm).
11. Connect the heater hoses to the core tubes.
12. Connect the negative battery cable, then properly refill the engine cooling system.
13. Run the engine at normal operating temperature, then check for leaks.

1998–99 Vehicles

PICK-UP MODELS

1. Disconnect the negative battery cable.

✳✳ CAUTION

Never open, service or drain the radiator or cooling system when hot; serious burns can occur from the steam and hot coolant. Also, when draining engine coolant, keep in mind that cats and dogs are attracted to ethylene glycol antifreeze and could drink any that is left in an uncovered container or in puddles on the ground. This will prove fatal in sufficient quantities. Always drain coolant into a sealable container. Coolant should be reused unless it is contaminated or is several years old.

2. Drain the engine coolant into a suitable container.
3. Disconnect the heater hoses at the firewall in the engine compartment.
4. Remove the instrument panel assembly. Refer to Section 10 of this manual for this procedure.
5. Remove the air inlet assembly as follows:
   a. If necessary, tag and disconnect the vacuum connectors.
   b. Remove the air inlet studs, the inlet assembly and if necessary the gasket.
6. Tag and disconnect all necessary vacuum lines.
7. From inside the engine compartment, remove the heater assembly studs.
8. Remove the blower motor resistor as follows:
   a. Unplug the resistor electrical connection.
   b. Unfasten the screws and remove the resistor.
9. Once the resistor is removed it will uncover a stud inside the heater core housing. Remove this stud.
10. Remove the rear case screws, the heater assembly and the seals.

To install:

11. Install the seals, the heater assembly and the rear case screws.
12. Install the stud inside the heater core housing and tighten to 17 inch lbs. (1.9 Nm).
13. Install the blower motor resistor as follows:
   a. Place the resistor in position and tighten the screws to 17 inch lbs. (1.9 Nm).
   b. Attach the electrical connector to the resistor.
14. Working inside the engine compartment, install the heater assembly studs. Tighten the studs to 17 inch lbs. (1.9 Nm).
15. Attach and disconnected vacuum lines.
16. Install the air inlet assembly as follows:
   a. If removed, install the inlet assembly gasket.
   b. Install the inlet assembly and the studs. Tighten the studs to 40 inch lbs. (4.5 Nm).
   c. Attach all unplugged vacuum connectors.
17. Install the instrument panel assembly.
18. Attach the heater hoses to the core tubes at the engine compartment firewall.
19. Refill the engine cooling system.
20. Connect the negative battery cable, start the vehicle and check for coolant leaks.

UTILITY MODELS

➡**Be sure to consult the laws in your area before servicing the air conditioning system. In most areas, it is illegal to perform repairs involving refrigerant unless the work is done by a certified technician. Also, it is quite likely that you will not be able to purchase refrigerant without proof of certification.**

Discharging, evacuating and charging the air conditioning system must be performed by a properly trained and certified mechanic in a facility equipped with refrigerant recovery/recycling equipment that meets SAE standards for the type of system to be serviced.

If you don't have access to the necessary equipment, we recommend that you take your vehicle to a reputable service station to have the work done. If you still wish to perform repairs on the vehicle, have them discharge the system, then take your vehicle home and perform the necessary work. When you are finished, return the vehicle to the station for evacuation and charging. Just be sure to cap ALL A/C system fittings immediately after opening them and keep them protected until the system is recharged.

1. Have the A/C system evacuated by a certified technician using approved equipment.

2. Disconnect the negative battery cable.

3. Remove the instrument panel. Refer to Section 10 of this manual for this procedure.

4. Remove the cowls, unplug the washer lines from the hood.

5. Unplug the underhood lamp electrical, if equipped, then remove the hood.

6. Remove the antenna and the PCM.

✳✳ CAUTION

Never open, service or drain the radiator or cooling system when hot; serious burns can occur from the steam and hot coolant. Also, when draining engine coolant, keep in mind that cats and dogs are attracted to ethylene glycol antifreeze and could drink any that is left in an uncovered container or in puddles on the ground. This will prove fatal in sufficient quantities. Always drain coolant into a sealable container. Coolant should be reused unless it is contaminated or is several years old.

7. Drain the coolant into a suitable container and remove the coolant recovery reservoir.

8. Disconnect the coolant hoses from the heater core at the firewall in the engine compartment.

9. Remove the right headlamp assembly. Tag and unplug all necessary electrical connections.

10. Remove right side fender.

11. Remove the battery, battery tray, and the wheel house panel.

12. Disconnect the A/C lines from the evaporator.

13. Unfasten the heater box shield retainers and remove the shield.

14. Unfasten the heater core mounting bolts from the engine compartment and remove the heater core fasteners from inside the vehicle.

15. With the aid of an assistant inside the vehicle, gently pry back on the heater box while removing the evaporator housing assembly to ensure clearance of the stud.

16. Remove the heater case, core and the seals.

To install:

17. Install the seals, core and case.

18. With the aid of an assistant inside the vehicle, pull forward on the heater box to make sure the evaporator core is in the correct position.

19. Install the heater case fasteners. Tighten the bolt/screw to 40 inch lbs. (4.5 Nm) and the stud to 40 inch lbs. (4.5 Nm).

20. Install the evaporator housing mounting bolts and tighten the bolt/screw to 40 inch lbs. (4.5 Nm).

21. Install the heater box shield and tighten the retainers to 19 inch lbs. (2.2 Nm).

22. Attach the A/C lines to the evaporator.

23. Install the wheel house panel, the battery tray and the battery. Do not connect the battery cables just yet.

24. Install the outer fender and attach all electrical connections that were disconnected.

25. Install the right headlamp assembly.

26. Attach the heater hoses to the heater core and install the coolant recovery reservoir.

27. Fill the cooling system.

28. Install the PCM and the antenna.

29. Install the hood, attach the hood lamp electrical connection and the washer lines. Install the cowls.

30. Install the instrument panel.

31. Connect the batter cables, start the vehicle and check for leaks.

Air Conditioning Components

REMOVAL & INSTALLATION

Repair or service of air conditioning components is not covered by this manual, because of the risk of personal injury or death, and because of the legal ramifications of servicing these components without the proper EPA certification and experience. Cost, personal injury or death, environmental damage, and legal considerations (such as the fact that it is a federal crime to vent refrigerant into the atmosphere), dictate that the A/C components on your vehicle should be serviced only by a Motor Vehicle Air Conditioning (MVAC) trained, and EPA certified automotive technician.

➡**If your vehicle's A/C system uses R-12 refrigerant and is in need of recharging, the A/C system can be converted over to R-134a refrigerant (less environmentally harmful and expensive). Refer to Section 1 for additional information on R-12 to R-134a conversions, and for additional considerations dealing with your vehicle's A/C system.**

Control Panel and Blower Switch

REMOVAL & INSTALLATION

▸ **See Figures 26, 27 and 28**

1. Disconnect the negative battery cable.
2. If equipped, remove the instrument panel trim plate.

Fig. 26 Remove the trim plate from the instrument panel

Fig. 27 Unfasten the retainers and remove the control head from the instrument panel

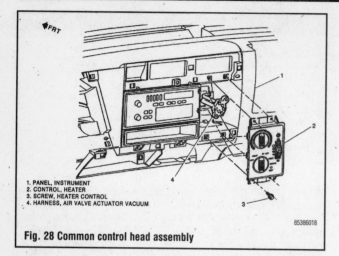

1. PANEL, INSTRUMENT
2. CONTROL, HEATER
3. SCREW, HEATER CONTROL
4. HARNESS, AIR VALVE ACTUATOR VACUUM

85386018

Fig. 28 Common control head assembly

➡**Most dash trim plates on these vehicles are retained by screws and/or snap fasteners. Make sure all screws are removed before attempting to remove the trim plate. If retained by snap fasteners, it may be necessary to pry the plate loose, BUT take care not to force and break the usually fragile plastic pieces.**

3. Remove the control panel-to-instrument panel screws, then pull the control panel from the instrument panel.

4. If equipped, disconnect the temperature cable from the control panel. Remove the control panel.

5. Unplug the vacuum hoses and electrical connectors from the control panel. Make sure each connection may be only made 1 way, or tag hoses/wires and cables before removal.

6. Remove the control panel assembly from the vehicle.

7. If necessary, remove the blower switch by removing the switch knob and spring clip, then remove the blower switch.

To install:

8. If removed, install the heater switch by holding the switch in position and installing the spring clip, then attach the switch knob.

9. If equipped, attach the temperature cable.

10. Attach the electrical connections and vacuum lines to the control panel.

11. Install the control panel and fasten the retaining screws.

12. If equipped, install the trim plate by either fastening the retaining screws or snapping the clips back into place.

13. Connect the negative battery cable and check for proper panel operation.

Temperature Control Cable

REMOVAL & INSTALLATION

1994 Utility Models

1. Remove the control panel assembly from the instrument panel.
2. Remove the radio.
3. Unfasten the cable retainers, then disconnect the cable from the control assembly and the heater module.
4. After all the control cable retainers and clips have been removed or disconnected, remove the cable.

To install:

5. Install the cable making sure it is routed correctly.
6. Attach the control cable to the control panel and the heater module.
7. Install all remaining cable retainers and clips.
8. Install the radio and control panel.

CRUISE CONTROL

General Information

EXCEPT 1994 UTILITY MODELS

▶ **See Figure 29**

The cruise control systems used in these vehicles use a electronic stepper system. The main components of theses systems are, the multi-function switch, cruise control module, vehicle Speed Sensor (VSS), VSS calibrator module, release switches and an electrical harness.

The control module contains a electronic controller and a electric stepper motor. The controller monitor the vehicle speed and operates the stepper motor. The motor moves a band or ribbon and the throttle linkage in response to the controller to maintain desired speed.

The cruise control module has a low speed limit that prevents the system from becoming active at speeds below 25 mph (40 kph).

The release switches are usually located on the brake or clutch pedal bracket. When the clutch or brake is depressed, the system is electrically disengaged.

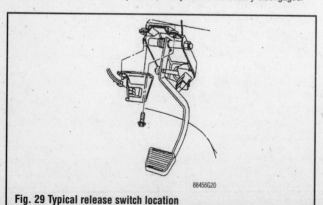

88456G20

Fig. 29 Typical release switch location

1994 UTILITY MODELS

▶ **See Figures 30, 31 and 32**

The cruise control systems used in these vehicles are a vacuum operated servo system. The main components of theses system are, the multi-function

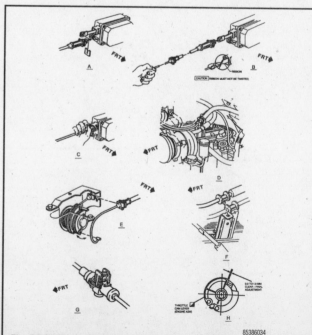

85386034

Fig. 30 Cruise control cable installation and adjustment—2.2L (VIN 4) engine

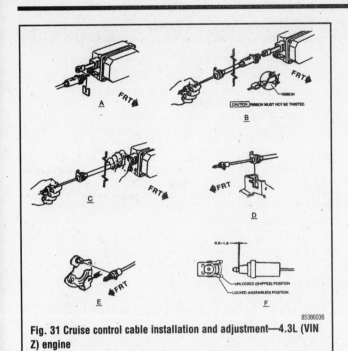

Fig. 31 Cruise control cable installation and adjustment—4.3L (VIN Z) engine

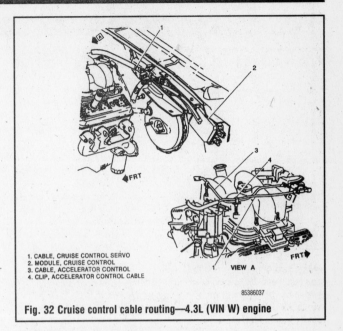

1. CABLE, CRUISE CONTROL SERVO
2. MODULE, CRUISE CONTROL
3. CABLE, ACCELERATOR CONTROL
4. CLIP, ACCELERATOR CONTROL CABLE

Fig. 32 Cruise control cable routing—4.3L (VIN W) engine

switch, cruise control module, servo, vehicle Speed Sensor (VSS), VSS buffer, vacuum supply, electrical and vacuum release switches and an electrical harness.

The system uses vacuum to operate a throttle servo. The servo maintains a desired speed by trapping vacuum in the servo at the proper servo position. The module monitors the vehicle speed and the servo position to operate the servo vacuum and vent valves to maintain vehicle speed.

The module has a low speed limit that prevents the system from becoming active at speeds below 25 mph (40 kph).

The release switch is usually located on the brake pedal bracket. When the clutch or brake is depressed, the system is disengaged.

A vacuum release valve, mounted on the brake or clutch pedal bracket, vents the trapped vacuum in the servo when either pedal is depressed, allowing the servo to quickly to the throttle idle position.

CRUISE CONTROL TROUBLESHOOTING

Problem	Possible Cause
Will not hold proper speed	Incorrect cable adjustment
	Binding throttle linkage
	Leaking vacuum servo diaphragm
	Leaking vacuum tank
	Faulty vacuum or vent valve
	Faulty stepper motor
	Faulty transducer
	Faulty speed sensor
	Faulty cruise control module
Cruise intermittently cuts out	Clutch or brake switch adjustment too tight
	Short or open in the cruise control circuit
	Faulty transducer
	Faulty cruise control module
Vehicle surges	Kinked speedometer cable or casing
	Binding throttle linkage
	Faulty speed sensor
	Faulty cruise control module
Cruise control inoperative	Blown fuse
	Short or open in the cruise control circuit
	Faulty brake or clutch switch
	Leaking vacuum circuit
	Faulty cruise control switch
	Faulty stepper motor
	Faulty transducer
	Faulty speed sensor
	Faulty cruise control module

Note: Use this chart as a guide. Not all systems will use the components listed.

TCCA6C01

ENTERTAINMENT SYSTEMS

Radio/Tape Player/CD Player

REMOVAL & INSTALLATION

All except 1994 Utility Models

▶ See Figures 33, 34 and 35

1. Disconnect the negative battery cable.
2. Remove the accessory trim plate.

➡Most dash trim plates on these vehicles are retained by screws and/or snap fasteners. Make sure all screws are removed before attempting to remove the trim plate. If retained by snap fasteners, it may be necessary to pry the plate loose, BUT take care not to force and break the usually fragile plastic pieces.

3. If necessary, remove the heating/air conditioning control head. For details, please refer to the procedure in this section.
4. Remove the radio bracket-to-instrument panel bracket screws or nuts, then carefully pull the instrument panel center compartment forward with the radio.
5. Unplug the antenna lead and electrical connectors, as necessary.
6. Remove the radio from the vehicle.
7. Remove the radio retaining nuts and separate the radio from the instrument panel center compartment.

To install:

8. Install the radio to the instrument panel center compartment.
9. Position the radio in front of the instrument panel, then attach the necessary electrical connectors and antenna lead.
10. Insert the radio into the dash, then secure using the retainers.
11. If removed, install the climate control head.
12. Install the accessory trim plate.

Fig. 33 Remove the trim plate from the instrument panel

➡In order to prevent damage to the receiver, always connect the speaker wire to the receiver before applying power to it.

13. Connect the negative battery cable and enjoy the tunes.

1994 Utility Models

1. Disconnect the negative battery cable.
2. Remove the ashtray and the accessory trim plate.

➡Most dash trim plates on these vehicles are retained by screws and/or snap fasteners. Make sure all screws are removed before attempting to remove the trim plate. If retained by snap fasteners, it may be necessary to pry the plate loose, BUT take care not to force and break the usually fragile plastic pieces.

3. Unfasten the radio bracket screws and slide the radio forward.
4. Unplug the antenna lead and all necessary electrical connections.
5. Unfasten the radio-to-brackets retainers, then separate the radio from the brackets.

To install:

6. Attach the brackets to the radio and install the retainers. Tighten the retainers to 25 inch lbs. (2.8 Nm).
7. Attach the antenna and all electrical connections to the radio.
8. Place the radio into position and install the radio bracket screws. Tighten the screws to 12 inch lbs. (1.4 Nm).
9. Install the accessory trim plate and the ashtray.
10. Connect the negative battery cable and check for proper radio operation.

Speakers

REMOVAL & INSTALLATION

Front

INSTRUMENT PANEL MOUNTED

▶ See Figures 36 thru 41

1. Disconnect the negative battery cable
2. Remove the front speaker grille screws, then lift and remove the grille.

➡On some models, the grille screws also retain the speaker. Always check to make sure that no additional fasteners are hidden under the grilles.

3. If equipped, remove the speaker-to-instrument panel retainers.
4. Lift the speaker and disengage the electrical connection(s), then remove the speaker from the vehicle.

To install:

5. Attach the speaker electrical connection(s), then install the speaker in the vehicle.
6. If equipped, install the speaker-to-instrument panel screws.

Fig. 34 Unfasten and remove the radio retainers

Fig. 35 Slide the radio forward, then disengage the electrical connections and the antenna

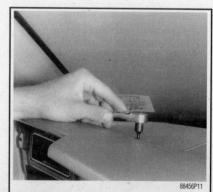

Fig. 36 Loosen and remove the speaker grille screws

Fig. 37 Remove the speaker grille

Fig. 38 Remove the speaker-to-instrument panel retainers

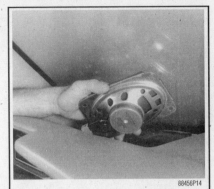

Fig. 39 Lift the speaker from the instrument panel . . .

Fig. 40 . . . then unplug the electrical connection and remove the speaker

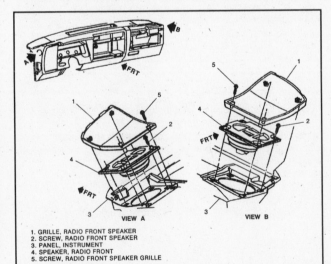

1. GRILLE, RADIO FRONT SPEAKER
2. SCREW, RADIO FRONT SPEAKER
3. PANEL, INSTRUMENT
4. SPEAKER, RADIO FRONT
5. SCREW, RADIO FRONT SPEAKER GRILLE

85386047

Fig. 41 Exploded view of the front (instrument panel) speaker mounting

of the panel is necessary before starting. If the grille fasteners are accessible with the trim panel installed, then panel removal may not be necessary.

1. Disconnect the negative battery cable
2. If necessary, remove the door trim panel. For details on door trim panel removal, please refer to the procedures in Section 10 of this manual.
3. Drill out the heads of the old speaker retaining rivets. Again, aftermarket systems may not contain rivets. If equipped with screws, unthread and remove them.
4. Pull the speaker from the door and unplug the electrical connectors, then remove the speaker from the vehicle.

To install:

5. Attach the speaker electrical connections, then install the speaker in the vehicle.
6. If equipped, install the screws. If equipped with rivets, install them.
7. If removed, install the door trim panel. Refer to Section 10 of this manual for this procedure.
8. Connect the negative battery cable.

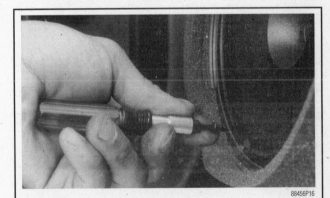

Fig. 42 Remove the speaker retaining screws

Fig. 43 Slide the speaker forward . . .

7. Install the speaker grille and tighten the screws.
8. Connect the negative battery cable.

DOOR MOUNTED SPEAKERS–PICK-UP MODELS

▶ See Figures 42, 43, 44 and 45

Some trucks may be equipped with door mounted radio speakers. Access to factory mounted speakers on some vehicles usually requires removal of inner door trim panel. Aftermarket speakers may be mounted in a variety of ways, but will often not require trim panel removal. In order to save time, be sure removal

Fig. 44 . . . then unplug the speaker electrical connection and remove the speaker

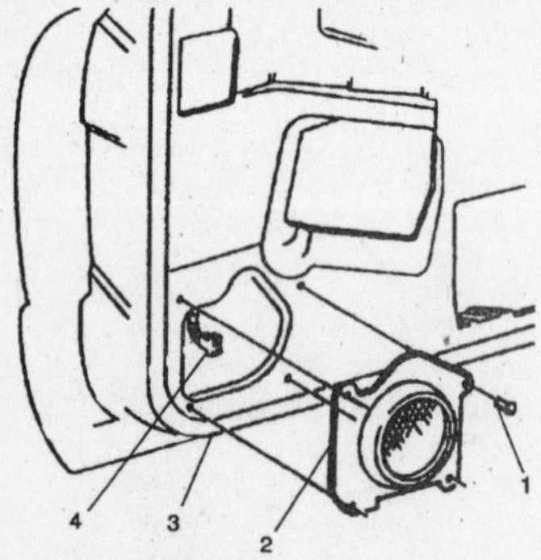

88456P18

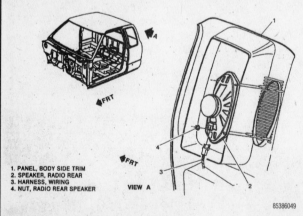

1. RIVET, RADIO FRT SIDE DOOR SPEAKER
2. SPEAKER, RADIO FRONT SIDE DOOR
3. DOOR, FRONT
4. HARNESS, WIRING

85386048

Fig. 45 View of the door panel mounted speakers

1. PANEL, BODY SIDE TRIM
2. SPEAKER, RADIO REAR
3. HARNESS, WIRING
4. NUT, RADIO REAR SPEAKER

VIEW A

85386049

Fig. 46 Common rear speaker mounting—late model extended cab shown

Rear

PICK-UP MODELS –EXTENDED CAB

♦ See Figure 46

1. Disconnect the negative battery cable
2. Remove the rear body side trim panel.
3. Unplug the necessary wiring.
4. Remove the speaker retaining nuts.
5. Remove the speaker from the vehicle.

To install:

6. Install the speaker and fasten retaining nuts to 11 inch lbs. (1.2 Nm).
7. Attach the speaker electrical connections.
8. Install the trim panel, then connect the negative battery cable.

TWO DOOR UTILITY VEHICLES—1994 MODELS

1. Disconnect the negative battery cable.
2. Unfasten the ashtray screws and remove the ashtray.
3. Unfasten the speaker cover screws and remove the cover.
4. Unplug any necessary electrical connections from the speaker.
5. Remove the speaker retaining nuts.
6. Remove the speaker from the cover.

To install:

7. Attach the speaker to the cover and fasten retaining nuts to 35 inch lbs. (4 Nm).
8. Attach the speaker electrical connections.
9. Install the speaker cover and its retainers. Tighten the retainers to 12 inch lbs. (1.4 Nm).
10. Install the ashtray and its retaining screws.
11. Connect the negative battery cable and check for proper operation.

TWO DOOR UTILITY VEHICLES—1995–99 MODELS

1. Disconnect the negative battery cable.
2. Remove the rear quarter trim panel.
3. Unfasten the speaker retainers and slide the speaker assembly forward.
4. Unplug the speaker electrical connections.
5. Remove the speaker from the vehicle.

To install:

6. Attach the speaker electrical connections and place the speaker into position.
7. Install the speaker retainers and the rear quarter trim panel.
8. Connect the negative battery cable and check for proper operation.

FOUR DOOR UTILITY VEHICLES

Access to factory mounted speakers on some vehicles usually requires removal of inner door trim panel. Aftermarket speakers may be mounted in a variety of ways, but will often not require trim panel removal. In order to save time, be sure removal of the panel is necessary before starting. If the grille fasteners are accessible with the trim panel installed, then panel removal may not be necessary.

1. Disconnect the negative battery cable.
2. Remove the rear side door trim panel.
3. Drill out the heads of the old speaker retaining rivets. Again, aftermarket systems may not contain rivets.
4. Pull the speaker from the door and unplug the electrical connectors, then remove the speaker from the vehicle.

To install:

5. Attach the speaker electrical connections, then install the speaker in the vehicle.
6. Install the rivets, or suitable self tapping screws.
7. Install the door trim panel.
8. Connect the negative battery cable.

WINDSHIELD WIPERS AND WASHERS

Windshield Wiper Blade and Arm

REMOVAL & INSTALLATION

Front Wiper Blade

EXCEPT 1994 UTILITY MODELS

1. Lift the wiper arm up into the serviceable position.
2. Press down on the locking tab of the blade assembly, then pull the assembly forward to disengage it from the wiper arm.
   To install:
3. Position the pivot of the blade assembly into the hook of the wiper arm assembly and pull upwards until the locking tab of the pivot engages the slot and in the hook. Make sure the blade assembly is firmly engaged.
4. Place the wiper arm back in its normal position.

1994 UTILITY MODELS

1. Turn the ignition switch **ON** and turn the wipers **ON**. Once the wipers reach the midway point, turn the ignition switch **OFF**. The wipers should stay in the middle of the windshield.
2. Press down on the blade retainer using a suitable tool, then pull the blade assembly off the wiper arm pin.
   To install:
3. Press the blade assembly into engagement by snapping it onto the wiper arm pin.

Rear Wiper Blade

1994 MODELS

1. Place the wiper in a position that they are easy to work on and move the arm up into a suitable position.
2. Press down on the blade retainer using a suitable tool, then pull the blade assembly off the wiper arm pin.
   To install:
3. Press the blade assembly into engagement by snapping it onto the wiper arm pin.

EXCEPT 1994 MODELS

1. Lift the wiper arm up into the serviceable position.
2. Press down on the locking tab of the blade assembly, then remove the blade assembly from the inside radius of the wiper arm.
3. Bring the wiper arm out through the opening in the blade assembly.
   To install:
4. Install the wiper blade on the arm assembly making sure the blade is fully seated and the locking tab engages.

Front Wiper Arm

▶ See Figures 47, 48, 49 and 50

1. To aid in installation, use a non-permanent marker and mark the position of the wiper arm assembly on the windshield.
2. Remove the cover from the wiper assembly.
3. Unfasten the arm retaining nut, then remove the arm.
   To install:
4. Install the arm assembly and tighten the retaining nut to 17 ft. lbs. (23 Nm).
5. Install the wiper arm cover and check the wiper operation.

Rear Wiper Arm

1994 MODELS

1. Disconnect the wiper arm hose from the connector above the roof trim panel.
2. Use a suitable non-permanent marker to indicate the proper park position of the wiper arm on the glass. This will aid during installation.
3. Remove the grommet on the washer hose from the hole in the glass.
4. Lift the wiper arm off the glass and insert a 1/8 inch diameter drift pin or an equivalent tool, through the wiper arm hole.
5. Remove the wiper arm from the shaft using a rocking motion.
6. Remove the drift pin.
   To install:
7. Straighten out the wiper arm and insert the drift pin into the hole.
8. Align the arm assembly with the park position assembly made on the glass during removal, then press down on the arm head casting until it seats and locks onto the shaft.
9. Remove the drift pin, then install the grommet and washer hose.

1995–99 MODELS

1. Make sure the wiper arm is in the park position.
2. Disconnect the hose assembly from the elbow from the vehicle connector.
3. Remove the cover from the wiper assembly.
4. Unfasten the arm retaining nut, then remove the arm.
   To install:
5. Install the arm assembly on the shaft in the park position with the arm resting on the wiper arm park ramp.
6. Install the nut and tighten to 17 ft. lbs. (23 Nm).
7. Install the wiper arm cover and connect the hose elbow.
8. Check for proper wiper operation.

Fig. 47 Remove the cover from the wiper assembly

Fig. 48 Unfasten and remove the wiper arm retainer

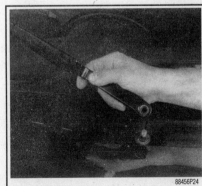

Fig. 49 Remove the wiper arm from the vehicle

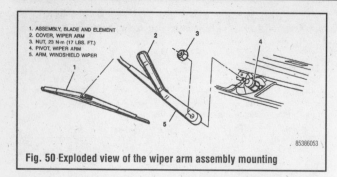

1. ASSEMBLY, BLADE AND ELEMENT
2. COVER, WIPER ARM
3. NUT, 23 N·m (17 LBS. FT.)
4. PIVOT, WIPER ARM
5. ARM, WINDSHIELD WIPER

85386053

Fig. 50 Exploded view of the wiper arm assembly mounting

Windshield Wiper Motor

REMOVAL & INSTALLATION

Front

EXCEPT 1994 UTILITY MODELS

♦ **See Figures 51 thru 56**

1. Disconnect the negative battery cable.
2. Remove the wiper arms from the linkage so the cowl may be removed.
3. Remove the cowl vent grille and screen. On some vehicles, the windshield washer hose may be connected to a hard plastic fitting located under the cowl grille. If the hose connection is very tight it may make removing the cowl grille difficult. Take your time if difficulty is encountered. If possible, reach underneath the grille to disconnect the hose from the fitting.
4. Remove the wiper transmission from the wiper motor drive link using J-39232 or an equivalent tool.
5. Unplug the wiring from the wiper motor.
6. Remove the wiper motor-to-cowl screws. Carefully rotate the motor and guide the drive link from the hole in the cowl, then remove the motor from the vehicle.

To install:

7. Guide the motor drive link through the hole in the cowl, then install the motor and secure using the retainers.
8. Install the drive link socket onto the crank arm ball using J-39529 or an equivalent tool. The wiper transmission assembly must be installed to the crank arm PAST the 2nd detent so that the seal is compressed to a maximum height of 1 in. (25.5mm)
9. Attach the wiring to the wiper motor.
10. Install the cowl vent grille and screen. On vehicles equipped with a plastic fitting attached to the cowl grille, the washer hose should be connected as the grille is positioned. Make sure the hose is not pinched or damaged as the grille is fastened.
11. Install the wiper arm and blade assemblies to the transmission linkage.
12. Connect the negative battery cable and verify proper operation.

1994 UTILITY MODELS

1. Disconnect the negative battery cable.
2. Remove the wiper arms from the linkage so the cowl may be removed.
3. Remove the cowl vent grille and screen. On some vehicles, the windshield washer hose may be connected to a hard plastic fitting located under the cowl grille. If the hose connection is very tight it may make removing the cowl grille difficult. Take your time if difficulty is encountered. If possible, reach underneath the grille to disconnect the hose from the fitting.
4. Unplug the wiper motor electrical connection.
5. Loosen, but do not remove, the two nuts from the transmission drive link socket.
6. Unfasten the three wiper motor-to-cowl retainers.
7. Remove the wiper motor assembly.

To install:

8. Place the wiper motor assembly into position and tighten the retaining screws.
9. Connect the drive link socket to the crank arm ball stud of the wiper motor. Tighten the drive link socket nuts to 62 inch lbs. (7 Nm).

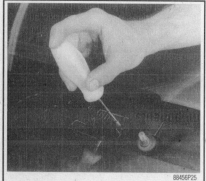

88456P25

Fig. 51 Remove the cowl vent grille and screen retainers

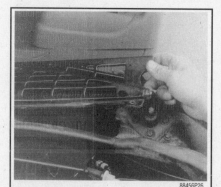

88456P26

Fig. 52 Remove the cowl vent grille and screen from the vehicle

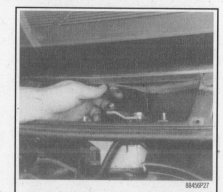

88456P27

Fig. 53 Disconnect the wiper linkage from the wiper transmission

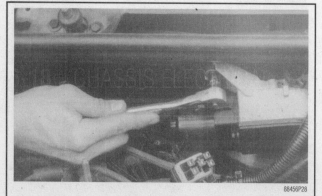

88456P28

Fig. 54 Unfasten the wiper motor retainers . . .

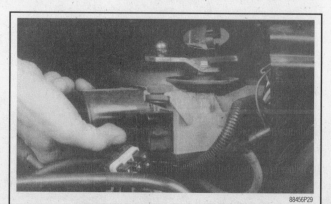

88456P29

Fig. 55 . . . then remove the wiper motor from the vehicle

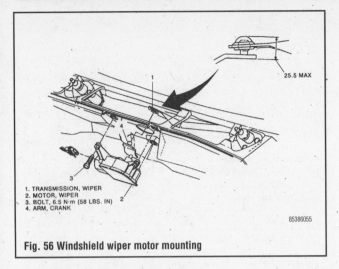

1. TRANSMISSION, WIPER
2. MOTOR, WIPER
3. BOLT, 6.5 N·m (58 LBS. IN)
4. ARM, CRANK

85386055

Fig. 56 Windshield wiper motor mounting

10. Attach the wiring to the wiper motor.

11. Install the cowl vent grille and screen. On vehicles equipped with a plastic fitting attached to the cowl grille, the washer hose should be connected as the grille is positioned. Make sure the hose is not pinched or damaged as the grille is fastened.

12. Install the wiper arm and blade assemblies to the transmission linkage.

13. Connect the negative battery cable and verify proper operation.

Rear

1994 MODELS

1. Disconnect the negative battery cable.
2. Unfasten the wiper motor cover screws, then remove the cover.
3. Remove the roof trim cover to access the wiper motor electrical connection.
4. Unplug the wiper motor electrical connection.
5. Remove the wiper arm assembly, then remove the nut and spacer from the wiper motor.
6. Unfasten the hinge assembly screw and remove the wiper motor assembly.

To install:

➡ **The wiper motor spacer is keyed to the driveshaft**

7. Place the wiper motor into position, then install the spacer and nut onto the wiper motor driveshaft on the outside of the glass.
8. Install the hinge assembly screw.
9. Make sure the endgate glass is properly aligned.
10. Tighten the wiper nut and the hinge cover screw to 57 inch lbs. (6 Nm).
11. Install the wiper arm assembly.
12. Attach the wiper motor electrical connection and install the roof trim panel.
13. Connect the negative battery cable and check for proper motor operation.

1995–99 MODELS

1. Disconnect the negative battery cable.
2. Remove the wiper arm assembly.
3. Remove the nut and washer from the wiper motor shaft.
4. Remove the inner trim panel from the end gate.
5. Unplug the wiper motor electrical connection.
6. Unfasten the two wiper motor retaining screws and remove the wiper motor.
7. Unplug the wiper motor harness from the controller, then remove the controller from the wiper motor.

To install:

8. Install the controller on the wiper motor and attach the motor wiring harness to the controller.

9. Place the wiper motor in position and install the two retaining screws. Do not tighten the screws until the wiper motor shaft is centered in the tailgate hole. Once the shaft is centered, tighten the screws to 57 inch lbs. (6.5 Nm).

10. Attach the wiper motor electrical connection, then install the end gate trim panel.

11. Install the spacer and nut onto the shaft and tighten the nut to 53 inch lbs. (6 Nm).

12. Install the wiper arm assembly and connect the negative battery cable. Check for proper motor operation.

Wiper Fluid Reservoir and Washer Motor

The vehicles covered by this manual utilize a small electric washer pump which is mounted to the bottom of the washer reservoir.

REMOVAL & INSTALLATION

▶ **See Figure 57**

1. Disconnect the negative battery cable.
2. Use a siphon or hand pump to drain the washer fluid from the reservoir. If you are using a siphon, be careful not to inhale or swallow the fluid. The stuff tastes nasty, and like with most fluids in your truck, can be harmful if swallowed.
3. Unplug the electrical connector(s) and washer hose(s) from the pump.
4. In some cases it may be necessary to remove the air filter housing by sliding it up and out of the way.
5. Unfasten the washer fluid reservoir mounting screws, then remove the reservoir from the vehicle.
6. Remove the washer pump from the reservoir.

To install:

7. Install the washer pump to the reservoir. Make sure the pump is fully inserted into the washer reservoir seal.
8. Install the reservoir to the vehicle and secure using the retaining screws.
9. If removed, install the air filter housing by sliding it down into position.
10. Attach the washer hose(s) and electrical connector(s) to the pump.
11. Refill the reservoir with fluid. Add just a little at first, and check for leaks. Refill the reservoir when you are certain the pump seal is secure.
12. Connect the negative battery cable and check for proper pump operation.

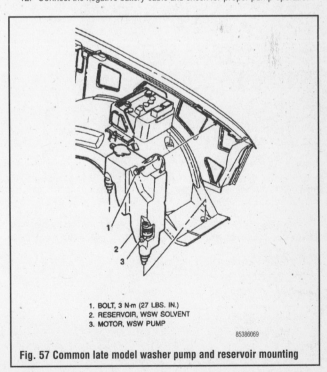

1. BOLT, 3 N·m (27 LBS. IN.)
2. RESERVOIR, WSW SOLVENT
3. MOTOR, WSW PUMP

85386069

Fig. 57 Common late model washer pump and reservoir mounting

INSTRUMENTS AND SWITCHES

❋❋ WARNING

Many solid state electrical components utilized in these vehicles can be damaged by Electrostatic Discharge (ESD). Some of these components will display a label informing you that they will be damaged by (ESD) and some will not have labels, but they may be damaged also. To avoid the possible damage to any of these components, follow the steps outlined in Handling Electrostatic Discharge (ESD) sensitive parts in this section.

Handling Electrostatic Discharge (ESD) Sensitive Parts

▶ See Figure 58

1. Body movement produces an electrostatic charge. To discharge personal static electricity, touch a ground point (metal) on the vehicle. This should be performed any time you:
   - slide across the vehicle seat
   - sit down or get up
   - do any walking
2. Do not touch any exposed terminals on components or connectors with your fingers or any tools.
3. Never use jumper wires, ground a terminal on a component, use test equipment on any component or terminal unless instructed to in a diagnosis or testing procedure. When using test equipment, always connect the ground lead first.
4. If installing a new component, never remove the replacement component from its protective packaging until you are ready to install it.
5. Always touch the component package to ground before opening it.
6. Solid state components may also be damaged if the are dropped, bumped, laid on any metal work bench or laid near any components that operate electrically such as a TV, radio, or an oscilloscope.

NOTICE

CONTENTS SENSITIVE
TO
STATIC ELECTRICITY

88456G21

Fig. 58 Electrostatic Discharge (ESD) label

Instrument Cluster

REMOVAL & INSTALLATION

1994 Pick-Up Models

▶ See Figures 59, 60 and 61

1. Disconnect the negative battery cable.
2. Remove the instrument cluster trim bezel. Since the light switch assembly is mounted to the bezel, once the bezel is released, pull it forward in order to disconnect the wiring, then the bezel may be removed.
3. If equipped disconnect the shift indicator cable from the lower shift bowl.

Fig. 59 Common instrument panel—1994 model

Fig. 60 Remove the trim plate to gain access to the instrument cluster retainers

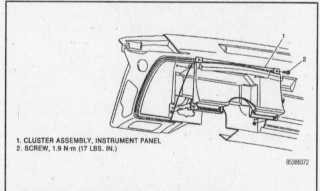

1. CLUSTER ASSEMBLY, INSTRUMENT PANEL
2. SCREW, 1.9 N·m (17 LBS. IN.)

85386072

Fig. 61 Instrument cluster mounting—1994 vehicles

4. Remove the 4 cluster-to-instrument panel retaining screws.
5. Carefully pull the cluster forward and from the multi-pin connector, then remove the cluster from the vehicle.

To install:

6. Carefully position the cluster in the vehicle, then firmly seat it onto the connector.
7. Install the cluster retaining screws and tighten to 17 inch lbs. (1.9 Nm).
8. If equipped, connect the shift indicator cable to the lower shift bowl and adjust, as necessary.
9. Install the instrument cluster bezel.
10. Connect the negative battery cable.

1994 Utility Models

1. Disconnect the negative battery cable.
2. Unfasten the lamp switch trim plate screws and remove the trim plate.
3. Disconnect the lamp switch electrical harness.
4. Unfasten the A/C and heater control assembly screws, remove the control assembly and unplug the assembly wiring harness.
5. Unfasten the filler panel screws and remove the filler panel.
6. If equipped, disconnect the shift indicator cable from the lower shift bowl.
7. Unfasten the cluster housing retainers and remove the cluster housing.
8. Remove the cluster assembly.

To install:

9. Carefully position the cluster in the vehicle.
10. Place the cluster housing into position and install the housing retainers.
11. If equipped, connect the shift indicator cable to the lower shift bowl.
12. Install the filler panel and tighten its retaining screws.
13. Attach the A/C and heater assembly wiring harness, place the assembly into position and tighten its retaining screws.
14. Attach the lamp switch harness, install the switch trim plate and tighten its retaining screws.
15. Connect the negative battery cable.

1995–99 Models

♦ **See Figure 62**

1. Disconnect the negative battery cable.
2. Remove the sound insulators/trim panels.
3. If necessary for access, unfasten the steering column nuts and if necessary, the bolts at the lower flange, then lower the column for access.
4. Unfasten the instrument cluster bezel screws located at the lower edge of the bezel. If no screws are present, then remove the bezel by pulling it straight out.
5. Unfasten the four screws retaining the instrument cluster to the instrument panel, unplug any necessary cluster electrical connections, then remove the cluster.

To install:

6. Install the cluster to the instrument panel making sure the cluster is firmly seated onto the connector, attach any necessary electrical connections and tighten the cluster fasteners to 17 inch. lbs. (1.9 Nm).
7. Install the instrument cluster panel bezel by snapping it into position, then if equipped, install the screws along the bottom of the bezel..
8. If lowered, re-position the steering column and tighten retaining nuts to 22 ft. lbs. (30 Nm) on 1995 models. On 1996–99 models tighten the nuts to 20 ft. lbs. (27 Nm). If removed, tighten lower flange bolts to 120 inch lbs. (13 Nm).
9. Install the sound insulators/trim panels.
10. Connect the negative battery cable.

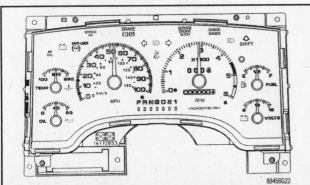

Fig. 62 Common instrument cluster found in 1995–97 "S" series Pick-ups

Gauges

REMOVAL & INSTALLATION

The gauges used on these models are an integral part of the cluster assembly. If any cluster is defective the whole cluster assembly must be replaced.

Front Windshield Wiper Switch

REMOVAL & INSTALLATION

The front windshield wiper switch is located deep inside the steering column assembly and is actuated by the multi-function lever on the left of the steering column. For details concerning removal and installation, please refer to the steering column procedures located in Section 8 of this manual.

Rear Windshield Wiper Switch

REMOVAL & INSTALLATION

1994 Models

♦ **See Figure 63**

1. Disconnect the negative battery cable.
2. Unfasten the switch-to-instrument panel screws.
3. Remove the switch trim plate from the instrument panel, then unplug the switch electrical harness.
4. Separate the switch from the trim plate.

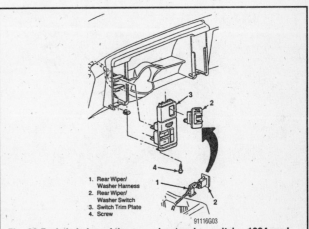

1. Rear Wiper/Washer Harness
2. Rear Wiper/Washer Switch
3. Switch Trim Plate
4. Screw

Fig. 63 Exploded view of the rear wiper/washer switch—1994 models

To install:

5. Attach the switch to the trim plate.
6. Attach the switch electrical harness, then position the switch trim plate on the instrument panel.
7. Install and tighten the switch-to-instrument panel retaining screws.
8. Connect the negative battery cable and check the switch for proper operation.

1995–99 Models

♦ **See Figure 64**

1. Disconnect the negative battery cable.
2. Remove the switch from the trim plate, then unplug the switch electrical harness.

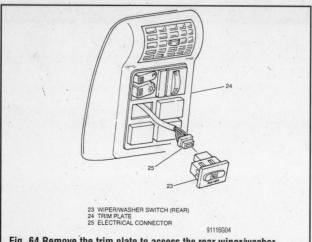

23 WIPER/WASHER SWITCH (REAR)
24 TRIM PLATE
25 ELECTRICAL CONNECTOR

91116G04

Fig. 64 Remove the trim plate to access the rear wiper/washer switch electrical connection—1995–99 models

To install:

3. Attach the switch electrical harness, then position the press the switch into the trim plate.

4. Connect the negative battery cable and check the switch for proper operation.

Headlight Switch

▶ See Figure 65

88456P32

Fig. 65 Headlight switch location (arrow)—1994 model

REMOVAL & INSTALLATION

1994 Pick-Up Models And All 1995–96 Models

▶ See Figure 66

1. Disconnect the negative battery cable.
2. Remove the instrument cluster trim bezel.
3. Unplug the electrical connector.
4. Remove the switch-to-bezel retaining screws.
5. Remove the switch from the bezel.

To install:

6. Engage the switch to the bezel and tighten the switch-to-bezel retaining screws.
7. Engage the electrical connector.
8. Install the instrument cluster trim panel.
9. Connect the negative battery cable.
10. Check the switch for proper operation.

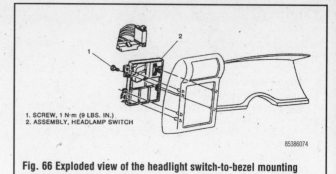

1. SCREW, 1 N·m (9 LBS. IN.)
2. ASSEMBLY, HEADLAMP SWITCH

85386074

Fig. 66 Exploded view of the headlight switch-to-bezel mounting

1994 Utility Models

1. Disconnect the negative battery cable.
2. Unfasten the trim plate screws.
3. Remove the trim plate by pivoting it out at the bottom, then pull the plate down.
4. Unplug any electrical connections that will facilitate switch removal.
5. Unfasten the screws from the switch trim plate, the remove the switch from the bracket.

To install:

6. Place the switch onto the bracket, then install and tighten the switch trim plate screws.
7. Attach any electrical connections that were unplugged.
8. Install the switch trim plate by pivoting it outward at the bottom and pulling the plate downward until it is aligned.
9. Install the trim plate screws.
10. Connect the negative battery cable and check for proper switch operation.

1997–99 Models

1. Disconnect the negative battery cable.
2. Make sure the headlight switch is **OFF** and the ignition switch is in the **LOCK** position.
3. Remove the instrument panel accessory trim plate as follows:

a. Remove the left instrument panel insulator by unfastening the screws that attach the Data Link Connector (DLC) to the insulator, then feed the DLC through the hole in the insulator. Unfasten the screws that attach the insulator to the knee bolster and the cowl panel and the nut that attaches the insulator to the accelerator pedal bracket. Unplug the remote control lock module electrical connector and remove the module from the insulator.

b. Remove the knee bolster by setting the parking brake and blocking the wheels. Release the parking brake release cable from the parking brake lever. Remove the center sound insulator, by unfastening the screws that attach it to the knee bolster, instrument panel, heater assembly and floor duct. Unfasten the screw that attaches the courtesy lamp to the knee bolster and the knee bolster-to-instrument panel screws. Disconnect the lap cooler duct and lighter outlet electrical connector. Remove the knee bolster.

c. Disable the air bag system. Refer to the procedure in this section.

d. Unfasten the steering column-to-instrument panel nuts and lower the column for clearance.

e. Unfasten the accessory trim plate-to-instrument panel screws, unplug all necessary electrical connections and remove the trim plate.

4. Unplug the electrical connection and unfasten the switch-to-accessory trim plate screws.

5. Disconnect the switch panel from the accessory trim plate.

6. Remove the switch from the switch panel.

To install:

7. Connect the switch to the switch panel.
8. Attach the switch panel to the accessory trim plate.
9. Install the switch-to-accessory trim plate screws and attach the electrical connection.
10. Install the instrument panel accessory trim plate as follows:

a. Attach all necessary electrical connections to the trim plate, place the trim plate into position and install the plate-to-instrument panel screws. Tighten the screws to 17 inch lbs. (1.9 Nm).

   b. Place the steering column into position and install the column retaining nuts. Tighten the nuts to 22 ft. lbs. (30 Nm).

   c. Enable the air bag system. Refer to the procedure in this section.

   d. Attach the lighter outlet and cooler duct to the knee bolster, place the knee bolster in position and tighten the Torx head screws to 80 inch lbs. (9 Nm) and the hex head screws to 17 inch lbs. (1.9 Nm). Place the courtesy light in position and tighten its retaining screw to 17 inch lbs. (1.9 Nm). Install the center sound insulator and tighten the screws that attach it to the knee bolster, instrument panel, heater assembly and floor duct to 17 inch lbs. (1.9 Nm). Attach the parking brake release cable to the brake lever.

   e. Attach the remote control door lock module to the left instrument panel sound insulator and attach the module electrical connection. Install the nut that attaches the insulator panel to the accelerator pedal bracket. Tighten the nut to 35 inch lbs. (4 Nm). Install the screws that attach the insulator panel to the cowl panel and the knee bolster. Tighten the screws to 17 inch lbs. (1.9 Nm). Feed the DLC through the hole in the insulator panel and install its retaining screws. Tighten the screws to 21 inch lbs. (2.4 Nm).

11. Connect the negative battery cable and check for proper switch operation.

Back-Up Light/Neutral Safety Switch

REMOVAL & INSTALLATION

Automatic Transmission

▶ **See Figure 67**

   The back-up light switch on automatic transmission vehicles also acts as the neutral safety switch. The switch will activate the reverse lights when the gear shift lever is placed in the Reverse position, and it will prevent the engine from starting unless the shifter is in Neutral or Park. The switch on 1994 models is mounted to the steering column. Refer to Section 7 of this manual for column mounted switch removal. On 1995 and later models, the switch is mounted on the transmission.

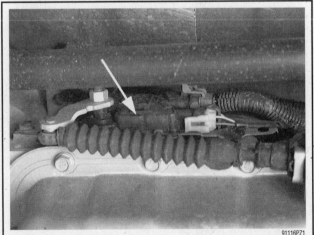

91116PZ1

Fig. 67 The neutral safety switch is located on the side of the transmission

1. Apply the parking brake and place the transmission in **Neutral**.
2. Disconnect the negative battery cable.
3. Raise the vehicle and support it with jackstands.
4. Remove the transmission control lever-to-manual shaft nut and disconnect the control lever from the manual shaft. Let the cable and control lever drop out of the way.
5. Unplug the switch electrical connection.
6. Unfasten the switch retainers and slide the switch off the shaft to remove it from the vehicle.

To install:

7. Install neutral safety switch alignment tool J 1364 or its equivalent onto the switch. Make sure that the two detents on the switch (where the manual shaft is inserted) are lined up with the lower tabs of the tool. Rotate the tool until the upper locator pin on the tool is aligned with the locator on the switch.

➡**Before sliding the switch onto the transmission it may be necessary to remove any burrs on the shaft by lightly filing the outer edge of the shaft.**

8. Align the switch hubs flats with the flats on the manual shaft, then slide the switch onto the shaft until the switch bracket contacts the mounting bosses on the transmission.

9. Install the switch retaining bolts and tighten them to 20 ft. lbs. (27 Nm), then remove the alignment tool and attach the switch electrical connection.

10. Connect the control lever to the manual shaft, install the nut and tighten to 20 ft. lbs. (27 Nm).

11. Lower the vehicle and connect the negative battery cable.

12. Check that vehicle starts in the **Park** and **Neutral** positions only. If the vehicle starts in any other position, loosen the switch bolts and rotate the switch slightly and tighten the bolts. Repeat this procedure until the vehicle will start in the desired positions only.

Manual Transmission

▶ **See Figure 68**

1. Disconnect the negative battery cable.
2. Raise the vehicle and support it with jackstands,
3. Locate the switch on the left or right rear of the transmission housing (depending on the application), the back-up light switch is threaded into the transmission case. The speed sensor is held in with a separate bracket. Unplug the electrical connector from the back-up light switch.
4. Remove the back-up light switch from the transmission.
5. To install, reverse the removal procedures and lower the vehicle.
6. With the engine NOT running (for safety), place the gear shift lever in the reverse position and check the back-up lights work.

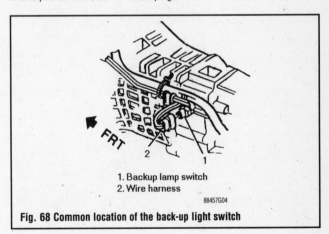

1. Backup lamp switch
2. Wire harness

88457G04

Fig. 68 Common location of the back-up light switch

LIGHTING

Headlights

REMOVAL & INSTALLATION

Sealed Beam

▶ See Figure 69

➡If some or all of the headlight bulbs being replaced still operate, refer to the headlight aiming procedure later in this section to ease checking or adjustment of the headlights after installation.

1994–95 MODELS

▶ See Figures 70, 71 and 72

1. If necessary, remove the grille from the vehicle. Refer to Section 10 of this manual for the proper procedure.
2. Unfasten the headlamp retaining ring fasteners, then remove the ring.
3. Grasp the headlamp and rotate it to the right and remove the headlamp.
4. Unplug the electrical connection from the rear of the lamp.
To install:
5. Attach the electrical connection to the rear of the headlamp.
6. Install the headlamp in the vehicle.
7. Install the retaining ring and tighten the retaining fasteners.
8. If removed, install the grille. Refer to Section 10 of this manual for the proper procedure.

1996–97 MODELS

1. Unfasten the headlamp retaining ring fasteners, then remove the ring.
2. Remove the headlamp.
3. Unplug the electrical connection from the rear of the lamp.

To install:
4. Attach the electrical connection to the rear of the headlamp.
5. Install the headlamp in the vehicle.
6. Install the retaining ring and tighten the retaining fasteners.

Composite Beam

Some vehicles covered by this manual were equipped with composite headlight assemblies. The composite headlight assembly houses the headlamp and side marker lamp bulbs. In most cases, the assembly is bolted in a fixed position so no adjustment is necessary or possible. Also, due to space constraints, no access may be provided to withdraw the bulbs, so the replacement usually requires removal of the composite assembly.

➡The composite headlight assemblies use Halogen bulbs which contain a gas under pressure. Handling a bulb improperly could cause it to shatter into flying glass fragments. To help avoid personal injury follow the precautions closely.

Whenever handling Halogen bulb ALWAYS follow these precautions:
• Do not directly touch the glass of the bulb. The oil from your skin can cause the bulb to explode when it is turned on.
• Turn the lamp switch OFF and allow the bulb to cool before changing it. Leave the switch OFF until the change is complete.
• ALWAYS wear eye protection when changing a Halogen bulb.
• DO NOT drop or scratch the bulb. Keep moisture away.
• Place the used bulb in the new bulb's carton and dispose of it properly.

1994–95 MODELS

▶ See Figure 73

1. Disconnect the negative battery cable.
2. If replacing the right side bulb, remove the battery from the vehicle.

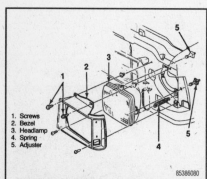

1. Screws
2. Bezel
3. Headlamp
4. Spring
5. Adjuster

85386080

Fig. 69 Exploded view of a common sealed beam headlight mounting (with separate headlight bezel shown)

88456P33

Fig. 70 Loosen the retaining ring fasteners . . .

88456P34

Fig. 71 . . . then remove the retaining ring

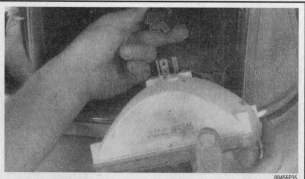

88456P35

Fig. 72 Slide the headlamp forward and disengage the electrical connection

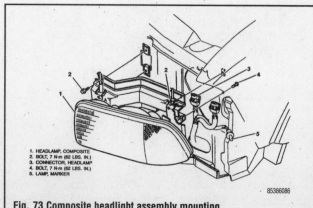

1. HEADLAMP, COMPOSITE
2. BOLT, 7 N•m (62 LBS. IN.)
3. CONNECTOR, HEADLAMP
4. BOLT, 7 N•m (62 LBS. IN.)
5. LAMP, MARKER

85386086

Fig. 73 Composite headlight assembly mounting

3. If replacing the left side bulb, remove the intake air box.

4. Remove the grille from the front of the vehicle.

5. Remove the retaining screw from the engine side of the radiator support, then remove the headlight capsule-to-radiator support screws.

6. Pull the composite headlight assembly forward slightly, then unplug the headlamp and side marker lamp wiring connectors.

7. Remove the headlight assembly from the vehicle. Remove the necessary bulb(s) from the assembly.

To install:

8. Install new bulbs, as necessary to the composite headlight assembly.

9. Position the assembly to the vehicle and attach the connectors.

10. Install the assembly retaining screws and tighten to 62 inch lbs. (7 Nm).

11. Install the grille to the front of the vehicle.

12. Install the air intake box and/or battery, as applicable.

13. Connect the negative battery cable and verify proper lamp operation.

1996–99 MODELS NOT RETAINED BY A LOCKING TAB

▶ See Figures 74 and 75

1. Disconnect the negative battery cable.

2. On 1996–97 models remove the lens assembly as follows:

a. If equipped, remove the plastic caps that cover the headlight retaining pins or screws, then remove the pins or screws while supporting the lens assembly.

3. On 1998–99 models remove the lens assembly as follows:

a. Open the hood and locate the headlight retainers (usually two). The headlight retainers are plastic or metal strips with an elongated hole in it. Grasp the retainers and pull them up until the pin is located at the largest part of the hole and remove the retainers while supporting the lens assembly.

4. Unplug the bulb electrical connection(s). Remove the bulb from the headlight by pushing them in and turning the ¼ turn counterclockwise.

To install:

5. Install the bulbs in the headlight assembly by pushing in rotating it ¼ turn clockwise.

6. Attach the electrical connectors for the headlight and side marker assemblies.

7. On 1996–97 models install the lens assembly as follows:

a. Place the lens in position, install the retaining pins or screws and tighten the pins or screws to 62 inch lbs. (7 Nm). If equipped, install the plastic caps.

8. On 1998–99 models install the lens assembly as follows:

a. Install the lens assembly, then place the largest hole of the retainer over the pin and push the retainer down until the pin is at the top of the elongated hole.

9. Connect the negative battery cable and check for proper light operation.

1996–99 MODELS RETAINED BY LOCKING TAB

▶ See Figures 76 thru 82

1. Disconnect the negative battery cable.

2. If necessary to access the locking tab, remove the grille assembly.

3. Turn the locking tab (usually red) upward to the unlocked position. The unlocked position should be marked on the back of the lens assembly.

4. Gently pull the top of the lens forward to disconnect it from the retainer.

5. Pull gently on the fender side of the lens to disconnect it from the second retaining pin, then slide the lens sideways to disconnect it from the third and last retaining pin

6. Unplug the bulb electrical connection(s). Remove the bulb from the headlight by pushing them in and turning the ¼ turn counterclockwise.

To install:

7. Install the bulbs in the headlamp assembly by pushing in rotating it ¼ turn clockwise.

8. Attach the electrical connectors.

➡ **When connecting the lens assembly to the retainers, make sure the headlight electrical harness is being pinched.**

9. Connect the lens assembly to the lower retainers.

10. Align the top retainer with the hole in the lens assembly and gently push in on the top of the assembly until it is firmly seated on the retainer.

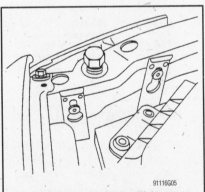

Fig. 74 Some composite headlight assembly retainers are located under the hood

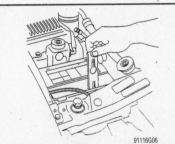

Fig. 75 These retainers can be removed by grasping the retainers and pulling them up until the pin is located at the largest part of the hole, then remove the retainers while supporting the lens assembly

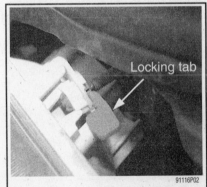

Fig. 76 The headlamp assembly may use one or more locking tabs

Fig. 77 Turn the locating tab until it releases, then pull forward to disconnect the lens assembly from the top retaining pin

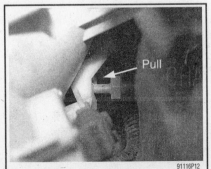

Fig. 78 Pull gently on the fender side of the lens to disconnect it from the second retaining pin . . .

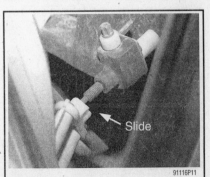

Fig. 79 . . . then slide the lens sideways to disconnect it from the third and last retaining pin

Fig. 80 Tilt the lens forward to access the bulb assemblies

Fig. 81 Unplug the halogen bulb electrical connector

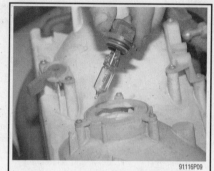

Fig. 82 Turn the bulb assembly to the left to remove it from the lens. Do not touch the bulb glass

11. Push the locking tab downward until the tab is in the locked position
12. If removed for access, install the grille assembly.
13. Connect the negative battery cable and check for proper light operation.

HEADLIGHT AIMING

▶ See Figures 83 and 84

The headlights must be properly aimed to provide the best, safest road illumination. The lights should be checked for proper aim and adjusted as necessary. Certain state and local authorities have requirements for headlight aiming; these should be checked before adjustment is made.

Headlight adjustment may be temporarily made using a wall, as described below, or on the rear of another vehicle. When adjusted, the lights should not glare in oncoming car or truck windshields, nor should they illuminate the passenger compartment of vehicles driving in front of you. These adjustments are rough and should always be fine-tuned by a repair shop which is equipped with headlight aiming tools. Improper adjustments may be both dangerous and illegal.

For most S/T vehicles, horizontal and vertical aiming of each sealed beam unit is provided by two adjusting screws which move the retaining ring and adjusting plate against the tension of a coil spring. There is no adjustment for focus; this is done during headlight manufacturing.

➥Because the composite headlight assembly is bolted into position, no adjustment should be necessary or possible. Some applications however may be bolted to an adjuster plate or may be retained used adjusting screws. If so, follow this procedure when adjusting the lights, BUT always have the adjustment checked by a reputable shop.

Before removing the headlight bulb or disturbing the headlamp in any way, note the current settings in order to make adjusting the headlights upon

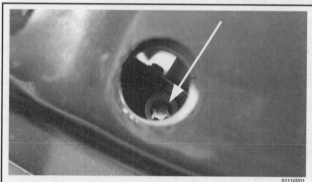

Fig. 84 The composite headlight adjustment screw can be accessed through a hole in the radiator support—1996 2.2L Hombre

reassembly easier. If the high or low beam setting of the old lamp still works, this can be done using the wall of a garage or a building:

1. Park the truck on a level surface, with the fuel tank no more than ½ full and with the vehicle empty of all extra cargo (unless normally carried). The vehicle should be facing a wall which is no less the 6 feet (1.82 m) high and 12 feet (3.96 m) wide. The front of the vehicle should be about 25 feet (7.62 m) from the wall.

➥The truck's fuel tank should be about half full when adjusting the headlights. Tires should be properly inflated, and if a heavy load is normally carried in the bed, it should remain there.

2. If this is be performed outdoors, it is advisable to wait until dusk in order to properly see the headlight beams on the wall. If done in a garage, darken the area around the wall as much as possible by closing shades or hanging cloth over the windows.
3. Turn the headlights **ON** and mark the wall at the center of each light's low beam, then switch on the brights and mark the center of each light's high beam. A short length of masking tape which is visible from the front of the truck may be used. Although marking all 4 positions is advisable, marking 1 position from each light should be sufficient.
4. If neither beam on 1 side of the vehicle is working, park another like-sized truck in the exact spot where the truck was and mark the beams using the same side light on that truck. Then switch the trucks so the S/T is back in the original spot. The truck must be parked no closer to or farther away from the wall than the second vehicle.
5. Perform the necessary repairs, but make sure the truck is not moved or is returned to the exact spot from which the lights were marked. Turn the headlights **ON** and adjust the beams to match the marks on the wall.
6. Have the headlight adjustment checked as soon as possible by a reputable repair shop.

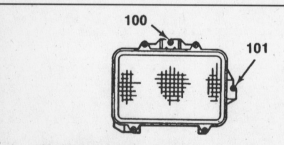

100. Vertical Adjusting Screw
101. Horizontal Adjusting Screw

Fig. 83 Headlight adjustment screw locations for most sealed beam headlight adjusting plates

Signal and Marker Lights

REMOVAL & INSTALLATION

Front Turn Signal and Parking Lights

1994–95 PICK-UP MODELS

▶ **See Figures 85 and 86**

1. Disconnect the negative battery cable.
2. Check for access to the rear of the lens. If none can be found, remove the grille from the front of the vehicle. Then remove the front bumper.
3. Twist the bulb socket to the left to release it, then remove the socket from the lens.
4. Remove the bulb from the socket.
To install:
5. Insert the bulb in the socket, then install the socket in the lens and turn it to the right to engage it.
6. If removed, install the front bumper and lens.
7. Connect the negative battery cable.

1994 UTILITY MODELS

1. Disconnect the negative battery cable.
2. From under the vehicle, reach behind the lens, grasp the bulb socket and turn it ¼ turn to remove it from the lens.
3. Remove the bulb from the socket.
4. Installation is the reverse of removal.

1996–99 MODELS

▶ **See Figure 87**

Most of the vehicles in this manual use the following procedure for the replacement of the bulb. However, to access and remove the turn signal bulbs on some of these models, the headlight assembly must be removed. If the headlight assembly must be removed, refer to the appropriate procedure in this section.

1. Disconnect the negative battery cable.
2. From under the vehicle, reach behind the lens, grasp the bulb socket and turn it ¼ turn to remove it from the lens.
3. Remove the bulb from the socket.
4. Installation is the reverse of removal.

Front and Side Marker Lights

1994–96 MODELS

▶ **See Figures 88, 89, 90, 91 and 92**

➡ **On vehicles equipped with composite headlights, the front marker light bulb is mounted in the composite assembly. Please refer to the headlight procedure earlier in this section for marker bulb replacement on these vehicles.**

Vehicles equipped with sealed beam headlights use a similar marker lens assembly. The difference comes in that the lens screws are easily accessible with the grille/bezel assembly installed. To replace marker lights on these vehicles, use the following procedure. Composite headlight vehicles should refer to that procedure located earlier in this section.

Fig. 85 Twist and remove the bulb socket from the rear of the lens housing . . .

Fig. 86 . . . then pull the bulb from the socket

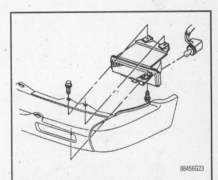
Fig. 87 Exploded view of the turn signal/parking lamp assembly—1996 and later models

Fig. 88 Remove the side marker lens retaining screws

Fig. 89 Remove the lens from its housing . . .

Fig. 90 . . . then twist the socket ¼ turn to the left and remove the socket from the lamp housing

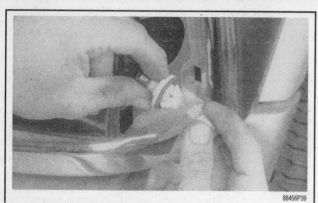

Fig. 91 Remove the bulb from the socket

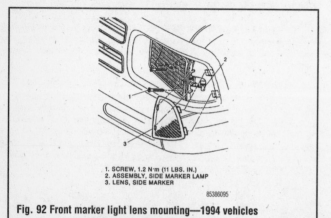

1. SCREW, 1.2 N·m (11 LBS. IN.)
2. ASSEMBLY, SIDE MARKER LAMP
3. LENS, SIDE MARKER

Fig. 92 Front marker light lens mounting—1994 vehicles

1. Disconnect the negative battery cable.
2. Remove the retaining screws from the marker light lens.
3. Carefully pull the lens forward from the grille/bezel assembly for access to the bulb. Turn the twist socket ¼ turn to left in order to release it.
4. Remove the bulb from the socket and replace, if necessary, with a new bulb.
5. Installation is the reverse of removal.

1997–99 MODELS

♦ **See Figures 93, 94, 95, 96 and 97**

The side marker lens on some of these models may be incorporated into the headlight assembly. If this is the case the headlight assembly must be removed, to access the bulb assembly. Refer to the appropriate headlight assembly removal procedure in this section.

On models where the bulb is not part of the headlight assembly, the bulb is replaceable by removing a lens. The lens may be retained in one of two ways, by screws or by locking tabs. Before attempting to remove the lens, check the lens assembly to see how it is being retained.

1. Disconnect the negative battery cable.
2. On models where the lens is retained by screws, remove the lens as follows:
    a. Locate the screws (usually two) and unfasten them, then slide the lens forward.
3. On models where the lens is retained by locking tabs, remove the lens as follows:
    a. Remove the headlight assembly and set it aside.
    b. Using a suitable prytool, push down on the locking tab and pull the lens forward.
4. Remove the bulb from the headlight by pushing them in and turning the ¼ turn counterclockwise.

To install:

5. Install the bulbs in the headlamp assembly by pushing in rotating it ¼ turn clockwise.
6. On models where the lens is retained by screws, place the lens in position and install its retaining screws.

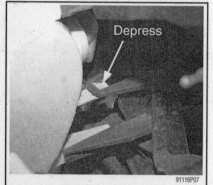

Fig. 93 Depress the center tab to unfasten the side marker lens assembly

Fig. 94 . . . and slide the side marker lens assembly forward to remove it

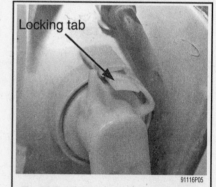

Fig. 95 The bulb socket is retained using a locking tab

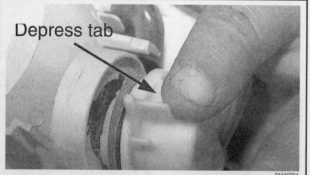

Fig. 96 Press the locking tab and turn the socket assembly to the left

Fig. 97 Gently pull the bulb from the socket

7. On models where the lens is retained by locking tabs, place the lens in position, align the tabs at the rear of the lens, then slide the lens back until the locking tab engages.

8. If removed, install the headlight assembly and connect the negative battery cable.

Rear Turn Signal, Brake, Parking and Reverse Lights

♦ **See Figures 98 thru 104**

Most vehicles covered by this manual us 2 tail light assemblies (1 on either side) to house the rear turn signal, brake, parking and reverse lights. A few models may also be equipped with a center high-mounted brake light (covered later in this section) on the top of the cab. To replace any of the bulbs housed in the rear tail light assemblies, then lens must be removed for access.

1. Disconnect the negative battery cable.
2. Lower the tailgate or open the liftgate.
3. Remove the rear lamp assembly-to-vehicle screws, then carefully pull

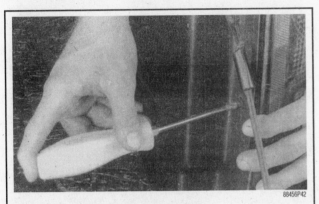

Fig. 98 Unfasten the rear lens retaining screws

the lamp housing away from the vehicle for access to the bulb twist sockets. On most vehicles, lamp screws can be found on the outer edge of the lamp and behind the tailgate or liftgate. Make sure all screws are removed and DO NOT force the lens.

4. Turn the bulb twist socket ¼ turn to the left and remove the socket from the lamp housing.
5. Remove the bulb from the bulb socket; if necessary, replace the bulb.

To install:

6. Insert the bulb in the socket.
7. Install the bulb twist socket in the lamp housing and turn it$FR 1/4 turn to the right to engage it properly.
8. Install the lamp assembly and tighten the retaining screws.
9. Close the tail gate or liftgate assembly.
10. Connect the negative battery cable and check for proper lamp operation.

Center High-Mount Brake Light

REMOVAL & INSTALLATION

Pick-Up Models

♦ **See Figure 105**

1. Disconnect the negative battery cable.
2. Remove the outer high-mount brake lens retaining screws. Remove the bulb.
3. From inside the cab, remove the dome lamp lens, then remove the bulb. Unplug the dome lamp connectors by squeezing and sliding them out of the dome lamp assembly.
4. With the dome lamp components out of the way, remove the 4 dome lamp-to-high mount lens screws
5. If necessary, remove the headliner from inside the vehicle.
6. Unplug the wiring connector from the dome lamp harness.
7. Remove the center high-mount lamp from the vehicle.

Fig. 99 Carefully remove the lens from its housing

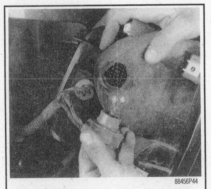

Fig. 100 Removing the brake lamp socket from the lens

Fig. 101 Removing the brake lamp bulb from its socket

Fig. 102 Removing the reverse lamp socket from the lens

Fig. 103 Removing the reverse lamp bulb from its socket

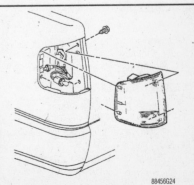

Fig. 104 Exploded view of a common pick-up tail light assembly mounting

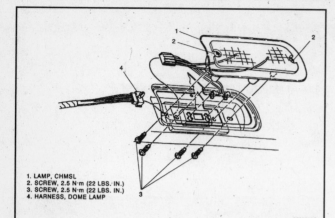

1. LAMP, CHMSL
2. SCREW, 2.5 N·m (22 LBS. IN.)
3. SCREW, 2.5 N·m (22 LBS. IN.)
4. HARNESS, DOME LAMP

85386106

Fig. 105 Exploded view a typical pick-up center high-mounted brake light assembly

To install:

8. Install the dome lamp and center high-mount lamp assembly to the vehicle.

9. Install the dome lamp bulb connectors to the lamp housing.

10. If removed, install the headliner.

11. Attach the connector to the dome lamp harness.

12. Install the inner and outer lens retaining screws and tighten to 22 inch lbs. (2.5 Nm).

13. Connect the negative battery cable and verify proper operation.

1994 Utility Models

1. Disconnect the negative battery cable.

2. Remove the rear dome lamp assembly as follows:

    a. Remove the lens.

    b. Remove the push nuts and the lamp housing.

    c. Remove the push nuts and the bulb, then disconnect the wire assembly from the studs.

3. Unplug the electrical connection from the dome lamp harness.

4. Unfasten the lamp assembly screws and remove the assembly.

To install:

5. Feed the brake light assembly wire through the hole in the roof panel and attach it to the dome lamp harness.

6. Attach the brake light assembly screws.

7. Install the rear dome lamp assembly as follows:

    a. Connect the wire assembly to the studs and install new push nuts onto the studs.

    b. Install the bulb and push nuts.

    c. Install the lamp housing onto the studs and install new push nuts.

    d. Install the lens assembly.

8. Connect the negative battery cable.

1995–99 Utility Models

ROOF MOUNTED

1. Unfasten the brake light assembly retaining screws.

2. Remove the assembly from the roof, pull the electrical connector through the hole in the roof and unplug the electrical connection.

3. Installation is the reverse of removal.

WINDOW MOUNTED

1. Unfasten the brake light assembly retaining screws.

2. Remove the assembly from its mounting, pull the rubber grommet from the body at the top of the end gate, pull the electrical connection through the hole and unplug it.

3. Installation is the reverse of removal.

Dome Light

REMOVAL & INSTALLATION

▶ See Figures 106, 107 and 108

1. Remove the lens assembly.
2. Remove the bulb by pulling it gently from the connector.

To install:

3. Install a new bulb in the connector.
4. Install the lens assembly.

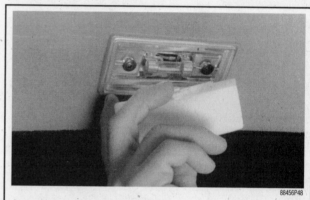

88456P48

Fig. 106 Remove the dome light cover

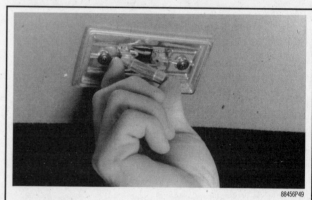

88456P49

Fig. 107 Remove the bulb from the dome light

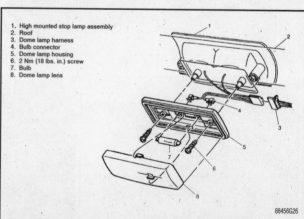

1. High mounted stop lamp assembly
2. Roof
3. Dome lamp harness
4. Bulb connector
5. Dome lamp housing
6. 2 Nm (18 lbs. in.) screw
7. Bulb
8. Dome lamp lens

88456G26

Fig. 108 Exploded view of a common dome lamp assembly

License Plate Light

REMOVAL & INSTALLATION

Pick-Up Models—Except Sportside

1994–96 MODELS WITH A STEP BUMPER

♦ See Figure 109

1. Disconnect the negative battery cable.
2. Remove the step bumper pads.
3. Remove the bumper bolts, then rotate the bumper for access. An assistant to steady the bumper will be helpful here.
4. Unplug the electrical wiring connector.
5. Remove the lamp-to-bumper screws, then remove the lamp from the vehicle.

To install:

6. Install the lamp to the bumper, then tighten the retaining screws to 14 inch lbs. (1.6 Nm).
7. Attach the wiring connector.
8. Install the bumper and step pad to the vehicle.
9. Connect the negative battery cable.

1997–99 MODELS WITH A STEP BUMPER

1. Make sure the headlight switch is off and the ignition switch is in the lock position.
2. If necessary, lift the lamp up and tilt the bottom away from the bumper to release the lamp retainer.
3. Disconnect the bulb socket from the license plate lamp by rotating it ¼ of a turn counterclockwise.

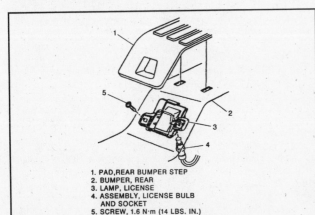

1. PAD, REAR BUMPER STEP
2. BUMPER, REAR
3. LAMP, LICENSE
4. ASSEMBLY, LICENSE BULB AND SOCKET
5. SCREW, 1.6 N·m (14 LBS. IN.)

85386111

Fig. 109 License plate lamp mounting on vehicles with a step bumper

4. Pull the bulb from the socket.
5. If necessary, remove the step bumper pad, the screws that attach the lamp to the bumper and remove the lamp assembly.
6. Installation is the reverse of removal. Tighten the lamp assembly-to-bumper screws to 14 inch lbs. (1.6 Nm).

1994–96 MODELS WITHOUT A STEP BUMPER

♦ See Figures 110, 111 and 112

1. Disconnect the negative battery cable.
2. Remove the socket from the lens by turning it ¼ turn to the left.
3. Remove the bulb from the socket.

To install:

4. Install the bulb in the socket.
5. Install the socket in the lens and engage it by turning it a ¼ turn to the right.
6. Connect the negative battery cable.

1997–99 MODELS WITHOUT A STEP BUMPER

1. Make sure the headlight switch is off and the ignition switch is in the lock position.
2. Disconnect the bulb socket from the license plate lamp by rotating it ¼ of a turn counterclockwise.
3. Pull the bulb from the socket.
4. If necessary, remove the lens retaining clip and the lens from the filler panel.
5. Installation is the reverse of removal.

UTILITY AND SPORTSIDE PICK-UP MODELS

1. Make sure the headlight switch is off and the ignition switch is in the lock position.
2. Unfasten the screws retaining the lens, then remove the lens.
3. Disconnect the bulb socket from the license plate lamp by rotating it ¼ of a turn counterclockwise.
4. Remove the bulb from the socket.
5. Installation is the reverse of removal.

Cargo Light

REMOVAL & INSTALLATION

♦ See Figure 113

Some vehicles may be equipped with a cargo light mounted to the top rear of the cab. On most applications, the bulb is easily accessible once the lens is removed.

1. Disconnect the negative battery cable.
2. If equipped, unfasten the lens-to-housing screws or use a small screwdriver and carefully remove the lens.
3. Remove the bulb from the cargo light housing; if necessary, replace the bulb.

88456P50

Fig. 110 Remove the socket from the lens by turning it slightly to the left

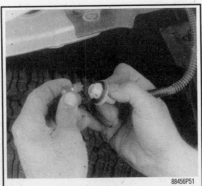

88456P51

Fig. 111 Remove the license plate light bulb from its socket

88456G25

Fig. 112 License plate lamp mounting on vehicles without a step bumper

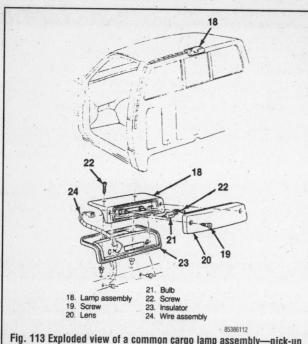

18. Lamp assembly
19. Screw
20. Lens
21. Bulb
22. Screw
23. Insulator
24. Wire assembly

85386112

Fig. 113 Exploded view of a common cargo lamp assembly—pick-up models

To install:

4. Install the bulb in the housing.
5. Install the lens and if equipped, tighten the retaining screws.
6. Connect the negative battery cable.

Fog Lamps

REMOVAL & INSTALLATION

♦ **See Figure 114**

Most fog lamp bulbs are easily replaced by removing the lens cover (standard bulbs) or lens trim panels (halogen bulbs) for access. Most later model vehicles are equipped with Halogen bulbs which require extra care. Handling a Halogen bulb improperly could cause it to shatter into flying glass fragments. To help avoid personal injury follow the precautions closely.

Whenever handling Halogen bulb ALWAYS follow these precautions:

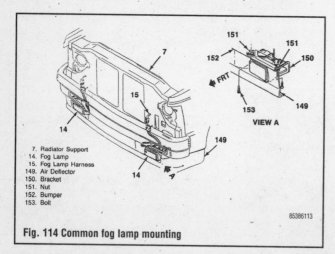

7. Radiator Support
14. Fog Lamp
15. Fog Lamp Harness
149. Air Deflector
150. Bracket
151. Nut
152. Bumper
153. Bolt

85386113

Fig. 114 Common fog lamp mounting

• Turn the lamp switch OFF and allow the bulb to cool before changing it. Leave the switch OFF until the change is complete.
• ALWAYS wear eye protection when changing a Halogen bulb.
• DO NOT drop or scratch the bulb. Keep moisture away.
• Place the use bulb in the new bulb's carton and dispose of it properly.
1. Disconnect the negative battery cable.
2. Remove the lens trim panel screws from the front of the lamp, then pull the lamp and lens assembly forward from the case and turn it over.
3. Unplug the white wire connector inside the braided insulator (leave the ground wire connected). Note the position of the wire clip at the lamp and lens assembly, then squeeze the edges of the clip together and remove it.
4. Lift out the wire and the halogen bulb assembly.

To install:

5. Install the white wire connector to the wiring in the brained insulator.
6. Install the bulb into the back of the lamp and lens assembly.
7. Install the wire clip to hold the bulb in place. Make sure the clip is firmly in position and the bulb is not loose.
8. Install the lens and lamp assembly into the case, then secure the trim panels using the retaining screws.
9. Connect the negative battery cable and check for proper operation.

INSTALLING AFTERMARKET AUXILIARY LIGHTS

➡**Before installing any aftermarket light, make sure it is legal for road use. Most acceptable lights will have a DOT approval number. Also check your local and regional inspection regulations. In certain areas, aftermarket lights must be installed in a particular manner or they may not be legal for inspection.**

1. Disconnect the negative battery cable.
2. Unpack the contents of the light kit purchased. Place the contents in an open space where you can easily retrieve a piece if needed.
3. Choose a location for the lights. If you are installing fog lights, below the bumper and apart from each other is desirable. Most fog lights are mounted below or very close to the headlights. If you are installing driving lights, above the bumper and close together is desirable. Most driving lights are mounted between the headlights.
4. Drill the needed hole(s) to mount the light. Install the light, and secure using the supplied retainer nut and washer. Tighten the light mounting hardware, but not the light adjustment nut or bolt.
5. Install the relay that came with the light kit in the engine compartment, in a rigid area, like a fender. Always install the relay with the terminals facing down. This will prevent water from entering the relay assembly.
6. Using the wire supplied, locate the ground terminal, or terminal with the number 85 next to it on the relay, and connect a length of wire from this terminal to a good ground source. You can drill a hole and screw this wire to an inside piece of metal; just scrape the paint away from the hole to ensure a good connection.
7. Locate the light terminal, or terminal with the number 87 next to it on the relay; and attach a length of wire between this terminal and the fog/driving lamps.
8. Locate the ignition terminal, or terminal with the number 86 next to it on the relay, and connect a length of wire between this terminal and the light switch.
9. Find a suitable mounting location for the light switch and install. Some examples of mounting areas are a location close to the main light switch, auxiliary light position in the dash panel, if equipped, or in the center of the dash panel.
10. Depending on local and regional regulations, the other end of the switch can be connected to a constant power source like the battery, an ignition opening in the fuse panel, or a parking or headlight wire.
11. Locate the power terminal, or terminal with the No. 30 next to it on the relay, and connect a wire with a fuse of at least 10 amperes in it between the terminal and the battery.
12. With all the wires connected and tied up neatly, connect the negative battery cable.
13. Turn the lights **ON** and adjust the light pattern if needed.

TRAILER WIRING

Wiring the vehicle for towing is fairly easy. There are a number of good wiring kits available and these 7should be used, rather than trying to design your own.

All trailers will need brake lights and turn signals as well as tail lights and side marker lights. Most areas require extra marker lights for overwide trailers. Also, most areas have recently required back-up lights for trailers, and most trailer manufacturers have been building trailers with back-up lights for several years.

Additionally, some Class I, most Class II and just about all Class III trailers will have electric brakes. Add to this number an accessories wire, to operate trailer internal equipment or to charge the trailer's battery, and you can have as many as seven wires in the harness.

Determine the equipment on your trailer and buy the wiring kit necessary. The kit will contain all the wires needed, plus a plug adapter set which includes the female plug, mounted on the bumper or hitch, and the male plug, wired into, or plugged into the trailer harness.

When installing the kit, follow the manufacturer's instructions. The color coding of the wires is usually standard throughout the industry. One point to note: some domestic vehicles, and most imported vehicles, have separate turn signals. On most domestic vehicles, the brake lights and rear turn signals operate with the same bulb. For those vehicles with separate turn signals, you can purchase an isolation unit so that the brake lights won't blink whenever the turn signals are operated, or, you can go to your local electronics supply house and buy four diodes to wire in series with the brake and turn signal bulbs. Diodes will isolate the brake and turn signals. The choice is yours. The isolation units are simple and quick to install, but far more expensive than the diodes. The diodes, however, require more work to install properly, since they require the cutting of each bulb's wire and soldering in place of the diode.

One, final point, the best kits are those with a spring loaded cover on the vehicle mounted socket. This cover prevents dirt and moisture from corroding the terminals. Never let the vehicle socket hang loosely; always mount it securely to the bumper or hitch.

CIRCUIT PROTECTION

Fuse Block and Fuses

▶ See Figures 115, 116 and 117

If the panel is not visible, check for a removable compartment door or trim panel which may used on later models to hide the block. This panel is usually located on the left end of the instrument panel.

The convenience center is located just below the instrument panel on the drivers side. It contains individual relays such as the seat belt and ignition key alarm, and flasher.

On newer model vehicles there is an underhood fuse/relay center contains both mini and maxi fuses, as well as some relays.

If a fuse blows, the cause should be investigated and corrected before the installation of a new fuse. This, however, is easier to say than to do. Because each fuse protects a limited number of components, your job is narrowed down somewhat. Begin your investigation by looking for obvious fraying, loose connections, breaks in insulation, etc. Use the techniques outlined at the beginning of this section. Electrical problems are almost always a real headache to solve,

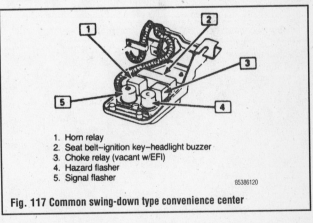

Fig. 116 The convenience center is usually located just below the instrument panel on the driver's side

1. Horn relay
2. Seat belt–ignition key–headlight buzzer
3. Choke relay (vacant w/EFI)
4. Hazard flasher
5. Signal flasher

Fig. 117 Common swing-down type convenience center

but if you are patient and persistent, and approach the problem logically (that is, don't start replacing electrical components randomly), you will eventually find the solution.

Each fuse block uses miniature fuses (normally plug-in blade terminal-type for these vehicles) which are designed for increased circuit protection and greater reliability. The compact plug-in or blade terminal design allows for fingertip removal and replacement.

Although most fuses are interchangeable in size, the amperage values are not. Should you install a fuse with too high a value, damaging current could be allowed to destroy the component you were attempting to protect by using a fuse in the first place. The plug-in type fuses have a volt number molded on them and are color coded for easy identification. Be sure to only replace a fuse with the proper amperage rated substitute.

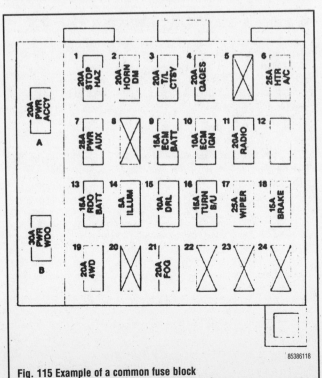

Fig. 115 Example of a common fuse block

A blown fuse can easily be checked by visual inspection or by continuity checking.

➡**A special heavy duty turn signal flasher is required to properly operate the turn signals when a trailer's lights are connected to the system.**

FUSE REPLACEMENT

◆ **See Figures 118, 119 and 120**

1. Pull the fuse from the fuse block.
2. Inspect the fuse element (through the clear plastic body) to the blade terminal for defects.

Fig. 118 Remove the fuse panel cover or trim panel (note the spare fuses and fuse puller on the cover)

Fig. 119 Removing a fuse using the fuse puller

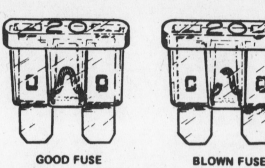

Fig. 120 Visual examination will reveal a blown fuse, but it should not be replaced until repairs are made

➡**When replacing the fuse, DO NOT use one of a higher amperage.**

3. Once repairs are completed, install a replacement fuse of the same amperage.

Fusible Links

A fusible link is a protective device used in an electrical circuit and acts very much like a standard fuse. The major difference lies in that fusible links are larger and capable of conducting a higher amperage than most fuses. When the current increases beyond the rated amperage for a given link, the fusible metal of the wire link will melt, thus breaking the electrical circuit and preventing further damage to any other components or wiring. Whenever a fusible link is melted because of a short circuit, correct the cause before installing a new one. There are 4 different gauge sizes commonly used and they are usually color coded so that they may be easily installed in their original positions.

Circuit Breakers

One device used to protect electrical components from burning out due to excessive current is a circuit breaker. Circuit breakers open and close the flow path for the electricity rapidly in order to protect the circuit if current is excessive. A circuit breaker is used on components which are more likely to draw excessive current such as a breaker often found in the light switch that protects the headlight circuit. Circuit breakers may be found in various locations on the vehicle including on/in the protected component, on a firewall bracket, the convenience center and/or the fuse block.

Flashers

The convenience center is used to centrally locate various buzzers, relays, flashers and/or circuit breakers. The turn signal and hazard flasher units are usually located in the convenience center located just below the instrument panel on the drivers side. Replace the flasher by unplugging the old one and plugging in the new one. Confirm proper flasher operation.

WIRING DIAGRAMS

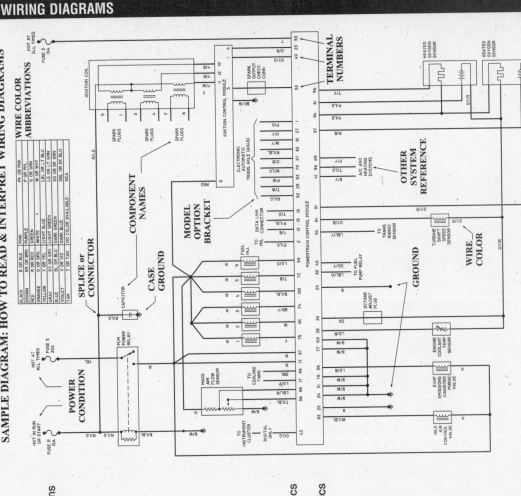

DIAGRAM 1

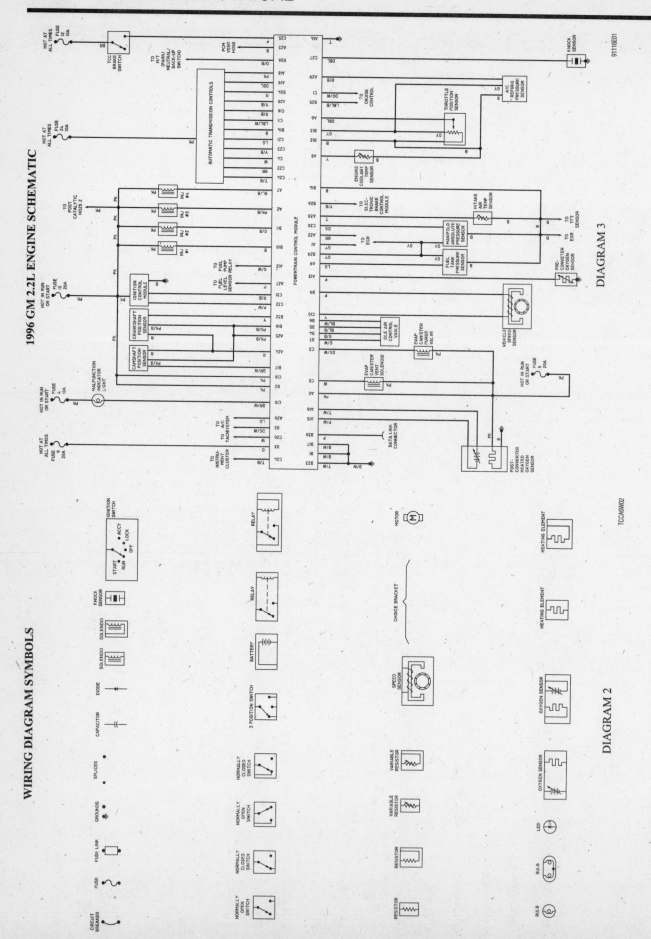

1996 GM 2.2L ENGINE SCHEMATIC

DIAGRAM 3

WIRING DIAGRAM SYMBOLS

DIAGRAM 2

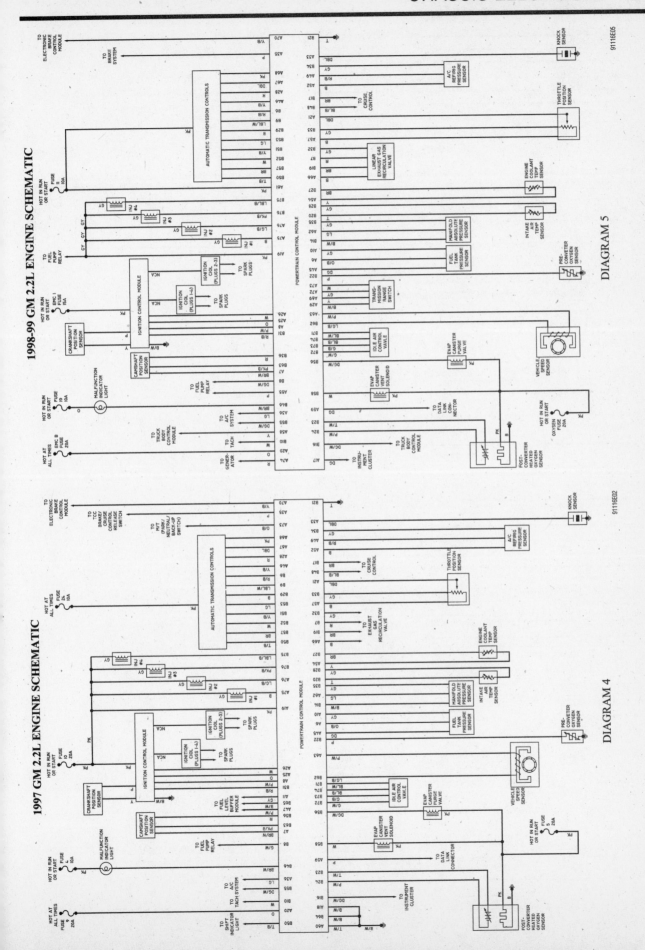

1998-99 GM 2.2L ENGINE SCHEMATIC

DIAGRAM 5

1997 GM 2.2L ENGINE SCHEMATIC

DIAGRAM 4

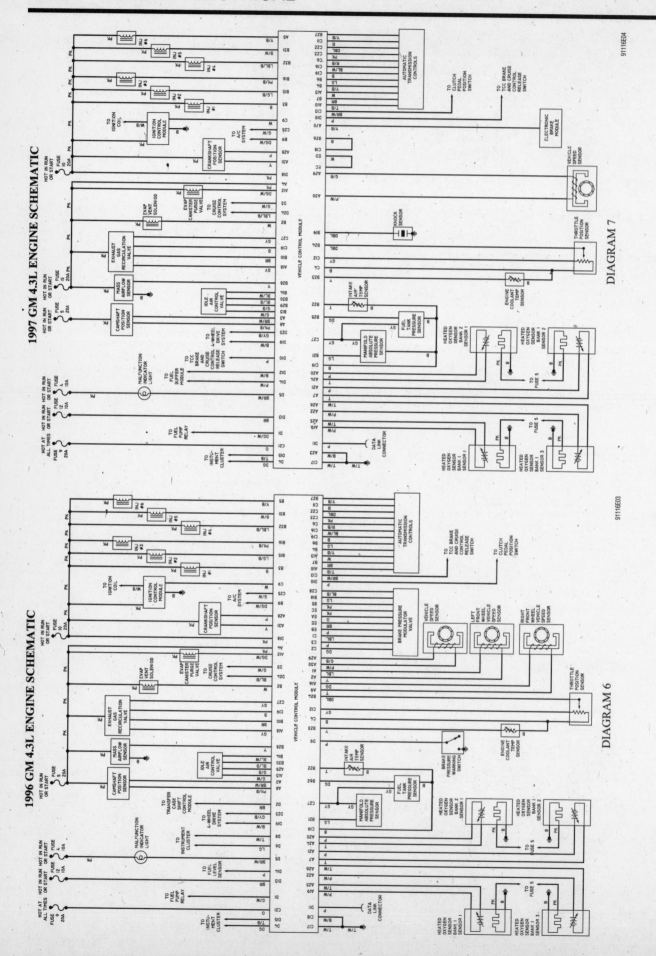

1997 GM 4.3L ENGINE SCHEMATIC

DIAGRAM 7

1996 GM 4.3L ENGINE SCHEMATIC

DIAGRAM 6

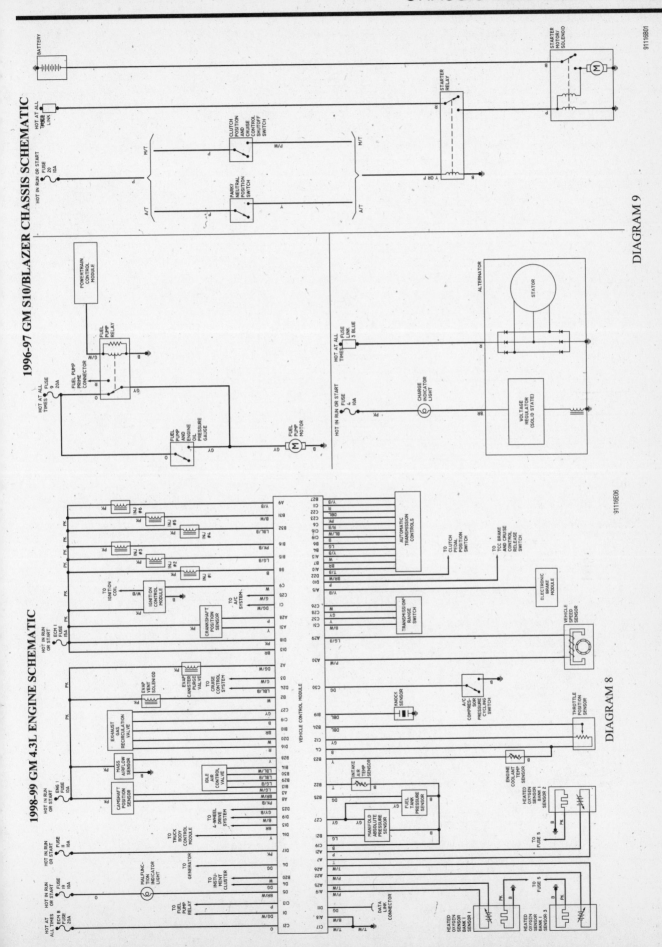

1996-97 GM S10/BLAZER CHASSIS SCHEMATIC

DIAGRAM 9

1998-99 GM 4.3L ENGINE SCHEMATIC

DIAGRAM 8

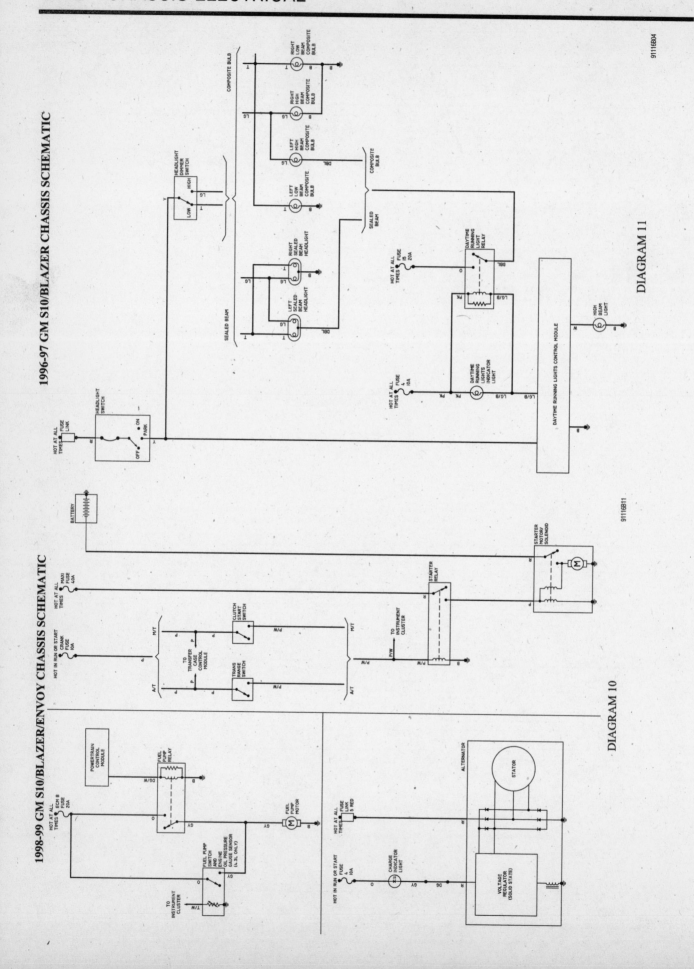

1996-97 GM S10/BLAZER CHASSIS SCHEMATIC

DIAGRAM 11

1998-99 GM S10/BLAZER/ENVOY CHASSIS SCHEMATIC

DIAGRAM 10

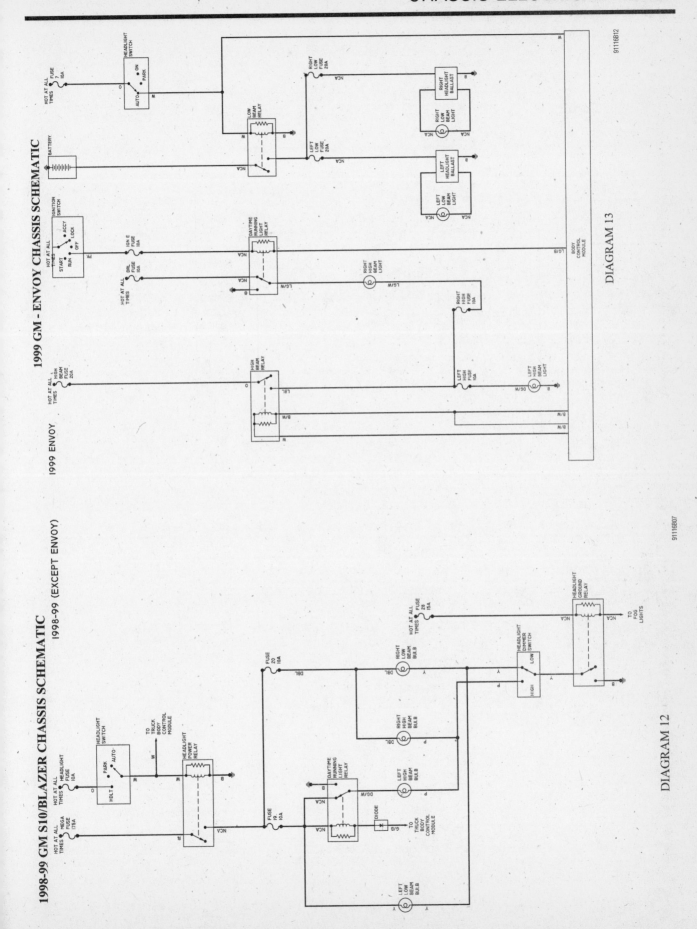

1999 GM - ENVOY CHASSIS SCHEMATIC

DIAGRAM 13

1998-99 GM S10/BLAZER CHASSIS SCHEMATIC

DIAGRAM 12

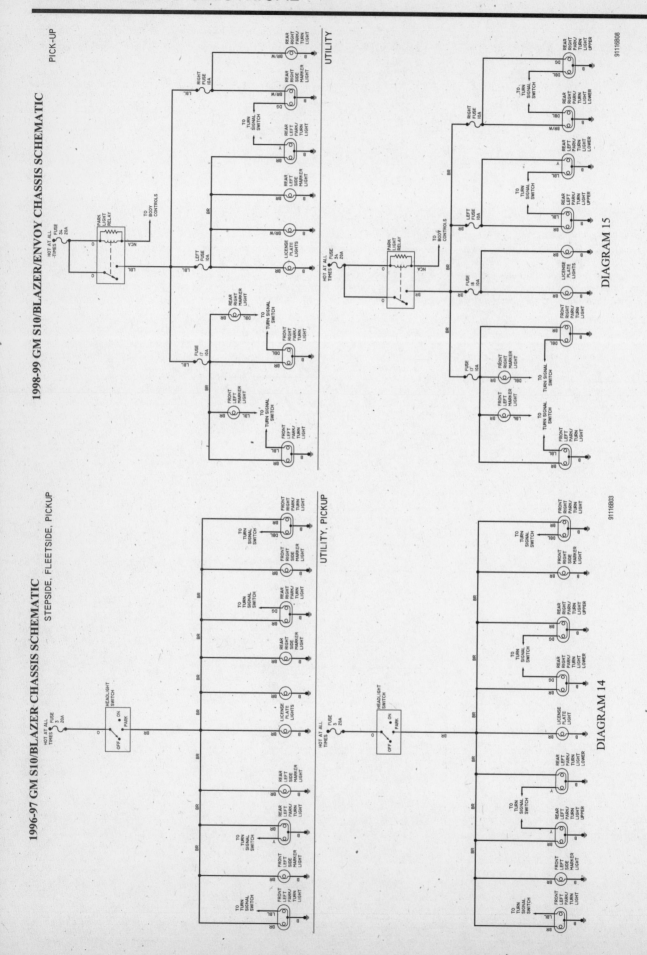

1998-99 GM S10/BLAZER/ENVOY CHASSIS SCHEMATIC

PICK-UP

UTILITY

DIAGRAM 15

91116B08

1996-97 GM S10/BLAZER CHASSIS SCHEMATIC

STEPSIDE, FLEETSIDE, PICKUP

UTILITY, PICKUP

DIAGRAM 14

91116B03

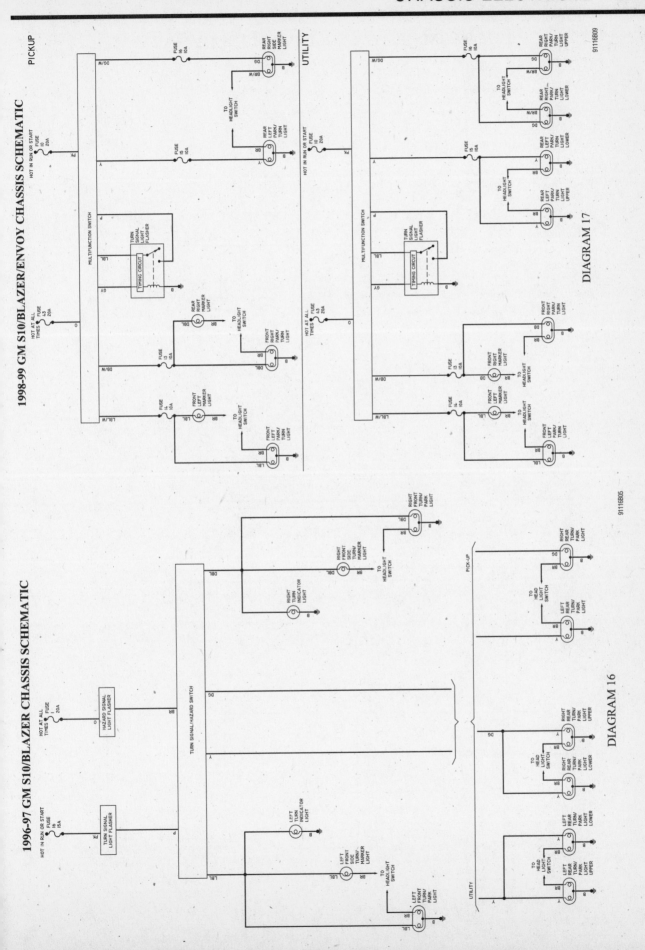

1998-99 GM S10/BLAZER/ENVOY CHASSIS SCHEMATIC

DIAGRAM 17

1996-97 GM S10/BLAZER CHASSIS SCHEMATIC

DIAGRAM 16

1996-97 GM S10/BLAZER CHASSIS SCHEMATIC

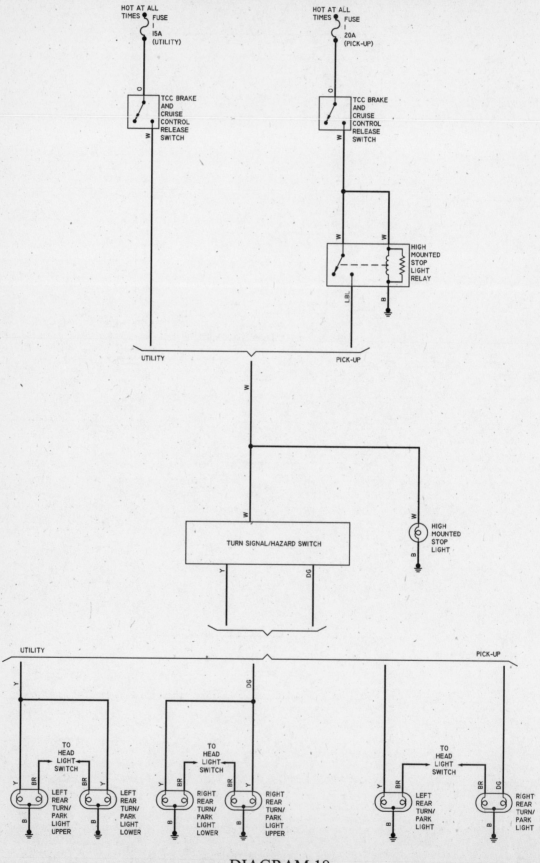

DIAGRAM 18

91116B06

1998-99 GM S10/BLAZER/ENVOY CHASSIS SCHEMATIC

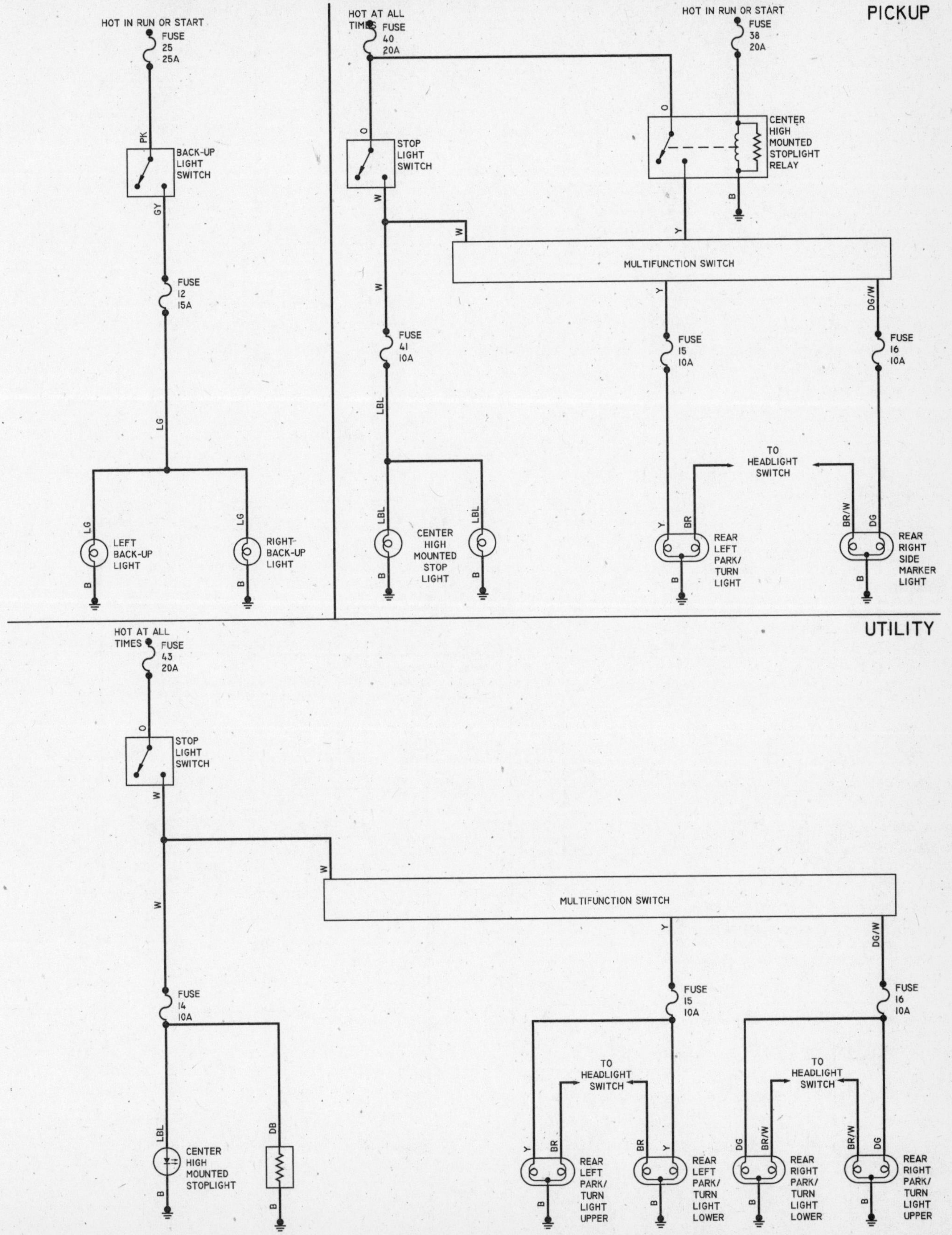

PICKUP

HOT IN RUN OR START

FUSE 25 25A

PK

BACK-UP LIGHT SWITCH

GY

FUSE 12 15A

LG

LG — LEFT BACK-UP LIGHT

B

LG — RIGHT BACK-UP LIGHT

B

HOT AT ALL TIMES   FUSE 40 20A

O

STOP LIGHT SWITCH

W

W

W

FUSE 41 10A

LBL

LBL — CENTER HIGH MOUNTED STOP LIGHT

B

LBL

B

HOT IN RUN OR START

FUSE 38 20A

O

CENTER HIGH MOUNTED STOPLIGHT RELAY

B

Y

MULTIFUNCTION SWITCH

Y

FUSE 15 10A

TO HEADLIGHT SWITCH

Y   BR — REAR LEFT PARK/ TURN LIGHT

B

DG/W

FUSE 16 10A

BR/W   DG — REAR RIGHT SIDE MARKER LIGHT

B

UTILITY

HOT AT ALL TIMES   FUSE 43 20A

O

STOP LIGHT SWITCH

W

W

W

FUSE 14 10A

LBL — CENTER HIGH MOUNTED STOPLIGHT

B

DB

B

MULTIFUNCTION SWITCH

Y

FUSE 15 10A

TO HEADLIGHT SWITCH

Y   BR — REAR LEFT PARK/ TURN LIGHT UPPER

B

BR   Y — REAR LEFT PARK/ TURN LIGHT LOWER

B

DG/W

FUSE 16 10A

TO HEADLIGHT SWITCH

DG   BR/W — REAR RIGHT PARK/ TURN LIGHT LOWER

B

BR/W   DG — REAR RIGHT PARK/ TURN LIGHT UPPER

B

DIAGRAM 19

91116B10

1996-99 GM S10/BLAZER CHASSIS SCHEMATIC

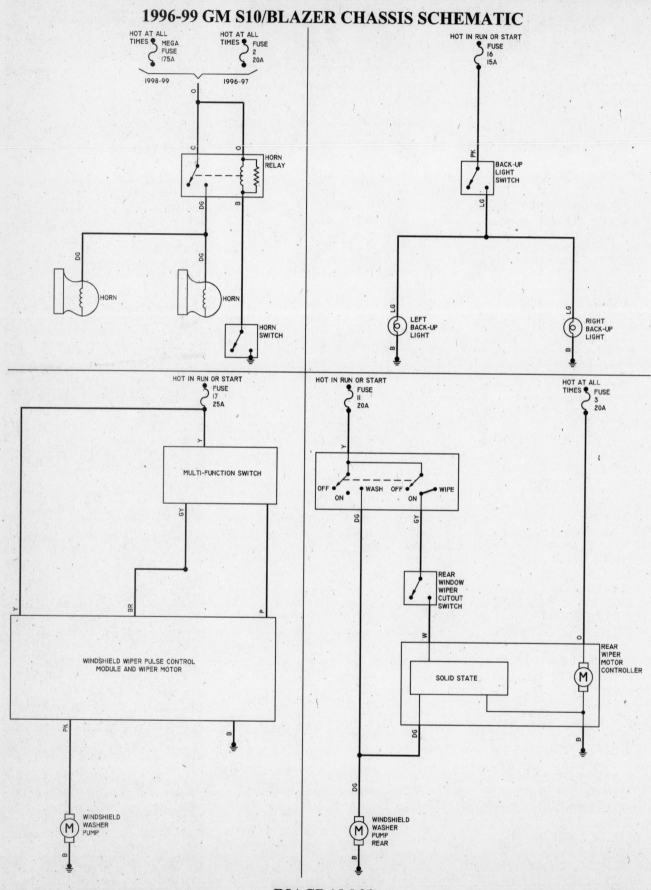

DIAGRAM 20

91116B02

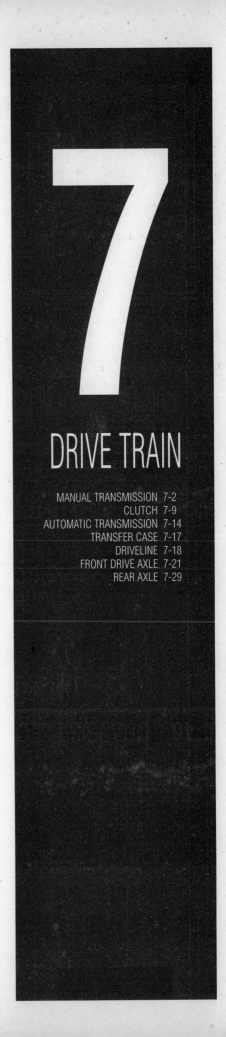

7

DRIVE TRAIN

MANUAL TRANSMISSION

Understanding the Manual Transmission

Because of the way an internal combustion engine breathes, it can produce torque (or twisting force) only within a narrow speed range. Most overhead valve pushrod engines must turn at about 2500 rpm to produce their peak torque. Often by 4500 rpm, they are producing so little torque that continued increases in engine speed produce no power increases.

The torque peak on overhead camshaft engines is, generally, much higher, but much narrower.

The manual transmission and clutch are employed to vary the relationship between engine RPM and the speed of the wheels so that adequate power can be produced under all circumstances. The clutch allows engine torque to be applied to the transmission input shaft gradually, due to mechanical slippage. The vehicle can, consequently, be started smoothly from a full stop.

The transmission changes the ratio between the rotating speeds of the engine and the wheels by the use of gears. 4-speed or 5-speed transmissions are most common. The lower gears allow full engine power to be applied to the rear wheels during acceleration at low speeds.

The clutch driveplate is a thin disc, the center of which is splined to the transmission input shaft. Both sides of the disc are covered with a layer of material which is similar to brake lining and which is capable of allowing slippage without roughness or excessive noise.

The clutch cover is bolted to the engine flywheel and incorporates a diaphragm spring which provides the pressure to engage the clutch. The cover also houses the pressure plate. When the clutch pedal is released, the driven disc is sandwiched between the pressure plate and the smooth surface of the flywheel, thus forcing the disc to turn at the same speed as the engine crankshaft.

The transmission contains a mainshaft which passes all the way through the transmission, from the clutch to the driveshaft. This shaft is separated at one point, so that front and rear portions can turn at different speeds.

Power is transmitted by a countershaft in the lower gears and reverse. The gears of the countershaft mesh with gears on the mainshaft, allowing power to be carried from one to the other. Countershaft gears are often integral with that shaft, while several of the mainshaft gears can either rotate independently of the shaft or be locked to it. Shifting from one gear to the next causes one of the gears to be freed from rotating with the shaft and locks another to it. Gears are locked and unlocked by internal dog clutches which slide between the center of the gear and the shaft. The forward gears usually employ synchronizers; friction members which smoothly bring gear and shaft to the same speed before the toothed dog clutches are engaged.

Shift Handle

Most vehicles covered by this manual utilize a 2-piece shift lever assembly. The upper portion of the shift lever is threaded to the lower portion and locked in position using a jamnut. If equipped, the upper portion may removed without unbolting the rest of the shifter lever/housing from the top of the transmission housing.

REMOVAL & INSTALLATION

▶ See Figures 1 thru 20

1. Disconnect the negative battery cable.
2. On 4wd pick-up models, remove the transfer case shift lever knob retaining clip, then remove the knob.
3. On 4wd utility models, unfasten the transfer case shifter locknut and unscrew the lever.
4. If equipped, remove the console assembly or cup holder.
5. Remove the shifter knob and nut from the lever.

➡On some models, to access the shift lever boot retaining screws the carpet will either have to be removed or cut. When we removed the shift lever we choose not to cut the carpet, instead we took the time to remove the seats and various trim pieces until the carpet could be pulled over the shifter assembly, then we removed the shift lever boot screws. If you choose to cut the carpet, we suggest that you cut the carpet in small amounts at all four sides of the shifter so that the carpet can be peeled back just enough to access the screws. Once the job is complete, the carpet can be held in place using Velcro.

6. Unfasten the boot retaining screws and remove the boot from the lever.
7. Unfasten the shift lever nut by turning it clockwise, then remove the lever by unscrewing it counterclockwise.

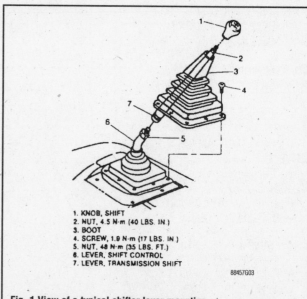

1. KNOB, SHIFT
2. NUT, 4.5 N·m (40 LBS. IN.)
3. BOOT
4. SCREW, 1.9 N·m (17 LBS. IN.)
5. NUT, 48 N·m (35 LBS. FT.)
6. LEVER, SHIFT CONTROL
7. LEVER, TRANSMISSION SHIFT

88457G03

Fig. 1 View of a typical shifter lever mounting

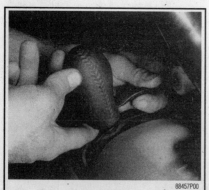

Fig. 2 Use an appropriate tool to locate the shift knob retainer clip—4WD vehicles

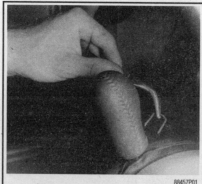

Fig. 3 After the retainer clip is removed, the knob can be removed—4WD vehicles

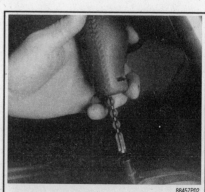

Fig. 4 Pull the knob up and off—4WD vehicles

Fig. 5 Remove the shifter cover—4WD vehicles

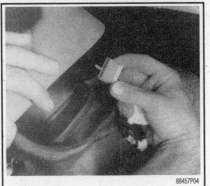
Fig. 6 Unplug the electrical harness—4WD vehicles

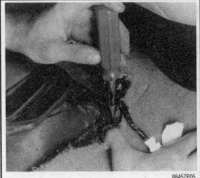
Fig. 7 Remove the shifter boot retainer screws—4WD vehicles

Fig. 8 Pull the shifter boot cover over the shifter and remove—4WD vehicles

Fig. 9 Once the boot is out of the way the shifter lever can be removed—4WD vehicles

Fig. 10 If the carpet has to be removed to access the gear shifter boot screws, first remove the cup holder by pulling up the disengage the clips—2WD vehicles

Fig. 11 Sometimes the clips will remain on the cup holder bracket when the cup holder is pulled up. If this happens, use pliers to remove the clips from the bracket and reinstall them in their original positions—2WD vehicles

Fig. 12 Unfasten the cup holder bracket retainers and then remove the bracket—2WD vehicles

Fig. 13 Unsnap the door sill trim plate clips (arrows) to remove it—2WD vehicles

Fig. 14 Remove the cowl kick panels. On models equipped with an air bag, the passenger side kick panels has the air bag system Diagnostic Energy Reserve Module (DERM) attached to it, so be careful not to damage it—2WD vehicles

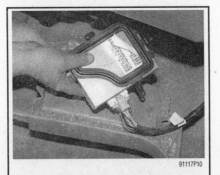
Fig. 15 Unfasten the DERM retainers and wire it to the door without unplugging any electrical connections—2WD vehicles

Fig. 16 After all the necessary trim pieces have been removed (including the seats), peel the carpet back to access the shifter boot retainers—2WD vehicles

Fig. 17 Unfasten all of the boot retainers and . . .

Fig. 18 . . . remove the boot from the shifter—2WD vehicles

Fig. 19 Loosen the shift lever retaining nut . . .

To install:

8. Install the lever and tighten the shift lever nut up against the lever.

9. Install the shifter nut and knob. Back the knob off until the shift pattern is aligned.

10. If removed, install the carpet. If you decided to cut the carpet, use Velcro to hold it in place.

11. If removed, install the console or cup holder assembly.

12. On 4wd utility models, install the transfer case lever and tighten the shifter locknut.

13. On 4wd pick-up models, connect the transfer case shift control cable to the knob and install the retaining clip.

Fig. 20 . . . then unscrew the shift lever—2WD vehicles

Extension Housing Seal

REMOVAL & INSTALLATION

1994—97 Models

▶ **See Figures 21, 22 and 23**

The extension housing seal (located in the tail section of the transmission assembly) controls oil leakage around the driveshaft. Continued failure of this seal usually indicates a worn output shaft bushing. If so, there will be signs of the same wear on the driveshaft, at the point where it contacts the seal and bushing. The seal is a fairly simple component to install, but it requires the proper driver tool to assure proper installation and prevent the danger of component damage.

1. Raise and support the rear of the truck safely using jackstands. If the rear of the vehicle is supported sufficiently, transmission oil loss will be minimized during the procedure. Keep a drain pan handy though, just to be sure.

2. Matchmark and remove the driveshaft from the truck. Refer to the procedure later in this section for details.

3. Pry the seal out of the transmission extension housing. Be careful not to score and damage the housing sealing surface when removing the seal.

To install:

4. Coat the outside of the replacement seal using a suitable locking compound.

5. On 1994—95 models, fill between the seal lips with chassis grease. On 1996 and later models, fill between the seal lips with transmission fluid, then drive the seal into position using J-21426, J-36503 or an equivalent seal installation tool.

6. Align and install the driveshaft.

7. Lower the rear of the truck or raise and support the front as well so the vehicle is level, then check the transmission fluid and add, as necessary. Remove the jackstands and carefully lower the vehicle.

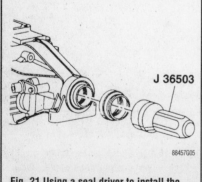

Fig. 21 Using a seal driver to install the extension housing seal

Fig. 22 A seal puller can be used to remove the transmission rear seal

Fig. 23 A seal driver or large socket with the same size diameter as the seal can be used to install the rear seal

Transmission

REMOVAL & INSTALLATION

▶ **See Figures 24 thru 68**

1. On Borg Warner and 1994—95 NVG 3500 models, shift the transmission into neutral.
2. On NVG 1500 and 1996—99 NVG models, shift the transmission into 3rd or 4th gear position.
3. Disconnect the negative battery cable.

✳✳ WARNING

Refer to the Shift Lever removal and installation procedures before attempting to remove the shift lever housing.

4. Remove the shift lever and the if necessary, the shift housing.
5. Raise and safely support the vehicle on jackstands.
6. Remove the parking brake cable for clearance.
7. Remove the propeller shaft.
8. If equipped, remove the skid plate.
9. On 4WD vehicles, remove the transfer case and shift lever. For details, please refer to the procedure later in this section.
10. Tag and disconnect all wiring harness that would interfere with transmission removal.
11. For 1994–95 4.3L engines properly relieve the fuel system pressure, then disconnect the fuel lines at the engine.
12. For 1994–95 2.2L engines, disconnect the fuel lines from the top cover.
13. For 1996–99 vehicles, disconnect the fuel line retainers from the rear crossmember.
14. Detach the muffler from the catalytic converter.
15. Disconnect the exhaust pipes from the exhaust manifold.
16. If necessary, remove the catalytic converter hanger.

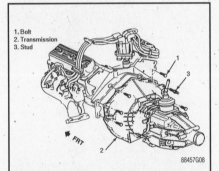

Fig. 24 Common transmission-to-engine mounting—New Venture Gear 3500 model shown

Fig. 25 Move the starter motor back out of the way so that inspection over can be removed—NVG 3500 transmission

Fig. 26 Remove the inspection plate—NVG 3500 transmission

Fig. 27 With the transmission supported securely with a jack, remove the cross-member-to-frame bolts—NVG 3500 transmission

Fig. 28 With the transmission supported securely with a jack, remove the mount-to-frame bolts—NVG 3500 transmission

Fig. 29 With the transmission supported securely with a jack, the crossmember can be safely removed —NVG 3500 transmission

Fig. 30 Remove the remaining section of the exhaust system—NVG 3500 transmission

Fig. 31 Loosen and remove the bell housing bolts—NVG 3500 transmission

Fig. 32 Carefully pull the transmission away from the engine to clear the input shaft and lower it down—NVG 3500 transmission

Fig. 33 Remove the insulator from the case using a suitable pry tool to access the shift housing retainers

Fig. 34 Unfasten the shift housing retainers

Fig. 35 Remove the shift housing assembly. Do not disassemble any of its components

Fig. 36 Place a clean rag or paper towels in the transmission shift housing cavity to prevent dirt from entering the transmission

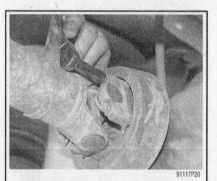

Fig. 37 Unfasten the bolts that attach the driveshaft retainers to the pinion flange . . .

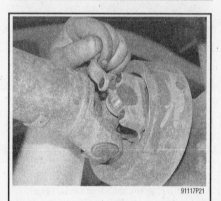

Fig. 38 . . . and remove the retainers

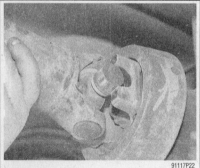

Fig. 39 Separate the yoke and cross assembly from the pinion flange by sliding the driveshaft forward

Fig. 40 Lower the rear end of the driveshaft and slide the shaft out of the transmission

Fig. 41 Install a plug in the transmission to avoid both fluid leaking out and dirt from getting in

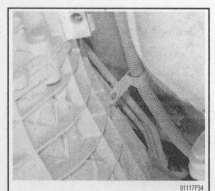

Fig. 42 Unfasten any wiring harness clip retainers attached to the transmission

Fig. 43 If equipped, unplug the downstream oxygen sensor electrical connection and unfasten the sensor harness retaining clip (arrow) from the crossmember

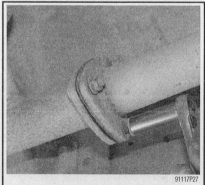

Fig. 44 Unfasten the nuts that attach the muffler to the catalytic converter

Fig. 45 Using a long extension, unfasten the exhaust pipe-to-manifold retaining bolts

Fig. 46 Unfasten the catalytic converter hanger retaining bolts . . .

Fig. 47 . . . and remove the catalytic converter and exhaust pipe

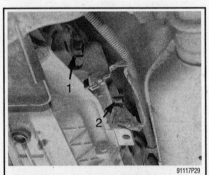

Fig. 48 Unplug the electrical connections from the speed sensor (1) and the back-up switch (2)

Fig. 49 Unfasten any fuel line retaining clips from the side of the transmission . .

Fig. 50 . . . and any clip retainer that attaches the fuel lines to the crossmember

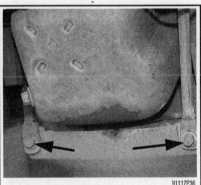

Fig. 51 Unfasten the bolts that attach the braces to the transmission

Fig. 52 The concentric slave cylinder fitting may be disconnected using two screw drivers at 180 degrees apart to depress the white plastic sleeve on the fitting

Fig. 53 After the sleeve is disengaged, separate the fitting from the slave cylinder

17. Remove the exhaust section.

18. Remove the bolts and nuts attaching any transmission braces to the engine and transmission.

19. On models equipped with the NVG transmission, detach the hydraulic clutch quick-connect from the concentric slave cylinder following 1 of the 2 steps:

a. Use 2 small prytools at 180 degrees from each other to depress the white plastic sleeve on the quick connect to separate the clutch line from the concentric slave cylinder quick connect.

b. Use special tool J–36221 to depress the white plastic sleeve on the quick connect to separate the clutch line end from the concentric slave cylinder quick connect.

20. On models equipped with the Borg Warner transmission, remove the slave cylinder from the transmission. If the cylinder can be repositioned with the hydraulics intact, simply support it out of the way, but make sure the line is not stretched, kinked or otherwise damaged. If necessary, disconnect the line and remove the cylinder completely.

21. If equipped, remove the bolts securing the clutch housing cover to the transmission.

22. If necessary, remove the clutch plate and clutch cover.

23. Support the transmission with a suitable jack.

24. Remove the rear crossmember from the frame rail.

25. If equipped, detach the wiring harness from the front crossmember. Move the wiring harness away from the transmission oil pan. Lower the transmission enough to gain access to the top of the transmission.

26. Remove the fuel line retainers or wiring harness's from the top of the transmission.

27. If necessary, remove the bolt, washer, and nut securing the wiring harness ground wires to the engine block.

28. Unfasten the bolts retaining the transmission to the engine. Pull the transmission straight back on the clutch hub splines.

29. Lower the transmission using the transmission jack.

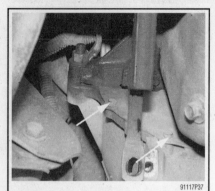

Fig. 54 Location of the clutch cover bolts on the drivers side

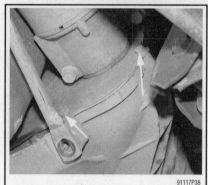

Fig. 55 Location of the clutch cover bolts on the passenger side

Fig. 56 After unfastening the cover bolts, remove both pieces of the cover

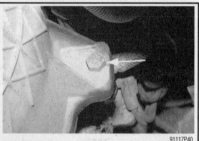

Fig. 57 Location of the lower transmission mounting bolt (passenger side). This bolt also retains a ground strap and has a nut on the other side. A back-up wrench will be needed to loosen this bolt

Fig. 58 The lower transmission bolt on the passenger side is located in front of the starter motor casting on the transmission

Fig. 59 Location of one of the transmission upper mounting bolts (passenger side). The top bolts are accessible using a long extension with a swivel socket and lowering the rear of the transmission

Fig. 60 The passenger side of the transmission crossmember is retained by four nuts and bolts. A back-wrench is required to unfasten these bolts

Fig. 61 The drivers side of the transmission crossmember is retained by a series of nuts and bolts. A back-up wrench is needed to unfasten the bolts indicated by the arrows

Fig. 62 The transmission rear mount is retained by a nut

Fig. 63 Before removing the crossmember, support the transmission with a suitable jack

Fig. 64 Unfasten the transmission mount-to-crossmember retaining nut

Fig. 65 Using a back-up wrench unfasten the crossmember retaining bolts on the drivers side

Fig. 66 Unfastening the passenger side crossmember retaining bolts using a back-up wrench

Fig. 67 After all the crossmember retainers have been unfastened, remove the crossmember from the vehicle

Fig. 68 After all the transmission-to-engine bolts have been unfastened, slide the transmission backwards until the shaft is clear of the clutch assembly

To install:

Installation is the reverse of removal, but please note the following important steps.

30. Place a THIN coat of high-temperature grease on the main drive gear (input shaft) splines.

31. Secure the transmission to the floor jack and raise the transmission into position.

➡On some models that use the NVG 3500 transmission, it may be necessary to rotate the transmission clockwise while inserting it into the clutch hub.

32. Slowly insert the input shaft through the clutch. Rotate the output shaft slowly to engage the splines of the input shaft into the clutch while pushing the transmission forward into place. Do not force the transmission into position, the transmission should easily fall into place once everything is properly aligned.

33. Tighten the transmission mounting bolts as follows:
- Borg Warner transmission: 55 ft. lbs. (75 Nm)
- NVG transmissions: 35 ft. lbs. (47 Nm)

34. Do not remove the transmission jack until the crossmembers have been installed.

35. Check the transmission fluid level and replenish as necessary.

CLUTCH

Clutch Disc and Pressure Plate

REMOVAL & INSTALLATION

▶ See Figures 69 thru 82

✱✱ CAUTION

The clutch plate may contain asbestos, which has been determined to be a cancer causing agent. Never clean the clutch surfaces with compressed air! Avoid inhaling any dust from any clutch surface! When cleaning clutch surfaces, use a commercially available brake cleaning fluid. If a spray cleaning fluid is not available, use a water dampened (NOT SOAKED) cloth to wipe away dust from the assembly.

1. Remove the manual transmission assembly from the vehicle.

2. If not performed for transmission removal, disconnect the slave cylinder from the clutch release fork and move it aside.

3. If the bell housing was not removed with the transmission, remove the inspection cover (if equipped), then loosen the retaining bolts and remove the bell housing from the rear of the engine assembly.

4. Remove the clutch fork from the ball stud (by carefully prying it free) and the dust boot (if applicable). Except for vehicles equipped with a New Venture Gear transmission, carefully pry the retainer out of the clutch fork (if it is not damaged). If necessary, remove the ball stud.

➡A used clutch drive gear may be used as an alignment tool. This may be available inexpensively from a junk yard or a transmission rebuilding shop.

5. Insert a clutch alignment tool such as No. J-33169, into the crankshaft pilot bearing to support the clutch assembly.

6. Check for an "X" or other painted mark on the pressure plate and fly-

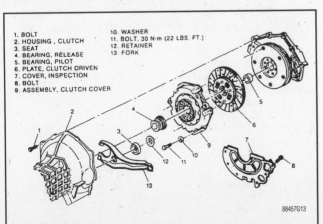

1. BOLT
2. HOUSING , CLUTCH
3. SEAT
4. BEARING, RELEASE
5. BEARING, PILOT
6. PLATE, CLUTCH DRIVEN
7. COVER, INSPECTION
8. BOLT
9. ASSEMBLY, CLUTCH COVER
10. WASHER
11. BOLT, 30 N·m (22 LBS. FT.)
12. RETAINER
13. FORK

Fig. 69 Exploded view of a common clutch assembly—New Venture Gear 3500 transmission shown

Fig. 70 Location of the six clutch pressure plate retaining bolts

Fig. 71 Install a suitable clutch alignment tool to support the clutch

Fig. 72 Mark the pressure plate to ensure proper alignment during installation

Fig. 73 Use a flywheel holding tool when loosening the pressure plate bolts

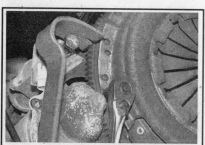

Fig. 74 If a flywheel holding tool is not available install one of the transmission retaining bolts, then use a crowbar to prevent the flywheel from turning while loosening the pressure plate bolts

Fig. 75 After unfastening all bolts, remove the pressure plate and clutch assembly

Fig. 76 Remove the clutch from the pressure plate

Fig. 77 Inspect the flywheel contact surface for wear and/or damage

Fig. 78 A dial indicator mounted on a magnetic base can be used to check flywheel run-out

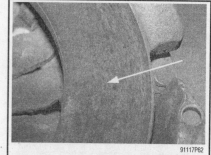

Fig. 79 Inspect the pressure plate for wear and/or damage. A straightedge should also be used to check the contact surface for scoring and flatness

wheel. If no marks are readily visible, matchmark the flywheel, clutch cover and pressure plate lug for installation purposes.

7. Loosen the pressure plate-to-flywheel bolts, evenly and alternately, a little at a time, until the spring tension is released. Remove the pressure plate, driven clutch plate and alignment tool.

To install:

8. Check the flywheel for cracks, wear, scoring or other damage. Check the pilot bearing for wear. If necessary, replace the bearing by removing it with a slide-type bearing puller and driving in a new one with a wood or plastic hammer. Lubricate the new pilot bearing with a few drops of machine oil.

9. If available, check the driven plate for run-out using a dial gauge. Run-out should not exceed 0.02 in. (5.08mm).

10. Using the clutch alignment tool to support the clutch, align and install the clutch plate and cover assembly. If a new clutch is being installed align the manufacturer's marks as directed.

11. Install the washers and bolts, then tighten each bolt one turn at a time to avoid warping the clutch cover. If spring washers were used, new ones should be installed. Once the bolts are fully threaded, tighten each one to 28 ft. lbs. (38 Nm) On 1994–95 2.2L models, 33 ft. lbs. (45 Nm) on 1996–99 2.2L models, or 29 ft. lbs. (40 Nm) on all 4.3L models. Refer to torque specification chart for correct application. Remove the clutch alignment tool.

12. If removed, install the ball stud. Pack the seat and coat the rounded end of the ball stud with high temperature (wheel-bearing) grease.

➡The clutch release bearing used on most vehicles covered by this manual is permanently packed with lubricant and should NOT be soaked in cleaning solvent as this will dissolve the lubricant.

13. Install the release bearing and the clutch fork. Pack the inside recess (A) and coat the outside groove (B) of the release bearing with high-temperature wheel-bearing grease. Please refer to the illustration for lubrication points.

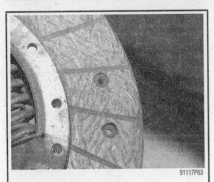

Fig. 80 Check the clutch for scoring, gouges, loose rivets and oil contamination. Replace as necessary

Fig. 81 Disengage the clutch cable from release lever

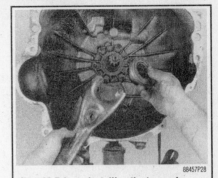

Fig. 82 Prior to installing the transmission, remove the release bearing lever and replace the release bearing

14. If separate, install the flywheel housing and install the retaining bolts.
15. If removed, install the inspection cover.
16. Reposition and secure the slave cylinder.
17. Install the manual transmission assembly.

Master Cylinder and Reservoir

The clutch master cylinder is located in the engine compartment, on the left-side of the firewall, above or near the steering column.

REMOVAL & INSTALLATION

1994 Utility Models

➡The master cylinder assembly is non serviceable and the entire unit should be replaced as an assembly.

1. Remove the lower filler panel.
2. If necessary, remove the lower left side air conditioning duct.
3. Unfasten the push rod retainer at the clutch pedal, then disconnect the push rod and washer from the pedal.
4. Using a suitable hydraulic clutch line separator tool such as J-36221 or its equivalent, disconnect the slave cylinder hydraulic line coupling.
5. Disconnect the slave cylinder hydraulic line from the cowl retaining clip.
6. Unfasten the master cylinder retaining nuts and remove the master cylinder from the engine compartment.
7. Unfasten the reservoir bolts and remove the reservoir.
To install:
8. Place the reservoir in position, install the bolts and tighten them to 25 inch lbs. (2.8 Nm).
9. Pre-fill the master cylinder and bleed it prior to installation.
10. Place the master cylinder into position, install the retaining nuts and tighten them to 13 ft. lbs. (18 Nm).
11. Connect the slave cylinder hydraulic line coupling and attach the line to the cowl retaining clip.
12. Connect the push rod and washer to the clutch pedal, then install and tighten the push rod retainer.
13. If removed, install the lower left side air conditioning duct.
14. Install the lower filler panel.
15. Properly refill the master cylinder reservoir, then bleed the system of air and check for fluid leaks.

1994–95 Pick-Up and 1995 Utility Models

♦ See Figure 83

➡On the 2.2L engine, individual components of the clutch actuating system (master cylinder/slave cylinder) may not be available for service. If so it is recommended that a complete, pre-filled and pre-bled unit should be installed and NO attempts should be made to disconnect the hydraulic lines.

1. Disconnect the negative battery cable.
2. Remove lower filler panel from under the dash.

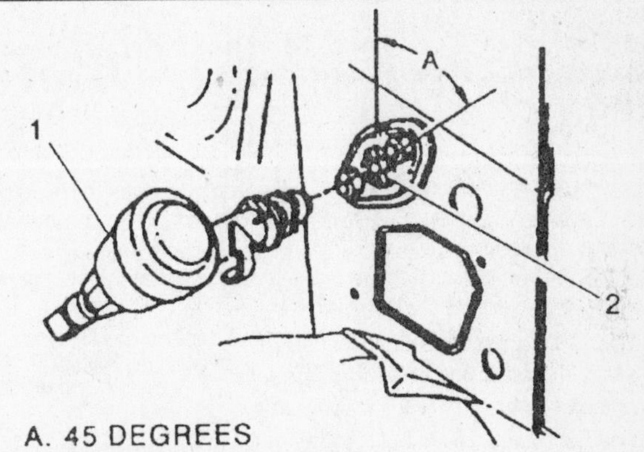

A. 45 DEGREES
1. CYLINDER, MASTER
2. ROD, PUSH

Fig. 83 Typical clutch master cylinder mounting—pick-up models

3. If necessary, remove the lower left A/C duct.
4. Remove the pushrod retainer, then disconnect pushrod from clutch pedal.

➡To expedite the hydraulic clutch bleeding, loose as little fluid as possible when disconnecting hydraulic lines. All openings should be immediately capped or plugged to prevent system contamination or excessive fluid loss.

5. Disconnect the slave cylinder hydraulic line from the master cylinder. Drive out the retaining pin holding the hydraulic tube to the master cylinder using a 7/64 in. (3mm) punch.
6. Remove the master cylinder from the cowl panel by grasping the cylinder body and rotating it about 45 degrees clockwise, then withdrawing it from the opening.
To install:
7. Hold the master cylinder assembly at a 45 degree angle (as during removal), then install the master cylinder to the cowl by inserting and twisting counterclockwise 45 degrees. Be sure not to over rotate the cylinder assembly or damage will occur.

➡Use a new retaining pin and quad seal during hydraulic line installation.

8. Remove the caps, then connect the slave cylinder hydraulic line to the master cylinder assembly.
9. Connect the pushrod to the pedal and secure using the retainer.
10. If removed, install the lower left A/C duct.
11. Install the lower filler panel.
12. Connect the negative battery cable.
13. Properly refill the master cylinder reservoir, then bleed the system of air and check for fluid leaks.

1996–99 Models

1. Disconnect the negative battery cable.
2. Remove lower filler panel from under the dash.
3. If necessary, remove the lower left A/C duct.

➡ **To expedite the hydraulic clutch bleeding, loose as little fluid as possible when disconnecting hydraulic lines. All openings should be immediately capped or plugged to prevent system contamination or excessive fluid loss.**

4. Detach the hydraulic clutch quick-connect from the concentric slave cylinder following 1 of the 2 steps:
   a. Use 2 small prytools at 180 degrees from each other to depress the white plastic sleeve on the quick connect to separate the clutch line from the concentric slave cylinder quick connect.
   b. Use special tool J–36221 to depress the white plastic sleeve on the quick connect to separate the clutch line end from the concentric slave cylinder quick connect.
5. Disconnect the tubes clips from the wiring harness bracket and sheet metal.
6. Remove the master cylinder from the cowl panel by grasping the cylinder body and rotating it about 45 degrees clockwise, then withdrawing it from the opening.

To install:
7. Hold the master cylinder assembly at a 45 degree angle (as during removal), then install the master cylinder to the cowl by inserting and twisting counterclockwise 45 degrees. Be sure not to over rotate the cylinder assembly or damage will occur.
8. Connect the clutch line to the slave cylinder. On some 4.3L models, a special band tie is used to attach the tubing to the body.
9. Connect the tubes clips to the wiring harness bracket and sheet metal.
10. Connect the pushrod to the pedal and secure using the retainer.
11. If removed, install the lower left A/C duct.
12. Install the lower filler panel.
13. Connect the negative battery cable.
14. Properly refill the master cylinder reservoir, then bleed the system of air and check for fluid leaks.

Slave (Secondary) Cylinder

On 1994–95 vehicles the slave cylinder is a conventional hydraulic actuator. It is located on the left side of the bell housing and controls the clutch release fork operation.

On 1996–99 vehicles the slave cylinder is called a concentric slave cylinder. It is located on the inside of the transmission bell housing on the input shaft. Removal of the transmission is required to replace it. It directly engages the clutch release bearing.

REMOVAL & INSTALLATION

1994 Utility Models

1. Disconnect the master cylinder pushrod from the clutch pedal assembly.

➡ **The master cylinder pushrod should be disconnected to protect the slave cylinder while it is removed from the bell housing. If not, any attempt to depress the clutch pedal while the slave cylinder is withdrawn from the bell housing will cause permanent damage to the slave cylinder assembly.**

2. Unfasten the slave cylinder-to-clutch housing nuts and separate the cylinder from the clutch housing.
3. Using a suitable hydraulic clutch line separator tool such as J-36221 or its equivalent, disconnect the slave cylinder hydraulic line coupling. Immediately cap or plug all openings to prevent system contamination or excessive fluid loss.
4. Disconnect the slave cylinder hydraulic line from the retaining clips.

To install:
5. Uncover the hydraulic line openings.
6. Pre-fill and bleed the slave cylinder. Attach the slave cylinder to the clutch housing and make sure the slave cylinder push rod is seated in the clutch fork.

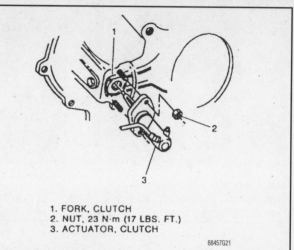

1. FORK, CLUTCH
2. NUT, 23 N·m (17 LBS. FT.)
3. ACTUATOR, CLUTCH

88457G21

Fig. 84 Slave cylinder mounting—1994–95 vehicles equipped with the Borg-Warner transmission

7. Connect the slave cylinder hydraulic line coupling and attach the line retaining clips.
8. Install the slave cylinder-to-clutch housing nuts and tighten to 18 ft. lbs. (24 Nm).
9. attach the master cylinder push rod to the clutch pedal.

1994–95 Pick-up and 1995 Utility Models

▶ **See Figures 84 and 85**

➡ **On the 2.2L engine, individual components of the clutch actuating system (master cylinder/slave cylinder) may not be available for service. If so it is recommended that a complete, pre-filled and pre-bled unit should be installed and NO attempts should be made to disconnect the hydraulic lines.**

1. Disconnect the master cylinder pushrod from the clutch pedal assembly.

➡ **The master cylinder pushrod should be disconnected to protect the slave cylinder while it is removed from the bell housing. If not, any attempt to depress the clutch pedal while the slave cylinder is withdrawn from the bell housing will cause permanent damage to the slave cylinder assembly.**

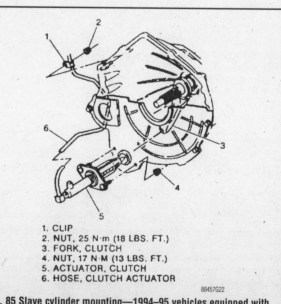

1. CLIP
2. NUT, 25 N·m (18 LBS. FT.)
3. FORK, CLUTCH
4. NUT, 17 N·M (13 LBS. FT.)
5. ACTUATOR, CLUTCH
6. HOSE, CLUTCH ACTUATOR

88457G22

Fig. 85 Slave cylinder mounting—1994–95 vehicles equipped with the New Venture Gear transmission

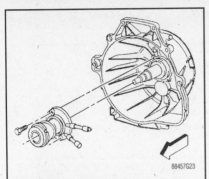

Fig. 86 Concentric slave cylinder mounting—1996–99 vehicles equipped with the New Venture Gear transmission

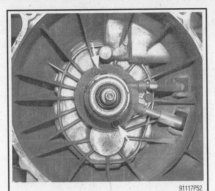

Fig. 87 The concentric slave cylinder is retained by two bolts

Fig. 88 Unfasten the concentric slave cylinder bolts . . .

Fig. 89 . . . and remove the slave cylinder from the transmission by sliding it off the shaft

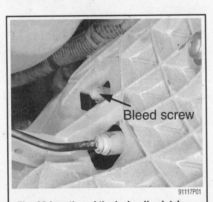

Bleed screw

Fig. 90 Location of the hydraulic clutch bleed screw

Fig. 91 Have an assistant fully depress and hold the clutch pedal, then open the bleeder screw of the slave cylinder or concentric cylinder using a box-end wrench

2. Using a 7/64 in. (3mm) punch to drive out the roll pin, disconnect the hydraulic line from the slave cylinder assembly. Immediately cap or plug all openings to prevent system contamination or excessive fluid loss.

➡To expedite the hydraulic clutch bleeding process, loose as little fluid as possible.

3. Remove the slave cylinder-to-bell housing retaining nuts.
4. Remove the slave cylinder from the bell housing and from the vehicle.
To install:
5. Install the slave cylinder to the bell housing, then tighten the retaining nuts to 18 ft. lbs. (24 Nm).
6. Uncover the hydraulic line openings, then connect the hydraulic line to the slave cylinder using a new O-ring (lightly lubricated with fluid) and a new roll pin.
7. Connect the master cylinder pushrod to the clutch pedal assembly.
8. Properly bleed the hydraulic system, then check for leaks.

1996–99 Models

▶ See Figures 86, 87, 88 and 89

1. Remove the transmission.
2. Remove the 2 bolts securing the concentric slave cylinder to the transmission and input shaft.
3. Remove the concentric slave cylinder from the input shaft.
To install:
4. Install the concentric slave cylinder over the transmission input shaft making sure the bleed screw and coupling are properly positioned and install 2 bolts.
5. Tighten the bolts to 80 inch lbs. (9 Nm).
6. Install the transmission.
7. Bleed the clutch hydraulic system.

HYDRAULIC SYSTEM BLEEDING

▶ See Figures 90 and 91

Bleeding air from the hydraulic clutch system is necessary whenever any part of the system has been disconnected or the fluid level (in the reservoir) has been allowed to fall so low, that air has been drawn into the master cylinder.
1. Fill master cylinder reservoir with new brake fluid conforming to DOT 3 specifications. Check manufactures recommendations for each vehicle.

✳✳ CAUTION

Never, under any circumstances, use fluid which has been bled from a system to fill the reservoir as it may be aerated, have too much moisture content and possibly be contaminated.

2. Raise and safely support the vehicle high enough to work comfortable under it.
3. Have an assistant fully depress and hold the clutch pedal, then open the bleeder screw of the slave cylinder or concentric cylinder.
4. Close the bleeder screw and have your assistant release the clutch pedal.
5. Repeat the procedure until all of the air is evacuated from the system. Check and refill master cylinder reservoir as required to prevent air from being drawn through the master cylinder.

➡Never release a depressed clutch pedal with the bleeder screw open or air will be drawn into the system.

6. Lower the vehicle and test clutch operation.
7. If the previous steps do not result in satisfactory pedal feel, remove the reservoir cap and pump the clutch pedal very fast for 30 seconds. Stop to let the air escape, then repeat the procedure as necessary to purge all remaining air.
8. Check the master cylinder fluid level and replenish as necessary.

AUTOMATIC TRANSMISSION

The automatic transmission allows engine torque and power to be transmitted to the rear wheels within a narrow range of engine operating speeds. It will allow the engine to turn fast enough to produce plenty of power and torque at very low speeds, while keeping it at a sensible rpm at high vehicle speeds (and it does this job without driver assistance). The transmission uses a light fluid as the medium for the transmission of power. This fluid also works in the operation of various hydraulic control circuits and as a lubricant.

Back-Up Lamp/Neutral Safety Switch

The back-up lamp/neutral safety switch assembly is mounted either on the steering column or on the floor shifter assembly, under the console, depending on the vehicle and application. Most 1994 models utilize a steering column mounted shifter for the automatic transmission, therefore the switch will be found on the steering column for those vehicles covered by this manual. For the removal, installation and adjustment procedures on transmission mounted switches (1995–99 models), please refer to the back-up lamp/neutral safety switch procedures in Section 6, of this manual.

COLUMN MOUNTED SWITCH

▶ See Figures 92 and 93

Two types of switches are generally found on these vehicles. Some early models will be equipped with adjustable switches which are bolted into position. Most vehicles covered by this manual should be equipped with ratcheting self-adjusting switches.

1. Disconnect the negative battery cable.
2. If necessary for access, remove the steering column insulator/filler panel for access to the switch.
3. Unplug the electrical harness connector from the switch.
4. Remove the switch by grasping and pulling it straight out of the steering column jacket.

To install:

5. If equipped with an early model switch which is bolted into position, the switch should be equipped with a gauge hole for adjustment. If equipped, loosely install the switch to the column and adjust following the procedures in the illustration.
6. Most vehicles covered by this manual utilize a self-adjusting (ratcheting) switch. To adjust:
   a. Align the actuator on the switch with the holes in the shift tube.
   b. Set the parking brake and place the gear selector in Neutral.
   c. Press down on the front of the switch until the tangs snap into the rectangular holes in the steering column jacket.
   d. Adjust the switch by moving the gear selector to **P**. The main housing and the housing back should ratchet, providing the proper switch adjustment.
7. Attach the harness connector to the switch.
8. Connect the negative battery cable, then verify proper switch operation.

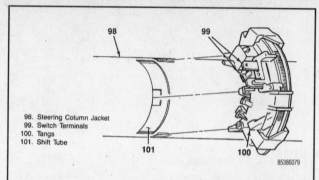

```
98                    99
98. Steering Column Jacket
99. Switch Terminals
100. Tangs
101. Shift Tube
101          100
                              85386079
```

Fig. 93 Ratcheting type back-up lamp/neutral safety switch mounting

Make sure the reverse lights work and that the ignition will only work in the **N** or **P** positions. If necessary, readjust the switch. For ratcheting type switches, move the gear selector all the way to the **L** position, then repeat the adjustment.

9. If applicable, install the steering column insulator/filler panel.

FLOOR CONSOLE MOUNTED SWITCH

1. Disconnect the negative battery cable.
2. Remove the center console for access to the switch assembly.
3. Disengage the switch electrical connector.
4. Remove the retaining nuts, then remove the switch from the vehicle.
5. If necessary, remove the gauge pin from the switch.
6. If installing a new switch:
   a. Place the shift control lever in **N**.
   b. Align the carrier tang on the back-up lamp/neutral safety switch with the slot on the shifter.

➡**Replacement switches are pinned in the N position to ease installation. If the switch has been rotated or the switch is broken, install the switch using the "old switch" installation and adjustment procedure.**

   c. Tighten the switch retaining nuts to 30 inch lbs. (3.4 Nm), then engage the switch connector.
   d. Move the shift control lever out of Neutral in order to shear the plastic pin, then remove the accessible piece(s) of the gauge pin.
7. If installing an old switch, install and adjust the switch to assure proper operation:
   a. Place the shift control lever in **N**.
   b. Align the carrier tang on the switch with the slot on the shifter.
   c. Loosely install the retaining switch nuts and engage the wiring connector.
   d. Rotate the switch to align the service adjustment hole with the carrier tang hold, then use a 0.09 in. (2.34mm) gauge pin to complete adjustment. Insert the pin in the service adjustment hole and rotate the switch until it drops to a depth of 0.59 in. (15mm). Hold the switch in this position and tighten the retaining nuts to 30 inch lbs. (3.4 Nm).
8. Install the center console.
9. Connect the negative battery cable.
10. Verify proper switch operation.

Extension Housing Seal

REMOVAL & INSTALLATION

▶ See Figure 94

1. Raise and support the vehicle safely using jackstands. If the rear of the vehicle is supported significantly higher than the front of the truck, the transmission fluid may not have to be drained for this service.
2. Remove the transmission fluid pan and drain the fluid from the vehicle. This step is recommended, but may not be necessary if the rear of the vehicle is

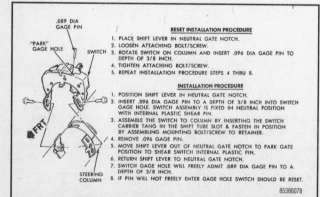

```
        .089 DIA
        GAGE PIN

"PARK"
GAGE HOLE

                    SWITCH

                                    RESET INSTALLATION PROCEDURE
                            1. PLACE SHIFT LEVER IN NEUTRAL GATE NOTCH.
                            2. LOOSEN ATTACHING BOLT/SCREW.
                            3. ROTATE SWITCH ON COLUMN AND INSERT .096 DIA GAGE PIN TO
                               DEPTH OF 3/8 INCH.
                            4. TIGHTEN ATTACHING BOLT/SCREW.
                            5. REPEAT INSTALLATION PROCEDURE STEPS 4 THRU 8.

                                      INSTALLATION PROCEDURE
                            1. POSITION SHIFT LEVER IN NEUTRAL GATE NOTCH.
                            2. INSERT .096 DIA GAGE PIN TO A DEPTH OF 3/8 INCH INTO SWITCH
                               GAGE HOLE. SWITCH ASSEMBLY IS FIXED IN NEUTRAL POSITION
                               WITH INTERNAL PLASTIC SHEAR PIN.
                            3. ASSEMBLE THE SWITCH TO COLUMN BY INSERTING THE SWITCH
                               CARRIER TANG IN THE SHIFT TUBE SLOT & FASTEN IN POSITION
                               BY ASSEMBLING MOUNTING BOLT/SCREW TO RETAINER.
FRT                         4. REMOVE .096 GAGE PIN.
                            5. MOVE SHIFT LEVER OUT OF NEUTRAL GATE NOTCH TO PARK GATE
                               POSITION TO SHEAR SWITCH INTERNAL PLASTIC PIN.
                            6. RETURN SHIFT LEVER TO NEUTRAL GATE NOTCH.
                            7. SWITCH GAGE HOLE WILL FREELY ADMIT .089 DIA GAGE PIN TO A
        STEERING              DEPTH OF 3/8 INCH.
        COLUMN              8. IF PIN WILL NOT FREELY ENTER GAGE HOLE SWITCH SHOULD BE RESET.

                                                                        85386078
```

Fig. 92 Installation and adjustment of the early model bolt-on back-up lamp/neutral safety switch

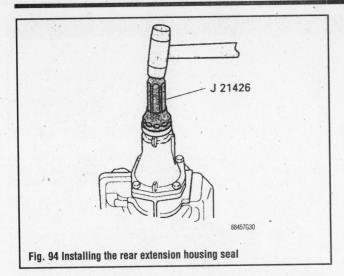

Fig. 94 Installing the rear extension housing seal

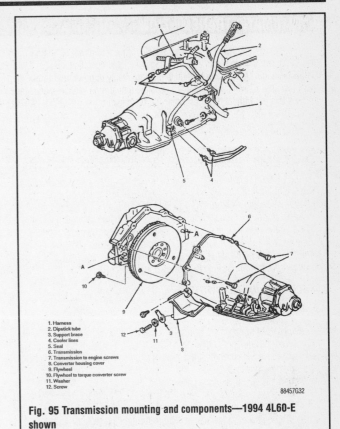

1. Harness
2. Dipstick tube
3. Support brace
4. Cooler lines
5. Seal
6. Transmission
7. Transmission to engine screws
8. Converter housing cover
9. Flywheel
10. Flywheel to torque converter screw
11. Washer
12. Screw

88457G32

Fig. 95 Transmission mounting and components—1994 4L60-E shown

held higher than the front. What is important is that the sealing surface in the extension housing may be cleaned of fluid and debris before installing the new seal. If fluid continues to run out of the housing once the old seal is removed, then the fluid should be drained to allow for proper seal installation.

3. Matchmark and remove the driveshaft. Most vehicles covered in this manual should be equipped with a slip yoke and the front of the driveshaft. In order to remove the shaft, disconnect it from the rear axle, and then carefully withdraw the splined yoke from the rear of the transmission.

4. Carefully distort the seal using a punch, then pry the seal from the rear of the transmission housing. Be careful not to damage the sealing surface of the housing.

To install:

5. Clean and DRY the sealing surface in the rear of the transmission housing.

6. Coat the outside of the new seal with a non-hardening sealing compound.

7. Carefully drive the new seal into position using a proper seal installation tool. Be careful not to damage the housing or the transmission output shaft upon installation.

8. Align and install the driveshaft assembly.

9. Remove the jackstands and carefully lower the vehicle.

10. Immediately check and, if necessary, add fresh transmission fluid.

Transmission

REMOVAL & INSTALLATION

On many of the vehicles covered by this manual, the upper transmission-to-engine bolts (especially the upper left) may be difficult to access and withdraw due to the close proximity of the cowl sheet metal. Even if a wrench fits over the bolt, there may be insufficient room to fully unthread it. The factory recommended procedure to access these bolts is to remove the left body mount bolt(s) from under the cab and loosen the radiator support mounting, then carefully jack the body up off the frame until sufficient clearance exists. Place wooden blocks between the body and frame to support the body (this is to prevent damage and for SAFETY) during service. In some cases, this may be unnecessary if the engine will pivot downward sufficiently on the motor mount to allow bolt access or if the motor mounts are removed and the engine is supported using a lifting device. BUT DO NOT try this if it appears that the mounts will be damaged by the stress. Also, be sure the engine is properly supported at ALL times and that no components will be damaged. Watch that the distributor does not contact the cowl and that the cooling fan remains clear of the radiator and shroud assembly. When in doubt, unbolt and raise the body for access.

1994–95 Vehicles

▶ **See Figure 95**

1. Properly relieve the fuel system pressure, then disconnect the negative battery cable.

2. Raise and support the vehicle safely using jackstands.

3. Drain the transmission fluid. For details, please refer to the pan procedure located in Section 1 of this manual.

4. On 1994 vehicles, disconnect the shift linkage from the transmission.

5. On 1995 vehicles, disconnect the shift cable from the transmission.

6. Matchmark and remove the rear driveshaft.

7. For 4WD vehicles, remove the transfer case assembly. For details, please refer to the procedure located later in this section.

8. Disconnect the fuel lines.

9. Remove the transmission crossmember-to-frame retaining bolts and member-to-transmission retainer(s), then remove the crossmember from the vehicle. Take care not to stretch or damage any cables or wiring when attempting to remove the crossmember.

10. Disconnect the exhaust pipe(s) from the manifold(s).

11. Remove the flywheel inspection cover and matchmark the flywheel-to-torque converter relationship, then remove the flywheel-to-torque converter bolts.

12. Remove the fuel lines and wiring harness from the transmission.

13. Make sure the transmission is properly supported by a floor jack, then remove the transmission-to-engine bolts. Note the positioning of any brackets, clips or harnesses as they are removed.

14. Remove the dipstick tube and seal, then plug or cover the opening in the transmission housing in order to prevent system contamination.

15. Disconnect the cooler lines. Plug or cover all openings in order to prevent system contamination or excessive fluid spillage.

16. Support the engine using a jackstand and a block of wood.

17. On 4WD vehicles, remove the transfer case shifter and set it aside.

18. Using the floor jack to support the transmission, pull it straight back and disengage it from the engine. Carefully lower the transmission and remove it from the vehicle. If possible, install a torque converter retaining strap before attempting to lower the transmission. This will prevent the converter from possibly falling and causing damage and/or personal injury.

To install:

Installation is the reverse of removal, but please note the following inportant steps

19. Make sure the torque converter is properly seated and a retaining strap is installed.

20. Using the floor jack, carefully raise the transmission into position in the vehicle, then remove the converter retaining strap. Slide the transmission straight onto the locating pins while aligning the marks on the flywheel and torque converter.

➡ **The converter must be flush on the flywheel and rotate freely by hand.**

21. Install the transmission-to-engine retainers, taking care to properly reposition all brackets, clips and harness, as noted during removal. Do NOT install the dipstick tube or transmission support brace screws at this time.
22. Tighten the transmission-to-engine retainers to 23 ft. lbs. (32 Nm).
23. Tighten the flywheel-to-converter bolts 46 ft. lbs. (63 Nm).
24. Tighten the transmission crossmember-to-frame bolts to 56 ft. lbs. (77 Nm).
25. Refill the transmission with the proper amount and type of fluid.
26. Connect the negative battery cable. Start the vehicle and allow to warm while checking for leaks. Road test the vehicle to check for shift quality.

1996–99 Vehicles

▶ **See Figures 96 and 97**

1. Disconnect the negative battery cable.
2. Raise and support the vehicle safely using jackstands.
3. Drain the transmission fluid.
4. Remove the driveshaft from the transmission (2WD) and transfer case, if equipped (4WD).
5. Support the transmission with a suitable transmission jack.
6. Remove the shift cable from the transmission control lever and bracket.
7. Remove the nut and washer securing the transmission mount to the crossmember.
8. Remove the bolts and washers securing the mount to the transmission.
9. Disconnect the exhaust pipe from the exhaust manifold(s).
10. If equipped, remove the bolts securing the converter pan cover to the transmission.
11. Remove the 3 bolts securing the torque converter to the flywheel.
12. Remove the bolt, clip, and strap securing the three fuel lines and transmission vent hose to the transmission case.
13. Remove the bolts and nut securing the transmission to the engine.
14. Remove the oil filler tube and seal from the transmission.
15. Disconnect the transmission cooler lines from the transmission. Plug the lines and the ports in the transmission.
16. Unplug the wiring harness connectors from the transmission.
17. Inspect for any other wiring, brackets etc. which may interfere with the removal of the transmission.

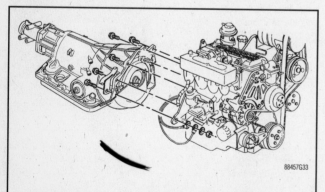

Fig. 96 Transmission mounting on 1996–99 2.2L engines

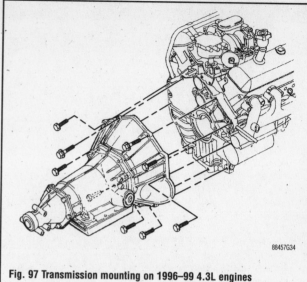

Fig. 97 Transmission mounting on 1996–99 4.3L engines

18. Since the transmission acts as a rear engine mount, properly support the rear of the engine with an underbody support of other suitable support before attempting to remove the transmission. Otherwise the rear of the engine may pitch downward and components on the rear of the engine and on the firewall may be damaged.
19. Remove the transmission from the engine by pulling the transmission rearward to disengage it from the locator dowel pins on the back of the block. Carefully lower the transmission from the vehicle. Use care that the torque converter does not fall out of the front of the transmission.

➡ **Use converter holding strap tool No. J-21366, or equivalent, to secure the torque converter to the transmission during removal and installation procedures.**

To install:
Installation is the reverse of removal, but please note the following important steps.

20. Make sure the torque converter is fully seated in the pump drive. If not, the transmission will not fit tightly to the rear of the engine block.
21. Raise the transmission into position and remove the torque converter holding strap and carefully. Slide the transmission forward until the dowel pins are engaged.
22. The torque converter should be flush with the flywheel and turn freely by hand.
23. Install the transmission–to–engine bolts. Tighten the bolts to 66 ft. lbs. (90 Nm) on 1996 2.2L models and 34 ft. lbs. (47 Nm) on 1996–99 4.3L vehicles and 1997–99 2.2L vehicles.
24. Tighten the torque converter-to-flywheel bolts to 46 ft. lbs. (63 Nm).
25. If equipped, tighten the converter pan cover to the transmission bolts to 37 ft. lbs. (50 Nm)
26. Tighten the bolts and washers securing the transmission mount to 35 ft. lbs. (47 Nm).
27. Tighten the nut and washer securing the transmission mount to the crossmember to 38 ft. lbs. (52 Nm).
28. Refill the transmission with the proper amount and type of fluid.
29. Connect the negative battery cable. Start the vehicle and allow to warm while checking for leaks. Road test the vehicle to check for shift quality.

TRANSFER CASE

Transfer Case Output Shaft Seal

REMOVAL & INSTALLATION

▶ **See Figure 98**

1. Raise and support the vehicle safely using jackstands.
2. Matchmark and remove the front or rear driveshaft, as applicable.
3. For front shaft seal on vehicles applicable, remove the shaft yoke nut and washers, then remove the yoke and shield for access to the seal.
4. For front shaft seal removal on models with the BW4472 transfer case, remove the flange nut, washers, then remove the output flange for access to the seal.
5. Pry out the old seal using a small suitable prytool. Be careful not to damage the seal bore.

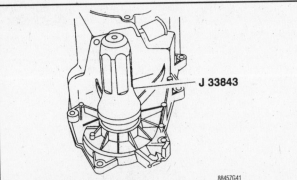

J 33843

Fig. 98 Install the shaft seal using a suitable installation tool or driver—NV231 and NV233 shown

To install:

6. Lubricate the lips of the new seal using automatic transmission fluid or petroleum jelly, whichever is at hand.
7. On models with the BW4472 transfer case, align the water hole in the rear output shaft oil seal with the drain hole in the extension housing, then using seal driver J-37668 or its equivalent, install the seal.
8. On all other models, position the seal and carefully drive it into position using a suitable seal installer tool.
9. As applicable, install the shield and shaft yoke, then install the washers and yoke nut. On 1994 vehicles, tighten the nut to 110 ft. lbs. (149 Nm). On 1995–99 vehicles, tighten the flange nut to 80 ft. lbs. (108 Nm).
10. Align and install the driveshaft to the vehicle.
11. Remove the jackstands and carefully lower the vehicle.

Transfer Case

REMOVAL & INSTALLATION

▶ **See Figures 99 thru 105**

1. Disconnect the negative battery cable.
2. Shift the transfer case into the 4WD High range.
3. Raise and support the vehicle safely using jackstands.
4. Remove the transfer case shield bolts, then remove the shield from under the transfer case assembly.
5. Remove the plug and drain the transfer case fluid.
6. Matchmark and remove the front and rear driveshafts from the transfer case.
7. Tag and disconnect the vacuum lines and/or the electrical connectors, as equipped.
8. Disconnect the transfer case shift rod or cable from the case, if applicable.

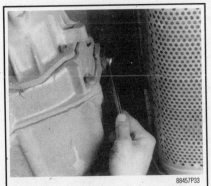

Fig. 99 If equipped, disconnect the shift cable linkage

Fig. 100 Unplug the vacuum harness

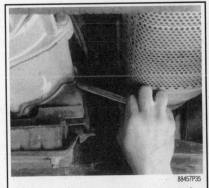

Fig. 101 With the transfer case supported, remove the transfer case retainer bolts

Fig. 102 Carefully lower the transfer case from the vehicle on a transmission jack

Fig. 103 Prior to installation, remove the old gasket from the mating surfaces

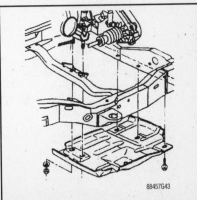

Fig. 104 View of the transfer case shield

9. If applicable, remove the support brace-to-transfer case bolts.

10. Support the transfer case using a floor jack, then remove the transfer case-to-transmission retaining bolts

11. Slide the transfer case rearward and off the transmission output shaft, then careful lower it from the vehicle.

12. Remove all traces of old gasket material from the mating surfaces.

To install:

13. Installation is the reverse of removal, but please pay special attention to the following important steps.

14. Using the floor jack, carefully raise the transfer case into position behind the transmission. Position a new gasket, using sealer to hold it in position, then slide the transfer case onto the transmission output shaft.

15. Tighten the transfer case-to-transmission retaining bolts to 24 ft. lbs. (33 Nm) on 1994 vehicles, 41 ft. lbs. (55 Nm) on 1995–98 vehicles or 33–35 ft. lbs. (45–47 Nm) on 1999 models.

16. If equipped, tighten the support brace bolts to 35 ft. lbs. (47 Nm) on 1994–95 vehicles, or 35–37 ft. lbs. (47–50 Nm) on 1996–99 vehicles.

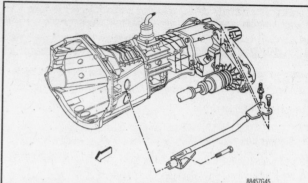

Fig. 105 Removing the left side support brace from the transmission/transfer case assembly—manual unit shown

DRIVELINE

Front Driveshaft and U-Joints

REMOVAL & INSTALLATION

♦ **See Figures 106, 107 and 108**

➡**DO NOT pound on the original driveshaft ears (unless the U-joints are being replaced) or the injected nylon U-joints may fracture.**

1. Raise and support the front of the truck safely using jackstands.

2. Matchmark the relationship of the driveshaft to the front axle and the transfer case flanges.

3. On 1994 vehicles, remove the driveshaft-to-retainer bolts and the retainers, first from the transfer case, then from the front axle.

4. On 1995–99 vehicles, remove the driveshaft-to-retainer bolts and the retainers front axle yoke.

5. On 1994 vehicles, collapse the driveshaft so it may be disengaged from the transfer case flange then from the front axle.

6. On 1995–99 vehicles, collapse the driveshaft and tilt it downward away from front axle end, then slide it out from the transfer case shaft.

➡**Use care when handling the driveshaft to avoid dropping the U-joint cap assemblies and loosing portions of the bearing assemblies.**

7. Wrap a length of tape around the loose caps to hold them in place.

To install:

8. Carefully insert the driveshaft into position in the vehicle.

9. Align the matchmarks made earlier, then remove the tape from the U-joints cap assemblies and position them to the flanges. Loosely install the retainers to hold the shaft in position.

10. Verify that the marks are properly aligned then tighten the retainers as follows:

- On 1994 vehicles, tighten the transfer case flange bolts and to 92 ft. lbs. (125 Nm) and the front axle flange bolts to 53 ft. lbs. (72 Nm).

- On 1995 vehicles, tighten the front axle flange bolts to 55 ft. lbs. (75 Nm).

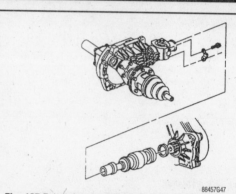

Fig. 107 Removing the driveshaft from the transfer case and front axle assembly—1995–97 vehicles

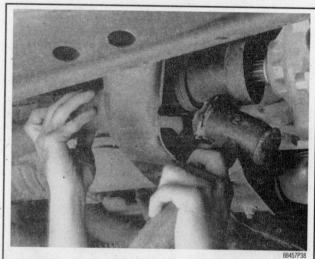

Fig. 108 It may be necessary to use a mallet to loosen the driveshaft from the transfer case shaft

- On 1996–99 vehicles, tighten the front axle flange bolts to 15 ft. lbs. (20 Nm).

11. Remove the jackstands and carefully lower the vehicle.

U-JOINT REPLACEMENT

With the exception of the size socket/pipe which must be used to support the trunnion yoke on some driveshafts, U-joint replacement is identical between the

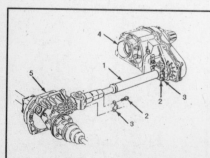

1. Front-Drive Propeller Shaft
2. Bolt
3. Retainer
4. Transfer Case
5. Front Axle

Fig. 106 Front axle and driveline assembly—1994 vehicles

front and rear driveshaft assemblies. Please refer to the procedure found later for the rear driveshaft to service the U-joints. Make sure an appropriately sized socket is used as a support. These driveshafts require a 1⅛ in. socket used by most front and rear driveshafts.

Rear Driveshaft and U-Joints

REMOVAL & INSTALLATION

◆ **See Figures 109, 110 and 111**

➥**DO NOT pound on the original propeller shaft yoke ears (unless the U-joints are being replaced) or the injected nylon joints may fracture.**

1. Raise and support the rear of the truck safely using jackstands.
2. Matchmark relationship of the driveshaft-to-pinion flange and the slip yoke-to-front driveshaft or transmission/transfer case housing, as necessary.

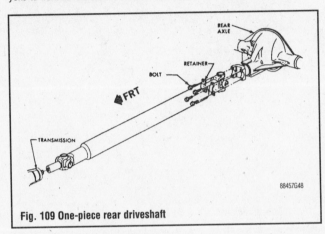

Fig. 109 One-piece rear driveshaft

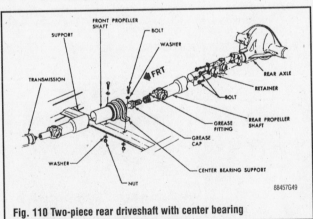

Fig. 110 Two-piece rear driveshaft with center bearing

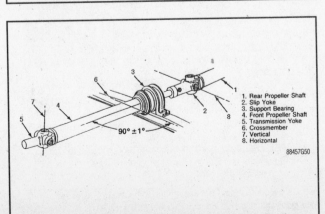

1. Rear Propeller Shaft
2. Slip Yoke
3. Support Bearing
4. Front Propeller Shaft
5. Transmission Yoke
6. Crossmember
7. Vertical
8. Horizontal

Fig. 111 Center bearing alignment or phasing to prevent vibrations

ALL shaft components which are being removed should be installed in their original positions, this includes slip yokes and U-joints ears. Disconnect the rear universal joint by removing retainers. If the bearing caps are loose, tape them together to prevent dropping and loss of bearing rollers.

3. If equipped with a one-piece driveshaft, perform the following procedures:
   a. Slide the driveshaft forward to disengage it from the rear axle flange.
   b. Move the driveshaft rearward to disengage it from the transmission slip-joint, passing it under the axle housing.
4. If equipped with a two-piece driveshaft, perform the following procedures:
   a. Slide the rear driveshaft half forward to disengage it from the rear axle flange.
   b. Slide the driveshaft rearward to disengage it from slip-joint of the front driveshaft half passing it under the axle housing.
   c. Remove the center bearing support nuts and bolts.
   d. Slide the front driveshaft half rearward to disengage it from the transfer case/transmission slip-joint.

➥**DO NOT allow the driveshaft to drop or allow the universal joints to bend to extreme angles, as this might fracture injected joint internally. Support propeller shaft during removal.**

To install:

5. Inspect the slip-joint splines for damage, burrs or wear, for this will damage the transmission seal. Apply engine oil to all splined propeller shaft yokes.
6. DO NOT use a hammer to force the driveshaft into place. Check for burrs on transmission output shaft spline, twisted slip yoke splines or possibly the wrong U-joint. Make sure the splines agree in number and fit. To prevent trunnion seal damage, DO NOT place any tool between yoke and splines.
7. If installing a one-piece driveshaft, perform the following procedures:
   a. Align the matchmarks made during removal, then slide driveshaft into the transmission/transfer case.
   b. Align the rear universal joint-to-rear axle pinion flange, make sure the bearings are properly seated in the pinion flange yoke.
   c. Install the rear driveshaft-to-pinion fasteners and verify all marks are aligned. Tighten the fasteners to 15 ft. lbs. (20 Nm) on 1994–99 2.2L models and 1994 4.3L models. On 1995–99 4.3L models, tighten the fasteners to 33 ft. lbs. (45 Nm).
8. If installing a two-piece driveshaft, perform the following procedures:
   a. Install the front driveshaft half into the transmission/transfer case (aligning the marks made during removal) and bolt the center bearing support in position. Tighten the center bearing to support nuts and bolts to 25 ft. lbs. (34 Nm) on 1994–95 models and 50 ft. lbs. (70 Nm) on 1996–99 models.

➥**In most cases, the yoke on the front driveshaft half must be bottomed out in the transmission (fully forward) before installation to the support.**

   b. Rotate the shaft as necessary so the front U-joint trunnion is in the correct position to align the matchmarks for the rear driveshaft half.

➥**Before installing the rear driveshaft, align the U-joint trunnions using the matchmarks made earlier (in some cases a "key" in the output spline of the front driveshaft half will align with a missing spline in the rear yoke).**

   c. Attach the rear U-joint to the axle, then tighten the retainers to 15 ft. lbs. (20 Nm).
9. Remove the jackstands and carefully lower the vehicle.
10. Road test the vehicle.

U-JOINT REPLACEMENT

◆ **See Figures 112 thru 118**

As mentioned earlier in this section, these vehicles utilize 2 different types of U-joint assemblies. At the factory, most vehicles are equipped with a nylon injected assembly. Because these assemblies contain no snapring grooves, and the very action of removing them destroys their retainers, they cannot be reused. Once removed, nylon injected U-joints should be discarded. If your vehicle has already received U-joint service, then it will be equipped with a snapring retained assembly. Once properly removed, these assemblies may be reused if they are in good condition.

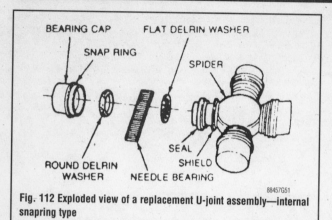

Fig. 112 Exploded view of a replacement U-joint assembly—internal snapring type

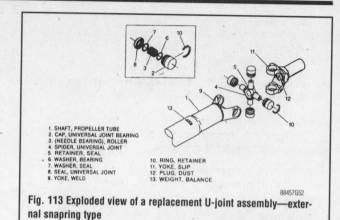

1. SHAFT, PROPELLER TUBE
2. CAP, UNIVERSAL JOINT BEARING
3. (NEEDLE BEARING), ROLLER
4. SPIDER, UNIVERSAL JOINT
5. RETAINER, SEAL
6. WASHER, BEARING
7. WASHER, SEAL
8. SEAL, UNIVERSAL JOINT
9. YOKE, WELD
10. RING, RETAINER
11. YOKE, SLIP
12. PLUG, DUST
13. WEIGHT, BALANCE

Fig. 113 Exploded view of a replacement U-joint assembly—external snapring type

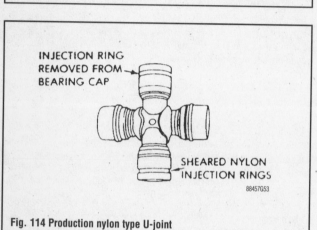

Fig. 114 Production nylon type U-joint

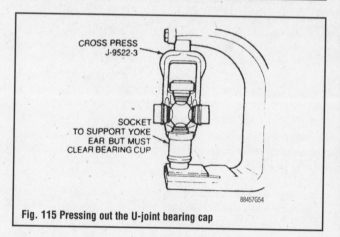

Fig. 115 Pressing out the U-joint bearing cap

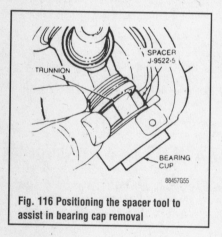

Fig. 116 Positioning the spacer tool to assist in bearing cap removal

Fig. 117 Installing the snaprings

Fig. 118 Tapping the yoke in order to seat the retaining clip

Snapring Type

1. Matchmark and remove the driveshaft assembly from the vehicle. Refer to the procedure earlier in this section.

> ※※ **WARNING**

NEVER clamp the driveshaft tube in a vise, for this may dent the tube. Support the driveshaft horizontally and clamp on the yokes of the universal joints using a soft-jawed vise or blocks of wood to protect the yokes.

2. Remove the snaprings from the yoke by pinching the ends together with a pair of pliers. If the snapring is difficult to remove, tap the end of the bearing cap lightly to relieve pressure from snapring.

3. Support the propeller shaft horizontally in line with the base plate of a bench vise, but never clamp the driveshaft tube.

4. Place the universal joint so the lower ear of the yoke is supported on a 1⅛ inch socket (or ID pipe), depending on the application. Most driveshafts require the 1⅛ in. support. Press the trunnion bearing against the socket/pipe in order to partially press it from the yoke. A cross press such as tool J-9522-3 should be used for this.

5. Grasp the cap and work it out, if necessary use tool J–9522–5 or equivalent spacer to further push the bearing cap from the trunnion, then grasp and work it free.

6. Rotate the shaft and support the other side of the yoke, then press the bearing cap from the yoke as in previous steps.

7. Remove the trunnion from the driveshaft yoke.

8. Clean and check the condition of all parts. Use U-joint repair kits to replace all the worn parts or replace the assembly using a new U-joint.

➡**If the used universal joints are going to be reinstalled, repack with new grease.**

To install:

9. Repack the bearings with chassis grease and replace the trunnion dust seals after any operation that requires disassembly of the U-joint. Be sure the lubricant reservoir at the end of the trunnion is full of lubricant. Fill the reservoirs with lubricant from the bottom.

10. Partially insert the cross into the yoke so one trunnion seats freely in the bearing cap, then rotate the shaft so this trunnion is on the bottom.

11. Install the opposite bearing cap part way. Be sure both trunnions are started straight into the bearing caps.

12. Press against opposite bearing caps, working the cross constantly to be sure the trunnions are free in the bearings. If binding occurs, check the needle rollers to be sure 1 or more needles have not become lodged under an end of the trunnion.

13. As soon as one bearing retainer groove is exposed, stop pressing and install the bearing retainer snapring.

➡It may be necessary to strike the yoke with a hammer to align the seating of the bearing retainers.

14. Continue to press until the opposite bearing retainer can be installed. If difficulty installing the snaprings is encountered, tap the yoke with a hammer to spring the yoke ears slightly.

15. Once the driveshaft and U-joints are properly assembled, align the matchmarks and install the driveshaft to the vehicle.

Nylon Injected Type

➡Don't disassemble these joints unless replacing the complete U-joint. These factory installed joints cannot be reused and should instead be replaced by snapring type U-joints.

1. Matchmark and remove the driveshaft assembly from the vehicle. Refer to the procedure earlier in this section.

✳✳ WARNING

NEVER clamp the driveshaft tube in a vise, for this may dent the tube. Support the driveshaft horizontally and clamp on the yokes of the universal joints using a soft-jawed vise or blocks of wood to protect the yokes.

2. Support the propeller shaft horizontally in line with the base plate of a bench vise, but never clamp the driveshaft tube.

3. Place the universal joint so the lower ear of the yoke is supported on a 1⅛ inch socket (or ID pipe), depending on the application. Most driveshafts driveshafts require the 1⅛ in support.

FRONT DRIVE AXLE

Halfshafts (Drive Axle)

REMOVAL & INSTALLATION

1994–96 Models

▶ **See Figures 119 thru 126**

1. Disconnect the negative battery cable.

2. Unlock the steering column so the linkage is free to move, then raise and support the front of the vehicle safely using jackstands.

3. If equipped, remove the front skid plate for access

4. Remove the tire and wheel assembly.

5. Insert a drift through the brake caliper into one of the brake rotor vanes to prevent the drive axle from turning.

6. Remove the cotter pin and retainer from the hub end of the shaft. Hold the hub from turning and loosen the axle nut. Once the nut is loosened unthread it and remove the washer.

7. Matchmark the inner shaft flange, then loosen (but DO NOT remove) the bolts retaining the inner joint flange to the output shaft companion flange.

4. Press the lower bearing cap out of the yoke ear, this will shear the nylon injected ring retaining the lower bearing cap.

5. If the bearing cap is not completely removed, lift the cross (J–9522–3) and insert J–9522–5 or equivalent spacer, then press the cap completely out.

6. Rotate the driveshaft, shear the opposite plastic retainer, and press the other bearing cap out in the same manner.

7. Remove the cross from the yoke.

➡**Production U-joints cannot be reassembled. There are no bearing retainer grooves in the caps. Discard all parts that were removed and substitute those in the overhaul kit.**

8. If the front U-joint is being removed, separate the bearing caps from the slip yoke in the same manner.

9. Remove the sheared plastic bearing retainer from the yoke. If necessary, drive a small pin or punch through the injection holes to aid removal.

10. Install the new snapring U-joints. Refer to the snapring type installation procedure found earlier in this section.

Center Support Bearing

REMOVAL & INSTALLATION

On vehicles covered by this manual that are equipped with a two-piece rear driveshaft assembly, the center support bearing may be removed for replacement. To be sure if your driveshaft may be serviced, check with your local parts supplier or dealer for parts availability information.

1. Matchmark and remove the rear driveshaft assembly. For details, please refer to the procedure located earlier in this section.

2. Remove the strap retaining the rubber cushion from the bearing support.

3. Pull the support bracket from the rubber cushion and the cushion from the bearing.

4. Press the bearing assembly from the halfshaft.

To install:

5. Assemble the center support bearing to the driveshaft:

   a. If removed, install the inner deflector onto the front shaft half and prick punch the deflector at 2 opposite points to make sure it is tight on the shaft.

   b. Fill the space between the inner dust shield and bearing with lithium soap grease.

   c. Start the bearing and slinger assembly straight onto the shaft journal. Support the shaft and using a length of pipe over the splined end of the shaft, press the bearing and inner slinger against the shoulder of the front shaft half.

   d. Install the bearing retainer, the rubber cushion onto bearing, the bracket onto the cushion and the retaining strap.

6. Align and install the driveshaft assembly to the vehicle.

8. Remove the brake line support bracket from the upper control arm in order to allow for additional knuckle travel. If necessary, remove the brake caliper and support aside.

9. Remove the cotter pin and nut from the outer tie rod end, then disengage the tie rod at the steering knuckle using J–24319–B, or an equivalent jawed tie rod puller. Push the linkage out toward the opposite side of the vehicle, then support the outer tie rod out of the way to provide the necessary clearance for shaft removal.

10. Remove the lower shock absorber retainers, then compress the shock and secure it out of the way using safety wire.

11. Position a jackstand between the spring seat and lower control arm ball joint for maximum leverage, then use the vehicle's weight to relieve the spring tension on the upper control arm.

12. Remove the cotter pin and retainer, then loosen and remove the upper ball joint stud nut away from the knuckle. Tip the knuckle out and toward the rear of the vehicle. Suspend the knuckle from the upper control arm or frame in order to prevent straining and damaging the brake line.

13. Using a suitable axle remover such as J–28733–B or equivalent, drive the axle shaft from the hub.

14. Remove the inboard flange bolts which were removed earlier.

15. Remove the axle from the vehicle. If the boots are not being serviced, take care not to damage or rip the CV-boots during removal.

Fig. 119 Remove the cotter pin from the hub end of the shaft

Fig. 120 Remove the retainer for access to the end nut

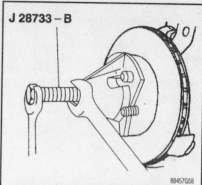

Fig. 121 Use a suitable axle shaft removal tool to drive the shaft from the hub

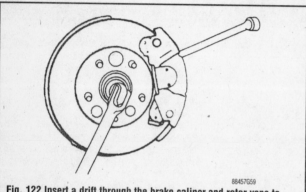

Fig. 122 Insert a drift through the brake caliper and rotor vane to prevent turning

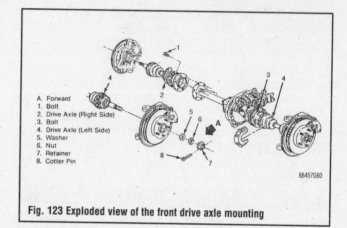

A. Forward
1. Bolt
2. Drive Axle (Right Side)
3. Bolt
4. Drive Axle (Left Side)
5. Washer
6. Nut
7. Retainer
8. Cotter Pin

Fig. 123 Exploded view of the front drive axle mounting

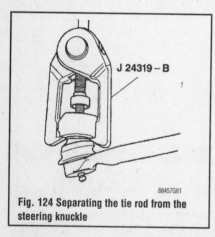

Fig. 124 Separating the tie rod from the steering knuckle

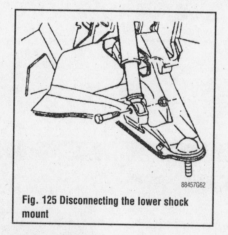

Fig. 125 Disconnecting the lower shock mount

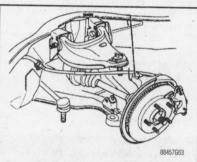

Fig. 126 Once the upper ball joint is disconnected, support the knuckle from the upper control arm or frame to prevent damage to the brake line and/or lower ball joint

⁂ CAUTION

DO NOT allow the vehicle's weight to load the front wheels or attempt to operate the vehicle when the drive axle(s) or hub nut(s) are removed. To do so may cause the front wheel bearing inner races to separate resulting in damage to the front brake and suspension components and/or personal injury.

To install:

16. Prior to shaft installation, cover the shock mounting bracket, lower control arm ball stud and ALL other sharp edges with a cloth or rag to help protect the boot.

17. Install the axle to the vehicle taking care not to damage the CV-boots. Insert the shaft end into the hub making sure to properly align the shaft splines.

18. Install the washer and retaining nut, if the nut can be fully threaded, it may be used to help draw the shaft into position in the hub.

19. Align the inboard flange to the output shaft companion flange, then loosely install the retainers.

➡ Neither the flange retainers or the axle end nut should be fully tightened at this time. Thread the retainers to hold the axle shaft in position and reassemble the other components.

20. Install the upper ball joint to the steering knuckle, then install the nut and tighten to 61 ft. lbs. (83 Nm). Install a new cotter pin, but DO NOT back of the specified torque. Lube the ball joint until grease appears at the seals, then remove the support from underneath the lower control arm.

21. Reposition and secure the lower shock absorber fasteners. Tighten the nut and bolt to 54 ft. lbs. (73 Nm).

22. Install the tie rod end to the steering knuckle, then tighten the nut to 35 ft. lbs. (47 Nm) on 1994–95 models and 39 ft. lbs. (53 Nm) on 1996 models. Align the cotter pin hole by rotating the retainer, DO NOT back off the specified torque OR exceed specification in order to install the cotter pin. Install the new cotter pin once the retainer is aligned.

23. Install the brake line support bracket and tighten the retainer(s) to 13 ft. lbs. (17 Nm). Make sure the brake hose is not twisted, kinked or otherwise damaged before securing the bracket.

24. Insert a drift through the brake caliper to prevent the drive axle from turning, then tighten the inboard flange bolts to 60 ft. lbs. (80 Nm).

25. Tighten the hub nut on the end of the axle to 180 ft. lbs. (245 Nm), then install the retainer and a new cotter pin. Rotate the retainer, as necessary to install the cotter pin. DO NOT back off or exceed specification to install the cotter pin.

26. If removed, reposition and secure the caliper.

27. Install the tire and wheel assembly.

28. If applicable, install the skid plate.

29. Remove the jackstands and carefully lower the vehicle.

30. Make sure the ignition is **OFF**, then connect the negative battery cable.

1997–99 Models

1. Disconnect the negative battery cable.

2. Unlock the steering column so the linkage is free to move, then raise and support the front of the vehicle safely using jackstands.

3. Remove the tire and wheel assembly.

4. Insert a drift through the brake caliper into one of the brake rotor vanes to prevent the drive axle from turning.

5. Remove the axle nut and washer from the hub end of the shaft. Hold the hub from turning and loosen the axle nut. Once the nut is loosened unthread it and remove the washer.

6. Remove the brake caliper and support it with a piece of wire to avoid damaging the brake hose. Remove the brake rotor.

7. Remove the ABS and brake line brackets from the top of the upper control arm.

➡Be careful when supporting the lower control arm that any components are damaged with the supporting device.

8. Place a jackstand or jack under the lower control arm.

9. Separate the axle shaft from the hub by placing a block of wood against the outer edge of the axle (to protect the threads), then strike the block of wood sharply with a hammer. Do not remove the axle at this time.

10. Remove the cotter pin and retainer, then loosen and remove the upper ball joint stud nut away from the knuckle. Tip the knuckle out and toward the rear of the vehicle. Suspend the knuckle from the upper control arm or frame in order to prevent straining and damaging the brake line.

11. Remove the lower shock absorber retainers, then compress the shock and secure it out of the way using safety wire.

➡Once the lower ball joint is separated from the knuckle, simultaneously push the axle shaft in towards the differential to allow room for the knuckle and assembly to be removed.

12. Remove the cotter pin and retainer, then loosen and remove the lower ball joint stud nut away from the knuckle.

13. Lower the safety stand or jack at the lower control arm to relieve pressure on the torsion bar, then separate the axle from the knuckle.

14. Remove the differential carrier shield, being very careful not to damage the axle seal.

15. To remove the shaft from the differential carrier, place a block of wood or a

brass drift against the tripot housing, then strike it outwards using a hammer. You will have to hit it hard enough to overcome the snapring pressure retaining it.

16. Support the drive axle, then pull the axle straight out from the carrier being careful not to tear the boot.

To install:

➡It is essential that the differential carrier and axle seals are not lubricated or damaged during installation. Prior to shaft installation, cover the shock mounting bracket, lower control arm ball stud and ALL other sharp edges with a cloth or rag to help protect the boot.

17. Install the axle into the carrier. With both hands on the tripot housing, align the splines on the shaft with the carrier. Then center the axle into the carrier seal and push the shaft straight into the carrier until the snapring is properly seated.

➡Be careful when supporting the lower control arm that any components are damaged with the supporting device.

18. Raise the lower control arm using a jackstand or jack until the full weight of the arm is supported.

➡It is necessary to slightly start the knuckle onto the axle while at the same time guiding the lower ball joint into position on the knuckle.

19. Install the lower ball joint, the lower shock absorber and the upper ball joint.

20. Install the axle washer and nut. Tighten the nut to 103 ft. lbs. (140 Nm).

21. Attach the ABS and brake line brackets to the top of the upper control arm.

22. Install the caliper and rotor.

23. Install the tire and wheel assembly.

24. Install the differential carrier shield.

25. Remove the jackstands and lower the vehicle.

CV-JOINT OVERHAUL

Outer CV-Joint

⬧ See Figures 127 thru 137

1. Remove the drive axle from the vehicle.

2. Place the axle in a vise using a protective covering on the vise jaws to prevent axle damage.

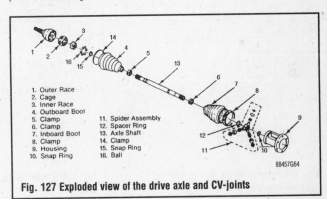

1. Outer Race
2. Cage
3. Inner Race
4. Outboard Boot
5. Clamp
6. Clamp
7. Inboard Boot
8. Clamp
9. Housing
10. Snap Ring
11. Spider Assembly
12. Spacer Ring
13. Axle Shaft
14. Clamp
15. Snap Ring
16. Ball

Fig. 127 Exploded view of the drive axle and CV-joints

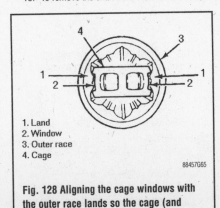

1. Land
2. Window
3. Outer race
4. Cage

Fig. 128 Aligning the cage windows with the outer race lands so the cage (and inner race) may be removed

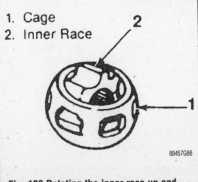

1. Cage
2. Inner Race

Fig. 129 Rotating the inner race up and out of the cage

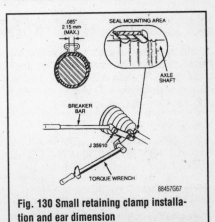

Fig. 130 Small retaining clamp installation and ear dimension

❋❋ CAUTION

Because the retaining clamps are under tension, use care when cutting and removing them. Wear gloves and safety goggles to protect you should the clamp spring loose upon releasing the tension.

3. Cut and remove the CV-boot retaining clamps. If the boot is not being replaced, use care not to cut or damage the boot.

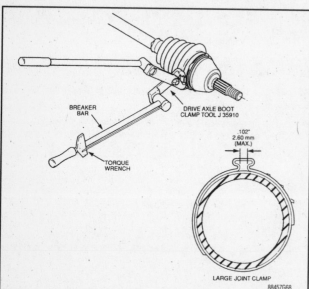

Fig. 131 Large retaining clamp installation and ear dimension—outer joint shown (inner joint uses same dimension)

➥Some vehicles are equipped with a swage ring. In order to remove the ring, use a hand grinder to cut through the ring. Take care not to damage the outer race while cutting the swage ring free.

4. Once the clamps are removed, reposition the boot and wipe the grease away in order to locate the snapring.
5. Remove the snapring using a suitable pair of snapring pliers, such as J-8059 or equivalent.
6. Remove the joint assembly from the axle shaft.
7. Using a brass drift and hammer, tap the cage until it tilts sufficiently to remove the first ball, remove the remaining balls in the same manner.
8. Pivot the cage so the inner race is 90 degrees to the centerline of the outer race, then align the cage windows with the outer race lands and lift the cage (along with the inner race) from the outer race. Please refer to the illustration for clarification.
9. Rotate the inner race up and out of the cage.
10. Thoroughly clean all parts in an approved solvent, then check for wear or damage and replaces, as necessary.

To install:

11. Apply a suitable grease to the ball grooves of the inner and outer races.
12. Install the inner race to the cage by inserting and rotating.
13. Align the cage windows with the outer race lands, then install the cage (along with the inner race) to the outer race. Make sure the retaining ring side of the inner race faces outward.
14. Use the brass drift to tap the cage to a tilted position, then install the balls.
15. Pack the joint using a suitable grease.
16. Position the small boot clamp onto the outboard boot, then install the boot the axle shaft. Tighten the small clamp securely using a suitable clamp tool such as J-35910 or equivalent. If the tool has a torque wrench fitting, secure the clamp using 100 ft. lbs. (136 Nm) of torque.
17. Check the clamp ear gap dimension (distance that the inner bends of the crimp should be from each other), it should be a maximum of 0.085 in. (2.15mm). Please refer to the illustration for clarification.
18. Install the joint assembly to the shaft and secure using the snapring. Pack the boot and outer joint assembly with the premeasured amount of the

Fig. 132 Before removal check the CV-boot for wear or damage

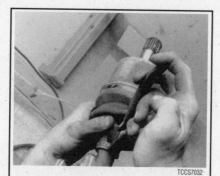

Fig. 133 In most cases, use a pair of side cutters to release clamp tension—inner band shown

Fig. 134 Remove the outer band from the CV-boot once the clamp tension has been released

Fig. 135 Clean the CV-joint housing prior to removing the boot, but be careful not to damage the boot

Fig. 136 With the clamps removed, carefully pull the CV-boot from the joint housing

Fig. 137 Pull the housing from the spider and shaft assembly—inner joint shown

grease supplied with the service kit, then snap the boot onto the outer joint assembly and manipulate it to remove excess air.

19. Install the large retaining clamp using the clamp tool and torque wrench. Secure the clamp using 130 ft. lbs. (176 Nm) of torque. Again, check the clamp ear dimension, it should be a maximum of 0.102 in. (2.60mm)

20. Install the drive axle to the vehicle.

Inner CV-Joint

▶ See Figures 138 thru 145

1. Remove the drive axle from the vehicle.
2. Place the axle in a vise using a protective covering on the vise jaws to prevent axle damage.

✳✳ CAUTION

Because the retaining clamps are under tension, use care when cutting and removing them. Wear gloves and safety goggles to protect you should the clamp spring loose upon releasing the tension.

3. Cut and remove the CV-boot retaining clamps. If the boot is not being replaced, use care not to cut or damage the boot.

➡ **Some vehicles are equipped with a swage ring. In order to remove the ring, use a hand grinder to cut through the ring. Take care not to damage the outer race while cutting the swage ring free.**

4. Remove the axle shaft with spider assembly from the housing.

➡ **Handle the spider assembly with care. The tripot needle rollers may separate from the spider trunnions.**

5. Grasp the space ring using J-8059, or an equivalent pair of snapring pliers, then slide the ring back on the axle shaft in order to provide clearance to move the spider assembly.

6. Move the spider assembly back on the shaft in order to expose the retaining snapring.

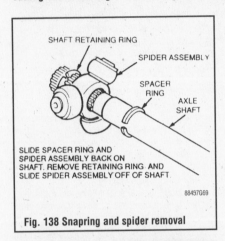

Fig. 138 Snapring and spider removal

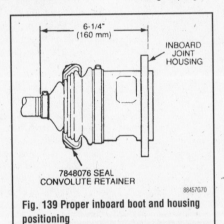

Fig. 139 Proper inboard boot and housing positioning

Fig. 140 On the inner CV-joint, be careful not to loose the spider assembly components

Fig. 141 Remove the CV-joint housing and check for wear or damage

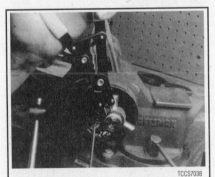

Fig. 142 With the spacer and spider pushed back, grasp the snapring using a pair of snapring pliers

Fig. 143 Remove the snapring from the shaft so the spider assembly may be removed

Fig. 144 With the snapring removed, the spider is free to be pulled from the shaft

Fig. 145 If necessary, remove the spacer ring from the shaft

7. Remove the snapring using a suitable pair of snapring pliers, such as J-8059 or equivalent.

8. Remove the spider assembly.

9. Thoroughly clean all grease from the housing. Check for rust at the boot mounting grooves, if found remove with a wire brush.

To install:

10. Install the small boot clamp and inboard boot to the axle shaft.

11. If the spacer ring was removed, make sure it is positioned up on the shaft leaving room for spider and snapring installation.

12. Install the spider assembly to the axle shaft, making sure the snapring counterbore faces the housing end of the axle.

13. Install the snapring to the shaft, then properly position the spider and space ring.

14. Position the small boot clamp and tighten securely using a suitable clamp tool such as J-35910 or equivalent. If the tool has a torque wrench fitting, secure the clamp using 100 ft. lbs. (136 Nm) of torque.

15. Check the clamp ear gap dimension (distance that the inner bends of the crimp should be from each other), it should be a maximum of 0.085 in. (2.15mm). Please refer to the illustration for clarification.

16. Repack the housing using about half of the premeasured grease supplied with the service kit, then place the remainder of grease in the boot. Coat the inside of the boot sealing lips with grease.

17. Make sure the joint/boot are assembled to the proper dimension of 6 ¼ in. (160mm) between the clamps. Please refer to the illustration for clarification.

18. Install the large retaining clamp using the clamp tool and torque wrench. Secure the clamp using 130 ft. lbs. (176 Nm) of torque. Again, check the clamp ear dimension, it should be a maximum of 0.102 in. (2.60mm).

19. Install the drive axle to the vehicle.

Axle Tube and Output Shaft Assembly

REMOVAL & INSTALLATION

◆ **See Figures 146, 147 and 148**

➡**The following procedure requires the use of the shift cable housing seal Installer tool No. J-33799 or equivalent.**

1. Disconnect the battery cables (negative cable first), then remove the battery and battery tray.

2. Disconnect the shift cable from the vacuum actuator by disengaging the locking spring. Then push the actuator diaphragm in to release the cable.

3. Unlock the steering wheel at steering column so the linkage is free to move.

4. Raise and support the front of the truck safely using jackstands.

5. Remove the front wheel assemblies.

6. If equipped, remove the front axle skid plate.

7. If necessary, remove the right side caliper and support using safety wire.

8. Place a support under right-side lower control arm and if equipped, unload the torsion bar.

9. Disconnect right-side upper ball joint, then remove the support so the control arm will hang free.

➡**To keep the axle from turning, insert a drift through the opening in the top of the brake caliper, into the corresponding vane of the brake rotor.**

10. Matchmark the right-side drive axle to the output shaft. Remove the right-side drive axle shaft-to-tube assembly bolts and separate the drive axle from the tube assembly, then remove the drift from the brake caliper and rotor.

11. Unplug the 4WD indicator lamp electrical connector from the switch.

12. Remove the three bolts securing the cable and switch housing-to-carrier and pull the housing away to gain access to the cable locking spring. DO NOT unscrew the cable coupling nut unless the cable is being replaced.

13. Disconnect the cable from the shift fork shaft by lifting the spring over the slot in the shift fork.

14. Remove the 2 bolts securing the tube bracket to the frame.

15. Remove the remaining 2 upper bolts securing the tube assembly to the carrier. The other 3 were removed with the shift cable housing.

16. Remove the tube assembly by working around the drive axle. Be careful not to allow the sleeve, thrust washers, connector and output shaft to fall out of carrier or be damaged when removing the tube.

To install:

17. Apply a bead of sealant on the tube-to-carrier mating surface.

18. Make sure the sleeve, thrust washers, connector and output shaft are in position in the carrier. Apply grease to the thrust washer to hold it in place during assembly, then position the washer to the tube.

19. Install the tube and shaft assembly-to-carrier, then thread and finger-tighten a bolt at the one o'clock position but DO NOT torque. Pull the assembly down, then install the cable/switch housing and the remaining bolts. Tighten the bolts to 36 ft. lbs. (48 Nm).

20. Install the tube-to-frame nuts/bolts and tighten to 55 ft. lbs. (75 Nm) on 1994 models and 72 ft. lbs. (98 Nm) on 1995–99 models.

21. Using the hub engagement tool No. J-33798 or equivalent, check the operation of the 4WD mechanism. Insert tool into the shift fork and check for the rotation of the axle shaft.

22. Remove the engagement tool, then install the shift cable switch housing by pushing the cable through into fork shaft hole. The cable will automatically snap into place. Please refer to shift cable replacement, later in this section for details.

23. Attach the 4WD indicator light wiring connector to the switch.

24. Install the support under the right-side lower control arm to raise arm and connect upper ball joint. For details, please refer to Section 8 of this manual.

25. Align and install right-side drive axle to the axle tube output shaft by installing one bolt first, then, rotate the axle to install and finger-tighten the remaining bolts. Tighten the bolts to 60 ft. lbs. (80 Nm).

➡**To hold the axle from turning, insert a drift through the opening in the top of the brake caliper into the corresponding vane of the brake rotor. If the caliper was removed, either temporarily install it or use a prybar across 2 installed lug nuts.**

26. If removed, reposition and secure the right side caliper.
27. If equipped, install the front axle skid plate.
28. Install the front wheel assemblies.
29. Remove the jackstands and carefully lower the vehicle.
30. Connect the shift cable-to-vacuum actuator by pushing the cable end

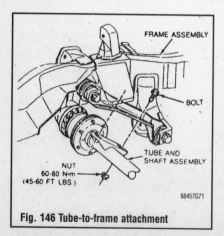

Fig. 146 Tube-to-frame attachment

FRAME ASSEMBLY

BOLT

TUBE AND SHAFT ASSEMBLY

NUT
60-80 N·m
(45-60 FT LBS)

88457G71

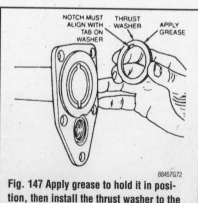

NOTCH MUST ALIGN WITH TAB ON WASHER

THRUST WASHER

APPLY GREASE

88457G72

Fig. 147 Apply grease to hold it in position, then install the thrust washer to the output shaft tube

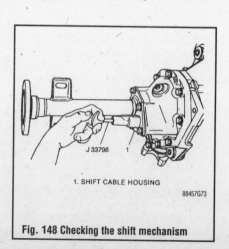

J 33798

1. SHIFT CABLE HOUSING

88457G73

Fig. 148 Checking the shift mechanism

into the vacuum actuator shaft hole. The cable will snap into place, automatically. For details, please refer to shift cable replacement, in this section.

31. Install the battery tray and battery.

32. Make sure the ignition is **OFF**, then connect the battery cables (negative cable first).

Output Shaft Pilot Bearing

REMOVAL & INSTALLATION

▶ See Figure 149

➡The following procedures requires the use of the pilot bearing remover tool No. J-34011 and the pilot bearing installer tool No. J-33842, or equivalents.

1. Remove the axle tube and output shaft assembly from the vehicle. For details, please refer to the procedure located earlier in this section.

2. Remove the pilot bearing from the tube using J-34011 or an equivalent pilot bearing remover tool.

To install:

3. Lubricate the new seal lips and the new bearing using fresh axle lubricant.

4. Install the new bearing using a pilot bearing installer tool such as J-33842, or equivalent.

5. Install the new seal using J-33893, or an equivalent seal installer.

6. Install the axle tube and output shaft assembly.

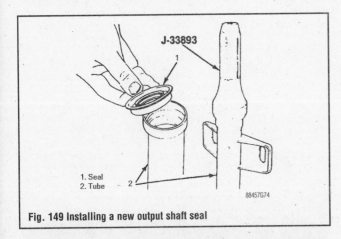

1. Seal
2. Tube

88457G74

Fig. 149 Installing a new output shaft seal

Differential Carrier

REMOVAL & INSTALLATION

▶ See Figures 150 and 151

1. Unlock the steering column so the linkage is free to move.

2. Remove the battery and battery tray from the vehicle.

3. Disconnect the shift cable from the vacuum actuator. For details, please refer to the procedure located later in this section.

4. Raise and support the front of the vehicle safely using jackstands, then remove the front wheels.

5. If equipped, remove the skid plate.

6. Remove the drain plug and flat washer, then drain the fluid from the carrier.

7. Remove the right lower shock retainer, then push the shock upward and wire it out of the way for access to the output shaft bolts.

8. Unplug the wire from the indicator switch.

9. Disconnect the shift cable housing and/or shift cable from the carrier housing, as necessary. Refer to the shift cable procedure later in this section for details.

10. Disconnect the vent hose.

11. Remove the steering relay rod from the idler arm and pitman arm, then pull the linkage forward for access.

12. Align the drive axles to their flanges. Hold the drive axles from turning

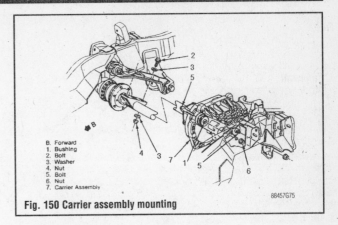

B. Forward
1. Bushing
2. Bolt
3. Washer
4. Nut
5. Bolt
6. Nut
7. Carrier Assembly

88457G75

Fig. 150 Carrier assembly mounting

by inserting a brass drift through the calipers into the rotor vanes, then remove the drive axle to output shaft retaining bolts.

13. Remove the nuts and washers holding the axle tube to the frame.

14. Matchmark and remove the front driveshaft.

15. Support both lower control arms using jackstands at the edge of the stabilizer shaft. Lower the vehicle until the font weight is resting on the stands.

16. Remove the bolts and nuts retaining the carrier assembly to the vehicle. Use an 18mm wrench inserted through the frame to keep the upper nut from turning.

17. Roll the carrier assembly counterclockwise while lifting upward to gain the necessary clearance from the mounting ears and remove the carrier from the vehicle.

To install:

18. Install the carrier assembly to the vehicle and secure using the retaining nuts and bolts. Tighten the bolts to 65 ft. lbs. (90 Nm) on 1994 models and 76 ft. lbs. (103 Nm) on 1995–99 models. Tighten the nuts to 55 ft. lbs. (75 Nm).

19. Install the nuts and washers holding the axle tube to the frame, then tighten to 36 ft. lbs. (48 Nm).

20. Install the front driveshaft assembly.

21. Align and install the drive axles to the carrier/output shaft flanges.

22. Connect the vent hose.

23. Connect the idler and pitman arms to the steering relay rod. For more information, please refer to Section 8 of this manual.

24. Connect the shift cable housing and/or cable, as applicable.

25. Engage the indicator switch wiring.

26. Remove the safety wire, then reposition and secure the shock.

27. If not done already, install the drain plug and flat washer, then check the fluid level and add as necessary. Remember that the vehicle must be level when checking or adding fluid.

28. If equipped, install the skid plate.

29. Install the front wheels, then remove the jackstands and carefully lower the vehicle.

30. Connect the shift cable to the vacuum actuator.

31. Install the battery tray and the battery to the vehicle.

Shift Cable

REMOVAL & INSTALLATION

▶ See Figures 152 and 153

1. Disconnect the shift cable from the vacuum actuator by disengaging the locking spring (bend the tang on the spring as shown in the illustration), then, push the actuator diaphragm in to release the cable. Using a pair of pliers, squeeze the two cable locking fingers, then pull the cable out of the bracket hole.

2. Raise and safely support the front of the truck safely using jackstands.

3. Remove the cable housing-to-carrier bolts and pull the housing away to gain access to the cable locking spring.

➡DO NOT unscrew the coupling nut at this time.

4. Disconnect the cable from the shift fork shaft by lifting the spring over shift fork slot.

5. Unscrew the cable from the housing by unscrewing the coupling nut.

6. Remove the cable from the truck.

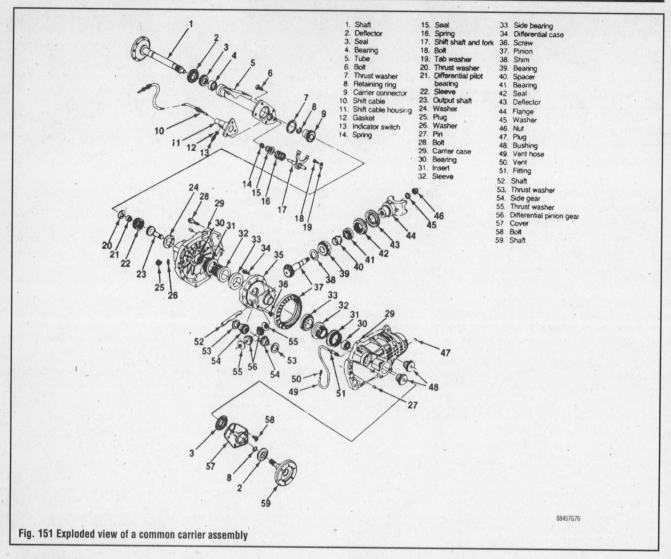

1. Shaft
2. Deflector
3. Seal
4. Bearing
5. Tube
6. Bolt
7. Thrust washer
8. Retaining ring
9. Carrier connector
10. Shift cable
11. Shift cable housing
12. Gasket
13. Indicator switch
14. Spring
15. Seal
16. Spring
17. Shift shaft and fork
18. Bolt
19. Tab washer
20. Thrust washer
21. Differential pilot bearing
22. Sleeve
23. Output shaft
24. Washer
25. Plug
26. Washer
27. Pin
28. Bolt
29. Carrier case
30. Bearing
31. Insert
32. Sleeve
33. Side bearing
34. Differential case
35. Screw
36. Pinion
37. Shim
38. Bearing
39. Spacer
40. Bearing
41. Bearing
42. Seal
43. Deflector
44. Flange
45. Washer
46. Nut
47. Plug
48. Bushing
49. Vent hose
50. Vent
51. Fitting
52. Shaft
53. Thrust washer
54. Side gear
55. Thrust washer
56. Differential pinion gear
57. Cover
58. Bolt
59. Shaft

Fig. 151 Exploded view of a common carrier assembly

To install:

7. Install the cable housing-to-carrier bolts. Tighten the bolts to 36 ft. lbs. (48 Nm).

8. Guide the cable through the housing into the fork shaft hole and push the cable inward; the cable will automatically snap into place. Start turning the coupling nut by hand, to avoid cross threading, then tighten the nut to 90 inch lbs. (10 Nm). DO NOT over tighten the nut as this will cause thread damage to the housing.

9. Carefully route the cable, then remove the jackstands and lower the vehicle.

10. Connect the shift cable-to-vacuum actuator by pressing the cable into the bracket hole. The cable and housing will snap into place, automatically.

11. Check the cable operation.

A. Bend lock spring as shown to release cable end.
B. Squeeze here with pliers to release cable.

1. Shift Cable
2. Vacuum Actuator
3. Lock Spring
4. Bracket
5. Cable Ferrule

Fig. 152 Disconnecting the shift cable from the vacuum actuator

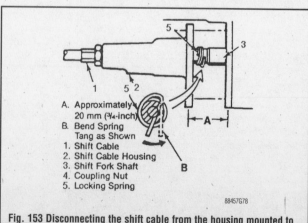

A. Approximately 20 mm (¾-inch)
B. Bend Spring Tang as Shown

1. Shift Cable
2. Shift Cable Housing
3. Shift Fork Shaft
4. Coupling Nut
5. Locking Spring

Fig. 153 Disconnecting the shift cable from the housing mounted to the carrier

REAR AXLE

Axle Shaft, Bearing and Seal

REMOVAL & INSTALLATION

▶ **See Figures 154 thru 162**

Although the axle shaft is easily removed using common hand tools, special tools are required if the bearings are also to be serviced.
1. Raise and support the rear of the vehicle safely using jackstands.
2. Remove the rear wheel and brake drum.

Fig. 154 Loosen pinion shaft lockscrew

❊❊ CAUTION

Brake shoes may contain asbestos, which has been determined to be a cancer causing agent. Never clean the brake surfaces with compressed air! Avoid inhaling any dust from any brake surface! When cleaning brake surfaces, use a commercially available brake cleaning fluid.

3. Using a wire brush, clean the dirt/rust from around the rear axle cover. This should be done to help prevent foreign material from entering the rear axle and possibly damaging the differential.
4. Place a catch pan under the differential, then unscrew the retaining bolts and remove the rear cover. When removing the cover, a small prytool may be used at the base of the cover to gently pry it back from the axle housing, breaking the gasket seal and allowing the lubricant to drain out into the container. Be careful not to use excessive force and damage the cover or housing.
5. Remove the rear pinion shaft lockbolt and the pinion shaft from the differential.
6. Push the axle shaft inward, then remove the C-lock from the button end of the axle shaft.
7. Remove the axle shaft from the axle housing by pulling straight back on the shaft hub, be careful not to damage the oil seal with the shaft splines.

➡ **It is recommended, when the axle shaft is removed, to replace the oil seal.**

8. If the bearing and/or oil seal is being replaced, use a medium pry bar to carefully pry the old oil seal from the end of the rear axle housing. DO NOT score or damage the housing oil seal surface.
9. If the wheel bearing is being removed, use the GM slide hammer tool No. J-2619, along with adapter No. J-2619-4 and the axle bearing puller No. J-22813-01, or the equivalent tools to pull the bearing from the tube. Be sure to install the tool assembly so that the tangs engage the outer race of the bearing,

Fig. 155 Remove the lockscrew in order to free the pinion shaft

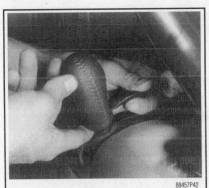

Fig. 156 Once the shaft is freed, withdraw it from the differential

Fig. 157 Push the axle shaft to expose the C-lock, then remove the lock in order to free the axle shaft

Fig. 158 Remove the shaft by pulling it straight back and from the housing tube

Fig. 159 Remove the old seal, but be careful not to damage the sealing surface

Fig. 160 Install a new seal using a suitable installation tool or driver

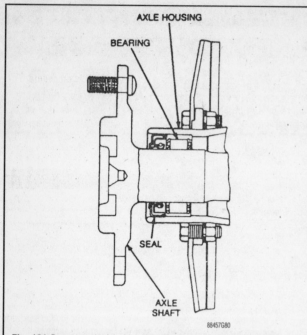

Fig. 161 Cross-sectional view of a common axle bearing and seal assembly

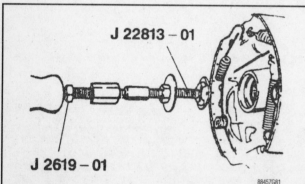

Fig. 162 Use a slide hammer, bearing puller and adapter to remove the old axle bearing

then use the action of the slide hammer to withdraw the wheel bearing from the axle housing.

To install:

10. Clean and inspect the axle tube housing.

11. If the bearing was removed, thoroughly clean the wheel bearing using solvent, then blow dry with compressed air. DO NOT spin the bearing with the compressed air or damage may occur. Inspect the wheel bearing for excessive wear or damage. If it feels rough, replace it.

12. With a new or the reused bearing, place a blob of heavy grease in the palm of your hand, then work the bearing into the grease until it is thoroughly lubricated. Using an axle shaft bearing installer such as No. J-34974, J-23765 or equivalents, drive the bearing into the axle housing until it bottoms against the seat.

13. If the bearing and/or seal was removed, use an axle shaft seal installer tool such as No. J-33782, J-23771 or equivalents to drive the new seal into the housing until it is flush with the axle tube. If a seal installer is not available, a suitably sized driver or socket may be used, just make sure the surface in contact with the seal is smooth so that it won't damage the seal.

14. Using gear oil, lubricate the new seal lips.

15. Using a putty knife, clean the gasket mounting surfaces on the housing and cover. Take care to keep material out of the differential housing. If necessary, place a rag or paper towels over the differential while cleaning the housing flange.

➡**When installing the axle shaft(s), be careful not to cut the oil seal lips.**

16. Slide the axle shaft into the rear axle housing, taking care not to damage the seal, then engage the splines of the axle shaft with the splines of the rear axle side gear.

17. Install the C-lock retainer on the axle shaft button end. After the C-lock is installed, pull the axle shaft outward to seat the C-lock retainer in the counterbore of the side gears.

18. Install the pinion shaft through the case and the pinions, then install a new pinion shaft lockbolt. Tighten the new lockbolt to 27 ft. lbs. (36 Nm).

➡**When adding oil to the rear axle, be aware that some locking differentials require the use of a special gear lubricant additive.**

19. Install the rear cover using a new gasket and sealant. Tighten the retaining bolts using a crosswise pattern to 20 ft. lbs. (27 Nm).

➡**Make sure the vehicle is level before attempting to add fluid to the rear axle or an incorrect fluid level will result.**

20. Refill the rear axle housing using the proper grade and quantity of lubricant as detailed in Section 1 of this manual. Install the filler plug, operate the vehicle and check for any leaks.

Pinion Oil Seal

REPLACEMENT

▸ **See Figures 163, 164 and 165**

➡**The following procedure requires the use of the pinion holding tool No. J-8614-10 or equivalent, the pinion flange removal tool No. J-8614-1, J-8614-2, J-8614-3 or equivalent, and the pinion oil seal installation tool No. J-23911 or equivalent.**

1. Matchmark the driveshaft and pinion flange to assure they are reassembled in the same position.

2. Disconnect the driveshaft from rear axle pinion flange and support the shaft up in body tunnel by wiring the driveshaft to the exhaust pipe. If the U-joint bearings are not retained by a retainer strap, use a piece of tape to hold bearings on their journals.

3. Mark the position of the pinion stem, flange and nut for reference.

4. Use an inch lbs. torque wrench to measure the amount of torque necessary to turn the pinion, then note this measurement as it is the combined pinion bearing, seal, carrier bearing, axle bearing and seal preload.

5. Using a pinion holding tool such as No. J-8614-10, and the appropriate pinion flange removal tool No. J-8614-1, J-8614-2, J-8614-3 (as applicable) or equivalents, remove the pinion flange nut and washer.

6. With suitable container in place to hold any fluid that may drain from rear axle, remove the pinion flange.

7. Remove the oil seal by driving it out of the differential with a blunt chisel; DO NOT damage the carrier.

To install:

8. Examine the seal surface of pinion flange for tool marks, nicks or damage, such as a groove worn by the seal. If damaged, replace flange as outlined later in this section.

9. Examine the carrier bore and remove any burrs that might cause leaks around the O.D. of the seal.

10. Apply GM seal lubricant No. 1050169 or equivalent to the outside diameter of the pinion flange and sealing lip of new seal. Drive the new seal into place using a correctly sized installation tool.

11. Install the pinion flange and tighten nut to the same position as marked

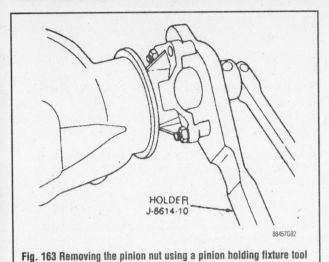

Fig. 163 Removing the pinion nut using a pinion holding fixture tool

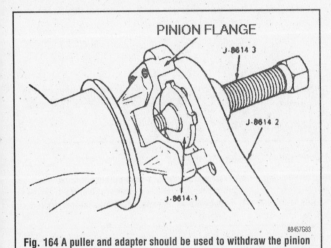

Fig. 164 A puller and adapter should be used to withdraw the pinion from the housing

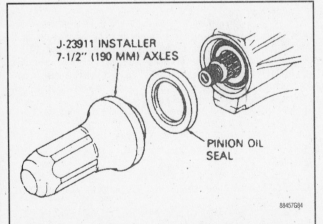

Fig. 165 Use the appropriately sized installation tool to drive the new seal into position.

in Step 3. Tighten the nut a little at a time and turn the pinion flange several times after each tightening in order to set the rollers.

12. Measure the torque necessary to turn the pinion and compare this to the reading taken during removal. Tighten the nut additionally, as necessary to achieve the same preload as measured earlier.

➡ If fluid was lost from the differential housing during this procedure, be sure to check and add additional fluid, as necessary. For details, please refer to Section 1 of this manual.

13. Remove the support then align and secure the driveshaft assembly to the pinion flange. The original matchmarks MUST be aligned to assure proper shaft balance and prevent vibration.

Pinion Flange Replacement

REMOVAL & INSTALLATION

1. Raise and safely support the rear of the truck safely using jackstands.
2. Remove both rear wheels and drums.
3. Matchmark the driveshaft and pinion flange, then disconnect the rear U-joint and support the driveshaft out of the way. If the U-joint bearings are not retained by a retainer strap, use a piece of tape to hold bearing caps on their journals.
4. The pinion rides against a tapered roller bearing. Check the pre-load by reading how much torque is required to turn the pinion. Use an inch pound torque wrench on the pinion flange nut and record the reading. This will give combined pinion bearing, carrier bearing, axle bearing and seal pre-load.
5. Remove pinion flange nut and washer. A suitable pinion holding tool should be used keep the flange from turning when loosening the nut.
6. With a suitable container in place to hold any fluid that may drain from the rear axle, remove the pinion flange.

To install:

7. Apply GM seal lubricant No. 1050169 or equivalent, to the outside diameter of the new pinion flange, then install the pinion flange.

➡ DO NOT hammer on the pinion flange in order to install it to the stem.

8. Install the washer and a new pinion flange nut finger-tight.
9. While holding the pinion flange, tighten the nut a little at a time and turn the drive pinion several revolutions after each tightening to set the rollers. Check the pre-load of bearings each time with an inch pound torque wrench until the same pre-load is achieved as the reading that was obtained in Step 4.
10. Remove the support then align and secure the driveshaft assembly to the pinion flange. The original matchmarks MUST be aligned to assure proper shaft balance and prevent vibration.

➡ If fluid was lost from the differential housing during this procedure, be sure to check and add additional fluid, as necessary. For details, please refer to Section 1 of this manual.

11. Install the rear drums and wheels.
12. Remove the jackstands and carefully lower the vehicle.

TORQUE SPECIFICATIONS

Components	Ft. Lbs.	Nm
Manual Transmission		
Transmission mounting bolts		
Borg Warner transmission	55	75
NVG transmissions	35	47
Clutch		
Clutch plate and cover bolts		
2.2L engines		
1994-95 models	28	38
1996-99 models	33	45
4.3L engines	29	40
Master cylinder and reservoir		
1994 utility models	25 inch lbs.	2.8
Reservoir bolts	13	18
Master cylinder nuts		
Slave (secondary) cylinder		
1994-95 models	18	24
Slave cylinder nuts		
1996-99 models		
Concentric slave cylinder bolts 80 inch lbs. (9).	80 inch lbs.	9
Automatic Transmission		
Back-up lamp/neutral safety switch		
Floor console mounted switch		
Switch retaining nuts	30 inch lbs.	3.4
Transmission		
1994-95 models		
Transmission-to-engine retainers	23	32
Flywheel-to-converter bolts	46	63
Transmission crossmember-to-frame bolts	56	77
1996-99 models		
Transmission-to-engine bolts	66	90
1996 2.2L models 66 (90)		
1996-99 4.3L models and 1997-99 2.2L models	34	47
Torque converter-to-flywheel bolts	46	63
Converter pan cover-to-transmission bolts	37	50
Transmission mount bolts	35	47
Transmission mount-to-crossmember nuts	38	52
Transfer Case		
Output shaft seal		
Yoke nut	110	149
Flange nut	80	108
Transfer case		
Transfer case-to-transmission retaining bolts		
1994 models	24	33
1995-98 models	41	55
1999 models	33-35	45-47
Support brace bolts		
1994-95 models	35	47
1996-99 models	35-37	47-50
Driveline		
Front Driveshaft and U-Joints		
1994 models		
Transfer case flange bolts	92	125
Front axle flange bolts	53	72

TORQUE SPECIFICATIONS

Components	Ft. Lbs.	Nm
Driveline (cont.)		
Front Driveshaft and U-Joints (cont.)		
1995 models		
Front axle flange bolts	55	75
1996-99 models		
Front axle flange bolts	15	20
Rear driveshaft and U-Joints		
Rear driveshaft-to-pinion fasteners		
1994-99 2.2L and 1994 4.3L models	15	20
1995-99 4.3L models	33	45
Center bearing-to-support nuts and bolts		
1994-95 models	25	34
1996-99 models	50	70
Rear U-joint-to-axle retainers	15	20
Front drive axle		
Halfshafts (drive axle)		
1994-96 models		
Upper ball joint-to-steering knuckle nut	61	83
Lower shock absorber nut and bolt	54	73
Tie rod end-to-steering knuckle nut		
1994-95 models	35	47
1996 models	39	53
Brake line support bracket retainer(s)	13	17
Inboard flange bolts	60	80
Hub nut		
1994-95 models	180	245
1997-99 Models	103	140
Axle nut		
Axle tube and output shaft assembly		
Cable/switch housing bolts	36	48
Tube-to-frame nuts/bolts		
1994 models	55	75
1995-99 models	72	98
Drive axle-to-axle tube output shaft bolts	60	80
Differential carrier		
Carrier assembly		
1994 models		
Bolts	65	90
Nuts	55	75
1995-99 models		
Bolts	76	103
Nuts	55	75
Axle tube-to-frame nuts	36	48
Shift Cable		
Cable housing-to-carrier bolts	36	48
Rear Axle		
Axle Shaft, Bearing and Seal		
Pinion shaft lockbolt		
Rear cover bolts		
Axle housing		
Leaf spring U-bolt nuts		
1994-95 models	41	55
1996-99 models	74	100

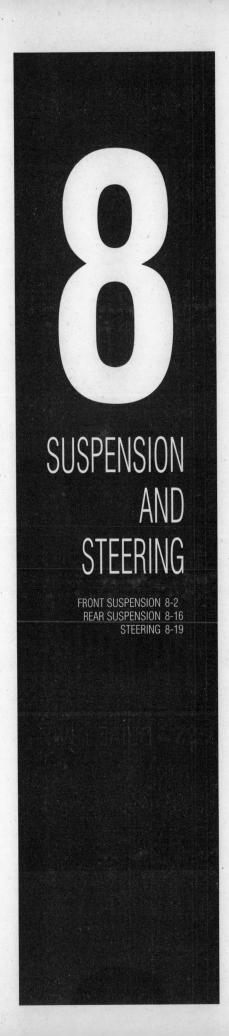

8

SUSPENSION AND STEERING

FRONT SUSPENSION

FRONT SUSPENSION COMPONENT LOCATIONS—TWO WHEEL DRIVE VEHICLES

1. Stabilizer shaft (sway bar)
2. Upper control arm
3. Pitman arm
4. Idler arm
5. Relay rod
6. Stabillizer bar link bolt, grommets, retainers and spacer
7. Coil spring
8. Outer tie rod
9. Lower ball joint
10. Shock absorber
11. Lower control arm
12. Tie rod clamp
13. Inner tie rod

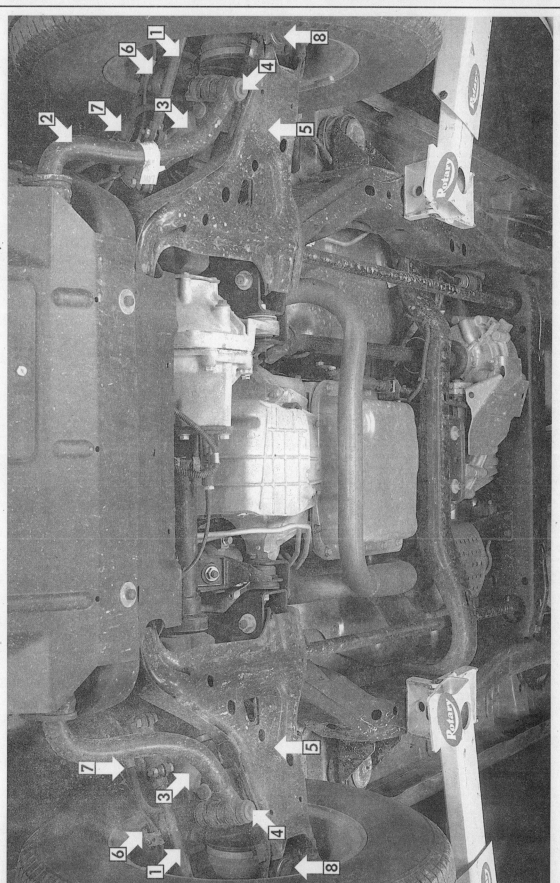

FRONT SUSPENSION COMPONENT LOCATIONS—FOUR WHEEL DRIVE VEHICLES

1. Tie rod
2. Stabilizer shaft (sway bar)
3. Shock absorber
4. Stabilizer shaft link bolt, spacer and insulator
5. Lower control arm
6. Upper ball joint
7. Upper control arm
8. Lower ball joint

Coil Spring

The 2WD vehicles covered by this manual use a coil spring support for the front suspension.

REMOVAL & INSTALLATION

▶ **See Figures 1 and 2**

➡ **The following procedure requires the use of a coil spring removal and installation tool such as No. J-23038-01 or equivalent.**

1. Raise and support the front of the vehicle safely using jackstands so that the front wheels hang free.
2. Remove the shock absorber-to-lower control arm bolts, then push the shock up through the control arm and into the spring.
3. Secure a coil spring tool (such as J-23038-01 or equivalent), to the end of a jack, then position it to cradle the inner control arm bushings.
4. Remove the stabilizer bar link from the lower control arm.
5. Properly remove the lower control arm pivot bolts in order to pivot the arm and remove spring:
   a. Raise the jack to remove the tension from the lower control arm pivot bolts.
   b. Install a chain around the spring and through the control arm as a safety measure.

➡ **During removal, note the direction in which the pivot bolts are mounted.**

   c. Remove the lower control arm-to-frame pivot nuts and bolts—unfasten the rear pivot bolt first.
   d. Lower the control arm by slowly lowering the jack.
6. When all of the compression is removed from the spring, remove the safety chain and the spring.

➡ **DO NOT apply force to the lower control arm and/or ball joint to remove the spring. Proper maneuvering of the spring will allow for easy removal.**

To install:

7. Apply adhesive into the insulators groove, then position the insulators onto the top and bottom of the spring.

✳✳ CAUTION

Use extreme care when installing and compressing the spring. Be sure the spring tool and jack and properly installed and the spring is securely seated.

8. Secure the coil spring tool, then position the coil spring and insulators on the lower control arm. Raise the control arm and spring assembly into position.
9. Install the pivot bolts, starting with the front bolt first, and secure using new nuts. Both bolts should be installed in the direction they were facing when removed, which usually means they are inserted from the front of the vehicle.

10. Install and secure the stabilizer bar link to the lower control arm.
11. Position and secure the shock absorber.
12. Remove the jackstands and carefully lower the vehicle.

Torsion Bar

Instead of the coil spring used on the front suspension of 2WD vehicles, the 4WD vehicles covered by this manual are equipped with a torsion bar.

REMOVAL & INSTALLATION

1994 Models

▶ **See Figures 3, 4 and 5**

➡ **The following procedure requires the use of the torsion bar unloader tool J-36202 or equivalent.**

1. Raise and safely support the front of the vehicle safely using jackstands.
2. Install a torsion bar unloader tool to relax the tension on the torsion bar adjusting arm screw; record the number of turns necessary to properly install the tool. Remove the adjusting screw.
3. Move the torsion bar forward and leave it in place.
4. Remove the adjuster arms.
5. Unfasten the nut and square washer (raise the support out of the way) from the retainer, then remove the retainer bolts from underneath the frame.
6. Slide the insulator off the support and remove it from the vehicle.
7. Disconnect the muffler flange from the converter, loosen the rear exhaust hanger and lower the rear exhaust.
8. Remove the torsion support from the frame.
9. Remove the torsion bars from the lower control arms.

To install:

10. Position the torsion bars with the lower control arms. If installing a replacement component, be sure the tag is facing forward.
11. Install the support.
12. Install and secure the rear exhaust system to the proper height, then connect the muffler flange to the converter.
13. Install the insulator, making sure the mount studs are positioned through the support and the insulator locator tabs are indexed to the support (facing forward).
14. Install and finger-tighten the square washer and nut.
15. Install the insulator mounting retainers, then tighten the bolts to 26 ft. lbs. (35 Nm) and/or the nuts to 25 ft. lbs. (34 Nm).
16. Install the adjuster arms, then connect the torsion bars to the arms. With the torsion bars installed, check for an assembled clearance from the end of the bar to the support of 0.236 in. (6.0mm).
17. Lubricate the top of the adjusting arm and the adjusting bolt, then install the nuts and adjuster bolts.
18. Check and adjust the **Z** height as outlined in the wheel alignment section of this section.

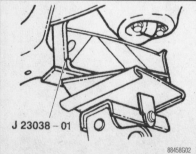

Fig. 1 With the spring tool secured to a jack, raise the control arm in order to relieve tension from the control arm pivot bolts

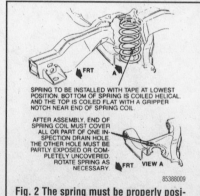

SPRING TO BE INSTALLED WITH TAPE AT LOWEST POSITION. BOTTOM OF SPRING IS COILED HELICAL AND THE TOP IS COILED FLAT WITH A GRIPPER NOTCH NEAR END OF SPRING COIL.

AFTER ASSEMBLY, END OF SPRING COIL MUST COVER ALL OR PART OF ONE INSPECTION DRAIN HOLE THE OTHER HOLE MUST BE PARTLY EXPOSED OR COMPLETELY UNCOVERED. ROTATE SPRING AS NECESSARY

Fig. 2 The spring must be properly positioned during installation

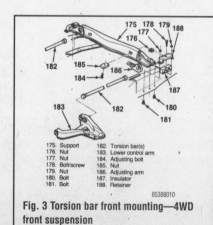

175. Support	182. Torsion bar(s)
176. Nut	183. Lower control arm
177. Nut	184. Adjusting bolt
178. Bolt/screw	185. Nut
179. Nut	186. Adjusting arm
180. Bolt	187. Insulator
181. Bolt	188. Retainer

Fig. 3 Torsion bar front mounting—4WD front suspension

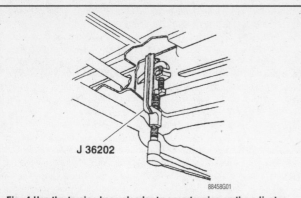

Fig. 4 Use the torsion bar unloader to ease tension so the adjuster bolt may be removed

6. Remove the lower link mount, upper link mount nut, upper link mount and then unfasten the torsion bar from the frame.

To install:

7. Install the torsion bar and support.

8. Install the upper link mount and mount nut. Tighten the nut to 33 ft. lbs. (45 Nm) on 1995–96 models and 48 ft. lbs. (68 Nm) on 1997–99 models.

9. Place a jack under the torsion bar to release tension, then install the lower link mount bushing and nut. Tighten the nut to 13 ft. lbs. (18 Nm) on 1995 models, 50 ft. lbs. (68 Nm) on 1996–98 models and 37 ft. lbs. (50 Nm) on 1999 models.

10. Install the torsion bar unloader tool and tighten the tool against the adjusting arm the same number turns recorded earlier, then remove the tool. This loads the torsion bars.

11. Install the transmission shield, if removed.

12. Remove the jackstands and lower the vehicle.

13. Check and adjust the **Z** height as outlined in the wheel alignment portion of this section.

Shock Absorbers

REMOVAL & INSTALLATION

2WD Vehicles

▶ **See Figure 6**

1. Raise and support the front of the vehicle safely using jackstands.

2. Using an open end wrench, hold the shock absorber upper stem to prevent it from turning, then remove the upper stem retaining nut, the retainer and rubber grommet.

3. Remove the shock absorber-to-lower control arm retaining bolts and lower the shock absorber assembly from the bottom of the control arm.

4. Inspect and test the shock absorber; replace it, if necessary.

To install:

5. Fully extend the shock absorber stem, then push it up through the lower control arm and spring so that the upper stem passes through the mounting hole in the upper control arm frame bracket.

6. Install the upper shock absorber nut and tighten to 100 inch. lbs. (11 Nm) on 1994 models 145 inch lbs. (16 Nm) on 1995 models, 54 ft. lbs. (73 Nm) on 1996 models, or 106 inch lbs. (12 Nm) on 1997–99 models while holding the stem with an open end wrench. Be careful not to crush the rubber bushing.

7. Install the shock absorber-to-lower control arm retaining bolts and tighten to 20 ft. lbs. (27 Nm) on 1994–95 models and 54 ft. lbs. (73 Nm) on 1996 models, or 22 ft. lbs. (30 Nm) on 1997–99 models.

8. Remove the jackstands and carefully lower the vehicle.

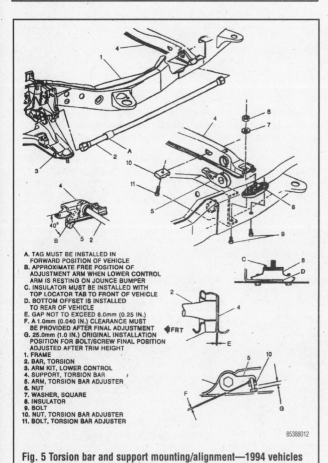

A. TAG MUST BE INSTALLED IN FORWARD POSITION OF VEHICLE
B. APPROXIMATE FREE POSITION OF ADJUSTMENT ARM WHEN LOWER CONTROL ARM IS RESTING ON JOUNCE BUMPER
C. INSULATOR MUST BE INSTALLED WITH TOP LOCATOR TAB TO FRONT OF VEHICLE
D. BOTTOM OFFSET IS INSTALLED TO REAR OF VEHICLE
E. GAP NOT TO EXCEED 6.0mm (0.25 IN.)
F. A 1.0mm (0.040 IN.) CLEARANCE MUST BE PROVIDED AFTER FINAL ADJUSTMENT
G. 25.0mm (1.0 IN.) ORIGINAL INSTALLATION POSITION FOR BOLT/SCREW FINAL POSITION ADJUSTED AFTER TRIM HEIGHT
1. FRAME
2. BAR, TORSION
3. ARM KIT, LOWER CONTROL
4. SUPPORT, TORSION BAR
5. ARM, TORSION BAR ADJUSTER
6. NUT
7. WASHER, SQUARE
8. INSULATOR
9. BOLT
10. NUT, TORSION BAR ADJUSTER
11. BOLT, TORSION BAR ADJUSTER

Fig. 5 Torsion bar and support mounting/alignment—1994 vehicles

1995–99 Models

➡ **The following procedure requires the use of the torsion bar unloader tool No. J-36202 or equivalent.**

1. Raise and safely support the front of the vehicle safely using jackstands.

2. Remove the transmission shield, if equipped.

3. Install a torsion bar unloader tool to relax the tension on the torsion bar adjusting arm screw; record the number of turns necessary to properly install the tool. Remove the adjusting screw and the unloader tool.

4. Unfasten the lower link mount nut from one side, then disengage the torsion bars.

➡ **Note the direction of the forward end and side of the torsion bar being removed**

5. Remove the lower link nut from the opposite side.

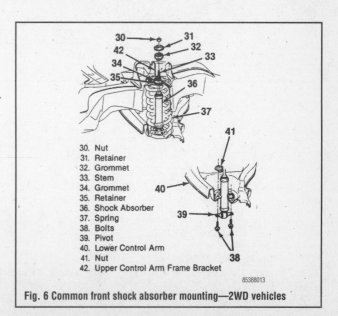

30. Nut
31. Retainer
32. Grommet
33. Stem
34. Grommet
35. Retainer
36. Shock Absorber
37. Spring
38. Bolts
39. Pivot
40. Lower Control Arm
41. Nut
42. Upper Control Arm Frame Bracket

Fig. 6 Common front shock absorber mounting—2WD vehicles

4WD Vehicles

▶ **See Figures 7 and 8**

1. Raise and support the front of the vehicle safely using jackstands.
2. Remove the tire and wheel assembly to ease access.
3. Remove the shock absorber-to-lower control arm nut and bolt (using a backup wrench), then collapse the shock absorber.
4. Remove the upper shock absorber-to-frame nut and bolt (again, using a backup wrench).
5. Inspect and test the shock absorber; replace it, if necessary.

To install:

6. Position the shock absorber to the mounting brackets.
7. Install the upper and lower retaining bolts (inserted from the front of the vehicle).
8. Install the retaining nuts to the bolts, then tighten the retainers to 54 ft. lbs. (73 Nm).
9. Install the tire and wheel assembly, then remove the jackstands and carefully lower the vehicle.

TESTING

▶ **See Figure 9**

The purpose of the shock absorber is simply to limit the motion of the spring during compression and rebound cycles. If the vehicle is not equipped with these motion dampers, the up and down motion would multiply until the vehicle was alternately trying to leap off the ground and to pound itself into the pavement.

Contrary to popular rumor, the shocks do not affect the ride height of the vehicle. This is controlled by other suspension components such as springs and tires. Worn shock absorbers can affect handling; if the front of the vehicle is rising or falling excessively, the "footprint" of the tires changes on the pavement and steering is affected.

The simplest test of the shock absorber is simply push down on one corner of the unladen vehicle and release it. Observe the motion of the body as it is released. In most cases, it will come up beyond it original rest position, dip back below it and settle quickly to rest. This shows that the damper is controlling the spring action. Any tendency to excessive pitch (up-and-down) motion or failure to return to rest within 2-3 cycles is a sign of poor function within the shock absorber. Oil-filled shocks may have a light film of oil around the seal, resulting from normal breathing and air exchange. This should NOT be taken as a sign of failure, but any sign of thick or running oil definitely indicates failure. Gas filled shocks may also show some film at the shaft; if the gas has leaked out, the shock will have almost no resistance to motion.

While each shock absorber can be replaced individually, it is recommended that they be changed as a pair (both front or both rear) to maintain equal response on both sides of the vehicle. Chances are quite good that if one has failed, its mate is weak also.

Ball Joints

REMOVAL & INSTALLATION

2WD Vehicles

UPPER

▶ **See Figures 10, 11, 12, 13 and 14**

➡ **The following procedure requires the use of a ball joint separator tool such as J-23742 and J-9519-E ball joint remover and installer set or their equivalents.**

1. Raise and support the front of the vehicle safely by placing jackstands securely under the lower control arms. Because the vehicle's weight is used to relieve spring tension on the upper control arm, the floor stands must be positioned between the spring seats and the lower control arm ball joints for maximum leverage.

Fig. 7 Loosen and remove the shock absorber lower mounting bolt

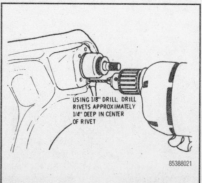
Fig. 8 Then loosen the upper mounting bolt and remove the shock from the vehicle

Fig. 9 When fluid is seeping out of the shock absorber, it's time to replace it

Fig. 10 Use a ball joint separator tool to drive the upper ball joint from the steering knuckle

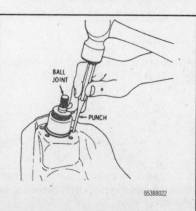
Fig. 11 Drill a small guide hole into each ball joint rivet

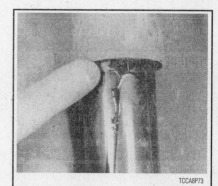
Fig. 12 Then drill off the rivet heads

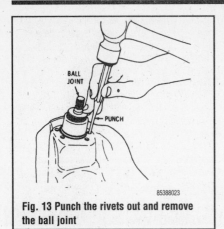

Fig. 13 Punch the rivets out and remove the ball joint

Fig. 14 Service ball joints are bolted to the control arm

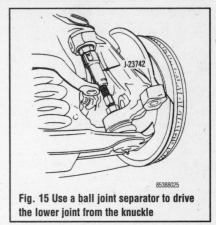

Fig. 15 Use a ball joint separator to drive the lower joint from the knuckle

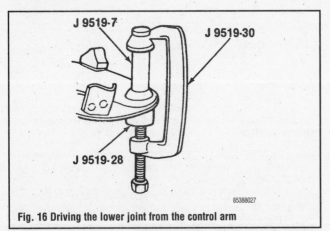

Fig. 16 Driving the lower joint from the control arm

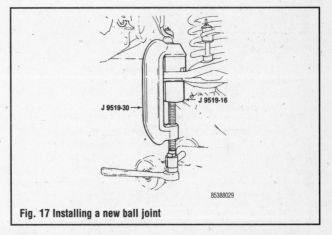

Fig. 17 Installing a new ball joint

✳✳ CAUTION

With components unbolted, the jackstand is holding the lower control arm in place against the coil spring. Make sure the jackstand is firmly positioned and cannot move, or personal injury could result.

2. Remove the tire and wheel assembly.
3. Remove the brake caliper and support it from the vehicle using a coat hanger or wire. Make sure the brake line is not stretched or damaged and that the caliper's weight is not supported by the line.
4. Remove the cotter pin and retaining nut from the upper ball joint.
5. If equipped, remove the anti-lock brake sensor wire bracket.
6. Position J-23742 or an equivalent ball joint separator tool between upper joint stud and the lower joint/control arm. Use the tool to separate the upper ball joint from the steering knuckle. Pull the steering knuckle free of the ball joint after removal.

➡**After separating the steering knuckle from the upper ball joint, be sure to support the steering knuckle/hub assembly to prevent damaging the brake hose.**

7. Remove the riveted upper ball joint from the upper control arm:
   a. Drill a ⅛ in. (3mm) hole, about ¼ in. (6mm) deep into each rivet.
   b. Then use a ½ in. (13mm) drill bit, to drill off the rivet heads.
   c. Using a pin punch and the hammer, drive out the rivets in order to free the upper ball joint from the upper control arm assembly, then remove the upper ball joint.
8. Clean and inspect the steering knuckle hole. Replace the steering knuckle if the hole is out of round.

To install:
9. Position the joint in the upper control arm, then install the joint retaining nuts and bolts. Position the bolts threaded upward from under the control arm. Tighten the ball joint retainers to 17 ft. lbs. (23 Nm).
10. If removed, install the anti-lock brake sensor wire bracket.
11. Remove the support from the steering knuckle, then install the ball joint

to the knuckle. Make sure the joint is seated, then install the stud nut and tighten to 61 ft. lbs. (83 Nm). Insert a new cotter pin.

➡**When installing the cotter pin, never loosen the castle nut to expose the cotter pin hole.**

12. If not installed already, thread the grease fitting into the ball joint. Use a grease gun to lubricate the upper ball joint until grease appears at the seal.
13. Reposition and secure the brake caliper.
14. Install the tire and wheel assembly.
15. Remove the jackstands and carefully lower the vehicle.
16. Check and adjust the front end alignment, as necessary.

LOWER

♦ **See Figures 15, 16 and 17**

➡**The following procedure requires the use of a ball joint remover/installer set (the particular set may vary upon application but must include a clamping-type tool with the appropriately sized adapters) and a ball joint separator tool, such as J-23742 or equivalent.**

1. Raise and support the front of the vehicle safely using jackstands under the frame so the control arms hang free.
2. Remove the tire and wheel assembly.
3. Position a floor jack under the spring seat of the lower control arm, then raise the jack to support the arm.

✳✳ CAUTION

The floor jack MUST remain under the lower control arm, during the removal and installation procedures, to retain the arm and spring positions. Make sure the jack is securely positioned and will not slip or release during the procedure or personal injury may result.

4. Remove the brake caliper and support it aside using a hanger or wire. Make sure the brake line is not stressed or damaged.

Fig. 18 Remove the cotter pin from the ball joint . . .

Fig. 19 . . . then unfasten the retaining nut

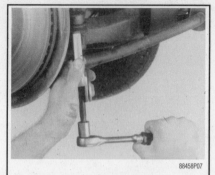

Fig. 20 Position a suitable ball joint separator tool and carefully loosen the joint in the steering knuckle . . .

Fig. 21 . . . then remove the tool and the retaining nut, then separate the joint from the knuckle

5. Remove and discard the lower ball joint cotter pin, then loosen and remove the stud nut.

6. Position J-23742 or an equivalent ball joint separator tool between lower joint stud and the upper joint/control arm. Use the tool to separate the lower ball joint from the steering knuckle.

7. Carefully guide the lower control arm out of the opening in the splash shield using a putty knife. Position a block of wood between the frame and upper control arm to keep the knuckle out of the way.

8. Remove the grease fitting.

9. Use the ball joint remover set along with the appropriate adapters to drive the ball joint from the control arm.

To install:

10. Clean the tapered hole in the steering knuckle of any dirt or foreign matter, then check the hole to see if it is out of round, deformed or otherwise damaged. If a problem is found, then knuckle must be replaced.

11. Using a suitable installation set, press the new ball joint (with grease fitting pointing inward) until it bottoms in the control arm. Make sure the grease seal is facing inboard.

12. Position the ball joint stud into the steering knuckle, then install the retaining nut and tighten to 83 ft. lbs. (113 Nm) on 1994 models and 79 ft. lbs. (108 Nm) on 1995–99 models. Insert a new cotter pin.

➡When installing the cotter pin, never loosen the castle nut to expose the cotter pin hole.

13. If not installed already, thread the grease fitting into the ball joint, then use a grease gun to lubricate the joint until grease appears at the seal.

14. Reposition and secure the brake caliper.

15. Install the tire and wheel assembly.

16. Remove the jackstands and carefully lower the vehicle.

17. Check and adjust the front end alignment, as necessary.

4WD Vehicles

▶ **See Figures 18, 19, 20 and 21**

On 4WD vehicles both the upper and lower ball joints are removed in the same manner. Once the joint is separated from the steering knuckle the rivets are drilled and punched to free the joint from the control arm. Service joints are bolted into position with the retaining bolts threaded upward from beneath the control arm. In this manner, the joint is replaced in an almost identical fashion to the upper joints on 2WD vehicles.

1. Raise and support the front of the vehicle safely using jackstands.

2. Remove the tire and wheel assembly.

3. When removing the upper ball joint, unplug the wheel speed sensor wiring connector from the upper control arm.

4. Remove the cotter pin from the ball joint, then loosen the retaining nut.

5. Position a suitable ball joint separator tool such as J-36607, or equivalent, then carefully loosen the joint in the steering knuckle. Remove the tool and the retaining nut, then separate the joint from the knuckle.

➡After separating the steering knuckle from the upper ball joint, be sure to support the steering knuckle/hub assembly to prevent damaging the brake hose.

6. Remove the riveted ball joint from the control arm:
   a. Drill a ⅛ in. (3mm) hole, about ¼ in. (6mm) deep into each rivet.
   b. Then use a ½ in. (13mm) drill bit, to drill off the rivet heads.
   c. Using a pin punch and the hammer, drive out the rivets in order to free the ball joint from the control arm assembly, then remove the ball joint.

To install:

7. Position the joint in the control arm, then install the joint retaining nuts and bolts. Position the bolts threaded upward from under the control arm. Tighten the ball joint retainers to 17 ft. lbs. (23 Nm).

8. Remove the support from the steering knuckle, then install the ball joint to the knuckle. Make sure the joint is seated, then install the stud nut and tighten both nuts to 70 ft. lbs. (95 Nm) on 1994 models. On 1995–99 models tighten the lower nut to 79 ft. lbs. (108 Nm) and the upper nut to 61 ft. lbs. (83 Nm). Install a new cotter pin.

➡When installing the cotter pin, never loosen the castle nut to expose the cotter pin hole, but DO NOT tighten more than an additional ⅙ turn.

9. Use a grease gun to lubricate the upper ball joint.

10. If the upper ball joint was removed, attach the wheel speed sensor wiring connector to the upper control arm.

11. Install the tire and wheel assembly.

12. Remove the jackstands and carefully lower the vehicle.

13. Check and adjust the front end alignment, as necessary.

INSPECTION

▶ **See Figures 22, 23, 24 and 25**

➡ **Before performing this inspection, make sure that the wheel bearings are adjusted correctly and that the control arm bushings are in good condition.**

1. Make sure the vehicle is parked on a level surface.

2. Raise and support the front of the vehicle safely by placing jackstands under each lower control arm as close as possible to each lower ball joint (as far outboard as possible). Make sure that the vehicle is stable and the control arm bumpers are not contacting the frame.

3. Wipe the ball joints clean and check the seals for cuts or tears. If a seal is cut or torn, then the ball joint must be replaced.

4. If necessary on 2WD vehicles, adjust the wheel bearings before proceeding.

5. Check the ball joints for horizontal deflection (looseness):

 a. Position a dial indicator against the lowest outboard point on the rim.

 b. Grasp the tire (top and bottom), then pull outward on the top and push inward on the bottom; record the reading on the dial indicator.

 c. Grasp the tire (top and bottom), then pull outward on the bottom and push inward on the top; record the reading on the dial indicator.

 d. The difference in the dial indicator reading is the horizontal deflection of both joints. If the reading exceeds 0.125 in. (3.2mm), the lower ball joint should be checked for wear in order to determine what component(s) must be replaced.

➡ **The lower ball joints used on 2WD vehicles use wear indicators.**

6. On 4WD vehicles (no wear indicators), check the lower ball joint for wear:

 a. With the vehicle still supported by jackstands, place a dial indicator against the spindle in order to measure vertical movement.

➡ **DO NOT pry between the lower control arm and the drive axle seal or damage to the seal will result.**

 b. Pry between the lower control arm and the outer bearing race while reading the dial indicator. This reading will show vertical deflection (looseness).

 c. The lower ball joint is not a pre-loaded joint and may show some looseness, but it should be replaced if movement exceeds 0.125 in. (3.2mm).

7. For 2WD vehicles check for lower ball joint wear using the indicators:

 a. Visually inspect the positioning of the grease fitting on the ball joint. The fitting is threaded into a small housing nub which projects approximately 0.050 in. (1.27mm) beyond the surface of the ball joint cover on new parts. As the joint wears, the nub will slowly retreat inward. If the housing nub is visible above the cover, then the joint is still good.

 b. If necessary, scrape a screwdriver or fingernail across the ball joint cover and feel for the housing nub. If the housing is flush or inside the cover surface, the joint is worn and should be replaced.

8. Finally, if the joints failed the initial combined test, but the lower joint is found good, the upper ball joint should be checked for looseness as it is probably the culprit:

 a. Disconnect the upper ball joint from the steering knuckle.

 b. Check for any looseness or if the stud can be twisted by hand. If so, the joint should be replaced.

Stabilizer Bar

REMOVAL & INSTALLATION

2WD Vehicles

▶ **See Figure 26**

1. Raise and support the front of the vehicle safely using jackstands.

2. If necessary, remove the front wheels for additional access.

3. Loosen the nut from the top of one of the link bolts, then remove the retainer and grommet so the stabilizer may be separated from the link bolt.

4. If necessary, remove the link bolt, washers and grommets, but make

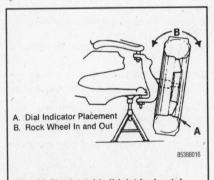

A. Dial Indicator Placement
B. Rock Wheel In and Out

85388016

Fig. 22 Check total ball joint horizontal deflection by rocking the wheel (a dial indicator is used to measure play)

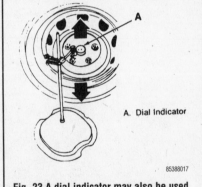

A. Dial Indicator

85388017

Fig. 23 A dial indicator may also be used to check lower joint vertical deflection

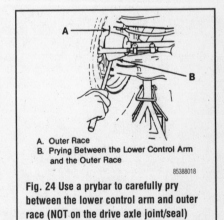

A. Outer Race
B. Prying Between the Lower Control Arm and the Outer Race

85388018

Fig. 24 Use a prybar to carefully pry between the lower control arm and outer race (NOT on the drive axle joint/seal)

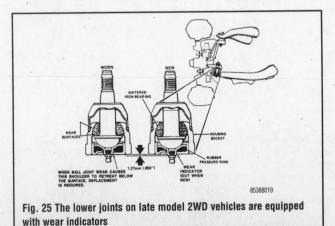

85388019

Fig. 25 The lower joints on late model 2WD vehicles are equipped with wear indicators

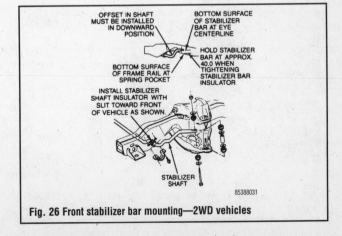

85388031

Fig. 26 Front stabilizer bar mounting—2WD vehicles

sure all components remain in order on the link bolt once it is removed in order to ease installation.

5. Loosen the nut from the top of the other link bolt and separate it from the stabilizer in the same fashion. If the link bolt and components are completely removed, be sure to tag or arrange everything to assure installation on the same side.

6. Unfasten the bolts retaining the stabilizer brackets to the frame, then remove the stabilizer bar from the vehicle.

7. If necessary, remove the rubber bushings (insulators).

To install:

8. If removed, install the rubber bushings to the stabilizer bar, making sure they are positioned with the slits facing toward the front of the vehicle.

9. Position the stabilizer shaft, then install the brackets over the bushings to retain the shaft. Tighten the bracket bolts to 24 ft. lbs. (33 Nm) on 1994–96 models and 26 ft. lbs. (36 Nm) on 1997–99 models.

10. Install the link bolts making sure the positioning of the grommets, retainers and washers is correct. If necessary, refer to the illustration for classification. But keep in mind the grommets are normally surrounded by washers/retainers or components (control arm or stabilizer).

11. Install the upper grommet, retainer and nut to the top of each link bolt, then tighten to 13 ft. lbs. (17 Nm).

12. If removed, install the front wheels.

13. Remove the jackstands and carefully lower the vehicle.

4WD Vehicles

▸ **See Figures 27, 28 and 29**

➥Installation of the stabilizer bar requires that the torsion bar be unloaded using a special unloader tool used during tension bar

removal. Do not attempt this procedure without the unloader. For details on the unloader and its use, please refer to the torsion bar procedure found earlier in this section.

1. Raise and support the front of the vehicle safely using jackstands.

2. Remove the stabilizer bar clamp-to-control arm retaining bolts, then remove the clamps.

3. Remove the stabilizer bar clamp-to-frame retaining bolts/nuts, then remove the clamps and carefully lower the stabilizer bar from the vehicle.

4. If necessary remove the bushings (insulators).

To install:

5. Using a torsion bar unloader tool, properly unload the torsion bar.

6. If removed, install the insulators to the stabilizer bar, making sure the slits in the insulators face forward.

7. Position the stabilizer bar to the frame and lower control arm, then loosely install the clamps and retaining bolts.

8. Tighten the bar clamp-to-control arm retaining bolts to 24 ft. lbs. (33 Nm) on 1994–95 models and 124 inch lbs. (14 Nm) on 1996 models and 11 ft. lbs. (15 Nm) on 1997–99 models.

9. Install the frame clamps to the insulators and frames, then tighten the retaining bolts/nuts to 35 ft. lbs. (48 Nm) on 1994–95 models and 48 ft. lbs. (65 Nm) on 1996–99 models.

10. Remove the jackstands and carefully lower the vehicle.

11. Check and/or adjust the vehicle trim (**Z**) height, as necessary.

Upper Control Arm and Bushing

REMOVAL & INSTALLATION

2WD Vehicles

▸ **See Figures 30, 31 and 32**

➥The following procedure requires the use of a ball joint separator tool such as J-23742 or equivalent.

1. Raise and support the front of the vehicle safely by placing jackstands securely under the lower control arms. Because the vehicle's weight is used to relieve spring tension on the upper control arm, the floor stands must be positioned between the spring seats and the lower control arm ball joints for maximum leverage.

✳✳ CAUTION

With components unbolted, the jackstand is holding the lower control arm in place against the coil spring. Make sure the jackstand is firmly positioned and cannot move, or personal injury could result.

2. Remove the tire and wheel assembly.

3. If equipped, remove the ABS wire and brake hose bracket(s) from the upper control arm.

4. Remove the brake caliper and support it from the vehicle using a coat hanger or wire. Make sure the brake line is not stretched or damaged and that the caliper's weight is not supported by the line.

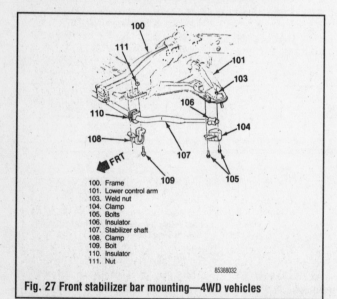

100. Frame
101. Lower control arm
103. Weld nut
104. Clamp
105. Bolts
106. Insulator
107. Stabilizer shaft
108. Clamp
109. Bolt
110. Insulator
111. Nut

85388032

Fig. 27 Front stabilizer bar mounting—4WD vehicles

88458P09

Fig. 28 When removing the 4WD stabilizer bar, first loosen the control arm clamp bolts

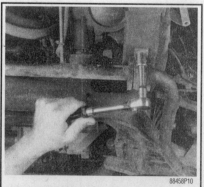

88458P10

Fig. 29 Loosen and remove the frame clamp retainers

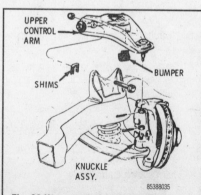

85388035

Fig. 30 Upper control arm mounting— 2WD vehicles

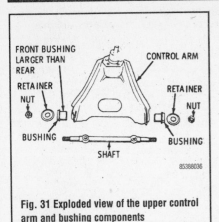

Fig. 31 Exploded view of the upper control arm and bushing components

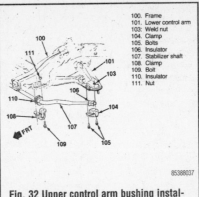

Fig. 32 Upper control arm bushing installation—2WD vehicles

100. Frame
101. Lower control arm
103. Weld nut
104. Clamp
105. Bolts
106. Insulator
107. Stabilizer shaft
108. Clamp
109. Bolt
110. Insulator
111. Nut

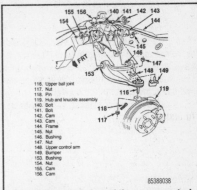

116. Upper ball joint
117. Nut
118. Pin
119. Hub and knuckle assembly
140. Bolt
141. Bolt
142. Cam
143. Cam
144. Frame
145. Nut
146. Bushing
147. Nut
148. Upper control arm
149. Bumper
153. Bushing
154. Nut
155. Cam
156. Cam

Fig. 33 Exploded view of the upper control arm mounting—4WD vehicles

5. Remove the cotter pin and retaining nut from the upper ball joint.

6. Position J-23742 or an equivalent ball joint separator tool between upper joint stud and the lower joint/control arm. Use the tool to separate the upper ball joint from the steering knuckle. Pull the steering knuckle free of the ball joint after removal.

➡ After separating the steering knuckle from the upper ball joint, be sure to support the steering knuckle/hub assembly to prevent damaging the brake hose.

➡ Before and during removal of the control arm-to-frame nuts and bolts, note the location of any shims.

7. Unfasten the upper control arm-to-frame nuts and bolts, then lift and remove the upper control arm from the vehicle.

8. Clean and inspect the steering knuckle hole. Replace the steering knuckle if any out of roundness is noted.

9. If replacement is necessary, mount the control arm in a vise, then remove the pivot shaft nuts and washers. Use a control arm bushing fixture (C-clamp like tool) along with a slotted washer and a piece of pipe (slightly larger than the bushing) to remove the old bushings.

To install

10. If removed, position the pivot shaft to the control arm and install the bushing using the fixture tool, washer and a length of pipe with the same outer diameter as the bushing.

11. Tighten the tool until the bushing is positioned on the shaft as shown in the illustration. Loosely install the bushing retaining nuts and washers. Tighten the bushing nuts to 85 ft. lbs. (115 Nm).

12. Loosely install the control arm to the frame using the bolts and nuts. Position the shims as noted during removal, then tighten the retainers to 67 ft. lbs. (90 Nm) on 1994–95 models and 85 ft. lbs. (115 Nm) on 1996–99 models.

➡ On most vehicles, the left upper control arm shaft must have the depression facing inboard.

13. Remove the support from the steering knuckle, then install the ball joint to the knuckle. Make sure the joint is seated, then install the stud nut. Install a new cotter pin.

➡ When installing the cotter pin, never loosen the castle nut to expose the cotter pin hole.

14. Reposition and secure the brake caliper.

15. If equipped, attach the ABS wire and brake hose bracket(s) from the upper control arm.

16. Install the tire and wheel assembly.

17. Remove the jackstands and carefully lower the vehicle.

18. Check and adjust the front end alignment, as necessary.

4WD Vehicles

▶ See Figures 33, 34 and 35

1. Raise and support the front of the vehicle safely using jackstands.

2. Remove the tire and wheel assembly.

3. Remove the cotter pin from the ball joint, then loosen the retaining nut.

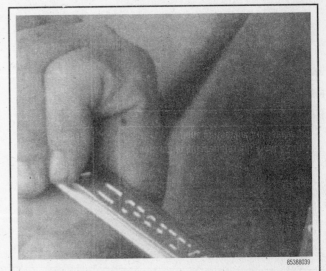

Fig. 34 Matchmark the cams to the control arm before removal

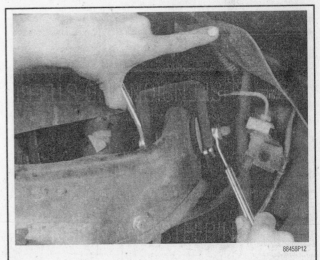

Fig. 35 Loosen the end retaining nuts from the upper control arm bolts

➡ After separating the steering knuckle from the upper ball joint, be sure to support the steering knuckle/hub assembly to prevent damaging the brake hose.

4. Position a suitable ball joint separator tool such as J-36607 or equivalent, then carefully loosen the joint in the steering knuckle. Dis-

engage the tool and the retaining nut, then remove the joint from the knuckle.

➡The 4WD vehicles covered by this manual do not use shims to adjust the front wheel alignment. Instead, the upper control arm bolts are equipped with cams, which are rotated to achieve caster and camber adjustments. In order to preserve adjustment and ease installation, matchmark the cams to the control arm before removal. If the control arm is being replaced, transfer the alignment marks to the new component before installation.

5. Unfasten the front and rear nuts retaining the control arm retaining bolts to the frame, then remove the outer cams from the bolts.

6. Remove the bolts and inner cams, then remove the control arm from the vehicle.

7. If necessary, remove the retaining nut and the bumper from the control arm.

8. If the bushings are being replaced, use a suitable bushing service set to remove the bushings from the arm.

To install:

9. If removed, use the bushing service set to drive the new bushings into the control arm.

10. If removed, install the bumper and retaining nut to the control arm. Tighten the bumper retaining nut to 20 ft. lbs. (27 Nm).

11. Position the control arm to the vehicle, then install the retaining bolts (from the inside of the frame brackets facing outward) and the inner cams. The inner cams must be positioned on the bolts before they are inserted through the control arm and frame brackets.

12. Position the outer cams over the retaining bolts, then install the nuts to the ends of the bolts at the front and rear of the control arm.

13. Align the cams to the reference marks made earlier, then tighten the end nuts to 70 ft. lbs. (95 Nm) on 1994 models. On 1995–99 models tighten the nuts to 85 ft. lbs. (115 Nm).

14. Remove the support from the steering knuckle, then install the ball joint to the knuckle. Make sure the joint is seated, then install the stud nut and tighten to 70 ft. lbs. (95 Nm) on 1994 models and 61 ft. lbs. (83 Nm) on 1995–99 models. Install a new cotter pin.

➡When installing the cotter pin, never loosen the castle nut to expose the cotter pin hole, but DO NOT tighten more than an additional ⅙ turn.

15. Install the tire and wheel assembly.
16. Remove the jackstands and carefully lower the vehicle.
17. Check and adjust the front end alignment, as necessary.

Lower Control Arm and Bushing

REMOVAL & INSTALLATION

2WD Vehicles

▶ **See Figure 36**

1. Remove the coil spring from the vehicle. For details, please refer to the procedure located earlier in this section.

2. If not done already, remove the tire and wheel assembly.

3. Remove the brake caliper and support it from the vehicle using a coat hanger or wire. Make sure the brake line is not stretched or damaged and that the caliper's weight is not supported by the line.

4. Remove the cotter pin and retaining nut from the upper ball joint.

5. Position J-23742 or an equivalent ball joint separator tool between upper joint stud and the upper joint/control arm. Use the tool to separate the ball joint from the steering knuckle. Pull the steering knuckle free of the ball joint after removal.

➡After separating the steering knuckle from the upper ball joint, be sure to support the steering knuckle/hub assembly to prevent damaging the brake hose. Also, support the lower control arm and guide it out of the opening in the splash shield.

6. Remove the jam nuts from the back of each lower control arm pivot bolt.

7. Unfasten the pivot bolts (noting the direction in which they are facing), then remove the control arm from the vehicle.

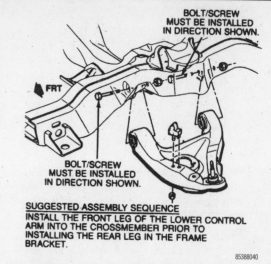

BOLT/SCREW MUST BE INSTALLED IN DIRECTION SHOWN.

FRT

BOLT/SCREW MUST BE INSTALLED IN DIRECTION SHOWN.

SUGGESTED ASSEMBLY SEQUENCE
INSTALL THE FRONT LEG OF THE LOWER CONTROL ARM INTO THE CROSSMEMBER PRIOR TO INSTALLING THE REAR LEG IN THE FRAME BRACKET.

85388040

Fig. 36 Lower control arm mounting—2WD vehicles

8. If the bushings are beings replaced, use a suitable bushing service set to remove the bushings from the control arm. The front bushing is normally flared and the flare must be driven down flush with the rubber using a blunt chisel before attempting removal.

To install:

9. If the bushings were removed, use the bushing service set to install them to the control arms. If the front bushing is the flared type, use a flaring tool to produce an approximate flare of 45 degrees.

10. Position the control arm to the vehicle.

11. Install the pivot bolts as noted during removal. For most vehicles covered by this manual, that means they should be installed with the heads forward, facing the rear.

12. Install the jam nuts and tighten to 67 ft. lbs. (90 Nm) on both nuts on 1994 models. On 1995–99 models tighten the front nut to 85 ft. lbs. (115 Nm) and the rear nut to 72 ft. lbs. (98 Nm).

13. Remove the support from the steering knuckle, then install the ball joint to the knuckle. Make sure the joint is seated, then install the stud nut. Install a new cotter pin.

➡When installing the cotter pin, never loosen the castle nut to expose the cotter pin hole.

14. Reposition and secure the brake caliper.
15. Install the coil spring.
16. Install the tire and wheel assembly.
17. Remove the jackstands and carefully lower the vehicle.
18. Check and adjust the front end alignment, as necessary.

4WD Vehicles

▶ **See Figure 37**

1. Raise and support the front of the vehicle safely using jackstands.

2. Remove the tire and wheel assembly.

3. If necessary, remove the drive axle nut. This will allow for more clearance when you are removing the control arm.

4. Remove the stabilizer bar. For details, please refer to the procedures earlier in this section. Installation of the stabilizer bar will require use of a torsion bar unloader tool.

5. Remove the shock absorber.

6. Unfasten the lower control arm-to-frame nuts, then withdraw the bolts, noting the direction they were facing for installation purposes.

7. If necessary, separate the ball joint stud from the steering knuckle. Remove the lower control arm from the vehicle.

8. If necessary, use a suitable bushing service set to remove the bushings from the lower control arm.

To install:

9. If removed, use the service set to install new bushings to the lower control arm.

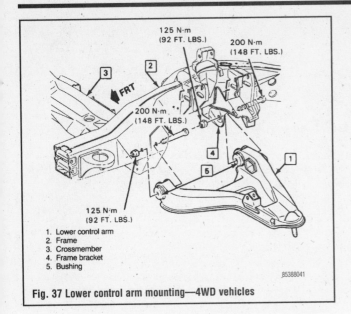

125 N·m
(92 FT. LBS.)

200 N·m
(148 FT. LBS.)

200 N·m
(148 FT. LBS.)

125 N·m
(92 FT. LBS.)

1. Lower control arm
2. Frame
3. Crossmember
4. Frame bracket
5. Bushing

85388041

Fig. 37 Lower control arm mounting—4WD vehicles

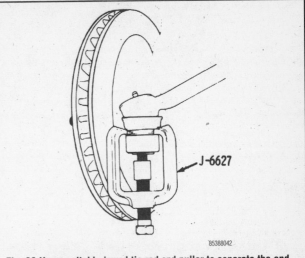

J-6627

85388042

Fig. 38 Use a suitable jawed tie rod end puller to separate the end from the steering knuckle

10. Position the control arm in the vehicle, installing the front leg of the lower control arm into the crossmember before installing the rear leg into the frame bracket.

11. Insert the control arm retaining bolts in the direction noted during removal. For most vehicles, they should be inserted from the rear of the vehicle facing forward.

12. Install the lower control arm retaining nuts and tighten them with the suspension at normal trim height to 70 ft. lbs. (95 Nm) for 1994 models for both nuts. On 1995–99 models tighten both nuts to 81 ft. lbs. (110 Nm).

13. If removed, attach the ball joint stud to the steering knuckle.

14. Install the shock absorber.

15. If removed, install and tighten the drive axle nut to specification.

16. Properly unload the torsion bar, then install the stabilizer bar. Adjust the torsion bar, as necessary. For details, please refer to the procedures located earlier in this section.

17. Install the tire and wheel assembly.

18. Remove the jackstands and carefully lower the vehicle.

Steering Knuckle and Spindle

REMOVAL & INSTALLATION

2WD Vehicles

▶ See Figure 38

1. Raise and support the front of the vehicle frame using jackstands.

➡When supporting the vehicle on jackstands, DO NOT place the jackstands under the lower control arms as spring tension will be used to help separate the ball joint studs from the knuckle. Place the jackstands under the frame and use a suitable floor jack under the control arm for safety.

2. Remove the tire and wheel assembly.

3. Remove the brake caliper from the steering knuckle and hang it from the vehicle using wire or a coat hanger. Make sure the brake line is not stretched or otherwise damaged.

4. Remove the grease cup, the cotter pin, the castle nut and the hub-and-rotor assembly. For details, please refer to the brake rotor (disc) procedure located in Section 9 of this manual.

5. Remove the splash shield-to-steering knuckle bolts and separate the shield from the knuckle.

6. At the tie rod end-to-steering knuckle stud, remove the cotter pin and the nut. Using suitable jawed tie rod end puller tools such as J-6627, J-24319-01 or their equivalent, separate the tie rod end from the steering knuckle.

7. Position a floor jack under the spring seat of the lower control arm in order to retain the spring seat. Raise the floor jack until it just contacts the arm.

Keep the jack in position during removal and installation to ensure the spring and control arm remain in position.

8. Remove the cotter pins from the upper and lower ball joint studs, then loosen the retaining nuts.

9. Use a ball joint separator such as J-23742 or equivalent to separate the upper ball joint from the steering knuckle. Remove the nut and pivot the upper control arm free of the knuckle.

10. Use the ball joint tool to separate the lower ball joint from the steering knuckle, then remove the nuts and lift the steering knuckle from the lower control arm.

11. Clean and inspect the steering knuckle and spindle for signs of wear or damage; if necessary, replace the steering knuckle. If any out-of-roundness is found in the tapered knuckle hole it must be replaced.

To install:

12. Position the steering knuckle onto the lower ball joint stud, then using the jack, lift the upper control arm to insert the upper ball joint stud into the steering knuckle. Loosely install both ball joint stud nuts to hold the components in position.

13. Properly tighten the upper and lower ball joint stud nuts, then install new cotter pins. For details, please refer to the procedures located earlier in this section.

➡When installing a cotter pin, never loosen the castle nut to expose the cotter pin hole.

14. If equipped, position a new steering knuckle gasket.

15. Install the splash shield to the knuckle and secure the retaining bolts.

16. Install the tie rod end to the steering knuckle, then tighten the stud nut to specification and install a new cotter pin.

17. Install the hub and rotor assembly and castle nut. Properly adjust the wheel bearings, then install a new cotter pin followed by the grease cup. For wheel bearing adjustment procedures, please refer to Section 1 of this manual.

18. Remove the support, then reposition and secure the brake caliper.

19. Install the tire and wheel assembly.

20. Remove the jackstands and carefully lower the vehicle.

21. Check and/or adjust the front end alignment, as necessary.

4WD Vehicles

▶ See Figures 39, 40, 41 and 42

➡The following procedure requires the use a universal steering linkage puller J-24319-01, an axle shaft boot seal protector J-28712, a ball joint separator tool J-36607 and a steering knuckle seal installation tool J-28574 or their equivalents.

1. Raise and support the front of the vehicle safely using jackstands.

2. Properly unload the torsion bar. For details, please refer to the torsion bar procedure located earlier in this section.

3. Remove the tire and wheel assembly.

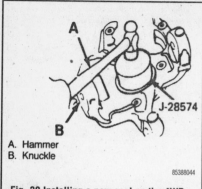

A. Hammer
B. Knuckle

85388044

Fig. 39 Installing a new seal on the 4WD steering knuckle

88458P13

Fig. 40 Remove the cotter pin from the drive axle end nut and retainer

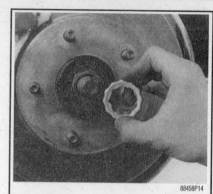

88458P14

Fig. 41 Remove the retainer for access to the end nut

88458P15

Fig. 42 Loosen the drive axle nut—here the caliper is installed so a drift could be inserted to keep the disc from spinning

4. Install an axle shaft boot seal protector to the tri-pot axle joint.

5. At the wheel hub, remove the cotter pin and retainer, then loosen and remove the castle nut and the thrust washer. In order to hold the hub from turning when loosening the nut, insert a drift through the caliper and into the rotor vanes.

6. Remove the brake caliper and support it aside using wire or a coat hanger. Make sure the brake line is not stretched or damaged.

7. Remove the brake rotor from the wheel hub.

8. Remove the bolts retaining the hub/bearing assembly to the knuckle, then carefully pull the assembly from the splined end of the halfshaft. If available, use J-28733-A or B, or an equivalent spindle remover to prevent damage to the shaft or hub/bearing assembly.

➡**When removed, lay the hub and bearing assembly on the hub bolt (outboard) side in order to prevent damage or contamination of the bearing seal.**

9. Remove the splash shield.

10. Remove the cotter pin and castle nut from the tie rod end, then separate the end from the knuckle using a suitable steering linkage puller.

11. Remove the cotter pins from the ball joints, then loosen the stud nuts.

12. Use the ball joint separator tool J-36607 or equivalent to loosen the ball joints in the steering knuckle.

13. Unfasten the ball joint nuts, then separate the ball joints from the knuckle and remove the knuckle from the vehicle.

14. Remove the spacer and the seal from the steering knuckle.

15. Clean and inspect the parts for nicks, scores and/or damage, then replace them as necessary.

To install:

16. Install a new seal into the steering knuckle, using a knuckle seal installation tool such as J-28574 or equivalent.

17. Install the spacer, then position the knuckle and insert the upper and lower ball joints.

18. Install the upper and lower ball joint stud nuts and tighten to specification, then install new cotter pins. For details, please refer to the ball joint procedures located earlier in this section.

19. Align the splash shield to the knuckle, then install the hub and bearing assembly, aligning the threaded holes.

20. Install the retaining bolts and tighten to 77 ft. lbs. (105 Nm).

21. Install the tie rod end of the steering knuckle, then secure using the retaining nut and a new cotter pin.

22. Install the brake rotor.

23. Reposition and secure the brake caliper.

24. Install the washer and retaining nut to the end of the halfshaft. Insert a brass drift to keep the rotor and hub from turning, then tighten the shaft nut to 180 ft. lbs. (245 Nm) on 1994–96 models and 103 ft. lbs. (140 Nm) on 1997–99 models.

25. Install the retainer and a new cotter pin, but DO NOT back off specification in order to insert the cotter pin.

26. Remove the torsion bar unloader tool and the drive axle boot protector.

27. Install the tire and wheel assembly.

28. Remove the jackstands and carefully lower the vehicle.

29. Check and/or adjust the vehicle trim (**Z**) height, as necessary.

Front Wheel Bearings

REMOVAL & INSTALLATION

2WD Vehicles

For wheel bearing removal, packing, installation and adjustment procedures on 2WD vehicles, please refer to

4WD Vehicles

➡**The wheel bearing is installed in the wheel hub assembly and is serviced by replacement only.**

Please refer to the appropriate portion of the steering knuckle procedure earlier in this section in order to replace the wheel hub assembly.

Wheel Alignment

If the tires are worn unevenly, if the vehicle is not stable on the highway or if the handling seems uneven in spirited driving, the wheel alignment should be checked. If an alignment problem is suspected, first check for improper tire inflation and other possible causes. These can be worn suspension or steering components, accident damage or even unmatched tires. If any worn or damaged components are found, they must be replaced before the wheels can be properly aligned. Wheel alignment requires very expensive equipment and involves minute adjustments which must be accurate; it should only be performed by a trained technician. Take your vehicle to a properly equipped shop.

Following is a description of the alignment angles which are adjustable on most vehicles and how they affect vehicle handling. Although these angles can apply to both the front and rear wheels, usually only the front suspension is adjustable.

CASTER

▶ **See Figure 43**

Looking at a vehicle from the side, caster angle describes the steering axis rather than a wheel angle. The steering knuckle is attached to a control arm or strut at the top and a control arm at the bottom. The wheel pivots around the line between these points to steer the vehicle. When the upper point is tilted back, this is described as positive caster. Having a positive caster tends to make the wheels self-centering, increasing directional stability. Excessive positive caster makes the wheels hard to steer, while an uneven caster will cause a pull to one side. Overloading the vehicle or sagging rear springs will affect caster, as will raising the rear of the vehicle. If the rear of the vehicle is lower than normal, the caster becomes more positive.

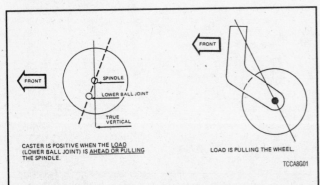

Fig. 43 Caster affects straight-line stability. Caster wheels used on shopping carts, for example, employ positive caster

CAMBER

▶ **See Figure 44**

Looking from the front of the vehicle, camber is the inward or outward tilt of the top of wheels. When the tops of the wheels are tilted in, this is negative camber; if they are tilted out, it is positive. In a turn, a slight amount of negative camber helps maximize contact of the tire with the road. However, too much negative camber compromises straight-line stability, increases bump steer and torque steer.

TOE

▶ **See Figure 45**

Looking down at the wheels from above the vehicle, toe angle is the distance between the front of the wheels, relative to the distance between the back of the wheels. If the wheels are closer at the front, they are said to be toed-in or to have negative toe. A small amount of negative toe enhances directional stability and provides a smoother ride on the highway.

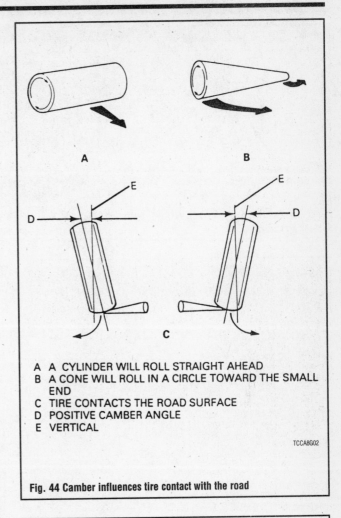

A   A CYLINDER WILL ROLL STRAIGHT AHEAD
B   A CONE WILL ROLL IN A CIRCLE TOWARD THE SMALL END
C   TIRE CONTACTS THE ROAD SURFACE
D   POSITIVE CAMBER ANGLE
E   VERTICAL

Fig. 44 Camber influences tire contact with the road

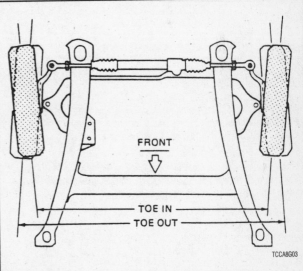

Fig. 45 With toe-in, the distance between the wheels is closer at the front than at the rear

REAR SUSPENSION

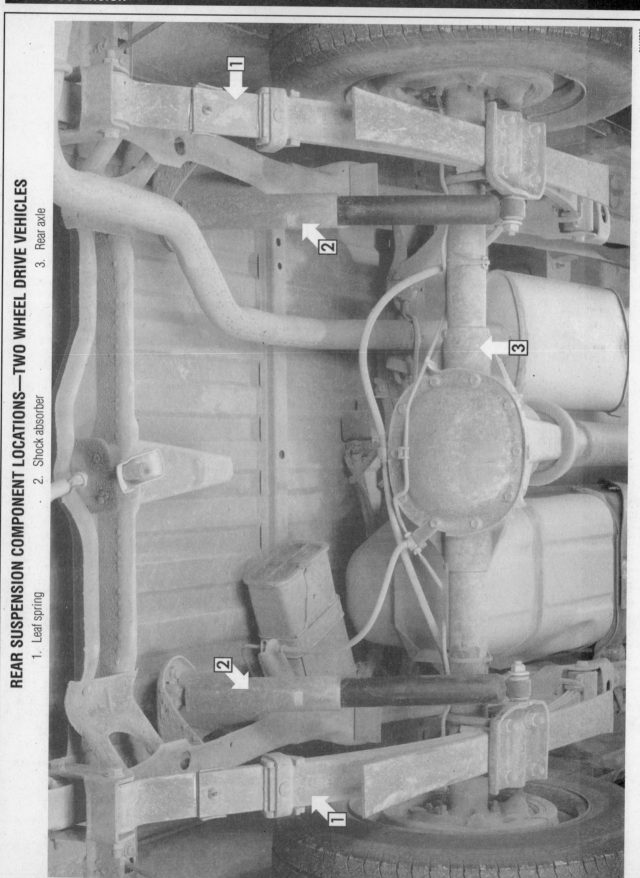

REAR SUSPENSION COMPONENT LOCATIONS—TWO WHEEL DRIVE VEHICLES

1. Leaf spring   2. Shock absorber   3. Rear axle

REAR SUSPENSION COMPONENT LOCATIONS—FOUR WHEEL DRIVE VEHICLES

1. Stabilizer shaft (sway bar)
2. Stabilizer shaft links
3. Leaf spring
4. Shock absorber
5. Rear axle

Leaf Springs

REMOVAL & INSTALLATION

▶ **See Figures 46 and 47**

➡ **The following procedure requires the use of two sets of jackstands.**

1. Raise and support the rear frame of the vehicle safely using jackstands. Support the rear axle with the second set of jackstands.

➡ **When supporting the rear of the vehicle, support the axle and the body separately in order to relieve the load on the rear spring.**

2. Remove the tire and wheel assembly.
3. Remove the shock absorber.
4. Remove the U-bolt nuts, washers, anchor plate and bolts.
5. Remove the spare tire, if equipped.
6. If necessary, unfasten the rear exhaust hangers and lower the rear exhaust.
7. Remove the shackle-to-frame bolt, washers and nut.
8. Remove the fuel tank, if necessary. For details, please refer to Section 5 of this manual.
9. Remove the front bracket nut, washers and bolt.
10. Carefully remove the spring from the vehicle.
11. If necessary, unfasten the shackle-to-spring nut, washers and bolts, then remove the shackle from the spring.

To install:

12. If removed, install the shackle to the rearward spring eye using the bolt, washers and nut, but do not fully tighten at this time.
13. Position the spring assembly to the vehicle.
14. Install the spring to the front bracket using the retaining bolt, washers and nut, but do not fully tighten at this time.
15. If removed, install the fuel tank.
16. Install the shackle-to-frame bolt, washers and nut, but do not fully tighten at this time. If used, remove the spring support.

17. Install the U-bolts, anchor plate, washers and U-bolt nuts. Tighten the U-bolt nuts using 2 passes of a diagonal sequence. On 1994 models, first tighten the nuts to 18 ft. lbs. (25 Nm), then tighten them to 85 ft. lbs. (115 Nm) in the sequence illustrated. On 1995–99 models, first tighten the nuts to 18 ft. lbs. (25 Nm), then tighten them to 73 ft. lbs. (100 Nm) in the sequence illustrated.
18. Position the axle to achieve an approximate gap of 6.46–6.94 in. (164–176mm) between the axle housing tube and the metal surface of the rubber frame bumper bracket. Measure from the housing between the U-bolts to the metal part of the rubber bump stop on the frame.
19. While supporting the axle in this position, tighten the front and rear spring mounting fasteners to 92 ft. lbs. (125 Nm) on 1994–95 models and 89 ft. lbs. (122 Nm) on 1996–99 models.
20. If removed, place the rear exhaust in position and tighten the hangers.
21. Install the spare tire.
22. Install the shock absorber.
23. Remove the jackstands and carefully lower the vehicle.

Shock Absorbers

REMOVAL & INSTALLATION

▶ **See Figures 48, 49 and 50**

1. Raise and support the rear of the vehicle safely using jackstands. Support the rear axle securely using jackstands or a floor jack. The axle must be supported to prevent overextension and damage to the brake lines once the shock is removed.
2. If equipped, disconnect the automatic level control air lines from the shock absorber.
3. Remove the shock absorber-to-frame retainers at the top of the shock.
4. Remove the shock-to-axle retainers at the bottom of the shock.
5. Remove the shock absorber from the vehicle.

To install:

6. Position the shock in the vehicle and loosely install the upper mounting fasteners to retain it.

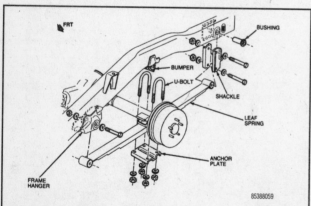

Fig. 46 Typical rear leaf spring and axle mounting—pick-up models

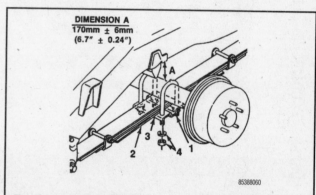

Fig. 47 Leaf spring U-bolts tighten sequence and axle tube-to-bumper bracket dimension

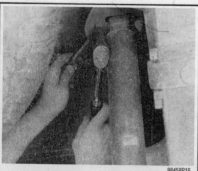

Fig. 48 Loosen the retainers from the upper shock mount—a backup wrench is usually needed

Fig. 49 Unfasten the lower shock retainer

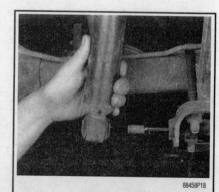

Fig. 50 Loosen and remove the shock from the lower mount

7. Align the lower-end of the shock absorber with the axle mounting, then loosely install the retainers.

8. On 1994 models, tighten the upper shock absorber retainers to 17 ft. lbs. (23 Nm). Then tighten lower shock absorber fastener to 47 ft. lbs. (64 Nm).

9. On 1995 models, tighten the upper shock absorber retainers 22 ft. lbs. (30 Nm). Then tighten the lower shock absorber fastener to 73 ft. lbs. (100 Nm).

10. On 1996–98 models, tighten the upper shock absorber retainers 22 ft. lbs. (30 Nm). Then tighten the lower shock absorber fastener to 62 ft. lbs. (84 Nm).

11. On 1999 models, tighten the upper shock retainers to 18 ft. lbs. (25 Nm). Tighten the lower shock retainers to 62 ft. lbs. (84 Nm) on pick-up and two door utility models and 74 ft. lbs. (100 Nm) on four door utility models.

12. If equipped, attach the automatic level control air lines to the shock absorber.

13. Remove the jackstands and carefully lower the vehicle.

TESTING

Refer to the shock absorber testing procedures in the front suspension portion of this manual.

Sway Bar

REMOVAL & INSTALLATION

1. Raise and support the rear of the vehicle safely using jackstands.
2. Remove the lower nuts, washers and bolts from the sway bar links.
3. Remove the nuts from the U-bolts, the U-bolts, the clamps and the insulators.
4. Remove the sway bar from the vehicle.

To install:

5. Place the sway bar in position.
6. Install the sway bar insulators, clamps, U-bolts and the U-bolt nuts. Tighten the nuts to 44 ft. lbs. (60 Nm).
7. On four door utility models, install the sway bar-to-link mounting bolt.
8. Install the sway bar-to-link nut. On 1994 models, tighten the nut to 50 ft. lbs. (68 Nm) on two door utility models and 28 ft. lbs. (35 Nm) on four door utility models.
9. On 1995–97 models, tighten the nuts as follows:
• Upper link nuts on pick-up, two and four door utility models: 25 ft. lbs. (35 Nm)
• Lower link nuts on pick-up, two and four door utility models: 50 ft. lbs. (68 Nm)
10. On 1998–99 models, tighten the upper link nuts on all models to 25 ft. lbs. (35 Nm)
11. Lower the vehicle.

Track Bar (Tie Rod)

REMOVAL & INSTALLATION

▶ See Figures 51 and 52

The track bar (tie rod assembly) is used only on models equipped with the ZR2 suspension.

STEERING

Steering Wheel

REMOVAL & INSTALLATION

Except Air Bag Models

▶ See Figures 53 thru 60

1. Disconnect the negative battery cable.
2. Position the steering wheel so that it is in the horizontal position and the front wheel are straight.

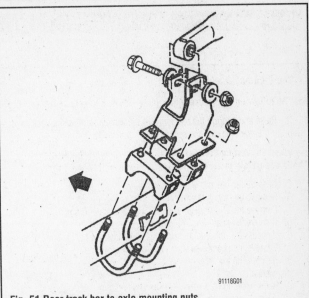

Fig. 51 Rear track bar-to-axle mounting nuts

1. Raise and support the rear of the vehicle safely using jackstands. Support the rear axle securely using jackstands or a floor jack.

2. Remove the track bar mounting bolts, washers and nuts at the axle bracket and frame bracket.

3. Remove the track bar from the vehicle.

To install:

4. Place the track bar in position and loosely install the bolts, washers and nuts.

5. Once the track bar is properly positioned, tighten the retainers as follows:
• Axle bracket nut: 84 ft. lbs. (115 Nm) on 1994–96 models and 44 ft. lbs. (61 Nm) on 1997–99 models
• Frame bracket bolt: 44 ft. lbs. (61 Nm) on all models
6. Remove the jackstands and lower the vehicle.

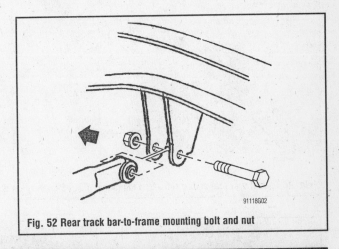

Fig. 52 Rear track bar-to-frame mounting bolt and nut

3. If equipped, remove the horn cap from the center of the steering wheel.

➡**If the horn cap or shroud is equipped with an electrical connector it must be unplugged in order to remove the cap/shroud from the steering column.**

4. Remove the steering wheel-to-steering shaft retainer clip (snapring), then loosen and remove the nut.

➡**Since the steering column is designed to collapse upon impact, NEVER hammer on it!**

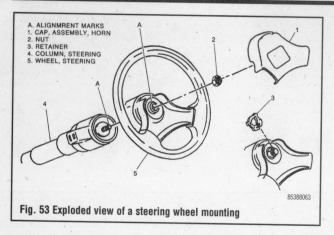

A. ALIGNMRENT MARKS
1. CAP, ASSEMBLY, HORN
2. NUT
3. RETAINER
4. COLUMN, STEERING
5. WHEEL, STEERING

Fig. 53 Exploded view of a steering wheel mounting

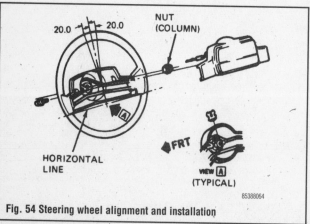

Fig. 54 Steering wheel alignment and installation

5. Matchmark the relationship of the steering wheel to the steering shaft. Some models may already be equipped with one or more alignment marks. If not, make your own using a permanent marker.

6. Using a suitable steering wheel puller, such as No. J-1859-03 or equivalent, carefully draw the wheel from the steering column.

To install:

➡ **Before installing the steering wheel, be sure that the turn signal switch is in the Neutral position. DO NOT mis-align the steering wheel more than 0.8 in. (20mm) from the horizontal centerline.**

7. Align the matchmarks and carefully fit the wheel onto the steering shaft splines.

8. Install the retaining nut and tighten to 30 ft. lbs. (40 Nm).

9. If equipped, install the horn pad.

10. Connect the negative battery cable.

Air Bag Models

▸ **See Figures 61 thru 78**

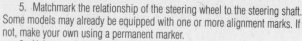

✳✳ CAUTION

These models are equipped with a Supplemental Restraint System (SRS), which uses an air bag. Whenever working near any of the SRS components, such as the impact sensors, the air bag module, steering column and instrument panel, disable the SRS, as described in Section 6.

1. Disconnect the negative battery cable.

2. Disable the Supplemental Inflatable Restraint System (SIR). Refer to Section 6 of this manual for this procedure.

3. Position the steering wheel so that it is in the horizontal position and the front wheel are straight.

4. Remove the air bag system inflator module as follows:

a. Make sure the air bag system is disabled and the negative battery disconnected.

Fig. 55 Remove the horn pad

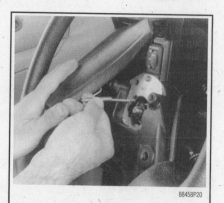

Fig. 56 Unplug the horn wire

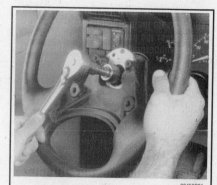

Fig. 57 Loosen and remove the wheel retaining nut

Fig. 58 Use a suitable threaded puller to loosen the steering wheel from the shaft

Fig. 59 Remove the steering wheel

Fig. 60 Matchmark the relationship of the steering wheel to the steering shaft

Fig. 61 Remove the fuse panel cover

Fig. 62 Look at the diagram on the back of the fuse panel cover to identify the location of the air bag fuse

Fig. 63 Once located, remove the air bag fuse from the panel

Fig. 64 Remove the lower left hand instrument panel knee bolster to access the Connector Position Assurance (CPA) 2-way connector located at the base of the steering column

Fig. 65 Remove the clip that prevents the CPA from being accidentally disconnected . . .

Fig. 66 Unplug the CPA connector

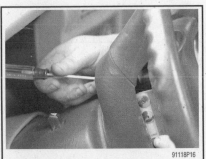

Fig. 67 Insert a screw driver into the shroud holes at the rear of the steering wheel and push the leaf spring to release the pin

Fig. 68 Once all the clips have been released, carefully move the inflator module forward to gain access to the rear of the module

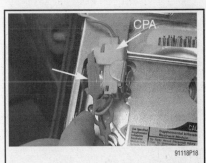

Fig. 69 Remove the inflator module Connector Position Assurance (CPA) retaining clip. This clip prevents the CPA connector becoming accidentally unplugged

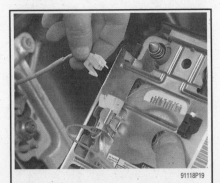

Fig. 70 Unplug the inflator module CPA connector

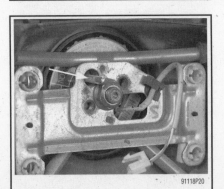

Fig. 71 Location of the horn plunger contact

Fig. 72 Remove the horn plunger contact and set aside

Fig. 73 Mark the relationship of the steering wheel to the steering shaft

Fig. 74 Unfasten the steering wheel retaining nut using a ratchet, short extension (for clearance) and a suitable size socket . . .

Fig. 75 . . . then remove the retaining nut

Fig. 76 Use a suitable steering wheel puller to separate the wheel from the shaft

Fig. 77 Once loosened the wheel is easily removed

Fig. 78 A torque wrench should be used to tighten the steering wheel nut to the proper specification

b. Turn the steering wheel 90 degrees, this will enable you to gain access to the rear shroud holes-to-inflator module.

c. Insert a prytool and push the leaf spring to release the pin.

d. Turn the steering wheel 180 degrees to access the remaining shroud holes, then repeat the procedure to release the pin using the prytool.

e. Tilt the inflator module rearward from the top to access the module electrical wiring, then disengage the wiring from the module and the steering wheel.

f. Unplug the Connector Position Assurance (CPA) and retainer from the module.

5. Remove the steering wheel retaining nut and the horn plunger contact.

➡️Since the steering column is designed to collapse upon impact, NEVER hammer on it!

6. Matchmark the relationship of the steering wheel to the steering shaft. Some models may already be equipped with one or more alignment marks. If not, make your own using a permanent marker.

7. Using a suitable steering wheel puller, such as No. J-1859-03 or equivalent, carefully draw the wheel from the steering column.

To install:

8. Align the matchmarks and carefully fit the wheel onto the steering shaft.

9. Install the retaining nut and tighten to 30 ft. lbs. (40 Nm).

10. Install the inflator module as follows:

a. Attach the Connector Position Assurance (CPA) and retainer to the module.

b. Attach the inflator module wiring to the steering wheel and to the module.

c. Install the inflator module by pressing it into the steering wheel enough to engage and latch all four notched pins in the leaf spring. Make sure the wires are not pinched.

11. Connect the negative battery cable.

12. Enable the air bag system. Refer to Section 6 of this manual for this procedure.

Turn Signal (Combination) Switch

REMOVAL & INSTALLATION

➡️When servicing any components on the steering column, should any fasteners require replacement, be sure to use only nuts and bolts of the same size and grade as the original fasteners. Using screws that are too long could prevent the column from collapsing during a collision.

1994 Vehicles

▶ See Figure 79

➡️The following procedures require the use of a lockplate compressor tool such as J-23653 or equivalent.

1. Disconnect the negative battery cable.

2. Matchmark and remove the steering wheel. Please refer to the procedure earlier in this section for details.

3. Remove the shaft lock cover.

4. Push downward on the shaft lock assembly until the snapring is exposed using the shaft lock compressor tool.

5. Remove the shaft lock retaining snapring, then carefully release the tool and remove the shaft lock from the column.

6. Remove the turn signal canceling cam assembly.

7. For standard columns, remove the upper bearing spring and thrust washer.

8. For tilt columns, remove the upper bearing spring, inner race seat and inner race.

9. Move the turn signal lever upward to the "Right Turn" position.

10. Remove the access cap and disengage the multi-function lever harness connector, then grasp the lever and pull it from the column.

11. Loosen and remove the hazard knob retaining screw, then remove the screw, button, spring and knob.

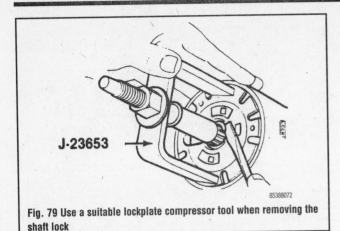

Fig. 79 Use a suitable lockplate compressor tool when removing the shaft lock

12. Remove the screw and the switch actuator arm.

13. Remove the turn signal switch retaining screws, then pull the switch forward and allow it to hang from the wires. If the switch is only being removed for access to other components, this may be sufficient.

14. If the switch is being completely removed, disengage the wiring at the base of the column. Attach a length of mechanic's wire to the switch harness connector, then pull the harness through the column, leaving the mechanic's wire in place for installation purposes.

➡**On some vehicles access to the connector may be difficult. If necessary, remove the column support bracket assembly and properly support the column, and/or remove the wiring protectors.**

15. Remove the switch and wiring harness from the vehicle.

To install:

16. Install the switch and wiring harness to the vehicle. If the switch was completely removed, use the length of mechanic's wire to pull the switch harness through the column, then engage the connector.

➡**If the column support bracket or wiring protectors were removed, install them before proceeding.**

17. Position the switch in the column and secure using the retaining screws. Tighten the screws to 30 inch lbs. (3.4 Nm).

18. Install the switch actuator arm and retaining screw, then tighten the screw to 20 inch lbs. (2.3 Nm).

19. Install the hazard knob assembly, then install the multi-function lever.

20. Install the thrust washer and upper bearing spring (standard columns) or the inner race, upper bearing race seat and upper bearing spring (tilt columns), as applicable.

21. Lubricate the turn signal canceling cam using a suitable synthetic grease (usually included in the service kit), then install the cam assembly.

22. Position the shaft lock and a NEW snaping, then use the lock compressor to hold the lock down while you seat the new snapring. Make sure the ring is firmly seated in the groove, then carefully release the tool.

23. Install the shaft lock cover.

24. Align and install the steering wheel.

25. Make sure the ignition is **OFF**, then connect the negative battery cable.

1995–99 Vehicles

▶ **See Figure 80**

※ CAUTION

These models are equipped with a Supplemental Restraint System (SRS), which uses an air bag. Whenever working near any of the SRS components, such as the impact sensors, the air bag module, steering column and instrument panel, disable the SRS, as described in Section 6.

1. Disconnect the negative battery cable.

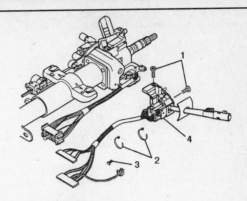

1. Pan hd tapping screw
2. Wire harness strap
3. Axial posn assur connector
4. T/S & multifunc switch asm

Fig. 80 Exploded view of the combination switch—1996 and later models

➡**Make sure that the turn signal switch is in the OFF (center) position.**

2. Disable the Supplemental Inflatable Restraint (SIR) system. For details, please refer to the procedure located in Section 6 of this manual.

3. Remove the steering wheel.

4. Remove the two pan head tapping screws from the lower steering column cover, then tilt the cover down and slide it back to disengage the locking tabs.

5. Remove the lower steering column cover.

6. Using a Torx® screwdriver, remove the two Torx head screws from the upper steering column cover, then remove the cover.

7. Remove the wire harness strap, then remove the two harness straps from the steering column wire harness.

8. Remove the screw and disengage the steering column bulkhead connector from the vehicle wiring harness.

9. Unplug the gray and black connectors of the switch from the steering column bulkhead connector.

10. Remove the two pan head tapping screws.

11. Grasp the lever/multi-function turn signal switch assembly, then remove it by carefully pulling it straight outward.

To install:

12. Install the lever/multi-function turn signal switch assembly, using a small blade screwdriver to compress the electrical contact and move the assembly into position.

➡**The electrical contact MUST rest on the canceling cam assembly.**

13. Connect the two pan head tapping screws, then tighten the screws to 53 inch lbs. (6 Nm).

14. Attach the gray and black connectors of the switch to the column bulkhead connector.

15. Connect the steering column bulkhead connector to the vehicle wiring harness.

16. Connect the two wire harness straps to the steering column wire harness, then install the wire harness strap.

17. Install the upper steering column cover, then using a Torx® screwdriver, connect the two Torx head screws to the upper column cover, tighten to 12 inch lbs. (1.4 Nm).

18. Install the lower steering column cover, then connect using the two pan head tapping screws, tighten to 53 inch lbs. (6 Nm).

19. Make sure that the lever is in the **OFF** (center) position.

20. Install the steering wheel.

21. If equipped, install the horn pad.

22. Activate the Supplemental Inflatable Restraint (SIR) system. For details, please refer to the procedure located in Section 6.

23. Connect the negative battery cable.

Ignition Switch

REMOVAL & INSTALLATION

1994 Vehicles

For anti-theft reasons, the ignition switch is located on top of the steering column assembly and is completely inaccessible without first lowering the steering column. The switch is actuated by a rod and rack assembly. A gear on the end of the lock cylinder engages the toothed upper end of the actuator rod.

1. Disconnect the negative battery cable.
2. Remove the lower column trim panel, then remove the steering column-to-instrument panel fasteners and carefully lower the column for access to the switch.
3. Remove the turn signal switch from the column and allow it to hang from the wires (leaving them connected). For details, please refer to the procedure located earlier in this section.
4. Remove the buzzer switch assembly.
5. Carefully remove the lock cylinder screw and the lock cylinder. If possible, use a magnetic tipped screwdriver on the screw in order to help prevent the possibility of dropping it.

❊❊ CAUTION

If the screw is dropped upon removal, it could fall into the steering column, requiring complete disassembly in order to retrieve the screw and prevent damage.

6. Unfasten the steering column support bracket assembly hex head bolts and remove the bracket.
7. Unfasten the dimmer switch assembly screws and remove the switch.
8. Place the ignition switch in the **OFF-LOCK** position.
9. Remove the ignition switch-to-steering column retainers, then remove the assembly.

To install:

10. Before installing the ignition switch, place it in the **OFF-LOCK** position, then make sure that the lock cylinder and actuating rod are in the Locked position (1st detent from the top or 1st detent to the right of far left detent travel).

➡**Most replacement switches are pinned in the OFF-LOCK position for installation purposes. If so, the pin MUST be removed after installation or damage may occur.**

11. Install the activating rod into the ignition switch and assemble the switch onto the steering column. Once the switch is properly positioned, tighten the ignition switch-to-steering column retainers to 35 inch lbs. (4.0 Nm).

❊❊ CAUTION

When installing the ignition switch, use only the specified screws since over length screws could impair the collapsibility of the column.

12. Install the dimmer switch and the steering column support bracket.
13. Align and install the lock cylinder set.
14. Push the lock cylinder all the way in, then carefully install the retaining screw. Tighten the screw to 22 inch lbs. (2.5 Nm) on tilt columns or to 40 inch lbs. (4.5 Nm) on standard non-tilt columns.
15. If necessary, install the buzzer switch assembly.
16. Reposition and secure the turn signal switch assembly
17. Raise the column into position and secure, then install any necessary trim plates.
18. Make sure the ignition is **OFF**, then connect the negative battery cable.

1995–99 Vehicles

▶ **See Figure 81**

1. Remove the column shroud halves.
2. Remove the column-to-dash attaching bolts and slowly lower the steering column, making sure that it is supported.

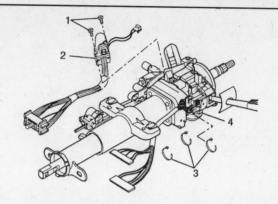

1. Tapping screw
2. Ign & key alarm switch asm
3. Wire harness strap
4. Strg column housing asm

88458G07

Fig. 81 Exploded view of the ignition and key alarm switch

3. Remove the multifunction switch if necessary.
4. Remove the key alarm switch, if equipped by gently prying the alarm switch retaining clip with a small screwdriver. Rotate the alarm switch ¼ in. (6mm) turn and remove.

❊❊ WARNING

Extreme care is necessary to prevent damage to the collapsible column.

5. Make sure that the switch is in the **LOCK** position. If the lock cylinder is out, pull the switch rod up to the stop, then go down one detent.
6. Remove the two screws and the switch.

To install:

7. Before installation, make sure the switch is in the **LOCK** position.
8. Install the switch using the original screws. Tighten the screws to 12 inch. lbs. (1.4 Nm).
9. Install the key alarm switch, if equipped . Make sure the retaining clip is parallel to the lock cylinder. Rotate the alarm switch ¼ in. (6mm) turn until locked in place.
10. Install the multifunction switch if removed.

❊❊ CAUTION

Use of screws that are too long could prevent the column from collapsing on impact.

11. Replace the column. Tighten the nuts to 22 ft. lbs. (29 Nm); the bolts to 20 ft. lbs. (27 Nm).
12. Install the column shroud halves.

Lock Cylinder

REMOVAL & INSTALLATION

1994 Vehicles

1. Disconnect the negative battery cable.
2. Matchmark and remove the steering wheel.
3. Remove the turn signal switch from the column and allow it to hang from the wires (leaving them connected). For details, please refer to the procedure located earlier in this section.
4. Remove the buzzer switch assembly.
5. Carefully remove the lock cylinder screw and the lock cylinder. If possible, use a magnetic tipped screwdriver on the screw in order to help prevent the possibility of dropping it.

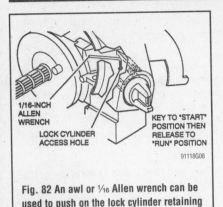

Fig. 82 An awl or 1/16 Allen wrench can be used to push on the lock cylinder retaining pin

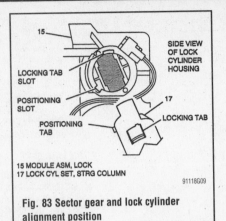

Fig. 83 Sector gear and lock cylinder alignment position

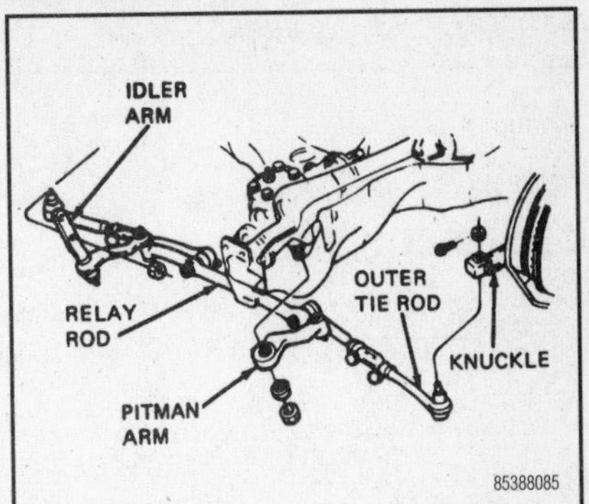

Fig. 84 Common steering linkage components

❋❋ CAUTION

If the screw is dropped upon removal, it could fall into the steering column, requiring complete disassembly in order to retrieve the screw and prevent damage.

To install:

6. Align and install the lock cylinder set.

7. Push the lock cylinder all the way in, then carefully install the retaining screw. Tighten the screw to 22 inch lbs. (2.5 Nm) on tilt columns or to 40 inch lbs. (4.5 Nm) on standard non-tilt columns.

8. If necessary, install the buzzer switch assembly.

9. Reposition and secure the turn signal switch assembly

10. Align and install the steering wheel.

11. Make sure the ignition is **OFF**, then connect the negative battery cable.

1995–99 Vehicles

◆ See Figures 82 and 83

1. Disconnect the negative battery cable.

❋❋ CAUTION

These models are equipped with a Supplemental Restraint System (SRS), which uses an air bag. Whenever working near any of the SRS components, such as the impact sensors, the air bag module, steering column and instrument panel, disable the SRS, as described in Section 6.

2. Disconnect the negative battery cable.

3. Disable the Supplemental Inflatable Restraint System (SIR). Refer to Section 6 of this manual for this procedure.

4. Unfasten the steering column-to-instrument panel retainers and lower the column.

5. Unfasten the pan head screws from the upper column shroud and the Torx head screws from the lower column screws, then remove lower shroud by tilting it down to disengage the locking tabs. Lift up the upper shroud to access the cylinder hole.

6. Hold the key in the **START** position.

7. Insert a 1/16 Allen wrench or an awl into the lock cylinder access hole and push down on the cylinder retaining pin.

8. Release the key to the **RUN** position and pull the lock cylinder from the column.

To install:

9. Install the upper shroud and lock cylinder as follows:

   a. Install the key in the cylinder and hold in it the **RUN** position.

   b. Make sure the sector in the lock module is in the **RUN** position.

   c. Engage the cylinder to the upper shroud, line up the locking tab and

positioning tab with the slots in the lock module assembly, then push the cylinder into position.

10. Install the upper shroud Torx head screws and tighten to 12 inch lbs. (1.4 Nm).

11. Install the lower shroud, making sure the slots in the lower shroud engage the tabs on the upper shroud, then tilt the lower shroud up to snap the halves together. Install the lower shroud screws and tighten to 53 inch lbs. (6 Nm).

12. Place the steering column into position and tighten the retainers.

13. Activate the Supplemental Inflatable Restraint (SIR) system. For details, please refer to the procedure located in Section 6.

14. Connect the negative battery cable.

Steering Linkage

◆ See Figures 84 and 85

The steering linkage consists of: a forward mounted linkage, crimp or prevailing torque nuts at the inner pivots, castellated nuts at the steering knuckle arm, an idler arm, a steering gear pitman arm, a relay rod and a steering damper (4WD vehicles). Grease fittings are equipped with each joint, for durability. Depending on the application, the relay rod may only be equipped with holes to accept ball studs, or the rod may itself contain ball studs for connection with the pitman/idler arms.

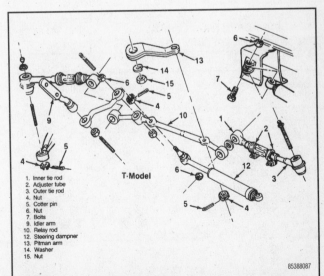

1. Inner tie rod
2. Adjuster tube
3. Outer tie rod
4. Nut
5. Cotter pin
6. Nut
7. Bolts
9. Idler arm
10. Relay rod
12. Steering dampner
13. Pitman arm
14. Washer
15. Nut

T-Model

Fig. 85 Common 4WD steering linkage components (with steering damper)

REMOVAL & INSTALLATION

Pitman Arm

TWO WHEEL DRIVE MODELS

♦ **See Figures 86, 87, 88, 89 and 90**

1. Raise and support the front of the vehicle safely using jackstands.
2. Remove the nut from ball stud at the relay rod-to-pitman arm connection. Discard the nut.
3. Using a suitable universal steering linkage puller, such as J-24319-01 or equivalent, separate the relay rod from the pitman arm. Pull down on the relay rod and separate the stud.
4. Remove the Pitman arm-to-Pitman shaft nut, then matchmark the relationship of the arm to the shaft to assure proper alignment during assembly.

➡**When separating the pitman arm from the shaft, DO NOT use a hammer or apply heat to the arm.**

5. Using a pitman arm remover such as J-6632 or equivalent, separate the pitman arm from the pitman shaft and remove it from the vehicle.

To install:

➡**If the pitman arm is being replaced, transfer the alignment mark to the new component.**

6. Install the pitman arm while aligning the arm-to-pitman shaft matchmark. Use a steering linkage installer such as J-29193 (12mm), J-29194 (14mm) or equivalent (as applicable) to properly seat the arm on the shaft, install the correct one onto the shaft and torque it to 40 ft. lbs. (54 Nm) to seat the taper.

7. Remove the installer tool, then install the pitman shaft nut and tighten to 185 ft. lbs. (250 Nm).
8. Connect the Pitman arm to the relay rod (make sure that the seal is on the stud). Use a steering linkage installer such as J-29193 (12mm), J-29194 (14mm) or equivalent (as applicable), install the correct one onto the ball stud and tighten it to 48 ft. lbs. (62 Nm) to seat the taper.
9. After seating, remove the tool, install the lockwasher and nut and tighten to 60 ft. lbs. (82 Nm). A NEW nut MUST be installed.
10. Remove the jackstands and carefully lower the vehicle.
11. Check and adjust toe, as necessary.

FOUR WHEEL DRIVE MODELS

1. Slide the intermediate shaft cover off the clamp and matchmark the relationship of the intermediate shaft.
2. Raise the front of the vehicle and support it with jackstands and disconnect the intermediate shaft.
3. Remove the oil filter pipes from the crossmember bracket.
4. Remove the splash shield.
5. Remove the nut from ball stud at the relay rod-to-Pitman arm connection. Discard the nut.
6. If necessary, remove the front differential carrier shield.
7. Using a suitable universal steering linkage puller, such as J-24319-01 or equivalent, separate the relay rod from the Pitman arm. Pull down on the relay rod and separate the stud.
8. Remove the Pitman arm-to-Pitman shaft nut, then matchmark the relationship of the arm to the shaft to assure proper alignment during assembly.
9. If necessary, remove the power steering gear.

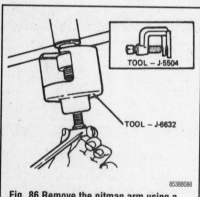

Fig. 86 Remove the pitman arm using a suitable pitman puller tool

Fig. 87 Loosen the pitman arm-to-relay rod nut

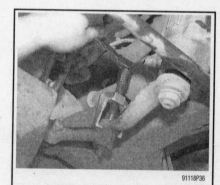

Fig. 88 Use a suitable puller to separate the pitman arm from the relay rod

Fig. 89 Loosen the pitman arm nut . . .

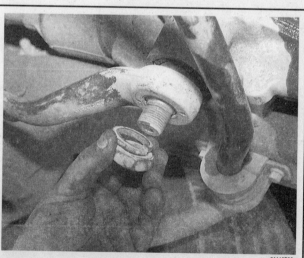

Fig. 90 . . . then remove the nut and washer

➡**When separating the Pitman arm from the shaft, DO NOT use a hammer or apply heat to the arm.**

10. Using a Pitman arm remover such as J-6632 or equivalent, separate the Pitman arm from the Pitman shaft and remove it from the vehicle.

To install:

➡**If the Pitman arm is being replaced, transfer the alignment mark to the new component.**

11. Install the Pitman arm while aligning the arm-to-Pitman shaft matchmark. Use a steering linkage installer such as J-29193 (12mm), J-29194 (14mm) or equivalent (as applicable) to properly seat the arm on the shaft, install the correct one onto the shaft and torque it to 40 ft. lbs. (54 Nm) to seat the taper.

12. Remove the installer tool, then install the Pitman shaft nut and tighten to 185 ft. lbs. (250 Nm).

13. If removed, install the steering gear.

14. If removed, install the front differential carrier shield.

15. Connect the Pitman arm to the relay rod (make sure that the seal is on the stud). Use a steering linkage installer such as J-29193 (12mm), J-29194 (14mm) or equivalent (as applicable), install the correct one onto the ball stud and tighten it to 48 ft. lbs. (62 Nm) to seat the taper.

16. After seating, remove the tool, install the lockwasher and nut and tighten to 60 ft. lbs. (82 Nm) on 1994–96 models and 79 ft. lbs. (108 Nm) on 1997–99 models. A NEW nut MUST be installed.

17. Attach the oil filter pipes to the crossmember bracket and install the splash shield.

18. Install the intermediate shaft making sure to align the marks made before removal.

19. Remove the jackstands and carefully lower the vehicle.

20. Check and adjust toe, as necessary.

Idler Arm

▶ **See Figures 91, 92, 93, 94 and 95**

1. Raise and support the front of the vehicle safely using jackstands under the frame so the wheels are free to turn.

➡**Jerking the right wheel assembly back and forth is not an acceptable testing procedure; there is no control on the amount of force being applied to the idler arm. Before suspecting idler arm shimmying complaints, check the wheels for imbalance, run-out, force variation and/or road surface irregularities.**

2. To inspect for a defective idler arm:
   a. Position the wheels in the straight ahead position.
   b. Position a spring scale near the relay rod end of the idler arm, then exert 25 ft. lbs. (110 Nm) of force upward and then downward. Measure the distance between the upward and downward directions that the idler arm moves. The allowable deflection is ⅛ in. (3.18mm) for each direction for a total difference of ¼ in. (6.35mm); if the idler arm deflection is beyond the allowable limits, replace it.

3. If equipped and if necessary, remove the steering linkage and differential carrier shields.

4. Remove the idler arm-to-frame bolts/nuts.

5. Remove the nut from the idler arm-to-relay rod ball joint.

6. Use a suitable steering linkage puller such as J-24319-B or equivalent to separate the relay rod from idler arm.

7. Remove the idler arm assembly from the vehicle.

To install:

8. Install the idler arm, then tighten the arm assembly-to-frame bolts to 60 ft. lbs. (82 Nm) on 1994 models and 79 ft. lbs. (108 Nm) on 1995–99 models.

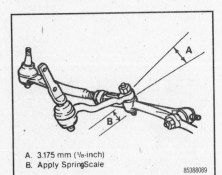

A. 3.175 mm (⅛-inch)
B. Apply Spring Scale

85388089

Fig. 91 Checking the idler arm for wear or damage

91118P28

Fig. 92 Using a back-up wrench and a ratchet and socket, remove the idler arm-to-frame nuts and bolts

91118P29

Fig. 93 Remove the nut from the idler arm ball stud

91118P30

Fig. 94 Use a suitable steering linkage to separate the relay rod from idler arm . . .

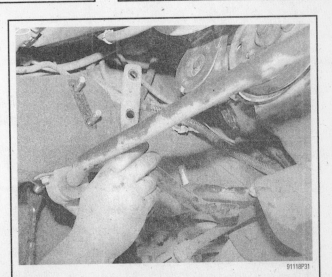

91118P31

Fig. 95 . . . then remove the idler arm

9. Connect the relay rod to the idler arm. Use a steering linkage installer such as J-29193 (12mm), J-29194 (14mm) or equivalent (as applicable) to seat the relay rod-to-idler arm ball joint stud. Tighten the tool to 40 ft. lbs. (54 Nm), then remove the tool.

10. Install the idler arm-to-relay rod stud nut and tighten it to 35 ft. lbs. (47 Nm) for 2WD vehicles or 60 ft. lbs. (82 Nm) for 4WD vehicles.

11. If removed, install the steering linkage and differential carrier shields.

12. Remove the jackstands and carefully lower the vehicle.

13. Check and/or adjust the toe-in, as necessary.

Relay Rod (Centerlink)

◆ See Figures 96, 97, 98, 99 and 100

1. Raise and support the vehicle safely using jackstands.

2. If equipped and if necessary, remove the steering linkage and differential carrier shields.

3. Remove the inner tie rod stud nuts, then separate the tie rods from the relay rod using a suitable linkage puller. For details, please refer to the tie rod procedure located later in this section.

4. On vehicles equipped with a steering damper, remove the shock absorber ball stud nut, then separate the shock from the relay rod using a suitable linkage puller, such as J-24319-01 or equivalent.

5. Remove the ball stud nut from the pitman arm-to-relay rod connection, then use a suitable steering linkage puller, such as J-24319-01 or equivalent, to disconnect the pitman rod from the idler arm.

6. Remove the ball stud nut from the idler arm-to-relay rod connection, then use a suitable steering linkage puller, such as J-24319-01 or equivalent, to disconnect the relay rod from the idler arm.

7. Once the linkage components have been removed from the relay rod, it is free to be removed from the vehicle.

To install:

8. Clean and inspect the threads on the tie rod, the tie rod ends and the ball joints for damage, and replace them (if necessary). Inspect the ball joint seals for excessive wear, and replace them (if necessary).

9. Connect the relay rod to the idler arm. Use a steering linkage installer such as J-29193 (12mm), J-29194 (14mm) or equivalent (as applicable) to seat the relay rod-to-idler arm ball joint stud. Tighten the tool to 40 ft. lbs. (54 Nm), then remove the tool.

10. Install the idler arm-to-relay rod stud nut and tighten it to 35 ft. lbs. (47 Nm) on 2WD models or 60 ft. lbs. (82 Nm) on 4WD models.

11. Connect the pitman arm to the relay rod (make sure that the seal is on the stud). Use a steering linkage installer such as J-29193 (12mm), J-29194 (14mm) or equivalent (as applicable), install the correct one onto the ball stud and tighten it to 40 ft. lbs. (54 Nm) to seat the taper.

12. After seating, remove the tool, install the lockwasher and nut and tighten to 35 ft. lbs. (47 Nm) on 2WD models or 60 ft. lbs. (82 Nm) on 4WD models. A NEW nut MUST be installed.

13. If equipped, install the steering shock absorber.

14. Install the inner tie rods to the relay rod, then install the mounting nuts and tighten to specification. For details, please refer to the tie rod procedure located later in this section.

15. If removed, install the steering linkage and differential carrier shields.

16. Remove the jackstands and carefully lower the vehicle, then check the steering linkage for proper operation.

Tie Rod

◆ See Figures 101 thru 110

➡The following procedure may be used to remove the entire tie rod assembly. If only one tie rod end of an assembly is being replaced, the entire assembly does not have to be removed from the vehicle. The opposite tie rod end (the end not being replaced) may remain attached to the steering linkage/knuckle, as applicable.

1. Raise and support the front frame of the vehicle safely using jackstands.

2. Remove the cotter pin from the tie rod-to-steering knuckle stud, then loosen and remove the retaining nut.

3. Remove the nut from the tie rod-to-relay rod connection.

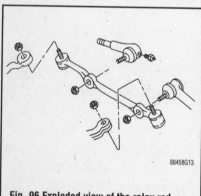
Fig. 96 Exploded view of the relay rod—2WD model shown

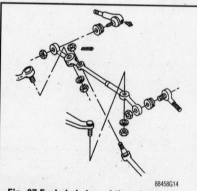
Fig. 97 Exploded view of the relay rod—4WD model shown

Fig. 98 Unfasten the relay rod-to-inner tie rod nuts

Fig. 99 Use a suitable puller to separate the relay rod from the inner tie rod

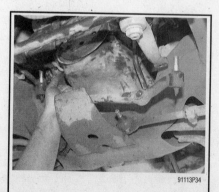
Fig. 100 Remove the relay rod from the vehicle

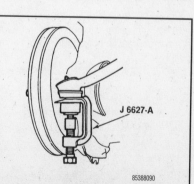
Fig. 101 A proper tools such as the wheel stud remover/tie rod separator tool should be used to free the tie rod ends

Fig. 102 Matchmark the tie rod before removal, this will aid during installation

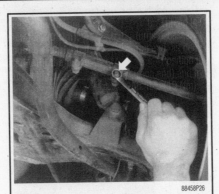

Fig. 103 Loosen the adjuster clamp bolt . . .

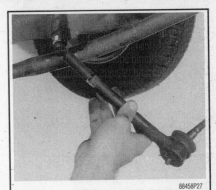

Fig. 104 . . . then remove the tie rod from the vehicle

Fig. 105 When removing a tie rod end, first straighten the ends of the old cotter pin . . .

Fig. 106 . . . then pull the cotter pin from the ball stud and retaining nut

Fig. 107 Loosen and remove the stud nut

Fig. 108 Use a suitable tool to push the tie rod end free. DO NOT use a wedge-type tool

Fig. 109 Once the ball stud has be unseated, withdraw the tie rod end from the component

Fig. 110 If replacing a tie rod end (in this case still on the vehicle), loosen the adjuster clamp bolt/nut

➡DO NOT attempt to separate the tie rod-to-steering knuckle joint by driving a wedge type tool between the joint and knuckle or seal damage could result.

4. Using a suitable tie rod remover such as the wheel stud/tie rod tool No. J-6627-A or equivalent, separate the outer tie rod stud from the steering knuckle and the inner tie from the relay rod.

5. Remove the tie rod from the vehicle.

6. If one or both of the tie rod ends are being replaced:

➡Tie rod adjustment components tend to rust in service. If the torque required to remove the nut from the bolt exceeds 62 inch lbs. (9 Nm), the nuts should be replaced. Also, the components should be lubricated with a penetrating oil, then the clamps should be rotated until the move freely. Pay attention to the clamp positioning before loosening or removing them.

a. Measure the installed length of the tie rod end(s) for installation purposes.

b. Loosen the adjuster tube clamp bolt(s).

c. Unscrew the tie rod end from the adjuster tube; count the number of turns necessary to remove the tie rod end. This can be used to help preserve the toe adjustment during installation.

To install:

7. If one or both of the tie rod ends were removed:

a. Clean, inspect and lubricate the adjuster tube threads.

b. Thread the tie rod end into the adjuster tube using the same number of turns necessary to remove it. Once installed, measure the length of the tie rod end, as done during removal to help assure toe adjustment.

c. Position the clamp bolts between the adjuster tube dimples (located at each end) and in the proper location. Tighten the adjuster tube clamp bolt 14 ft. lbs. (19 Nm).

8. Position the tie rod ends to the steering knuckle and/or the relay rod. Use a steering linkage installer such as J-29193 (12mm), J-29194 (14mm) or equivalent (as applicable), install the correct one onto the ball stud and tighten it to 40 ft. lbs. (54 Nm) to seat the taper(s).

9. Once the ends are properly seated, remove the tool and install the retaining nut(s).

10. Tighten the inner and/or outer tie rod end retaining nuts to 35 ft. lbs. (47 Nm) on 1994 models. On 1995–99 models tighten the inner nut to 35 ft. lbs. (47 Nm) and the outer nut to 39 ft. lbs. (53 Nm).

11. Install a new cotter pin to the castle nut(s), as applicable.

12. Check and adjust the toe, as necessary.

13. Remove the jackstands and carefully lower the vehicle, then check the steering linkage for proper operation.

Damper Assembly

The damper assembly is used to remove steering wheel vibration and vehicle wander; not all vehicles are equipped with it, though most 4WD vehicles should come with a damper assembly.

1. Raise and support the front frame of the vehicle safely using jackstands.

2. If equipped, remove the differential carrier shield.

3. Remove the damper assembly-to-relay rod cotter pin and nut.

4. Use a suitable universal steering linkage puller such as J-24319-01 or equivalent to separate the damper assembly from the relay rod.

5. Remove the cotter pin (if equipped) and the damper assembly-to-frame bracket nut/bolt, then disengage the damper assembly from the vehicle.

To install:

6. Install the damper assembly to the frame bracket, then secure using the retainers. Tighten the bolt/nut to 26 ft. lbs. (35 Nm) on 1994 models and 44 ft. lbs. (60 Nm) on 1995–99 models. If equipped, install a new cotter pin.

7. Position the damper assembly to the relay rod. Use a steering linkage installer such as J-29193 (12mm), J-29194 (14mm) or equivalent (as applicable), install the correct one onto the stud and tighten it to 40 ft. lbs. (54 Nm) to seat the taper.

8. Remove the installation tool, then install retaining nut and tighten to 45 ft. lbs. (62 Nm). Install a new cotter pin.

9. If removed, install the differential carrier shield.

10. Remove the jackstands and carefully lower the vehicle.

Manual Steering Gear

The recirculating ball type manual steering gear found on most of vehicles covered by this manual is manufactured by Saginaw and is equipped with a mechanical ratio of 24:1.

REMOVAL & INSTALLATION

▶ **See Figure 111**

1. Disconnect the negative battery cable.

2. Raise and safely support the front of the vehicle using jackstands under the frame. Turn the wheels so they are facing in the straight ahead position.

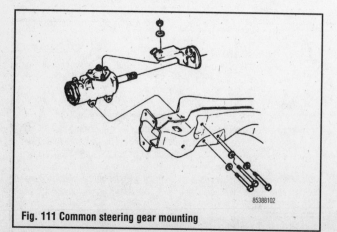

85388102

Fig. 111 Common steering gear mounting

3. If equipped, remove the retainers and the shield from the base of the intermediate shaft.

4. Matchmark the intermediate shaft-to-steering gear connection in order to assure proper installation.

5. Remove the intermediate shaft-to-steering gear pinch bolt.

6. Matchmark and remove the pitman arm from the pitman shaft. For details, please refer to the procedure located earlier in this section. It may be easier to save this step for later as access to the pitman arm/shaft may be difficult unless the gear is loosened or removed.

➡ **When separating the pitman arm from the shaft, DO NOT use a hammer or apply heat to the arm.**

7. Unfasten the steering gear-to-frame mounting bolts and washers, then remove the gear from the vehicle.

8. If not done already and, if necessary, remove the pitman shaft from the gear at this time.

To install:

9. If necessary, align and install the pitman shaft to the gear.

10. Position the steering gear to the frame and secure by threading the retaining bolts. On some late model vehicles, if not done already, it will be necessary to align and install the pitman arm to the shaft at this time.

11. Install the gear retaining bolts and tighten to 55 ft. lbs. (75 Nm).

➡ **When installing the steering gear, be sure that the intermediate shaft bottoms on the worm shaft, so that the pinch bolt passes through the undercut on the worm shaft. Check and/or adjust the alignment of the pitman arm-to-pitman shaft.**

12. Align and install the intermediate shaft coupling using the pinch bolt. Tighten the bolt to 30 ft. lbs. (41 Nm).

13. If not done already, align and install the pitman arm to the shaft. Refer to the procedure earlier in this section for details.

14. If applicable, install the coupling shield over the intermediate shaft-to-gear coupling.

15. Remove the jackstands and carefully lower the vehicle.

16. Connect the negative battery cable.

Power Steering Gear

The recirculating ball type power steering gear used on these vehicles is basically the same as the manual steering gear, except that it uses a hydraulic assist on the rack piston.

The power steering gear control valve directs the power steering fluid to either side of the rack piston, which rides up and down the worm shaft. The steering rack converts the hydraulic pressure into mechanical force. Should the vehicle loose the hydraulic pressure, it can still be controlled mechanically.

REMOVAL & INSTALLATION

1. Raise and support the front of the vehicle safely using jackstands.

2. Position a fluid catch pan under the power steering gear.

3. Disconnect the feed and return fluid hoses from the steering gear. Immediately cap or plug all openings to prevent system contamination or excessive fluid loss.

➡ **Be sure to plug the pressure hoses and the openings of the power steering pump to keep dirt out of the system.**

4. If equipped, remove the intermediate shaft lower coupling shield.

5. Remove the intermediate shaft-to-steering gear bolt. Matchmark the intermediate shaft-to-power steering gear and separate the shaft from the gear.

6. Matchmark and remove the pitman arm from the gear pitman shaft. For details, please refer to the procedure earlier in this section.

7. Remove the power steering gear-to-frame bolts and washers, then carefully remove the steering gear from the vehicle.

To install:

8. Position the steering gear to the vehicle and secure by finger-tightening the fasteners. For some vehicles, the pitman arm must be connected to the gear while it is still removed from the vehicle or while it is partially installed and lowered for access. If necessary, align and install the pitman arm to the shaft at this time.

9. Tighten the power steering gear-to-frame bolts to 55 ft. lbs. (75 Nm).

10. Align and install the intermediate shaft to the power steering, then secure using the pinch bolt.

11. If equipped, install the shield over the intermediate shaft lower coupling.

12. Remove the caps, then connect the feed and return hoses to the power steering gear. Refill the pump reservoir.

13. Remove the jackstands and carefully lower the vehicle.

14. Properly bleed the power steering system.

15. Road test the vehicle.

Power Steering Pump

▶ See Figure 112

Two types of power steering pumps are commonly found on these vehicles; the submerged and the non-submerged types. The submerged pump has a housing and internal parts which are inside the reservoir and operate submerged in oil. The non-submerged pump functions the same as the submerged pump except the reservoir is separate from the housing and internal parts.

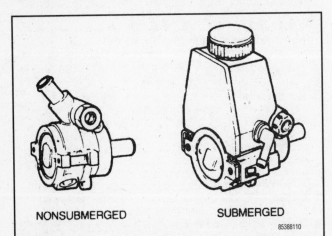

NONSUBMERGED   SUBMERGED

Fig. 112 Two types of power steering pumps are commonly found on these vehicles

REMOVAL & INSTALLATION

▶ See Figures 113, 114 and 115

1. Position a fluid catch pan under the power steering pump.

2. Disconnect the feed and return hoses from the power steering pump, then drain the excess fluid into the catch pan.

➡ On models equipped with a remote fluid reservoir, disconnect and plug the hose(s) in order to prevent system contamination or excessive fluid loss.

3. Remove the drive belt from the pulley.

4. Install a puller tool such as J-25034, or equivalent onto the power steering pump pulley. While holding the pilot bolt, turn the tool nut counterclockwise in order to press the drive pulley from the pump.

➡ When installing the puller tool onto the power steering pump pulley, be sure that the pilot bolt bottoms in the pump shaft by turning the head of the pilot bolt.

5. On most models, it may be necessary to unplug the electrical connection from the A/C compressor, unfasten the compressor mounting bolts and set the compressor to one side without disconnecting the lines.

6. If equipped, unfasten the power steering filler tube bolt and remove the filler tube.

7. Remove the rear brace retainers and the brace.

8. Remove the power steering pump-to-bracket bolts and then remove the pump from the vehicle.

To install:

9. Position the pump to the vehicle and secure using the front retaining bolts to 22 ft. lbs. (30 Nm) 2.2L engines. (50 Nm). On 4.3L engines tighten the bolts to 37 ft. lbs. (50 Nm).

10. If equipped, install the rear brace and tighten the retainers to 22 ft. lbs. (30 Nm) on 1994–98 2.2L engines. On 1999 2.2L engines, tighten the brace retainers to 37 ft. lbs. On 1994 4.3L models tighten the retainers to 24 ft. lbs. (33 Nm). On 1995–99 4.3L models, tighten the retainers to 31 ft. lbs. (41 Nm).

11. If removed, install the A/C compressor.

12. If removed, install the filler tube and its retainer. Tighten the retainer to 15 ft. lbs. (20 Nm).

13. Use a pulley installer such as J-25033 or equivalent to press the drive pulley onto the power steering pump. While holding the pilot bolt, turn the tool nut clockwise in order to press the drive pulley onto the pump. Check that the pulley is flush within 0.010 in. (0.25mm) of the shaft end.

➡ When positioning the installer tool onto the power steering pump pulley, be sure that the pilot bolt bottoms in the pump shaft by turning the head of the pilot bolt.

14. Properly install the drive belt and, if applicable, adjust the tension.

➡ Be sure to secure any hoses which may get in the way or rub other components.

15. Remove the caps, then connect the feed and return hoses to the pump.

16. Properly refill and bleed the power steering system.

17. Test drive the vehicle.

SYSTEM BLEEDING

1994 Models

1. Add fluid to the reservoir until the proper level is reached, then allow the fluid to settle for at least 2 minutes. Start the engine and let it run for a few seconds, then turn it off and check if the level has changed. Repeat this until the level remains constant.

2. Raise and support the front of the vehicle safely using jackstands under the frame to the wheels are free to turn.

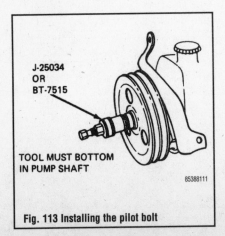

J-25034
OR
BT-7515

TOOL MUST BOTTOM
IN PUMP SHAFT

Fig. 113 Installing the pilot bolt

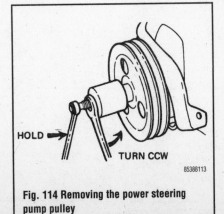

HOLD ▶   TURN CCW

Fig. 114 Removing the power steering pump pulley

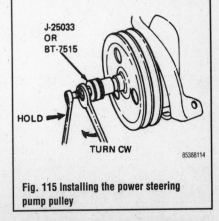

J-25033
OR
BT-7515

HOLD ▶   TURN CW

Fig. 115 Installing the power steering pump pulley

3. Start and run the engine, then slowly turn the wheels in both directions (lightly hitting the stops) several times.

4. Stop the engine and check the fluid level. If necessary, add power steering fluid to obtain the level indicated on the reservoir.

➡**Maintain the fluid level just above the internal pump casting. Fluid with air in it will have a light tan or milky appearance. This air must be eliminated from the fluid before normal steering action can be obtained.**

5. Remove the jackstands and carefully lower the vehicle.

6. Start and run the engine while turning the wheel slowly from stop to stop.

7. Stop the engine and check the fluid level. If necessary, add fluid in order to obtain the proper indicated level.

8. If the fluid is extremely foamy, allow the vehicle to stand for a few minutes, then repeat the procedure through this step.

9. Road test the vehicle to make sure the steering functions normally and is free from noise.

10. Allow the vehicle to stand for 2–3 hours, then recheck the power steering fluid.

1995–98 Models

1. Turn the ignition **OFF**, then turn the wheel to the full left position.

2. Fill the reservoir to the **FULL COLD** level and leave the cap off.

3. Raise the front of the vehicle and support it with jackstands.

4. With the ignition still in the **OFF** position, turn the wheel lock-to-lock at least 20 times (on models with long return lines perform this procedure at least 40 times).

5. Ensure that the fluid level remains at the **FULL COLD** position. and that there is no spilled fluid or air bubbles that could indicate a loose connection or leaking O-ring seal.

6. Turn the ignition **ON** and with the engine idling check the fluid level. If the level is correct install the cap.

7. Return the wheels to the center position and lower the vehicle.

8. With the engine still running turn the wheel from side-to-side. If there is a smooth, noiseless and leak free operation the procedure is complete.

9. If there is a problem, check that the fluid is free of bubbles and that the O-rings and clamps are in good condition. If not replace the worn or damaged part(s) and repeat the bleeding procedure.

1999 Models

◆ **See Figure 116**

A Mity Vac and power steering bleeder adapter J 43485 are required to perform the bleeding procedure. Make sure none of the power steering hoses are touching any part of the vehicle and that all connections are tight.

1. Remove the power steering pump reservoir cap.

2. Fill the reservoir to the **FULL COLD** level and leave the cap off.

3. Attach the bleeder adapter to the Mity Vac, then position the adapter to the reservoir cap opening.

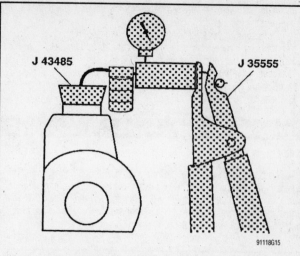

Fig. 116 Attach the bleeder adapter and Mity vac to the power steering pump as shown and apply 20 in. Hg. (67 kPa) vacuum

4. Apply 20 in. Hg. (67 kPa) and wait five minutes. The typical vacuum drop over this time period is 2–3 in. Hg. (6–10 k Pa).

5. If there is a bigger vacuum drop, perform the following procedure:

a. Disconnect the pressure and return hoses from the pump.

b. Install the two plugs that were supplied with the bleeder adapter kit into the hose ports on the pump.

c. Apply 20 in. Hg. (67 kPa) and wait five minutes. If the vacuum drops again, repair or replace the pump.

6. Remove the adapter and reinstall the reservoir cap.

7. Start the engine and allow it to idle, then turn the engine off and check the fluid level.

8. If the fluid level is low, bring it to the proper level and repeat steps 3 through 6 until the fluid level stabilizes.

9. Start the engine and allow it to idle.

➡**Do not turn the steering wheel lock-to-lock.**

10. Turn the steering wheel 180–360 degrees in both directions five times.

11. Turn the engine off and check the fluid level.

12. Remove the power steering pump reservoir cap.

13. Attach the bleeder adapter to the Mity Vac, then position the adapter to the reservoir cap opening.

14. Apply 20 in. Hg. (67 kPa) of vacuum and wait five minutes.

15. Make sure the fluid level is correct and reinstall the reservoir cap.

TORQUE SPECIFICATIONS

Components	Ft. Lbs.	Nm
Wheels		
Lug nuts		
1994-97 models	95	130
1998-99 models	103	140
Front Suspension		
Torsion bar		
1994 models		
Insulator mounting retainers		
Bolts	26	35
Nuts	25	34
Except 1994 models		
Upper link mount nut		
1995-96 models	33	45
1997-99 models	48	65
Lower link mount nut		
1995 models	13	18
1996-98 models	50	68
1999 models	37	50
Shock absorbers		
2WD models		
Upper shock absorber nut		
1994 models	100 inch lbs.	11
1995 models	145 inch lbs.	16
1996 models	54	73
1997-99 models	106 inch lbs.	12
Shock absorber-to-lower control arm retaining bolts		
1994-95 models	20	27
1996 models	54	73
1997-99 models	23	30
4WD models		
Upper and lower retaining bolts/nuts	54	73
Ball joints		
2WD models		
Upper ball joint		
Ball joint retainers	17	23
Ball joint stud nut	61	83
Lower ball joint		
Ball joint stud nut		
1994 models	83	113
1995-99 models	79	108

91118C01

TORQUE SPECIFICATIONS

Components	Ft. Lbs.	Nm
Front Suspension (cont.)		
Ball joints (cont.)		
4WD models		
Ball joint retainers	17	23
Ball joint stud nut		
1994 models	70	95
1995-97 models	79	108
Lower nut	61	83
Upper nut		
Stabilizer bar		
2WD models		
Bracket bolts		
1994-96 models	24	33
1997-99 models	26	36
Link bolt	13	17
4WD models		
Clamp-to-control arm bolts		
1994-95 models	24	33
1996 models	124 inch lbs.	14
1997-99 models	11	15
Frame clamps-to-insulators/frame		
Bolts/nuts		
1994-95 models	35	48
1996-99 models	48	65
Upper control arm and bushing		
2WD models		
Bushing nuts	85	115
Control arm-to-frame bolts/nuts		
1994-95 models	67	90
1996-99 models	85	115
4WD models		
Bumper nut	20	27
1994 models		
End nuts	70	95
1996-99 models	85	115
Lower control arm and bushing		
2WD models		
Jam nuts		
1994 models	67	90
1995-99 models		
Front nut	85	115
Rear nut	72	98

91118C02

TORQUE SPECIFICATIONS

Components	Ft. Lbs.	Nm
Front Suspension (cont.)		
Lower control arm and bushing (cont.)		
4WD models		
Lower control arm and bushing		
Lower control arm nuts		
1994 models	70	95
1995-99 models	81	110
Steering knuckle and spindle		
4WD models	77	105
Hub and bearing bolts		
Halfshaft nut		
1994-96 models	180	245
1997-99 models	103	140
Rear Suspension		
Leaf springs		
U-bolt nuts		
1994 models		
First pass	18	25
Final pass	85	115
1995-99 models		
First pass	18	25
Final pass	73	100
Front and rear spring mounting fasteners		
1994-95 models	92	125
1996-99 models	89	122
Shock absorbers		
1994 models		
Upper shock absorber retainers	17	23
Lower shock absorber retainer	47	64
1995 models		
Upper shock absorber retainers	22	30
Lower shock absorber retainer	73	100
1996-98 models		
Upper shock absorber retainers	22	30
Lower shock absorber retainer	62	84
1999 models		
Upper shock absorber retainers	18	25
Lower shock absorber retainer		
Pick-up and two door utility models	62	84
Four door pick-up models	74	100

91118C03

TORQUE SPECIFICATIONS

Components	Ft. Lbs.	Nm
Rear Suspension		
Sway bar		
1994 models		
Sway bar-to-link nut		
Two door utility models	50	68
Four door utility models	28	35
1995-97 models		
Upper link nuts	25	35
Lower link nuts	50	68
1998-99 models		
Upper link nuts	25	35
Track bar (tie rod)		
Axle bracket nut		
1994-96 models	84	115
1997-99 models	44	61
Frame bracket bolt		
1994-99 models	44	61
Steering		
Steering wheel		
Wheel retaining nut	30	40
Turn signal (combination) switch		
1994 models		
Switch retaining screws 30 inch lbs. 3.4	30 inch lbs.	3.4
Switch actuator arm screw	20 inch lbs.	2.3
1995-99 models		
Pan head tapping screws	53 inch lbs.	6
Upper steering column cover		
Torx head screws	12 inch lbs.	1.4
Ignition switch		
1994 models		
Ignition switch retainers	35 inch lbs.	4
1995-99 models		
Switch screws	12 inch lbs.	1.4
Lock cylinder		
1994 models		
Steering column		
Nuts	22	29
Bolts	20	27
Lock cylinder screw		
Tilt columns	22 inch lbs.	2.5
Standard non-tilt columns	40 inch lbs.	4.5

91118C04

TORQUE SPECIFICATIONS

Components	Ft. Lbs.	Nm
Steering (cont.)		
Steering linkage		
Pitman arm		
2WD models		
Pitman shaft nut	185	250
Pitman arm-to-relay rod nut	60	82
4WD models		
Pitman shaft nut	185	250
Pitman arm-to-relay rod nut		
1994-96 models	60	82
1997-99 models	79	108
Idler arm		
Idler arm-to-frame bolts		
1994 models	60	82
1995-99 models	79	108
Relay rod-to-idler arm nut		
2WD models	35	47
4WD models	60	82
Relay rod (centerlink)		
Relay rod-to-idler arm nut		
2WD models	35	47
4WD models	60	82
Pitman arm-to-idler arm nut		
2WD models	35	47
4WD models	60	82
Tie rod		
Adjuster tube clamp bolt	14	19
Inner and/or outer tie rod end nuts		
1994 models	35	47
1995-99 models		
Inner nut	35	47
Outer nut	39	53
Damper assembly		
Damper assembly-to-frame bracket retainers		
1994 models	26	35
1995-99 models	44	60
Damper assembly-to-relay rod nut	45	62
Manual steering gear		
Gear retaining bolts	55	75
Intermediate shaft coupling pinch bolt	30	41

91118C05

TORQUE SPECIFICATIONS

Components	Ft. Lbs.	Nm
Power steering gear		
Power steering gear-to-frame bolts	55	75
Power steering pump		
Pump retaining bolts		
2.2L engines	20	30
4.3L engines	37	50
Rear brace retainers		
2.2L engines		
1994-98 models	22	30
1999 models	37	50
4.3L engines		
1994 models	24	33
1995-99 models	31	41
Filler tube retainer	15	20

91118C06

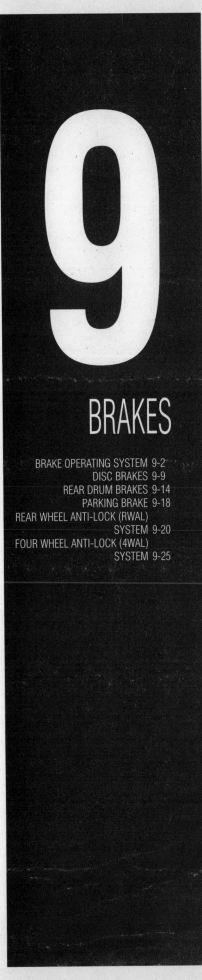

9

BRAKES

BRAKE OPERATING SYSTEM

Brake Light Switch

REMOVAL & INSTALLATION

Except 1994 Utility Models

▶ See Figure 1

1. Disconnect the negative battery cable.
2. Unplug the switch electrical connector.
3. Disengage the retainer from the brake pedal pin, then remove the switch by unsnapping it from the pushrod.

To install:

4. Install the switch by snapping it onto the pushrod, then secure using the retainer on the pedal pin.
5. Attach the switch connector.
6. Connect the negative battery cable and verify proper switch operation.

1994 Utility Models

▶ See Figure 2

1. Disconnect the negative battery cable.
2. Remove the lower trim panel to allow clearance to access the switch.
3. Unplug the switch electrical connector.
4. Remove the switch by pulling it from its retainer and then remove the retainer from the pedal assembly.

To install:

5. Install the switch retainer, then push the switch into the retainer.
6. Adjust the switch as follows:

a. Apply the brake pedal and press the switch until it is fully seated in the retainer. A number of clicks should be heard as the threaded part of the switch is pushed into the retainer.
b. Pull the pedal against the pedal stop until no more clicks are heard.
7. Attach the switch connector.
8. Install the trim panel.
9. Connect the negative battery cable and verify proper switch operation.

Master Cylinder

REMOVAL & INSTALLATION

▶ See Figures 3, 4, 5, 6 and 7

➡A scan tool is absolutely necessary to bleed the brake hydraulic system on models equipped with an Anti-lock Brake System (ABS). If your vehicle is equipped with ABS, be sure to refer to the ABS bleeding procedures in this section before performing any work on your vehicle's brake hydraulic system.

✳✳ WARNING

Clean, high quality brake fluid is essential to the safe and proper operation of the brake system. You should always buy the highest quality brake fluid that is available. If the brake fluid becomes contaminated, drain and flush the system, then refill the master cylinder with new fluid. Never reuse any brake fluid. Any brake fluid that is removed from the system should be discarded.

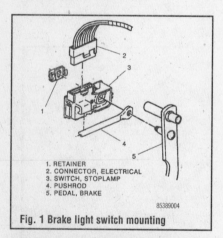

1. RETAINER
2. CONNECTOR, ELECTRICAL
3. SWITCH, STOPLAMP
4. PUSHROD
5. PEDAL, BRAKE

85389004

Fig. 1 Brake light switch mounting

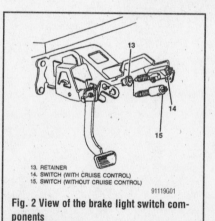

13. RETAINER
14. SWITCH (WITH CRUISE CONTROL)
15. SWITCH (WITHOUT CRUISE CONTROL)

91119G01

Fig. 2 View of the brake light switch components

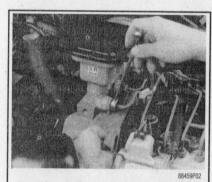

88459P02

Fig. 3 Place a rag under the line wrench to help minimize spillage when disconnecting the brake lines

88459P03

Fig. 4 Once the line nut is loosened, carefully pull the fitting away from the master cylinder

88459P04

Fig. 5 Once the lines are disconnected and plugged, loosen and remove the master cylinder retaining nuts

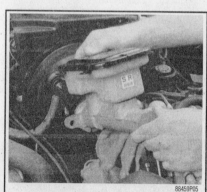

88459P05

Fig. 6 Carefully pull the master cylinder from the mounting studs

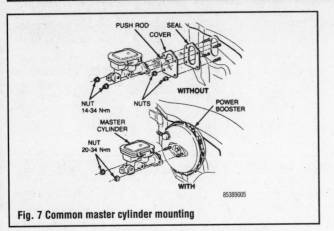

Fig. 7 Common master cylinder mounting

1. Apply the parking brakes and block the drive wheels.
2. Use a line wrench to loosen and disconnect the hydraulic lines from the master cylinder. Immediately plug the lines to prevent system contamination or excessive fluid loss.
3. If equipped with non-power brakes, disconnect the pushrod from the brake pedal.
4. Remove the master cylinder attachment nuts, then separate the combination valve/bracket from the master cylinder.
5. Remove the master cylinder and, as equipped, the gasket and/or rubber boot from the vehicle.

To install:

6. In order to ease installation, bench bleed the master cylinder before installation:
   a. Plug the master cylinder outlet ports. This can be done using rubber or plastic plugs or, more effectively, using a single length of brake line with appropriately sized flares/flare nuts on each end.
   b. Mount the cylinder in a soft-jawed vise with the front end tilted slightly downward.
   c. Fill the reservoir with clean brake fluid, then use a tool with a smooth rounded end (such as a wooden dowel or pencil eraser) to stroke the primary piston about 1 in. (25mm) several times. As air is bled from the cylinder, the primary piston will no longer travel the full distance.
   d. Reposition the master cylinder in the vise with the front end tilted slightly up, then continue stroking the primary piston to further bleed air.
   e. Reposition the master cylinder so it is level, then loosen the plugs one at a time and push the piston into the bore forcing air from the cylinder. DO NOT allow the piston to return with the plugs loosened or air will be drawn back into the master cylinder.
   f. Make sure the plugs are tightly sealed, then check and refill the reservoir.
7. Position the master cylinder to the cowl or brake booster (as applicable), then reposition the combination valve bracket over the studs.
8. Install the master cylinder/combination valve bracket retaining nuts and tighten to 20 ft. lbs. (27 Nm) on 1994 models and 27 ft. lbs. (36 Nm) on 1995–99 models.
9. Working on one line at a time, remove the plugs and quickly connect the brake lines to the master cylinder. Tighten each of the line nuts to 20–22 ft. lbs. (27–30 Nm).

➡ **If equipped with manual brakes, be sure to reconnect the pushrod to the brake pedal.**

10. Refill the master cylinder with clean brake fluid, then properly bleed the hydraulic brake system and check the brake pedal travel.
11. When all service is finished, remove the blocks from the drive wheels.

Power Brake Booster

The power brake booster is a tandem vacuum suspended unit. Some models may be equipped with a single or dual function vacuum switch which activates a brake warning light should low booster vacuum be present. Under normal operation, vacuum is present on both sides of the diaphragms. When the brakes are applied, atmospheric air is admitted to one side of the diaphragms to provide power assistance.

REMOVAL & INSTALLATION

1994–97 Models

▶ **See Figures 8 and 9**

1. Apply the parking brake and block the drive wheels.
2. Remove the master cylinder-to-power brake booster nuts, then reposition the master cylinder and combination valve out of the way; if necessary, support the master cylinder on a wire to prevent damaging the brake lines.

➡ **When removing the master cylinder from the power brake booster, it is not necessary to disconnect the hydraulic lines, therefore the brake system should not have to be bled.**

3. Disconnect the vacuum hose from the power brake booster.
4. From under the dash, remove the retainer and washer from the brake pedal on 1994 utility models. On all other models, remove the retainer and brake switch from the brake pedal.
5. Disconnect the pushrod from the brake pedal.
6. From under the dash, remove the power brake booster-to-cowl retaining nuts.
7. Back under the hood, remove the power brake booster and the gasket from the cowl.

To install:

8. Position the booster to the cowl using a new gasket.
9. Install the booster retaining nuts and tighten to 16 ft. lbs. (22 Nm) 1994 utility models, 24 ft. lbs. (32 Nm) on 1994 pick-up models and 27 ft. lbs. (36 Nm) on all 1995–97 models.
10. Connect the pedal pushrod and install the washer or switch and the retainer.
11. Connect the vacuum hose.
12. For all vehicles covered in this manual, gauge the booster rod:
   a. Apply 25 in. Hg (85 kPa) of vacuum using a hand held vacuum pump or apply maximum engine vacuum.
   b. Check the maximum and minimum rod lengths using J-37839 or an equivalent pushrod height gauge.

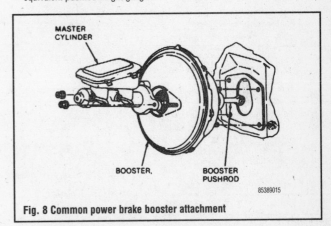

Fig. 8 Common power brake booster attachment

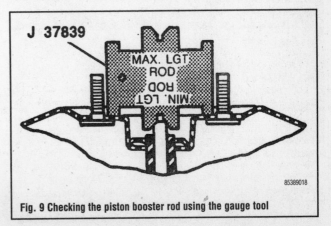

Fig. 9 Checking the piston booster rod using the gauge tool

c. If the piston is not within limits, install a service adjustable piston rod and adjust it to the correct length.

13. Reposition the master cylinder and combination valve bracket to the booster studs, then secure using the retaining nuts. For details, please refer to the master cylinder procedure located earlier in this section.

14. Start and run the engine, then check for proper booster operation.

1998–99 Models

▶ See Figure 9

1. Apply the parking brake and block the drive wheels.
2. Remove the master cylinder-to-power brake booster nuts, then reposition the master cylinder and combination valve out of the way; if necessary, support the master cylinder on a wire to prevent damaging the brake lines.

➡When removing the master cylinder from the power brake booster, it is not necessary to disconnect the hydraulic lines, therefore the brake system should not have to be bled.

3. Disconnect the vacuum hose from the power brake booster.
4. From under the dash, remove the retainer and brake switch from the brake pedal.
5. Remove the magnesium beam as follows:
   a. Remove the instrument panel as outlined in Section 8 of this manual.
   b. Disconnect the pushrod from the brake pedal.
   c. Unfasten the four large flange nuts and the two bolts retaining the magnesium beam.
   d. Unfasten the brake pedal bolts, remove the bushings and the spacer, and then separate the pedal from the magnesium beam.
6. From under the dash, remove the power brake booster-to-cowl retaining nuts.
7. Back under the hood, remove the power brake booster and the gasket from the cowl.

To install:

8. Position the booster to the cowl using a new gasket.
9. Install the booster retaining nuts and tighten to 30 ft. lbs. (40 Nm).
10. Install the magnesium beam as follows:
    a. Install the brake pedal bushings into the brake pedal and position the pedal onto the beam. Install the pedal retainer and tighten to 19 ft. lbs. (25 Nm).
    b. Place the beam into position and tighten the nuts and bolts to 18 ft. lbs. (25 Nm).
11. Connect the pedal pushrod and install the switch and the retainer.
12. Connect the vacuum hose.
13. For all vehicles covered in this manual, gauge the booster rod:
    a. Apply 25 in. Hg (85 kPa) of vacuum using a hand held vacuum pump or apply maximum engine vacuum.
    b. Check the maximum and minimum rod lengths using J-37839 or an equivalent pushrod height gauge.
    c. If the piston is not within limits, install a service adjustable piston rod and adjust it to the correct length.
14. Reposition the master cylinder and combination valve bracket to the booster studs, then secure using the retaining nuts. For details, please refer to the master cylinder procedure located earlier in this section.
15. Start and run the engine, then check for proper booster operation.

Combination Valve

▶ See Figure 10

The combination valve is located in the engine compartment, directly under the master cylinder. It is usually mounted to a bracket, which shares the master cylinder mounting studs on the brake booster. The valve consists of three sections: the metering valve, the warning switch and the proportioning valve.

The metering section limits the pressure to the front disc brakes until a predetermined front input pressure is reached. The specific pressure is enough to overcome the rear shoe retractor springs. Under 30 psi (200 kPa), there are no restrictions of the inlet pressures; this way pressures are allowed to equalize during the no brake period.

The proportioning section controls the outlet pressure to the rear brakes after a predetermined rear input pressure has been reached; this feature is provided for vehicles with light loads, to help prevent rear wheel lock-up. The by-pass feature of this valve assures full system pressure to the rear brakes in the event

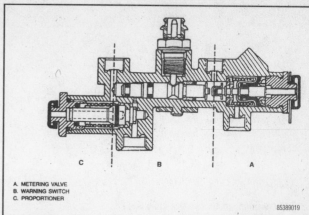

A. METERING VALVE
B. WARNING SWITCH
C. PROPORTIONER

85389019

Fig. 10 Cross-sectional view of a combination valve assembly

of a front brake system malfunction. Also, full front pressure is retained if the rear system malfunctions.

The pressure differential warning switch is designed to constantly compare the front and the rear brake pressures; if one circuit should malfunction, the warning light (on the dash) will turn on. The valve and switch are designed to lock in the warning position once the malfunction has occurred. The only way the light can be turned off is to repair the malfunction and apply a brake line force of 450 psi (3100 kPa).

REMOVAL & INSTALLATION

1994–95 Models

▶ See Figure 11

➡A scan tool is absolutely necessary to bleed the brake hydraulic system on models equipped with an Anti-lock Brake System (ABS). If your vehicle is equipped with ABS, be sure to refer to the ABS bleeding procedures in this section before performing any work on your vehicle's brake hydraulic system.

1. Disconnect the negative battery cable.
2. Disconnect the hydraulic lines from the combination valve one at a time. Immediately plug all openings to prevent system contamination or excessive fluid loss.
3. Unplug the electrical connector from the combination valve pressure switch.
4. If equipped with Rear Wheel Anti-Lock (RWAL) brakes, unplug the RWAL pressure valve connector.
5. On most vehicles, remove the master cylinder/combination valve-to-bracket retaining nuts, then remove the valve from the vehicle. On some early model vehicles the combination valve may be removed from the bracket by removing the retaining bolt. If desired, remove the bolt and valve leaving the bracket and master cylinder secured to the booster.
6. If used, remove the RWAL pressure valve.

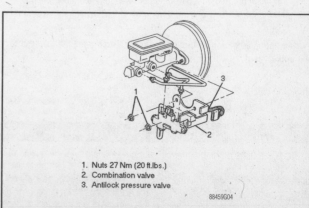

1. Nuts 27 Nm (20 ft.lbs.)
2. Combination valve
3. Antilock pressure valve

88459G04

Fig. 11 View of the combination valve mounting (RWAL)

➡The combination valve is not repairable and must be replaced as a complete assembly.

To install:

7. If applicable, install the RWAL pressure valve.

8. Install the combination valve and bracket assembly, then install and tighten the master cylinder/valve bracket retaining nuts to specification. For details, please refer to the master cylinder procedure located earlier in this section.

9. If used, attach the RWAL pressure valve connector.

10. Engage the pressure switch electrical connector.

11. Remove the caps (one at a time) and connect the brake lines to the combination valve, then tighten the fittings.

12. Check and refill the master cylinder reservoir, then properly bleed the hydraulic brake system.

1996–97 Models

▶ See Figure 12

➡A scan tool is absolutely necessary to bleed the brake hydraulic system on models equipped with an Anti-lock Brake System (ABS). If your vehicle is equipped with ABS, be sure to refer to the ABS bleeding procedures in this section before performing any work on your vehicle's brake hydraulic system.

1. Disconnect the hydraulic lines from the combination valve one at a time. Immediately plug all openings to prevent system contamination or excessive fluid loss.

2. Unplug the electrical connector from the combination valve pressure switch.

3. Unfasten the combination valve retaining nuts and remove the valve.

To install:

4. Install the combination valve and tighten the retaining nuts to 27 ft. lbs. (36 Nm).

5. Attach the combination valve pressure switch electrical connector.

6. Connect the hydraulic lines to the combination valve and tighten the fittings to 21 ft. lbs. (29 Nm).

7. Bleed the brake system as outlined later in this section.

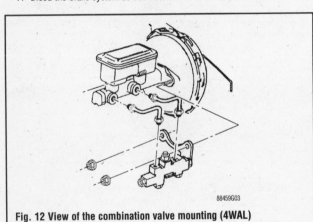

Fig. 12 View of the combination valve mounting (4WAL)

1998–99 Models

▶ See Figure 13

➡A scan tool is absolutely necessary to bleed the brake hydraulic system on models equipped with an Anti-lock Brake System (ABS). If your vehicle is equipped with ABS, be sure to refer to the ABS bleeding procedures in this section before performing any work on your vehicle's brake hydraulic system.

➡Prior to replacing the combination valve, note the identification code on the valve. You must have the proper code when replacing the valve so that you can replace it with the correct replacement part.

1. Refer to the accompanying illustration when performing this procedure.

2. Disconnect the negative batter cable.

3. Unplug the valve electrical connection (10).

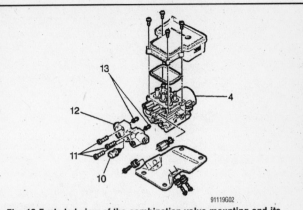

Fig. 13 Exploded view of the combination valve mounting and its related components

4. Disconnect the front and rear brake pipes from the valve. Immediately plug all openings to prevent system contamination or excessive fluid loss.

5. Unfasten the three Allen head bolts (11) which attach the combination valve to the (BPMV) Brake Pressure Modulator Valve (12).

6. Separate the combination valve from the BPMV (4).

7. Remove the two transfer tubes (13).

➡Do not reuse the transfer tubes. Always install new ones.

To install:

8. Check that new combination valve has the same code as the old one.

9. Install two new transfer tubes (13) into the new valve (12) until they are fully seated.

10. Attach the valve to the BPMV (4).

11. Install the Allen head bolts and tighten them to 6 ft. lbs. (8 Nm).

12. Remove the caps from the brake lines and attach them to the valve. Tighten the line fittings to 18 ft. lbs. (24 Nm).

13. Attach the valve electrical connection.

14. Connect the negative battery cable.

15. Bleed the brake system. Refer to the ABS brake bleeding procedure outlined later in this section.

Brake Hoses and Lines

▶ See Figures 14, 15 and 16

Metal lines and rubber brake hoses should be checked frequently for leaks and external damage. Metal lines are particularly prone to crushing and kinking under the vehicle. Any such deformation can restrict the proper flow of fluid and therefore impair braking at the wheels. Rubber hoses should be checked for cracking or scraping; such damage can create a weak spot in the hose and it could fail under pressure.

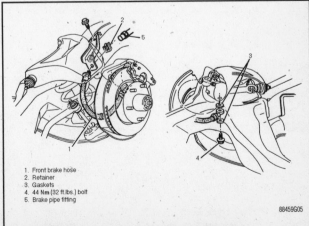

1. Front brake hose
2. Retainer
3. Gaskets
4. 44 Nm (32 ft.lbs.) bolt
5. Brake pipe fitting

Fig. 14 Common front brake hose routing—2WD models

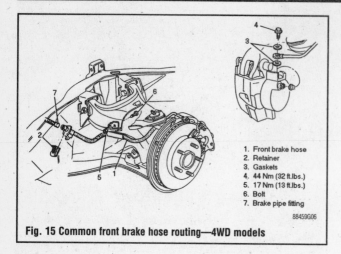

Fig. 15 Common front brake hose routing—4WD models

1. Front brake hose
2. Retainer
3. Gaskets
4. 44 Nm (32 ft.lbs.)
5. 17 Nm (13 ft.lbs.)
6. Bolt
7. Brake pipe fitting

88459G06

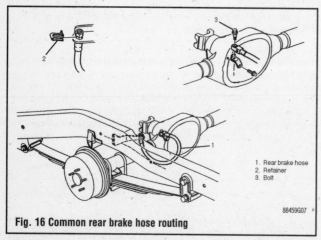

Fig. 16 Common rear brake hose routing

1. Rear brake hose
2. Retainer
3. Bolt

88459G07

Any time the lines are removed or disconnected, extreme cleanliness must be observed. Clean all joints and connections before disassembly (use a stiff bristle brush and clean brake fluid); be sure to plug the lines and ports as soon as they are opened. New lines and hoses should be flushed clean with brake fluid before installation to remove any contamination.

REMOVAL & INSTALLATION

♦ See Figures 17, 18, 19 and 20

➡A scan tool is absolutely necessary to bleed the brake hydraulic system on models equipped with an Anti-lock Brake System (ABS). If your vehicle is equipped with ABS, be sure to refer to the ABS bleeding procedures in this section before performing any work on your vehicle's brake hydraulic system.

1. Disconnect the negative battery cable.
2. Raise and safely support the vehicle on jackstands.
3. Remove any wheel and tire assemblies necessary for access to the particular line you are removing.
4. Thoroughly clean the surrounding area at the joints to be disconnected.
5. Place a suitable catch pan under the joint to be disconnected.
6. Using two wrenches (one to hold the joint and one to turn the fitting), disconnect the hose or line to be replaced.
7. Disconnect the other end of the line or hose, moving the drain pan if necessary. Always use a back-up wrench to avoid damaging the fitting.
8. Disconnect any retaining clips or brackets holding the line and remove the line from the vehicle.

➡If the brake system is to remain open for more time than it takes to swap lines, tape or plug each remaining clip and port to keep contaminants out and fluid in.

To install:

9. Install the new line or hose, starting with the end farthest from the master cylinder. Connect the other end, then confirm that both fittings are correctly threaded and turn smoothly using finger pressure. Make sure the new line will not rub against any other part. Brake lines must be at least 1/2 in. (13mm) from the steering column and other moving parts. Any protective shielding or insulators must be reinstalled in the original location.

❄❄ WARNING

Make sure the hose is NOT kinked or touching any part of the frame or suspension after installation. These conditions may cause the hose to fail prematurely.

10. Using two wrenches as before, tighten each fitting.
11. Install any retaining clips or brackets on the lines.
12. If removed, install the wheel and tire assemblies, then carefully lower the vehicle to the ground.

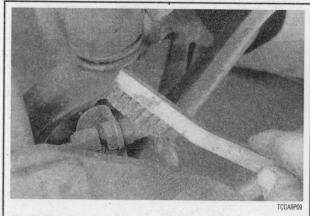

Fig. 17 Use a brush to clean the fittings of any debris

TCCA9P09

Fig. 18 Use two wrenches to loosen the fitting. If available, use flare nut type wrenches

TCCA9P10

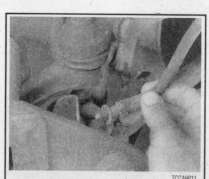

Fig. 19 Any gaskets/crush washers should be replaced with new ones during installation

TCCA9P11

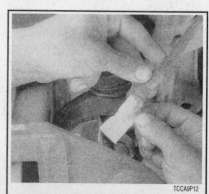

Fig. 20 Tape or plug the line to prevent contamination

TCCA9P12

13. Refill the brake master cylinder reservoir with clean, fresh brake fluid, meeting DOT 3 specifications. Properly bleed the brake system.

14. Connect the negative battery cable.

Bleeding the Hydraulic Brake System

➡A scan tool is absolutely necessary to bleed the brake hydraulic system on models equipped with an Anti-lock Brake System (ABS). If your vehicle is equipped with ABS, be sure to refer to the ABS bleeding procedures in this section before performing any work on your vehicle's brake hydraulic system.

This brake bleeding procedure is for models that are not equipped with ABS. If your vehicle is equipped with an ABS system, refer to the ABS bleeding procedure later in this section.

The hydraulic brake system must be bled any time one of the lines is disconnected or any time air enters the system. If a point in the system, such as a wheel cylinder or caliper brake line is the only point which was opened, the bleeder screws down stream in the hydraulic system are the only ones which must be bled. If however, the master cylinder fittings are opened, or if the reservoir level drops sufficiently that air is drawn into the system, air must be bled from the entire hydraulic system. If the brake pedal feels spongy upon application, and goes almost to the floor but regains height when pumped, air has entered the system. It must be bled out. If no fittings were recently opened for service, check for leaks that would have allowed the entry of air and repair them before attempting to bleed the system.

As a general rule, once the master cylinder is bled, the remainder of the hydraulic system should be bled starting at the furthest wheel from the master cylinder and working towards the nearest wheel. Therefore, the correct bleeding sequence is: master cylinder, , right rear wheel cylinder, left rear, right front caliper and left front. Most master cylinder assemblies on these vehicles are NOT equipped with bleeder valves, therefore air must be bled from the cylinders using the front brake pipe connections.

MANUAL BLEEDING

◆ See Figures 21 and 22

For those of us who are not fortunate enough to have access to a power bleeding, the manual brake bleeding procedure will quite adequately remove air from the hydraulic system. The major difference between the pressure and manual bleeding procedures is that the manual method takes more time and will require help from an assistant. One person must depress the brake pedal, while another opens and closes the bleeder screws.

Fig. 21 Position a bleeder wrench over the wheel cylinder bleeder screw (rear wheels)

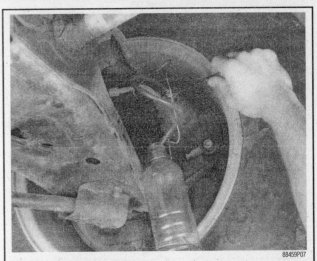

Fig. 22 Attach a hose to the screw and submerge the other end in a container of clean brake fluid

➡In addition to a length of clear neoprene bleeder hose, bleeder wrenches and a clear bleeder bottle (old glass jar or drink bottle will suffice), bleeding late-model ABS systems may also require the use of one or more relatively inexpensive combination valve pressure bleeding tools (which are used to depress one or more valves in order to allow component/system bleeding). To fully bleed the late model ABS systems, a scan tool should also be used to run the system through functional tests.

1. Clean the top of the master cylinder, remove the cover and fill the reservoirs with clean fluid. To prevent squirting fluid, and possibly damaging painted surfaces, install the cover during the procedure, but be sure to frequently check and top off the reservoirs with fresh fluid.

✳✳ WARNING

Never reuse brake fluid, which has been bled from the system.

2. The master cylinder must be bled first if it is suspected to contain air. If the master cylinder was removed and bench bled before installation it must still be bled, but it should take less time and effort. Bleed the master cylinder as follows:

a. Position a container under the master cylinder to catch the brake fluid.

✳✳ WARNING

Do not allow brake fluid to spill on or come in contact with the vehicle's finish as it will remove the paint. In case of a spill, immediately flush the area with water.

b. Loosen the front brake line at the master cylinder and allow the fluid to flow from the front port.

c. Have a friend depress the brake pedal slowly and hold (air and/or fluid should be expelled from the loose fitting). Tighten the line, then release the brake pedal and wait 15 seconds. Loosen the fitting and repeat until all air is removed from the master cylinder bore.

d. When finished, tighten the line fitting to 20 ft. lbs. (27 Nm).

e. Repeat the sequence at the master cylinder rear pipe fitting.

➡During the bleeding procedure, make sure your assistant does NOT release the brake pedal while a fitting is loosened or while a bleeder screw is opening. Air will be drawn back into the system.

3. Check and refill the master cylinder reservoir.

➡**Remember, if the reservoir is allowed to empty of fluid during the procedure, air will be drawn into the system and bleeding procedure must be restarted at the master cylinder assembly.**

4. On late model ABS equipped vehicles, perform the special ABS procedures as described later in this section. On 4 wheel ABS systems the Brake Pressure Modulator Valve (BPMV) must be bled (if it has been replaced or if it is suspected to contain air) and on most Rear Wheel Anti-Lock (RWAL) systems the combination valve must be held open. In both cases, special combination valve depressor tools should be used during bleeding and a scan tool must be used for ABS function tests.

5. If a single line or fitting was the only hydraulic line disconnected, then only the caliper(s) or wheel cylinder(s) affected by that line must be bled. If the master cylinder required bleeding, then all calipers and wheel cylinders must be bled in the proper sequence:
   a. Right rear
   b. Left rear
   c. Right front
   d. Left front
6. Bleed the individual calipers or wheel cylinders as follows:
   a. Place a suitable wrench over the bleeder screw and attach a clear plastic hose over the screw end. Be sure the hose is seated snugly on the screw or you may be squirted with brake fluid.

➡**Be very careful when bleeding wheel cylinders and brake calipers. The bleeder screws often rust in position and may easily break off if forced. Installing a new bleeder screw will often require removal of the component and may include overhaul or replacement of the wheel cylinder/caliper. To help prevent the possibility of breaking a bleeder screw, spray it with some penetrating oil before attempting to loosen it.**

   b. Submerge the other end of the tube in a transparent container of clean brake fluid.
   c. Loosen the bleed screw, then have a friend apply the brake pedal slowly and hold. Tighten the bleed screw to 62 inch lbs. (7 Nm), release the brake pedal and wait 15 seconds. Repeat the sequence (including the 15 second pause) until all air is expelled from the caliper or cylinder.
   d. Tighten the bleed screw to 62 inch lbs. (7 Nm) when finished.
7. Check the pedal for a hard feeling with the engine not running. If the pedal is soft, repeat the bleeding procedure until a firm pedal is obtained.
8. If the brake warning light is on, depress the brake pedal firmly. If there is no air in the system, the light will go out.
9. After bleeding, make sure that a firm pedal is achieved before attempting to move the vehicle.

Pressure Bleeding

▶ **See Figures 23 and 24**

For the lucky ones with access to a pressure bleeding tool, this procedure may be used to quickly and efficiently remove air from the brake system. This procedure may be used as guide, but be careful to follow the tool manufacturer's directions closely. Any pressure bleeding tool MUST be of the diaphragm-type. A proper pressure bleeder tool will utilize a rubber diaphragm between the air source and brake fluid in order to prevent air, moisture oil and other contaminants from entering the hydraulic system.

1. Prepare a pressure bleeder tool such as J-29567 or equivalent by making sure the pressure tank is at least ⅔ full of fresh, clean brake fluid. In most cases, the bleeder must be bled each time fluid is added. Charge the bleeder tool to 20–25 psi (140–170 kPa).
2. Install a suitable combination valve depressor tool such J-39177 or equivalent, to the combination valve in order to hold the valve open during the bleeding operation.
3. Install the pressure bleeder tool to the master cylinder reservoir.
4. On 4 wheel ABS systems, refer to the ABS bleeding procedures later in this section to bleed the Brake Pressure Modulator Valve (BPMV) of air.

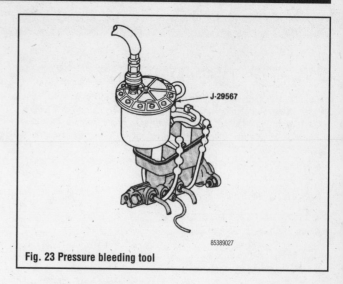

Fig. 23 Pressure bleeding tool

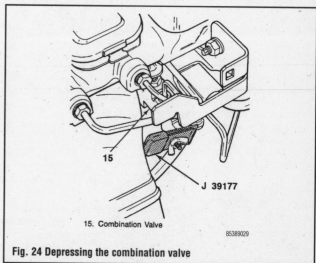

Fig. 24 Depressing the combination valve

5. Bleed each wheel cylinder or caliper in the proper sequence:
   a. Right rear
   b. Left rear
   c. Right front
   d. Left front
6. Connect a hose from the bleeder tank to the adapter at the master cylinder, then open the tank valve.
7. Attach a clear vinyl hose to the brake bleeder screw, then immerse the opposite end into a container partially filled with clean brake fluid.
8. Open the bleeder screw ¾ turn and allow the fluid to flow until no air bubbles are seen in the fluid, then close the bleeder screw and tighten to 62 inch lbs. (7 Nm).
9. Repeat the bleeding process at each wheel.
10. Inspect the brake pedal for sponginess and if necessary, repeat the entire bleeding procedure.
11. Remove the depressor tool from the combination valve and the bleeder adapter from the master cylinder.
12. Refill the master cylinder to the proper level with brake fluid.
13. DO NOT attempt to move the vehicle unless a firm brake pedal is obtained.

DISC BRAKES

✳✳ CAUTION

Brake pads may contain asbestos, which has been determined to be a cancer causing agent. Never clean the brake surfaces with compressed air! Avoid inhaling any dust from any brake surface! When cleaning brake surfaces, use a commercially available brake cleaning fluid.

Brake Pads

INSPECTION

♦ **See Figures 25, 26 and 27**

Brake pads should be inspected once a year or at 6000 miles (9600 km), whichever occurs first or every time the wheel is removed. Check both ends of the outboard pad, looking in at each end of the caliper; then check the lining thickness of the inboard pad, looking down through the inspection hole. On riveted pads, the lining should be more than 0.030 in. (0.76mm) thick above the rivet (so that the lining is thicker than the metal backing in most cases) in order to prevent the rivet from scoring the rotor. On bonded brake pads, a minimum lining thickness of 0.030 in. (0.76mm) above the backing plate should be used to determine necessary replacement intervals. Keep in mind that any applicable state inspection standards that are more stringent take precedence. All four pads MUST be replaced as a set if one shows excessive wear.

➡ **All models should be equipped with a wear indicator that makes a noise when the linings have worn to a degree where replacement is necessary. The spring clip is an integral part of the inboard pad and lining. When the brake pad reaches a certain degree of wear, the clip will contact the rotor and produce a warning noise.**

REMOVAL & INSTALLATION

♦ **See Figures 28 thru 44**

➡ The following procedure requires the use of a C-clamp and on front disc brakes a pair of channel lock pliers.

1. If the fluid reservoir is full, siphon off about ⅔ of the brake fluid from the master cylinder reservoirs in order to prevent the possibility of spillage when the caliper pistons are bottomed. A common kitchen turkey baster may also be used to remove brake fluid, but make sure the tool is clean before inserting it in the reservoir.

✳✳ WARNING

The insertion of thicker replacement pads will push the piston back into its bore and will cause a full master cylinder reservoir to overflow, possibly causing paint damage. In addition to siphoning off fluid, keep the reservoir cover on during pad replacement.

2. Raise and support the vehicle safely using jackstands.
3. Remove the necessary tire and wheel assemblies.

➡ **Replacing the pads on just one wheel may cause uneven braking; always replace the pads on both wheels.**

4. Install a C-clamp on the caliper so that the solid frame side of the clamp rests against the back of the caliper and the driving screw end rests against the metal part (center backing plate) of the outboard pad.
5. Tighten the clamp until the caliper moves sufficiently to bottom the piston in its bore, then remove the clamp.
6. On models equipped with front disc brakes, perform the following steps for pad removal:

Fig. 25 The brake lining can be checked through a opening in the brake caliper housing

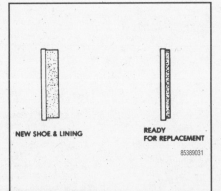

NEW SHOE & LINING
READY FOR REPLACEMENT
85389031

Fig. 26 Relative size differences between a new and worn pad lining

91119P25

Fig. 27 The brake pads have a wear indicator which touches the brake rotor when the pad lining is worn and makes a loud metal-to-metal squealing noise. Once this happens the pads should be replaced

88459P01

Fig. 28 If the fluid reservoir is full, siphon some fluid from the reservoirs to prevent spillage

88459P08

Fig. 29 View of a common front disc brake system

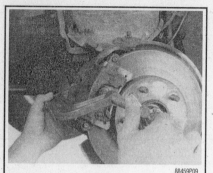

Fig. 30 On front disc brakes, use a C-clamp to bottom the piston in the caliper bore

Fig. 31 On front disc brakes, loosen the caliper mounting bolts/pins

Fig. 32 On front disc brakes, remove the caliper mounting bolts

Fig. 33 On front disc brakes, after removing the caliper, support the weight of the caliper with mechanics wire or a coat hanger

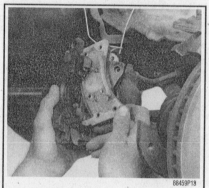

Fig. 34 On front disc brakes, remove the outboard pad from the caliper

Fig. 35 On front disc brakes, remove the inboard pad from the caliper piston

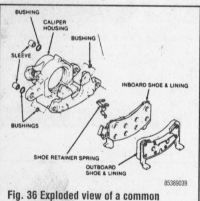

Fig. 36 Exploded view of a common caliper and brake pad assembly

Fig. 37 On rear disc brakes, using a back-up wrench, loosen the top caliper mounting bolt and remove the bottom bolt . . .

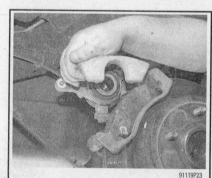

Fig. 38 . . . then grasp the bottom of the caliper and rotate the caliper upwards to access the brake pads

Fig. 39 On rear disc brakes, once the caliper is out of the way, the pads are easily removed

Fig. 40 On rear disc brakes, the spring clip must be properly installed on the inboard pad

Fig. 41 On rear disc brakes, install the inboard pad to the caliper by carefully inserting the spring clip in the piston

Fig. 42 On rear disc brakes, position the outboard pad over the caliper ears

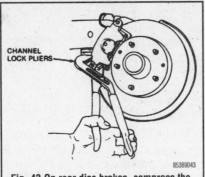

Fig. 43 On rear disc brakes, compress the brake pad ears using a pair of channel lock pliers

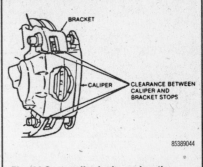

Fig. 44 On rear disc brakes, when the caliper is installed, check for proper caliper-to-knuckle bracket clearance

a. Remove the two Allen head caliper mounting bolts from the back of the caliper.

b. Remove the caliper from the mounting bracket and support from the vehicle's suspension using a coat hanger or length of wire. Do not allow the brake line to support the caliper's weight and be sure the line is not otherwise kinked or damaged.

c. Remove the inboard and outboard pads from the caliper.

d. Remove the inboard pad spring clip from the piston or pad. Remove the spring clip carefully as it must be reused upon installation of the new pads.

e. Remove the bolt ear sleeves and rubber bushings for cleaning, inspection and lubrication.

7. On models equipped with rear disc brakes, perform the following steps for pad removal:

a. Using a back-up wrench, loosen the top caliper mounting bolt and remove the bottom bolt.

b. Grasp the bottom of the caliper and rotate the caliper upwards to access the brake pads. In some cases it may be necessary to unfasten both caliper retaining bolts and remove the caliper. If the caliper must be removed, support it from the vehicle's suspension or frame using a coat hanger or length of wire. Do not allow the brake line to support the caliper's weight and be sure the line is not otherwise kinked or damaged.

c. Remove the inboard and outboard pads from the caliper.

d. Remove the pad spring shim, if equipped.

8. Check the rotor for cracks, excessive scoring and lateral run-out. Refer to the procedure outlined in this section.

To install:

9. Check the inside of the caliper for leakage and the condition of the piston dust boot. If necessary, remove the caliper and overhaul or replace it.

10. Lubricate the sleeves and bushings using a suitable silicone lubricant, and if removed, then install them.

11. Make sure the piston is fully bottomed in the caliper providing clearance for the new brake pads. If the piston is not compressed, install the old inboard pad and use the C-clamp on the pad and back on the caliper to bottom the piston. Be careful not to pinch and damage the piston boot.

12. On models equipped with front disc brakes, install the pad assembly as follows:

a. Install the spring clip to the inboard pad, then install the pad to the caliper.

➡ **Make sure that the wear sensor is facing in the proper direction. On most vehicles it should face toward the rear of the caliper.**

b. Place the outboard pad in the caliper with its top ears over the caliper ears and the bottom tab engaged in the caliper cutout.

c. Place the caliper over the disc, lining up the hole in the caliper ears with the holes in the mounting bracket. Make sure that the brake hose is not twisted or kinked.

d. Carefully insert the mounting bolts through the bracket and caliper (bushing and sleeves), then tighten to 37 ft. lbs. (50 Nm) on all except 1998–99 4 wheel disc models. On 4 wheel disc models, tighten the bolts to 77 ft. lbs. (105 Nm).

13. Use a pair of channel lock pliers to compress the pad ears so no clearance exists between the pad ears and the caliper.

14. Check the clearance between the caliper and steering knuckle. Clearance at each end of the caliper should be measured individually and the results added together. Clearance should not exceed 0.010–0.024 in. (0.026–0.60mm).

15. On models equipped with rear disc brakes, install the pads as follows:

a. If removed, install the pad spring shim, then install the pads.

b. If removed, place the caliper over the disc, lining up the hole in the caliper ears with the holes in the mounting bracket. Make sure that the brake hose is not twisted or kinked.

c. If the caliper was not removed, rotate it back into position and install the mounting bolt. Tighten the bolt(s) to 23 ft. lbs. (31 Nm).

16. Pump the brake pedal a few times to seat the linings against the rotors.

17. Install the wheels, then remove the jackstands and carefully lower the vehicle.

18. Check and refill the master cylinder reservoirs with brake fluid.

❖❖❖ CAUTION

DO NOT attempt to move the vehicle until a firm brake pedal is obtained.

19. Pump the brake pedal to make sure that it is firm. If necessary, bleed the brakes.

Brake Caliper

REMOVAL & INSTALLATION

Front Caliper

➡ **A scan tool is absolutely necessary to bleed the brake hydraulic system on models equipped with an Anti-lock Brake System (ABS). If your vehicle is equipped with ABS, be sure to refer to the ABS bleeding procedures in this section before performing any work on your vehicle's brake hydraulic system.**

1. If the fluid reservoir is full, siphon off about ⅔ of the brake fluid from the master cylinder reservoirs in order to prevent the possibility of spillage when the caliper pistons are bottomed. A common kitchen turkey baster may also be used to remove brake fluid, but make sure the tool is clean before inserting it in the reservoir.

2. Raise and support the vehicle safely using jackstands.

3. Remove the tire and wheel assemblies.

4. If equipped, remove the ABS sensor wire retainer.

5. Install a C-clamp on the caliper so that the solid frame side of the clamp rests against the back of the caliper and the driving screw end rests against the metal part (center backing plate) of the outboard pad. Tighten the clamp until the caliper moves sufficiently to bottom the piston in its bore, then remove the clamp.

6. Remove the two caliper mounting bolts from the back of the caliper. If the caliper is not being completely removed from the vehicle, remove it from the

mounting bracket and support it from the suspension using a coat hanger or length of wire. Do not allow the hose to be stretched, twisted, kinked or otherwise damaged.

7. If the caliper is being completely removed from the vehicle, disconnect the flexible brake hose-to-caliper banjo-bolt, discard the pressure fitting washers (they must be replaced with new ones during assembly), then remove the brake caliper from the vehicle and place it on a work bench.

8. To inspect the caliper assembly, perform the following procedures:

a. Check the inside of the caliper assembly for pitting or scoring. If heavy scoring or pitting is present, caliper replacement is recommended.

b. Check the mounting bolts and sleeves for signs of corrosion; if necessary, replace the bolts.

➡**If the mounting bolts have signs of corrosion, DO NOT attempt to polish away the corrosion. Instead the bolts must be replaced to assure proper caliper sliding and prevent the possibility of brake drag or locking.**

To install:

9. Lubricate and position the caliper bushings and sleeves. Apply Delco® silicone lube or equivalent to lubricate the mounting bolts.

10. With both pads installed to the caliper, place the caliper over the disc, lining up the hole in the caliper ears with the holes in the mounting bracket.

11. If the caliper was completely removed, install the flexible hose to the caliper and secure using the banjo bolt and new washers. Make sure that the brake hose is not twisted or kinked, then tighten the bolt to 32 ft. lbs. (44 Nm).

12. Carefully insert the mounting bolts through the bracket and caliper (bushing and sleeves), then tighten to 37 ft. lbs. (50 Nm) on all except 1998–99 4 wheel disc models. On 4 wheel disc models, tighten the bolts to 77 ft. lbs. (105 Nm).

13. If removed, install the ABS sensor wire retainer and tighten the bolt to 13 ft. lbs. (17 Nm).

14. Pump the brake pedal a few times to seat the linings against the rotors.

15. Use a pair of channel lock pliers to compress the pad ears so no clearance exists between the pad ears and the caliper.

16. Check the clearance between the caliper and steering knuckle. Clearance at each end of the caliper should be measured individually and the results added together. Clearance should not exceed 0.010–0.024 in. (0.026–0.60mm).

17. Install the wheels, then remove the jackstands and carefully lower the vehicle.

18. Check and refill the master cylinder reservoirs with brake fluid.

❊❊ CAUTION

DO NOT attempt to move the vehicle until a firm brake pedal is obtained.

19. Properly bleed the hydraulic brake system. If only a caliper fitting was disconnected, bleeding of the entire system should not be required. Bleed air from the system at the caliper that was disconnected. Check the system for proper operation. If air remains in the system, bleeding at all points in the system may be required.

Rear Caliper

➡**A scan tool is absolutely necessary to bleed the brake hydraulic system on models equipped with an Anti-lock Brake System (ABS). If your vehicle is equipped with ABS, be sure to refer to the ABS bleeding procedures in this section before performing any work on your vehicle's brake hydraulic system.**

1. Raise and support the vehicle safely using jackstands.

2. Remove the tire and wheel assemblies.

3. Remove the two caliper mounting bolts from the back of the caliper. If the caliper is not being completely removed from the vehicle, remove it from the mounting bracket and support it from the suspension using a coat hanger or length of wire. Do not allow the hose to be stretched, twisted, kinked or otherwise damaged.

4. If the caliper is being completely removed from the vehicle, disconnect the flexible brake hose-to-caliper banjo-bolt, discard the pressure fitting washers (they must be replaced with new ones during assembly), then remove the brake caliper from the vehicle and place it on a work bench.. Plug the hole in the caliper and the cap the brake line to prevent contamination of the system.

5. To inspect the caliper assembly, perform the following procedures:

a. Check the inside of the caliper assembly for pitting or scoring. If heavy scoring or pitting is present, caliper replacement is recommended.

➡**If the mounting bolts have signs of corrosion, DO NOT attempt to polish away the corrosion. Instead the bolts must be replaced to assure proper caliper sliding and prevent the possibility of brake drag or locking.**

To install:

6. With both pads installed to the caliper, place the caliper over the disc, lining up the hole in the caliper ears with the holes in the mounting bracket.

7. If the caliper was completely removed, install the flexible hose to the caliper and secure using the banjo bolt and new washers. Make sure that the brake hose is not twisted or kinked, then tighten the bolt to 27 ft. lbs. (20 Nm).

8. Carefully insert the mounting bolts through the bracket and caliper (bushing and sleeves), then tighten to 23 ft. lbs. (31 Nm).

9. Pump the brake pedal a few times to seat the linings against the rotors.

10. Install the wheels, then remove the jackstands and carefully lower the vehicle.

11. Check and refill the master cylinder reservoirs with brake fluid.

❊❊ CAUTION

DO NOT attempt to move the vehicle until a firm brake pedal is obtained.

12. Properly bleed the hydraulic brake system if a brake hose fitting was disconnected. If no hoses were disconnected, no bleeding should be required. Bleed air from the system at the caliper that was disconnected. Check the system for proper operation. If air remains in the system, bleeding at all points in the system may be required.

Brake Disc (Rotor)

REMOVAL & INSTALLATION

Front

2WD MODELS

1. Raise and support the front of the vehicle safely using jackstands.

2. Remove the tire and wheel assembly.

3. Remove the brake caliper mounting bolts and carefully remove the caliper (along with the brake pads) from the rotor. Do not disconnect the brake line; instead wire the caliper out of the way with the line still connected.

➡**Once the rotor is removed from the vehicle the wheel bearings may be cleaned and repacked or the bearings and races may be replaced. For more information, please refer to the wheel bearing procedures in Section 1 of this manual.**

4. Carefully pry out the grease cap, then remove the cotter pin, spindle nut, and washer.

5. Remove the hub, being careful not to drop the outer wheel bearings. As the hub is pulled forward, the outer wheel bearings will often fall forward and they may easily be removed at this time.

To install:

6. Carefully install the wheel hub over the spindle.

7. Using your hands, firmly press the outer bearing into the hub.

8. Loosely install the spindle washer and nut, but do not install the cotter pin or dust cap at this time.

9. Install the brake caliper.

10. Install the tire and wheel assembly.

11. Properly adjust the wheel bearings:

a. Spin the wheel forward by hand and tighten the nut to 12 ft. lbs. (16 Nm) in order to fully seat the bearings and remove any burrs from the threads.

b. Back off the nut until it is just loose, then finger-tighten the nut.

c. Loosen the nut ¼-½ turn until either hole in the spindle lines up with a slot in the nut, then install a new cotter pin. This may appear to be too loose, but it is the correct adjustment.

d. Proper adjustment creates 0.001–0.005 in. (0.025–0.127mm) end-play.

12. Install the dust cap.

13. Install the wheel/hub cover, then remove the supports and carefully lower the vehicle.

4WD MODELS

▶ See Figure 45

1. Raise and support the front of the vehicle safely using jackstands under the frame.

2. Remove the tire and wheel assembly.

3. Remove the brake caliper mounting bolts and carefully remove the caliper (along with the brake pads) from the rotor. Do not disconnect the brake line; instead wire the caliper out of the way with the line still connected.

4. If equipped, remove the lockwashers from the hub studs in order to free the rotor.

5. Remove the brake disc (rotor) from the wheel hub.

To install:

6. Inspect the disc for nicks, scores and/or damage, then replace if necessary.

7. Install the disc over the wheel hub studs.

8. If used, install the lockwashers over the studs.

9. Install the brake caliper and pads. For details, please refer to the caliper procedure located earlier in this section.

10. Install the tire and wheel assembly.

11. Remove the jackstands and carefully lower the vehicle. DO NOT attempt to move the vehicle unless a firm brake pedal is felt.

Fig. 45 Removing the rotor from the vehicle

Rear

1. Raise and support the front of the vehicle safely using jackstands under the frame.

2. Remove the tire and wheel assembly.

3. Unfasten the caliper anchor bracket bolts, then remove the brake caliper mounting and anchor assembly from the mounting plate. Do not disconnect the brake line; instead wire the caliper out of the way with the line still connected.

4. Remove the brake disc (rotor) from the wheel hub. It my help to slowly turn the rotor to ease in removal.

To install:

5. Inspect the disc for nicks, scores and/or damage, then replace if necessary.

6. Install the disc over the wheel hub studs.

7. Install the brake caliper and anchor plate assembly onto the rotor and mounting plate. Tighten the anchor bracket bolts to 52 ft. lbs. (70 Nm).

8. Install the tire and wheel assembly.

9. Remove the jackstands and carefully lower the vehicle. DO NOT attempt to move the vehicle unless a firm brake pedal is felt.

INSPECTION

▶ See Figure 46

Check the disc brake rotor for scoring, cracks or other damage. Rotor run-out should be measured while the rotor is installed, while rotor thickness/thick-

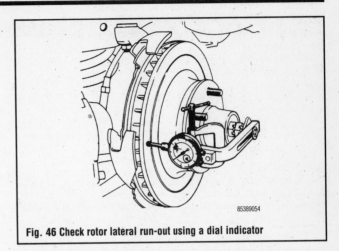

Fig. 46 Check rotor lateral run-out using a dial indicator

ness variation may be checked with the rotor installed or removed. Use a dial gauge to check rotor run-out. Check the rotor thickness to make sure it is greater than minimum thickness and check for thickness variations using a caliper micrometer.

1. Raise and support the front of the vehicle safely using jackstands.

2. Remove the front wheels.

3. Visually inspect the rotor for cracks, excessive scoring or other damage. A light scoring of the surface which does not exceed 0.06 in. (1.5mm) in depth is normal and should not be considered detrimental to brake operation.

➡**Before attempting to check rotor run-out on 2WD vehicles, make sure the wheel bearings are properly adjusted. On all vehicles, the bearings must be in good condition and not contain excessive play.**

4. Check the disc for excessive run-out using a dial indicator:

a. On 2WD models only, tighten the wheel bearings to eliminate all freeplay.

b. Position and secure a dial indicator so that the button contacts the rotor about 1 in. (25.4mm) on front rotors or 0.5 in. (13mm) on rear rotors from the outer edge of the rotor. Set the dial indicator to zero. On rear rotors, push in on the axle while setting the dial indicator to zero.

c. Rotate the disc one complete revolution. The lateral run-out reading should not exceed 0.003 in. (0.08mm) on front rotors and 0.004 in. (0.10mm) on rear rotors. If the reading is excessive, recondition or replace the disc.

d. After checking the run-out reset the freeplay adjustment on the 2WD models.

5. Check the disc minimum thickness and the disc parallelism (thickness variation):

a. Use a micrometer to check the disc thickness at 4 locations around the disc. Make sure the measuring point is at the same distance from the edge at all locations.

b. The thickness should be greater than the minimum specification (which is normally cast onto the disc) and should not vary more than 0.0005 in. (0.013mm) on front rotors and 0.0003 in. (0.010mm) on rear rotors.

6. On rear rotors, the lateral run-out still exceeds specification can be rectified by indexing the rotor, then move the rotor one or two wheel bolt positions from its original position and recheck the run-out.

7. If the run-out is still excessive, check the axle shaft flange for excessive lateral run-out or looseness as follows:

a. Remove the rotor and position the dial indicator so that the button contacts the surface of the axle shaft flange.

b. Push the axle shaft inwards while turning shaft flange one full turn.

c. Continue to push on the shaft flange while setting the dial indicator to zero.

d. While maintaining inward pressure on the shaft, rotate the shaft flange and note the run-out reading.

e. If the shaft flange run-out exceeds 0.002 in. (0.05mm), replace the rear axle shaft.

f. If the axle shaft run-out is within specification, refinish or replace the rotor.

8. If the variations are excessive, recondition or replace the disc. A disc which is smaller than the discard dimension MUST be replaced for safety.

REAR DRUM BRAKES

REAR DRUM BRAKE COMPONENTS

1. Primary brake shoe
2. Adjusting screw assembly
3. Actuator lever
4. Actuator lever return spring
5. Actuator lever pivot
6. Hold-down pin
7. Hold-down spring
8. Parking brake strut spring
9. Adjusting screw spring
10. Wheel cylinder
11. Parking brake strut
12. Shoe guide
13. Return spring
14. Return spring
15. Actuator link
16. Secondary brake shoe

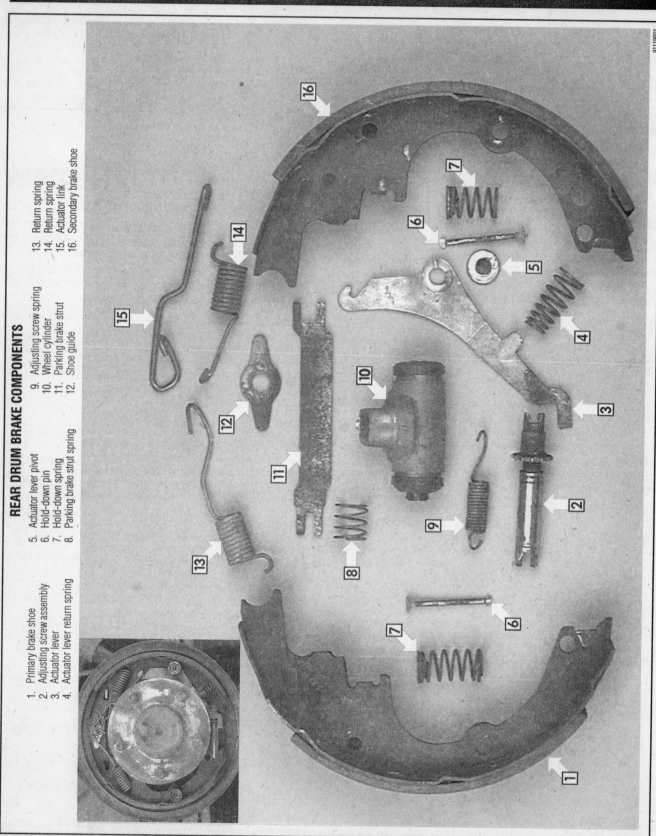

91119P01

✳✳ CAUTION

Brake shoes may contain asbestos, which has been determined to be a cancer causing agent. Never clean the brake surfaces with compressed air! Avoid inhaling any dust from any brake surface! When cleaning brake surfaces, use a commercially available brake cleaning fluid.

Brake Drums

REMOVAL & INSTALLATION

▶ **See Figures 47 and 48**

1. Raise and support the rear of the vehicle safely using jackstands.
2. Remove the rear tire and wheel assemblies.
3. Matchmark the drum to the hub or hub studs for installation purposes.
4. Pull the brake drum from the hub studs. It may by necessary to gently tap the rear edges of the drum using a rubber mallet to start it off the studs.
5. If the drum will not come off past the shoes, it will be necessary to retract the adjusting screw. Remove the access hole cover from the backing plate and turn the adjuster to retract the linings away from the drum.

To install:

➡ **The rear wheel bearings are not adjustable, they are serviced by replacement only. If necessary to replace the rear wheel bearings, please refer to the axle shaft, bearing and seal, removal and installation procedures located in Section 7 of this manual.**

6. If removed, install a rubber adjustment hole cover before reinstalling the drum.
7. Install the drum in the same position on the hub as removed.
8. Install the rear tire and wheel assemblies.
9. Remove the jackstands and carefully lower the vehicle.

88459P19

Fig. 47 View of a common brake drum used on the S-series pickups

INSPECTION

Clean all grease, brake fluid, and other contaminants from the brake drum using brake cleaner. Visually check the drum for scoring, cracks, or other damage and replace, if necessary.

Check the drum inner diameter using a brake shoe clearance gauge. There are 2 important specifications when discussing rear drum diameters. The refinish diameter is the maximum diameter to which the drum may be machined. This diameter allows room for drum wear after is has been machined and is returned to service. The discard diameter is the point at which the drum becomes unsafe to use and must be discarded. NEVER refinish a drum to the discard diameter. If after refinishing the drum the diameter is within 0.030 in. (0.76mm) of the discard diameter, the drum MUST be replaced.

Brake Shoes

INSPECTION

Brake shoes should be inspected once a year or at 6000 miles (9600 km), whichever occurs first or every time the wheel is removed. Remove the drum and inspect the lining thickness of both brake shoes. The rear brake shoes should be replaced if the lining is less than 0.030 in. (0.76mm) thick above the rivet (so that the lining is thicker than the metal shoe backing in most cases) in order to prevent the rivet from scoring the drum. On bonded shoes the same specification should be used and the thickness of the bonded lining should be 0.030 in. (0.76mm) thick above the metal shoe backing plate. As with all brake service, keep in mind that local regulations take precedence over these specifications. Always check with your local authorities to be sure you are in compliance with local laws.

➡ **Brake shoes should always be replaced in sets.**

REMOVAL & INSTALLATION

▶ **See Figures 49 thru 60**

1. Raise and support the rear of the vehicle safely using jackstands.
2. Remove the rear wheels.
3. Matchmark and remove the brake drums.
4. Remove the shoe return springs and disconnect the actuator link (the link may be removed at this time), then remove the shoe guide from the stud at the top of the backing plate.

➡ **Special brake spring tools are available from the auto supply stores, which will ease the removal and installation of the return springs and the shoe hold-down spring and anchor pin.**

5. Remove the shoe hold-down springs and pins.
6. Remove the actuator lever, pivot and return spring.
7. If not done earlier, remove the actuator link.
8. Remove the parking brake strut and strut spring, then remove the parking brake lever from the shoe (it may be easier to wait until the shoe is being removed to separate the lever).

88459P20

Fig. 48 Removing the brake drum from the vehicle

88459P21

Fig. 49 Use an evaporative spray brake cleaner to remove brake dust from the components

88459P22

Fig. 50 Use a brake tool to release the return springs

Fig. 51 When the first spring is released, pivot it and remove it from the shoe

Fig. 52 Remove the second return spring . . . .

Fig. 53 . . . then remove the actuator link

Fig. 54 Remove the shoe guide from the stud at the top of the backing plate

Fig. 55 Use the brake tool to compress the hold-down spring and twist the plate to free the pin

Fig. 56 Once the pin and the slot on top of the plate are aligned, separate the hold-down spring and pin

Fig. 57 Remove the actuator lever and return spring

Fig. 58 Remove the parking brake strut and spring

Fig. 59 Remove the shoes from the backing plate

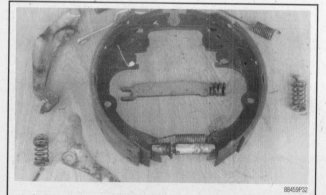

Fig. 60 Exploded view of the drum brake components

9. Remove the brake shoes, the adjuster screw assembly and the adjuster spring.
10. Clean and inspect all of the brake parts.
11. Check the wheel cylinders for seal condition and leaking.
12. Inspect the axle seal for leakage and replace, if necessary.
To install:
13. Inspect the replacement shoes for nicks or burrs, lightly lubricate the backing plate contact points, the brake cable, the levers and adjusting screws with a white lithium brake grease.
14. Make sure that the right and left hand adjusting screws are not mixed. You can prevent this by working on one side at a time. This will also provide you with a reference for reassembly, just keep in mind that the assembly on one side of the vehicle is the mirror image of the assembly on the other side. The star wheel should be nearest to the secondary shoe when correctly installed.
15. Install the adjusting screw assembly and spring to both shoes, then position the shoes to the backing plate.
16. Install the parking brake lever to the secondary shoe.

17. Install the strut spring to the parking brake strut, then position the strut.

18. Install the actuator lever, lever pivot and the link. Install the lever return spring.

19. Install the shoe hold-down pins and springs.

20. Install the shoe guide over the stud at the top of the backing plate.

21. Install the return springs.

22. Lightly sandpaper the shoes to make sure they are clean, then align and install the drum.

23. Install the rear tire and wheel assemblies.

24. Adjust the brakes as described in this section.

25. Remove the jackstands and carefully lower the vehicle, then road test the vehicle.

ADJUSTMENTS

♦ **See Figure 61**

Normal adjustments of the rear drum brakes are automatic and are made during the reverse applications of the brakes. The following procedure should be used ONLY if the linings have been replaced.

1. Raise and support the rear of the vehicle safely using jackstands.

2. Using a punch and a hammer on the rear of the backing plates, knock out the lanced metal areas near the starwheel assemblies on each plate. The metal areas may already have been removed and covered with rubber adjustment plugs, if so remove the plugs by grasping and pulling with a pair of pliers.

➡ **After knocking out the lanced metal areas from the backing plate, the wheels must be removed and all of the metal pieces discarded, then the wheels should be reinstalled for adjustment.**

3. Insert a suitable brake adjustment tool such as J-4735 or equivalent, into the breaking plate slots and engage the lowest possible tooth on the starwheel. Move the end of the brake tool downward to move the starwheel upward and expand the adjusting screw. Repeat this operation until the wheels can JUST be turned by hand. This is a position immediately before the brakes lock.

➡ **The brake drag should be equal at both wheels.**

4. Back off the adjusting screws 24 notches (clicks). By the time you have backed off the adjustment 12 clicks, the brakes should have no drag. If a heavy drag is still present, the parking brake cable is likely in need of adjustment.

5. Make sure both sides of the brakes are properly adjusted. When backing off the brakes on the other side, the adjusting lever must be backed off the same number of turns to prevent side-to-side brake pull.

6. After the brakes are adjusted, install a rubber hole cover into each of the backing plate slots. To complete the brake adjustment operation, make several stops while backing the vehicle to fully equalize the adjustment.

7. Road test the vehicle.

Wheel Cylinders

REMOVAL & INSTALLATION

♦ **See Figure 62**

➡ **A scan tool is absolutely necessary to bleed the brake hydraulic system on models equipped with an Anti-lock Brake System (ABS). If your vehicle is equipped with ABS, be sure to refer to the ABS bleeding procedures in this section before performing any work on your vehicle's brake hydraulic system.**

1. Raise and support the rear of the vehicle safely using jackstands.

2. Remove the tire and wheel assembly.

3. Matchmark and remove the brake drum for access to the wheel cylinder assembly.

4. Remove the brake shoes.

5. Clean away all dirt, crud and foreign material from around wheel cylinder. It is important that dirt be kept away from the brake line when the cylinder is disconnected.

6. Disconnect the inlet tube line from the back of the wheel cylinder. Immediately plug or cap the line to prevent system contamination or excessive fluid loss.

7. Loosen and remove the bolts from the back side of the backing plate, then remove the wheel cylinder assembly.

To install:

8. Place the cylinder into position, then install the retaining bolts and tighten to 115 inch lbs. (13 Nm).

9. Remove the cap or plug, then connect and secure the hydraulic inlet line.

10. Install the brake shoes.

11. Align and install the brake drum, then install the tire and wheel assembly.

12. Bleed the wheel cylinder and adjust the brakes (if necessary).

13. Remove the jackstands and carefully lower the vehicle.

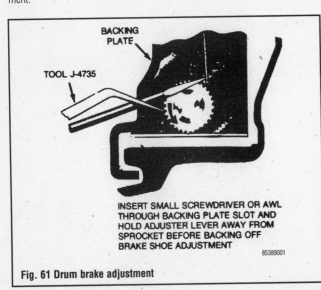

INSERT SMALL SCREWDRIVER OR AWL THROUGH BACKING PLATE SLOT AND HOLD ADJUSTER LEVER AWAY FROM SPROCKET BEFORE BACKING OFF BRAKE SHOE ADJUSTMENT

85389001

Fig. 61 Drum brake adjustment

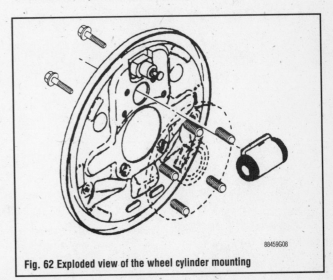

88459G08

Fig. 62 Exploded view of the wheel cylinder mounting

PARKING BRAKE

Front Cable

REMOVAL & INSTALLATION

▶ See Figure 63

1. Raise and support the front of the vehicle safely using jackstands.

➡The parking brake equalizer threads will often rust in service making adjustment or removal difficult. If necessary, spray a penetrating lubricant on the nut and equalizer threads, then allow time for the lubricant to work.

2. Loosen the nut on the cable equalizer assembly.
3. Separate the front cable from the equalizer.
4. If applicable, remove the front-cable retaining bolts and clips.
5. Bend or squeeze the frame retainer fingers and release the cable from the frame.

➡On some models, it may be necessary to remove the dash trim panels to gain access to the brake pedal.

6. If necessary for access, remove the lower trim panel from the left side of the dash.
7. Release the cowl retainer and grommet, then disconnect the front cable from the parking pedal assembly.
8. Attach a length of wire to the cable, then carefully pull it through the cowl leaving the wire in place for installation purposes. Remove the cable from the vehicle.

To install:

9. Use the wire left in the cowl opening to pull the cable into position.
10. Seat the retainer and grommet to the cowl, making sure the retaining fingers are completely through the hole.

11. Attach the cable to the lever, then if removed for access, install the lower trim panel.
12. Install the cable retainer to the frame, then if applicable, secure any retaining clips.
13. Connect the cable to the equalizer, then properly adjust the parking brake. For details, please refer to the procedure located later in this section.
14. Remove the jackstands and carefully lower the vehicle.

Rear Cables

REMOVAL & INSTALLATION

Except All Wheel Drive Models

▶ See Figures 64, 65, 66, 67 and 68

1. Raise and support the rear of the vehicle safely using jackstands.
2. Remove the rear tire and wheel assembly, then matchmark and remove the brake drum.

➡The parking brake equalizer threads will often rust in service making adjustment or removal difficult. If necessary, spray a penetrating lubricant on the nut and equalizer threads, then allow time for the lubricant to work.

3. Loosen the nut on the cable equalizer assembly.
4. Separate the cable from the equalizer.
5. If equipped, release the rear cable retainer from the frame rail.
6. Remove the brake shoes and disconnect the parking brake cable from the shoe lever.
7. Remove the cable retainer from the backing plate by squeezing all of the

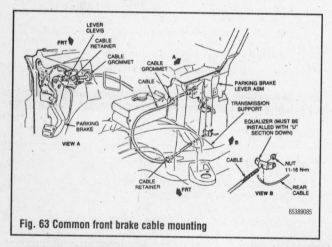

Fig. 63 Common front brake cable mounting

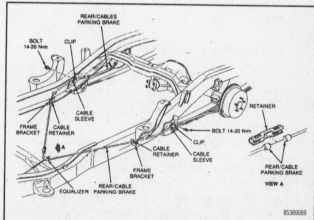

Fig. 64 Common rear parking brake cable mounting

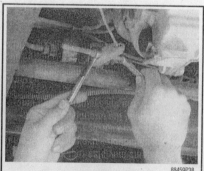

Fig. 65 Hold the adjuster rod from turning while you loosen the nut using a box wrench

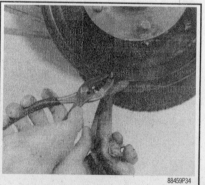

Fig. 66 Use pliers or vise grips when disconnecting the cable from the shoe lever

Fig. 67 To release the cable retainer, position a box wrench over the retainer in order to squeeze the fingers

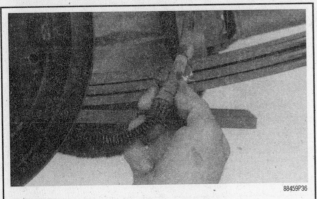

Fig. 68 Pull the cable through the backing plate

retainer fingers and pulling the cable/retainer out of the plate. One easy way of accomplishing this is to position a box wrench (which is slightly smaller than the cable retainer) over the retainer to squeeze the fingers, then gently tap the wrench with a hammer to free the cable.

8. If equipped, remove the cable bolt and clip from the frame.
9. Remove the cable from the vehicle.

To install:

10. Position the cable under the vehicle and insert it through the brake backing plate. Seat the retainer on the plate making sure all of the fingers are locked in position. Route the cable and, if equipped, secure the frame retainer in the same manner.

11. Install the brake shoes, attaching the cable to the parking brake lever.

12. When installing the cable, attach it to the brake shoe lever and assemble the brakes. Before installing the drums, pull the cable by hand and watch the parking brake action for smooth operation.

13. Align and install the brake drum, then install the tire and wheel assembly.

14. If equipped, install the retaining clip and bolt. Tighten the bolt to 13 ft. lbs. (17 Nm).

15. Properly adjust the parking brake cable. For details, please refer to the procedure located later in this section.

16. Remove the jackstands and carefully lower the vehicle.

All Wheel Drive Models

1. Raise and support the rear of the vehicle safely using jackstands.

➡The parking brake equalizer threads will often rust in service making adjustment or removal difficult. If necessary, spray a penetrating lubricant on the nut and equalizer threads, then allow time for the lubricant to work.

2. Loosen the front cable nut at the equalizer assembly.
3. Disconnect the front cable connector from the rear parking brake cable.
4. Disconnect the cable from the parking brake lever at the rear axle.

5. Unclip the cable from the rear axle differential carrier.
6. Remove the cable by routing it through the cable bracket and remove the cable from the vehicle..

To install:

7. Route the cable through the bracket and connect the cable to the lever at the rear axle.

8. Attach the clips that retain the cable to the rear axle.
9. Attach the front cable to the equalizer.
10. Properly adjust the parking brake cable. For details, please refer to the procedure located later in this section.
11. Remove the jackstands and carefully lower the vehicle.

ADJUSTMENT

▶ **See Figures 69, 70 and 71**

The parking brake cables must be adjusted any time one of the cables have been disconnected or replaced. Another indication of a need for cable adjustment is if under heavy foot pressure the pedal travel is less than 9 ratchet clicks or more than 13. Remember that the brake shoes must be properly adjusted before attempting to adjust the parking brake cable.

➡**Before adjusting the parking brakes, check the condition of the brake shoes and components; replace any necessary parts.**

1. Block the front wheels.
2. Raise and support the rear of the vehicle safely using jackstands.

➡**The parking brake equalizer threads will often rust in service making adjustment or removal difficult. If necessary, spray a penetrating lubricant on the nut and equalizer threads, then allow time for the lubricant to work.**

3. Loosen the nut on the cable equalizer assembly.
4. Fully release the parking brake pedal.
5. Tighten the cable equalizer nut until the rear wheel cannot be turned forward by hand without excessive force.
6. Loosen the equalizer nut until there is just moderate drag when the rear wheels are rotated forward.
7. Release the parking brake and verify that there is no brake drag in either direction.
8. If equipped, tighten the equalizer locknut.
9. Remove the jackstands and carefully lower the vehicle.

Parking Brake Shoes

REMOVAL & INSTALLATION

▶ **See Figure 72**

1. Raise and support the rear of the vehicle safely using jackstands.
2. Remove the rear tire and wheel assembly.
3. Remove the caliper and rotor.
4. Disconnect the parking brake cable from the parking brake lever.

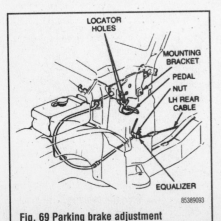

Fig. 69 Parking brake adjustment

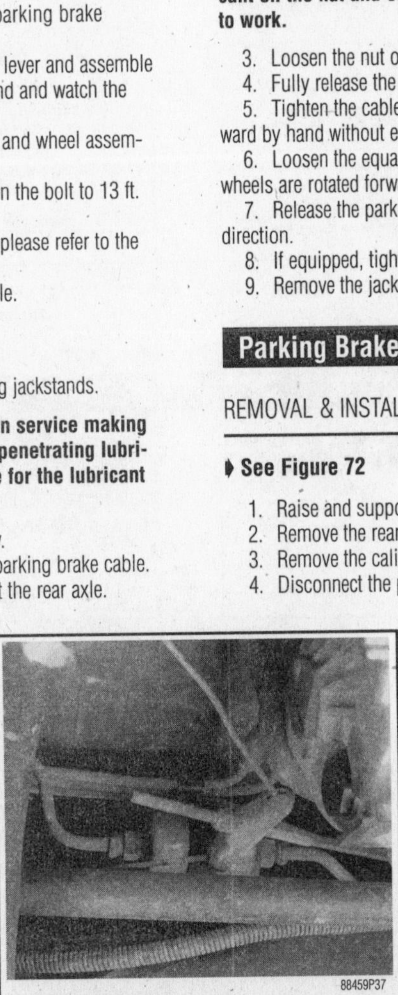

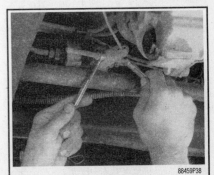

Fig. 70 View of the parking cable equalizer assembly

Fig. 71 Be careful when attempting to turn the equalizer nut; rusted threads may release without warning

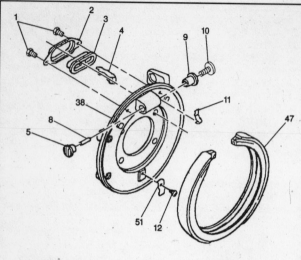

(1) Bolt/Screw, Retainer   (11) Pawl, Adjuster
(2) Retainer, Boot   (12) Bolt/Screw
(3) Boot   (38) Mounting Plate
(4) Lever   (47) Shoe and Lining
(8) Tappet   (49) Actuator
(9) Pushrod   (51) Clip
(10) Nut/Adjuster

Fig. 72 Exploded view of the rear parking brake assembly components

5. Remove the parking brake shoes assembly by sliding the shoe towards the hold-down spring until the shoe is disconnected from the spring.

6. Remove the shoe from the actuation mechanism.

7. Clean all dirt, debris and dust from the parking brake assembly components using a clean rag.

8. Turn the adjustment screw to the fully home position in the notched adjustment nut, then back it off ¼ of a turn.

9. Align the slots in both the adjusting screw and the tappet to be parallel with the backing plate face.

To install:

10. Install a new parking brake shoe.

11. Position the shoe on the inboard side of the actuation mechanism.

12. Clip the shoe onto the hold-down spring. Make sure the shoe is central on the backing plate and has both tips located in the slots.

13. Manually check the parking brake for proper operation.

14. Attach the parking brake cable to the lever.

15. Adjust the parking brake shoe as outlined later in this section.

16. Install the caliper and the rotor.

17. Install the wheel and tire assembly.

18. Lower the vehicle and check for proper operation.

ADJUSTMENT

▶ **See Figure 73**

1. Raise and support the rear of the vehicle safely using jackstands.

2. Remove the rear tire and wheel assembly.

3. Remove the caliper and rotor.

4. Disconnect the parking brake cable from the parking brake lever.

5. Adjust the shoe diameter using the adjuster nut. Turn the nut clockwise to increase the diameter until the rear wheel will not rotate forward without using excessive force. For location of the nut as refer to the accompanying illustration.

6. Attach the parking brake cable to the lever.

7. Install the caliper and the rotor.

8. Install the wheel and tire assembly.

9. Adjust the rear parking brake cables as outlined earlier in this section.

10. Lower the vehicle and check for proper operation.

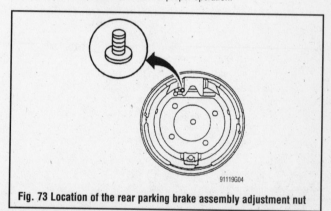

Fig. 73 Location of the rear parking brake assembly adjustment nut

REAR WHEEL ANTI-LOCK (RWAL) SYSTEM

General Description

▶ **See Figures 74 and 75**

The RWAL system may be found on 1994–95 2.2L pick-up models covered by this manual. The system is particularly useful because of the wide variations of loading the vehicle may experience. Preventing rear wheel lock-up often makes the difference in controlling the vehicle during hard or sudden stops.

Found on both 2WD and 4WD vehicles, the RWAL system is designed to regulate rear hydraulic brake line pressure, preventing rear wheel lock-up during hard braking. On most 4WD vehicles, the system is deactivated when operating in four wheel drive. In this case the braking system acts as a normal hydraulic system. Pressure regulation is managed by the control valve, located under the master cylinder. The control valve is capable of holding, increasing or decreasing brake line pressure based on electrical commands from the Electronic Brake Control Module (EBCM), originally known as the RWAL Electronic Control Unit (ECU).

The control valve holds pressure when the control module energizes the isolation solenoid. This isolates the rear hydraulic circuit and prevents fluid from entering or leaving, therefore holding constant at a given pressure. Pressure is decreased when the module keeps the isolation solenoid energized and then energizes a dump solenoid which allows fluid from the rear hydraulic circuit to enter an accumulator, thereby reducing pressure and preventing wheel lockup. Pressure may be increased (though never over the driver's input) when both the isolation and dump solenoids are de-energized allowing the rear hydraulic circuit to function normally from full master cylinder pressure.

The RWAL ECU/EBCM is a separate and dedicated microcomputer mounted next to the master cylinder; it is not to be confused with the engine management computers also found in these vehicles. The ECU/EBCM receives signals from the speed sensor. The speed sensor sends its signals to the Vehicle Speed Sen-

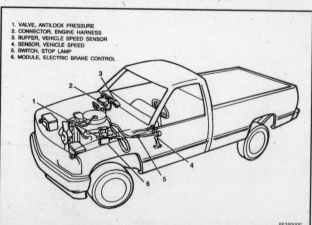

1. VALVE, ANTILOCK PRESSURE
2. CONNECTOR, ENGINE HARNESS
3. BUFFER, VEHICLE SPEED SENSOR
4. SENSOR, VEHICLE SPEED
5. SWITCH, STOP LAMP
6. MODULE, ELECTRIC BRAKE CONTROL

Fig. 74 Component locations for the Rear Wheel Anti-Lock (RWAL) brake system

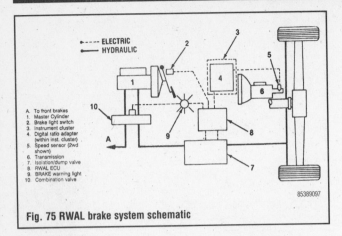

A. To front brakes
1. Master Cylinder
2. Brake light switch
3. Instrument cluster
4. Digital ratio adapter (within inst. cluster)
5. Speed sensor (2wd shown)
6. Transmission
7. Isolation/dump valve
8. RWAL ECU
9. BRAKE warning light
10. Combination valve

85389097

Fig. 75 RWAL brake system schematic

sor (VSS) buffer (previously known as the Digital Ratio Adapter Controller or DRAC) usually found within the instrument cluster. The buffer translates the sensor signal into a form usable by the computer module. The brake control module reads this signal and commands the control valve to function.

The RWAL system is connected to the brake warning lamp on the instrument cluster. A RWAL self-check and a bulb test are performed every time the ignition switch is turned to **ON**. The brake warning lamp should illuminate for about 2 seconds and then go off. Problems within the RWAL system will be indicated by the brake warning lamp remaining illuminated after this initial test period.

If a fault is detected within the system, the control module will assign a diagnostic fault code and store the code in memory. The code may be read to aid in diagnosis, much in the same way codes are used in the engine emission control systems used by these vehicles.

SYSTEM COMPONENTS

No component of the RWAL system can be disassembled or repaired. Should the control module, control valve containing the isolation/dump valves or the speed sensor fail, each failed component must be replaced as an assembly. If the axle ratio or tire size is changed on the vehicle, the VSS buffer must be replaced with one of the appropriate calibration.

CIRCUIT MAINTENANCE

All electrical connections must be kept clean and tight. Make certain that all connectors are properly seated and all of the sealing rings on weather–proof connectors are in place. The low current and/or voltage found in some circuits require that every connection be the best possible. Special tools are required for servicing the GM Weather–Pack and Metric–Pack connectors. Use terminal remover tool J–28742 or equivalent for Weather–Pack and J–35689–A or equivalent for Metric–Pack connectors.

If removal of a terminal is attempted with a regular pick, there is a good chance the terminal will be bent or deformed. Once damaged, these connectors cannot be straightened.

Use care when probing the connections or replacing terminals; it is possible to short between adjacent terminals, causing component damage. Always use jumper wires between circuit connectors for testing circuits; never probe through weather–proof seals on connectors.

Oxidation or terminal misalignment may be hidden by the connector shell. When diagnosing open or intermittent circuits, wiggling the wire harness at the connector or component may reveal or correct the condition. When the location of the fault is identified, the connector should be separated and the problem connected. Never disconnect a harness connector with the ignition **ON**.

➡ **When working with the RWAL ECU/EBCM connectors, do not touch the connections or pins with the fingers. Do not allow the connectors or pins to contact brake fluid; internal damage to the RWAL ECU/EBCM may occur.**

SYSTEM PRECAUTIONS

• Certain components within the RWAL system are not intended to be serviced or repaired. Only those components with removal & Installation proce-

dures should be serviced. Do not attempt to disassemble or overhaul RWAL system components.

• Do not use rubber hoses or other parts not specifically specified for the RWAL system. When using repair kits, replace all parts included in the kit. Partial or incorrect repair may lead to functional problems.

• Lubricate rubber parts with clean, fresh brake fluid to ease assembly. Do not use lubricated shop air to clean parts; damage to rubber components may result.

• Use only brake fluid from an unopened container. Use of suspect or contaminated brake fluid can reduce system performance and/or durability.

• A clean repair area is essential. Perform repairs after components have been thoroughly cleaned; use only denatured alcohol to clean components. Do not allow components to come into contact with any substance containing mineral oil; this includes used shop rags.

• The RWAL ECU/EBCM is a microprocessor similar to other computer units in the vehicle. Insure that the ignition switch is **OFF** before removing or installing controller harnesses. Avoid static electricity discharge at or near the controller.

• Never disengage any electrical connection with the ignition switch **ON** unless instructed to do so in a test.

• Always wear a grounded wrist strap when servicing any control module or component labeled with a Electrostatic Discharge (ESD) symbol.

• Avoid touching module connector pins.

• Leave new components and modules in the shipping package until ready to install them.

• To avoid static discharge, always touch a vehicle ground after sliding across a vehicle seat or walking across carpeted or vinyl floors.

• Never allow welding cables to lie on, near or across any vehicle electrical wiring.

• Do not allow extension cords for power tools or drop lights to lie on, near or across any vehicle electrical wiring.

System Diagnosis

READING CODES

▶ **See Figure 76**

The RWAL (ECU/EBCM) will assign a code to the first fault found in the system. If there is more than 1 fault, only the first recognized code will the stored and transmitted.

Trouble codes may be read either though the use of Tech-1 or equivalent scan tool or by connecting a jumper wire from pin H on the ALDL/DLC to pin A. If the jumper method is used, the fault code will be displayed through the flashing of the BRAKE warning lamp on the dash. The terminals must be connected for about 20 seconds before the display begins. The display will begin with 1 long flash followed by shorter ones—count the long flash as part of the display.

➡ **Sometimes the first display sequence will be inaccurate or short; subsequent displays will be accurate.**

If using a hand scanner, note if a soft code is stored, only the last recognized code will be retained and displayed on the scanner. Soft fault Codes 2, 3, 4, 6, 7, 8, 9, and 10 can only be read with a scan tool. On some models, Codes 1, 11 and 12 will not read on the scan tool and must be read using the jumper wire method.

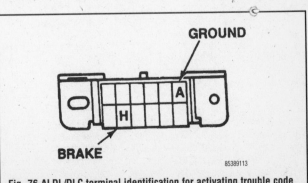

GROUND

BRAKE

85389113

Fig. 76 ALDL/DLC terminal identification for activating trouble code read out

➥Never ground terminal H of the ALDL to terminal A if the BRAKE warning lamp is not lit. Doing so will usually set a false code 9 and illuminate the BRAKE warning lamp. With the brake lamp on, the RWAL system will be disabled.

The following is a list of Diagnostic Trouble Codes (DLCs) for the RWAL system.

- Code 2: Open isolation solenoid or EBCM malfunction
- Code 3: Open dump solenoid or EBCM malfunction
- Code 4: Grounded anti-lock pressure valve reset switch
- Code 5: Excessive dump valve actuations during an anti-lock stop
- Code 6: Erratic speed signal
- Code 7: Shorted isolation solenoid or EBCM malfunction
- Code 8: Shorted dump solenoid or EBCM malfunction
- Code 9: Open or grounded speed signal circuit
- Code 10: Brake switch circuit
- Codes 1, 11 or 13: Invalid diagnostic trouble codes
- Codes 13, 14 or 15: Electric brake control module malfunction

CLEARING CODES

Stored trouble codes must be cleared with the ignition switch **OFF**. NEVER attempt to clear codes while the ignition switch is in the **ON** position or the computer module will likely be destroyed. Remove the ECM B fuse for at least 5 seconds, then reinstall the fuse.

TESTING

♦ **See Figures 77 thru 84**

Before reading trouble codes, perform the Function Test according to the appropriate charts for your vehicle. The charts are located in this section. This test will aid in separating RWAL system problems from common problems in the hydraulic brake system. The diagnostic circuit check will direct the reading of trouble codes as necessary.

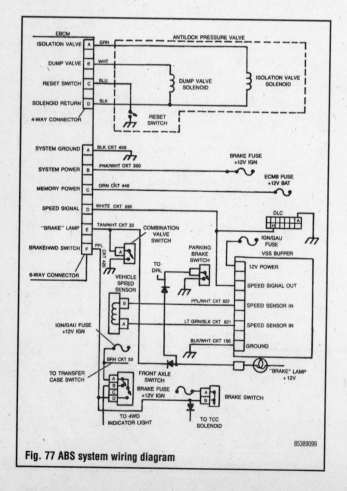

Fig. 77 ABS system wiring diagram

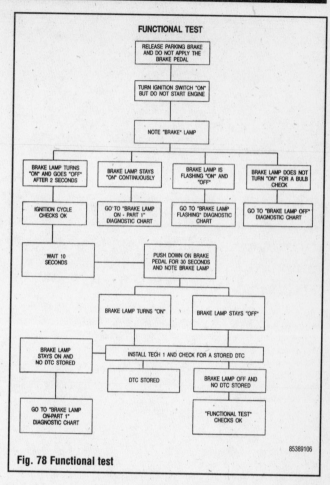

Fig. 78 Functional test

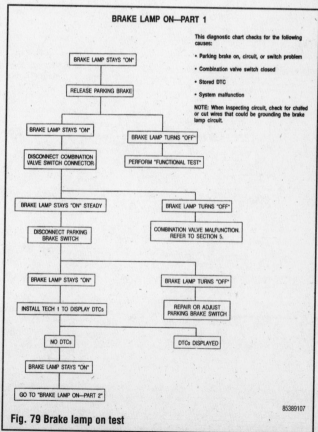

Fig. 79 Brake lamp on test

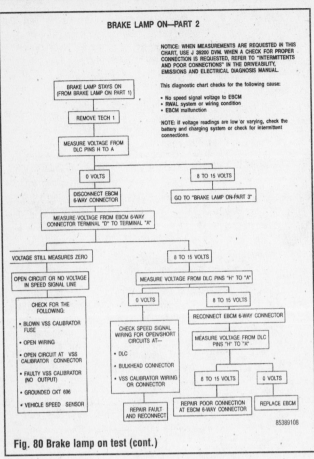

Fig. 80 Brake lamp on test (cont.)

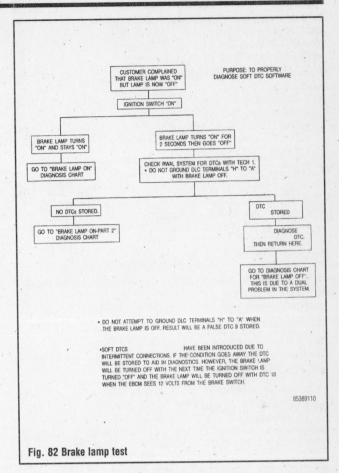

Fig. 82 Brake lamp test

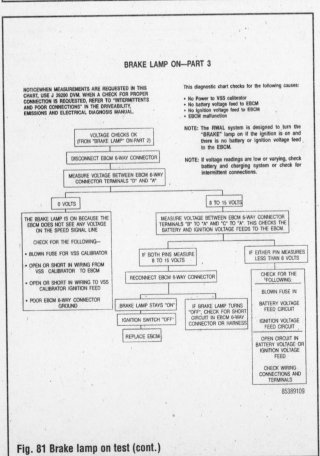

Fig. 81 Brake lamp on test (cont.)

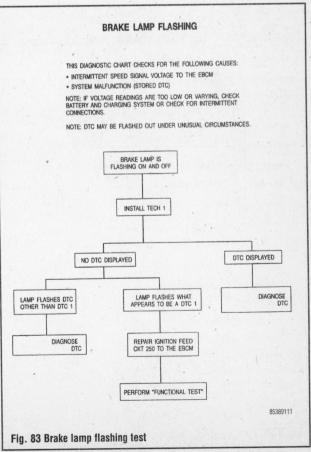

Fig. 83 Brake lamp flashing test

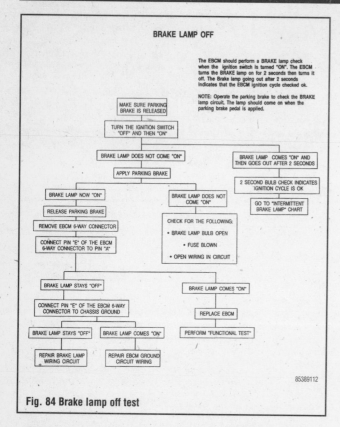

Fig. 84 Brake lamp off test

DO NOT ground the brake trouble code terminal of the ALDL/DLC if the BRAKE lamp is not on indicating a stored trouble code. Attempting to activate trouble code read out with the BRAKE lamp off may set a false Code 9. This will turn the BRAKE lamp ON and disable the anti-lock brake system.

Component Replacement

RWAL ECU/EBCM

▶ **See Figure 85**

The Electronic Brake Control Module (EBCM), formerly known as the RWAL Electronic Control Unit (ECU), is a non-serviceable unit. It must be replaced when diagnosis indicates it is faulty. Because it is expensive and normally non-returnable, be absolutely sure the module is at fault before replacement.

1. Turn the ignition switch **OFF**. The switch MUST be **OFF** whenever you are connecting/disconnecting power from the module. Failure to do this may destroy the computer.

2. Disengage the wiring harness connector(s) from the computer control module.

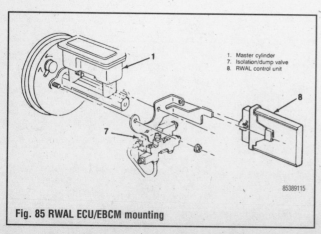

1. Master cylinder
7. Isolation/dump valve
8. RWAL control unit

Fig. 85 RWAL ECU/EBCM mounting

3. Grasp the module and remove it by pulling toward the front of the vehicle. If necessary, gently pry the tab at the rear of the module while pulling.

➡**Do not touch the electrical connectors or pins; do not allow them to contact brake fluid. If contaminated with brake fluid, clean them with water followed by isopropyl alcohol.**

To install:

4. Install the computer module by aligning it and carefully sliding it into the bracket until the tab locks into the hole.

5. Engage the wiring harness connector(s) to the module.

6. Turn the ignition **ON**, then verify proper system operation.

ANTI-LOCK PRESSURE CONTROL VALVE

➡**A scan tool is absolutely necessary to bleed the brake hydraulic system on models equipped with an Anti-lock Brake System (ABS). Be sure to refer to the ABS bleeding procedures in this section before performing any work on your vehicle's brake hydraulic system.**

The Anti-Lock Pressure Valve (APV), formerly known as the isolation/dump or control valve assembly is not serviceable. The entire component must be replaced as an assembly should a malfunction be confirmed.

1. Turn the ignition switch **OFF**. The switch MUST be **OFF** whenever you are connecting/disconnecting power from the module (as will done later in this procedure). Failure to do this may destroy the computer.

2. Disconnect the brake line fittings at the valve, then immediately cap or plug all openings to prevent system contamination or excessive fluid loss. Remember to protect the surrounding paint work from damage by fluid spillage.

3. Disengage the bottom connector from the RWAL ECU/EBCM. At no time should you allow the APV to hang by the wiring.

➡**Do not touch the electrical connectors or pins; do not allow them to contact brake fluid. If contaminated with brake fluid, clean them with water followed by isopropyl alcohol.**

4. Remove the bolts holding the valve to the bracket.

5. Remove the valve from the vehicle.

To install:

6. Place the valve in position and install the retaining bolts. Tighten the bolts to 21 ft. lbs. (29 Nm).

7. Engage the electrical connector to the RWAL ECU/EBCM.

➡**Before engaging the electrical connector, double check to be sure there is no brake fluid on the terminals or the control module may be damaged. If necessary, clean the terminals with water, followed by denatured alcohol.**

8. Remove the caps or plugs, then install the brake lines and tighten the fittings to 18 ft. lbs. (24 Nm).

9. Properly bleed the RWAL hydraulic brake system at all 4 wheels.

SPEED SENSOR

▶ **See Figure 86**

The speed sensor is not serviceable and must replaced if malfunctioning. The sensor is usually located in the left rear of the transmission case on 2WD vehicles and on the transfer case of 4WD vehicles.

The speed sensor may be tested with an ohmmeter; the correct resistance is normally 900–2000 ohms. To remove the speed sensor:

1. Raise and support the vehicle safely using jackstands.

2. Disengage the electrical connector from the speed sensor.

3. If used, remove the sensor retaining bolt.

4. Remove the speed sensor; have a container handy to catch transmission fluid when the sensor is removed.

➡**If equipped with the 4L60-E automatic transmission, use J-38417 or an equivalent speed sensor remover/installer tool whenever the sensor is serviced.**

5. Recover the O-ring used to seal the sensor; inspect it for damage or deterioration.

To install:

6. When installing, coat the new O-ring with a thin film of transmission fluid.

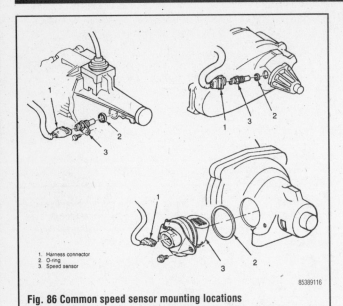

1. Harness connector
2. O-ring
3. Speed sensor

85389116

Fig. 86 Common speed sensor mounting locations

7. Install the O-ring and speed sensor.
8. If a retaining bolt is used, tighten the bolt to 97 inch lbs. (11 Nm) in automatic transmissions or 107 inch lbs. (12 Nm) for manual transmissions.
9. If the sensor is a screw-in unit tighten it to 32 ft. lbs. (43 Nm).
10. Engage the wire harness to the sensor.
11. Remove the jackstands and carefully lower the vehicle.

Bleeding the RWAL Brake System

On RWAL a few steps (listed below) should be added to the bleeding sequence in order to ease the procedure and assure all air is removed from the system. If you have access to the additional tools required, you may use these extra steps on all RWAL vehicles to assure proper bleeding.

The use of a power bleeder is recommended, but the system may also be bled manually. If a power bleeder is used, it must be of the diaphragm type and provide isolation of the fluid from air and moisture.

Do not pump the pedal rapidly when bleeding; this can make the circuits very difficult to bleed. Instead, press the brake pedal slowly 1 time and hold it down while bleeding takes place. Tighten the bleeder screw, release the pedal and wait 15 seconds before repeating the sequence. Because of the length of the brake lines and other factors, it may take 10 or more repetitions of the sequence to bleed each line properly. When necessary to bleed all 4 wheels, the correct order is right rear, left rear, right front and left front.

✳✳ CAUTION

Do not move the vehicle until a firm brake pedal is achieved. Failure to properly bleed the system may cause impaired braking and the possibility of injury and/or property damage

On all RWAL equipped vehicles, use the non-ABS system bleeding procedures found earlier in this section, with the following additions:
1. Make sure the ignition is in the **OFF** position to prevent setting false trouble codes.
2. After properly bleeding the master cylinder, install J-39177 or an equivalent combination valve depressor tool to the combination valve. This tool is used to hold the internal valve open allowing the entire system to be completely bled.

➥This tool is relatively inexpensive and should be available from various aftermarket companies. Although a homemade tool may suffice, DO NOT attempt to fabricate a homemade tool unless you are CERTAIN it will not damage the valve by over-extension.

3. Recheck the master cylinder fluid level and add, as necessary.
4. Bleed the wheel cylinders as described in the non-ABS system bleeding procedures earlier in this section.
5. Attach the Tech-1 or an equivalent scan tool, then perform 3 RWAL function tests.
6. Re-bleed the rear wheel cylinders.
7. Check for a firm brake pedal, if necessary repeat the entire bleeding procedure.
8. Once you are finished, be sure to remove the combination valve depressor tool.

FOUR WHEEL ANTI-LOCK (4WAL) SYSTEM

General Description

♦ **See Figures 87, 88, 89 and 90**

There are some slightly different four wheel anti-lock brake systems used on the pick up models. One system utilizes a separate EBCM, like the RWAL and some 4WAL systems; while the other system utilizes a Vehicle Control Module (VCM). On the VCM equipped model, the computer control module (which is mounted in the engine compartment) controls both the ABS system and the engine emission control/fuel injection systems.

All versions of the four wheel anti-lock system are designed to reduce brake lock-up during severe brake application. The basic function of each system is similar to the RWAL system described earlier in this manual, the major difference simply being that the 4 wheel system monitors and controls wheel spin/lockup on the front wheels as well as the rear.

Instead of the APV (control valve) used on RWAL systems, the 4WAL systems utilize a Brake Pressure Modulator Valve (BPMV), formerly known as the Electro-Hydraulic Control Unit (EHCU). The EHCU/BPMV is located near the master cylinder and controls the hydraulic pressure within the brake lines.

SYSTEM OPERATION

In a severe brake application, the EHCU/BPMV valve will, depending on the circumstance: allow pressure to increase within the system, maintain (isolate)

the pressure within the system, or release existing pressure through the dump valves into the accumulators.

The EHCU/BPMV valve operates by receiving signals from the speed sensors, located at each wheel, and from the brake lamp switch. The speed sensors connect directly to the EHCU/BPMV valve through a multi-pin connector.

The system is connected to the ANTI-LOCK warning lamp on the dashboard. The warning lamp will illuminate for about 2 seconds every time the vehicle is started as a lamp check. The warning lamp will illuminate if the computer detects a problem within the anti-lock system during vehicle operation. If the warning light comes on when the vehicle is started and does not go out, or if the light comes on and remains on during vehicle operation, trouble has been detected by the computer module.

SYSTEM COMPONENTS

EHCU/BPMV Valve

♦ **See Figures 91 and 92**

The BPMV valve (formerly referred to as the EHCU) is mounted near or under the master cylinder and combination valve assemblies. The valve is not serviceable and must be replaced if malfunctioning. The valve is also the sight for the only additional attention required to properly bleed the 4WAL hydraulic system.

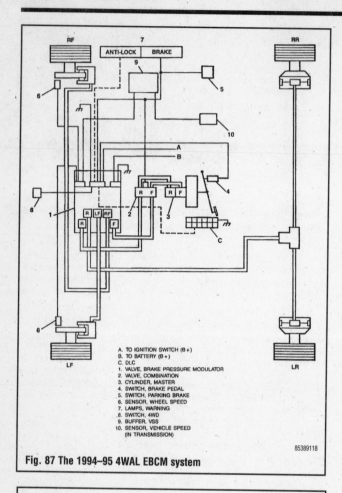

A. TO IGNITION SWITCH (B+)
B. TO BATTERY (B+)
C. DLC
1. VALVE, BRAKE PRESSURE MODULATOR
2. VALVE, COMBINATION
3. CYLINDER, MASTER
4. SWITCH, BRAKE PEDAL
5. SWITCH, PARKING BRAKE
6. SENSOR, WHEEL SPEED
7. LAMPS, WARNING
8. SWITCH, 4WD
9. BUFFER, VSS
10. SENSOR, VEHICLE SPEED
   (IN TRANSMISSION)

85389118

Fig. 87 The 1994–95 4WAL EBCM system

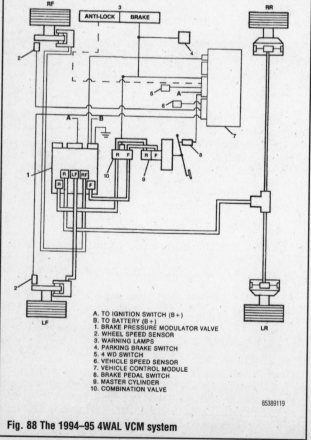

A. TO IGNITION SWITCH (B+)
B. TO BATTERY (B+)
1. BRAKE PRESSURE MODULATOR VALVE
2. WHEEL SPEED SENSOR
3. WARNING LAMPS
4. PARKING BRAKE SWITCH
5. 4 WD SWITCH
6. VEHICLE SPEED SENSOR
7. VEHICLE CONTROL MODULE
8. BRAKE PEDAL SWITCH
9. MASTER CYLINDER
10. COMBINATION VALVE

85389119

Fig. 88 The 1994–95 4WAL VCM system

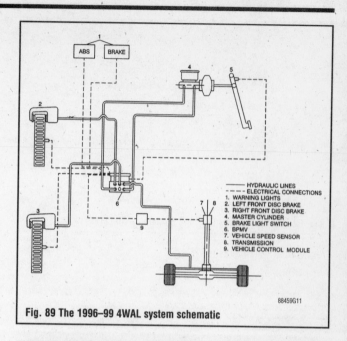

——— HYDRAULIC LINES
------- ELECTRICAL CONNECTIONS
1. WARNING LIGHTS
2. LEFT FRONT DISC BRAKE
3. RIGHT FRONT DISC BRAKE
4. MASTER CYLINDER
5. BRAKE LIGHT SWITCH
6. BPMV
7. VEHICLE SPEED SENSOR
8. TRANSMISSION
9. VEHICLE CONTROL MODULE

88459G11

Fig. 89 The 1996–99 4WAL system schematic

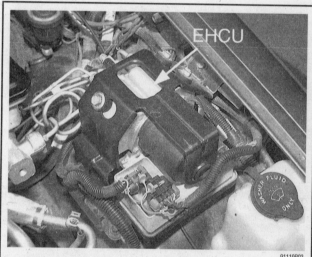

91119P03

Fig. 90 The Electro-Hydraulic Control Unit (EHCU) is located near the master cylinder and controls the hydraulic pressure within the brake lines

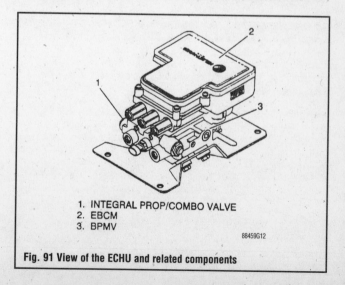

1. INTEGRAL PROP/COMBO VALVE
2. EBCM
3. BPMV

88459G12

Fig. 91 View of the ECHU and related components

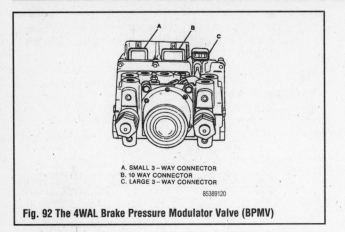

A. SMALL 3 — WAY CONNECTOR
B. 10 WAY CONNECTOR
C. LARGE 3 — WAY CONNECTOR

85389120

Fig. 92 The 4WAL Brake Pressure Modulator Valve (BPMV)

Front Wheel Speed Sensors

▶ **See Figure 93**

On most 2 and 4WD vehicles covered by this manual, the front wheel speed sensors are permanently mounted to the brake rotor splash shield which must be replaced as an assembly should the sensor fail. On 2WD vehicles, the rotor must be removed for access. On 4WD vehicles, the hub and bearing assembly must be removed.

The front wheel speed sensors operate with the help of sensor tone wheels. The tone wheels are metal rings equipped with teeth on their outer diameter. The AC voltage is produced as the teeth come into and leave alignment with the sensor. The tone wheels are attached to the rotor on 2WD vehicles and the front hub and bearing assembly on 4WD vehicles.

A properly operating speed sensor should have a resistance value of 900–2000 ohms.

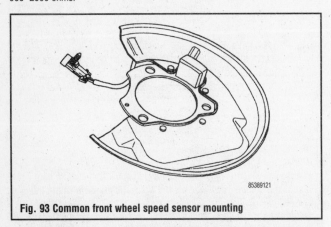

85389121

Fig. 93 Common front wheel speed sensor mounting

Diagnosis and Testing

READING CODES

▶ **See Figure 94**

On 1994 models not equipped with a VCM and 4WAL ABS system, stored trouble codes may be transmitted through the flashing of the ANTI-LOCK dash warning lamp. On these vehicles, the system may be placed in diagnostic mode using a jumper wire, however, the use of an OBD I compliant scan tool is highly recommended. On all VCM and 4WAL equipped vehicles, an OBD I compliant scan tool for 1994–96 models or an OBD II compliant scan tool for 1997–99 models must be used to display trouble codes. For all systems, the scan tool will allow performance of the specific system tests called for by the trouble tree for each code.

On vehicles where flash-diagnosis is possible, trouble code read out may be started using a jumper wire to connect Terminal H on the ALDL/DLC (diagnostic connector located under the instrument panel—refer to self-diagnostics in Section 4 of this manual for more information) to either body ground or to terminal

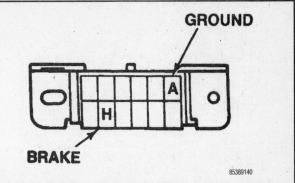

85389140

Fig. 94 The 1994 Non-VCM and 4WAL equipped vehicles may activate trouble code flash diagnosis using the ALDL/DLC

A (internal ground). The terminals must be connected for a few seconds before the code will transmit. Observe the ANTI-LOCK light on the dash and count the flashes in groups: a group of 4 flashes, a pause and a group of 3 flashes indicates Code 43.

Remember that trouble codes cannot specify the exact cause of the problem, but may only relate which circuit is affected by the problem. Before replacing any component, be sure that it is the cause of the problem, especially when dealing with a control module fault. Control modules are quite expensive and are usually not returnable.

The following is a list of trouble codes on 1994–96 models equipped with EBCM, VCM or 4WAL ABS systems

- Code 21: Right front wheel speed sensor or circuit open
- Code 22: Missing right front speed signal
- Code 23: Erratic right front wheel speed sensor
- Code 25: Left front wheel speed sensor or circuit open
- Code 26: Missing left front speed signal
- Code 27: Erratic left front wheel speed sensor
- Code 29: Simultaneous drop-out of front wheel speed sensors
- Code 35: Open or grounded rear speed signal circuit—EBCM models only
- Code 36: Missing rear speed signal
- Code 37: Erratic rear speed signal
- Code 38: Wheel speed error
- Codes 41–54: Control valves—EBCM models only
- Code 41: Right front isolation solenoid or circuit open—VCM or 4WAL models only
- Code 42: Right front pulse-width modulated solenoid or circuit open—VCM or 4WAL models only
- Code 43: Right front isolation solenoid or circuit open—VCM or 4WAL models only
- Code 44: Right front pulse-width modulated solenoid or circuit shorted—VCM or 4WAL models only
- Code 45: Left front isolation solenoid or circuit open—VCM or 4WAL models only
- Code 46: Left front pulse-width modulated solenoid or circuit open—VCM or 4WAL models only
- Code 47: Left front isolation solenoid or circuit shorted—VCM or 4WAL models only
- Code 48: Left front pulse-width modulated solenoid or circuit shorted—VCM or 4WAL models only
- Code 51: Rear isolation solenoid or circuit open—VCM or 4WAL models only
- Code 52: Rear pulse-width modulated solenoid or circuit open—VCM or 4WAL models only
- Code 53: Rear isolation solenoid or circuit shorted—VCM or 4WAL models only
- Code 54: Rear pulse-width modulated solenoid or circuit shorted—VCM or 4WAL models only
- Code 64: VCM/4WAL system voltage low—VCM or 4WAL models only
- Codes 65–66: Open or shorted pump motor relay—EBCM models only
- Code 65: Pump motor relay or circuit open—VCM or 4WAL models only
- Code 66: Pump motor relay or circuit shorted—VCM or 4WAL models only
- Code 67: Open motor circuit or shorted BPMV output—EBCM models only

- Code 67: Open motor circuit or shorted VCM output—VCM or 4WAL models only
- Code 68: Locked motor or shorted motor circuit—EBCM models only
- Codes 71–74: memory errors—EBCM models only
- Code 74: Excessive isolation time—VCM or 4WAL models only
- Code 81: Brake switch circuit shorted or open
- Code 86: Shorted anti-lock indicator lamp
- Code 88: Shorted brake warning lamp—EBCM models only

The following is a list of trouble codes on 1997–99 models equipped with 4WAL ABS systems

- Code C0021: Right front wheel speed sensor circuit open or shorted to battery
- Code C0022: Missing right front speed signal
- Code C0023: Erratic right front wheel speed sensor
- Code C0025: Left front wheel speed sensor circuit open or shorted to battery
- Code C0026: Missing left front speed signal
- Code C0027: Erratic left front wheel speed sensor
- Code C0029: Simultaneous drop-out of front wheel speed sensors
- Code C0035: Open or grounded rear speed signal circuit
- Code C0036: Missing rear speed signal
- Code C0037: Erratic rear speed signal
- Code C0038: Wheel speed signal malfunction
- Codes C0041: Right front isolation solenoid or circuit open
- Code C0042: Right front dump solenoid circuit open
- Code C0043: Right front isolation solenoid circuit shorted
- Code C0044: Right front dump solenoid circuit shorted
- Code C0045: Left front isolation solenoid circuit open
- Code C0046: Left front dump solenoid circuit open
- Code C0047: Left front isolation solenoid circuit shorted
- Code C0048: Left front dump solenoid circuit shorted
- Code C0051: Rear isolation solenoid circuit open
- Code C0052: Rear dump solenoid circuit open
- Code C0053: Rear isolation solenoid circuit shorted
- Code C0054: Rear dump solenoid circuit shorted
- Codes C0065: Pump motor relay circuit open
- Code C0066: Pump motor relay circuit shorted
- Code C0067: Open pump motor circuit
- Code C0068: Locked pump motor or shorted pump motor circuit
- Codes C0071–74: EBCM internal fault
- Code C0081: Stoplamp switch always closed or open
- Code C0086: Anti-lock indicator lamp circuit shorted to battery
- Code C0088: Brake warning lamp circuit shorted to battery

CLEARING CODES

Stored codes may be erased with the hand scanner if available or, on 1994 models not equipped with a VCM or 4WAL ABS system vehicles using a jumper wire:

1. If a hand scanner is available, use it to erase the computer module code memory.

2. For VCM or 4WAL equipped vehicles, a code cannot clear on the same ignition cycle it was set. Before attempting to clear the code (using a scan tool as this is the only way to access codes on these vehicles) it may be necessary to cycle the ignition to the **OFF** position for at least 10 seconds, then back to **ON** again to start another cycle.

3. On 1994 models not equipped with a VCM or 4WAL system, codes may be cleared without a scan tool as follows:

   a. Turn the ignition switch **ON** but do not start the engine.

   b. Use a jumper wire to ground ALDL/DLC terminal H to terminal A for 2 seconds.

   c. Remove the jumper wire for 1 second.

   d. Repeat the grounding for 2 more seconds.

   e. When the trouble codes are cleared, the ANTI-LOCK and BRAKE lamps should both illuminate and then extinguish.

PRELIMINARY DIAGNOSIS

Please refer to the charts located in this section. If the chart is used correctly, it will aid in elimination of simple, non-system problems such as blown fuses, failed bulbs or non-ABS related brake failures. The chart will prompt the reading of codes at the proper point in the diagnosis.

➡ Some of the diagnostic or repair procedures refer to the performance of a Function Test. This test is performed with the scan tool; it operates all components of the EHCU/BPMV and checks their function. The test cannot be performed without the scan tool.

1994 EBCM Equipped Vehicles

◆ See Figures 95 thru 101

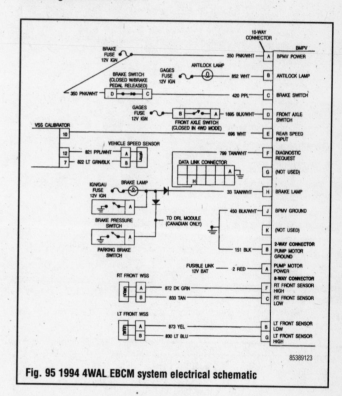

Fig. 95 1994 4WAL EBCM system electrical schematic

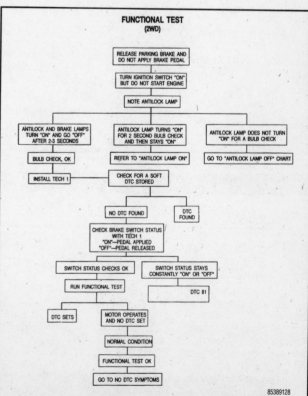

Fig. 96 1994 4WAL EBCM system functional test—2WD models

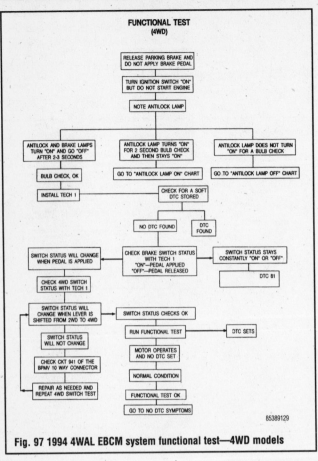

Fig. 97 1994 4WAL EBCM system functional test—4WD models

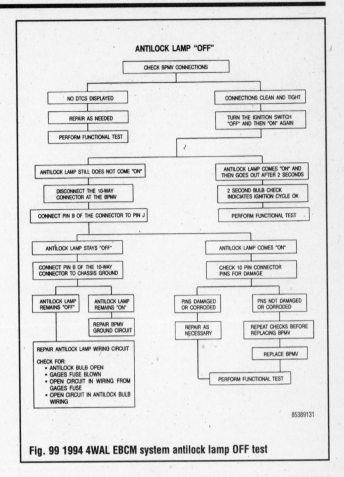

Fig. 99 1994 4WAL EBCM system antilock lamp OFF test

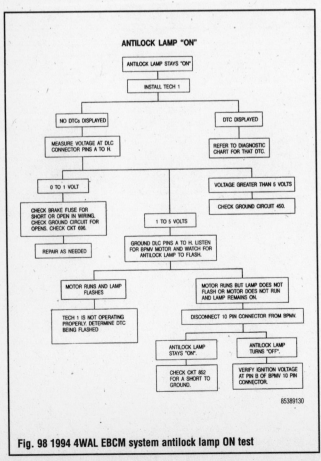

Fig. 98 1994 4WAL EBCM system antilock lamp ON test

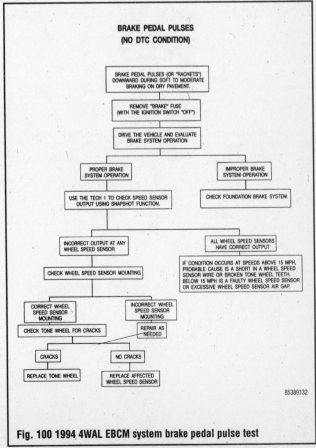

Fig. 100 1994 4WAL EBCM system brake pedal pulse test

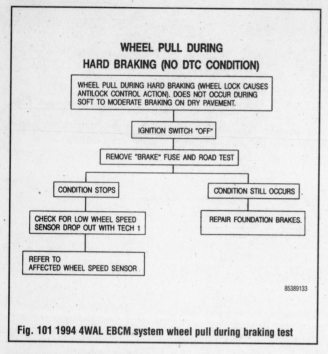

Fig. 101 1994 4WAL EBCM system wheel pull during braking test

1994–96 VCM Equipped Vehicles

▶ **See Figures 102 thru 112**

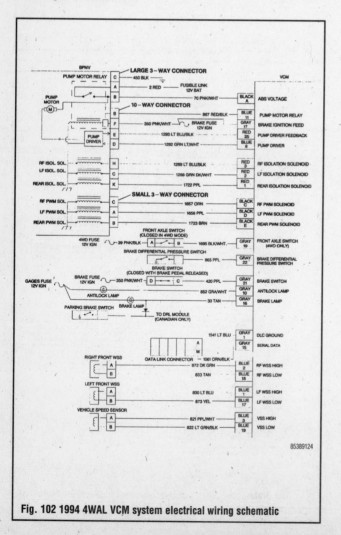

Fig. 102 1994 4WAL VCM system electrical wiring schematic

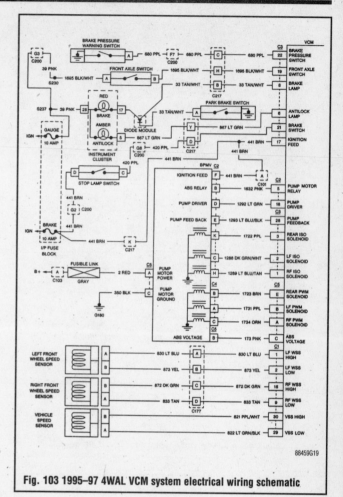

Fig. 103 1995–97 4WAL VCM system electrical wiring schematic

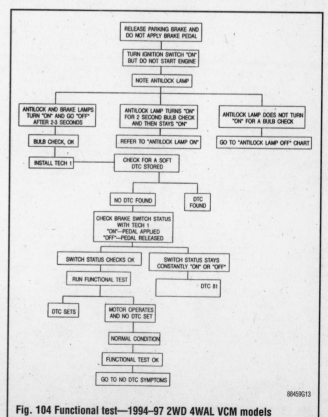

Fig. 104 Functional test—1994–97 2WD 4WAL VCM models

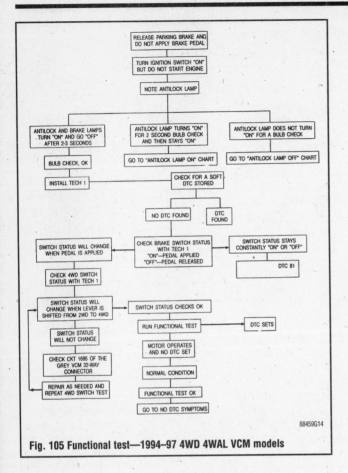

Fig. 105 Functional test—1994–97 4WD 4WAL VCM models

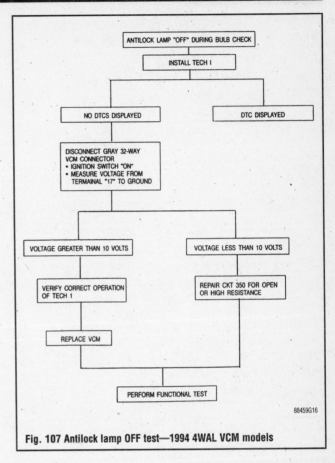

Fig. 107 Antilock lamp OFF test—1994 4WAL VCM models

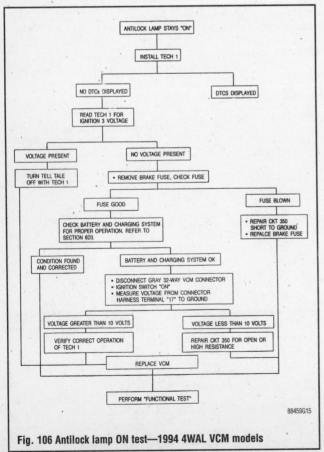

Fig. 106 Antilock lamp ON test—1994 4WAL VCM models

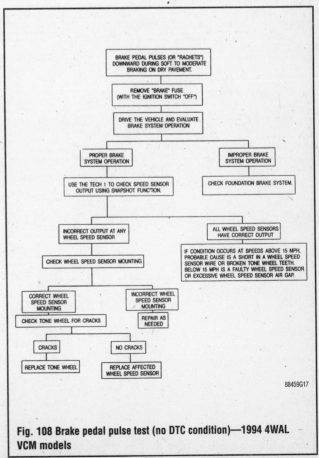

Fig. 108 Brake pedal pulse test (no DTC condition)—1994 4WAL
VCM models

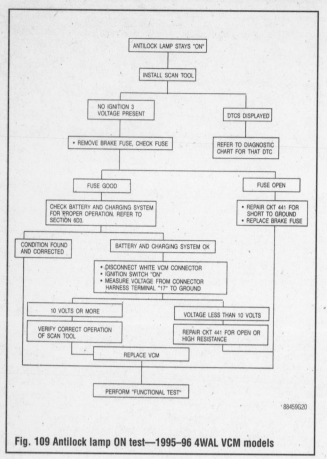

Fig. 109 Antilock lamp ON test—1995–96 4WAL VCM models

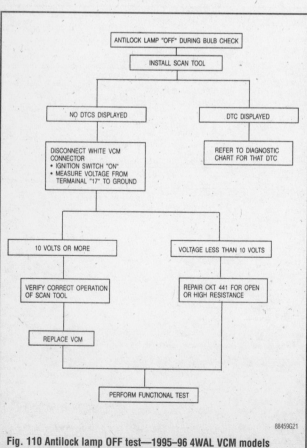

Fig. 110 Antilock lamp OFF test—1995–96 4WAL VCM models

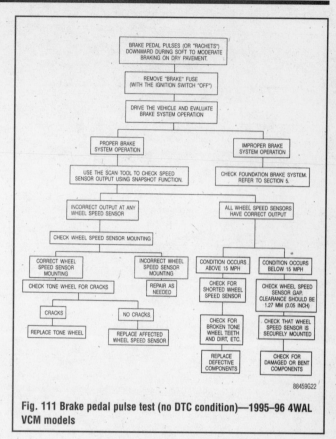

Fig. 111 Brake pedal pulse test (no DTC condition)—1995–96 4WAL VCM models

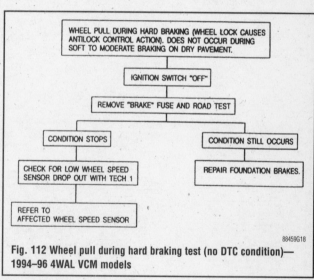

Fig. 112 Wheel pull during hard braking test (no DTC condition)—1994–96 4WAL VCM models

1997–99 4WAL Equipped Vehicles

▶ See Figures 113, 114, 115, 116 and 117

Wheel Speed Sensor

TESTING

1994 EBCM and 1994–96 VCM Equipped Vehicles

For wheel speed sensor testing on these models, refer to and follow the appropriate flow chart(s) for the ABS system used on your vehicle in this section.

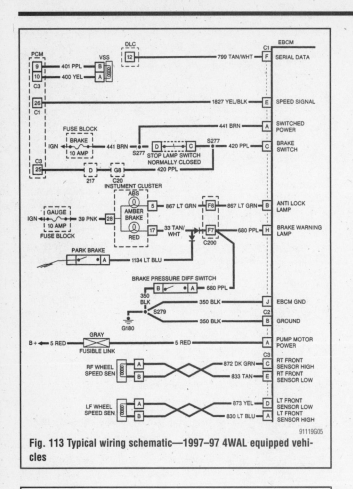

Fig. 113 Typical wiring schematic—1997–97 4WAL equipped vehicles

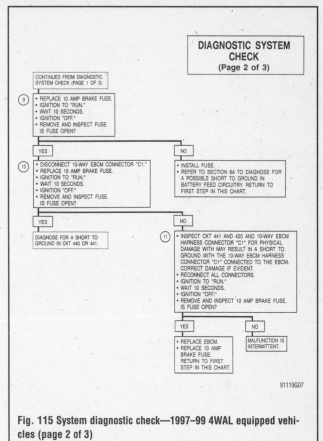

Fig. 115 System diagnostic check—1997–99 4WAL equipped vehicles (page 2 of 3)

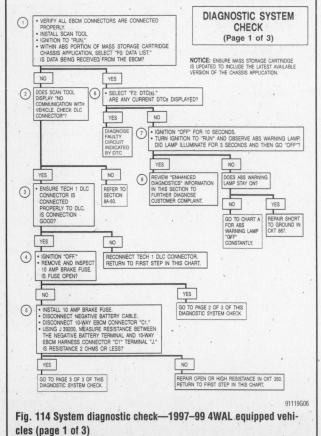

Fig. 114 System diagnostic check—1997–99 4WAL equipped vehicles (page 1 of 3)

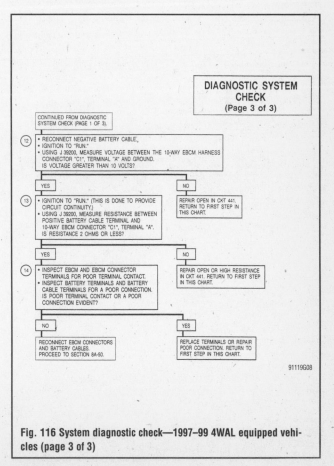

Fig. 116 System diagnostic check—1997–99 4WAL equipped vehicles (page 3 of 3)

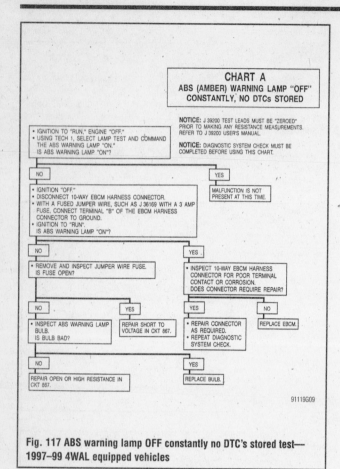

CHART A
ABS (AMBER) WARNING LAMP "OFF" CONSTANTLY, NO DTCs STORED

NOTICE: J 39200 TEST LEADS MUST BE "ZEROED" PRIOR TO MAKING ANY RESISTANCE MEASUREMENTS. REFER TO J 39200 USER'S MANUAL.

NOTICE: DIAGNOSTIC SYSTEM CHECK MUST BE COMPLETED BEFORE USING THIS CHART.

- IGNITION TO "RUN," ENGINE "OFF."
- USING TECH 1, SELECT LAMP TEST AND COMMAND THE ABS WARNING LAMP "ON."
  IS ABS WARNING LAMP "ON"?

YES → MALFUNCTION IS NOT PRESENT AT THIS TIME.

NO
- IGNITION "OFF."
- DISCONNECT 10-WAY EBCM HARNESS CONNECTOR.
- WITH A FUSED JUMPER WIRE, SUCH AS J 36169 WITH A 3 AMP FUSE, CONNECT TERMINAL "B" OF THE EBCM HARNESS CONNECTOR TO GROUND.
- IGNITION TO "RUN."
  IS ABS WARNING LAMP "ON"?

NO → REMOVE AND INSPECT JUMPER WIRE FUSE. IS FUSE OPEN?

YES → INSPECT 10-WAY EBCM HARNESS CONNECTOR FOR POOR TERMINAL CONTACT OR CORROSION. DOES CONNECTOR REQUIRE REPAIR?

NO → INSPECT ABS WARNING LAMP BULB. IS BULB BAD?

YES → REPAIR SHORT TO VOLTAGE IN CKT 867.

YES → • REPAIR CONNECTOR AS REQUIRED. • REPEAT DIAGNOSTIC SYSTEM CHECK.

NO → REPLACE EBCM.

NO → REPAIR OPEN OR HIGH RESISTANCE IN CKT 867.

YES → REPLACE BULB.

91119G09

Fig. 117 ABS warning lamp OFF constantly no DTC's stored test— 1997–99 4WAL equipped vehicles

1997–97 4WAL Equipped Vehicles

♦ See Figure 118

Some speed sensor intermittent malfunctions may be difficult to locate. Care should be taken not to disturb any electrical connections prior to an indicated step in the following procedure. This will ensure that an intermittent connection will not be corrected before the source of the malfunction is found.

1. Make sure the ignition is **OFF**.
2. Raise the vehicle and support it with jackstands.
3. Using a 5% salt water solution (two tablespoons of salt and 12 ounces of water), thoroughly spray the wheel speed sensor.
4. Unplug the five-way EBCM harness connector.
5. Using a Digital Volt Ohmmeter (DVOM) set to read resistance, probe terminals **C** and **E** of the five-way EBCM harness connector.
6. Compare your readings to the accompanying temperature versus resistant chart shown.
7. If the resistance was within specification, inspect the harness connector for signs of damage and/or corrosion. Perform all necessary repairs, clear all DTC's and repeat the test.
8. If the resistance was not within specification, unplug the sensor harness from the sensor.
9. Using a fused jumper wire, jumper terminals **A** and **B** of the two-way EBCM-to-Wheel Speed Sensor (WSS) harness connector.
10. Using the DVOM, measure the resistance between terminals **C** and **E** of the five-way EBCM harness connector.
11. If the resistance reading is not less than two Ohms. Repair an open or high resistance in wires coming from the speed sensor (these wires are usually dark green and tan).
12. If the resistance is less than two Ohms, measure the resistance between terminal **A** and terminal **B** of the sensor connector and compare your readings with the temperature versus resistance chart shown.
13. If the resistance is not within specification, replace the sensor.
14. If the resistance is within specification, check all connectors and harnesses for damage and repair as necessary.

WHEEL SPEED SENSOR TEMPERATURE VS. SENSOR RESISTANCE (APPROXIMATE)		
TEMP. (°C)	TEMP. (°F)	RESISTANCE (OHMS)
-40 TO 4	-40 TO 40	920 TO 1387
5 TO 43	41 TO 110	1125 TO 1620
44 TO 93	111 TO 200	1305 TO 1900
94 TO 150	201 TO 302	1530 TO 2200

91119G10

Fig. 118 Wheel speed sensor temperature versus resistance chart— 1997–99 4WAL ABS systems

Component Replacement

EHCU/BPMV VALVE

♦ See Figures 119 and 120

The EHCU/BPMV valve is not serviceable and must never be disassembled or repaired. If tests indicate the unit is faulty, the entire assembly must be replaced.

1. Tag and disconnect the brake lines from the EHCU/BPMV. Immediately cap or plug all openings to prevent system contamination or excessive fluid loss.
2. Tag and unplug the electrical connectors from the EHCU/BPMV.
3. Remove the retainers holding the EHCU/BPMV upper bracket to the lower bracket and vehicle. Remove the upper bracket and hydraulic unit as an assembly.
4. If necessary, once they are removed from the vehicle, separate the bracket from the EHCU/BPMV.

To install:

5. If removed, assemble the EHCU/BPMV to its bracket. Install the retainers and tighten to 84 inch lbs. (9 Nm). Be careful as overtightening these bolts can cause excessive noise transfer during system operation.
6. Install the assembly into the vehicle, then tighten the retainers 18 ft. lbs. (25 Nm).
7. Engage the electrical connectors as tagged during removal. Make certain each is squarely seated and secure.
8. Remove the caps or plugs, then connect the brake lines to their original locations, as tagged during removal. Tighten the fittings to 21 ft. lbs. (29 Nm).
9. Properly bleed the hydraulic brake system, including the EHCU/BPMV valve.

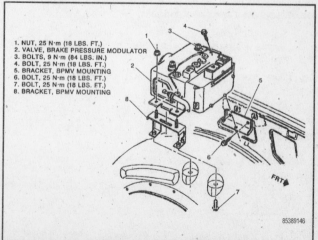

1. NUT, 25 N·m (18 LBS. FT.)
2. VALVE, BRAKE PRESSURE MODULATOR
3. BOLTS, 9 N·m (84 LBS. IN.)
4. BOLT, 25 N·m (18 LBS. FT.)
5. BRACKET, BPMV MOUNTING
6. BOLT, 25 N·m (18 LBS. FT.)
7. BOLT, 25 N·m (18 LBS. FT.)
8. BRACKET, BPMV MOUNTING

FRT

85389146

Fig. 119 Brake Pressure Modulator Valve (BPMV) mounting

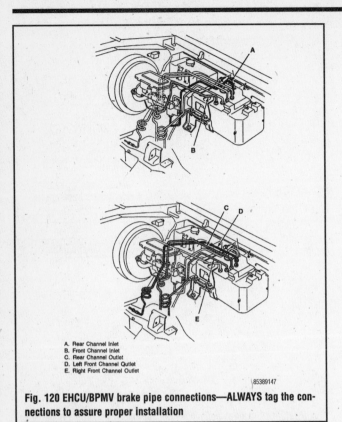

A. Rear Channel Inlet
B. Front Channel Inlet
C. Rear Channel Outlet
D. Left Front Channel Outlet
E. Right Front Channel Outlet

85389147

Fig. 120 EHCU/BPMV brake pipe connections—ALWAYS tag the connections to assure proper installation

Electronic Brake Control Module (EBCM)

REMOVAL & INSTALLATION

1. Disconnect the negative battery cable.
2. Unplug the electrical connections from the Electronic Brake Control Module (EBCM) and the combination valve.
3. Tag and disconnect the brake lines from the combination valve and the hydraulic lines from the three tube adapters on the Brake Pressure Modulator Valve (BPMV).
4. Unfasten the three 10mm bolts that attach the Electro-Hydraulic Control Unit (EHCU) to the vehicle mounting bracket.
5. Remove the EHCU from the engine compartment.
6. Remove the four T-25 Torx® bolts that attach the EBCM to the BPMV.

➡Do not pry on the EBCM or the BPMV using a mechanical aid or you may damage the EBCM. Do not reuse the EBCM gasket or retaining bolts. Always use a new gasket and bolts.

7. Separate the EBCM from the BPMV using a light amount of force.
8. Clean the EBCM using a clean dry cloth.
To install:

➡Do not use RTV or any other type of sealant on the gasket mating surfaces.

9. Position a new EBCM gasket on the BPMV.
10. Position the EBCM onto the BPMV. Make sure the gasket and the components are all perfectly aligned. Install the EBCM-to-BPMV bolts and tighten them to 39 inch lbs. (5 Nm) using an X pattern.
11. Position the EHCU onto the vehicle bracket and install the retaining bolts.
12. Attach the brake lines to the combination valve and tighten the fittings to 18 ft. lbs. (24 Nm).
13. Attach the hydraulic lines to the tube adapters and tighten them until they are snug.
14. Attach all electrical connections to the assembly.
15. Connect the negative battery cable and bleed the brake system.

FRONT WHEEL SPEED SENSORS

▸ **See Figures 121, 122 and 123**

1. Raise and support the front of the vehicle safely using jackstands.
2. Remove the tire and wheel assembly.
3. Remove the brake caliper from the mounting bracket and support aside from the suspension using a coat hanger or wire. Make sure the brake line is not stretched, kinked or otherwise damaged. The line should never support the weight of the caliper.
4. For 2WD vehicles, remove the hub and rotor assembly. For details, please refer to the brake disc procedure found earlier in this section.
5. For 4WD vehicles, remove the brake disc (please refer to the procedure

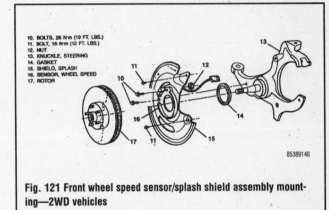

10. BOLTS, 26 N·m (19 FT. LBS.)
11. BOLT, 16 N·m (12 FT. LBS.)
12. NUT
13. KNUCKLE, STEERING
14. GASKET
15. SHIELD, SPLASH
16. SENSOR, WHEEL SPEED
17. ROTOR

85389148

Fig. 121 Front wheel speed sensor/splash shield assembly mounting—2WD vehicles

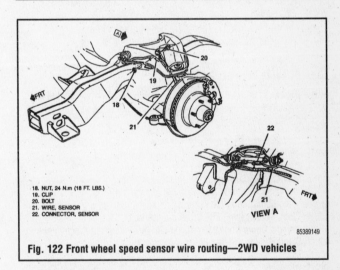

18. NUT, 24 N·m (18 FT. LBS.)
19. CLIP
20. BOLT
21. WIRE, SENSOR
22. CONNECTOR, SENSOR

VIEW A

85389149

Fig. 122 Front wheel speed sensor wire routing—2WD vehicles

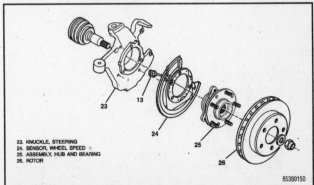

23. KNUCKLE, STEERING
24. SENSOR, WHEEL SPEED
25. ASSEMBLY, HUB AND BEARING
26. ROTOR

85389150

Fig. 123 Front wheel speed sensor/splash shield assembly mounting—4WD vehicles

9-36 BRAKES

earlier in this section), then remove the hub and bearing assembly. For details on hub and bearing removal, please refer to the steering knuckle procedure in Section 8 of this manual.

6. Unplug the sensor wiring connector.

7. Disconnect the sensor wire from the clip(s) on the upper control arm. On most vehicles this will involve removing the retaining bolt/nut in order to free the clip, then separating the wire from the clip. 4WD vehicles tend to utilize more clips than the 2WD vehicles due to the difference in the front suspension.

8. Remove the splash shield retaining bolts, then remove the shield and sensor assembly.

To install:

9. Mount the sensor and splash shield assembly to the steering knuckle. Install the retaining bolts and tighten them to 19 ft. lbs. (26 Nm) for the outer bolts and 12 ft. lbs. (16 Nm) for the inner bolts.

10. Connect the wiring to the clip(s) on the upper control arm. Check the wiring for correct routing. If removed, install and tighten the clip retaining bolt/nuts. The wiring on some vehicles/components may be marked at the appropriate clip mounting position, look for a paint stripe on the sensor wire.

11. Engage the wiring connector.

12. On 4WD vehicles, install the hub and bearing assembly.

13. Install the brake disc.

14. Remove the support, then reposition and secure brake caliper.

15. Install the tire and wheel assembly, then adjust the wheel bearings on 2WD vehicles.

16. Remove the jackstands and carefully lower the vehicle.

REAR WHEEL SPEED SENSOR

The sensor is usually located in the left rear of the transmission case on 2WD vehicles and on the transfer case of 4WD vehicles.

The speed sensor may be tested with an ohmmeter; the correct resistance is normally 900–2000 ohms. To remove the speed sensor:

1. Raise and support the vehicle safely using jackstands.

2. Unplug the electrical connector from the speed sensor.

3. If used, remove the sensor retaining bolt.

4. Remove the speed sensor; have a container handy to catch transmission fluid when the sensor is removed.

➡️If equipped with the 4L60-E automatic transmission, use J-38417 or an equivalent speed sensor remover/installer tool whenever the sensor is serviced.

5. Recover the O-ring used to seal the sensor; inspect it for damage or deterioration.

To install:

6. When installing, coat the new O-ring with a thin film of transmission fluid.

7. Install the O-ring and speed sensor.

8. If a retaining bolt is used, tighten the bolt to 97 inch lbs. (11 Nm) in automatic transmissions or 107 inch lbs. (12 Nm) for manual transmissions.

9. Engage the wire harness to the sensor.

10. Remove the jackstands and carefully lower the vehicle.

Bleeding the Brake System

1994–96 VCM-ABS SYSTEMS AND 1994–95 4WAL ABS SYSTEMS

▶ See Figures 124 and 125

The EHCU/BPMV module is the one component which adds to the complexity of bleeding the 4WAL brake systems. For the most part the system is bled in the same manner as the non-ABS vehicles. Refer to the non-ABS system brake bleeding procedure earlier in this section for details. But because of the EHCU/BPMV's complex internal valving additional steps are necessary if the unit has been replaced or if it is suspected to contain air. These bleeding steps are not necessary if the only connection/fitting(s) opened were downstream of the unit. These steps may or may not be necessary after master cylinder replacement. If in doubt (or without the necessary special tools) thoroughly bleed the system and see if a firm brake pedal can be obtained, if not, the EHCU/BPMV must be bled as well.

As with the RWAL brake system, the use of a power bleeder is recommended, but the system may also be bled manually. If a power bleeder is used, it must be of the diaphragm type and provide isolation of the fluid from air and moisture.

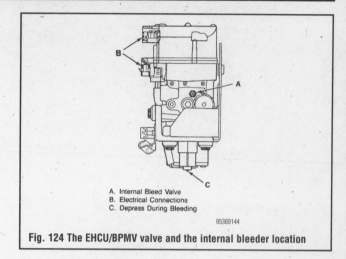

A. Internal Bleed Valve
B. Electrical Connections
C. Depress During Bleeding

Fig. 124 The EHCU/BPMV valve and the internal bleeder location

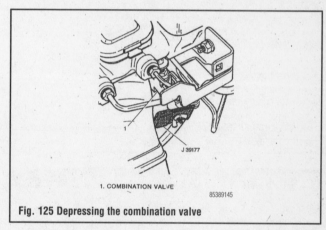

1. COMBINATION VALVE

Fig. 125 Depressing the combination valve

Do not pump the pedal rapidly when bleeding; this can make the circuits very difficult to bleed. Instead, press the brake pedal slowly 1 time and hold it down while bleeding takes place. Tighten the bleeder screw, release the pedal and wait 15 seconds before repeating the sequence. Because of the length of the brake lines and other factors, it may take 10 or more repetitions of the sequence to bleed each line properly. When necessary to bleed all 4 wheels, the correct order is right rear, left rear, right front and left front.

✳✳ CAUTION

Do not move the vehicle until a firm brake pedal is achieved. Failure to properly bleed the system may cause impaired braking and the possibility of injury and/or property damage

If the EHCU/BPMV requires bleeding, the following procedures may be used to free all trapped air from the component. The combination valve depressor tools are used to hold the internal passages (combination valve and EHCU/BPMV bleed accumulator bleed stems open allowing the entire system to be completely bled.

➡️The combination valve tools are relatively inexpensive and should be available from various aftermarket companies. Although a homemade tool may suffice, DO NOT attempt to fabricate a homemade tool unless you are CERTAIN it will not damage the valve/bleed stem by over-extension.

Finally, remember to always bleed the 4WAL brake system with the ignition **OFF** to prevent setting false trouble codes.

1. Make sure the ignition is in the **OFF** position to prevent setting false trouble codes.

2. If necessary, properly bleed the master cylinder assembly as directed in the hydraulic brake bleeding procedure found earlier in this section. Check and add additional fluid, as necessary.

3. Open the internal bleed valves ¼–½ turn each.

4. Install one J–39177 or equivalent combination valve depressor tool on the left accumulator bleed stem of the EHCU. Install one tool on the right accumulator bleed stem and install the third tool on the combination valve.

5. Properly bleed the wheel cylinders and calipers. For details, please refer to the hydraulic brake bleeding procedure located earlier in this section.

6. Remove the 3 special tools.

7. Check the master cylinder fluid level, refilling as necessary.

8. Switch the ignition **ON** (engine not running) and use a hand scanner to perform 6 function tests on the system.

9. Repeat the wheel cylinder and caliper bleeding procedure to remove all air that was purged from the BPMV during the function tests.

10. Check for a firm brake pedal. If necessary, repeat the entire procedure until a firm pedal is obtained.

11. Carefully test drive the vehicle at moderate speeds; check for proper pedal feel and brake operation. If any problem is noted in feel or function, repeat the entire bleeding procedure.

1996–99 4WAL ABS SYSTEM

➡**The manual bleeding procedure is preferred on these models. Pressure bleeding may be used may be used for base brake bleeding only and is not suitable on these ABS systems.**

➡**To bleed the system, a length of clear neoprene bleeder hose, bleeder wrenches and a clear bleeder bottle (old glass jar or drink bottle will suffice). A scan tool should also be used to run the system through functional tests.**

1. Clean the top of the master cylinder, remove the cover and fill the reservoirs with clean fluid. To prevent squirting fluid, and possibly damaging painted surfaces, install the cover during the procedure, but be sure to frequently check and top off the reservoirs with fresh fluid.

❋❋ WARNING

Never reuse brake fluid, which has been bled from the system.

2. The master cylinder must be bled first if it is suspected to contain air. If the master cylinder was removed and bench bled before installation it must still be bled, but it should take less time and effort. Bleed the master cylinder as follows:
   a. Position a container under the master cylinder to catch the brake fluid.

❋❋ WARNING

Do not allow brake fluid to spill on or come in contact with the vehicle's finish as it will remove the paint. In case of a spill, immediately flush the area with water.

   b. Loosen the front brake line at the master cylinder and allow the fluid to flow from the front port.
   c. Have a friend depress the brake pedal slowly and hold (air and/or fluid should be expelled from the loose fitting). Tighten the line, then release the brake pedal and wait 15 seconds. Loosen the fitting and repeat until all air is removed from the master cylinder bore.

   d. When finished, tighten the line fitting.
   e. Repeat the sequence at the master cylinder rear pipe fitting.

➡**During the bleeding procedure, make sure your assistant does NOT release the brake pedal while a fitting is loosened or while a bleeder screw is opening. Air will be drawn back into the system.**

3. Check and refill the master cylinder reservoir.

➡**Remember, if the reservoir is allowed to empty of fluid during the procedure, air will be drawn into the system and bleeding procedure must be restarted at the master cylinder assembly.**

4. All calipers and wheel cylinders must be bled in the proper sequence:
   a. Right rear
   b. Left rear
   c. Right front
   d. Left front

5. Check the master cylinder after every four-to-six strokes of the brake pedal and replenish as necessary. This will avoid running the system dry.

6. Bleed the individual calipers or wheel cylinders as follows:
   a. Place a suitable wrench over the bleeder screw and attach a clear plastic hose over the screw end. Be sure the hose is seated snugly on the screw or you may be squirted with brake fluid.

➡**Be very careful when bleeding wheel cylinders and brake calipers. The bleeder screws often rust in position and may easily break off if forced. Installing a new bleeder screw will often require removal of the component and may include overhaul or replacement of the wheel cylinder/caliper. To help prevent the possibility of breaking a bleeder screw, spray it with some penetrating oil before attempting to loosen it.**

   b. Submerge the other end of the tube in a transparent container of clean brake fluid.
   c. Loosen the bleed screw, then have a friend apply the brake pedal slowly through its full travel and hold. Tighten the bleed screw, release the brake pedal and wait 15 seconds. Repeat the sequence (including the 15 second pause) until all air is expelled from the caliper or cylinder.
   d. Tighten the bleed screw when finished.

7. Repeat the procedure at each wheel until approximately one pint of fluid has been bled from each wheel. Clean fluid should be present at each wheel bleed screws.

➡**On 1997 and later models, do not run the function test after combination valve or tube adapter replacement except on S/T trucks.**

8. If any component is replaced, which may have caused air to enter the BPMV, use a suitable scan tool to run the function tests four times while applying the brake pedal firmly.

➡**Set the parking brake when running the function tests.**

9. Re-bleed all four wheels using the procedures described above after running the function tests so that all air is expelled from the brake system.

10. Check the pedal feel before attempting to move the vehicle and re-bleed the system as often as necessary to obtain the proper pedal feel.

BRAKE SPECIFICATIONS

All specifications given in inches unless otherwise indicated

Year	Model		Brake Disc			Brake Drum Diameter			Minimum Lining Thickness	
			Original Thickness	Minimum Thickness	Maximum Run-out	Original Inside Diameter	Max. Wear Limit	Maximum Machine Diameter	Front	Rear
1994	S10 Blazer/Jimmy/Bravada	F	1.030	0.980	0.002	—	—	—	0.030	0.030
		R	—	—	—	9.50	9.59	9.56	0.030	0.030
	S10/S15 Pick-up/Sonoma	F	1.030	0.980	0.002	—	—	—	0.030	0.030
		R	—	—	—	9.50	9.59	9.56	0.030	0.030
1995	S10 Blazer/Jimmy/Bravada	F	1.030	0.980	0.002	—	—	—	0.030	0.030
		R	—	—	—	9.50	9.59	9.56	0.030	0.030
	S10/S15 Pick-up/Sonoma	F	1.030	0.980	0.002	—	—	—	0.030	0.030
		R	—	—	—	9.50	9.59	9.56	0.030	0.030
1996	S10 Blazer/Jimmy/Bravada	F	1.030	0.965	0.003	—	—	—	0.030	0.030
		R	—	—	—	9.50	9.59	9.56	0.030	0.030
	S10/S15 Pick-up/Sonoma/Hombre	F	1.030	0.965	0.003	—	—	—	0.030	0.030
		R	—	—	—	9.50	9.59	9.56	0.030	0.030
1997	S10 Blazer/Jimmy/Bravada/Envoy	F	1.030	0.965	0.003	—	—	—	0.030	0.030
		R	0.787	0.728	0.004	9.50	9.59	9.56	0.030	0.030
	S10/S15 Pick-up/Sonoma/Hombre	F	1.030	0.965	0.003	—	—	—	0.030	0.030
		R	0.787	0.728	0.004	9.50	9.59	9.56	0.030	0.030
1998	S10 Blazer/Jimmy/Bravada/Envoy	F	1.03	0.965	0.003	—	—	—	0.030	0.030
		R	0.787	0.728	0.004	9.50	9.59	9.56	0.030	0.030
	S10/S15 Pick-up/Sonoma/Hombre	F	1.030	0.965	0.003	—	—	—	0.030	0.030
		R	0.787	0.728	0.004	9.50	9.59	9.56	0.030	0.030
1999	S10 Blazer/Jimmy/Bravada/Envoy	F	1.030	0.965	0.003	—	—	—	0.030	0.030
		R	0.787	0.728	0.004	9.50	9.59	9.56	0.030	0.030
	S10/S15 Pick-up/Sonoma/Hombre	F	1.030	0.965	0.003	—	—	—	0.030	0.030
		R	0.787	0.728	0.004	9.50	9.59	9.56	0.030	0.030

F: Front disc brakes

R: Rear disc brakes

91119C01

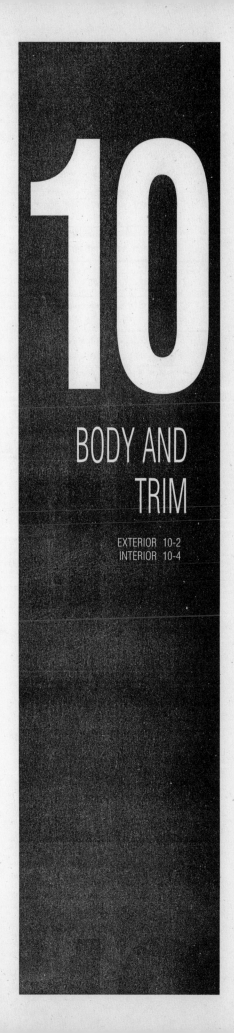

10

BODY AND TRIM

EXTERIOR

Door Hinges

ADJUSTMENT

Factory installed hinges are welded in place, so no adjustment of the system is necessary or recommended. Service replacement hinges are bolted in position and may be adjusted. If your vehicle is equipped with service replacement hinges, please refer to the door hinge adjustment procedure located later in this section.

➡The ½ in. (13mm) drill hinge holes with the service replacement bolt-on door hinges provide for some adjustment.

1. Loosen the striker and door hinge bolts, then adjust the door up, down, forward, rearward, in or out (as necessary) at the door hinges.
2. Hold the door in position (an assistant is helpful here) and tighten the hinge bolts slightly, then check the for the following specified gaps:
   • Door-to-rocker panel—0.21–0.27 in. (5–7mm)
   • Door-to-roof panel—0.21–0.27 in. (5–7mm)
   • Rear of door-to-rear of pillar—0.16–0.22 in. (4–6mm)
   • Forward edge of door-to-front fender—0.16–0.22 in. (4–6mm)
   • Door surface flush with other panels to within—0.03 in. (1mm)
3. Make sure that the striker properly engages the lock fork bolt.
4. When all adjustments are complete, tighten the hinge bolts to 26 ft. lbs. (35 Nm), then tighten the striker bolts securely.

Hood

ALIGNMENT

Align the hood so that the gaps between all of the components are equal; it must be flush with the fender and the cowl vent grille. Center the hood in the opening between the fenders, the cowl and the radiator grille. If it is difficult to center the hood or if the hood appears to be out of square, the front end sheet metal may need to be adjusted.

Most of the hood adjustment is achieved through the hinge-bolts, though on some vehicles adjustment may also be obtained through repositioning the striker and/or through the used of bump stops.

Grille

REMOVAL & INSTALLATION

♦ See Figures 1 and 2

1. Loosen and remove the grille-to-fender, grille-to-radiator support or grille-to-center support retainers.
2. Pull the grille forward sufficiently and unplug any necessary wiring (such as side marker wiring and bulb sockets).

Fig. 1 Location of the grill-to-radiator support bolts

91110P13

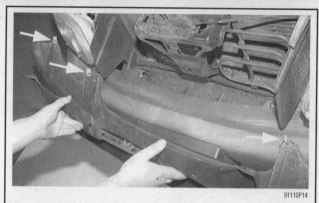

Fig. 2 Unsnap the four grill-to-body clips

91110P14

3. Remove the grille from the vehicle.
4. Installation is the reverse of removal. Be careful not to overtighten any of the fasteners as the grille, bezel and fasteners are all easily damaged. Most fasteners should be tightened to no more than 12 inch lbs. (1.4 Nm).

Outside Mirrors

REMOVAL & INSTALLATION

Except 1994 Utility Models

♦ See Figure 3

➡A damaged mirror glass face may be replaced by placing a large piece or multiple strips of tape over the glass then breaking the mirror face. Adhesive back mirror faces should be available for most applications.

1. Remove the door trim panel and the water deflector in order to access the mirror retaining nuts.
2. If equipped, remove the access hole plugs, then unfasten the mirror nuts.
3. If equipped, unplug the mirror electrical connection.
4. Remove the mirror assembly from the vehicle.

To install:

5. Place the mirror into position and install the retaining nuts. Tighten the nuts to 53 inch lbs. (6 Nm).
6. If equipped, attach the mirror electrical connection.
7. If equipped, install the access hole plugs.
8. Install the water deflector. The water deflector is secured by a strip of adhesive between the deflector and door, as well as waterproof sealing tape. Upon installation, make sure a good seal is achieved to keep water from entering into the body. If necessary, use strip caulking as a sealant between the deflector and door.
9. Install the door trim panel.

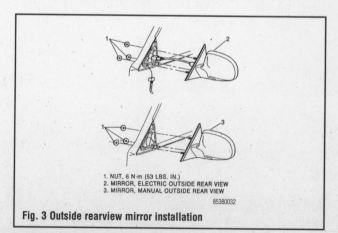

1. NUT, 6 N·m (53 LBS. IN.)
2. MIRROR, ELECTRIC OUTSIDE REAR VIEW
3. MIRROR, MANUAL OUTSIDE REAR VIEW

85380032

Fig. 3 Outside rearview mirror installation

1994 Utility Models

1. Unfasten the screws that attach the mirror to the door.
2. Remove the mirror from the door and if equipped, unplug the mirror electrical connection.
3. Installation is the reverse of removal. Tighten the mirror retainers to 53 inch lbs. (6 Nm).

Antenna

REMOVAL & INSTALLATION

Except 1994 Utility Models

▶ **See Figures 4, 5 and 6**

1. Disconnect the negative battery cable.
2. Remove the mast retaining nut, mast and bezel.
3. Disconnect the antenna cable from the receiver cable.
4. Remove the screw and star washer attaching the antenna to the fender.
5. Remove the antenna.

➡ **When installing the antenna to the fender make sure the retaining nut is tight. A loose antenna or one that does not make good contact at the fender can cause radio interference.**

6. Installation is the reverse of removal.

1994 Utility Models

1. Remove the antenna mast, cable nut and bezel.
2. Remove the wiper arms and the cowl vent grille.
3. Disconnect the antenna cable from the radio extension cable.
4. Remove the antenna retainers and washers.
5. Remove the antenna.

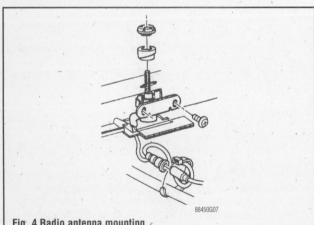

Fig. 4 Radio antenna mounting

➡ **When installing the antenna to the fender make sure the retaining nut is tight. A loose antenna or one that does not make good contact at the fender can cause radio interference.**

6. Installation is the reverse of removal.

Fenders

REMOVAL & INSTALLATION

▶ **See Figure 7**

Right

1. Disconnect the negative battery cable.
2. Remove the radiator grille.
3. On 1994–95 utility models, remove the bumper.
4. On models equipped, the bumper end cap must be removed.
5. Matchmark and remove the hood from the vehicle.
6. Remove the battery, battery tray and radiator coolant bottle (if present).
7. If equipped, remove the VCM/PCM.
8. Remove the antenna mast and base. For details, please refer to the procedure earlier in this section.
9. On 1994–95 utility models, remove the wiper arms and the cowl vent grille.
10. On 1994–95 utility models, remove the hood hinge-to-fender nut and bolt.
11. Remove the fender retaining bolts. Locations should include all or some of the following, radiator support, reinforcement, wheelhouse panel, door frame and/or door hinge. Keep track of any shim washers which may come lose after removing fender bolts. The shim washers should be installed in their original locations during assembly.
12. Separate any necessary wiring or vacuum hoses from the fender, then remove it from the vehicle.
13. Installation is the reverse of the removal. Tighten all fender retaining bolts to 21 ft. lbs. (29 Nm) on all pick-up models and 1996–99 utility models. On 1994–95 utility models tighten the bolts to 18 ft. lbs. (25 Nm).

Left

1. Remove the radiator grille.
2. On 1994–95 utility models, remove the bumper.
3. On models equipped the bumper end cap must be removed.
4. Matchmark and remove the hood from the vehicle.
5. If present on this side, remove the coolant reservoir bottle.
6. Remove the windshield wiper bottle from the fender.
7. Remove the horn from the fender.
8. Remove the hood latch cable.
9. On 1994–95 utility models, remove the wiper arms and the cowl vent grille.
10. If equipped with 4 wheel ABS, remove the BPMV from the fender. If the assembly cannot be repositioned slightly and supported with the lines attached, the unit must be removed completely from the vehicle. DO NOT kink or damage the brake lines, brake failure and serious personal injury could result.

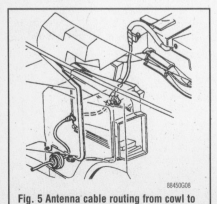

Fig. 5 Antenna cable routing from cowl to radio

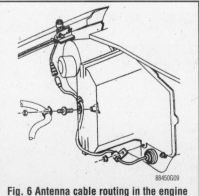

Fig. 6 Antenna cable routing in the engine compartment

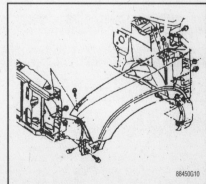

Fig. 7 Fender to radiator support and cowl bolts

11. On 1994–95 utility models, remove the hood hinge-to-fender nut and bolt.

12. Remove the fender retaining bolts. Locations should include all or some of the following: radiator support, reinforcement, wheelhouse panel, door frame and/or door hinge. Keep track of any shim washers which may come lose after removing fender bolts. The shim washers should be installed in their original locations during assembly.

13. Separate any necessary wiring or vacuum hoses from the fender, then remove it from the vehicle.

14. Installation is the reverse of the removal. Tighten all fender retaining bolts to 21 ft. lbs. (29 Nm) on all pick-up models and 1996–99 utility models. On 1994–95 utility models tighten the bolts to 18 ft. lbs. (25 Nm).

Power Sunroof

REMOVAL & INSTALLATION

Glass

1. Close the sunroof and open the sunshade.
2. If the piece of glass being removed is to be reinstalled, mark the location of the screws, this will ensure proper alignment during installation.
3. Unfassten the screw that attach the sunroof glass to the sunroof assembly.
4. Remove the glass from the vehicle.
To install:
5. Place the glass into position and install the screws that retain the glass. Do not fully tighten the screws just yet.
6. Adjust the glass so that the fit between the glass and the opening is equal at all four sides. The rear edge of the glass may be slightly higher than the front edge to reduce the wind noise.
7. After the glass has been adjusted, tighten the screws to 31 inch lbs. (3.5 Nm).
8. Check the operation and fit of the glass.

Motor

1. Disconnect the negative battery cable.
2. Remove the sunroof opening trim by starting at the butt joint and pulling the trim strip from the sunroof opening.
3. Remove the headlines as follows:
   a. If equipped, remove the overhead or sunroof console.
   b. If equipped, remove the dome lamp.
   c. Remove the coat hooks and the assist handles.
   d. Remove the sunshade-to-roof screws, while pulling down on the sunshade base, push in on the extended screws, loosen the screw that attaches sunshade to the roof and pull down on the sunshade retainer while pushing in on the extended screw. Remove the retainer.
   e. Remove the windshield garnish moldings using trim removal tool J 38778 or its equivalent. Pull the molding away from the pillar and up to remove it.
   f. On four door models, remove the body lock pillar trim panels.
   g. Remove the roof rear header garnish molding using the trim removal

tool. Insert the tool into the front edge of the trim and work along the front of the panel, from one end to the other. Unplug the cargo lamp electrical connection and remove the trim.
   h. On two door models, remove the rear seat upper seat belt anchor bolts.
   i. Remove the upper and lower front seat belt anchor bolts.
   j. Remove the rear seat belt lower anchor nut (two door models only).
   k. Remove the end gate or liftgate opening sill plate.
   l. Remove the jack storage cover (left side).
   m. Remove the upper body side trim panel screw (left side).
   n. Remove the upper body side trim panel and the body side front lower trim panel.
   o. Remove the headliner from the vehicle.
4. Remove the sunroof console mounting bracket.
5. Remove the straps that retain the wiring harness.
6. Tag and unplug any necessary electrical connections.
7. Unfasten the screws that attach the motor to the sunroof assembly.
8. Remove the motor from the vehicle. Make sure that you do not move the sunroof mechanism while the motor is not in place.
To install:
9. Place the motor into position and install the retaining screws. Tighten the screws to 31 inch lbs. (3.5 Nm).
10. Attach all electrical connections that were unplugged.
11. Attach the straps that retain the wiring harness.
12. Install the sunroof console mounting bracket.

➡**New headliners must be pierced to accommodate actual vehicle accessories.**

13. Install the headliner as follows:
   a. Install the body side front lower trim panel and the upper body side trim panel.
   b. Install the upper body side trim panel screw (left side).
   c. Install the jack storage cover (left side).
   d. Install the end gate or liftgate opening sill plate.
   e. Install the rear seat belt lower anchor nut (two door models only). Tighten to 59 ft. lbs. (80 Nm).
   f. Install the upper and lower front seat belt anchor bolts. Tighten the bolts to 52 ft. lbs. (70 Nm).
   g. On two door models, install the rear seat upper seat belt anchor bolts. Tighten the bolts to 52 ft. lbs. (70 Nm).
   h. Install the roof rear header garnish molding. Attach the cargo lamp electrical connection, place the trim in position and engage the molding retainers.
   i. On four door models, install the body lock pillar trim panels.
   j. Install the windshield garnish moldings. Place the molding into position, align the retainer clips with the slots and press into place.
   k. Place the sunshade retainer in position, install the screw and tighten to 10 inch lbs. (1.1 Nm). Position the sunshade, install the screws and tighten to 10 inch lbs. (1.1 Nm).
   l. Install the coat hooks and the assist handles.
   m. If equipped, install the dome lamp.
   n. If equipped, install the overhead or sunroof console.
14. Install the sunroof opening trim. Start the trim in the center of the front of the sunroof opening and work around the perimeter.

INTERIOR

Instrument Panel and Pad

REMOVAL & INSTALLATION

1994 Pick-Up Models

1. Disconnect the negative battery cable.
2. Unfasten the lower shroud insulator screws and remove the lower sound insulator panels from the vehicle.
3. Unfasten the courtesy lamp screws and allow the lamp to hang.
4. Remove the front speaker grills and the speakers.

5. Unfasten the Data Link Connectors (DLC) and separate the DLC from the steering column panel.
6. Remove the steering column filler panel.
7. Remove the instrument panel accessory trim plate.
8. Remove the instrument cluster and the heater and/or A/C controls from the instrument panel.
9. Remove the radio, and then pry the defroster from the grille using a suitable tool.
10. Unfasten the box striker screws and remove the striker.
11. Unfasten the glove box screws and remove the glove box from the instrument panel.
12. Remove the door sill trim plates and the cowl side trim panels.

13. Remove the parking brake handle.

14. Unfasten the steering column nuts and lower the steering column.

15. Unfasten the four lower instrument panel screws. Three of the screws can be found along the bottom of the panel and the fourth next to the steering column.

16. Unfasten the four screws attaching the panel to the cowl, and then tilt the panel into the cab.

17. Unfasten the fuse block-to-panel screws.

18. Tag and unplug all wiring and vacuum connections. Feed the wires and vacuum hoses through the carrier opening.

19. Disconnect the heater and/or A/C ducts.

20. Remove the panel and carrier from the vehicle.

To install:

21. Position the panel and carrier in the vehicle, and attach the heater and/or A/C ducts.

22. Feed the vacuum hoses and wires through the carrier opening, then attach the hoses and wiring.

23. Position the fuse block to the panel and install the retaining screws.

24. Install the panel-to-cowl screws. Tighten the screws to 17 inch lbs. (1.9 Nm).

25. Install the lower panel screws and tighten them to 66 inch lbs. (7.5 Nm).

26. Position the steering column onto its mounting studs and tighten the nuts.

27. Install the parking brake handle.

28. Install the cowl side panels and the door sill trim plates.

29. Istall the glove box and its retaining screws.

30. Place the glove box striker in position and install its retaining screws.

31. Install the defroster grille, the radio and the heater and/or A/C controls.

32. Install the instrument cluster and the panel accessory trim plate.

33. Attach the DLC to steering column filler panel.

34. Install the steering column filler panel.

35. Install the front speakers and the speaker grilles.

36. Place the courtesy lamp in position and tighten its retaining screws.

37. Position the lower sound insulator panels, install the retainers. Tighten the screws to 17 inch lbs. (1.9 Nm) and the nut to 35 inch lbs. (4 Nm).

38. Connect the negative battery cable.

1994 Utility Models

1. Disconnect the negative battery cable.

2. Remove the ashtray.

3. Unfasten the accessory trim plate screws, then remove the accessory trim plate.

4. Remove the glove box door strap, then remove the glove box hinge screws.

5. Remove the glove box door frame.

6. Loosen the ashtray support screws, then remove the ashtray support.

7. Remove the glove box.

8. Unfasten the radio bracket bushing nut, then remove the radio.

9. Disconnect the speaker grille screws, then remove the speaker grilles.

10. Loosen the speaker retainers, then remove the front radio speakers.

11. Unfasten the sound insulation panel screws, then remove the sound insulation panels.

12. Loosen the steering column filler screws, then remove the steering column filler.

13. Disconnect the hood release cable.

14. Disconnect the shift indicator cable from the column bowl.

15. Disconnect the steering column support nuts, then lower the steering column.

16. Unfasten the switch plate trim screw, then remove the switch trim plate.

17. Disengage the electrical wiring harness from the rear defogger and the light switches.

18. Disconnect the heater and A/C control.

19. Disconnect the cluster housing bezel mounting nuts, then remove the bezel.

20. Remove the instrument cluster from the vehicle. Disconnect and allow to hang:

• The speedometer instrument panel electrical connector and the Vehicle Speed Sensor (VSS) connector

• The courtesy lamps and the cruise control module

• The horn relay, multifunction alarm and the flasher assembly

21. If necessary, remove the applicable computer control module.

22. Remove the instrument panel-to-cowl mounts:

a. Unfasten the screws from under the panel.

b. Remove the instrument panel support.

c. Unfasten the screws in the defroster outlets.

d. Remove the ductwork, dash plugs, wire looms, and heater cables attached to the panel.

23. Disengage any electrical connections/wires routed through the instrument panel, then remove the instrument panel from the vehicle.

To install:

24. Install the instrument panel assembly to the cowl, carefully routing and connecting the electrical wires and cables.

25. Connect the instrument panel-to-cowl mounts:

a. Connect the ductwork, dash plugs, wire looms, and heater cables to the instrument panel.

b. Secure the screws in the defroster outlets.

c. Install the instrument panel support, then fasten the screws (located under the panel).

26. Install the computer control module, if removed.

27. Install the instrument cluster. Reconnect and mount:

• The speedometer and VSS electrical connectors

• The flasher assembly, multifunction alarm, and horn relay

• The cruise control module and the courtesy lamps

28. Install the cluster housing bezel using the mounting nuts. Tighten the nuts to 12 inch lbs. (1.4 Nm).

29. Install the heater and A/C control.

30. Engage the rear defogger and light switch electrical harness.

31. Install the switch trim plate using the retaining screw. Tighten the screw to 12 inch lbs. (1.4 Nm).

32. Raise the steering column to the mounting bracket, then install the steering column support nuts.

33. Install the shift indicator column to the column bowl, making sure that the indicator is aligned.

34. Connect the hood release cable.

35. Install the steering column filler panel using the retaining screws. Tighten the screws to 14 inch lbs. (1.6 Nm).

36. Install the sound insulation panels using the retaining screws. Tighten the screws to 14 inch lbs. (1.6 Nm).

37. Install the front radio speakers and speaker retainers, then connect the speaker grilles using the retaining screws. Tighten the screws to 12 inch lbs. (1.4 Nm).

38. Install the radio and tighten the fastener to 12 inch lbs. (1.4 Nm).

39. Install the glove compartment, then install the ashtray support using the retaining screws. Tighten the screws to 12 inch lbs. (1.4 Nm).

40. Install the glove compartment door frame, door and door hinge screws. Tighten the screws to 12 inch lbs. (1.4 Nm).

41. Install the glove compartment door strap.

42. Install the accessory trim plate using the retaining screws. Tighten the screws to 12 inch lbs. (1.4 Nm).

43. Install the ashtray, then connect the negative battery cable.

1995–96 Models

▶ See Figures 8 thru 16

❄ CAUTION

When performing service around the air bag system components or wiring, the air bag system MUST be disabled. Failure to do so could result in possible air bag deployment, personal injury or unneeded air bag system repairs.

1. Disconnect the negative battery cable.

2. Disable the air bag system. Please refer to Supplemental Inflatable Restraint (SIR) System in Section 6.

3. Remove the two screws from the instrument cluster trim plate and remove the cluster trim plate from the instrument panel.

4. Unplug all electrical connectors, as necessary.

5. If equipped with a tilt steering column, move it to the down position.

6. Set the parking brake, block the wheels and place the automatic transmission in low, if equipped.

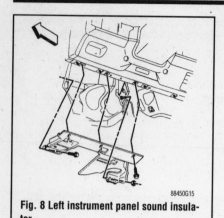

Fig. 8 Left instrument panel sound insulator

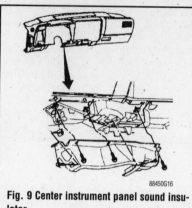

Fig. 9 Center instrument panel sound insulator

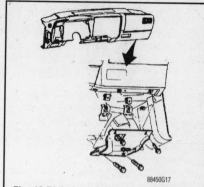

Fig. 10 Right instrument panel sound insulator

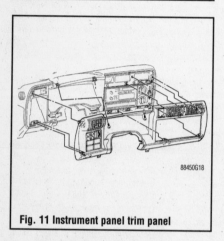

Fig. 11 Instrument panel trim panel

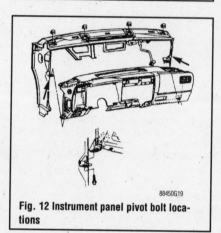

Fig. 12 Instrument panel pivot bolt locations

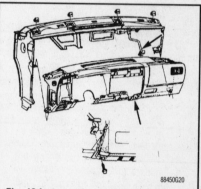

Fig. 13 Instrument panel lower support bolts locations

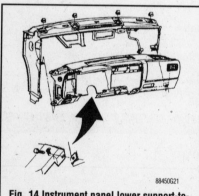

Fig. 14 Instrument panel lower support-to-brake pedal bracket bolt location

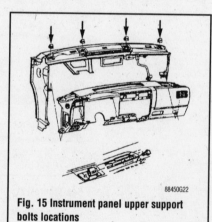

Fig. 15 Instrument panel upper support bolts locations

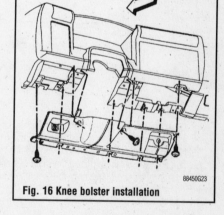

Fig. 16 Knee bolster installation

7. Remove the left instrument panel sound insulator.
8. Unplug the DLC connector.
9. Disengage the RKE/delay module.
10. Remove the center instrument panel sound insulator.
11. Disconnect the parking brake release cable by squeezing the retainers.
12. Disconnect the cable slug from the parking brake mechanism and remove the knee bolster.
13. Remove the right instrument panel sound insulator.
14. Remove the lighter and accessory power outlets, if equipped.
15. Remove the courtesy lamp.
16. Remove the knee bolster from the vehicle.
17. Remove the HVAC control assembly and set aside.
18. Remove the four radio screws, and through the storage compartment, reach behind the radio and unplug the antenna and three electrical connectors.
19. Using a 15 mm wrench, remove the four steering column screws.
20. Remove the following four lower instrument panel support bolts screws across the bottom of the instrument panel.

a. Remove the left and right instrument panel pivot bolts.
b. Remove the instrument panel lower support to brake pedal bracket.
c. Remove the instrument panel lower support bolt.
21. Remove the instrument panel upper support bolts.
22. Remove both speaker grilles.
23. Using a flat bladed tool, remove windshield defrost grilles.
24. Unplug all electrical connectors, as necessary.
25. Remove the instrument panel from the vehicle.
To install:
26. Position the instrument panel to the vehicle and rest onto the lower pivot studs.
27. Engage all electrical connectors, as necessary.
28. Install the upper instrument panel support screws, but do not tighten.
29. Install the right, center and left lower instrument panel support screws, but do not tighten.
30. Align the instrument panel for the lower screws.
31. Tighten the upper and lower support screws to 66 inch lbs. (7.5 Nm).

32. Install the steering column nuts and tighten to 22 ft. lbs. (30 Nm).
33. Install both speaker grilles.
34. Install the radio and plug the antenna and three electrical connectors.
35. Install the HVAC control assembly and vacuum and electrical connections.
36. Install the instrument cluster trim plate and align with the knee bolster.
37. Install the knee bolster to the vehicle.
38. Install the courtesy lamp.
39. Install the lighter and accessory power outlets, if equipped.
40. Install the parking brake cable.
41. Install the center instrument panel sound insulator.
42. Install the left instrument panel sound insulator.
43. Engage the RKE/delay module.
44. Plug in the DLC connector.
45. Install the nut to the accelerator stud and tighten to 35 inch lbs. (4 Nm).
46. Install the right instrument panel sound insulator.
47. Enable the air bag system. Please refer to Section 6.
48. Connect the negative battery cable.

1997–99 Models

⁎⁎ CAUTION

When performing service around the air bag system components or wiring, the air bag system MUST be disabled. Failure to do so could result in possible air bag deployment, personal injury or unneeded air bag system repairs.

1. Disconnect the negative battery cable.
2. Disable the air bag system. Please refer to Supplemental Inflatable Restraint (SIR) System in Section 6.
3. Set the parking brake and block the wheels.
4. Disconnect the parking brake release cable from the parking brake lever.
5. Unfasten the screws that retain the Data Link Connector (DLC) instrument panel left side sound insulator. Feed the DLC through the hole in the sound insulator.
6. Unfasten the right side sound insulator panel screws and remove the panel.
7. Unfasten the screws that attach the instrument panel left side sound insulator to the knee bolster and cowl panel.
8. Unfasten the nut that attaches the left side sound insulator to the accelerator pedal bracket.
9. Unplug the remote control door lock receiver module electrical connector.
10. Remove the door lock receiver module from the left side sound insulator. Remove the left side sound insulator.
11. Unfasten the screws that attach the instrument panel center sound insulator to the knee bolster, instrument panel, heater assembly and floor duct.
12. Remove the center sound insulator.
13. Unfasten the screws that attach the courtesy lamp to the knee bolster.
14. Unfasten the screws that attach the knee bolster to the instrument panel.
15. Disconnect the lap cooler duct from the knee bolster.
16. Unplug the lighter electrical connection and remove the knee bolster.
17. Unfasten the steering column-to-instrument panel nuts and lower the column.
18. Unfasten the screws that attach the instrument panel accessory trim plate to the instrument panel.
19. Remove the trim plate and unplug all necessary electrical connection.
20. Remove the heater and/or A/C control assembly.
21. Remove the radio and the storage compartment assembly (if equipped).
22. If necessary, remove the instrument cluster.
23. Unfasten the left and right instrument panel pivot bolts and the panel lower support bolt.
24. Unfasten the speaker grilles retaining screws and remove the speaker grilles.
25. Remove the windshield defroster grille using a flat-bladed prytool. Start at one end of the grille and work your way down the grille.
26. Unfasten the four instrument panel upper support screws.
27. Tag and unplug all necessary electrical connections.
28. Remove the instrument panel from the vehicle.
To install:
29. Rest the instrument panel on the lower pivot studs.
30. Attach the electrical connections.

31. Install but do not tighten the four upper instrument panel support screws.
32. Install the left and right panel pivot bolts. Tighten the bolts to 102 inch lbs. (11.5 Nm).
33. Install the panel lower support bolt. Tighten the bolt to 102 inch lbs. (11.5 Nm).
34. Tighten the upper support screws to 17 inch lbs. (1.9 Nm).
35. Install the windshield defroster grille and the speaker grilles.
36. Install the radio and storage compartment assembly (if equipped).
37. If removed, install the instrument cluster.
38. Install the heater and/or A/C control assembly.
39. Attach the electrical connections to the instrument panel accessory trim plate.
40. Place the trim plate in position and install its retaining screws. Tighten the screws to 17 inch lbs. (1.9 Nm).
41. Place the steering column into position and install its retaining nuts. Tighten the nuts to 22 ft. lbs. (30 Nm).
42. Attach the lighter electrical connection and the lap cooler duct to the knee bolster.
43. Place the knee bolster into position and install its retaining screws. Tighten the TorxÆ head screws to 80 inch lbs. (9 Nm) and the hex head screws to 17 inch lbs. (1.9 Nm).
44. Place the courtesy lamp in position and install its screws. Tighten the screws to 17 inch lbs. (1.9 Nm).
45. Place the instrument panel center sound insulator in position. Install the screws that attach the center sound insulator to the knee bolster, instrument panel and the floor duct. Tighten the screws to 17 inch lbs. (1.9 Nm).
46. Install the screw that attaches the center sound insulator to the heater assembly. Tighten the screw to 13 inch lbs. (1.5 Nm).
47. Install the remote control door lock receiver module to the instrument panel left side sound insulator.
48. Attach the door lock receiver electrical connection.
49. Install the nut that attaches the left side sound insulator to the accelerator pedal bracket. Tighten the nut to 35 inch lbs. (4 Nm).
50. Install the screw that attaches the left side sound insulator to cowl panel. Tighten the screw to 13 inch lbs. (1.5 Nm).
51. Install the screws that attach the left side sound insulator to knee bolster. Tighten the screw to 17 inch lbs. (1.9 Nm).
52. Feed the DLC through the hole in the sound insulator, place the DLC in position and install its retaining screws. Tighten the screws to 21 inch lbs. (2.4 Nm).
53. Install the right side sound insulator and tighten the screws
54. Connect the parking brake release cable to the lever.
55. Enable the air bag system. Please refer to Section 6.
56. Connect the negative battery cable.

Front Console

REMOVAL & INSTALLATION

♦ **See Figure 17**

1. Remove the transfer case shift lever knob, if equipped.
2. Remove the shift control lever (manual transmission) or floor shift knob (automatic transmissions).

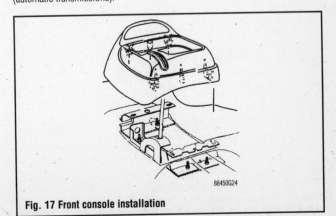

88450G24

Fig. 17 Front console installation

3. Lift up on the console to release the clips.
4. Unplug the electrical connector, if equipped, and remove the console from the vehicle.
5. Installation is the reverse of removal.

Floor Console

REMOVAL & INSTALLATION

1994 Models

1. Remove the transfer case shift lever knob, if equipped.
2. Remove the shift control lever (manual transmission) or floor shift knob (automatic transmissions).
3. Remove the cup holder.
4. Unfasten the trim bezel-to-console screws and remove the bezel.
5. Remove the console compartment tray and the console compartment.
6. Unfasten the console assembly-to-floor nuts.
7. Pull up on the front of the console to release the retaining clips, unplug the electrical connector (if equipped) and remove the console.
8. Installation is the reverse of removal.

1995–96 Models

▶ See Figures 18 and 19

1. Remove the cup holder and unfasten the one console retaining screw.
2. Remove the two screws and the upper console cover.
3. Remove the center nut.
4. Open the storage compartment cover, and remove the storage compartment.
5. Remove the two rear console nuts.
6. Lower the console from the vehicle.
7. Installation is the reverse of removal.

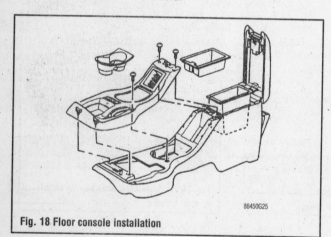

88450G25

Fig. 18 Floor console installation

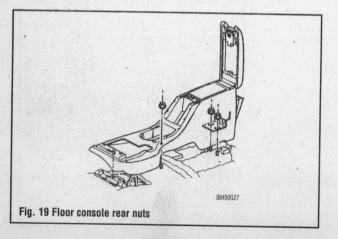

88450G27

Fig. 19 Floor console rear nuts

1997–99 Models

FULL LENGTH CONSOLE (EXCEPT AUTOMATIC TRANSMISSION FLOOR SHIFT)

1. Remove the transfer case shift lever knob, if equipped.
2. Remove the shift control lever (manual transmission).
3. On models equipped, with floor shift automatic transmission, remove the shift handle retaining clip at the front of the handle, then remove the handle
4. Remove the cup holder insert.
5. Unfasten the trim plate-to-console screws and remove the plate.
6. Open the console compartment cover and remove the storage compartment.
7. Unfasten the console assembly-to-floor nuts.
8. Lift the console up, unplug the electrical connector (if equipped) and remove the console.
9. Installation is the reverse of removal.

FULL LENGTH CONSOLE (AUTOMATIC TRANSMISSION FLOOR SHIFT)

1. Remove the shift handle retaining clip at the front of the handle, then remove the handle
2. Open the console compartment cover and remove the console insert screw.
3. Remove the console insert.
4. Unfasten the nuts that retain the rear of the console, then remove the cup holder insert.
5. Unfasten the screws that attach the front of the console.
6. Remove the console.
7. Installation is the reverse of removal.

Overhead Console

REMOVAL & INSTALLATION

1994 Models

1. Remove the dome lamp lens.
2. Unfasten the console-to-roof screws.
3. Lower the console, unplug any electrical connections and remove the console.
4. Installation is the reverse of removal.

1995–99 Models

▶ See Figure 20

1. Remove the screw from the windshield end of the console.
2. Unplug the electrical connector from the dome lamp harness.
3. Remove the console by swinging downward and pulling forward to clear the rear mounting tabs.

To install:

4. Insert the rear console mounting tabs into the roof panel.
5. Plug the electrical connector to the dome lamp harness.
6. Install the console by swinging upward and tightening the retaining screw.

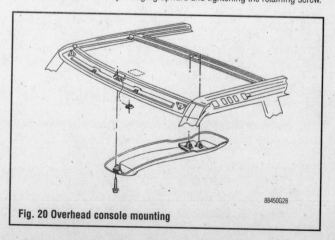

88450G28

Fig. 20 Overhead console mounting

Door Trim Panel

REMOVAL & INSTALLATION

▶ **See Figures 21 thru 30**

➡ **The following procedure requires the use of the Trim Pad Removal tool, J-38778 or equivalent, and the Window Regulator Clip Removal tool No. J-9886-01 or equivalent.**

1. Remove the door handle bezel-to-door screws and the bezel.
2. If removing the rear door trim panel, unfasten the upper molding screws, then using the trim pad removal tool, separate the molding from the door with the clips still left attached to the molding

3. Unless equipped with power windows, use a window regulator clip removal tool such as J-9886-01 or equivalent, to remove the window regulator clip and separate the handle from the door.
4. Carefully pry off the armrest screw cover and remove the armrest-to-door screw and the armrest.
5. If equipped with power windows, remove/disengage the switch mounting panel.
6. Check the panel for any additional screws and remove then as necessary.
7. Using a suitable trim pad removal tool, remove the nylon fasteners from their seats.
8. Remove the door panel from the vehicle.
9. Installation is the reverse of removal.

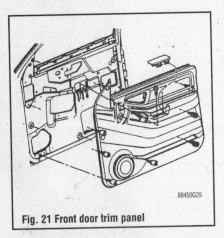
Fig. 21 Front door trim panel

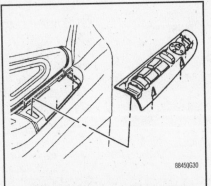
Fig. 22 Front door power accessory switch mounting panel

Fig. 23 Front door inside handle bezel

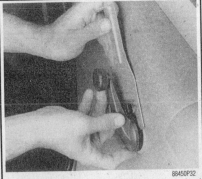
Fig. 24 Disengaging the window regulator handle retaining spring clip

Fig. 25 Removing the window regulator handle and retaining spring clip

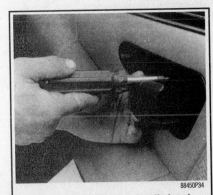
Fig. 26 Removing the door handle bezel-to-door screws

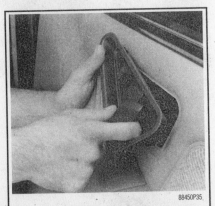
Fig. 27 Removing the door handle bezel

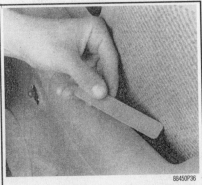
Fig. 28 Carefully pry off the armrest screw cover

Fig. 29 Carefully disconnect the trim panel retaining clips

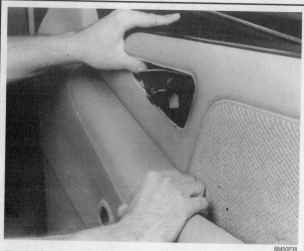

Fig. 30 Carefully lift up and disconnect the trim panel from the upper door frame

Door Locks

REMOVAL & INSTALLATION

Front Door Lock Assembly

1994 MODELS

1. Remove the door trim panel. For details, please refer to the procedure located earlier in this section.
2. If necessary, remove the water deflector.

➡The water deflector is secured by a strip of adhesive between the deflector and door, as well as waterproof sealing tape. Upon installation, make sure a good seal is achieved to keep water from entering into the body. If necessary, use strip caulking as a sealant between the deflector and door.

3. Remove the lock rods from the inner handle housing.
4. Remove the outside handle lock rod from the lock mechanism.
5. Remove the lock cylinder rod from the lock cylinder.
6. Remove the lock assembly-to-door retaining screws, then remove the assembly from the door.
7. Installation is the reverse of removal. Tighten the lock retainers to 62 inch lbs. (7 Nm) on utility models and 80 inch lbs. (9 Nm) on pick-up models. Be sure to check the operation of the lock assembly before installing the door water deflector (if equipped) and trim panel.

1995–99 MODELS

▶ See Figure 31

1. Disconnect the negative battery cable.
2. Remove the door trim panel. For details, please refer to the procedure located earlier in this section.
3. If necessary, remove the water deflector.

➡The water deflector is secured by a strip of adhesive between the deflector and door, as well as waterproof sealing tape. Upon installation, make sure a good seal is achieved to keep water from entering into the body. If necessary, use strip caulking as a sealant between the deflector and door.

4. Remove the inside handle rod from the lock assembly.
5. Remove the outside handle lock rod from the lock assembly.
6. Remove the inside lock lever rod from lock assembly.
7. Remove the outside lock cylinder rod from the lock assembly.
8. Unplug the power actuator wiring connector, if equipped.
9. Remove the lock assembly-to-door retaining screws, then remove the assembly from the door.

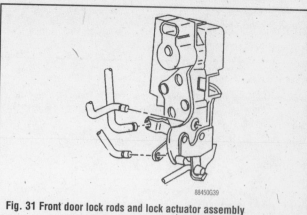

Fig. 31 Front door lock rods and lock actuator assembly

10. Installation is the reverse of removal. Tighten the lock retainers to 80 inch lbs. (9 Nm). Be sure to check the operation of the lock assembly before installing the door water deflector (if equipped) and trim panel.

Rear Door Lock Assembly

1994 MODELS

1. Remove the armrest and the trim panel.
2. Remove the armrest bracket and the sound deadener.
3. Disconnect the lock rods from the lock mechanism.
4. Unfasten the lock assembly retaining screws, and then remove the lock assembly.
5. Installation is the reverse of removal. Tighten the lock retaining screws to 62 inch lbs. (7 Nm).

1995–99 MODELS

1. Remove the door trim panel and the water deflector.
2. Disconnect the inside lock rod; inside handle rod and outside handle rod from the lock assembly.
3. If equipped, unplug the power actuator electrical connection.
4. Unfasten the lock assembly retainers and remove the assembly from the door.
5. Installation is the reverse of removal. Tighten the lock retainers to 80 inch lbs. (9 Nm).

Lock Cylinder Assembly

1994 MODELS

▶ See Figures 32 and 33

1. Remove the trim panel and the armrest bracket.
2. Remove the water deflectors. Roll the window up.
3. Remove the lock cylinder retainer.
4. Disconnect the lock cylinder from the linkage.

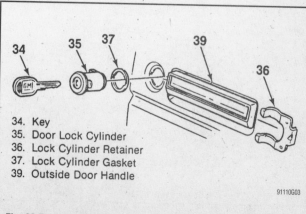

34. Key
35. Door Lock Cylinder
36. Lock Cylinder Retainer
37. Lock Cylinder Gasket
39. Outside Door Handle

Fig. 32 Front door lock cylinder components—1994 utility models

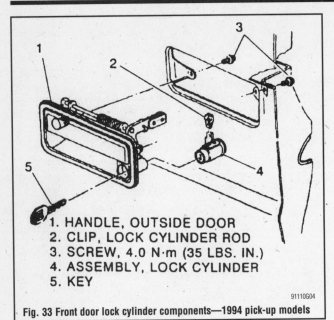

1. HANDLE, OUTSIDE DOOR
2. CLIP, LOCK CYLINDER ROD
3. SCREW, 4.0 N·m (35 LBS. IN.)
4. ASSEMBLY, LOCK CYLINDER
5. KEY

91110G04

Fig. 33 Front door lock cylinder components—1994 pick-up models

5. On utility models, remove the lock cylinder gasket.
6. Installation is the reverse of removal.

1995 MODELS

▶ See Figure 34

1. Raise the window to the closed position.
2. Remove the door trim panel. For details, please refer to the procedure located earlier in this section.
3. Remove the water deflector (if equipped) and roll up the window.

➡The water deflector is secured by a strip of adhesive between the deflector and door, as well as waterproof sealing tape. Upon installation, make sure a good seal is achieved to keep water from entering into the body. If necessary, use strip caulking as a sealant between the deflector and door.

4. If necessary, remove the outside door handle screw access hole plug.
5. Disconnect the outside handle rod from the rod clip.
6. Disconnect the lock cylinder rod from the rod clip.
7. Remove the outside handle mounting retainers.
8. Remove the door lock cylinder from the outside handle housing.

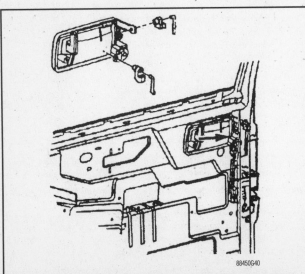

88450G40

Fig. 34 Front door lock cylinder and outside handle lock rod connections

9. Installation is the reverse of removal. Tighten the handle mounting retainers to 35 inch lbs. (4 Nm). Check the operation of the lock cylinder before installing the water deflector (if equipped) and the door trim panel.

Endgate/Liftgate Lock Cylinder

REMOVAL & INSTALLATION

Utility Models

1994 MODELS

▶ See Figure 35

1. Open the tailgate/endgate to the horizontal position.
2. Remove the tailgate trim panel, then remove the water deflector.
3. Remove the tailgate inner panel reinforcement from the endgate.
4. Remove the tailgate lock rods.
5. Remove the lock cylinder retainer by working it through the access hole.
6. Remove the lock cylinder through the outer panel.

To install:

7. If equipped, connect the actuator cable.
8. Work the lock cylinder through the inner panel and secure with the retainer.
9. Install the tailgate lock rods.
10. Connect the tailgate inner panel reinforcement to the endgate.
11. Install the water deflector, then the tailgate trim panel.

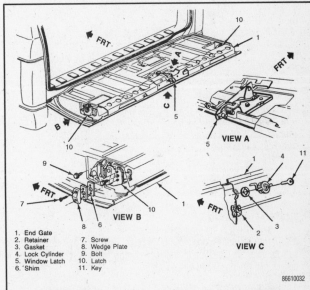

1. End Gate
2. Retainer
3. Gasket
4. Lock Cylinder
5. Window Latch
6. Shim
7. Screw
8. Wedge Plate
9. Bolt
10. Latch
11. Key

86610032

Fig. 35 Common late model lock cylinder and latch assemblies—except 1995 vehicles

1995–96 Models

▶ See Figure 36

➡New lock cylinders are available as replacement parts. If, for any reason, lock cylinders require replacement, apply a coat of GM No. 12345120 or equivalent lubricant inside the lock case and cylinder keyway prior to installation.

➡This procedure requires GM tool No. J-20922-A rivet installer, or equivalent tool.

1. Open the tailgate, then remove the tailgate handle by unfastening the retaining screws.
2. Remove the tailgate trim panel by unfastening the screws securing the panel to the endgate.
3. Remove the access panel cover:

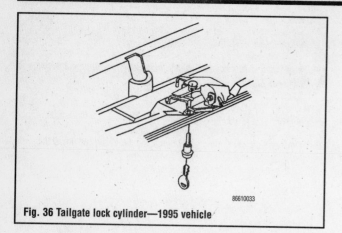

86610033

Fig. 36 Tailgate lock cylinder—1995 vehicle

  a. Remove the lock rods from the door handle.
  b. Drill out the access panel rivets.
  c. Remove the lock rods from the access panel, then remove the access panel cover.
  d. Unplug the electrical connector from the liftgate actuator.
  4. Remove the liftgate latch assembly by removing the latch-to-bracket bolts.
  5. Remove the liftgate striker assembly by removing the striker bracket bolts and bracket.
  6. If equipped, unplug the electrical connector.
  7. Disconnect the lock cylinder retaining clip, then remove the lock cylinder.

To install:
  8. Install the lock cylinder using the retaining clip.
  9. If equipped, attach the electrical connector.
  10. Install the liftgate striker assembly by installing the striker bracket with the retaining bolts.
  11. Install the liftgate latch assembly using the latch-to-bracket bolts.
  12. Install the access panel cover:
  a. Engage the electrical connector to the liftgate actuator.
  b. Install the access panel cover, then connect the lock rods to the cover.
  c. Using tool No. J-20922-A or equivalent, install rivets to the access panel and endgate.
  13. Install the tailgate trim panel using the retaining screws.
  14. Install the tailgate handle using the retaining screws.

1997–99 Models

ENDGATE

➡**New lock cylinders are available as replacement parts. If, for any reason, lock cylinders require replacement, apply a coat of GM No. 12345120 or equivalent lubricant inside the lock case and cylinder keyway prior to installation.**

  1. Open the endgate and unfasten screws that attach the inside handle to the endgate, then remove the handle.
  2. Unfasten the screw that attaches the endgate trim panel to the endgate latch support.
  3. Unfasten the screws that attach the trim panel to the endgate. If necessary, release the retaining clips from the upper edge and sides of the trim panel, then lift the panel up to release the tabs along the bottom edge.
  4. Mark the location of the endgate window latch, this will aid during installation.
  5. Disconnect the endgate bellcrank rod from the endgate inside handle assembly.
  6. Unfasten the screws that attach endgate cover to the endgate, release the endgate latch rods from the latch rod clips, then remove the endgate cover.
  7. Unplug the necessary electrical connections.
  8. Unfasten the endgate window latch retainers and remove the latch.
  9. Remove the cargo lamp switch.
  10. Mark the location of the endgate window latch support, this will aid during installation.
  11. Unfasten the endgate window latch support retainers and remove the latch support.

  12. Unplug any necessary electrical connections.
  13. Unfasten the clip that attaches lock cylinder to the endgate, and then remove the lock cylinder.

To install:
  14. Place the lock cylinder into position and install the lock cylinder retaining clip.
  15. Attach any electrical connections that were unplugged earlier.
  16. Align the endgate window latch support with the marks made prior to removal and install its retainers. Tighten the retainers to 80 inch lbs. (9 Nm).
  17. Install the cargo lamp switch.
  18. Align the endgate window latch with the marks made prior to removal, and then install its retainers. Tighten the retainers to 88 inch lbs. (10 Nm).
  19. Attach any electrical connectors unplugged earlier.
  20. Place the endgate cover in position and secure the endgate latch rods to the latch rod clips.
  21. Install the screws that attach the cover to the endgate. Tighten the screws to 11 inch lbs. (1.2 Nm).
  22. Attach the endgate bellcrank rod to the inside handle.
  23. Place the endgate trim panel in position and install its retaining screws. Tighten the screws to 17 inch lbs. (1.9 Nm).
  24. Install the screw that attaches the trim panel to the window latch support. Tighten the screw to 17 inch lbs. (1.9 Nm).
  25. Place the endgate inside handle into position, install the screws and tighten them to 25 inch lbs. (2.8 Nm).

LIFTGATE

  1. Open the liftgate window and unfasten the screw which attaches the liftgate trim panel to the liftgate window latch support.
  2. Open the liftgate and remove the trim panel.
  3. Mark the location of the liftgate window latch, this will aid during installation.
  4. Unplug the necessary electrical connections.
  5. Unfasten the liftgate window latch retainers and remove the latch.
  6. Remove the cargo lamp switch.
  7. Mark the location of the liftgate window latch support, this will aid during installation.
  8. Unfasten the liftgate window latch support retainers and remove the latch support.
  9. Unplug any necessary electrical connections.
  10. Unfasten the clip that attaches lock cylinder to the liftgate, and then remove the lock cylinder.

To install:
  11. Place the lock cylinder into position and install the lock cylinder retaining clip.
  12. Attach any electrical connections that were unplugged earlier.
  13. Align the liftgate window latch support with the marks made prior to removal and install its retainers. Tighten the retainers to 80 inch lbs. (9 Nm).
  14. Install the cargo lamp switch.
  15. Align the liftgate window latch with the marks made prior to removal, then install its retainers. Tighten the retainers to 88 inch lbs. (10 Nm).
  16. Attach any electrical connectors unplugged earlier.
  17. Place the liftgate trim panel in position and install the screw that attaches the trim panel to the window latch support. Tighten the screw to 17 inch lbs. (1.9 Nm).

Door Glass and Regulator

REMOVAL & INSTALLATION

❊❊ CAUTION

Always wear heavy gloves when handling glass to minimize the risk of injury.

Front Door Glass

1994 MODELS

  1. Remove the trim panel.
  2. Raise the glass to the closed position and apply cloth-backed tape to hold the glass in place.

3. Remove the armrest bracket-to-door screws and the bracket.

4. Remove the water deflector from the door.

➡**The water deflector is secured by a strip of adhesive between the deflector and door, as well as waterproof sealing tape. Upon installation, make sure a good seal is achieved to keep water from entering the body. If necessary, use strip caulking as a sealant between the deflector and door.**

5. Lower the window until it and the sash channel can be seen in the door panel opening, then remove the sash assembly-to-window bolts.

6. Remove the sash assembly and the window from the door.

7. Cut the clips from the glass in order to remove the glass from the door.

To install:

8. Install new clips, lower the glass into the door and rotate it into the run channel.

9. Install the bolts attaching the sash assembly to the window. Tighten the bolts to 53 inch lbs. (6 Nm).

10. Install the water deflector, armrest bracket and the trim panel.

1995–99 MODELS

1. Lower the window.

2. Remove the door trim panel.

3. Remove the water deflector from the door.

4. Remove the front glass run channel retaining screws and slide the channel from the glass.

5. Remove the weatherstrip.

6. Remove the glass from the regulator.

   a. Bend the glass sash panel retaining tabs.

   b. Raise the window halfway and push the window forward to remove the window sash from the regulator roller.

   c. Carefully tilt the glass vertically and pull the glass upward to remove the glass sash from the front regulator roller.

7. Remove the glass from the door.

To install:

8. Position the glass to the door.

9. Install the window sash to the regulator.

   a. Rotate the window vertically and slide the window sash downward into the front regulator roller.

   b. Push the glass forward to align to align the rear of the sash with the rear regulator roller.

   c. Bend the retaining tabs back to the original positions.

10. Install the weatherstrip.

11. Install the glass run channel and tighten the retaining screws to 18 inch lbs. (2 Nm).

12. Install the water deflector and trim panel.

➡**The water deflector is secured by a strip of adhesive between the deflector and door, as well as waterproof sealing tape. Upon installation, make sure a good seal is achieved to keep water from entering into the body. If necessary, use strip caulking as a sealant between the deflector and door.**

Rear Door Glass

1994 MODELS

1. Remove the trim panel and the armrest bracket.

2. Remove the sound deadener.

3. Remove the stationary window garnish molding and reveal (outside) molding.

4. Remove the stationary window.

5. Unfasten the inner handle housing screws, slide the housing towards the front of the door and pull it from the door.

6. Disconnect the lock linkage rods and swing the housing away.

7. Disconnect the outside handle linkage rod and the outside door handle.

8. Unfasten the rear run channel screws at the door header and the speed nuts at the inner door and move away.

9. Cut the glass guide clips to disengage the glass from the front run channel. Lower the glass until the sash channel and glass can be clearly seen in the door panel opening.

10. Remove the sash assembly and glass from the door.

To install:

11. Lower the glass into the door and rotate it into the run channel.

12. Attach the sash assembly to the glass.

13. Install new guide clips.

14. Install the rear run channel-to-inner door speed nuts and the run channel-to-door header screws.

15. Install the outside door handle and attach the linkage rod to the outside door handle.

16. Attach the lock rods to the inside door handle.

17. Install the stationary window and reveal molding.

18. Install the stationary glass garnish molding. Lubricate and adjust the molding as necessary.

19. Install the armrest bracket and trim panel.

1995–99 MODELS

1. Remove the trim panel.

2. Remove the water deflector.

3. Lower the window.

4. Unfasten the rear window run channel/stationary window weatherstrip bolts.

5. Pull the stationary window weatherstrip from the window frame.

6. If necessary, carefully pop the glass from the weatherstrip/run channel assembly.

7. Push the glass rearward and rotate it out of the regulator rollers.

8. Remove the glass from the door.

To install:

9. If necessary, move the regulator to the half way down to locate the front roller.

10. Install the glass into the door, rotate the glass sash assembly into the regulator rollers.

11. If removed, carefully insert the glass in the weatherstrip/run channel assembly.

12. Install the weatherstrip and run channel onto the door. Tighten the run bolts to 17 inch lbs. (1.9 Nm).

13. Press the weatherstrip firmly into the window frame.

14. Install the water deflector and the trim panel.

Door Glass Regulator

◆ See Figure 37

1. Remove the door trim panel. For details, please refer to the procedure earlier in this section.

2. Remove the water deflector from the door.

➡**The water deflector is secured by a strip of adhesive between the deflector and door, as well as waterproof sealing tape. Upon installation, make sure a good seal is achieved to keep water from entering into the body. If necessary, use strip caulking as a sealant between the deflector and door.**

3. If equipped, unplug the power window motor electrical connection.

4. Raise the window to the full up position. Using cloth backed tape, securely tape the glass to the door frame.

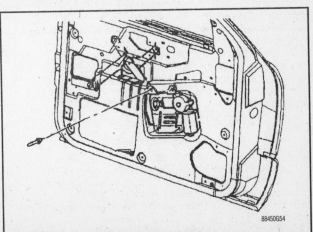

88450G54

Fig. 37 Front door window regulator and motor

5. Drill out the regulator-to-door or rivets and separate the regulator lift arm roller from the window sash, then remove the regulator and motor (if applicable) from the door.

6. Installation is the reverse of removal. Use new rivets (when applicable) unless the service kit contains replacement bolts. Be sure to check for proper regulator operation before installing the water deflector and trim panel.

Electric Window Motor

REMOVAL & INSTALLATION

♦ **See Figures 37 and 38**

The rear motor/regulator replacement parts are sold as an assembly. Do not attempt to separate the motor from the regulator before verify that separate replacement parts are available.

1. Remove the door trim panel. For details, please refer to the procedure earlier in this section.
2. Disconnect the negative battery cable.
3. Remove the armrest bracket-to-door screws and the bracket.
4. Remove the water deflector from the door.

➡The water deflector is secured by a strip of adhesive between the deflector and door, as well as waterproof sealing tape. Upon installation, make sure a good seal is achieved to keep water from entering into the body. If necessary, use strip caulking as a sealant between the deflector and door.

5. Raise the window to the full up position. Using cloth backed tape, tape the glass to the door frame.
6. Unplug the electrical wiring connector from the window regulator motor.
7. Separate the regulator lift arm roller from the window sash.
8. On 1994–96 models, the regulator can remain in the door, on 1997–99 models, remove the regulator before attempting to remove the motor.
9. To remove the window regulator motor from the door:
   a. Drill a hole through the regulator sector gear and backplate, then install a bolt/nut to lock the sector gear in position.

❋❋ CAUTION

The sector gear MUST be locked into position. The regulator lift arm is under tension from the counterbalance spring and could cause personal injury if the sector gear is not locked before the motor is disconnected.

   b. Using a ³⁄₁₆ in. (5mm) drill bit, drill out the motor-to-door rivets.
   c. Remove the motor from the door.
To install:
10. Position the motor to the regulator, then secure using ³⁄₁₆ in. (4.8mm) rivets.
11. After the motor is riveted to the door, remove the nut/bolt from the sector gear.
12. Install the regulator lift arm roller to the window mount sash.
13. The balance of installation is the reverse of removal. It is usually wise to check operation of the system before installing the water deflector and trim panel.

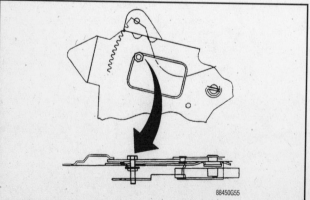

Fig. 38 Installation of the bolt to lock the sector gear

Endgate/Liftgate Glass

REMOVAL & INSTALLATION

1994–96 Models

1. Open the endgate and mark the position of the glass hinges.
2. If equipped, remove the rear wiper motor.
3. On Bravada models equipped with an air deflector, hold the deflector, unfasten its retaining screws, unplug the electrical connection from the deflector and remove the deflector.
4. Disconnect the rear brake light electrical connection
5. Unplug the rear defogger electrical connection, if equipped.
6. Carefully pry the clip from the window gas support at the glass side, then pull support end from the ball socket.
7. Support the rear window glass and disconnect the ball sockets from the body side.
8. Unfasten the hinge bolts and remove the glass.
To install:
9. Place the glass into position and align the hinges with the marks made prior to removal.
10. Install the glass hinge retaining bolts and tighten them to 54 inch lbs. (6 Nm).
11. Position the window gas support on the ball sockets and push them onto the ball.
12. Attach the window defogger wire and the brake light electrical connection, if removed.
13. If removed, install the rear wiper motor.
14. On Bravada models equipped with an air deflector, attach the deflector electrical connection, place the assembly in position and install its retaining screws. Tighten the screws to 62 inch lbs. (7 Nm).

1997–99 Models

1. Open the liftgate and mark the position of the glass hinges.
2. Unplug the rear defogger electrical connection, if equipped.
3. Open and support the liftgate.
4. Release the liftgate strut retaining clip from the lower end of the liftgate and disconnect the strut from the liftgate. Repeat the procedure at the upper end of the liftgate.
5. Remove the hinge pin retainers and discard them.
6. Remove the hinge pins, then remove the glass.
To install:
7. Place the glass into position and install the hinge pins.
8. Install new hinge pin retainers.
9. Attach the upper end on the liftgate strut to the ball stud on the liftgate and by pushing on the end of the strut. Attach the lower end of the strut in the same manner.
10. Attach the window defogger wire electrical connection, if removed.

Windshield and Fixed Glass

REMOVAL & INSTALLATION

If your windshield, or other fixed window, is cracked or chipped, you may decide to replace it with a new one yourself. However, there are two main reasons why replacement windshields and other window glass should be installed only by a professional automotive glass technician: safety and cost.

The most important reason a professional should install automotive glass is for safety. The glass in the vehicle, especially the windshield, is designed with safety in mind in case of a collision. The windshield is specially manufactured from two panes of specially-tempered glass with a thin layer of transparent plastic between them. This construction allows the glass to "give" in the event that a part of your body hits the windshield during the collision, and prevents the glass from shattering, which could cause lacerations, blinding and other harm to passengers of the vehicle. The other fixed windows are designed to be tempered so that if they break during a collision, they shatter in such a way that there are no large pointed glass pieces. The professional automotive glass technician knows how to install the glass in a vehicle so that it will function optimally during a collision. Without the proper experience, knowledge and tools, installing a piece of automotive glass yourself could lead to additional harm if an accident should ever occur.

Cost is also a factor when deciding to install automotive glass yourself. Performing this could cost you much more than a professional may charge for the same job. Since the windshield is designed to break under stress, an often life saving characteristic, windshields tend to break VERY easily when an inexperienced person attempts to install one. Do-it-yourselfers buying two, three or even four windshields from a salvage yard because they have broken them during installation are common stories. Also, since the automotive glass is designed to prevent the outside elements from entering your vehicle, improper installation can lead to water and air leaks. Annoying whining noises at highway speeds from air leaks or inside body panel rusting from water leaks can add to your stress level and subtract from your wallet. After buying two or three windshields, installing them and ending up with a leak that produces a noise while driving and water damage during rainstorms, the cost of having a professional do it correctly the first time may be much more alluring. We here at Chilton, therefore, advise that you have a professional automotive glass technician service any broken glass on your vehicle.

WINDSHIELD CHIP REPAIR

▶ See Figures 39 and 40

➡Check with your state and local authorities on the laws for state safety inspection. Some states or municipalities may not allow chip repair as a viable option for correcting stone damage to your windshield.

Although severely cracked or damaged windshields must be replaced, there is something that you can do to prolong or even prevent the need for replacement of a chipped windshield. There are many companies which offer windshield chip repair products, such as Loctite's® Bullseye™ windshield repair kit. These kits usually consist of a syringe, pedestal and a sealing adhesive. The syringe is mounted on the pedestal and is used to create a vacuum which pulls the plastic layer against the glass. This helps make the chip transparent. The adhesive is then injected which seals the chip and helps to prevent further stress cracks from developing

➡Always follow the specific manufacturer's instructions.

Inside Rear View Mirror

REPLACEMENT

Mirror

1. If applicable, remove the wire cover using a flat-blade tool.
2. If applicable, unplug the electrical connection.

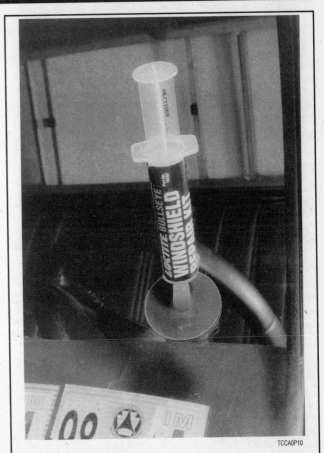
Fig. 40 Most kits use a self-stick applicator and syringe to inject the adhesive into the chip or crack

3. Slide the mirror off the support.
4. Installation is the reverse of removal.

Base

▶ See Figure 41

1. Determine the location of the rear view mirror and using a wax pencil, draw a centerline on the outside of the glass from the roof panel to the windshield base.
2. Draw a line intersecting the centerline approximately 23 1/8 in. (587mm) on 1994 models or 21 inches (53.4 cm) on 1995–99 models from the base of

Fig. 39 Small chips on your windshield can be fixed with an aftermarket repair kit, such as the one from Loctite®

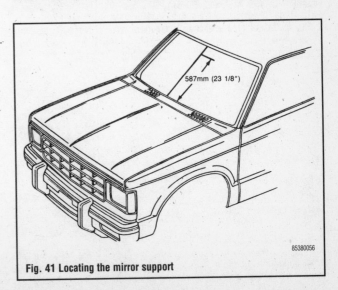
Fig. 41 Locating the mirror support

the glass. The base of the support will be located at the intersection of these lines.

3. Clean the inside glass within 3 in. (76mm) of the intersecting lines. Using a glass cleaning solution rub the area until completely dry. Reclean with a towel saturated with alcohol.

4. Sand the bonding surface of the rear view mirror support with 320 grit sandpaper. Remove all traces of the factory adhesive if reusing the old support. Wipe the mirror support with alcohol and allow to dry.

5. Apply Loctite® Minute Bond Adhesive 312, or equivalent to the mirror support bonding surfaces.

6. Place the bottom of the support at the premarked line. The rounded edge of the support should face upward.

7. Press the support against the glass for 30–60 seconds with a steady pressure. Allow the adhesive to dry 5 minutes before cleaning.

8. Clean all traces of adhesive and wax from the windshield with alcohol.

Seats

REMOVAL & INSTALLATION

▶ **See Figures 42 thru 49**

If your vehicle is equipped with power seats, disconnect the negative battery cable and unplug the motor electrical connection prior to removing the seat.

Most vehicles covered by this manual are equipped with bench seats. Removal of the bench seat assembly is a relatively simple process. Locate and remove the retainers (usually nuts), then carefully lift the seat and adjuster from the floor pan.

Removal of a bucket seat is also a relatively simple process, once you find the retainers. On some vehicles you will have to remove trim covers which are used to hide the seat adjuster mounting bolts. Also, power seats will have one or more electrical wiring connectors. Disconnect the negative battery cable then disengage the seat wiring connectors before attempting to remove the seat. Once the nuts are removed and any wiring has been dis-

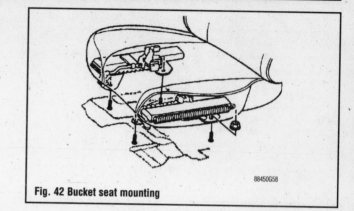

Fig. 42 Bucket seat mounting

88450G58

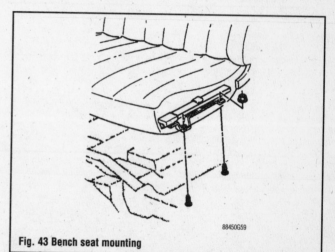

Fig. 43 Bench seat mounting

88450G59

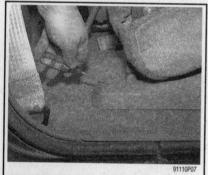

91110P07

Fig. 44 Unfasten the seat track trim retaining screw, then . . .

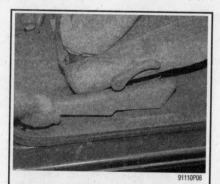

91110P08

Fig. 45 . . . unsnap the retaining clip from the seat track

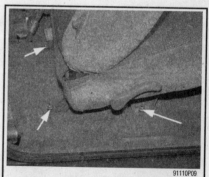

91110P09

Fig. 46 Location of three of the four seat-to-track retainers (drivers side shown)

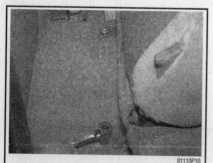

91110P10

Fig. 47 Slide the seat forwards or backwards as necessary to access the seat-to-track bolts

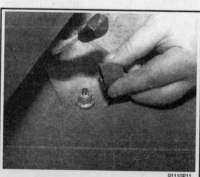

91110P11

Fig. 48 Some bolts may have a trim cap. Pull or pry the cap off the bolt

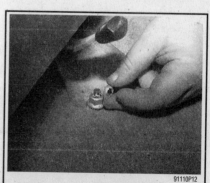

91110P12

Fig. 49 . . . and remove the clip to access the bolt

connected, lift the bucket seat and adjuster from the vehicle. When installing, all seat adjuster to floor pan nuts are tightened to 33 ft. lbs. (45 Nm).

To remove the jump seat on extended cab models, remove the trim panel and remove the bolts and nuts securing the seat support to the floor. Remove the seat from the vehicle. When installing, tighten the seat support to floor pan nuts and bolts to 35 ft. lbs. (47 Nm).

To remove the rear seats on utility models, remove the trim panel and unfasten the retainers securing the seat to the floor. To reach the rear retainers you may have to fold the seat forward to access them. Remove the seat from the vehicle. When installing, tighten the seat retainers to 59 ft. lbs. (40 Nm).

Power Seat Motor

REMOVAL & INSTALLATION

1. Remove the seat from the vehicle.
2. Tag and disconnect all necessary motor electrical connections and motor-to adjuster cables.
3. On newer model vehicles, unfasten the adjuster assembly retainers and remove the adjuster assembly.
4. Unfasten the motor assembly retainers and remove the motor assembly.
5. Installation is the reverse of removal.

TORQUE SPECIFICATIONS

Components	Ft. Lbs.	Nm
Exterior		
Doors		
Door hinge		
Bolts	26	35
Hood		
Hinge bolts	18	25
Endgate		
1994 models		
Cable support retaining bolts	25 inch lbs.	28
Torque rod bolts		
1995-96 models	89 inch lbs	10
1997-99 models		
Rod-to-vehicle body	89 inch lbs.	10
Rod-to-endgate	18	25
Grille		
Grille retainers	12 inch lbs.	1.4
Outside mirrors		
Mirror retaining nuts	53 inch lbs.	6
Fenders		
All pick-up and 1996-99 utility models	21	29
1994-95 utility models	18	25
Cab/body mounts		
Mount bolts	52-74	70-73
Power sunroof		
Glass		
Retaining screws	31 inch lbs.	3.5
Interior		
Instrument panel and pad		
1994 pick-up models		
Panel-to-cowl screws	17 inch lbs.	1.9
Lower panel screws	66 inch lbs.	7.5
Lower sound insulator panel		
Screws	17 inch lbs.	1.9
Nut	35 inch lbs.	4
1994 utility models		
Cluster housing bezel nuts	12 inch lbs.	1.4
Switch trim plate screw	12 inch lbs.	1.4
Steering column filler panel screws	14 inch lbs.	1.6
Sound insulation panels	14 inch lbs.	1.6
Speaker grille screws	12 inch lbs.	1.4
Ashtray support screws	12 inch lbs.	1.4
Glove compartment door frame, door and door hinge screws	12 inch lbs.	1.4
Accessory trim plate screws	12 inch lbs.	1.4

91110C01

TORQUE SPECIFICATIONS

Components	Ft. Lbs.	Nm
Instrument panel and pad (cont.)		
1995-96 models		
Upper and lower support screws	66 inch lbs.	7.5
Steering column nuts	22	30
1997-99 models		
Left and right panel pivot bolts	102 inch lbs.	11.5
Panel lower support bolt	102 inch lbs.	1.5
Upper support screws	17 inch lbs.	1.9
Instrument panel accessory trim plate screws	17 inch lbs.	1.9
Steering column nuts	22	30
Knee bolster		
Torx® head screws	80 inch lbs.	9
Hex head screws	17 inch lbs.	1.9
Courtesy lamp screws	17 inch lbs.	1.9
Instrument panel center sound insulator screws	17 inch lbs.	1.9
Center sound insulator-to-heater assembly screw	13 inch lbs.	1.5
Left side sound insulator-to-accelerator pedal bracket nut	35 inch lbs.	4
Left side sound insulator-to-cowl panel screw	13 inch lbs.	15
Left side sound insulator-to-knee bolster screw	17 inch lbs.	1.9
Data link connector screws	21 inch lbs.	2.4
Door locks		
Front door lock assembly		
1994 models		
Lock retainers		
Utility models	62 inch lbs.	7
Pick-up models	80 inch lbs.	9
1995-99 models		
Lock retainers	80 inch lbs.	9
Rear door lock assembly		
1994 models		
Lock retaining screws	62 inch lbs.	7
1995-99 models		
Lock retainers	80 inch lbs.	9
Endgate latch		
Pick-up models		
Endgate latches-to-endgate retainers	18	25
Endgate/liftgate lock cylinder		
1997-99 models		
Endgate		
Endgate window latch support retainers	80 inch lbs.	9
Endgate window latch retainers	88 inch lbs.	10
Endgate cover screws	11 inch lbs.	1.2
Endgate trim panel screws	17 inch lbs.	1.9
Trim panel-to-window latch support screw	17 inch lbs.	1.9
Endgate inside handle screws	25 inch lbs.	2.9
Liftgate		
Liftgate window latch support retainers	80 inch lbs.	9
Liftgate window latch retainers	88 inch lbs.	10
Liftgate trim panel screw	17 inch lbs.	1.9
Door glass and regulator		
Front door glass		
1994 models		
Sash assembly-to-window bolts	53 inch lbs.	6
1995-99 models		
Glass run channel screws	18 inch lbs.	2
Rear door glass		
1995-99 models		
Run channel bolts	17 inch lbs.	1.9
Seats		
All except rear seats		
Retainers	35	47
Rear seats		
Retainers	59	40

91110CA2

GLOSSARY

AIR/FUEL RATIO: The ratio of air-to-gasoline by weight in the fuel mixture drawn into the engine.

AIR INJECTION: One method of reducing harmful exhaust emissions by injecting air into each of the exhaust ports of an engine. The fresh air entering the hot exhaust manifold causes any remaining fuel to be burned before it can exit the tailpipe.

ALTERNATOR: A device used for converting mechanical energy into electrical energy.

AMMETER: An instrument, calibrated in amperes, used to measure the flow of an electrical current in a circuit. Ammeters are always connected in series with the circuit being tested.

AMPERE: The rate of flow of electrical current present when one volt of electrical pressure is applied against one ohm of electrical resistance.

ANALOG COMPUTER: Any microprocessor that uses similar (analogous) electrical signals to make its calculations.

ARMATURE: A laminated, soft iron core wrapped by a wire that converts electrical energy to mechanical energy as in a motor or relay. When rotated in a magnetic field, it changes mechanical energy into electrical energy as in a generator.

ATMOSPHERIC PRESSURE: The pressure on the Earth's surface caused by the weight of the air in the atmosphere. At sea level, this pressure is 14.7 psi at 32°F (101 kPa at 0°C).

ATOMIZATION: The breaking down of a liquid into a fine mist that can be suspended in air.

AXIAL PLAY: Movement parallel to a shaft or bearing bore.

BACKFIRE: The sudden combustion of gases in the intake or exhaust system that results in a loud explosion.

BACKLASH: The clearance or play between two parts, such as meshed gears.

BACKPRESSURE: Restrictions in the exhaust system that slow the exit of exhaust gases from the combustion chamber.

BAKELITE: A heat resistant, plastic insulator material commonly used in printed circuit boards and transistorized components.

BALL BEARING: A bearing made up of hardened inner and outer races between which hardened steel balls roll.

BALLAST RESISTOR: A resistor in the primary ignition circuit that lowers voltage after the engine is started to reduce wear on ignition components.

BEARING: A friction reducing, supportive device usually located between a stationary part and a moving part.

BIMETAL TEMPERATURE SENSOR: Any sensor or switch made of two dissimilar types of metal that bend when heated or cooled due to the different expansion rates of the alloys. These types of sensors usually function as an on/off switch.

BLOWBY: Combustion gases, composed of water vapor and unburned fuel, that leak past the piston rings into the crankcase during normal engine operation. These gases are removed by the PCV system to prevent the buildup of harmful acids in the crankcase.

BRAKE PAD: A brake shoe and lining assembly used with disc brakes.

BRAKE SHOE: The backing for the brake lining. The term is, however, usually applied to the assembly of the brake backing and lining.

BUSHING: A liner, usually removable, for a bearing; an anti-friction liner used in place of a bearing.

CALIPER: A hydraulically activated device in a disc brake system, which is mounted straddling the brake rotor (disc). The caliper contains at least one piston and two brake pads. Hydraulic pressure on the piston(s) forces the pads against the rotor.

CAMSHAFT: A shaft in the engine on which are the lobes (cams) which operate the valves. The camshaft is driven by the crankshaft, via a belt, chain or gears, at one half the crankshaft speed.

CAPACITOR: A device which stores an electrical charge.

CARBON MONOXIDE (CO): A colorless, odorless gas given off as a normal byproduct of combustion. It is poisonous and extremely dangerous in confined areas, building up slowly to toxic levels without warning if adequate ventilation is not available.

CARBURETOR: A device, usually mounted on the intake manifold of an engine, which mixes the air and fuel in the proper proportion to allow even combustion.

CATALYTIC CONVERTER: A device installed in the exhaust system, like a muffler, that converts harmful byproducts of combustion into carbon dioxide and water vapor by means of a heat-producing chemical reaction.

CENTRIFUGAL ADVANCE: A mechanical method of advancing the spark timing by using flyweights in the distributor that react to centrifugal force generated by the distributor shaft rotation.

CHECK VALVE: Any one-way valve installed to permit the flow of air, fuel or vacuum in one direction only.

CHOKE: A device, usually a moveable valve, placed in the intake path of a carburetor to restrict the flow of air.

CIRCUIT: Any unbroken path through which an electrical current can flow. Also used to describe fuel flow in some instances.

CIRCUIT BREAKER: A switch which protects an electrical circuit from overload by opening the circuit when the current flow exceeds a predetermined level. Some circuit breakers must be reset manually, while most reset automatically.

COIL (IGNITION): A transformer in the ignition circuit which steps up the voltage provided to the spark plugs.

COMBINATION MANIFOLD: An assembly which includes both the intake and exhaust manifolds in one casting.

COMBINATION VALVE: A device used in some fuel systems that routes fuel vapors to a charcoal storage canister instead of venting them into the atmosphere. The valve relieves fuel tank pressure and allows fresh air into the tank as the fuel level drops to prevent a vapor lock situation.

COMPRESSION RATIO: The comparison of the total volume of the cylinder and combustion chamber with the piston at BDC and the piston at TDC.

CONDENSER: 1. An electrical device which acts to store an electrical charge, preventing voltage surges. 2. A radiator-like device in the air conditioning system in which refrigerant gas condenses into a liquid, giving off heat.

CONDUCTOR: Any material through which an electrical current can be transmitted easily.

CONTINUITY: Continuous or complete circuit. Can be checked with an ohmmeter.

COUNTERSHAFT: An intermediate shaft which is rotated by a mainshaft and transmits, in turn, that rotation to a working part.

CRANKCASE: The lower part of an engine in which the crankshaft and related parts operate.

CRANKSHAFT: The main driving shaft of an engine which receives reciprocating motion from the pistons and converts it to rotary motion.

CYLINDER: In an engine, the round hole in the engine block in which the piston(s) ride.

CYLINDER BLOCK: The main structural member of an engine in which is found the cylinders, crankshaft and other principal parts.

CYLINDER HEAD: The detachable portion of the engine, usually fastened to the top of the cylinder block and containing all or most of the combustion chambers. On overhead valve engines, it contains the valves and their operating parts. On overhead cam engines, it contains the camshaft as well.

DEAD CENTER: The extreme top or bottom of the piston stroke.

DETONATION: An unwanted explosion of the air/fuel mixture in the combustion chamber caused by excess heat and compression, advanced timing, or an overly lean mixture. Also referred to as "ping".

DIAPHRAGM: A thin, flexible wall separating two cavities, such as in a vacuum advance unit.

DIESELING: A condition in which hot spots in the combustion chamber cause the engine to run on after the key is turned off.

DIFFERENTIAL: A geared assembly which allows the transmission of motion between drive axles, giving one axle the ability to turn faster than the other.

DIODE: An electrical device that will allow current to flow in one direction only.

DISC BRAKE: A hydraulic braking assembly consisting of a brake disc, or rotor, mounted on an axle, and a caliper assembly containing, usually two brake pads which are activated by hydraulic pressure. The pads are forced against the sides of the disc, creating friction which slows the vehicle.

DISTRIBUTOR: A mechanically driven device on an engine which is responsible for electrically firing the spark plug at a predetermined point of the piston stroke.

DOWEL PIN: A pin, inserted in mating holes in two different parts allowing those parts to maintain a fixed relationship.

DRUM BRAKE: A braking system which consists of two brake shoes and one or two wheel cylinders, mounted on a fixed backing plate, and a brake drum, mounted on an axle, which revolves around the assembly.

DWELL: The rate, measured in degrees of shaft rotation, at which an electrical circuit cycles on and off.

ELECTRONIC CONTROL UNIT (ECU): Ignition module, module, amplifier or igniter. See Module for definition.

ELECTRONIC IGNITION: A system in which the timing and firing of the spark plugs is controlled by an electronic control unit, usually called a module. These systems have no points or condenser.

END-PLAY: The measured amount of axial movement in a shaft.

ENGINE: A device that converts heat into mechanical energy.

EXHAUST MANIFOLD: A set of cast passages or pipes which conduct exhaust gases from the engine.

FEELER GAUGE: A blade, usually metal, or precisely predetermined thickness, used to measure the clearance between two parts.

FIRING ORDER: The order in which combustion occurs in the cylinders of an engine. Also the order in which spark is distributed to the plugs by the distributor.

FLOODING: The presence of too much fuel in the intake manifold and combustion chamber which prevents the air/fuel mixture from firing, thereby causing a no-start situation.

FLYWHEEL: A disc shaped part bolted to the rear end of the crankshaft. Around the outer perimeter is affixed the ring gear. The starter drive engages the ring gear, turning the flywheel, which rotates the crankshaft, imparting the initial starting motion to the engine.

FOOT POUND (ft. lbs. or sometimes, ft.lb.): The amount of energy or work needed to raise an item weighing one pound, a distance of one foot.

FUSE: A protective device in a circuit which prevents circuit overload by breaking the circuit when a specific amperage is present. The device is constructed around a strip or wire of a lower amperage rating than the circuit it is designed to protect. When an amperage higher than that stamped on the fuse is present in the circuit, the strip or wire melts, opening the circuit.

GEAR RATIO: The ratio between the number of teeth on meshing gears.

GENERATOR: A device which converts mechanical energy into electrical energy.

HEAT RANGE: The measure of a spark plug's ability to dissipate heat from its firing end. The higher the heat range, the hotter the plug fires.

HUB: The center part of a wheel or gear.

HYDROCARBON (HC): Any chemical compound made up of hydrogen and carbon. A major pollutant formed by the engine as a byproduct of combustion.

HYDROMETER: An instrument used to measure the specific gravity of a solution.

INCH POUND (inch lbs.; sometimes in.lb. or in. lbs.): One twelfth of a foot pound.

INDUCTION: A means of transferring electrical energy in the form of a magnetic field. Principle used in the ignition coil to increase voltage.

INJECTOR: A device which receives metered fuel under relatively low pressure and is activated to inject the fuel into the engine under relatively high pressure at a predetermined time.

INPUT SHAFT: The shaft to which torque is applied, usually carrying the driving gear or gears.

INTAKE MANIFOLD: A casting of passages or pipes used to conduct air or a fuel/air mixture to the cylinders.

JOURNAL: The bearing surface within which a shaft operates.

KEY: A small block usually fitted in a notch between a shaft and a hub to prevent slippage of the two parts.

MANIFOLD: A casting of passages or set of pipes which connect the cylinders to an inlet or outlet source.

MANIFOLD VACUUM: Low pressure in an engine intake manifold formed just below the throttle plates. Manifold vacuum is highest at idle and drops under acceleration.

MASTER CYLINDER: The primary fluid pressurizing device in a hydraulic system. In automotive use, it is found in brake and hydraulic clutch systems and is pedal activated, either directly or, in a power brake system, through the power booster.

MODULE: Electronic control unit, amplifier or igniter of solid state or integrated design which controls the current flow in the ignition primary circuit based on input from the pick-up coil. When the module opens the primary circuit, high secondary voltage is induced in the coil.

NEEDLE BEARING: A bearing which consists of a number (usually a large number) of long, thin rollers.

OHM: (Ω) The unit used to measure the resistance of conductor-to-electrical flow. One ohm is the amount of resistance that limits current flow to one ampere in a circuit with one volt of pressure.

OHMMETER: An instrument used for measuring the resistance, in ohms, in an electrical circuit.

OUTPUT SHAFT: The shaft which transmits torque from a device, such as a transmission.

OVERDRIVE: A gear assembly which produces more shaft revolutions than that transmitted to it.

OVERHEAD CAMSHAFT (OHC): An engine configuration in which the camshaft is mounted on top of the cylinder head and operates the valve either directly or by means of rocker arms.

OVERHEAD VALVE (OHV): An engine configuration in which all of the valves are located in the cylinder head and the camshaft is located in the cylinder block. The camshaft operates the valves via lifters and pushrods.

OXIDES OF NITROGEN (NOx): Chemical compounds of nitrogen produced as a byproduct of combustion. They combine with hydrocarbons to produce smog.

OXYGEN SENSOR: Use with the feedback system to sense the presence of oxygen in the exhaust gas and signal the computer which can reference the voltage signal to an air/fuel ratio.

PINION: The smaller of two meshing gears.

PISTON RING: An open-ended ring with fits into a groove on the outer diameter of the piston. Its chief function is to form a seal between the piston and cylinder wall. Most automotive pistons have three rings: two for compression sealing; one for oil sealing.

PRELOAD: A predetermined load placed on a bearing during assembly or by adjustment.

PRIMARY CIRCUIT: the low voltage side of the ignition system which consists of the ignition switch, ballast resistor or resistance wire, bypass, coil, electronic control unit and pick-up coil as well as the connecting wires and harnesses.

PRESS FIT: The mating of two parts under pressure, due to the inner diameter of one being smaller than the outer diameter of the other, or vice versa; an interference fit.

RACE: The surface on the inner or outer ring of a bearing on which the balls, needles or rollers move.

REGULATOR: A device which maintains the amperage and/or voltage levels of a circuit at predetermined values.

RELAY: A switch which automatically opens and/or closes a circuit.

RESISTANCE: The opposition to the flow of current through a circuit or electrical device, and is measured in ohms. Resistance is equal to the voltage divided by the amperage.

RESISTOR: A device, usually made of wire, which offers a preset amount of resistance in an electrical circuit.

RING GEAR: The name given to a ring-shaped gear attached to a differential case, or affixed to a flywheel or as part of a planetary gear set.

ROLLER BEARING: A bearing made up of hardened inner and outer races between which hardened steel rollers move.

ROTOR: 1. The disc-shaped part of a disc brake assembly, upon which the brake pads bear; also called, brake disc. 2. The device mounted atop the distributor shaft, which passes current to the distributor cap tower contacts.

SECONDARY CIRCUIT: The high voltage side of the ignition system, usually above 20,000 volts. The secondary includes the ignition coil, coil wire, distributor cap and rotor, spark plug wires and spark plugs.

SENDING UNIT: A mechanical, electrical, hydraulic or electro-magnetic device which transmits information to a gauge.

SENSOR: Any device designed to measure engine operating conditions or ambient pressures and temperatures. Usually electronic in nature and designed to send a voltage signal to an on-board computer, some sensors may operate as a simple on/off switch or they may provide a variable voltage signal (like a potentiometer) as conditions or measured parameters change.

SHIM: Spacers of precise, predetermined thickness used between parts to establish a proper working relationship.

SLAVE CYLINDER: In automotive use, a device in the hydraulic clutch system which is activated by hydraulic force, disengaging the clutch.

SOLENOID: A coil used to produce a magnetic field, the effect of which is to produce work.

SPARK PLUG: A device screwed into the combustion chamber of a spark ignition engine. The basic construction is a conductive core inside of a ceramic insulator, mounted in an outer conductive base. An electrical charge from the spark plug wire travels along the conductive core and jumps a preset air gap to a grounding point or points at the end of the conductive base. The resultant spark ignites the fuel/air mixture in the combustion chamber.

SPLINES: Ridges machined or cast onto the outer diameter of a shaft or inner diameter of a bore to enable parts to mate without rotation.

TACHOMETER: A device used to measure the rotary speed of an engine, shaft, gear, etc., usually in rotations per minute.

THERMOSTAT: A valve, located in the cooling system of an engine, which is closed when cold and opens gradually in response to engine heating, controlling the temperature of the coolant and rate of coolant flow.

TOP DEAD CENTER (TDC): The point at which the piston reaches the top of its travel on the compression stroke.

TORQUE: The twisting force applied to an object.

TORQUE CONVERTER: A turbine used to transmit power from a driving member to a driven member via hydraulic action, providing changes in drive ratio and torque. In automotive use, it links the driveplate at the rear of the engine to the automatic transmission.

TRANSDUCER: A device used to change a force into an electrical signal.

TRANSISTOR: A semi-conductor component which can be actuated by a small voltage to perform an electrical switching function.

TUNE-UP: A regular maintenance function, usually associated with the replacement and adjustment of parts and components in the electrical and fuel systems of a vehicle for the purpose of attaining optimum performance.

TURBOCHARGER: An exhaust driven pump which compresses intake air and forces it into the combustion chambers at higher than atmospheric pressures. The increased air pressure allows more fuel to be burned and results in increased horsepower being produced.

VACUUM ADVANCE: A device which advances the ignition timing in response to increased engine vacuum.

VACUUM GAUGE: An instrument used to measure the presence of vacuum in a chamber.

VALVE: A device which control the pressure, direction of flow or rate of flow of a liquid or gas.

VALVE CLEARANCE: The measured gap between the end of the valve stem and the rocker arm, cam lobe or follower that activates the valve.

VISCOSITY: The rating of a liquid's internal resistance to flow.

VOLTMETER: An instrument used for measuring electrical force in units called volts. Voltmeters are always connected parallel with the circuit being tested.

WHEEL CYLINDER: Found in the automotive drum brake assembly, it is a device, actuated by hydraulic pressure, which, through internal pistons, pushes the brake shoes outward against the drums.

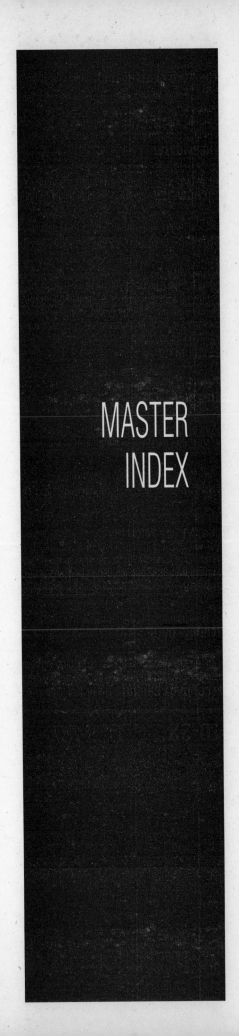

MASTER

INDEX